# CHARLESTON AND SAVANNAH

GEORGIA

SOUTH CAROLINA

Oak Park

Aiken

Claxton

Canoochee

Statesboro

Sylvania

Savannah River

Ogeechee River

Rincon

JERUSALEM EVANGELICAL LUTHERAN CHURCH

Garden City

Savannah

Hardeeville

Pinckney Island National Wildlife Refuge

Fort Pulaski National Monument

Tybee Island

Hilton Head

Beaufort

St. Helena

St. Helena Sound

Port Royal Sound

ACE Basin National Wildlife Refuge

Osborn

Edisto Beach State Park

CHARLESTON TEA PLANTATION

Wadmalaw Sound

Coosawhatchie River

Ulmer

Bamberg

Walterboro

Ashepoo River

Edisto River

Salkehatchie

Orangeburg

To Columbia

Congaree River

Lake Marion

Lake Moultrie

Francis Marion National Forest

Santee River

Salters

McClellanville

Bulls Bay

Georgetown

Moncks Corner

CHARLESTON INTERNATIONAL AIRPORT

CHARLESTON NAVYYARD

Charleston

Cooper River

BOONE HALL PLANTATION

FORT MOULTRIE

OCEAN

# Contents

# CHARLESTON
# & SAVANNAH

JIM MOREKIS

# Charleston & Savannah

**N**o doubt about it: The travel spotlight is shifting South. Taking their place alongside old favorites like Paris, New York, and San Francisco are the smaller but just as delectable destinations of Charleston and Savannah, each now enjoying an unprecedented boom in visitor interest.

As more and more people discover the subtle, compelling charms of these two Southern gems, the inevitable comparisons begin. Stereotypes abound, such as the famous adage "In Charleston they ask what your mother's maiden name is, and in Savannah they ask what you're drinking." But the truth is that Savannah can be just as obsessed with arcane genealogy, and anyone who's ever spent a weekend night in downtown Charleston knows that city is no stranger to a carousing good time.

The key difference between the two is mostly physical. Charleston's charms are more serendipitous, its architecture more Caribbean. The compact, winding downtown means a new surprise awaits you around every corner. That's the magic of Charleston.

Savannah, with its more spacious downtown, has more room to breathe, to walk, and to stretch out. And there are those matchless, tidy squares, still studied

**Clockwise from top left:** the John Rutledge House; South Carolina Aquarium; headstone in Magnolia Cemetery; Charleston's Pineapple Fountain; decorative iron horse hitch in Charleston; wild horse on Cumberland Island.

as marvels of urban design. Savannah's classically Anglophilic architecture tends more toward the stately. While both cities love a good time, Charleston—with its vast selection of nationally renowned restaurants—is definitely more of a foodie's paradise. Savannah, on the other hand, loves nothing more than a boisterous party.

Perhaps we should be talking instead about the things that tie the two together. Charleston and Savannah share a parallel history; stubborn individuality and defiance against the norm have been constants, as evidenced by their key roles in the American Revolution and the Civil War. The entire area has in common a rare natural beauty, with the South Carolina Lowcountry and the Georgia coast together composing the largest contiguous salt marsh in the world and one of the planet's unique ecosystems. Kayakers are at home paddling in the blackwater of the ACE Basin or the vast Okefenokee Swamp. Beachgoers are amazed at the underrated quality of the area's serene strands.

Most of all, however, the greatest treasure of this region is its people. The folks down here love a good story, a good conversation, and a good laugh. It's not just the fabled Southern hospitality; it's a joie de vivre born of great weather and proximity to the ever-invigorating rivers, marshes, and ocean.

**Clockwise from top left:** the waterfront at St. Simons Island; sunset on St. Helena Island; the Jekyll Island Club; Pirates Courtyard in Charleston.

# Planning Your Trip

## Where to Go

### Charleston

One of America's oldest cities and an early national center of **arts and culture**, Charleston's legendary taste for the high life is matched by its forward-thinking outlook. The **birthplace of the Civil War** is not just a city of museums resting on its historic laurels. Situated on a hallowed spit of land known as "the peninsula," the Holy City is now a **vibrant, creative hub** of the New South.

### Beaufort and the Lowcountry

The Lowcountry's **mossy, laid-back pace** belies its former status as the heart of American plantation culture and the original cradle of secession. Today it is a mix of **history** (Beaufort and Bluffton), **natural beauty** (the ACE Basin), **resort development** (Hilton Head), **military bases** (Parris Island), and **relaxed beaches** (Edisto and Hunting Islands).

### Savannah

Surprisingly **cosmopolitan** for a Deep South city, Savannah's quirky hedonism permeates any visit. The brainchild of General James Oglethorpe, the city's layout is studied even today as a **masterpiece of urban design.** Whether you're admiring an **antebellum home** from the cotton era or enjoying the sea breeze and a cocktail out on **Tybee Island,** a sense of fun imbues all parts of life here.

### The Golden Isles

Georgia's Golden Isles are home to one-third of

blooming azaleas and live oaks on Magnolia Plantation in Charleston

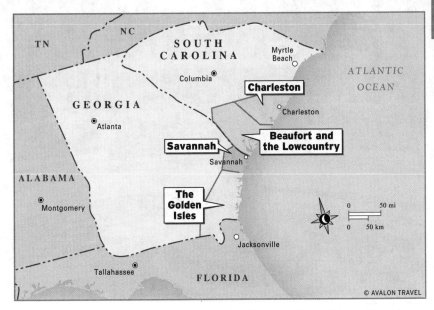

© AVALON TRAVEL

the East Coast's **salt marsh,** and their **natural beauty** is a testament to the Gilded Age millionaires who kept the area largely undeveloped over the years. Even today, this region evokes a **timeless mystique** redolent of Spanish missions, Native American shell ring ceremonies, insular but friendly shrimping communities, and lonely colonial English outposts.

# Know Before You Go

## High and Low Seasons

Springtime is for lovers, and it's no coincidence that spring is when most love affairs with the region begin. Unless you have severe pollen allergies—not a trivial concern given the explosion of plant life at this time—you should try to experience this area at its peak of natural beauty during the magical period from **mid-March to mid-May.** Not surprisingly, lodging is the most expensive and most difficult to secure at that time.

The **hardest time to get a room** in Charleston is during Spoleto from **Memorial Day through mid-June.** Hilton Head's busiest time is during the **RBC Heritage golf tournament** in mid-April. Savannah's tricky time of year is the **St. Patrick's Day** celebration, a multiday event clustering around March 17. While last-minute cancellations are always possible, the only real guarantee is to secure reservations as far in advance as possible (a full year in advance is not unusual for these peak times).

Activity here slows down noticeably in **July and August.** But overall, summertime in the South gets a bad rap and is often not appreciably worse than summers north of the Mason-Dixon Line—though it's certainly more humid.

My favorite time of year on the southeastern coast is the **middle of November,** when the tourist crush noticeably subsides. Not only are the days delightful and the nights crisp (but not frigid), you can get a room at a good price.

St. Patrick's Day in Savannah

## What to Pack

Unless you're coming in the winter to take advantage of lower rates or to enjoy the copious seasonal cheer, there's not much need for a heavy jacket. A **sweater or windbreaker** will do fine for chillier days. Also note that the ocean and the larger rivers can generate some surprisingly crisp breezes, even on what otherwise might be a warm day.

Because of the area's temperate climate, perspiration is likely to be a constant travel companion; pack accordingly. Whatever you wear, stay with **natural fabrics** such as cotton. The humidity and generally warm weather combine for a miserable experience with polyester and other synthetic fabrics.

Biting insects, such as mosquitos and sand gnats, are frequent unwelcome companions in this part of the country. Plan a trip to the drugstore or supermarket to buy some **bug spray** or Skin So Soft, an Avon product that keeps away the gnats.

autumn decorations in Savannah

# The Best of Charleston and Savannah

Both cities share an abiding respect for social manners and mores, for history, for making money, and for good food and strong drink. They differ in outlook: Charleston has one well-shod foot firmly in the global future, whereas Savannah tends to be more insular. The difference is also one of scale: Savannah's downtown is bigger and has more room to breathe and stretch out, whereas Charleston's charms are more compact and serendipitous. This "Best of" tour will allow you to come to your own conclusions.

## Day 1
### CHARLESTON

Begin your journey in Charleston, the Holy City, named not for its piety but for the steeples in its skyline. First, feel the pulse of the city by going to its bustling heart, **Marion Square.** Maybe do a little shopping on **King Street** and at **Old City Market** afterward. Take a sunset stroll around

The **Battery** and admire **Rainbow Row** before diving right into a great meal at one of the city's fine restaurants.

## Day 2

Today you put your historian's hat on and visit one of Charleston's great house museums, such as the **Aiken-Rhett House** or the **Edmondston-Alston House.** Have a hearty Southern-style lunch, and then take an afternoon trip to **Fort Sumter.** After another fantastic Charleston dinner, take a stroll or carriage ride through the French Quarter to close the evening.

## Day 3
### BEAUFORT

After a hearty breakfast, make the 20-minute drive over the Ashley River to gorgeous **Middleton Place,** where you'll tour the gardens. Then stop at adjacent **Drayton Hall** and see

Old City Market

Middleton Place

one of the oldest and best-preserved plantation homes in the nation. Make the hour-long drive into Beaufort and spend the afternoon walking around the beautifully preserved historic district. If you have time, go over the bridge to St. Helena Island and visit historic **Penn Center.**

## Day 4
### HILTON HEAD TO SAVANNAH
From Beaufort, drive to **Hilton Head Island,** where you can spend a few hours sunning or biking on the family-friendly beach, shop, or visit the free and informative **Coastal Discovery Museum at Honey Horn**. A half hour away, make a late-afternoon stop in **Old Town Bluffton** to shop for art, see the beautiful **Church of the Cross** on the May River, and have a light dinner. Another half hour's drive puts you into a cute B&B in Savannah to relax for the night, maybe stopping in a pub for a pint or two.

## Day 5
### SAVANNAH
Hit downtown Savannah hard today, starting with a walk down **River Street.** Then enjoy the aesthetic charms of the two adjacent museums, one traditional and one modern, composing the

Harbour Town Lighthouse on Hilton Head Island

# Southern Cooking: High Style and Homestyle

the peel 'n' eat shrimp at The Glass Onion in Charleston

## FRESH SEAFOOD

The best seafood places put a premium on freshly harvested fish and shellfish.

- **Bowens Island Restaurant,** Charleston (page 116): Gloriously unpretentious.

- **39 Rue de Jean,** Charleston (page 110): Amazing mussels and fish.

- **Desposito's,** Savannah (page 268): Shrimp and oysters dockside.

- **Red Fish,** Hilton Head Island (page 168): Stylish but always fresh.

- **Saltus River Grill,** Beaufort (page 141): Meeting and eating place.

- **Speed's Kitchen,** Shellman Bluff (page 316): Delicacies right off the boat.

## NEW SOUTHERN

The area is home to some adventurous chefs offering an updated take on Lowcountry classics.

- **The Grey,** Savannah (page 265): Savannah's new world-class restaurant, competitive with the best in the nation.

- **FIG,** Charleston (page 107): Three words: tomato tarte tatin.

- **Sapphire Grill,** Savannah (page 264): Closest thing to a Charleston restaurant in Savannah.

- **The Glass Onion,** Charleston (page 111): Farm-to-table goodness in an informal setting.

## CLASSIC SOUTHERN

Your best bets for fine old-school Southern cooking:

- **Hominy Grill,** Charleston (page 111): Comfort-food hit with locals and visitors alike.

- **See Wee Restaurant,** Charleston (page 114): Possibly the best she-crab soup on the planet.

- **Dixie Supply Bakery and Café,** Charleston (page 105): Diner-style brunch faves.

- **Mrs. Wilkes' Dining Room,** Savannah (page 266): Old-school "pass the plate" community seating in a historic home.

## BARBECUE

The pleasures of the pig are never far away in this region. Here are some of the best coastal 'cue joints:

- **Angel's BBQ,** Savannah (page 267): Hipsters do 'cue too.

- **Fiery Ron's Home Team,** Charleston (page 110): My favorite barbecue spot in the world, believe it or not.

- **JB's Smokeshack,** Charleston (page 115): Lowcountry classic on James Island.

- **Po Pigs Bo-B-Q,** Edisto Island (page 155): Great 'cue on a friendly island.

Driftwood Beach on Jekyll Island

**Telfair Museums.** Tour the exquisite **Owens-Thomas House Museum** and then take a walk through the squares, visiting the **Cathedral of St. John the Baptist** in Lafayette Square and the **Mercer-Williams House** on Monterey Square.

## Day 6

On your way out to Tybee Island, stop for a walk through amazing **Bonaventure Cemetery**—about 15 minutes outside of downtown—and pay your respects to native son Johnny Mercer. A half-hour drive takes you to scenic and historically important **Fort Pulaski National Monument.** Scoot on into Tybee another 10 minutes and climb to the top of the **Tybee Lighthouse** before dinner.

## Day 7
### THE GOLDEN ISLES

Drive down scenic U.S. 17 through the Altamaha River estuary, about an hour and a half south of Savannah, and stop by historic **Hofwyl-Broadfield Plantation,** near Brunswick, for a glimpse at an authentic old rice plantation. Make the five-minute trip over the causeway and enjoy the afternoon at **The Village** on St. Simons Island, with a visit to historic **Fort Frederica National Monument.**

## Day 8

This morning, a 20-minute drive takes you into the **Jekyll Island Historic District.** Tour the grounds and have lunch at any of the great restaurants on-site. Rent a bike and pedal up to the **Clam Creek Picnic Area,** checking out the **Horton House Tabby Ruins** along the way. Ride on the sand to **Driftwood Beach** and relax awhile.

## Day 9

This morning, drive an hour south to St. Marys and have a walk around the cute little downtown area before heading out on the ferry to **Cumberland Island National Seashore.** The 45-minute ferry ride takes you to a full day of biking or hiking the many trails among the ruins and dunes.

## Day 10

Make the half-hour drive into Folkston and the Suwanee Canal Recreation Area at **Okefenokee National Wildlife Refuge.** Take a guided tour up and down the blackwater canal, or walk the trails out to the swamp's prairie vistas and drink in this unique natural beauty.

# African American Heritage

The cities and Sea Islands of the Lowcountry and Georgia coast are integral to a full understanding of the experience of African Americans in the South. More than that, they are living legacies, with a thriving culture—called Gullah in South Carolina and Geechee in Georgia—whose roots can be traced directly back to West Africa.

## Charleston

Charleston is planning to build the $75 million International African American Museum, probably at Calhoun and Concord Streets not far from Museum Row. While building has yet to begin, there are plenty of other spots to enjoy in the meantime. Pay your respects to the victims of the 2015 mass shooting at **Emanuel AME Church** on Calhoun Street. Shop in **City Market;** it never hosted a slave auction, but during its heyday, it was home to a number of African American entrepreneurs and vendors. Don't forget to walk by **Cabbage Row,** inspiration for Catfish Row of the African American-themed George Gershwin opera *Porgy and Bess.* Visit the **Old Slave Mart** and learn more about the Middle Passage and

## Civil War History

Throughout the region there are plenty of military history sights that highlight the Civil War era.

- In Charleston, take the ferry out to **Fort Sumter** (page 48), where the Civil War began. There is also **Fort Moultrie** (page 73), which hosted a young Edgar Allan Poe in the years prior to the war.

- See the raised **CSS *Hunley*** (page 68) at the decommissioned Navy Yard (only open Fri.-Sat.).

- Visit historic **Drayton Hall** (page 63), the country's oldest standing plantation home, saved from the torch only because Union troops thought it might have been used to quarantine smallpox victims.

- Beaufort served as a medical center for Union occupation troops, who even used **St. Helena's Episcopal Church** (page 134) as a hospital.

- In Savannah, stop at the **Green-Meldrim House** (page 214) where General Sherman made his headquarters.

Drayton Hall

- Visit **Fort Pulaski** (page 230), which a young Lieutenant Robert E. Lee helped build. It was later defeated by the first use of rifled artillery in warfare.

- In Richmond Hill, stop by **Fort McAllister** (page 238), overrun by Union troops in 1864.

Fans of retro Americana and roadside kitsch will find a treasure trove of down-home sites along the old Coastal Highway, now known as U.S. 17. Before the arrival of the interstate highway system, U.S. 17 was by far the most traveled route in the region. While now just a shadow of its former self, it is still a vital roadway and contains a lot of interesting, little-known history. Here's a look at some of the highlights, beginning just north of Charleston and ending at Brunswick, Georgia. This is a fun road trip you could easily accomplish in a day, just checking out the sights along the way.

- **Sweetgrass Baskets** (page 84): A stretch of U.S. 17 in Mt. Pleasant north of Charleston has been dubbed the "Sweetgrass Basket Makers Highway" in honor of the many wooden stalls along its length hosting local African American artisans selling their homemade sweetgrass baskets, a centuries-old tradition with African roots.

- **Arthur Ravenel Jr. Bridge** (page 95): The longest cable-stayed bridge in the Western Hemisphere joins Mt. Pleasant with Charleston proper. It has a pedestrian and bike lane too.

weaving a sweetgrass basket

- **The Coburg Cow** (page 67): This nearly century-old dairy advertisement—a slowly rotating milk cow—was once amid pastureland outside the Charleston city limits. Find it in West Ashley on the portion of U.S. 17 known as the "Savannah Highway," just west of Charleston, about 15 minutes from the Ravenel Bridge.

- **Old Sheldon Church** (page 146): A very short drive off U.S. 17, the ruins of the Old Sheldon Church—burned by both the British during the Revolution and the Yankees during the Civil War—are huge, stark, and poignant. After going south on U.S. 17 for about an hour out of Charleston, take a right onto Old Sheldon Church Road.

- **Firework Stands** (page 181): About half an hour from the Old Sheldon Church, at the intersection of U.S. 17 and I-95 at Hardeeville, South Carolina, you'll find many garish, colorful stores selling enough fireworks to blow you to the moon and back.

- **Midway Church** (page 234): Forty-five minutes south of Savannah in the Liberty County town of Midway is this beautiful 1792 church, whose congregation once boasted two of Georgia's signers

of the Declaration of Independence. Don't miss the historic cemetery across the street.

- **Smallest Church in North America** (page 313): About 15 minutes south of Midway on the side of the road near South Newport is the miniscule and charming Memory Park Christ Chapel. The current building was rebuilt after arson sadly destroyed the original in 2015.

- **Butler Island** (page 315): In another 15 or so minutes, just south of Darien, Georgia, on the west side of U.S. 17, you'll find this tall chimney—the only remnant of the Butler plantation. English actress Fanny Kemble, who married a Butler heir, wrote the influential abolitionist work *Journal of a Residence on a Georgian Plantation* after witnessing the miserable life of the slaves who worked here. (Strangely, the nearby historical marker makes no mention of this.)

- **Brunswick Stew** (page 293): Allegedly the container in which the first batch of Brunswick stew was cooked up, you can find this cast-iron pot in Brunswick, Georgia, at the corner of U.S. 17 and the Torras Causeway to St. Simons Island, about 20 minutes south of Butler Island.

Emanuel AME Church in Charleston

Robert Smalls House in Beaufort

how Charleston's black population overcame the legacy of slavery. Browse the research library at the **Avery Research Center,** one of the main repositories of Gullah culture and history. Take the ferry out to **Fort Sumter,** where the Civil War began. From the fort you can see nearby undeveloped Morris Island, scene of the 1863 Battle of Battery Wagner. That battle included the first all-black regiment in the U.S. Army, the 54th Massachusetts, whose tale was recounted in the film *Glory.* Visit the wrought-iron garden of the noted black Charleston artisan **Philip Simmons.** Take a guided African American history tour of downtown Charleston or tour the **Aiken-Rhett House,** with its excellently and respectfully preserved artifacts of the African American servants who made the historic property run. Visit **Drayton Hall;** take the guided tour and pay respects at the African American cemetery.

## Beaufort and the Lowcountry

While walking around the scenic historic district, visit the **Robert Smalls House,** home of the African American Civil War hero Robert Smalls, as well as his burial site at the **Tabernacle**

**Baptist Church.** Drive by the **Berners Barnwell Sams House** to see where Harriet Tubman worked as a nurse and helped ferry slaves to freedom on the Underground Railroad. Visit **Beaufort National Cemetery** and see the memorial to the African American troops of the 54th and 55th Massachusetts Regiments of the U.S. Army in the Civil War. Make the short drive to St. Helena Island and visit the campus of the **Penn Center,** a key clearinghouse for the study and celebration of Gullah culture and the site of activism by Martin Luther King Jr. in the 1960s. Head on into Hilton Head, stop by the **Coastal Discovery Museum at Honey Horn,** and take an African American heritage tour, visiting the site of Mitchelville, the first community of freed slaves in the United States. An alternate plan is to make the trip inland to Walterboro to visit the **Tuskegee Airmen Memorial** at the regional airport.

## Savannah and the Golden Isles

Check out the **African American Monument** at Rousakis Plaza on River Street. Head over to the former center of black life in Savannah,

the Haitian Monument in Savannah

Martin Luther King Jr. Boulevard (once West Broad St.), and see the **Ralph Mark Gilbert Civil Rights Museum,** and then tour the **First African Baptist Church** in City Market, the oldest black congregation in North America. Nearby is the **Haitian Monument,** a nod to the volunteers who helped the cause of independence in the Revolutionary War. Visit the **Second African Baptist Church,** where Sherman announced the famous "40 acres and a mule" field order. Close by is the **Beach Institute,** a repository of African American art, culture, and history. Check out the restored schoolroom at **Massie Heritage Center,** Savannah's first African American school, and the **Carnegie Branch Library,** Savannah's first black library, where future Supreme Court Justice Clarence Thomas once studied. Pay your respects at **Laurel Grove Cemetery South,** a historic African American cemetery with stirring memorials to some of Savannah's most notable black figures. Head down to **Harris Neck National Wildlife Refuge,** once the site of an African American community displaced for a World War II airfield. Be sure to visit the vernacular **Gould Cemetery**

near the landing within the refuge. An alternate plan is to drive all the way down to little Meridian near Darien and ride the ferry out to **Sapelo Island,** taking a guided day tour of the island and its rich Gullah/Geechee history, including the community of Hog Hammock.

Massie Heritage Center

A bike rests on Hilton Head Island.

# Outdoors Odyssey

While Charleston and Savannah are globally renowned for their history and architecture, a short drive outside their historic districts will take you to a unique natural wonderland. The Lowcountry and Georgia coast is framed by the largest contiguous salt marsh in the world. It's not only a kayaker's paradise but also an amazing natural habitat for indigenous and migratory birds. Here are some highlights for an active outdoor journey.

## Biking

Ride 12 miles across the expansive hard-packed sand all around **Hilton Head Island,** which also offers a number of more strenuous adventures. **Sullivan's Island** offers a long stretch of easy beach bicycling just outside Charleston.

## Bird-Watching

October-March is the perfect time for bird-watchers to visit the 22-acre **Crab Bank Seabird Sanctuary** in Charleston Harbor. Serious bird-watchers can visit the **Bear Island** and **Donnelly Wildlife Management Areas** within the ACE Basin, as well as the impounded rice paddies at the **Ernest F. Hollings ACE Basin National Wildlife Refuge.** The **Savannah National Wildlife Refuge,** with parts in both South Carolina and Georgia, also has an excellent bird-watching (and gator-watching!) area.

## Camping

Head down to Tybee Island outside Savannah for a day trip across the Back River to undeveloped **Little Tybee Island,** where wilderness camping is allowed. **Skidaway State Park** also offers great camping.

## Fishing

Inshore **fishing charters** abound in these coastal waters and are a great way to pass a day or half day. Some standouts are Telecaster Charters in Savannah and Barrier Island Eco Tours out of Charleston.

# Seaside Romance

Bonaventure Cemetery in Savannah

Spanish moss, friendly beaches, sunsets over the water, sultry weather, moonlit carriage rides—what more could you ask for? The Lowcountry and Georgia coast pretty much wrote the book on romantic getaways. Here's a starter list of the most romantic spots.

## CHARLESTON

- Romantic B&Bs include the John Rutledge House Inn and Two Meeting Street Inn.

- Enjoy an Italian dinner at Fulton Five or a fantastic Southern dinner at Circa 1886.

- Don't forget a carriage ride or art gallery stroll through the French Quarter.

- Shopping can be sexy! Visit the great stores on King Street.

## BEAUFORT AND THE LOWCOUNTRY

- Take a walkable, picturesque stroll of historic Beaufort Homes.

- Visit the driftwood beach on nearby Hunting Island State Park and enjoy the stunning views from the top of the lighthouse.

- Edisto Island is a wonderful place for a relaxing, quiet, no-hassle beach getaway.

## SAVANNAH

- Relax on the grass at vast, scenic Forsyth Park, surrounded by Victorian architecture.

- Yes, cemeteries can be romantic, especially gorgeous Bonaventure Cemetery.

- Avoid the lines at The Lady & Sons and instead have a delightful dinner at Sapphire Grill. Share a coffee, sweet treat, or perhaps a signature martini at Lulu's Chocolate Bar.

- Have a nightcap at Rocks on the Roof on top of the Bohemian Hotel Savannah and watch the big cargo ships roll in and out on the river.

- Up for a crazy night of dancing? Club One Jefferson is the ticket.

## THE GOLDEN ISLES

- Stay at the Jekyll Island Club, former stomping ground of the world's richest people. Rent a bike and crisscross the whole island in the late afternoon, coming back to the club to enjoy a romantic dinner by the fireplace at the Courtyard at Crane.

- Take the ferry to Cumberland Island National Seashore, surely one of the most romantic locations on earth. Rent a bike on arrival and take your time pedaling among the ruins of the old mansions, making sure to visit the chapel at the First African Baptist Church, site of the wedding of John F. Kennedy Jr. and Carolyn Bessette. Before you board the ferry to conclude your journey, maybe you'll get lucky and encounter some of the island's famous wild horses, fitting symbols of passion and romance.

the entrance to Wormsloe State Historic Site

## Kayaking

**Cape Romain National Wildlife Refuge** is a delightful oasis of nearly pristine marsh habitat north of Charleston. Bull Island and Capers Island are highlights of this largely maritime preserve, which comprises 66,000 acres of kayaking opportunities. You can easily kayak for a full day or two in the **ACE Basin,** comprising the estuaries of the Ashepoo, Combahee, and Edisto Rivers (the latter being the largest and most traveled). Public landings and guided tours abound for trips on these nearly pristine blackwater runs.

## Surfing

Believe it or not, Charleston's **Folly Beach** offers some of the East Coast's best surfing. McKevlin's Surf Shop is your go-to source for gear and info.

## Scenic Walks

While the coast's particularly flat nature—not to mention the heat and humidity—doesn't lend itself to strenuous hiking, there are plenty of enjoyable outdoor strolls. In the Savannah area, the entire area surrounding **Fort Pulaski National Monument** features extensive maritime forest walking trails, including a converted railbed.

**Skidaway State Park** and nearby **Wormsloe State Historic Site** both offer walking trails along the marsh and river. For hiking in the Charleston area, try the **Awendaw Passage** in the Francis Marion National Forest north of town.

sanderlings at Cape Romain National Wildlife Refuge

# Life's a Beach

shells and a sand dollar on Edisto Beach

There are plenty of beaches to enjoy on the Georgia and South Carolina coast, many of them made even more enjoyable by the fact that they tend to get much less traffic than more touristy areas. Here's a quick guide to match the beach to the trip:

## FAMILY FRIENDLY

- **Hilton Head Island**'s beaches are roomy and spotlessly maintained. And because no alcohol is allowed on them, they're geared to families with children.

- **Isle of Palms** outside Charleston is home to the Wild Dunes Resort, which caters to beach-loving families.

- Quiet **Edisto Island** has absolutely none of the flash that young people tend to gravitate to, but it is extraordinarily safe and friendly.

- Popular state park **Hunting Island State Park** is a great place to enjoy family time on the beach. Don't miss the hike to the top of the lighthouse!

- A playground for the people of Georgia by order of the state legislature, **Jekyll Island** is a safe, roomy, and friendly getaway.

## PEACE AND QUIET

- Romantic and isolated, **Cumberland Island** is virtually the mossy picture of the old Sea Island South.

- The total lack of chain hotels and high-rises on **Edisto Island** means a laid-back and thoroughly noncommercial beach experience.

- Low-traffic **Sapelo Island** offers friendly folks and a really beautiful beach.

- Even lower-traffic **Daufuskie Island** is where you want to go when only the most laid-back will do.

## DOG FRIENDLY

- Easily the two most dog-friendly beaches in the area covered by this book are **Hunting Island State Park,** South Carolina, and **Jekyll Island,** Georgia. Just keep 'em on a leash and you're fine year-round.

- For a Charleston-area dog beach, go straight to **Isle of Palms.**

- **Hilton Head** doesn't allow canines at all Memorial Day-Labor Day, but you can take them on a leash 10am-5pm from April 1 until the day before Memorial Day.

- On **Edisto Island,** your pup must be on a leash May 1-October 31 and under voice command or on a leash at all other times.

- Sorry, Rover can't come over to Tybee Island, Georgia, at all.

# Charleston

Look for ★ to find recommended sights, activities, dining, and lodging.

# Highlights

Lake Moultrie

Huger

Summerville

**Middleton Place** ★

**Drayton Hall** ★

North Charleston

**CSS *Hunley*** ★

Walterboro

Charleston

**Fort Sumter** ★

The Battery
Rainbow Row
South Carolina Aquarium
St. Philip's Episcopal Church
Aiken-Rhett House

Beaufort

ATLANTIC

OCEAN

0     15 mi

0     15 km

© AVALON TRAVEL

★ **The Battery:** Tranquil surroundings combine with beautiful views of Charleston Harbor, historical points key to the Civil War, and amazing mansions (page 39).

★ **Rainbow Row:** Painted in warm pastels, these old merchant homes near the cobblestoned waterfront take you on a journey to Charleston's antebellum heyday (page 40).

★ **South Carolina Aquarium:** Experience the state's surprising breadth of habitat (page 46).

★ **Fort Sumter:** Take the ferry to this historic place where the Civil War began, and take in the gorgeous views along the way (page 48).

★ **St. Philip's Episcopal Church:** A sublimely beautiful sanctuary and two historic graveyards await you in the heart of the evocative French Quarter (page 52).

★ **Aiken-Rhett House:** There are certainly more ostentatious house museums in Charleston, but none that provide such a virtually intact glimpse into real antebellum life (page 60).

★ **Drayton Hall:** Don't miss Charleston's oldest surviving plantation home and one of the country's best examples of professional historic preservation (page 63).

★ **Middleton Place:** Wander around one of the world's most beautifully landscaped gardens—and the first in North America (page 65).

★ **CSS *Hunley*:** The first submarine to sink a ship in battle is a moving example of bravery and sacrifice (page 68).

**E**veryone who spends time in Charleston comes away with a story about the locals' courtesy and hospitality.

Mine came while walking through the French Quarter and admiring a handsome old single house on Church Street, one of the few that survived the fire of 1775. To my surprise, the woman chatting with a friend nearby turned out to be the homeowner. Noticing my interest, she invited me, a total stranger, inside to check out the progress of her renovation. This is a city that takes civic harmony seriously—it even boasts the country's only "Livability Court," a legally binding board that meets regularly to enforce local quality-of-life ordinances.

In 2015, however, Charleston gained national prominence when a white gunman murdered nine worshippers in the historically black Emanuel AME Church on Calhoun Street downtown. The nation was transfixed not only by the horror of the incident, but also by Charleston's community response, which was wholly in keeping with its character: hopeful, forgiving, resilient, and compassionate. Charleston's nickname, the "Holy City," derives from the skyline's abundance of church steeples rather than any excess of piety among its citizens, but its response to the Mother Emanuel tragedy seemed to lend a new meaning.

While many visitors come to see the historical south of Charleston—finding it and then some, of course—they leave impressed by the diversity of Charlestonian life. It's a surprisingly cosmopolitan mix of students, professionals, and longtime inhabitants—who discuss the finer points of Civil War history as if it were last year, party on Saturday night like there's no tomorrow, and go to church on Sunday morning dressed in their finest.

This city, so known for its history, is also quietly booming as one of the nation's key centers of tech and digital development. Highly educated and motivated millennials from all over the country are flocking to Charleston for its blend of startup-friendliness, great nightlife, eco-friendly sensibilities, and vibrant arts and cultural scene.

**Previous:** colorful buildings on Broad Street; the Angel Oak. **Above:** carriage tour on State Street.

# Map 1: Downtown Charleston

## SIGHTS

| | | | |
|---|---|---|---|
| 2 | South Carolina Aquarium | 37 | Old City Jail |
| 3 | Fort Sumter National Monument | 39 | Unitarian Church |
| 5 | Philip Simmons Garden | 48 | Confederate Museum |
| 18 | Kahal Kadosh Beth Elohim Reform Temple | 59 | Gibbes Museum of Art |
| 19 | William Rhett House | 60 | Circular Congregational Church |
| 25 | St. Mary of the Annunciation Church | 63 | Old Powder Magazine |
| 32 | Old City Market | 64 | St. Philip's Episcopal Church |
| | | 77 | Dock Street Theatre |

| | | | |
|---|---|---|---|
| 79 | French Huguenot Church | 99 | Cabbage Row |
| 80 | Old Slave Mart Museum | 100 | Heyward-Washington House |
| 84 | Waterfront Park | 101 | Nathaniel Russell House |
| 90 | Four Corners of Law | 102 | Miles Brewton House |
| 91 | St. Michael's Episcopal Church | 103 | The Battery |
| 97 | Rainbow Row | 104 | Calhoun Mansion |
| 98 | The Old Exchange and Provost Dungeon | 105 | Edmondston-Alston House |

## RESTAURANTS

| | | | |
|---|---|---|---|
| 22 | Black Tap Coffee | 41 | Fulton Five |
| 15 | Jestine's Kitchen | 54 | Dixie Supply Bakery and Cafe |
| 20 | Circa 1886 | 57 | Husk |
| 24 | Charleston Grill | 58 | Poogan's Porch |
| 26 | Hyman's Seafood | 66 | Magnolias |
| 27 | FIG | 69 | Slightly North of Broad |
| 29 | Cru Café | 71 | Cypress |
| 33 | Peninsula Grill | 81 | McCrady's |
| 34 | Kaminsky's | 89 | Gaulart & Maliclet |
| 38 | Queen Street Grocery | | |
| 40 | City Lights Coffeehouse | | |

## NIGHTLIFE

| | | | |
|---|---|---|---|
| 21 | Vickery's Bar and Grill | 68 | The Gin Joint |
| 52 | Tommy Condon's Irish Pub | 82 | Rooftop Bar and Restaurant |

## ARTS AND CULTURE

| | | | |
|---|---|---|---|
| 13 | The Have Nots! | 78 | Charleston Stage |
| 44 | Sylvan Gallery | 85 | City Gallery at Waterfront |
| 45 | The Audubon Gallery | 92 | Ann Long Fine Art |
| 49 | Gallery Chuma | 93 | Pink House Gallery |
| 61 | Corrigan Gallery | 95 | Charleston Renaissance Gallery |
| 65 | The Footlight Players | 96 | Helena Fox Fine Art |
| 70 | Robert Lange Studios | | |

## SPORTS AND ACTIVITIES

| | | | |
|---|---|---|---|
| 1 | Spiritline Cruises | 53 | Original Charleston Walks |
| 4 | Sandlapper Water Tours | 74 | Charleston Strolls |
| 35 | Bulldog Tours | 94 | Charleston Art Tours |
| 36 | Ed Grimball's Walking Tours | | |

## SHOPS

| | | | |
|---|---|---|---|
| 6 | Bob Ellis Shoe Store | 42 | George C. Birlant & Co. |
| 7 | Oops! | 43 | Joint Venture Estate Jewelers |
| 8 | Phillips Shoes | 50 | City Market |
| 9 | Copper Penny Shooz | 55 | Preservation Society of Charleston Book and Gift Shop |
| 10 | Art Jewelry by Mikhail Smolkin | 56 | Alexandra AD |
| 11 | Croghan's Jewel Box | 62 | Curiosity |
| 12 | The Trunk Show | 67 | Charleston Cooks! |
| 14 | Half Moon Outfitters | 72 | Indigo |
| 16 | Rangoni of Florence | 76 | Shops of Historic Charleston Foundation |
| 17 | Worthwhile | 88 | Berlins Men's and Women's |
| 23 | Pauline Books and Media | | |
| 30 | Belmond Charleston Place | | |

© AVALON TRAVEL

COMING ST

WENTWORTH ST

**20**

PITT ST

BEAUFAIN ST

**NORTH OF BROAD**

MAGAZINE ST

**37**

**Old City Jail**

QUEEN ST

**Unitarian Church**

**38**

LOCUST ST

BROAD ST

**86**

**87**

TRADD ST

LENWOOD ST

LEGARE ST

GIBBES ST

**Miles Brewton House** **102**

KING ST

LAMBOLL ST

**The Battery** **103**

MURRAY BLVD

S BATTERY ST

*White Point Gardens*

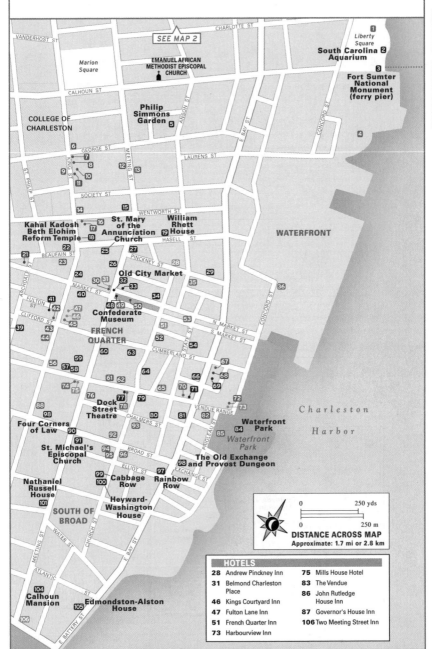

SEE MAP 2

Liberty Square 1

South Carolina Aquarium 2

3

Fort Sumter National Monument (ferry pier)

4

VANDERHOST ST
CHARLOTTE ST

Marion Square

EMANUEL AFRICAN METHODIST EPISCOPAL CHURCH

CALHOUN ST

COLLEGE OF CHARLESTON

Philip Simmons Garden 5

6 GEORGE ST

7

8

9 10

11

12 13

LAURENS ST

SOCIETY ST

15

14

WENTWORTH ST

Kahal Kadosh Beth Elohim Reform Temple

16 17 18

St. Mary of the Annunciation Church

William Rhett House 19

HASELL ST

WATERFRONT

22

21

BEAUFAIN ST

23

25 27

26

PINCKNEY ST

28

24

29

Old City Market

30 31 32 33

34

35

36

MARKET ST

40

41

42

47

48 49 50

Confederate Museum

46

45

39

43

44

FRENCH QUARTER

60

63

51

52

53

N MARKET ST

S MARKET ST

CONCORD ST

CUMBERLAND ST

54

56

57 58

59

64

67

61 62

65

66

68

69

74

75

70 71

76

77 78

79

72

73

Charleston

88

98

Dock Street Theatre

80

81

82

Harbor

Four Corners of Law

90

CHALMERS ST

93

92

Waterfront Park

84

85

St. Michael's Episcopal Church

91

94 95

96

BROAD ST

Waterfront Park

Nathaniel Russell House

101

99 100

Cabbage Row

ELLIOT ST

97

Rainbow Row

98

EXCHANGE ST

The Old Exchange and Provost Dungeon

SOUTH OF BROAD

Heyward-Washington House

MEETING ST

WATER ST

CHURCH ST

E BAY ST

ATLANTIC ST

104

Calhoun Mansion

105

Edmondston-Alston House

106

E BATTERY ST

| 0 | | 250 yds |
| 0 | | 250 m |

**DISTANCE ACROSS MAP**
Approximate: 1.7 mi or 2.8 km

| HOTELS | | |
|---|---|---|
| 28 Andrew Pinckney Inn | | 75 Mills House Hotel |
| 31 Belmond Charleston Place | | 83 The Vendue |
| 46 Kings Courtyard Inn | | 86 John Rutledge House Inn |
| 47 Fulton Lane Inn | | 87 Governor's House Inn |
| 51 French Quarter Inn | | 106 Two Meeting Street Inn |
| 73 Harbourview Inn | | |

# Map 2: Upper King and Hampton Park

© AVALON TRAVEL

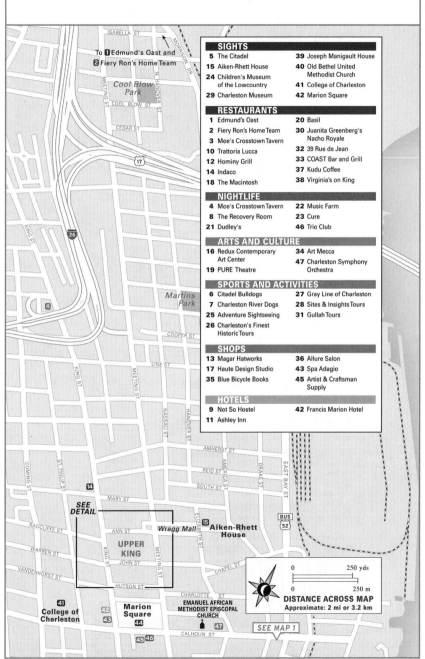

To **1** Edmund's Oast and
**2** Fiery Ron's Home Team

ISABELLA ST
MORRISON DR
N HANOVER ST
Cool Blow Park
MEETING ST
COOL BLOW ST
CEDAR ST
17
KING ST
26
Martins Park
8
COOPER ST
LINE ST
KING ST
MEETING ST
NASSAU ST
HANOVER ST
COMING ST
ST PHILIP ST
14
AMHERST ST
REID ST
AMERICA ST
DRAKE ST
EAST BAY ST
SOUTH ST
MARY ST
SEE DETAIL
RADCLIFFE ST
ANN ST
Wragg Mall **15** Aiken-Rhett House
ELIZABETH ST
BUS 52
UPPER KING
WARREN ST
KING ST
JOHN ST
MEETING ST
CHAPEL ST
VANDERHORST ST
HUTSON ST
CHARLOTTE ST
COMING ST
**41** College of Charleston
**42** **43** Marion Square **44**
EMANUEL AFRICAN METHODIST EPISCOPAL CHURCH
**47**
**45** **46**
CALHOUN ST
SEE MAP 1

## SIGHTS
**5** The Citadel
**15** Aiken-Rhett House
**24** Children's Museum of the Lowcountry
**29** Charleston Museum
**39** Joseph Manigault House
**40** Old Bethel United Methodist Church
**41** College of Charleston
**42** Marion Square

## RESTAURANTS
**1** Edmund's Oast
**2** Fiery Ron's Home Team
**3** Moe's Crosstown Tavern
**10** Trattoria Lucca
**12** Hominy Grill
**14** Indaco
**18** The Macintosh
**20** Basil
**30** Juanita Greenberg's Nacho Royale
**32** 39 Rue de Jean
**33** COAST Bar and Grill
**37** Kudu Coffee
**38** Virginia's on King

## NIGHTLIFE
**4** Moe's Crosstown Tavern
**8** The Recovery Room
**21** Dudley's
**22** Music Farm
**23** Cure
**46** Trio Club

## ARTS AND CULTURE
**16** Redux Contemporary Art Center
**19** PURE Theatre
**34** Art Mecca
**47** Charleston Symphony Orchestra

## SPORTS AND ACTIVITIES
**6** Citadel Bulldogs
**7** Charleston River Dogs
**25** Adventure Sightseeing
**26** Charleston's Finest Historic Tours
**27** Gray Line of Charleston
**28** Sites & Insights Tours
**31** Gullah Tours

## SHOPS
**13** Magar Hatworks
**17** Haute Design Studio
**35** Blue Bicycle Books
**36** Allure Salon
**43** Spa Adagio
**45** Artist & Craftsman Supply

## HOTELS
**9** Not So Hostel
**11** Ashley Inn
**42** Francis Marion Hotel

0        250 yds
0        250 m
**DISTANCE ACROSS MAP**
Approximate: 2 mi or 3.2 km

# Map 3: West Ashley and North Charleston

To ❶Colonial Dorchester
State Historic Site

DORCHESTER RD

RICHARDSON AVE
W 5TH N ST
DOTY AVE
MAIN ST
4
78
5
6
7
Summerville
Summerville-Dorchester Museum
CENTRAL AVE
CAROLINA AVE
5TH
8 Azalea Park
BERLIN G MYERS PKWY
LINCOLN AVE

9 10
11
Middleton Place
Ashley River
642
Joint Base Charleston

61
DORCHESTER RD

Magnolia Plantation and Gardens
12
13 Drayton Hall

ASHLEY RIVER RD

**RESTAURANTS**
4 Alex's Restaurant
6 Guerin's Pharmacy
10 Middleton Place Restaurant
19 EVO Pizzeria
27 Boxcar Betty's

28 Fiery Ron's Home Team BBQ
29 Glass Onion
31 Al Di La
33 Gene's Haufbrau

**NIGHTLIFE**
18 Madra Rua Irish Pub
30 Voodoo Lounge

34 Gene's Haufbrau

**SPORTS AND ACTIVITIES**
2 Carolina Ice Palace
16 South Carolina Stingrays

36 Charleston Scuba
37 West Ashley Greenway

**SHOPS**
3 The Guitar Center
14 Tanger Outlet
17 Fox Music House
25 Stella Nova

26 Monster Music and Movies
35 ESD, Elizabeth Stuart Design

**HOTELS**
5 Woodlands Resort & Inn

11 The Inn at Middleton Place

BEES FERRY RD

GLENN MCCONNELL PKY

17
MAIN RD
17

To ㉔ Caw Caw
Interpretive Center

0                    1 mi
0          1 km
**DISTANCE ACROSS MAP**
Approximate: 13 mi or 21 km

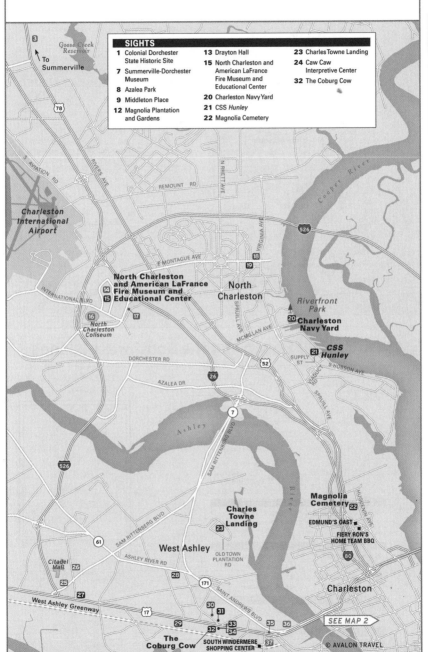

**SIGHTS**

1 Colonial Dorchester State Historic Site
7 Summerville-Dorchester Museum
8 Azalea Park
9 Middleton Place
12 Magnolia Plantation and Gardens
13 Drayton Hall
15 North Charleston and American LaFrance Fire Museum and Educational Center
20 Charleston Navy Yard
21 CSS *Hunley*
22 Magnolia Cemetery
23 Charles Towne Landing
24 Caw Caw Interpretive Center
32 The Coburg Cow

© AVALON TRAVEL

# Map 4: Mount Pleasant and East Cooper

# Map 5: Folly Beach and the Southwest Islands

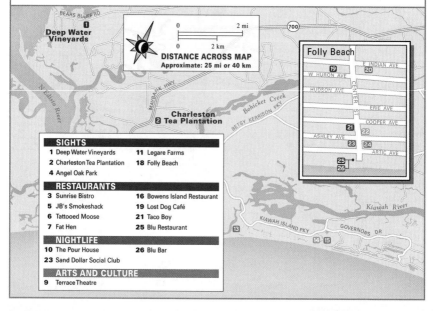

**SIGHTS**
1 Deep Water Vineyards
2 Charleston Tea Plantation
4 Angel Oak Park
11 Legare Farms
18 Folly Beach

**RESTAURANTS**
3 Sunrise Bistro
5 JB's Smokeshack
6 Tattooed Moose
7 Fat Hen
16 Bowens Island Restaurant
19 Lost Dog Café
21 Taco Boy
25 Blu Restaurant

**NIGHTLIFE**
10 The Pour House
23 Sand Dollar Social Club
26 Blu Bar

**ARTS AND CULTURE**
9 Terrace Theatre

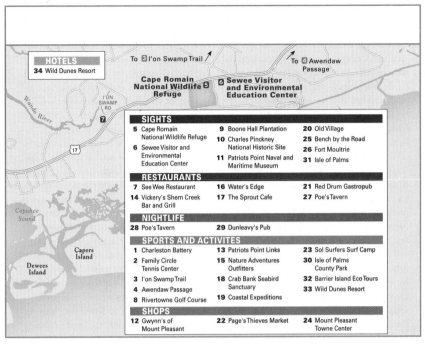

### HOTELS
**34** Wild Dunes Resort

To **3** I'on Swamp Trail

To **4** Awendaw Passage

**Cape Romain National Wildlife 5** Refuge

**6 Sewee Visitor and Environmental Education Center**

### SIGHTS
**5** Cape Romain National Wildlife Refuge
**6** Sewee Visitor and Environmental Education Center
**9** Boone Hall Plantation
**10** Charles Pinckney National Historic Site
**11** Patriots Point Naval and Maritime Museum
**20** Old Village
**25** Bench by the Road
**26** Fort Moultrie
**31** Isle of Palms

### RESTAURANTS
**7** See Wee Restaurant
**14** Vickery's Shem Creek Bar and Grill
**16** Water's Edge
**17** The Sprout Cafe
**21** Red Drum Gastropub
**27** Poe's Tavern

### NIGHTLIFE
**28** Poe's Tavern
**29** Dunleavy's Pub

### SPORTS AND ACTIVITES
**1** Charleston Battery
**2** Family Circle Tennis Center
**3** I'on Swamp Trail
**4** Awendaw Passage
**8** Rivertowne Golf Course
**13** Patriots Point Links
**15** Nature Adventures Outfitters
**18** Crab Bank Seabird Sanctuary
**19** Coastal Expeditions
**23** Sol Surfers Surf Camp
**30** Isle of Palms County Park
**32** Barrier Island Eco Tours
**33** Wild Dunes Resort

### SHOPS
**12** Gwynn's of Mount Pleasant
**22** Page's Thieves Market
**24** Mount Pleasant Towne Center

Wando River

I'ON SWAMP RD

Copahee Sound

Capers Island

Dewees Island

---

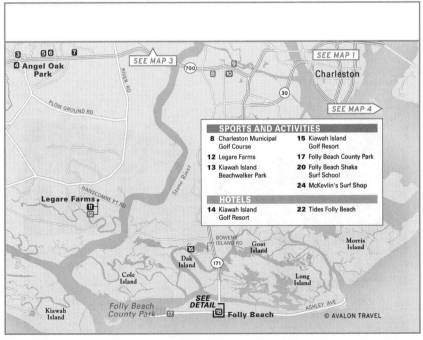

**3** **5 6** **7**
**4 Angel Oak Park**

RIVER RD

SEE MAP 3

700

**9**

**8** **10**

Charleston

**30**

SEE MAP 1

SEE MAP 4

PLOW GROUND RD

HANSCOMBE PT RD

**Legare Farms** **11**
**12**

Stono River

### SPORTS AND ACTIVITIES
**8** Charleston Municipal Golf Course
**12** Legare Farms
**13** Kiawah Island Beachwalker Park
**15** Kiawah Island Golf Resort
**17** Folly Beach County Park
**20** Folly Beach Shaka Surf School
**24** McKevlin's Surf Shop

### HOTELS
**14** Kiawah Island Golf Resort
**22** Tides Folly Beach

BOWENS ISLAND RD

Goat Island

Morris Island

**16**
Oak Island

171

Cole Island

Long Island

Kiawah Island

**Folly Beach County Park** **17**

SEE DETAIL **18** **Folly Beach**

ASHLEY AVE

© AVALON TRAVEL

# HISTORY

Unlike the many English colonies in America that were based on freedom from religious persecution, Carolina was strictly a commercial venture from the beginning. The tenure of the Lords Proprietors—the eight English aristocrats who literally owned the colony—began in 1670 when the *Carolina* finished its journey from Barbados to Albemarle Creek on the west bank of the Ashley River.

Those first colonists set up a small fortification called Charles Towne, named for Charles II, the first monarch of the Restoration. In a year they were joined by settlers from the prosperous but overcrowded British colony of Barbados, who brought a Caribbean sensibility that exists in Charleston to this day.

Finding the first Charles Towne not very fertile and vulnerable to attack from Native Americans and the Spanish, they moved to the peninsula and down to "Oyster Point," what Charlestonians now call White Point Gardens. Just above Oyster Point they set up a walled town, bounded by modern-day Water Street to the south (then a marshy creek, as the name indicates), Meeting Street to the west, Cumberland Street to the north, and the Cooper River on the east.

Growing prosperous as a trading center for deerskin from the great American interior, Charles Towne came into its own after two nearly concurrent events in the early 1700s: the decisive victory of a combined force of Carolinians and Native American allies against the fierce Yamasee people, and the final eradication of the pirate threat with the deaths of Blackbeard and Stede Bonnet.

Flush with a new spirit of independence, Charles Towne threw off the control of the anemic, disengaged Lords Proprietors, tore down the old defensive walls, and was reborn as an outward-looking, expansive, and increasingly cosmopolitan city that came to be called Charleston. With safety from hostile incursion came the time of the great rice and indigo plantations. Springing up all along the Ashley River soon after the introduction of the crops, they turned the labor and expertise of imported Africans into enormous profit for their owners. However, the planters preferred the pleasures and sea breezes of Charleston, and gradually summer homes became year-round residences.

It was during this colonial era that the indelible Charlestonian character was stamped: a hedonistic aristocracy that combined a love of carousing with a love of the arts; a code of

colonial dancing at Middleton Place

chivalry meant to both reflect a genteel spirit and reinforce the social order; and, ominously, an ever-increasing reliance on slave labor.

As the storm clouds of civil war gathered in the early 1800s, the majority of Charleston's population was of African descent, and the city had long been America's main importation point for the transatlantic slave trade. The worst fears of white Charlestonians seemed confirmed during the alleged plot by slave leader Denmark Vesey in the early 1820s to start a rebellion. The Lowcountry's reliance on slave labor put it front and center in the coming national confrontation over abolition, which came to a head with the bombardment of Fort Sumter in Charleston Harbor in April 1861.

By war's end, not only did the city lay in ruins—mostly from a disastrous fire in 1861, as well as from a 545-day Union siege—so did its way of life. Pillaged by Northern troops and freed slaves, the great plantations along the Ashley became the sites of the first strip mining in the United States as poverty-stricken owners scraped away the layer of phosphate under the topsoil to sell—perhaps with a certain poetic justice—as fertilizer.

The Holy City didn't really wake up until the great "Charleston Renaissance" of the 1920s and 1930s, when the city rediscovered art, literature, and music in the form of jazz and the world-famous Charleston dance. This was also the time that the world rediscovered Charleston. In the 1920s, George Gershwin read local author DuBose Heyward's novel *Porgy* and decided to write a score around the story. Along with lyrics written by Ira Gershwin, the three men's collaboration became the first American opera, *Porgy and Bess,* which debuted in New York in 1935. It was also during this time that a new appreciation for Charleston's history sprang up, as the Preservation Society of Charleston spearheaded the nation's first historic preservation ordinance.

World War II brought the same economic boom that came to much of the South, most notably through an expansion of the Navy Yard and the addition of a military air base. By the 1950s, the automobile suburb and a thirst for "progress" had claimed so many historic buildings that the inevitable backlash inspired the formation of the Historic Charleston Foundation, which continues to lead the fight to keep intact the Holy City's architectural legacy.

Civil rights came to Charleston in earnest with a landmark suit to integrate the

Charles Towne Landing

Charleston Municipal Golf Course in 1960. The biggest battle, however, would be the 100-day strike in 1969 against the Medical University of South Carolina—then, as now, a large employer of African Americans.

Charleston's next great renaissance—still ongoing today—came with the redevelopment of its downtown and the fostering of the tourism industry under the nearly 40-year tenure of Mayor Joe Riley, during which so much of the current visitor-friendly infrastructure became part of daily life here. Today, Charleston is completing the transition away from a military and manufacturing base to a much more diversified economy, attracting high-end professionals and artists to town.

## PLANNING YOUR TIME

Even if you're just going to confine yourself to the peninsula, plan on spending at least **two nights** in Charleston. You'll want half a day for shopping on King Street and a full day for seeing various attractions and museums. Keep in mind that one of Charleston's key sights, Fort Sumter, takes almost half a day to see once you factor in ticketing and boarding time for the ferry out to the fort and back; plan accordingly.

If you have a car, there are several great places to visit off the peninsula, especially the three plantations along the Ashley—Drayton Hall, Magnolia Plantation, and Middleton Place—and Charles Towne Landing. They are all no more than 30 minutes from downtown, and because they're roughly adjacent, you can visit all of them in a single day if you get an early start. The sites and excellent down-home restaurants on Johns Island are about 45 minutes out of downtown.

While a good time is never far away in Charleston, keep in mind that this is the South, and Sundays can get pretty slow. While the finely honed tourist infrastructure here means that there will always be something to do, the selection of open shops and restaurants dwindles on Sundays, though most other attractions keep working hours.

But for those of us who love the old city,

there's nothing like a Sunday morning in Charleston—church bells ringing, families on their way to worship, and a beguiling slowness in the air, perhaps spiced with the anticipation of that particular Charleston specialty, a hearty and delicious Sunday brunch.

## ORIENTATION

Charleston occupies a peninsula bordered by the Ashley River to the west and the Cooper River to the east, which "come together to form the Atlantic Ocean," according to the haughty phrase once taught to generations of Charleston schoolchildren. Although the lower tip of the peninsula actually points closer to southeast, that direction is regarded locally as due south, and anything toward the top of the peninsula is considered due north.

The peninsula is ringed by islands, many of which have become heavily populated suburbs. Clockwise from the top of the peninsula, they are: Daniel Island, Mount Pleasant, Isle of Palms, Sullivan's Island, Morris Island, Folly Island, and James Island. The resort island of Kiawah and the less-developed Edisto Island are farther south down the coast.

North Charleston is not only a separate municipality, it's also a different state of mind. A sprawling combination of malls, light industry, and low-income housing, it also boasts some of the more cutting-edge urban redesign activity in the area.

While Charlestonians would scoff, the truth is that Charleston proper has a surprising amount in common with Manhattan. Both are on long spits of land situated roughly north-south. Both were settled originally at the peninsula's lower end behind walled fortifications—Charleston's walls came down in 1718, while Manhattan still has its Wall Street as a reminder. Both cityscapes rely on age-old north-south streets that run nearly the whole length—Charleston's King and Meeting Streets, with only a block between them, and Manhattan's Broadway and Fifth Avenue. And like Manhattan, Charleston also has its own "Museum Mile" just off of a major green space, in Charleston's case up near Marion

Square—though certainly its offerings are not as expansive as those a short walk from New York's Central Park.

Unfortunately, also like Manhattan, parking is at a premium in downtown Charleston. Luckily the city has many reasonably priced parking garages, which I recommend that you use. But cars should be used only when necessary. Charleston is best enjoyed on foot, both because of its small size and the cozy, meandering nature of its old streets, designed not for cars and tour buses but for boots, horseshoes, and carriage wheels.

Charleston is made up of many small neighborhoods, many of them quite old. The boundaries are confusing, so your best bet is to simply look at the street signs (signage in general is excellent in Charleston). If you're in a historic neighborhood, such as the French Quarter or Ansonborough, a smaller sign above the street name will indicate that.

Other key terms you'll hear are "the Crosstown," the portion of U.S. 17 that goes across the peninsula; "Savannah Highway," the portion of U.S. 17 that traverses "West Ashley," which is the suburb across the Ashley River; "East Cooper," the area across the Cooper River that includes Mount Pleasant, Isle of Palms, and Daniel and Sullivan's Islands; and "the Neck," up where the peninsula narrows. These are the terms that locals use, and hence what you'll see in this guide.

# Sights

Though most key sights in Charleston do indeed have some tie to the city's rich history, house museums are only a subset of the attractions here. Charleston's sights are excellently integrated into its built environment, and often the enjoyment of nearby gardens or a lapping river is part of the fun.

## SOUTH OF BROAD

Wander among these narrow streets and marvel at the lovingly restored old homes, but keep in mind that almost everything down here is in private hands. Don't wander into a garden or take photos inside a window unless you're invited to do so (and given Charleston's legendary hospitality, that can happen). This residential area has no nightlife to speak of and gets almost eerily quiet after hours.

### ★ THE BATTERY

For many, the Battery is the single most iconic Charleston spot, drenched in history and boasting dramatic views in all directions. A look to the south gives you the sweeping expanse of the Cooper River with views of Fort Sumter, Castle Pinckney, Sullivan's Island, and, off to the north, the old carrier *Yorktown*

moored at Mount Pleasant. A landward look gives you a view of the adjoining peaceful **White Point Gardens,** the sumptuous mansions lining South and East Battery, and a beguiling peek behind them into some of the oldest neighborhoods in Charleston.

If you had been one of the first European visitors to this tip of the peninsula about 400 years ago, you'd have seen how it got its first name, Oyster Point: This entire area was once home to an enormous outcropping of oysters. Their shells glistened bright white in the harsh Southern sun as a ship approached from sea, hence its subsequent name, White Point. Although the oysters are long gone and much of the area you're walking on is actually reclaimed marsh, the Battery and White Point Gardens are still a balm for the soul.

Once the bustling (and sometimes seedy) heart of Charleston's maritime activity, the Battery was where "the gentleman pirate" Stede Bonnet and 21 of his men were hanged in 1718. As you might imagine, the area got its name for hosting cannons during the War of 1812, with the current distinctive seawall structure built in the 1850s.

Contrary to popular belief, no guns fired

from here on Fort Sumter, as they would have been out of range. However, many thankfully inoperable cannons, mortars, and piles of shot still reside here, much to the delight of kids of all ages. This is where Charlestonians gathered in a giddy, party-like atmosphere to watch the shelling of Fort Sumter in 1861, blissfully ignorant of the horrors to come. A short time later, the North would return the favor as the Battery and all of Charleston up to Broad Street would bear the brunt of shelling during the long siege of the city (the rest was out of reach of Union guns).

Now, the Battery is a place to relax, not fight. The relaxation starts with the fact that there's usually plenty of free parking all along Battery Street. A promenade all around the periphery is a great place to stroll or jog. Add the calming, almost constant sea breeze and the meditative influence of the wide, blue Cooper River and you'll see why this land's end—once so martial in nature—is now a favorite place for after-church family gatherings, travelers, love-struck couples, and weddings (about 200 a year at the gazebo in White Point Gardens).

Still, military history is never far away in Charleston, and one of the chief landmarks at the Battery is the USS *Hobson* Memorial, which remembers the sacrifice of the men of that vessel when it sank after a collision with the carrier USS *Wasp* in 1952.

Look for the three-story private residence where East Battery curves northward. You won't be taking any tours of it, but you should be aware that it's the **DeSaussure House** (1 E. Battery St.), best known in Charleston history for hosting rowdy celebratory crowds on the roof and the piazzas to watch the 34-hour shelling of Fort Sumter in 1861.

**MAP 1**: S. Battery St. and Murray Blvd., 843/724-7321; daily 24 hours; free

## EDMONDSTON-ALSTON HOUSE

The most noteworthy single attraction on the Battery is the 1825 Edmondston-Alston House, the only Battery home open to the public for tours. This is one of the most unique and well-preserved historic homes in the United States, thanks to the ongoing efforts of the Alston family, who acquired the house from shipping merchant Charles Edmondston for $15,500 after the Panic of 1837 and still lives on the third floor (tours only visit the first two stories).

Over 90 percent of the home's furnishings are original items from the Alston era, a percentage that's almost unheard of in the world of house museums. (Today, the house is owned and administered by the Middleton Place Foundation, best known for its stewardship of Middleton Place along the Ashley River.) You can still see the original paper bag used to store the house's deeds and mortgages. There's also a copy of South Carolina's Ordinance of Secession and some interesting memorabilia from the golden days of Race Week, that time in February when all of Charleston society came out to bet on horses, carouse, and show off their finery. The Edmondston-Alston House has withstood storms, fires, earthquakes, and Yankee shelling, due in no small part to its sturdy construction; its masonry walls are two bricks thick, and it features both interior and exterior shutters. Originally built in the Federal style, second owner Charles Alston added several Greek Revival elements, notably the parapet, balcony, and piazza, from which General P. G. T. Beauregard watched the attack on Fort Sumter.

**MAP 1**: 21 E. Battery St., 843/722-7171, www. middletonplace.org; Tues.-Sat. 10am-4:30pm, Sun.-Mon. 1pm-4:30pm; $12 adults, $8 students

## ★ RAINBOW ROW

At 79-107 East Bay Street, between Tradd and Elliot Streets, is one of the most photographed sights in the United States: colorful Rainbow Row. The reason for its name becomes obvious when you see the array of pastel-colored mansions, all facing the Cooper River. The bright, historically accurate colors—nine of them, to be exact—are one of the many vestiges you'll see around town of Charleston's Caribbean heritage, a legacy of the English settlers from

# Know Your Charleston Houses

Charleston's homes boast not only a long pedigree, but an interesting and unique one as well. Here are the basics of local architecture:

**Single House:** Thus named for its single-room width. With full-length piazzas, or long verandas, on the south side to take advantage of breezes, the single house is perhaps the nation's first sustainable house design. The house is lengthwise on the lot, with the entrance on the side. This means the "backyard" is actually the side yard. Church Street has great examples, including 90, 92, and 94 Church Street, and the oldest single house in town, the 1730 Robert Brewton House (71 Church St.).

**Double House:** This layout is two rooms wide with a central hallway and a porched facade facing the street. Double houses often had separate carriage houses. The Aiken-Rhett and Heyward-Washington Houses are good examples.

a Charleston single house

**Charleston Green:** This uniquely Charlestonian color—extremely dark green that looks pitch black in low light—has its roots in the aftermath of the Civil War. The government distributed surplus black paint to contribute to the reconstruction of the ravaged peninsula, but Charlestonians were too proud to use it as-is. So they added a tiny bit of yellow, producing Charleston green.

**Earthquake Bolt:** Due to structural damage after the 1886 earthquake, many buildings were retrofitted with one or more wall-to-wall iron rods to keep them stable. The rod was capped at both ends by a "gib plate," often disguised with a decorative element such as a lion's head, an S or X shape, or some other design. Notable examples are at 235 Meeting Street, 198 East Bay Street, 407 King Street, and 51 East Battery (a rare star design); 190 East Bay Street is unusual for having both an X and an S plate on the same building.

**Joggling Board:** This long (10-15 ft.) flexible plank of cypress, palm, or pine with a handle at each end served various recreational purposes. Babies were bounced to sleep, small children used it as a trampoline, and it was also a method of courtship. A couple would start out at opposite ends and bounce until they met in the middle.

**Carolopolis Award:** The Preservation Society of Charleston hands out these badges, to be mounted near the doorway, to local homeowners who have renovated historic properties downtown. On the award is "Carolopolis," the Latinized name of the city; "Condita AD 1670," the Latin word for "founding" with the date of Charleston's inception; and the date the award was given.

**Ironwork:** Wrought iron was a widely used ornament before the mid-1800s. Charleston's best-known blacksmith, Philip Simmons, worked in wrought iron. His masterpieces are visible most notably at the Philip Simmons Garden (91 Anson St.), a gate for the Visitors Center (375 Meeting St.), and the Philip Simmons Children's Garden at Josiah Smith Tennent House (Blake St. and E. Bay St.). Chevaux-de-frise are iron bars on top of a wall that project menacing spikes. They became popular after the Denmark Vesey slave revolt conspiracy of 1822. The best example is at the Miles Brewton House (27 King St.).

Rainbow Row

the colony of Barbados who were among the city's first citizens.

The homes are unusually old for this fire-, hurricane-, and earthquake-ravaged city, with most dating from 1730 to 1750. As you admire Rainbow Row from across East Battery, you're actually walking on what used to be water. These houses were originally right on the Cooper River, their lower stories serving as storefronts on the wharf. The street was created later on top of landfill, or "made land" as it's called locally. Besides its grace and beauty, Rainbow Row is of vital importance to American historic preservation. These were the first Charleston homes to be renovated and brought back from early-20th-century seediness. The restoration projects on Rainbow Row directly inspired the creation of the Preservation Society of Charleston, the first such group in the United States.

Continue walking up the High Battery past Rainbow Row and find Water Street. This aptly named little avenue was in fact a creek in the early days, acting as the southern border of the original walled city. The large brick building on the seaward side housing the Historic Charleston Foundation sits on the site of the old Granville bastion, a key defensive point in the wall.

**MAP 1**: 79-107 E. Bay St.

### NATHANIEL RUSSELL HOUSE

Considered one of Charleston's grandest homes despite being built by an outsider from Rhode Island, the Nathaniel Russell House is now a National Historic Landmark and one of the country's best examples of neoclassicism. Built in 1808 for the then-princely sum of $80,000 by Nathaniel Russell, aka "King of the Yankees," the home is furnished as accurately as possible to represent not only the lifestyle of the Russell family, but also the 18 African American servants who shared the premises. The house was eventually bought by the Allston family, who amid the poverty of the Civil War and Reconstruction decided in 1870 to sell it to the Sisters of Charity of Our Lady of Mercy for use as a school for young Catholic women.

Restorationists have identified 22 layers of paint within the home, which barely survived a tornado in 1811, got away with only minimal damage in the 1886 earthquake, and was damaged extensively by Hurricane Hugo in 1989 (and has since been repaired). As with fine antebellum homes throughout coastal South Carolina and Georgia, the use of faux finishes is prevalent throughout, mimicking surfaces such as marble, wood, and lapis lazuli. Visitors are often most impressed by the Nathaniel Russell House's magnificent "flying" spiral staircase, a work of such sublime carpentry and engineering that it needs no external support, twisting upward of its own volition.

When you visit, keep in mind that you're in the epicenter of not only Charleston's historic preservation movement but perhaps the nation's as well. In 1955, the Nathaniel Russell House was the first major project of the Historic Charleston Foundation, which raised $65,000 to purchase it. Two years later, admission fees from the house would support Historic Charleston's groundbreaking revolving fund for preservation, the prototype for many such successful programs. For an extra $6, you can gain admission to the Aiken-Rhett House farther uptown, also administered by the Historic Charleston Foundation.

MAP 1: 51 Meeting St., 843/724-8481, www. historiccharleston.org; Mon.-Sat. 10am-5pm, Sun. 2pm-5pm, last tour begins 4:30pm; $12 adults, $5 children

## CALHOUN MANSION

The single largest of Charleston's surviving grand homes, the 1876 Calhoun Mansion boasts 35 opulent rooms (with 23 fireplaces!) in a striking Italianate design taking up a whopping 24,000 square feet. The grounds feature some charming garden spaces. A 90-minute "grand tour" is available for $75 per person; call for an appointment. Though the interiors at this privately run house are packed with antiques and furnishings, not all of them are accurate for the period.

MAP 1: 16 Meeting St., 843/722-8205, www. calhounmansion.net; tours daily 11am-5pm; $16

## MILES BREWTON HOUSE

A short distance from the Nathaniel Russell House but much less viewed by visitors, the circa-1769 Miles Brewton House, now a private residence, is maybe the best example of Georgian-Palladian architecture in the world. The almost medieval wrought-iron fencing, or chevaux-de-frise, was added in 1822 after rumors of a slave uprising spread through town. This imposing double house was the site of not one but two headquarters of occupying armies, that of British general Henry Clinton in the Revolution and the federal garrison after the end of the Civil War. The great Susan Pringle Frost, principal founder of the Preservation Society of Charleston and a Brewton descendant, grew up here.

MAP 1: 27 King St.

## HEYWARD-WASHINGTON HOUSE

The Heyward-Washington House takes the regional practice of naming a historic home for the two most significant names in its pedigree to its logical extreme. Built in 1772 by the father of Declaration of Independence signer Thomas Heyward Jr., the house also hosted George Washington during the president's visit to Charleston in 1791. It's now owned and operated by the Charleston Museum. The main attraction at the Heyward-Washington House is its masterful woodwork, exemplified by the cabinetry of legendary Charleston carpenter Thomas Elfe. You'll see his work all over the house, from the mantles to a Chippendale chair. Look for his signature, a figure eight with four diamonds.

MAP 1: 87 Church St., 843/722-0354, www. charlestonmuseum.org; Mon.-Sat. 10am-5pm, Sun. noon-5pm; $12 adults, $5 children, combo tickets to Charleston Museum and Manigault House available

## CABBAGE ROW

You know the addresses that make up Cabbage Row better as "Catfish Row" in Gershwin's opera Porgy and Bess (itself based on the book Porgy by the great Charleston author DuBose Heyward, who lived at 76 Church St.). Today this complex—which once housed 10 families—next to the Heyward-Washington House is certainly upgraded from years past, but the row still has the humble appeal of the tenement housing it once was, primarily for freed African American slaves after the Civil War. The house nearby at 94 Church Street was where John C. Calhoun and others drew up the infamous Nullification Acts that eventually led to the South's secession.

MAP 1: 89-91 Church St.

## ST. MICHAEL'S EPISCOPAL CHURCH

The oldest church in South Carolina, St. Michael's Episcopal Church is actually the second sanctuary on this spot. The first church here was made out of black cypress and was called St. Philip's, or "the English Church," which was later rebuilt on Church Street. Although the designer is not known, we do know that work on this sanctuary in the style of Christopher Wren began in 1752 as a response to the overflowing congregation at the rebuilt St. Philip's, and it didn't finish until 1761. Other than a small addition on the southeast corner in 1883, the St. Michael's you see today is virtually unchanged, including the massive pulpit, outsized in the style of the time.

Services here over the years hosted such luminaries as the Marquis de Lafayette, George Washington, and Robert E. Lee, the latter two of whom are known to have sat in the "governor's pew." Two signers of the U.S. Constitution, John Rutledge and Charles Cotesworth Pinckney, are buried in the sanctuary. The 186-foot steeple, painted black during the Revolution in a futile effort to disguise it from British guns, actually sank eight inches after the earthquake of 1886. Inside the tower, the famous "bells of St. Michael's" have an interesting story to tell, having made seven transatlantic voyages for a variety of reasons. They were forged in London's Whitechapel Foundry and sent over in 1764, only to be brought back as a war prize during the Revolution, after which they were returned to the church. Damaged during the Civil War, they were sent back to the foundry of their birth to be recast and returned to Charleston. In 1989 they were damaged by Hurricane Hugo, sent back to Whitechapel yet again, and returned to St. Michael's in 1993. Throughout the life span of the bells, the clock tower has continued to tell time, although the minute hand wasn't added until 1849.

St. Michael's offers informal, free guided tours to visitors after Sunday services; contact the greeter for more information.

MAP 1: 71 Broad St., 843/723-0603; services Sun. 8am and 10:30am, tours available after services

## FOUR CORNERS OF LAW

No guidebook is complete without a mention of the famous intersection of Broad and Meeting Streets, nicknamed "Four Corners of Law" for its confluence of federal law (the Post Office building), state law (the state courthouse), municipal law (City Hall), and God's law (St. Michael's Episcopal Church). The phrase "Four Corners of Law" was actually popularized by *Ripley's Believe It or Not!* Still, there's no doubt that this intersection has been key to Charleston from the beginning. Meeting Street was laid out around 1672 and takes its name from the White Meeting House of early Dissenters, meaning non-Anglicans. Broad Street was also referred to as Cooper Street in the early days. Right in the middle of the street once stood the very first statue in the United States, a figure of William Pitt erected in 1766.

MAP 1: Broad St. and Meeting St.

# WATERFRONT
## THE OLD EXCHANGE AND PROVOST DUNGEON

The Old Exchange and Provost Dungeon at the intersection of East Bay and Meeting Streets is absolutely brimming with history. The last building erected by the British before the American Revolution, it's also one of the three most historically significant colonial buildings in the United States, along with Philadelphia's Independence Hall and Boston's Faneuil Hall.

This is actually the former Royal Exchange and Custom House, the cellar of which served as a British prison. The complex was built in 1771 over a portion of the original 1698 seawall, a portion of which you can see today during the short but fascinating tour of the "dungeon" (actually built as a warehouse). Three of Charleston's four signers of the Declaration of Independence did time downstairs for sedition against the crown. Later, happier times were experienced in

# The Great Charleston Earthquake

Note the 'earthquake bolts' on this Charleston building.

The Charleston peninsula is bordered by three faults: the Woodstock Fault above North Charleston, the Charleston Fault running along the east bank of the Cooper River, and the Ashley Fault to the west of the Ashley River. On August 31, 1886, one of them buckled, causing one of the most damaging earthquakes ever to hit the United States.

The earthquake of 1886 was signaled by foreshocks earlier that week. Residents of Summerville, 20 miles up the Ashley River, felt a small earthquake after midnight on Friday, August 27. Most slept through it. But soon after dawn a larger shock came, complete with a loud bang, causing many to run outside their houses. That Saturday afternoon another tremor hit Summerville, breaking windows and throwing a bed against a wall in one home. Still, Charlestonians remained unconcerned. Then, that Tuesday at 9:50pm came the big one. With an epicenter somewhere near the Middleton Place Plantation, the Charleston earthquake is estimated to have measured about 7 on the Richter scale. Tremors were felt across half the country, with the ground shaking in Chicago and a church damaged in Indianapolis. A dam 120 miles away in Aiken gave way, washing a train off the tracks. Cracks opened up parallel to the Ashley River, with part of the riverbank falling into the water. Thousands of chimneys all over the state fell or were rendered useless. A Charleston minister at his summer home in Asheville, North Carolina, described a noise like the sound of wheels driving straight up the mountain, followed by the sound of many railroad cars going by. A moment later, one corner of his house lifted off the ground and slammed back down again. The quake brought a series of "sand blows," a phenomenon where craters open and spew sand and water into the air. In Charleston's case, some of the craters were 20 feet wide, shooting debris another 20 feet into the air. The whole event lasted less than a minute.

In crowded Charleston, the damage was horrific: over 2,000 buildings destroyed, a quarter of the city's value gone, 27 killed immediately and almost 100 more to die from injuries and disease. Because of the large numbers of newly homeless, tent cities sprang up in every available park and green space. The American Red Cross's first field mission soon brought some relief, but the scarcity of food and especially fresh water made life difficult.

Almost every surviving building had experienced structural damage, in some cases severe. This led to the widespread use of the "earthquake bolt" now seen throughout older Charleston homes. Essentially acting as a very long screw with a washer on each end, the idea of the earthquake bolt is simple: Poke a long iron rod through two walls that need stabilizing, and cap the ends. Charleston being Charleston, the caps were often decorated with a pattern or symbol.

The seismic activity of Charleston's earthquake was so intense that more than 300 aftershocks occurred in the 35 years after the event. Geologists think that most seismic events measured in the region today are probably also aftershocks.

the ballroom upstairs, as it was here that the state selected its delegates to the Continental Congress and ratified the U.S. Constitution; it's also where George Washington took a spin on the dance floor during his raucous "Farewell Tour" in 1791. While the highlight for most is the basement dungeon, or provost, where the infamous "gentleman pirate" Stede Bonnet was imprisoned in 1718 before being hanged, visitors shouldn't miss the sunny upstairs ballroom and its selection of Washington-oriented history.

MAP 1: 122 E. Bay St., 843/727-2165, www. oldexchange.com; daily 9am-5pm; $10 adults, $5 children and students

## WATERFRONT PARK

Dubbing it "this generation's gift to the future," Mayor Joe Riley made this eight-acre project another part of his downtown renovation. Situated on Concord Street roughly between Exchange Street and Vendue Range, Waterfront Park was, like many waterfront locales in Charleston, built on what used to be marsh and water. This particularly massive chunk of "made land" juts about a football field's length farther out than the old waterline. Visitors and locals alike enjoy the relaxing vista of Charleston Harbor, often from the many swinging benches arranged in an unusual front-to-back, single-file pattern all down the pier. On the end you can find viewing binoculars to see the various sights out on the Cooper River, chief among them the USS *Yorktown* at Patriots Point and the big bridge to Mount Pleasant. Children will enjoy the large "Vendue" wading fountain at the park's entrance off Vendue Range, while a bit farther south is the large and quite artful Pineapple Fountain with its surrounding wading pool. Contemporary art lovers of all ages will appreciate the nearby **Waterfront Park City Gallery** (34 Prioleau St., www.citygalleryat-waterfrontpark.com, Tues.-Fri. 10am-6pm, Sat.-Sun. noon-5pm, free).

MAP 1: Concord St., 843/724-7327; daily dawn-dusk; free

## ★ SOUTH CAROLINA AQUARIUM

If you've been to the more expansive aquariums in Monterey or Boston, you might be disappointed at the breadth of offerings at the South Carolina Aquarium. Nonetheless, it's clean and well done and is a great place for the whole family to have some fun while getting educated about the rich aquatic life off the coast and throughout this small but ecologically diverse state.

the Old Exchange and Provost Dungeon

# Mayor Joe's Legacy

the entrance to Joseph P. Riley Jr. Park

Few cities anywhere have been as greatly influenced by one mayor as Charleston has by Joseph P. "Joe" Riley, who finally declined to run for reelection in 2015 after his 10th four-year term. "Mayor Joe," or just "Joe," as he's usually called, is not only responsible for the majority of redevelopment in the city; he also set the bar for its award-winning tourism industry.

Riley won his first mayoral race at the age of 32, the second Irish American mayor of the city. The lawyer, Citadel grad, and former member of the state legislature had a clear vision for his administration: to bring unprecedented numbers of women and minorities into city government, rejuvenate then-seedy King Street, and enlarge the city's tax base by annexing surrounding areas (during Riley's tenure the city grew from 16.7 square miles to over 100).

Here's only a partial list of the major projects and events Mayor Joe has made happen in Charleston:

- Charleston Maritime Center
- Charleston Place
- Children's Museum of the Lowcountry
- Hampton Park rehabilitation
- King Street-Market Street retail district
- Joseph P. Riley Jr. Park (named after the mayor at the insistence of city council, over his objections)

- MOJA Arts Festival
- Piccolo Spoleto
- South Carolina Aquarium
- Spoleto USA
- Waterfront Park
- West Ashley Bikeway & Greenway

When you enter you're greeted with the 15,000-gallon Carolina Seas tank, with placid nurse sharks and vicious-looking moray eels. Other exhibits highlight the five key South Carolina ecosystems: beach, salt marsh, coastal plain, piedmont, and mountain forest. Another neat display is the Touch Tank, a hands-on collection of invertebrates found along the coast, such as sea urchins and horseshoe crabs. The pièce de résistance, however, is certainly the three-story Great Ocean Tank with its hundreds of deeper-water marine creatures, including sharks, puffer fish, and sea turtles.

A key part of the aquarium's research and outreach efforts is the Turtle Hospital, which, in partnership with the state of South Carolina, attempts to rehabilitate and save sick and injured specimens. The hospital has saved many dozens of sea turtles, the first one being a 270-pound female affectionately known as "Edisto Mama." New in 2016, the Sea Turtle Rescue expansion showcases these efforts.

**MAP 1:** 100 Aquarium Wharf, 843/720-1990, www. scaquarium.org; Mar.-Aug. daily 9am-5pm, Sept.-Feb. daily 9am-4pm; $29.95 adults, $22.95 children, 4D film extra, combo tickets with Fort Sumter tour available

## ★ FORT SUMTER NATIONAL MONUMENT

This is it: the place that brought about the beginning of the Civil War, a Troy for modern times. Though many historians insist the war would have happened regardless of President Lincoln's decision to keep Fort Sumter in federal hands, the stated casus belli was Major Robert Anderson's refusal to surrender the fort when requested to do so in the early morning hours of April 12, 1861. A few hours later came the first shot of the war, fired from Fort Johnson by Confederate captain George James. That 10-inch mortar shell, a signal for the general bombardment to begin, exploded above Fort Sumter, and nothing in Charleston or the South or the United States would ever be the same again. Notorious secessionist Edmund Ruffin gets credit for firing the first

shot in anger, only moments after James's signal shell, from a battery at Cummings Point. Ruffin's 64-pound projectile scored a direct hit, smashing into the fort's southwest corner. The first return shot from Fort Sumter was fired by none other than Captain Abner Doubleday, the man once credited as the father of baseball. The first death of the Civil War also happened at Fort Sumter—not during the Confederate bombardment but on the day after. U.S. Army private Daniel Hough died when the cannon he was loading, to be fired as part of a 100-gun surrender salute to the Stars and Stripes, exploded prematurely. Today the battered but still-standing Fort Sumter remains astride the entrance to Charleston Harbor on an artificial 70,000-ton sandbar. Sumter was part of the so-called Third System of fortifications ordered after the War of 1812. Interestingly, the fort was still not quite finished when the Confederate guns opened up on it 50 years later, and it never enjoyed its intended full complement of 135 big guns.

As you might expect, you can only visit by boat, specifically boats run by the approved concessionaire **Fort Sumter Tours** (843/881-7337, www.fortsumtertours.com, $18 adults, $11 ages 6-11, $16 seniors). Once at the fort, there's no charge for admission. Ferries leave from Liberty Square at Aquarium Wharf on the peninsula three times a day during the high season (Apr.-Oct.); call or check the website for times. Make sure to arrive about 30 minutes before the ferry departs. You can also get to Fort Sumter by ferry from Patriots Point at Mount Pleasant through the same concessionaire.

Budget at least 2.5 hours for the whole trip, including an hour at Fort Sumter. At Liberty Square on the peninsula is the **Fort Sumter Visitor Education Center** (340 Concord St., www.nps.gov/fosu, daily 8:30am-5pm, free), so you can learn more about where you're about to go. Once at the fort, you can be enlightened by the regular ranger talks on the fort's history and construction (generally at 11am and 2:30pm), take in the interpretive

The ferry to Fort Sumter departs next door to the South Carolina Aquarium.

exhibits throughout the site, and enjoy the view of the spires of the Holy City from afar. For many, though, the highlight is the boat trip itself, with beautiful views of Charleston Harbor and the islands of the Cooper River estuary. If you want to skip Sumter, you can still take an enjoyable 90-minute ferry ride around the harbor and past the fort on the affiliated **Spiritline Cruises** (800/789-3678, www.spiritlinecruises.com, departs 2-3 times daily Mar.-Nov., $22 adults, $12 ages 6-11). Ferries depart from Liberty Square at Aquarium Wharf on the peninsula. Purchase tickets at the visitor center.

Some visitors are disappointed to find many of the fort's gun embrasures bricked over. This was done during the Spanish-American War, when the old fort was turned into an earthwork and the newer Battery Huger (Huge-EE) was built on top of it.
MAP 1: 843/883-3123, www.nps.gov/fosu; hours seasonal; free

## FRENCH QUARTER
### CIRCULAR CONGREGATIONAL CHURCH
The historic Circular Congregational Church has one of the most interesting pedigrees of any house of worship in Charleston, which

is saying a lot. Services were originally held on the site of the "White Meeting House," for which Meeting Street is named; they were moved here beginning in 1681 and catered to a polyglot mix of Congregationalists, Presbyterians, and Huguenots. For that reason it was often called the Church of Dissenters ("dissenter" being the common term at the time for anyone not an Anglican). As with many structures in town, the 1886 earthquake necessitated a rebuild, and the current edifice dates from 1891. Ironically, in this municipality called "the Holy City" for its many high spires, the Circular Church has no steeple and instead stays low to the ground in an almost medieval fashion. Look for the adjacent meetinghouse, a green-friendly addition that houses the congregation's Christian outreach, has geothermal heating and cooling, and boasts Charleston's only vegetative roof.
MAP 1: 150 Meeting St., 843/577-6400, www.circularchurch.org; services fall-spring Sun. 11am, summer Sun. 10:15am, tours Mon.-Fri. 10:30am

### DOCK STREET THEATRE
The Dock Street Theatre, right down the street from the Huguenot Church, is where any thespian or lover of the stage must pay homage to this incarnation of the first theater built

Dock Street Theatre

in North America. In a distressingly familiar Charleston story, the original 1736 Dock Street Theatre burned down. A second theater opened on the same site in 1754. That building was in turn demolished for a grander edifice in 1773, which, you guessed it, also burned down. The current building dates from 1809, when the Planter's Hotel was built near the site of the original Dock Street Theatre. (So why is the theater not actually on Dock Street? Because that street on the theater's north side was renamed Queen Street, the name it bears today.) To mark the theater's centennial, the hotel added a stage facility in 1835, and it's that building you see now. For the theater's second centennial, the Works Progress Administration completely refurbished Dock Street back into a working theater in time to distract Charlestonians from the pains of the Great Depression. In addition to a very active and well-regarded annual season from the resident Charleston Stage Company, the 464-seat venue has hosted umpteen events of the Spoleto Festival over the past three decades and since its renovation continues to do so.
**MAP 1:** 135 Church St., 843/720-3968, www.charlestonstage.com; box office Mon.-Fri. 1pm-5pm, tickets $63-67

## FRENCH HUGUENOT CHURCH

One of the oldest congregations in town, the French Huguenot Church also has the distinction of being the only remaining independent Huguenot Church in the country. Founded around 1681 by French Calvinists, the church had about 450 congregants by 1700. While they were refugees from religious persecution, they weren't destitute, as they had to pay for their passage to America. As is the case with so many historic churches in the area, the building you see isn't the original sanctuary. The first church was built on this site in 1687 and became known as the "Church of Tides" because at that time the Cooper River lapped at its property line. This sanctuary was deliberately destroyed as a firebreak during the great conflagration of 1796. The church was replaced in 1800, but that building was in turn demolished in favor of the picturesque, stucco-coated Gothic Revival sanctuary you see today, which was completed in 1845 and subsequently survived Union shelling and the 1886 earthquake. Does the church look kind of Dutch to you? There's a good reason for that. In their diaspora, French Huguenots spent a lot of time in Holland and became influenced by the tidy sensibilities of the Dutch

# French Huguenots

the French Huguenot Church

A visitor can't spend a few hours in Charleston without coming across many French-sounding names. Some are common surnames, such as Ravenel, Manigault (MAN-i-go), Gaillard, Laurens, or Huger (huge-EE). Some are street or place names, such as Mazyck or Legare (Le-GREE). The Gallic influence in Charleston was of the Calvinist Protestant variety. Known as Huguenots, these French immigrants—refugees from an increasingly intolerant Catholic regime in France—were numerous enough in the settlement by the 1690s that they were granted full citizenship and property rights if they swore allegiance to the British crown.

Unlike other colonies, Carolina never put much of a premium on religious conformity, a trait that exists to this day despite the area's overall conservatism. And unlike many who fled European monarchies to come to the New World, the French Huguenots were far from poverty-stricken. Most arrived already well educated and skilled in one or more useful trades. In Charleston's early days, they were mostly farmers or tar burners (makers of tar and pitch for maritime use). Their pragmatism and work ethic would lead them to higher positions in local society, such as lawyers, judges, and politicians. One of the wealthiest Charlestonians, the merchant Gabriel Manigault, was by some accounts the richest person in the American colonies during the early 1700s. South Carolina's most famous French Huguenot was Francis Marion, the "Swamp Fox" of Revolutionary War fame. Born on the Santee River, Marion grew up in Georgetown and is now interred near Moncks Corner.

The library of the **Huguenot Society of Carolina** (138 Logan St., 843/723-3235, www. huguenotsociety.org, Mon.-Fri. 9am-2pm) is a great research tool for anyone interested in French Protestant history and genealogy.

To this day, the spiritual home of Charleston's Huguenots is the same as always: the French Huguenot Church on Church Street, one of the earliest congregations in the city. The church still holds a liturgy in French every April.

people. The history of the circa-1845 organ is interesting as well. A rare "tracker" organ, so named for its ultrafast linkage between the keys and the pipe valves, it was built by famed organ builder Henry Erben. After the fall of Charleston in 1865, Union troops had begun dismantling the instrument for shipment to New York when the church organist, T. P. O'Neale, successfully pleaded with them to let it stay.

Sunday services are conducted in English now, but a single annual service in French is still celebrated in April. The unique Huguenot Cross of Languedoc, which you'll occasionally see ornamenting the church, is essentially a Maltese Cross, its eight points representing the eight beatitudes. Between the four arms of the cross are four fleurs-de-lis, the age-old French symbol of purity.

MAP 1: 44 Queen St., 843/722-4385, www. frenchhuguenotchurch.org; liturgy Sun. 10:30am

## OLD POWDER MAGAZINE

The Old Powder Magazine may be small, but the building is quite historically significant. The 1713 edifice is the oldest public building in South Carolina and the only one remaining from the days of the Lords Proprietors. As the name indicates, this was where the city's gunpowder was stored during the Revolution. The magazine is designed to implode rather than explode in the event of a direct hit. This is another labor of love of the Historic Charleston Foundation, which has leased the building—which from a distance looks curiously like an ancient Byzantine church—from The Colonial Dames since 1993. It was opened to the public as an attraction in 1997. Now directly across the street from a huge parking garage, the site has continuing funding issues, so occasionally the hours for tours can be erratic. Inside, you'll see displays, a section of the original brick, and an exposed earthquake rod. Next door is the privately owned, circa-1709 **Trott's Cottage**, the first brick dwelling in Charleston.

MAP 1: 79 Cumberland St., 843/722-9350, www. powdermag.org; Mon.-Sat. 10am-4pm, Sun. 1pm-4pm; $5 adults, $2 children

## OLD SLAVE MART MUSEUM

Slave auctions became big business in the South after 1808, when the United States banned the importation of slaves, thus increasing both price and demand. The auctions generally took place in public buildings where everyone could watch the wrenching spectacle. In the 1850s, public auctions in Charleston were put to a stop when city leaders discovered that visitors from European nations—all of which had banned slavery years before—were horrified at the practice. The slave trade was moved indoors to "marts" near the waterfront, where sales could be conducted out of the public eye. The last remaining such structure is the Old Slave Mart Museum. Built in 1859, and originally known as Ryan's Mart after the builder, it was only in service a short time before the outbreak of the Civil War. The last auction was held in November 1863. After the war, the Slave Mart became a tenement, and then in 1938 an African American history museum. The city of Charleston acquired the building in the 1980s and reopened it as a small museum in late 2007. There are two main areas: the orientation area, where visitors learn about the transatlantic slave trade and the architectural history of the building itself, and the main exhibit area, where visitors can see documents, tools, and displays recreating what happened inside during this sordid chapter in local history and celebrating the resilience of the area's African American population.

MAP 1: 6 Chalmers St., 843/958-6467, www. charleston-sc.gov; Mon.-Sat. 9am-5pm; $7 adults, $5 children, free under age 6

## ★ ST. PHILIP'S EPISCOPAL CHURCH

With a pedigree dating back to the colony's fledgling years, St. Philip's Episcopal Church is the oldest Anglican congregation south of Virginia. That pedigree gets a little complicated and downright tragic at times, but any connoisseur of Charleston history needs to be clear on the fine points: The first St. Philip's was built in 1680 at the corner of Meeting

St. Philip's Episcopal Church

Street and Broad Street, the present site of St. Michael's Episcopal Church. That first St. Philip's was badly damaged by a hurricane in 1710, and the city fathers approved the building of a new sanctuary dedicated to the saint on Church Street. However, that building was nearly destroyed by yet another hurricane during construction. Fighting with local Native Americans further delayed rebuilding in 1721. Alas, the second St. Philip's burned to the ground in 1835—a distressingly common fate for so many old buildings in this area. Construction immediately began on a replacement, and it's that building you see today. Heavily damaged by Hurricane Hugo in 1989, a $4.5 million renovation kept the church usable. So, to recap: St. Philip's was originally on the site of the present St. Michael's. And while St. Philip's is the oldest congregation in South Carolina, St. Michael's has the oldest physical church building in the state. Are we clear?

South Carolina's great statesman John C. Calhoun—who ironically despised Charlestonians for what he saw as their loose morals—was originally buried across Church Street in the former "stranger's churchyard," or West Cemetery, after his death in 1850. (Charles Pinckney and Edward Rutledge are two other notable South Carolinians buried here.) But near the end of the Civil War, Calhoun's body was moved to an unmarked grave closer to the sanctuary in an attempt to hide its location from Union troops, who it was feared would go out of their way to wreak vengeance on the tomb of one of slavery's staunchest advocates and the man who invented the doctrine of nullification. In 1880, with Reconstruction in full swing, the state legislature directed and funded the building of the large memorial to Calhoun in the West Cemetery.

**MAP 1:** 142 Church St., 843/722-7734, www.stphilipschurchsc.org; sanctuary Mon.-Fri. 10am-noon and 2pm-4pm, services Sun. 8:15am

# NORTH OF BROAD
## CONFEDERATE MUSEUM

Located on the second floor of City Market's iconic main building, Market Hall on Meeting Street, the small but spirited Confederate

Museum hosts an interesting collection of Civil War memorabilia, with an emphasis on the military side, and is the local headquarters of the United Daughters of the Confederacy. Perhaps its best contribution, however, is its research library.

MAP 1: 188 Meeting St., 843/723-1541; Tues.-Sat. 11am-3:30pm; $5 adults, $3 children, cash only

## GIBBES MUSEUM OF ART

The Gibbes Museum of Art is one of those rare Southern museums that manages a good blend of the modern and the traditional, the local and the international. It's even more impressive these days, coming off a multi-million-dollar renovation intended to restore it to its full beaux arts glory, and an expansion that will increase gallery space by a third. Begun in 1905 as the Gibbes Art Gallery—the final wish of James Shoolbred Gibbes, who willed $100,000 for its construction—the complex has grown through the years in size and influence. The key addition to the original beaux arts building came in 1978 with the addition of the modern wing in the rear, which effectively doubled the museum's display space. Shortly thereafter the permanent collection and temporary exhibit space was also expanded. Serendipitously, these renovations enabled the Gibbes to become the key visual arts venue for the Spoleto Festival, begun about the same time. The influential Gibbes Art School in the early 20th century formed a close association with the Woodstock School in New York, bringing important ties and prestige to the fledgling institution. Georgia O'Keeffe, who taught college for a time in Columbia, brought an exhibit here in 1955. The first solo show by an African American artist came here in 1974 with an exhibit of the work of William H. Johnson. Don't miss the nice little garden and its centerpiece, the 1972 fountain and sculpture of Persephone by Marshall Fredericks.

MAP 1: 135 Meeting St., 843/722-2706, www. gibbesmuseum.org; Tues.-Sat. 10am-5pm, Sun. 1pm-5pm; $9 adults, $7 students, $5 ages 6-12

## KAHAL KADOSH BETH ELOHIM REFORM TEMPLE

The birthplace of Reform Judaism in the United States and the oldest continuously active synagogue in the nation is Kahal Kadosh Beth Elohim Reform Temple. The congregation—*Kahal Kadosh* means "holy community" in Hebrew—was founded in 1749, with the current temple dating from 1840 and built in the Greek Revival style so popular at the time. The temple's Reform roots came about indirectly because of the great fire of 1838. In rebuilding, some congregants wanted to introduce musical instruments into the temple—previously a no-no—in the form of an organ. The Orthodox contingent lost the debate, and so the new building became the first home of Reform Judaism in the country, a fitting testament to Charleston's long-standing ecumenical spirit of religious tolerance and inclusiveness. Technically speaking, because all Reform temples in Europe were destroyed during the Holocaust, this is actually the oldest existing Reform synagogue in the world.

MAP 1: 90 Hasell St., 843/723-1090, www.kkbe.org; services Sat. 11am, tours Mon.-Fri. 10am-noon, Sun. 10am-4pm

## OLD CITY JAIL

If you were to make a movie called *Dracula Meets the Lord of the Rings*, the Old City Jail might make a great set. Built in 1802 on a lot set aside for public use since 1680, the edifice was indeed the Charleston County lockup until 1939. It was once even more imposing, but the top story and a large octagonal tower fell victim to the 1886 earthquake. Its history is also the stuff from which movies are made. Some of the last pirates were jailed here in 1822 while awaiting hanging, as was slave rebellion leader Denmark Vesey. (As a response to the aborted Vesey uprising, Charleston for a while required that all African sailors in port be detained at the jail.) During the Civil War, prisoners of both armies were held here at various times.

The Old City Jail currently houses the American College of the Building Arts. Unless

# The New Charleston Green

the Clemson wind turbine lab in North Charleston

Most people know "Charleston green" as a unique local color, the result of adding a few drops of yellow to post-Civil War surplus black paint. But these days the phrase also refers to environmentally friendly development in Charleston.

The most obvious example is the ambitious Navy Yard redevelopment, which seeks to repurpose the closed-down facility. That project is part of a larger civic vision for the 3,000-acre historic Noisette community of North Charleston, with an accompanying wetlands protection conservancy. From its inception in 1902 at the command of President Theodore Roosevelt through the end of the Cold War, the Charleston Navy Yard was one of the city's biggest employers. Though the yard was closed in 1995, a 340-acre section now hosts an intriguing mix of green-friendly design firms, small nonprofits, and commercial maritime companies. Clemson University—with the help of a massive federal grant, the largest in the school's history—will oversee one of the world's largest wind turbine research facilities, to be constructed in Building 69.

Also in North Charleston, local retail chain Half Moon Outfitters has a green-friendly warehouse facility in an old grocery store. The first LEED (Leadership in Energy and Environmental Design) Platinum-certified building in South Carolina, the warehouse features solar panels, rainwater reservoirs, and locally harvested or salvaged interiors. There's also the LEED-certified North Charleston Elementary School as well as North Charleston's adoption of a "dark skies" ordinance to cut down on light pollution. On the peninsula, the historic meetinghouse of the Circular Congregational Church has a green addition with geothermal heating and cooling, rainwater cisterns, and Charleston's first vegetative roof.

For many Charlestonians, the green movement manifests in simpler things: the pedestrian and bike lanes on the Ravenel Bridge, the thriving city recycling program, and the Sustainable Seafood Initiative, a partnership of local restaurants, universities, and conservation groups that brings the freshest, most environmentally responsible dishes to your table when you dine out in Charleston.

This forward-thinking mode doesn't just mean enhanced quality of life for Charleston residents. It also pays off in attracting tech businesses and other cutting-edge employers, and the well-educated millennial knowledge workers who founded and staff them.

Charleston's tech economy is among the fastest growing in the nation, 26 percent faster than the national average, faster even than Austin, Texas, and Raleigh/Durham, North Carolina. Nearly 100 firms are part of the public/private Charleston Digital Corridor (www.charlestondigitalcorridor.com). The growth has garnered so much attention that some are using the nickname "Silicon Harbor" for the Charleston region.

you're a student there, the only way to tour the Old Jail is through **Bulldog Tours** (18 Anson St., 843/722-8687, www.bulldogtours. com). Their Haunted Jail Tour ($20 adults, $10 children) starts daily at 7pm, 8pm, 9pm, and 10pm; all tours are paid for at 40 North Market Street, a short walking distance away, with jail tours starting at the jail itself.
**MAP 1:** 21 Magazine St., 843/577-5245

## OLD CITY MARKET

Part kitschy tourist trap, part glimpse into the Old South, part community gathering place, Old City Market remains Charleston's most reliable, if perhaps least flashy, attraction. It is certainly the practical center of the city's tourist trade, not least because so many tours originate nearby. Originally built on Daniel's Creek—claimed from the marsh in the early 1800s after the city's first marketplace at Broad and Meeting Streets burned in 1796—one of City Market's early features was a colony of vultures who hung around the many butcher stalls. Sensing that the carrion eaters would keep the area cleaner than any human could, officials not only allowed the buzzards to hang around, they were also protected by law, becoming known as "Charleston eagles" in tongue-in-cheek local jargon. No matter what anyone tries to tell you, Charleston's City Market never hosted a single slave auction. Indeed, when the Pinckney family donated this land to the city for a "Publick Market," one stipulation was that no slaves were ever to be sold here—or else the property would immediately revert to the family's descendants. A recent multimillion-dollar renovation has prettified the bulk of City Market into more of a big-city air-conditioned pedestrian shopping mall. It's not as shabbily charming as it once was, but it certainly offers a more comfortable stroll during the warmer months.
**MAP 1:** Meeting St. and Market St., 843/973-7236; daily 6am-11:30pm

## PHILIP SIMMONS GARDEN

Charleston's most beloved artisan is the late Philip Simmons. Born on nearby Daniel

Island in 1912, Simmons went through an apprenticeship to become one of the most sought-after decorative ironworkers in the United States. In 1982 the National Endowment for the Arts awarded him its National Heritage Fellowship. His work is on display at the Smithsonian Institution and the Museum of International Folk Art in Santa Fe, New Mexico, among many other places. In 1989, the congregation at Simmons's **St. John's Reformed Episcopal Church** voted to make the church garden a commemoration of the life and work of this legendary African American artisan, who died in 2009 at age 97. Completed in two phases, the Bell Garden and the Heart Garden, the project is a delightful blend of Simmons's signature graceful, sinuous style and fragrant flowers.
**MAP 1:** 91 Anson St., 843/722-4241, http:// philipsimmons.us

## ST. MARY OF THE ANNUNCIATION CHURCH

The oldest Roman Catholic church in the Carolinas, St. Mary of the Annunciation traces its roots to 1789, when the Irish priest Father Matthew Ryan was sent to begin the first Catholic parish in the colony. The original church was destroyed in the great Charleston fire of 1838, and the present sanctuary dates from immediately thereafter. While it did receive a direct hit from a Union shell during the siege of Charleston in the Civil War—taking out the organ—the handsome Greek Revival edifice has survived in fine form the 1886 earthquake, the great hurricane of 1893, and 1989's Hurricane Hugo. You can tour the interior most weekdays 9:30am-3:30pm.
**MAP 1:** 89 Hasell St., 843/722-7696, www. catholic-doc.org/saintmarys; mass Sun. 9:30am

## UNITARIAN CHURCH

In a town filled with cool old church cemeteries, the coolest belongs to the Unitarian Church. As a nod to the beauty and power of nature, vegetation and shrubbery in the cemetery have been allowed to take their natural

Church (5 Clifford St., 843/723-2426, www.
stjohnscharleston.org, worship Sun. 8:30am
and 11am), which had its origin in 1742 when
Dr. Henry Melchior Muhlenberg stopped in
town for a couple of days on his way to minister to the burgeoning Salzburger colony in
Ebenezer, Georgia. He would later be known
as the father of the Lutheran Church in
America. To see the sanctuary at times other
than Sunday mornings, go by the office next
door Monday-Friday 9am-2pm and they'll let
you take a walk through the interior.

MAP 1: 4 Archdale St., 843/723-4617, www.
charlestonuu.org; services Sun. 11am, free tours Sat.
10am-1pm

### WILLIAM RHETT HOUSE

The oldest standing residence in Charleston
is the circa-1713 William Rhett House, which
once belonged to the colonel who captured the
pirate Stede Bonnet. It's now a private residence, but you can admire this excellent pro-
totypical example of a Charleston single house
easily from the street and read the nearby historical marker.

MAP 1: 54 Hasell St.

## UPPER KING
### MARION SQUARE

While The Citadel moved lock, stock, and
barrel almost a century ago, the college's old
home, the South Carolina State Arsenal, still
overlooks 6.5-acre Marion Square, a reminder
of the former glory days when this was the institute's parade ground, the "Citadel Green"
(the old Citadel is now a hotel). Seemingly
refusing to give up on tradition—or perhaps
just attracted by the many female College of
Charleston students—uniformed cadets from
The Citadel are still chockablock in Marion
Square on any given weekend, a bit of local
flavor that reminds you that you're definitely
in Charleston. Marion Square is named for
the "Swamp Fox" himself, Revolutionary War
hero and father of modern guerrilla warfare
Francis Marion, for whom the hotel at the
square's southwest corner is also named.
The square's newest feature is the Holocaust

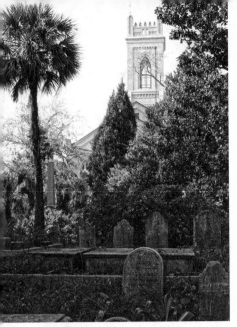
the Unitarian Church cemetery

course (walkways excepted). Virginia creeper
wraps around 200-year-old grave markers, honeybees feed on wildflowers, and tree
roots threaten to engulf entire headstones.
The whole effect is oddly relaxing, making it
one of my favorite places in Charleston. The
church itself—the second oldest such edifice in Charleston and the oldest Unitarian
sanctuary in the South—is pretty nice too.
Begun in 1776 because of overcrowding at
the Circular Congregational Church, the
brand-new building saw rough usage by
British troops during the Revolution. In 1787
the church was repaired, though it was not
officially chartered as a Unitarian church
until 1839. An extensive modernization happened in 1852. The church was spared in the
fire of 1861, which destroyed the old Circular
Church but stopped at the Unitarian Church's
property line. Sadly, it was not so lucky during the 1886 earthquake, which toppled the
original tower. The version you see today is a
subsequent and less grand design.

Directly next door is **St. John's Lutheran**

Memorial on Calhoun Street. However, the dominant monument is the towering memorial to John C. Calhoun. Its 1858 cornerstone includes one of the more interesting time capsules you'll encounter: $100 in Continental money, a lock of John Calhoun's hair, and a cannonball from the Fort Moultrie battle. Marion Square hosts many events, including the farmers market every Saturday mid-April-late December, the Food and Wine Festival, and, of course, some Spoleto events.

MAP 2: between King St. and Meeting St. at Calhoun St., 843/965-4104; daily dawn-dusk

## COLLEGE OF CHARLESTON

The oldest college in South Carolina and the first municipal college in the country, the College of Charleston boasts a fair share of history in addition to the way its 12,000-plus students bring a modern, youthful touch to so much of the city's public activities. Its services are no longer free, and despite its moniker the college is now a full-blown, state-supported university. Though the college has its share of modernistic buildings, a stroll around the gorgeous campus will uncover some historic gems. The oldest building on campus, the Bishop Robert Smith House, dates from the year of the college's founding, 1770, and is now the president's house; find it on Glebe Street between Wentworth and George. The large Greek Revival building dominating the college's old quad off George and St. Philip's Streets is the magnificent Randolph Hall (1828), the oldest functioning college classroom in the country and now host to the president's office. The huge circular feature directly in front of it is "The Cistern," a historic reservoir that's a popular place for students to sit in the grass and enjoy the sun filtering through the live oaks. The Cistern is also where then-candidate Barack Obama spoke at a rally in January 2008. Movies that have had scenes shot on campus include *Cold Mountain, The Patriot,* and *The Notebook.* If you have an iPhone or iPod Touch, you can download a neat self-guided tour, complete with video, from the iTunes App Store (www.

apple.com, search "College of Charleston Tour," free).

The college's main claims to academic fame are its outstanding Art History and Marine Biology departments and its performing arts program. The **Halsey Institute of Contemporary Art** (54 St. Philip St., 843/953-5680, www.halsey.cofc.edu, Mon.-Sat. 11am-4pm, free) focuses on modern visual art and offers film screenings and lectures. The groundbreaking **Avery Research Center for African American History and Culture** (843/953-7609, www.cofc.edu/avery, Mon.-Fri. 10am-5pm, Sat. noon-5pm, free) features rotating exhibits from its permanent archive collection.

MAP 2: 66 George St., 843/805-5507, www.cofc.edu

## EMANUEL AFRICAN METHODIST EPISCOPAL CHURCH

Known simply as "Mother Emanuel," Emanuel African Methodist Episcopal Church has a distinguished history as one of the South's oldest African American congregations. The church came under heavy scrutiny prior to the Civil War when one of its founders, Denmark Vesey, was implicated in planning a slave uprising. The existing edifice was burned as retaliation for Vesey's involvement (and the founding of The Citadel as a military academy nearby was directly related to white unrest over the plot). In the wake of the Nat Turner revolt in 1834, open worship by African Americans was outlawed in Charleston and went underground until after the Civil War. The congregation adopted the "Emanuel" name with the building of a new church in 1872, a wooden structure which unfortunately didn't survive the great earthquake of 1886. The simple, elegant, and deceptively large church you see today dates from 1891, and has hosted luminaries such as Booker T. Washington, Dr. Martin Luther King Jr., and Coretta Scott King. In 2015, the historically black church was the site of the horrific murders of nine worshippers—including its pastor, Clementa Pinckney—by a white racist. At Pinckney's memorial service,

President Barack Obama spoke and led the congregation in singing *Amazing Grace*.

**MAP 2:** 110 Calhoun St., www.emanuelamechurch.org; Sunday services 9:30am

## CHARLESTON MUSEUM

During its long history, the Charleston Museum has moved literally all over town. It's currently housed in a noticeably modern building, but make no mistake: This is the nation's oldest museum, founded in 1773. It strives to stay as fresh and relevant as any new museum, with a rotating schedule of special exhibits in addition to its very eclectic permanent collection. For a long time this was the only place to get a glimpse of the CSS *Hunley,* albeit just a fanciful replica in front of the main entrance. (Now you can see the real thing at its conservation site in North Charleston, and it's even smaller than the replica would indicate.) Much of the Charleston Museum's collection focuses on aspects of everyday life of Charlestonians, from the aristocracy to slaves, including items such as utensils, clothing, and furniture. There are quirks as well, such as the Egyptian mummy and the fine lady's fan made out of turkey feathers. A particular and possibly surprising specialty includes work and research by noted regional naturalists like John James Audubon, André Michaux, and Mark Catesby. There are also numerous exhibits chronicling the local history of Native Americans and African Americans. The location is particularly convenient, being close not only to the excellent Charleston Visitors Center and its equally excellent parking garage, but also to the Joseph Manigault House (which the museum runs), the Children's Museum of the Lowcountry, and the Gibbes Museum of Art.

**MAP 2:** 360 Meeting St., 843/722-2996, www.charlestonmuseum.org; Mon.-Sat. 9am-5pm, Sun. noon-5pm; $12 adults, $5 children, combo tickets to Heyward-Washington and Manigault Houses available

## JOSEPH MANIGAULT HOUSE

Owned and operated by the nearby Charleston Museum, the Joseph Manigault House is sometimes called the "Huguenot House." Its splendor is a good reminder of the fact that the French Protestants were far from poverty-stricken, unlike so many groups who came to America fleeing persecution. This circa-1803 National Historic Landmark was designed by wealthy merchant Gabriel Manigault for his brother, Joseph, a rice planter of local repute. (Gabriel, quite the crackerjack dilettante architect, also designed Charleston City Hall.)

Emanuel African Methodist Episcopal Church

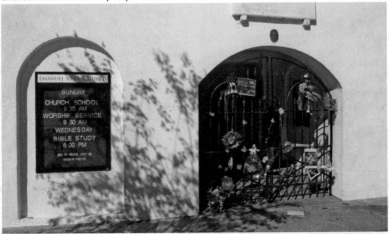

The three-story brick town house is a great example of Adams, or Federal, architecture. The furnishings are top-notch examples of 19th-century handiwork, and the rooms have been restored as accurately as possible. The foundations of various outbuildings, including a privy and slaves' quarters, are clustered around the picturesque little Gate Temple to the rear of the main house in the large enclosed garden. Each December, the Manigault House offers visitors a special treat, as the Garden Club of Charleston decorates it in period seasonal fashion, using only flowers that would have been used in the 19th century.

**MAP 2**: 350 Meeting St., 843/723-2926, www. charlestonmuseum.org; Mon.-Sat. 10am-5pm, Sun. noon-5pm, last tour 4:30pm; $12 adults, $5 children, combo tickets to Charleston Museum and Heyward-Washington House available

### ★ AIKEN-RHETT HOUSE

One of my favorite spots in all of Charleston and a comparatively recent acquisition of the Historic Charleston Foundation, the poignant Aiken-Rhett House shows another side of that organization's mission. Whereas the Historic Charleston-run Nathaniel Russell House seeks to re-create a specific point in time, work at the Aiken-Rhett House emphasizes conservation and research. Built in 1818 and expanded by South Carolina governor William Aiken Jr., after whom we know the house today, parts of this rambling, almost Dickensian house remained sealed from 1918 until 1975, when the family relinquished the property to the Charleston Museum. As you walk the halls, staircases, and rooms—seeing the remains of original wallpaper and the various fixtures added through the years—you can really feel the impact of the people who lived within these walls and get a great sense of the full sweep of Charleston history. While the docents are friendly and helpful, the main way to enjoy the Aiken-Rhett House is by way of a self-guided MP3 player audio tour, which is unique in Charleston. While you might think this isolates you from the others in your party, it's actually part of the fun—you can synchronize your players and move as a unit if you'd like.

**MAP 2**: 48 Elizabeth St., 843/723-1159, www. historiccharleston.org; Mon.-Sat. 10am-5pm, Sun. 2pm-5pm, last tour 4:15pm; $12 adults, $5 children

### CHILDREN'S MUSEUM OF THE LOWCOUNTRY

Yet another example of Charleston's savvy regarding the tourist industry is the Children's

the stables at the Aiken-Rhett House

Museum of the Lowcountry. Recognizing that historic homes and Civil War memorabilia aren't enough to keep a family with young children in town for long, the city established this museum in 2005 specifically to give families with kids aged 3 months to 12 years a reason to spend more time (and money) downtown. A wide variety of hands-on activities—such as a 30-foot shrimp boat replica and a medieval castle—stretch the definition of "museum" to its limit. In truth, this is just as much an indoor playground as a museum, but no need to quibble. The Children's Museum has been getting rave reviews since it opened, and visiting parents and their children seem happy with the city's investment.

**MAP 2:** 25 Ann St., 843/853-8962, www.explorecml. org; Tues.-Sat. 9am-5pm, Sun. noon-5pm; $12 non-SC residents

## OLD BETHEL UNITED METHODIST CHURCH

The history of the Old Bethel United Methodist Church, the third-oldest church building in Charleston, is a little confusing. Completed in 1807, the church once stood across Calhoun Street until a schism formed in the church community over whether black parishioners should be limited to sitting in the galleries (in those days in the South, all races attended church together far more frequently than during the Jim Crow era). The entire African American congregation wanted out, so in 1852 the original building was moved aside for the construction of a new church for Caucasians, and then entirely across the street in 1880. Look across the street and sure enough you'll see the circa-1853 **Bethel Methodist Church** (57 Pitt St., 843/723-4587, worship Sun. 9am and 11:15am).

**MAP 2:** 222 Calhoun St., 843/722-3470

# HAMPTON PARK
## THE CITADEL

Although for many its spiritual and historic center will always be at the Old State Arsenal in Marion Square, The Citadel has been at this 300-acre site farther up the peninsula along the Ashley River since 1922 and shows no signs of leaving. Getting there is a little tricky in that the entrance to the college is situated behind beautiful Hampton Park off Rutledge Avenue, a main north-south artery on the western portion of the peninsula. The Citadel (technically its full name is The Citadel, The Military College of South Carolina) has entered popular consciousness through the works of graduate Pat Conroy, especially his novel *Lords of Discipline,* starring a thinly disguised "Carolina Military Institute." Other famous Bulldog alumni include construction magnate Charles Daniel (for whom the school library is named); Ernest "Fritz" Hollings, South Carolina governor and longtime U.S. senator; and Charleston mayor Joe Riley. You'll see The Citadel's living legacy all over Charleston in the person of the ubiquitous cadet, whose gray-and-white uniform, ramrod posture, and impeccable manners all hark back to the days of the Confederacy. But to best experience The Citadel, you should go to the campus itself.

There's a lot for visitors to see, including **The Citadel Museum** (843/953-6779, daily noon-5pm, free), on your right just as you enter campus; the "Citadel Murals" in the Daniel Library; "Indian Hill," the highest point in Charleston and former site of an Indian trader's home; and the grave of U.S. general Mark Clark of World War II fame, who was Citadel president from 1954 to 1966. Ringing vast Summerall Field—the huge open space where you enter campus—are the many castle-like cadet barracks.

The most interesting single experience for visitors to The Citadel is the colorful Friday afternoon dress parade on Summerall Field, in which cadets pass for review in full dress uniform (the fabled "long gray line") accompanied by a marching band and pipers. Often called "the best free show in Charleston," the parade happens almost every Friday at 3:45pm during the school year; you might want to consult the website before your visit to confirm. Arrive well in advance to avoid parking problems.

# Family Fun in Charleston

Let's face it: A steady diet of house museums and long-ago history will bore anyone to tears, not just the young folks in your traveling party. Fortunately, Charleston has a range of options to please children of all ages. You just have to know where to look.

The South Carolina Aquarium is a must-visit for kids.

- **Children's Museum of the Lowcountry:** Conveniently located in the city's "Museum Row," this indoor playground offers a variety of hands-on activities for kids aged 3 months to 12 years.

- **Old Exchange and Provost Dungeon:** For a real-life Pirates of the Caribbean experience, take a guided tour of this spooky spot from colonial times, complete with animatronic-style figures of pirates and scoundrels.

- **Sewee Visitor and Environmental Education Center:** Visit a pack of red wolves (indigenous to the coastal area) at this center devoted to preserving the species and educating people about these magnificent little animals.

- **South Carolina Aquarium:** The closest thing to a zoo, this easily managed and very informative installation features aspects of every habitat in the ecologically diverse Palmetto State—from Lowcountry marshland to Upstate mountain rivers—anchored around an enormous three-floor central observation tank filled with marine life.

- **Waterfront Park:** These outdoor fountain sculptures are sure to please any carefree spirit in your group.

The institute was born out of panic over the threat of a slave rebellion organized in 1822 by Denmark Vesey. The state legislature passed an act establishing the school to educate the strapping young men picked to protect Charleston from a slave revolt. Citadel folks will proudly tell you they actually fired the first shots of the Civil War, when on January 9, 1861, two cadets fired from a battery on Morris Island at the U.S. steamer *Star of the West* to keep it from supplying Fort Sumter. After slavery ended—and with it the school's original raison d'être—The Citadel continued, taking its current name in 1910 and moving to the Ashley River site in 1922. While The Citadel is rightly famous for its pomp and circumstance—as well as its now-defunct no-lock "honor system," done away with after the Virginia Tech shootings—the little-known truth is that to be one of the 2,000 or so currently enrolled Citadel Bulldogs, you don't have to go through all that, or the infamous "Hell Week" either. You can just sign up for one of their many evening graduate school programs.

**MAP 2:** 171 Moultrie St., 843/953-3294, www.citadel.edu; grounds daily 8am-6pm

# WEST ASHLEY
## CHARLES TOWNE LANDING

Any look at West Ashley must start where everything began, with the 600-acre state historic site Charles Towne Landing. This is where Charleston's original settlers first arrived and camped in 1670, remaining only a few years before eventually moving to the more defensible peninsula where the Holy City now resides. For many years the site was in disrepair and borderline neglect, useful mainly as a place to ship busloads of local schoolchildren on field trips. However, a long-overdue upgrade came to fruition with a grand "reopening" of sorts in 2006, which has been very well received and has given the site a newfound sheen of respect. A beautiful and fully seaworthy replica of a settlers' ship is the main highlight, docked in the creek on the far side of the long and well-done exploration trail through the site. You can get on board, and a ranger will explain aspects of both the ship and the original settlement. Another highlight is the remnant of the original palisade wall (there's a reconstructed palisade to show what it looked like). Ranger-guided programs are available Wednesday-Friday at 10am; call ahead for reservations.

Not just a historic site, this is also a great place to bring the family. It has Charleston's only zoo, the "Animal Forest," featuring otters, bears, cougars, and buffalo, and 80 acres of beautiful gardens to relax in, many featuring fabulously ancient live oaks and other indigenous flora. An audio tour has been instituted, where you can rent an MP3 player ($5), but the self-guided approach works just fine. The outdoor highlights of Charles Towne Landing are obvious, but don't miss the fantastic exhibits inside the visitors center, which are particularly well done and give a comprehensive and informative look back at the time of the original settlers.

**MAP 3**: 1500 Old Town Plantation Rd., 843/852-4200, www.southcarolinaparks.com/ctl; daily 9am-5pm; $10 adults, $6 students, free under age 6

## ★ DRAYTON HALL

A mecca for historic preservationists all over the country, Drayton Hall is remarkable not only for its pedigree, but also for the way in which it has been preserved. This stately redbrick Georgian-Palladian building, the oldest plantation home in the country open to the public, is literally historically preserved—as in no electricity, heat, or running water. Since its construction in 1738 by John Drayton, son of Magnolia Plantation founder Thomas, Drayton Hall has survived almost completely intact through the ups and downs of Lowcountry history. In its heyday before the American Revolution, Drayton Hall was widely considered the finest home in all the

Drayton Hall

colonies, the very symbol of the extraordinary wealth of the South Carolina aristocracy.

John Drayton died while fleeing the British in 1779; subsequently his house served as the headquarters of British generals Henry Clinton and Charles Cornwallis. In 1782, however, American general "Mad Anthony" Wayne claimed the house as his own headquarters. During the Civil War, Drayton Hall escaped the depredations of the conquering Union army, one of only three area plantation homes to survive.

Three schools of thought have emerged to explain why it was spared the fate of so many other plantation homes: (1) A slave told the troops it was owned by "a Union Man," Drayton cousin Percival, who served alongside Admiral David Farragut of "damn the torpedoes" fame; (2) General William Sherman was in love with one of the Drayton women; and (3) one of the Draytons, a doctor, craftily posted smallpox warning flags at the outskirts of the property. Of the three scenarios, the last is considered most likely.

Visitors expecting the more typical approach to house museums, i.e., subjective renovation with period furnishings that may or may not have any connection with the actual house, might be disappointed. But for others the experience at Drayton Hall is quietly exhilarating, almost in a Zen-like way. Planes are routed around the house so that no rattles will endanger its structural integrity. There's no furniture to speak of; only bare rooms decorated with original paint, no matter how little remains. It can be jarring at first, but after you get into it, you might wonder why anyone does things any differently.

Another way the experience is different is in the professionalism of the National Trust for Historic Preservation, which has owned and administered Drayton Hall since 1974. The guides hold degrees in the field, and a tour of the house, which starts on the half hour, takes every bit of 50 minutes. A separate 45-minute program called "Connections: From Africa to America," chronicles the diaspora of the slaves who originally worked this plantation, from their capture to their eventual freedom. "Connections" is presented at 11:15am, 1:15pm, and 3:15pm.

The site comprises not only the main house, but two self-guided walking trails as well, one along the peaceful Ashley River and another along the marsh. Note also the foundations of the two "flankers," or guest wings, at each side of the main house. They survived the Yankees only for one to fall victim to the 1886 earthquake and the other to the 1893 hurricane. Also on-site is an African American cemetery with at least 33 known graves. It's kept deliberately untended and unlandscaped to honor the final wish of Richmond Bowens (1908-1998), the seventh-generation descendant of some of Drayton Hall's original slaves.

**MAP 3:** 3380 Ashley River Rd., 843/769-2600, www.draytonhall.org; Mon.-Sat. 9am-5pm, Sun. 11am-5pm, tours on the half hour; $22 adults, $10 ages 12-18, $6 ages 6-11, grounds only $10

## MAGNOLIA PLANTATION AND GARDENS

A different legacy of the Drayton family is Magnolia Plantation and Gardens. It claims not only the first garden in the United States, dating back to the 1680s, but also the first public garden, dating to 1872. Magnolia's history spans back two full centuries before that, however, when Thomas Drayton Jr.—scion of Norman aristocracy, son of a wealthy Barbadian planter—came from the Caribbean to build his own fortune. He immediately married the daughter of Stephen Fox, who began this plantation in 1676. Through wars, fevers, depressions, earthquakes, and hurricanes, Magnolia has stayed in the possession of an unbroken line of Drayton descendants to this very day.

As a privately run attraction, Magnolia has little of the academic veneer of other plantation sites in the area, most of which have long passed out of private hands. There's a slightly kitschy feel here, the opposite of the quiet dignity of Drayton Hall. And unlike Middleton Place a few miles down the road, the gardens here are anything but manicured, with a wild, almost playful feel. That said, Magnolia can claim fame to being one of the earliest bona fide tourist attractions in the United States and the beginning of Charleston's now-booming tourist industry. It happened after the Civil War, when John Grimke Drayton, reduced to near poverty, sold off most of his property, including the original Magnolia Plantation, just to stay afloat. (In a common practice at the time, as a condition of inheriting the plantation, Mr. Grimke, who married into the family, was required to legally change his name to Drayton.)

The original plantation home was burned during the war—either by Union troops or freed slaves—so Drayton barged a colonial-era summer house from Summerville down the Ashley River to this site and built the modern Magnolia Plantation around it specifically as an attraction. Before long, tourists regularly came here by crowded boat from Charleston (a wreck of one such ferry is still on-site). Magnolia's reputation became so exalted that at one point Baedecker's listed it as one of the three main attractions in North America, alongside the Grand Canyon and Niagara Falls. The family took things to the next level in the 1970s, when John Drayton Hastie bought out his brother and set about marketing Magnolia Plantation and Gardens a modern tourist destination. While spring remains the best—and the most crowded—time to come, a huge variety of camellias bloom in early winter, a time marked by a yearly Winter Camellia Festival.

Today Magnolia is a place to bring the whole family, picnic under the massive old live oaks, and wander the lush, almost overgrown grounds. Children will enjoy finding their way through "The Maze" of manicured camellia and holly bushes, complete with a viewing stand to look within the giant puzzle. Plant lovers will enjoy the themed gardens such as the Biblical Garden, the Barbados Tropical Garden, and the Audubon Swamp Garden, complete with alligators and named after John James Audubon, who visited here in 1851. House tours, the 45-minute Nature

Train tour, the 45-minute Nature Boat tour, and a visit to the Audubon Swamp Garden run about $8 pp extra for each offering.

Of particular interest is the poignant old Drayton Tomb, along the Ashley River. Look closely at the nose of one of the cherubs on the tomb; it was shot off by a vengeful Union soldier. Nearby you'll find a nice walking and biking trail along the Ashley among the old paddy fields.

**MAP 3**: 3550 Ashley River Rd., 843/571-1266, www.magnoliaplantation.com; daily 8:30am-4:30pm; $15 adults, $10 children, free under age 6

## ★ MIDDLETON PLACE

Not only the first landscaped garden in North America but still one of the most magnificent in the world, Middleton Place is a sublime, unforgettable combination of history and sheer natural beauty. Nestled along a quiet bend in the Ashley River, the grounds contain a historic restored home, working stables, and 60 acres of breathtaking gardens, all manicured to perfection. A stunning piece of modern architecture, the Inn at Middleton Place, completes the package in surprisingly harmonious fashion. First granted in 1675, Middleton Place is the culmination of the Lowcountry rice plantation aesthetic. That sensibility is most immediate in the graceful Butterfly Lakes at the foot of the green landscaped terrace leading up to the foundation of the Middleton Place House itself, the only surviving remnant of the vengeful Union occupation. In 1741 the plantation became the family seat of the Middleton's, one of the most notable surnames in U.S. history. The first head of the household was Henry Middleton, president of the First Continental Congress, who began work on the gardens. The plantation passed to his son Arthur, a signer of the Declaration of Independence; then on to Arthur's son Henry, governor of South Carolina; and then down to Henry's son Williams Middleton, a signer of the Ordinance of Secession. As the Civil War wound down, on February 22, 1865, the 56th New York Volunteers burned the main house and destroyed the gardens,

the scenic gardens at Middleton Place

leaving only the circa-1755 guest wing, which today is the Middleton Place House Museum. The great earthquake of 1886 added insult to injury by wrecking the Butterfly Lakes. It wasn't until 1916 that renovation began. In 1971 Middleton Place was named a National Historic Landmark, and 20 years later the International Committee on Monuments and Sites named Middleton Place one of six U.S. gardens of international importance.

All that's left of the great house are the remains of the foundation, still majestic in ruin. Today visitors can tour the excellently restored **Middleton Place House Museum** (4300 Ashley River Rd., 843/556-6020, www.middletonplace.org, guided tours Mon. 1:30pm-4:30pm, Tues.-Sun. 10am-4:30pm, $15)—actually the only remaining "flanker" building—and see furniture, silverware, china, and books belonging to the Middletons as well as family portraits by Thomas Sully and Benjamin West.

A short walk takes you to the Plantation Stableyards, where costumed craftspeople still work using historically authentic tools and methods surrounded by a happy family of domestic animals. The Stableyards is also home

to a pair of magnificent male water buffalo. Henry Middleton originally brought a pair in to work the rice fields—the first in North America—but today they're just there to relax and add atmosphere. They bear the Turkish names of Adem (the brown one) and Berk (the white one), or "Earth" and "Solid." Meet the fellas daily 9am-5pm. If you're like most folks, however, you'll best enjoy simply wandering and marveling at the gardens. "Meandering" is not the right word to describe them, since they're systematically laid out. "Intricate" is the descriptor I prefer, and that sums up the attention to detail that characterizes all the garden's portions, each with a distinct personality and landscape design template. To get a real feel for how things used to be here, for an extra $15 pp you can take a 45-minute carriage ride through the bamboo forest to an abandoned rice field. Rides start around 10am and run every hour or so, weather permitting.

The 53-room **Inn at Middleton Place** (www.theinnatmiddletonplace.com), besides being a wholly gratifying lodging experience, is also a quite self-conscious and largely successful experiment. Its bold Frank Lloyd Wright-influenced design, comprising four units joined by walkways, is modern. But both inside and outside it manages to blend quite well with the surrounding fields, trees, and riverbanks. The inn also offers kayak tours and instruction—a particularly nice way to enjoy the grounds from the waters of the Ashley—and features its own organic garden and labyrinth, intriguing modern counterpoints to the formal gardens of the plantation itself.

They still grow the exquisite Carolina Gold rice in a field at Middleton Place, harvested in the old style each September. You can sample some of it in many dishes at the **Middleton Place Restaurant** (843/556-6020, www.middletonplace.org, lunch daily 11am-3pm, dinner Tues.-Thurs. 6pm-8pm, Fri.-Sat. 6pm-9pm, Sun. 6pm-8pm, $15-25). You can tour the gardens for free if you arrive for a dinner reservation at 5:30pm or later.

MAP 3: 4300 Ashley River Rd., 843/556-6020, www.middletonplace.org; daily 9am-5pm; $28 adults, $15 students, $10 children, guided house tour $15 extra

### THE COBURG COW

The entire stretch of U.S. 17 (Savannah Hwy.) heading into Charleston from the west is redolent of a particularly Southern brand of retro Americana. The chief example is the famous Coburg Cow, a large, rotating dairy cow accompanied by a bottle of chocolate milk. The current installation dates from 1959, though a version of it was on this site as far back as the early 1930s, when this area was open countryside. During Hurricane Hugo the Coburg Cow was moved to a safe location. In 2001 the attached dairy closed down, and the city threatened to have the cow moved or demolished. But community outcry preserved the delightful landmark, which is visible today on the south side of U.S. 17 in the 900 block. You can't miss it—it's a big cow on the side of the road!

MAP 3: 900 block of U.S. 17

### CAW CAW INTERPRETIVE CENTER

About 10 minutes west of Charleston on U.S. 17 you'll find the unique Caw Caw Interpretive Center, a treasure trove for history buffs and naturalists wanting to learn more about the old rice culture of the South. With a particular emphasis on the expertise of those who worked on the rice plantations using techniques they brought with them from Africa, the county-run facility comprises 650 acres of land on an actual former rice plantation built on a cypress swamp, eight miles of interpretive trails, an educational center with exhibits, and a wildlife sanctuary with seven different habitats. Most Wednesday and Saturday mornings, guided bird walks are held at 8:30am ($5 pp). You can put in your own canoe for $10 October-April on Saturdays and Sundays. Bikes and dogs aren't allowed on the grounds.

MAP 3: 5200 Savannah Hwy., Ravenel, 843/889-8898, www.ccprc.com; Tues.-Sun. 9am-5pm; $2

# NORTH CHARLESTON

## MAGNOLIA CEMETERY

Although not technically in North Charleston, historic Magnolia Cemetery is on the way, well north of the downtown tourist district in the area called "the Neck." This historic burial ground, while not quite the aesthetic equal of Savannah's famed Bonaventure Cemetery, is still a stirring site for its natural beauty and ornate memorials as well as for its historic aspects. Here are buried the crewmen who died aboard the CSS *Hunley*, reinterred after their retrieval from Charleston Harbor. In all, over 2,000 Civil War dead are buried here, including 5 Confederate generals and 84 rebels who fell at Gettysburg and were moved here.

MAP 3: Cunnington Ave. at Huguenin Ave., 843/722-8638; Sept.-May daily 8am-5pm, June-Aug. daily 8am-6pm

### CHARLESTON NAVY YARD

A vast postindustrial wasteland to some and a fascinating outdoor museum to others, the Charleston Navy Yard is in the baby steps of rehabilitation from one of the Cold War era's major military centers to the largest single urban redevelopment project in the United States. The U.S. Navy's gone now, forced off the site during a phase of base realignment in the mid-1990s. But a 340-acre section, the **Navy Yard at Noisette** (1360 Truxtun Ave., 843/302-2100, daily 24 hours), now hosts an intriguing mix of homes, green design firms, nonprofits, and commercial maritime companies and was named the country's sixth-greenest neighborhood by *Natural Home* magazine in 2008. It has even played host to some scenes of the Lifetime TV series *Army Wives*. Enter on Spruill Avenue and you'll find yourself on wide streets lined with huge, boarded-up warehouse facilities, old machine shops, and dormant power stations. A notable project is the restoration of **10 Storehouse Row** (2120 Noisette Blvd., 843/302-2100, Mon.-Fri. 9am-5pm), which now hosts design firms, galleries, and a small café. Nearby, Clemson University will soon be administering one of the world's largest wind turbine research facilities. At the north end lies the new **Riverfront Park** (843/745-1087, daily dawn-dusk) in the old Chicora Gardens military residential area. There's a nifty little fishing pier on the Cooper River, an excellent naval-themed band shell, and many sleekly designed modernist sculptures paying tribute to the sailors and ships that made history here. From Charleston you get to the Navy Yard by taking I-26 north to exit 216B (you can reach the I-26 junction by just going north on Meeting Street). After exiting, take a left onto Spruill Avenue and a right onto McMillan Avenue, which takes you straight in.

**MAP 3**: west bank of Cooper River, south of Riverfront Park

### ★ CSS *HUNLEY*

For the longest time, the only glimpse of the ill-fated Confederate submarine afforded to visitors was a not-quite-accurate replica outside the Charleston Museum. But after maritime novelist and adventurer Clive Cussler and his team finally found the CSS *Hunley* in 1995 off Sullivan's Island, the tantalizing dream became a reality: We'd finally find out what it looked like, and perhaps even be lucky

enough to bring it to the surface. That moment came on August 8, 2000, when a team comprising the nonprofit **Friends of the Hunley** (Warren Lasch Conservation Center, 1250 Supply St., Bldg. 255, 866/866-9938, www.hunley.org, Sat. 10am-5pm, Sun. noon-5pm, $16 adults, $8 students, free under age 5), the federal government, and private partners successfully implemented a plan to safely raise the vessel. It was moved to its current home on the grounds of the old Navy Yard, named after Warren Lasch, chairman of the Friends of the Hunley. You can view the sub, see the life-size model from the TNT movie *The Hunley*, and look at artifacts such as the "lucky" gold piece of the commander. You can even see facial reconstructions of some of the eight sailors who died on board the sub that fateful February day in 1864, when it mysteriously sank right after successfully destroying the USS *Housatonic* with the torpedo attached to its bow. So that research and conservation can be performed during the week, tours only happen Saturday-Sunday. Because of this limited window of opportunity and the popularity of the site, reserve tickets ahead of time. (The remains of the crew lie in Magnolia Cemetery, where they were buried in 2004 with full military honors.) To get to the Warren Lasch Center from Charleston, take I-26 north to exit 216B. Take a left onto Spruill Avenue and a right onto McMillan Avenue. Once in the Navy Yard, take a right on Hobson Avenue, and after about one mile take a left onto Supply Street. The Lasch Center is the low white building on the left.

**MAP 3**: Warren Lasch Conservation Center, 1250 Supply St., Bldg. 255, 866/866-9938, www.hunley. org; Sat. 10am-5pm, Sun. noon-5pm; $16 adults, $8 students, free under age 5

### Park Circle

The focus of restoration in North Charleston is the old Park Circle neighborhood. The adjacent **Olde North Charleston** development has a number of quality shops, bars, and restaurants.

# Raising the *Hunley*

The raising of the Confederate submarine CSS *Hunley* from the muck of Charleston Harbor sounds like the plot of an adventure novel—which makes sense considering that the major player is an adventure novelist. For 15 years, undersea diver and best-selling author Clive Cussler looked for the final resting place of the *Hunley*. The sub was mysteriously lost at sea after sinking the USS *Housatonic* on February 17, 1864, with the high-explosive "torpedo" mounted on a long spar on its bow. It marked the first time a sub ever sank a ship in battle.

For over a century before Cussler, treasure seekers had searched for the sub, with P. T. Barnum even offering $100,000 to the first person to find it. But on May 3, 1995, a magnetometer operated by Cussler and his group, the National Underwater Marine Agency, discovered the *Hunley*'s final resting place—in 30 feet of water and under three feet of sediment about four miles off Sullivan's Island at the mouth of the harbor. A 19-person dive crew and a team of archaeologists began a process that would result in raising the vessel on August 8, 2000. But first a dilemma had to be solved. For 136 years saltwater had permeated its metallic skin. Exposure to air would rapidly disintegrate the entire thing. So the conservation team, with input from the U.S. Navy, came up with a plan to keep the vessel intact at the specially constructed **Warren Lasch Conservation Center** (1250 Supply St., Bldg. 255, 866/866-9938, www.hunley.org, Sat. 10am-5pm, Sun. noon-5pm, $16 adults, $8 students, free under age 5) in the old Navy Yard while research and conservation were performed on it piece by piece.

Upon seeing the tiny, cramped vessel—much smaller than most experts imagined it would be—visitors are often visibly moved at the bravery and sacrifice of the nine-man Confederate crew, who would have known that the *Hunley*'s two previous crews had drowned at sea in training accidents.

The Lasch Center is only open to the public on weekends. Archaeology continues apace during the week—inch by painstaking inch, muck and tiny artifacts are removed millimeter by millimeter. The process is so thorough that archaeologists have even identified an individual eyelash from one of the crew members. Other interesting artifacts include a threefold wallet with a leather strap, seven canteens, and a wooden cask in one of the ballast tanks.

The very first order of business once the sub was brought up was properly burying the sailors. In 2004, Charleston came to a stop as a ceremonial funeral procession took the remains of the nine to historic Magnolia Cemetery, where they were buried with full military honors.

## NORTH CHARLESTON AND AMERICAN LAFRANCE FIRE MUSEUM AND EDUCATIONAL CENTER

It's got a mouthful of a name, but the North Charleston and American LaFrance Fire Museum and Educational Center, right next to the huge Tanger Outlet Mall, does what it does with a lot of chutzpah—which is fitting considering that it pays tribute to firefighters and the tools of their dangerous trade. The museum, which opened in 2007 and shares a huge 25,000-square-foot space with the North Charleston Convention and Visitors Bureau, is primarily dedicated to maintaining and increasing its collection of antique American LaFrance firefighting vehicles and equipment. The 18 fire engines here date from 1857 to 1969. The museum's exhibits have taken on greater poignancy in the wake of the tragic loss of nine Charleston firefighters killed trying to extinguish a warehouse blaze on U.S. 17 in summer 2007—second only to the 9/11 attacks as the largest single loss of life for a U.S. firefighting department.

**MAP 3**: 4975 Centre Pointe Dr., North Charleston, 843/740-5550, www.legacyofheroes.org; Mon.-Sat. 10am-5pm, Sun. 1pm-5pm, last ticket 4pm; $6 adults, free under age 14

# SUMMERVILLE

The Dorchester County town of Summerville, population 30,000, is a friendly, scenic, and upscale suburb north of Charleston. Founded as Pineland Village in 1785, Summerville made its reputation as a place for plantation owners and their families to escape the insects and heat of the swampier areas of the Lowcountry. Summerville got a second wind at the turn of the 20th century, when it was recommended by doctors all over the world as a great place to recover from tuberculosis (supposedly all the turpentine fumes in the air from the pine trees were a big help).

Summerville boasts a whopping 700 buildings on the National Register of Historic Places. For a walking tour of the historic district, download the map at www.visitsummerville.com or pick up a hard copy at the **Summerville Visitors Center** (402 N. Main St., 843/873-8535, Mon.-Fri. 9am-5pm, Sat. 10am-3pm, Sun. 1pm-4pm). Alas, the grand old Pine Forest Inn, perhaps the greatest of all Summerville landmarks and the "winter White House" for presidents William Taft and Theodore Roosevelt, was torn down after World War II, a victim of the Florida vacation craze. Summerville is about 30 minutes from downtown Charleston; take I-26 north.

## AZALEA PARK

Much visitor activity in Summerville centers on Azalea Park, rather obviously named for its most scenic inhabitants. Several fun yearly events take place here, most notably the **Flowertown Festival** (www.flowertownfestival.com, free) each April, a three-day affair heralding the coming of spring and the blooming of the flowers. One of the biggest festivals in South Carolina, 250,000 people usually attend. Another event, **Sculpture in the South** (www.sculptureinthesouth.com) in May, takes advantage of the extensive public sculpture in the park.

MAP 3: S. Main St. and W. 5th St. S.; daily dusk-dawn; free

## COLONIAL DORCHESTER STATE HISTORIC SITE

Just south of Summerville on the way back to Charleston is the interesting Colonial Dorchester State Historic Site, chronicling a virtually unknown segment of Carolina history. A contingent of Massachusetts Puritans ("Congregationalists" in the parlance of time) were given special dispensation in 1697 to form a settlement of their own specifically to enhance commercial activity on the Ashley River. Today little is left of old Dorchester but the tabby walls of the 1757 fort overlooking the Ashley. Don't miss the unspectacular but still historically vital remains of the wooden wharf on the walking trail along the river, once the epicenter of a thriving port. The most-photographed thing on-site is the bell tower of the Anglican church of St. George—which actually wasn't where the original settlers worshipped and was in fact quite resented by them since they were forced to pay for its construction. The dispute with the Anglican Church became tense enough to cause many Congregationalists to leave and settle little Midway, Georgia, where many became key figures in the movement for American independence. The resulting Revolutionary War would be the downfall of Dorchester itself, abandoned during the upheaval.

MAP 3: 300 County Road S-18-373, 843/873-1740, www.southcarolinaparks.com; daily 9am-6pm; $2 adults, free under age 16

## SUMMERVILLE-DORCHESTER MUSEUM

To learn more about Summerville's interesting history, go just off Main Street to the Summerville-Dorchester Museum. Located in the former town police station, the museum has a wealth of good exhibits. The museum opened in 1992 thanks to a group of Summerville citizens who wanted to preserve the region's history.

MAP 3: 100 E. Doty Ave., 843/875-9666, www.summervilledorchestermuseum.org; Mon.-Sat. 9am-2pm; donations accepted

# MOUNT PLEASANT AND EAST COOPER

## PATRIOTS POINT NAVAL AND MARITIME MUSEUM

Directly across Charleston Harbor from the old city lies the Patriots Point Naval and Maritime Museum complex, one of the first chapters in Charleston's tourism renaissance. The project began in 1975 with what is still its main attraction, the World War II aircraft carrier USS *Yorktown,* named in honor of the carrier lost at the Battle of Midway. Much of "The Fighting Lady" is open to the public, and kids and nautical buffs will thrill to walk the decks and explore the many stations below deck on this massive 900-foot vessel, a veritable floating city. You can even have a full meal in the CPO Mess Hall just as the crew once did (except you'll have to pay $8.50 pp). And if you really want to get up close and personal, try the Navy Flight Simulator for a small additional fee. Speaking of planes, aviation buffs will be overjoyed to see that the *Yorktown* flight deck (the top of the ship) and the hangar deck (right below) are packed with authentic warplanes, not only from World War II but from subsequent conflicts the ship had participated in.

Other ships moored beside the *Yorktown* and open for tours are the Coast Guard cutter USCG *Ingham,* the submarine USS *Clamagore,* and the destroyer USS *Laffey,* which survived being hit by three Japanese bombs and five kamikaze attacks—all within an hour.

A big plus is the free 90-minute guided tour. If you really want to make a family history day out of it, you can hop on the ferry from Patriots Point to Fort Sumter and back. MAP 4: 40 Patriots Point Rd., 843/884-2727, www. patriotspoint.org; daily 9am-6:30pm; $20 adults, $12 ages 6-11, free for active-duty military

## OLD VILLAGE

It won't blow you away if you've seen Charleston or Beaufort, but Mount Pleasant's old town has its share of fine colonial and antebellum homes and historic churches. Indeed, Mount Pleasant's history is almost as old as Charleston's. First settled for farming in 1680, it soon acquired cachet as a great place for planters to spend the hot summers away from the mosquitoes inland. The main drag is Pitt Street, where you can shop and meander among plenty of stores and restaurants (try an ice cream soda at the historic Pitt Street Pharmacy). The huge meeting hall on the waterfront, Alhambra Hall, was the old ferry terminal. MAP 4: West of Royall Ave. to the waterfront, Mount Pleasant

## BOONE HALL PLANTATION

Visitors who've also been to Savannah's Wormsloe Plantation will see the similarity in the majestic, live oak-lined entrance avenue to Boone Hall Plantation. But this site is about half a century older, dating back to a grant to Major John Boone in the 1680s (the oaks of the entranceway were planted in 1743). Unusual for this area, where fortunes were originally made mostly on rice, Boone Hall's main claim to fame was as a cotton plantation as well as a noted brick-making plant. Boone Hall takes the phrase "living history" to its extreme; it's not only an active agricultural facility, it also lets visitors go on "u-pick" walks through its fields, which boast succulent strawberries, peaches, tomatoes, and even pumpkins in October—as well as free hayrides. Currently owned by the McRae family, who first opened it to the public in 1959, Boone Hall is called "the most photographed plantation in America." And photogenic it is, with natural beauty to spare in its scenic location on the Wando River and its adorable Butterfly Garden. But as you're clicking away with your camera, keep in mind that the plantation's "big house" is not original; it's a 1935 reconstruction. While Boone Hall's most genuine historic buildings include the big Cotton Gin House (1853) and the 1750 Smokehouse, to me the most poignant and educational structures by far are

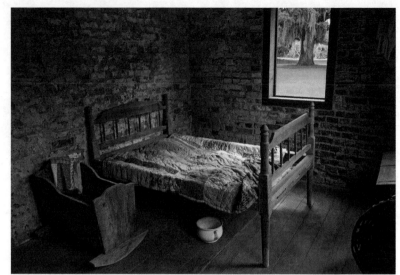

restored slave cabin at Boone Hall Plantation

the nine humble brick slave cabins from the 1790s, expertly restored and most fitted with interpretive displays. The cabins are the center of Boone Hall's educational programs, including an exploration of Gullah culture at the outdoor "Gullah Theatre." Summers see some serious Civil War reenacting going on. In all, three different tours are available: a 30-minute house tour, a tour of Slave Street, and a garden tour.

MAP 4: 1235 Long Point Rd., 843/884-4371, www. boonehallplantation.com; mid-Mar.-Labor Day, Mon.-Sat. 8:30am-6:30pm, Sun. noon-5pm, Labor Day.-mid-Mar. Mon.-Sat. 9am-5pm, Sun. noon-5pm; $20 adults, $10 children

## CHARLES PINCKNEY NATIONAL HISTORIC SITE

This is one of my favorite sights in Charleston, for its uplifting, well-explored subject matter as well as its tastefully maintained house and grounds. Though "Constitution Charlie's" old Snee Farm is down to only 28 acres from its original magnificent 700, the Charles Pinckney National Historic Site that encompasses it is still an important repository of local and national history. Sometimes called "the forgotten founder," Charles Pinckney was not only a hero of the American Revolution and a notable early abolitionist, but also one of the main authors of the U.S. Constitution. His great-aunt Eliza Lucas Pinckney was the first woman agriculturalist in the United States, responsible for opening up the indigo trade. Her son Charles Cotesworth Pinckney was one of the signers of the Constitution. The current main house, doubling as the visitors center, dates from 1828, 11 years after Pinckney sold Snee Farm to pay off debts. That said, it's still a great example of Lowcountry architecture. It replaces Pinckney's original home, where President George Washington slept and had breakfast under a nearby oak tree in 1791 while touring the South. Another highlight at this National Park Service-administered site is the 0.5-mile self-guided walk around the grounds, some of it on boardwalks over the marsh. No matter what anyone tells you, no one is buried underneath the tombstone in the grove of oak trees bearing the name of Constitution Charlie's father, Colonel Charles Pinckney. The marker incorrectly states the elder Pinckney's age; it was put here only as a monument. Another memorial to the colonel is in the churchyard of the 1840s-era Christ Church about one mile down Long Point Road.

MAP 4: 1240 Long Point Rd., 843/881-5516, www.nps. gov/chpi; daily 9am-5pm; free

## ISLE OF PALMS

This primarily residential area of about 5,000 people received the state's first "Blue Wave" designation from the Clean Beaches Council for its well-managed and preserved beaches. Like adjacent Sullivan's Island, there are pockets of great wealth here, but also a laid-back, windswept beach-town vibe. You get here from Mount Pleasant by taking the Isle of Palms Connector (Hwy. 517) off U.S. 17 (Johnnie Dodds/Chuck Dawley Blvd.). Aside from just enjoying the whole scene, the main self-contained attraction here is **Isle of Palms County Park** (14th Ave., 843/886-3863, www. ccprc.com, May-Labor Day daily 9am-7pm, Mar.-Apr. and Sept.-Oct. daily 10am-6pm, Nov.-Feb. daily 10am-5pm, $7 per vehicle, free for pedestrians and cyclists), with its ocean-front beach, complete with umbrella rental, a volleyball court, a playground, and lifeguards. Get here from the Isle of Palms Connector by going through the light at Palm Boulevard and taking the next left at the gate. The island's other claim to fame is the excellent (and surprisingly affordable) **Wild Dunes Resort** (5757 Palm Blvd., 888/778-1876, www.wild-dunes.com) with its two Fazio golf courses and 17 clay tennis courts. Breach Inlet, between Isle of Palms and Sullivan's Island, is where the Confederate sub *Hunley* sortied to do battle with the USS *Housatonic*. During 1989's Hurricane Hugo, the entire island was submerged.

MAP 4: off U.S. 17, via Hwy. 517

## Sullivan's Island

Part funky beach town, part ritzy getaway, Sullivan's Island has a certain timeless quality. While much of it was rebuilt after Hurricane Hugo's devastation, plenty of local character remains, as evidenced by some cool little bars in its tiny "business district" on the main drag of Middle Street. There's a ton of history on Sullivan's, but you can also just while the day away on the quiet, windswept beach on the Atlantic or ride a bike all over the island and back. Unless you have a boat, you can only get here from Mount Pleasant. From U.S. 17, follow the signs for Highway 703 and Sullivan's Island. Cross the Ben Sawyer Bridge, and then turn right onto Middle Street; continue for about 1.5 miles.

## FORT MOULTRIE

While Fort Sumter gets the vast bulk of the attention, the older Fort Moultrie on Sullivan's Island actually has a much more sweeping history. Furthering the irony, Major Robert Anderson's detachment at Fort Sumter at the opening of the Civil War was actually the Fort Moultrie garrison, reassigned to Sumter because Moultrie was thought too vulnerable from the landward side. Indeed, Moultrie's first incarnation, a perimeter of felled palm trees, didn't even have a name when it was unsuccessfully attacked by the British in the summer of 1776, the first victory by the colonists in the Revolution. The redcoat cannonballs bounced off those flexible trunks, and thus was born South Carolina's nickname, "The Palmetto State." The hero of the battle, Sergeant William Jasper, would gain immortality for putting the blue-and-white regimental banner—forerunner to the modern blue-and-white state flag—on a makeshift staff after the first one was shot away. Subsequently named for the commander at the time, William Moultrie, the fort was captured by the British in a later engagement. That first fort fell into decay and a new one was built over it in 1798 but was soon destroyed by a hurricane.

In 1809 a brick fort was built here; it soon gained notoriety as the place where the great chief Osceola was detained soon after his capture, and where he posed for the famous portrait by George Catlin. His captors got more than they bargained for when they jokingly asked the old guerrilla soldier for a rendition of the Seminole battle cry. According to accounts, Osceola's realistic performance scared some bystanders half to death. The chief died here in 1838, and his modest grave site is still on-site, in front of the fort on the landward side.

Other famous people to have trod on Sullivan's Island include Edgar Allan Poe, who was inspired by Sullivan's lonely, evocative environment to write *The Gold Bug* and other works. There's a Gold Bug Avenue and a Poe Avenue here today, and the local library is named after him as well. A young Lieutenant William Tecumseh Sherman was also stationed here during his Charleston stint in the 1830s before his encounter with history in the Civil War.

Moultrie's main Civil War role was as a target for Union shot during the long siege of Charleston. It was pounded so hard and for so long that its walls fell below a nearby sand hill and were finally unable to be hit anymore. A full military upgrade happened in the late 1800s, extending over most of Sullivan's Island (some private owners have even bought some of the old batteries and converted them into homes). It's the series of later forts that you'll visit on your trip to the Moultrie site, which is technically part of the Fort Sumter National Monument and administered by the National Park Service.

Most of the outdoor tours are self-guided, but ranger programs typically happen Memorial Day-Labor Day daily at 11am and 2:30pm There's a bookstore and visitors center across the street offering a 20-minute video on the hour and half hour 9am-4:30pm. Keep in mind there's no regular ferry to Fort Sumter from Fort Moultrie; the closest ferry to Sumter leaves from Patriots Point on Mount Pleasant. **MAP 4**: 1214 Middle St., 843/883-3123, www.nps.gov/fosu; daily 9am-5pm; $3, free under age 16

### BENCH BY THE ROAD

Scholars say that about half of all African Americans alive today had an ancestor who once set foot on Sullivan's Island. As the first point of entry for at least half of all slaves imported to the United States, the island's "pest houses" acted as quarantine areas so slaves could be checked for communicable diseases before going to auction in Charleston proper. But few people seem to know this. In a 1989 magazine interview, African American author and Nobel laureate Toni Morrison said about historic sites concerning slavery, "There is no suitable memorial, or plaque, or wreath or

*A Bench by the Road,* on Sullivan's Island

wall, or park or skyscraper lobby. There's no 300-foot tower, there's no small bench by the road." In 2008, that last item became a reality, as the first of several planned "benches by the road" was installed on Sullivan's Island to mark the sacrifice of enslaved African Americans. It's a simple black steel bench with an attached marker and a nearby plaque. The Bench by the Road is at the Fort Moultrie visitors center.

MAP 4: Fort Moultrie visitors center, 1214 Middle St.

## Awendaw and Points North

This area just north of Charleston along U.S. 17—named for the Sewee Indian village originally located here and known to the world chiefly as the place where Hurricane Hugo made landfall in 1989—is seeing some new growth but still hews to its primarily rural, nature-loving roots.

### CAPE ROMAIN NATIONAL WILDLIFE REFUGE

One of the best natural experiences in the area is about a 30-minute drive north of Charleston at Cape Romain National Wildlife Refuge. Essentially comprising four barrier islands, the 66,000-acre refuge—almost all of which is marsh—provides a lot of great paddling opportunities, chief among them **Bulls Island** (no overnight camping). A fairly lengthy trek from where you put in lies famous Boneyard Beach, where hundreds of downed trees lie on the sand, bleached by sun and salt. Slightly to the south within the refuge, **Capers Island Heritage Preserve** (843/953-9300, www.dnr.sc.gov, daily dawn-dusk, free) is still a popular camping locale despite heavy damage from 1989's Hurricane Hugo. Get permits in advance by calling the South Carolina Department of Natural Resources. You can kayak to the refuge yourself or take the only approved ferry service from **Coastal Expeditions** (514-B Mill St., Mount Pleasant, 843/881-4582, www.coastalexpeditions.com, $40 adults, $20 children, 30 minutes). **Barrier Island Eco Tours** (50 41st Ave., Isle of Palms, 843/886-5000, www.

nature-tours.com, 3.5-hour boat excursions $38 adults, $28 children) on Isle of Palms also runs trips to the area.

MAP 4: 5801 U.S. 17 N., 843/928-3264, www.fws.gov/caperomain; daily dawn-dusk

### SEWEE VISITOR AND ENVIRONMENTAL EDUCATION CENTER

Twenty miles north of Charleston you'll find the Sewee Visitor and Environmental Education Center. Besides being a gateway of sorts for the almost entirely aquatic Cape Romain National Wildlife Refuge, Sewee is primarily known for housing several rare red wolves, who were part of a unique release program on nearby Bull Island begun in the late 1970s. They're kept at the center to maintain the genetic integrity of the species.

MAP 4: 5821 U.S. 17, 843/928-3368, www.fws.gov/seweecenter; Wed.-Sat. 9am-5pm; free

## FOLLY BEACH AND THE SOUTHWEST ISLANDS
### FOLLY BEACH

A large percentage of the town of Folly Beach was destroyed by Hurricane Hugo in 1989, and erosion since then has increased and hit the beach itself pretty hard. All that said, enough of Folly's funky charm is left to make it worth visiting. Called "The Edge of America" during its heyday as a swinging resort getaway from the 1930s through the 1950s, Folly Beach is now a slightly beaten but enjoyable little getaway on this barrier island. As with all areas of Charleston, the cost of living here is rapidly increasing, but Folly Beach still reminds locals of a time that once was: a time of soda fountains, poodle skirts, stylish one-piece bathing suits, and growling hot rods. Folly's main claim to larger historic fame is playing host to George Gershwin, who stayed at a cottage on West Arctic Avenue to write the score for *Porgy and Bess*, set across the harbor in downtown Charleston. (Ironically, Gershwin's opera couldn't be performed in its original setting until 1970 because of segregationist Jim Crow laws.) Original *Porgy* author

DuBose Heyward stayed around the corner at a summer cottage on West Ashley Avenue that he dubbed "Follywood."

Called Folly Road until it gets to the beach, Center Street is the main drag here, dividing the beach into east and west. In this area you'll find the **Folly Beach Fishing Pier** (101 E. Arctic Ave., 843/588-3474, Apr.-Oct. daily 6am-11pm, Nov. and Mar. daily 7am-7pm, Dec.-Feb. daily 8am-5pm, $5-7 parking, $8 fishing fee), which replaced the grand old wooden pier-and-pavilion structure that tragically burned down in 1960.

Back in the day, restaurants, bars, and amusement areas with rides lined the way up to the old pavilion. As the premier musical venue in the region, the pavilion hosted legends like Tommy and Jimmy Dorsey, Benny Goodman, and Count Basie. The new fishing pier, while not as grand as the old one, is worth visiting—a massive, well-built edifice jutting over 1,000 feet into the Atlantic with a large diamond-shaped pavilion at the end. Fishing-rod holders and cleaning stations line the entire thing. Out on the "front beach," daytime activities once included boxing matches and extralegal drag races. In the old days, the "Washout" section on the far west end was where you went to go crabbing or fly-fishing or maybe even steal a kiss from your sweetie. Today, though, the Washout is known as the prime surfing area in the Carolinas, with a dedicated group of diehards.

To get to Folly Beach from Charleston, go west on Calhoun Street and take the James Island Connector. Take a left on Folly Road (Hwy. 171), which becomes Center Street on into Folly Beach.

At the far east end of Folly Island, about 300 yards offshore, you'll see the **Morris Island Lighthouse,** an 1876 beacon that was once surrounded by lush green landscape, now completely surrounded by water as the land has eroded around it. Now privately owned, there's an extensive effort to save and preserve the lighthouse (www.savethelight.org). There's also an effort to keep high-dollar condo development off of beautiful bird-friendly Morris Island itself (www.morrisisland.org). To get there while there's still something left to enjoy, take East Ashley Street until it dead-ends. Park in the lot and take a 0.25-mile walk to the beach.

**MAP 5**: south of Charleston via Hwy. 30 and Hwy. 171

## Kiawah Island and Seabrook Island

The beautiful island of Kiawah with a

For peaceful resort-style living in a relaxed atmosphere, Kiawah Island is the place to go.

beautiful beach to match—about 45 minutes away from downtown Charleston—has as its main attraction the sumptuous **Kiawah Island Golf Resort** (12 Kiawah Beach Dr., 800/654-2924, www.kiawahgolf.com, $600-800), a key location for PGA tournaments. But even if you don't play golf, the resort is an amazing stay. The main component is **The Sanctuary,** an upscale hotel featuring an opulent lobby complete with grand staircases, a large pool area overlooking the beach, tasteful Spanish Colonial-style architecture, and 255 smallish but excellently appointed guest rooms.

Several smaller private, family-friendly resorts also exist on Kiawah, with fully furnished homes and villas and every amenity you could ask for. Go to www.explorekiawah.com for a full range of options or call 800/877-0837.

Through the efforts of the **Kiawah Island Conservancy** (23 Beachwalker Dr., 843/768-2029, www.kiawahconservancy.org), over 300 acres of the island have been kept as an undeveloped nature preserve. The island's famous bobcat population has made quite a comeback; the bobcats are vital to the island ecosystem, since as top predator they help cull what would otherwise become untenably large populations of deer and rabbit.

The beach at Kiawah is a particular delight, set as it is on such a comparatively undeveloped island. No matter where you stay on Kiawah, a great thing about the island is the notable lack of light pollution—don't forget to look up at night and enjoy the stars!

Like its neighbor Kiawah, **Seabrook Island** is also a private resort-dominated island. In addition to offering miles of beautiful beaches, on its 2,200 acres are a wide variety of golfing, tennis, equestrian, and swimming facilities as well as extensive dining and shopping options. There are a lot of kids' activities as well. For information on lodging options and packages, go to www.seabrook.com or call 866/249-9934. Seabrook Island is about 45 minutes from Charleston. From downtown, take SC 30 West to Maybank Highway, then take a left onto Cherry Point Road.

## Johns Island
### ANGEL OAK PARK
The outlying community of Johns Island is where you'll find the inspiring Angel Oak Park, home of a massive live oak, 65 feet in circumference, that's over 1,000 years old and commonly considered the oldest tree east of the Mississippi River. As is the case with all live oaks, don't expect impressive height—when oaks age they spread *out*, not up. The sprawling, picturesque tree and the park containing it are owned by the city of Charleston, and the scenic grounds are often used for weddings and special events. Angel Oak Park is about 30 minutes from Charleston. Take U.S. 17 over the Ashley River, then Highway 171 to Maybank Highway. Take a left onto Bohicket Road, and then look for signs on the right.

**MAP 5**: 3688 Angel Oak Rd.; Mon.-Sat. 9am-5pm, Sun. 1pm-5pm; free

### LEGARE FARMS
Legare Farms is open to the public for various activities, including its annual pumpkin patch in October, its "sweet corn" festival in June, and bird walks (Sat. 8:30am, $6 adults, $3 children) in fall. To make the 20-minute drive from downtown Charleston, take SC 30 West to Maybank Highway, then a left onto River Road and a right onto Jenkins Farm Road.

**MAP 5**: 2620 Hanscombe Point Rd., 843/559-0763, www.legarefarms.com; hours vary

## Wadmalaw Island
### CHARLESTON TEA PLANTATION
Currently owned by the R. C. Bigelow Tea corporation, the Charleston Tea Plantation is no cute living-history exhibit: It's a big working tea plantation—the only one in the United States—with acre after acre of *Camellia sinensis* being worked by modern

farm machinery. Visitors get to see a sample of how the tea is made "from the field to the cup." Factory tours are free, and a trolley tour of the "Back 40" is $10. And, of course, there's a gift shop where you can sample and buy all types of teas and tea-related products. Growing season is April-October. The tea bushes, direct descendants of plants brought over in the 1800s from India and China, "flush up" two-three inches every few weeks during growing season. Charleston Tea Plantation is about 30 minutes from Charleston. Take the Ashley River Bridge, stay left to Folly Road (Hwy. 171), turn right onto Maybank Highway for 18 miles, and look for the sign on the left.

MAP 5: 6617 Maybank Hwy., 843/559-0383, www. charlestonteaplantation.com; Mon.-Sat. 10am-4pm, Sun. noon-4pm; free

### DEEP WATER VINEYARDS

South Carolina has several good wineries, among them Wadmalaw's own Deep Water, formerly Irvin House Vineyards, the Charleston area's only vineyard. They make several varieties of muscadine wine here, with $5 tastings and a gift shop. Every Saturday they host a "Wine-Down" party noon-4pm). Also on the grounds you'll find **Firefly Distillery** (6775 Bears Bluff Rd., 843/559-6867, www.fireflyvodka.com, Tues.-Sat. 10am-5pm), home of their signature Firefly Sweet Tea Vodka. To get here from Charleston, go west on Maybank Highway about 10 miles to Bears Bluff Road veering right. The vineyard entrance is on the left after about eight miles.

MAP 5: 6775 Bears Bluff Rd., 843/559-6867, www. deepwatervineyard.com; Tues.-Sat. 10am-5pm

# Entertainment and Nightlife

Unlike the locals-versus-tourists divide you find so often in other destination cities, in Charleston it's nothing for a couple of visitors to find themselves at a table next to four or five college students enjoying themselves in true Charlestonian fashion: loudly and with lots of good food and strong drink nearby. Indeed, the Holy City is downright ecumenical in its partying. The smokiest dives also have some of the best brunches. Tourist hot spots written up in all the guidebooks also have their share of local regulars. But through it all, one constant remains: Charleston's finely honed ability to seek out and enjoy the good life.

Bars close in Charleston at 2am, though there is a movement afoot to make the closing time earlier in some areas of town, mostly the Upper King neighborhood, the youngest and most vibrant nightlife area in Charleston. All hard-liquor sales stop at 7pm, with none at all on Sundays. You can buy beer and wine in grocery stores 24-7.

Charleston's live music scene is hit-or-miss. With the long-ago passing of the heyday of

Hootie & the Blowfish, there's no distinct "Charleston sound" to speak of (though Hootie frontman-turned-country-star Darius Rucker still plays frequently in the area), but they do a good job of bringing in well-regarded national and regional touring acts. The best place to find up-to-date music listings is the local free weekly *Charleston City Paper* (www.charlestoncitypaper.com).

## WATERFRONT
### Lounges
### ROOFTOP BAR AND RESTAURANT

The aptly named Rooftop Bar and Restaurant at newly restored The Vendue is a very popular waterfront happy hour spot from which to enjoy the sunset over the Charleston skyline.

MAP 1: 23 Vendue Range, 843/723-0485; Tues.-Sat. 6pm-2am

### THE GIN JOINT

If artisan cocktails are your thing, head straight to The Gin Joint, where you can get drinks with names like Thieve's Tonic (rum, turmeric, lime, coconut, ginger honey) and Studmuffin (Madeira, chicory liqueur, coffee liqueur, and bay leaf ice cubes). With most cocktails running about $11 each, they're actually bargains when you consider the curated ingredients going into each one. Got a big party? Order one of four signature punches to share, prepared tableside (about $40). Fair warning: These aren't your typical office party punches and pack a commensurately large, well, punch. Thankfully, there is a good little menu of tapas to soak up all the alcohol. **MAP 1:** 182 E. Bay St., 843/577-6111, www.theginjoint. com; Thurs.-Fri. 5pm-2am, Sat. 3pm-2am, Sun.-Wed. 5pm-midnight

## FRENCH QUARTER
### Bars and Pubs
#### TOMMY CONDON'S IRISH PUB
The Guinness flows freely at touristy Tommy Condon's Irish Pub—after the obligatory and traditional slow-pour, that is—as do the patriotic Irish songs performed live most nights. **MAP 1:** 160 Church St., 843/577-3818, www. tommycondons.com; Sun.-Thurs. 11am-2am, dinner until 10pm, Fri.-Sat. 11am-2am, dinner until 11pm

## NORTH OF BROAD
### Bars and Pubs
#### VICKERY'S BAR AND GRILL
If it's a nice day out, a good place to relax and enjoy happy hour outside is Vickery's Bar and Grill, actually part of a small regional chain based in Atlanta. Start with the oyster bisque and maybe try the turkey and brie sandwich or crab cakes for your entrée.

Though Vickery's Bar and Grill does not market itself as a gay and lesbian establishment, it has nonetheless become quite popular with that population—not least because of the good reputation its parent tavern in Atlanta has with that city's large and influential gay community. **MAP 1:** 15 Beaufain St., 843/577-5300, www. vickerysbarandgrill.com; Mon.-Sat. 11:30am-2am, Sun. 11am-1am, kitchen closes 1am

## Doin' the Charleston

It has been called the biggest song and dance craze of the 20th century. It first entered the American public consciousness via New York City in a 1923 Harlem musical called *Runnin' Wild*, but the roots of the dance soon to be known as the Charleston were indeed in the Holy City. No one is quite sure of the day and date, but local lore assures us that members of Charleston's legendary Jenkins Orphanage Band were the first to start dancing that crazy "Geechie step," a development that soon became part of the band's act. The Jenkins Orphanage was started in 1891 by the African American Baptist minister Reverend D. J. Jenkins and was originally housed in the Old Marine Hospital at 20 Franklin Street (which you can see today, although it's not open to the public). To raise money, Reverend Jenkins acquired donated instruments and started a band comprising talented orphans from the house. The orphans traveled as far away as London, where they were a hit with the locals but not with the constabulary, who unceremoniously fined them for stopping traffic. A Charleston attorney who happened to be in London at the time, Augustine Smyth, paid their way back home, becoming a lifelong supporter of the orphanage in the process.

From then on, playing in donated old citadel uniforms, the Jenkins Orphanage Band frequently took its act on the road. They played at the St. Louis and Buffalo expositions and even at President Taft's inauguration. They also frequently played in New York, and it was there that African American pianist and composer James P. Johnson heard the Charlestonians play and dance to their Gullah rhythms, considered exotic at the time. Johnson would incorporate what he heard into the tune "Charleston," one of many songs in the revue *Runnin' Wild*. The catchy song and its accompanying loose-limbed dance seemed tailor-made for the Roaring '20s and its liberated, hedonistic spirit. Before long the Charleston had swept the nation, becoming a staple of jazz clubs and speakeasies across the country and, indeed, the world.

## UPPER KING

### Bars and Pubs

#### RECOVERY ROOM

The hottest hipster dive bar is the Recovery Room on bustling Upper King. The drinks are cheap and stiff, and the bar food is addictively tasty (two words: Tater Tots!).

**MAP 2**: 685 King St., 843/727-0999; Mon.-Fri. 4pm-2am, Sat. 3pm-2am, Sun. noon-2am

### Dance Clubs

#### TRIO CLUB

The Trio Club, right off Marion Square, is a favorite place to make the scene. There's a relaxing outdoor area with piped-in music, an intimate sofa-filled upstairs bar for dancing and chilling, and the dark candlelit downstairs with frequent live music leaning toward hip-hop sounds.

**MAP 2**: 139 Calhoun St., 843/965-5333; Thurs.-Sat. 9pm-2am

### Gay and Lesbian

#### CURE

Charleston's hottest dance spot of any type, gay or straight, is Cure on Upper King, on the lower level of the parking garage across from the visitors center (375 Meeting St.). This space was for years known as Club Pantheon but has changed ownership. Cover charges are typically not cheap, but it's worth it for the great DJs, the dancing, and the people watching, not to mention the frequent drag cabaret shows.

**MAP 2**: 28 Ann St., 843/577-2582; Fri.-Sun. 10pm-2am

#### DUDLEY'S

Just down the street from Cure—and owned by the same people—is a totally different kind of gay bar, Dudley's. Mellower and more appropriate for conversation or a friendly game of pool, Dudley's is a nice contrast to the thumping pantheon a few doors down.

**MAP 2**: 42 Ann St., 843/577-6779; daily 4pm-2am

### Live Music

#### MUSIC FARM

The venerable Music Farm on Upper King isn't much to look at from the outside, but inside the cavernous space has played host to all sorts of bands over the past two decades. Recent concerts have included Fitz and the Tantrums, the Dropkick Murphys, and the Drive-By Truckers.

**MAP 2**: 32 Ann St., 843/722-8904, www.musicfarm.com

---

## Craft Breweries

The craft beer revolution has hit Charleston hard. No newcomer to the game, **Palmetto Brewing** (289 Huger St., 843/937-0903, www.palmettobrewery.com, tasting room Tues.-Wed. 3pm-7pm, Thurs. 3pm-9pm, Fri. 1pm-10pm, Sat. 1pm-7pm) actually has roots in Charleston going back before the Civil War and was the city's first post-Prohibition brewery. Known for their Nitro beers and Espresso Porter, among many others, they have an extensive outdoor seating area and often feature live music on weekends. Currently situated near a highway overpass, Palmetto is planning a move, likely up the road in North Charleston, but as of this writing no plans had been finalized.

**COAST Brewing** (1250 2nd St. North, 843/343-4727, www.coastbrewing.com, Thurs.-Fri. 4pm-7pm, Sat. 11am-4pm) in North Charleston focuses on sustainable and organic ingredients. Try the Blackbeerd Stout if it's available, and any Kolsch. This is more of a casual, all-outdoor tasting experience, so keep weather in mind.

**Holy City Brewing** (4155C Dorchester Rd., www.holycitybrewing.com, Mon.-Thurs. 11am-8pm, Fri.-Sat. 11am-9pm, Sun. 11am-5pm), also in North Charleston, is known for their porters and stouts. This is also a great choice if you're hungry, as they have a full menu. Try the namesake Holy City Burger.

## HAMPTON PARK
### Bars and Pubs
#### MOE'S CROSSTOWN TAVERN

One of Charleston's favorite neighborhood spots is Moe's Crosstown Tavern at Rutledge and Francis in the Wagener Terrace/Hampton Square area. A newer location, **Moe's Downtown Tavern** (5 Cumberland St., 843/577-8500, daily 11am-2am) offers a similar vibe and menu, but the original, and best, Moe's experience is at the Crosstown.
MAP 2: 714 Rutledge Ave., 843/722-3287; daily 11am-2am

## WEST ASHLEY
### Bars and Pubs
#### GENE'S HAUFBRAU

Located not too far over the Ashley River on U.S. 17, Charleston institution Gene's Haufbrau is worth making a special trip into West Ashley. Boasting the largest beer selection in Charleston—from the Butte Creek Organic Ale from California to a can of PBR—Gene's also claims to be the oldest bar in town, established in 1952.
MAP 3: 17 Savannah Hwy., 843/225-4363, www.geneshaufbrau.com; daily 11:30am-2am

### Lounges
#### VOODOO LOUNGE

Across the street from Gene's Haufbrau, the retro-chic Voodoo Lounge is another very popular West Ashley hangout. It has a wide selection of trendy cocktails and killer gourmet tacos.
MAP 3: 15 Magnolia Rd., 843/769-0228; Mon.-Fri. 4pm-2am, Sat.-Sun. 5:30pm-2am, kitchen until 1am

## NORTH CHARLESTON
### Bars and Pubs
#### MADRA RUA IRISH PUB

If you find yourself up in North Charleston, by all means stop by Madra Rua Irish Pub, an authentic watering hole with a better-than-average pub-food menu that's also a great place to watch a soccer game.
MAP 3: 1034 E. Montague Ave., 843/554-2522; daily 11am-1am

## MOUNT PLEASANT AND EAST COOPER
### Bars and Pubs
#### DUNLEAVY'S PUB

Though Sullivan's Island has a lot of high-dollar homes, it still has friendly watering holes like Dunleavy's Pub. Inside is a great bar festooned with memorabilia, or you can enjoy a patio table.
MAP 4: 2213-B Middle St., 843/883-9646; Sun.-Thurs. 11:30am-1am, Fri.-Sat. 11:30am-2am

#### POE'S TAVERN

The other Sullivan's watering hole of note is Poe's Tavern across the street, a nod to Edgar Allan Poe and his service on the island as a clerk in the U.S. Army. It's a lively, mostly locals scene, set within a fun but suitably dark interior (though you might opt for one of the outdoor tables on the raised patio). Simply put, no trip to Sullivan's is complete without a stop at one (or possibly both) of these two local landmarks, which are within a stone's throw of each other.
MAP 4: 2210 Middle St., 843/883-0083; www.poestavern.com; daily 11am-2am, kitchen closes 10pm

## FOLLY BEACH AND THE SOUTHWEST ISLANDS
### Bars and Pubs
#### BLU RESTAURANT AND BAR

If you're in Folly Beach, enjoy the great views and the great cocktails at Blu Restaurant and Bar inside the Holiday Inn Folly Beach Oceanfront. There's nothing like a Spiked Lemonade on a hot Charleston day at the beach.
MAP 5: 1 Center St., 843/588-6658, www.blufollybeach.com; daily 7am-10pm

#### SAND DOLLAR SOCIAL CLUB

A notable Folly Beach watering hole is the Sand Dollar Social Club, the kind of cash-only, mostly local dive you often find in little beach towns. You have to pony up for a "membership" to this private club, but it's only a buck. There's a catch, though: You can't get in until your 24-hour "waiting period" is over.
MAP 5: 7 Center St., 843/588-9498; Sun.-Fri. noon-1am, Sat. noon-2am

## Live Music

### THE POUR HOUSE

The hippest music spot in town is out on James Island at The Pour House, where the local characters are sometimes just as entertaining as the acts onstage.

**MAP 5**: 1977 Maybank Hwy., 843/571-4343, www.charlestonpourhouse.com; 9pm-2am on nights with music scheduled

# FESTIVALS AND EVENTS

Charleston is a festival-mad city, especially in the spring and early fall. And new festivals are being added every year, further enhancing the hedonistic flavor of this city that has also mastered the art of hospitality. Here's a look through the calendar at all the key festivals in the area.

## January

Held on a Sunday in late January at historic Boone Hall Plantation in Mount Pleasant, the **Lowcountry Oyster Festival** (www.charlestonlowcountry.com, 11am-5pm Sun., $8, food additional) features literal truckloads of the sweet shellfish for your enjoyment. Gates open at 10:30am, and there's plenty of parking. Oysters are sold by the bucket and served with crackers and cocktail sauce. Bring your own shucking knife or glove, or buy one on-site.

## February

One of the more unique events in town is the **Southeastern Wildlife Exposition** (various venues, 843/723-1748, www.sewe.com, $12.50 per day, $30 for 3 days, free under age 13). For the last quarter century, the Wildlife Expo has brought together hundreds of artists and exhibitors to showcase just about any kind of naturally themed art you can think of in over a dozen galleries and venues all over downtown. Kids will enjoy the live animals on hand as well.

Up in North Charleston is where **Brewvival** (adjacent to COAST Brewing, 1250 2nd St. North, www.brewvival.com, $75) is held. This day-long craft brew-tasting festival focuses heavily on featuring brewers from the rapidly growing South Carolina craft beer industry. There is live music and of course food vendors available as well.

## March

Generally straddling late February and the first days of March, the four-day **Charleston Food & Wine Festival** (www.charlestonfoodandwine.com, various venues and admission) is a glorious celebration of one of the Holy City's premier draws: its amazing culinary community. While the emphasis is on Lowcountry chefs, guest chefs from as far away as New York, New Orleans, and Los Angeles routinely come to show off their skills. Oenophiles, especially of domestic wines, will be in heaven as well. This event has boomed in recent years and downtown gets quite crowded. Tickets aren't cheap—an all-event pass is over $500 pp—but then again, this is one of the nation's great food cities.

Immediately before the Festival of Houses and Gardens is the **Charleston International Antiques Show** (40 E. Bay St., 843/722-3405, www.historiccharleston.org, admission varies), held at Historic Charleston's headquarters at the Missroon House on the High Battery. It features over 30 of the nation's best-regarded dealers and offers lectures and tours.

Mid-March-April, the perennial favorite **Festival of Houses and Gardens** (843/722-3405, www.historiccharleston.org, admission varies) is sponsored by the Historic Charleston Foundation and held at the very peak of the spring blooming season for maximum effect. In all, the festival goes into a dozen historic neighborhoods to view about 150 homes. Each day sees a different three-hour tour of a different area, at about $50 pp. This is a fantastic opportunity to peek inside some amazing old privately owned properties that are inaccessible to visitors at all other times. A highlight is a big oyster roast and picnic at Drayton Hall.

Not to be confused with the above festival, the **Garden Club of Charleston House and Garden Tours** (843/530-5164, www.

thegardenclubofcharleston.com, $35) are held over a weekend in late March. Highlights include the Heyward-Washington House and the private garden of the late great Charleston horticulturalist Emily Whaley.

One of Charleston's newest and most fun events, the five-night **Charleston Fashion Week** (www.charlestonfashionweek.com, admission varies) benefits local women's and children's charities. Mimicking New York's Fashion Week events under tenting in Bryant Park, Charleston's version features runway action under big tents in Marion Square—and, yes, past guests have included former contestants on *Project Runway*.

## April

The annual **Cooper River Bridge Run** (www. bridgerun.com) happens the first Saturday in April (unless that's Easter weekend, in which case it runs the week before) and features a six-mile jaunt across the massive new Arthur Ravenel Bridge over the Cooper River, the longest cable span in the Western Hemisphere. It's not for those with a fear of heights, but it's still one of Charleston's best-attended events—there are well over 30,000 participants. The whole crazy idea started when Dr. Marcus Newberry of the Medical University of South Carolina in Charleston was inspired by an office fitness trail in his native state of Ohio to do something similar in Charleston to promote fitness. Participants can walk the course if they choose, and many do. The start is signaled with the traditional cannon shot. The race still begins in Mount Pleasant and ends downtown, but over the years the course has changed to accommodate growth—not only in the event itself but in the city. Auto traffic, of course, is rerouted starting the night before the race. Each participant in the Bridge Run now must wear a transponder chip; new "Bones in Motion" technology allows you to track a favorite runner's exact position in real time during the race. The 2006 Run had wheelchair participants for the first time. There's now a Kid's Run in Hampton Square the Friday before, which also allows strollers.

Previously known as the Family Circle Cup, the **Volvo Car Open** (161 Seven Farms Dr., Daniel Island, 843/856-7900, www.volvocaropen.com, admission varies) is held at Daniel Island's Family Circle Tennis Center, specifically built for the event. Almost 100,000 people attend the multiple-week event. Individual session tickets go on sale the preceding January.

Mount Pleasant is the home of Charleston's shrimping fleet, and each April sees all the boats parade by the Alhambra Hall and Park for the **Blessing of the Fleet** (843/884-8517, www.townofmountpleasant.com). Family events and lots and lots of seafood are also on tap.

## May

Free admission and free parking are not the only draws at the outdoor **North Charleston Arts Festival** (5000 Coliseum Dr., www. northcharleston.org), but let's face it, that's important. Held beside North Charleston's Performing Arts Center and Convention Center, the festival features music, dance, theater, multicultural performers, and storytellers. There are a lot of kids' events as well.

Held over three days at the Holy Trinity Greek Orthodox Church up toward the Neck, the **Charleston Greek Festival** (30 Race St., 843/577-2063, www.charlestongreekfestival. com, $5 admission, food extra) offers a plethora of live entertainment, dancing, Greek wares, and, of course, fantastic Greek cuisine cooked by the congregation. Parking is not a problem, and there's even a shuttle to the church from the lot.

Indisputably Charleston's single biggest and most important event, **Spoleto Festival USA** (843/579-3100, www.spoletousa.org, admission varies) has come a long way since it was a sparkle in the eye of the late Gian Carlo Menotti three decades ago. Though Spoleto long ago broke ties with its founder, his vision remains indelibly stamped on the event from start to finish. There's plenty of music, to be sure, in genres that include orchestral, opera, jazz, and avant-garde, but you'll find something in every other performing art, such as dance, drama, and spoken word, in traditions from Western to African to Southeast Asian. For 17 days from Memorial Day weekend through early June, Charleston hops and hums nearly 24 hours a day to the energy of this vibrant, cutting-edge yet accessible, artistic celebration, which dominates everything and every conversation for those three weeks. Events happen in historic venues and churches all over downtown and as far as Middleton Place, which hosts the grand finale under the stars. If you want to come to Charleston during Spoleto—and everyone should, at least once—book your accommodations and your tickets far in advance. Tickets usually go on sale in early January for that summer's festival.

As if all the hubbub around Spoleto didn't give you enough to do, there's also **Piccolo Spoleto** (843/724-7305, www.piccolospoleto. com, various venues and admission), literally "little Spoleto," running concurrently. The intent of Piccolo Spoleto—begun just a couple of years after the larger festival came to town and run by the city's Office of Cultural Affairs—is to give local and regional performers a time to shine, sharing some of that larger spotlight on the national and international performers at the main event. Of particular interest to visiting families will be Piccolo's children's events, a good counter to some of the decidedly more adult fare at Spoleto USA.

## June

Technically part of Piccolo Spoleto but gathering its own following, the **Sweetgrass Cultural Arts Festival** (www.sweetgrass-festival.org) is held the first week in June in Mount Pleasant at the Laing Middle School (2213 U.S. 17 N.). The event celebrates the traditional sweetgrass basket-making skills of African Americans in the historic Christ Church Parish area of Mount Pleasant. If you want to buy some sweetgrass baskets made by the world's foremost experts in the field, this would be the time.

## July

Each year over 30,000 people come to see the **Patriots Point Fourth of July Blast** (866/831-1720), featuring a hefty barrage of fireworks shot off the deck of the USS *Yorktown* moored on the Cooper River in the Patriots Point complex. Food, live entertainment, and kids' activities are also featured.

## September

From late September into the first week of October, the city-sponsored **MOJA Arts Festival** (843/724-7305, www.mojafestival. com, various venues and admission) highlights the cultural contributions of African Americans and people from the Caribbean with dance, visual art, poetry, cuisine, crafts, and music in genres that include gospel, jazz, reggae, and classical. In existence since 1984, MOJA's name comes from the Swahili word for "one," and its diverse range of offerings in so many media have made it one of the Southeast's premier events. Some events are ticketed, while others, such as the kids' activities and many of the dance and film events, are free.

For five weeks from the last week of September into October, the Preservation Society of Charleston hosts the much-anticipated **Fall Tours of Homes & Gardens** (843/722-4630, www.preservationsociety. org, $45). The tour takes you into more than a dozen local residences and is the nearly 90-year-old organization's biggest fund-raiser. Tickets typically go on sale the previous June, and they tend to sell out very quickly.

Another great food event in this great food city, the **Taste of Charleston** (1235 Long Point Rd., 843/577-4030, www.charleston-restaurantassociation.com, 11am-5pm, $12) is held on a weekend in October at Boone Hall Plantation in Mount Pleasant and sponsored by the Greater Charleston Restaurant Association. Over 50 area chefs and restaurants come together so you can sample their wares, including a wine and food pairing, with proceeds going to charity.

# A Man, a Plan: Spoleto!

People gather in Marion Square to listen to music and enjoy Piccolo Spoleto.

Sadly, Gian Carlo Menotti is no longer with us, having died in 2007 at the age of 95. But the overwhelming success of the composer's brainchild and labor of love, **Spoleto Festival USA,** lives on, enriching the cultural and social life of Charleston and serving as the city's chief calling card to the world at large.

Menotti began writing music at age seven in his native Italy. As a young man he moved to Philadelphia to study music, where he shared classes—and lifelong connections—with Leonard Bernstein and Samuel Barber. His first full-length opera, *The Consul,* would garner him the Pulitzer Prize, as would 1955's *The Saint of Bleecker Street.* But by far Menotti's best-known work is the beloved Christmas opera *Amahl and the Night Visitors,* composed especially for NBC television in 1951. At the height of his fame in 1958, the charismatic and mercurial genius—fluent and witty in five languages—founded the "Festival of Two Worlds" in Spoleto, Italy, specifically as a forum for young American artists in Europe. But it wasn't until nearly two decades later, in 1977, that Menotti was able to make his long-imagined dream of an American counterpart a reality.

Attracted to Charleston because of its long-standing support of the arts, its undeniable good taste, and its small size—ensuring that his festival would always be the number-one activity in town while it was going on—Menotti worked closely with the man who was to become the other key part of the equation: Charleston mayor Joe Riley, then in his first term in office. Since then, the city has built on Spoleto's success by founding its own local version, **Piccolo Spoleto**—literally, "little Spoleto"—which focuses exclusively on local and regional talent.

Things haven't always gone smoothly. Menotti and the stateside festival parted ways in 1993, when he took over the Rome Opera. Making matters more uneasy, the Italian festival—run by Menotti's longtime partner (and later adopted son) Chip—also became estranged from what was intended to be its soul mate in South Carolina. (Chip was later replaced by the Italian Culture Ministry.) But perhaps this kind of creative tension is what Menotti intended all along. Indeed, each spring brings a Spoleto USA that seems to thrive on the inherent conflict between the festival's often cutting-edge offerings and the very traditional city that hosts it. Unlike so many of the increasingly generic arts "festivals" across the nation, Spoleto still challenges its audiences, just as Menotti intended it to. Depending on the critic and the audience member, that modern opera debut you see may be groundbreaking or gratuitous. The drama you check out may be exhilarating or tiresome.

Still, the crowds keep coming. Each year, a total of about 500,000 people attend both Spoleto and Piccolo Spoleto. Nearly one-third of the attendees are Charleston residents—the final proof that when it comes to supporting the arts, Charleston puts its money where its mouth is.

## October

Local company **Half Moon Outfitters** (280 King St., 843/853-0990; 425 Coleman Blvd., 843/881-9472, www.halfmoonoutfitters.com, Mon.-Sat. 10am-7pm, Sun. noon-6pm) sponsors an annual six-mile Giant Kayak Race at Isle of Palms Marina in late October benefiting the Coastal Conservation League.

## November

**Plantation Days at Middleton Place** (4300 Ashley River Rd., 843/556-6020, www.middletonplace.org, daily 9am-5pm, last tour 4:30pm, guided tour $10) happen each Saturday in November, giving visitors a chance to wander the grounds and see artisans at work practicing authentic crafts, as they would have done in antebellum days, with a special emphasis on the contributions of African Americans. A special treat comes on Thanksgiving, when a full meal is offered on the grounds at the Middleton Place Restaurant (843/556-6020, www.middletonplace.org, reservations strongly recommended).

One of Charleston's newest annual events is the **Charleston International Film Festival** (843/817-1617, www.charlestoniff.com, various venues and prices). Despite being a relative latecomer to the film-festival circuit, the event is pulled off with Charleston's usual aplomb.

Though the **Battle of Secessionville** actually took place in June 1862 much farther south, November is the time the battle is reenacted at Boone Hall Plantation (1235 Long Point Rd., 843/884-4371, www.boonehallplantation.com, $17.50 adults, $7.50 children) in Mount Pleasant. Call for specific dates and times.

## December

A yuletide in the Holy City is an experience you'll never forget, as the **Christmas in Charleston** (843/724-3705) events clustered around the first week of the month prove. For some reason—whether it's the old architecture, the friendly people, the churches, the carriages, or all of the above—Charleston feels right at home during Christmas. The festivities begin with the mayor lighting the city's 60-foot Tree of Lights in Marion Square, followed by a parade of brightly lit boats from Mount Pleasant all the way around Charleston up the Ashley River. The key event is the Sunday Christmas Parade through downtown, featuring bands, floats, and performers in the holiday spirit. The Saturday farmers market in the square continues through the middle of the month with a focus on holiday items.

# Arts and Culture

Unlike the (literally) more puritanical colonies farther up the North American coast, Charleston was an arts-friendly settlement from the beginning. The first theatrical production on the continent happened in Charleston in January 1735, when a nomadic troupe rented a space at Church and Broad Streets to perform Thomas Otway's *The Orphan*. The play's success led to the building of the Dock Street Theatre on what is now Queen Street. Notable thespians performing in town included Edwin Booth, Junius Booth Jr. (brothers of Lincoln's assassin John Wilkes), and Edgar Allan Poe's mother, Eliza.

While not considered a visual arts mecca, since native son Joseph Allen Smith began one of the country's first art collections in Charleston in the late 1700s, the Holy City has been fertile ground for visual artists. For most visitors, the center of gallery activity is in the French Quarter between South Market and Tradd Streets.

# SOUTH OF BROAD
## Art Galleries
### CHARLESTON RENAISSANCE GALLERY

Charleston Renaissance Gallery specializes in 19th- and 20th-century oils and sculpture and features artists from the American South, including some splendid pieces from the Charleston Renaissance.
**MAP 1:** 103 Church St., 843/723-0025, www.fineartsouth.com; Mon.-Sat. 10am-5pm

### HELENA FOX FINE ART

Helena Fox Fine Art deals in 20th-century representational art.
**MAP 1:** 106-A Church St., 843/723-0073, www.helenafoxfineart.com; Mon.-Sat. 10am-5pm

# WATERFRONT
## Art Galleries
### CITY GALLERY AT WATERFRONT

The City Gallery at Waterfront is funded by the city, with exhibits focusing on local and regional culture and folkways.
**MAP 1:** 34 Prioleau St., 843/958-6484, www.citygalleryatwaterfrontpark.com; Tues.-Fri. 10am-6pm, Sat.-Sun. noon-5pm

## Art Walks

The best way to experience visual art galleries in Charleston is to go on one of the popular and free **Charleston Gallery Association ArtWalks** (843/724-3424, www.charlestongalleryassociation.com, first Friday of March, May, October, and December 5pm-8pm), which features lots of wine, food, and, of course, art. Over 40 galleries throughout downtown, with a special focus on the French Quarter, are featured. You can download a map at the website and visit them all yourself, whether or not you're here for the ArtWalk.

# FRENCH QUARTER
## Art Galleries
### ANN LONG FINE ART

Right up the street from the Sylvan Gallery and incorporating works from the estate of Charleston legend Elizabeth O'Neill Verner is Ann Long Fine Art, which seeks to combine the painterly aesthetic of the Old World with the edgy vision of the New.
**MAP 1:** 54 Broad St., 843/577-0447, www.annlongfineart.com; Mon.-Sat. 11am-5pm

### CORRIGAN GALLERY

One of the French Quarter's most beloved galleries, the Corrigan deals in some of the best current local artists, along with a focus on the Charleston Renaissance and the Charleston printmaking tradition.
**MAP 1:** 62 Queen St., 843/722-9868, www.corrigangallery.com; daily 10am-5pm

### PINK HOUSE GALLERY

The Pink House Gallery is in the oldest tavern building in the South, built circa 1694. The exhibits here offer a glimpse into old Charleston, including exclusive antique prints.
**MAP 1:** 17 Chalmers St., 843/723-3608, http://pinkhousegallery.tripod.com; Mon.-Sat. 10am-5pm

### ROBERT LANGE STUDIOS

In the heart of the French Quarter, Robert Lange Studios is oriented toward modern art. It hosts not only the work of its owners, Robert and Megan Lange, but also a slate of up-and-coming regional artists. This is a great place to be on the regular first Friday monthly art walks and events.
**MAP 1:** 2 Queen St., 843/805-8052, www.robertlangestudios.com; daily 11am-5pm

## Performing Arts
### CHARLESTON STAGE

Several high-quality troupes continue to keep Charleston's proud theater tradition alive, chief among them being Charleston Stage, the resident company of the Dock Street

Theatre. In addition to its well-received regular season of classics and modern staples, Charleston Stage has debuted more than 30 original scripts over the years, a recent example being *Gershwin at Folly*, recounting the composer's time at Folly Beach working on *Porgy and Bess*.

MAP 1: Dock Street Theatre, 135 Church St., 843/577-7183, www.charlestonstage.com

### THE FOOTLIGHT PLAYERS

The Footlight Players are the oldest continuously active company in town, founded in 1931. This community-based amateur company performs a mix of crowd-pleasers (*Who's Afraid of Virginia Woolf?*) and creative adaptations (*Miracle in Bedford Falls*, a musical based on *It's a Wonderful Life*) at their space at 20 Queen Street.

MAP 1: Footlight Players Theatre, 20 Queen St., 843/722-4487, www.footlightplayers.net

## NORTH OF BROAD
### Art Galleries
#### SYLVAN GALLERY

For a more modern take from local artists, check out the Sylvan Gallery, which specializes in 20th- and 21st-century art and sculpture.

MAP 1: 171 King St., 843/722-2172, www.thesylvangallery.com; Mon.-Fri. 9am-5pm, Sat. 10am-5pm, Sun. 11am-4pm

#### THE AUDUBON GALLERY

Farther up King and specializing in original Audubon prints and antique botanical prints is The Audubon Gallery, the sister store of the Joel Oppenheimer Gallery in Chicago.

MAP 1: 190 King St., 843/853-1100, www.audubonart.com; Mon.-Sat. 10am-5pm

#### GALLERY CHUMA

Within City Market is Gallery Chuma, which specializes in the art of the Gullah people of the South Carolina coast. They put on lots of cultural and educational events about Gullah culture as well as display art on the subject.

MAP 1: 188 Meeting St., 843/722-1702, www.gallerychuma.com; daily 9:30am-6pm

## Performing Arts
### THE HAVE NOTS!

The city's most unusual players are The Have Nots!, with a total ensemble of 35 comedians who typically perform their brand of edgy improv every Friday night at Theatre 99.

MAP 1: Theatre 99, 280 Meeting St., 843/853-6687, www.theatre99.com; Wed. 8pm, Fri.-Sat. 8pm and 10pm; $5-12.50

## Chamber Music in Charleston

The excellent music department at the College of Charleston sponsors the annual **Charleston Music Fest** (Simons Center for the Arts, 54 St. Philip St., $25), a series of chamber music concerts at various venues around the beautiful campus, featuring many faculty members of the college as well as visiting guest artists. Other college musical offerings include the **College of Charleston Concert Choir** (www.cofc.edu/music), which performs at various venues, usually churches, around town during the fall; the **College of Charleston Opera,** which performs at least one full-length production during the school year and often takes the stage at Piccolo Spoleto; and the popular **Yuletide Madrigal Singers,** who sing in early December at a series of concerts in historic Randolph Hall.

**Chamber Music Charleston** (various locations, 843/763-4941, www.chambermusiccharleston.org), which relies on many core Charleston Symphony Orchestra musicians, continues to perform around town, including at Piccolo Spoleto. They play a wide variety of picturesque venues, including the **Sottile Theatre** (44 George St.) and Kiawah Island. They can also be found at private house concerts, which sell out quickly.

# UPPER KING
## Art Galleries
### ART MECCA

This inviting modernist space specializes in local and regional contemporary artists. It's a great place to get a flavor of what Charleston's younger up-and-coming artists are doing. MAP 2: 427 King St., 843/577-0603, www. artmeccaofcharleston.com; Mon.-Fri. 10am-6pm, Sat. 10am-7pm, Sun. 11am-5pm

### PURE THEATRE

The players of PURE Theatre perform in a black box space in the heart of the Upper King entertainment/nightlife district. Their shows emphasize compelling, mature drama, beautifully performed. This is where to catch less glitzy, grittier productions like *Rabbit Hole*, *American Buffalo*, and *Cold Tectonics*, a hit at Piccolo Spoleto. MAP 2: 477 King St., 843/723-4444, www. puretheatre.org

### REDUX CONTEMPORARY ART CENTER

One of the most important single venues, the nonprofit Redux Contemporary Art Center features modernistic work in a variety of media, including illustration, video installation, blueprints, performance art, and graffiti. Outreach is hugely important to this venture and includes lecture series, classes, workshops, and internships. MAP 2: 136 St. Philip St., 843/722-0697, www. reduxstudios.org; Tues.-Fri. 10am-6pm, Sat. noon-5pm

## Performing Arts
### CHARLESTON SYMPHONY ORCHESTRA

The Charleston Symphony Orchestra (CSO) performed for the first time on December 28, 1936, at the Hibernian Hall on Meeting Street. During that first season the CSO accompanied *The Recruiting Officer*, the inaugural show at the renovated Dock Street Theatre. For seven decades, the CSO continued to provide world-class orchestral music, gaining "Metropolitan" status in the 1970s, when they accompanied the first-ever local performance of *Porgy and Bess*, which despite its Charleston setting couldn't be performed locally before then due to segregation laws. Now under the direction of conductor Ken Lam, the CSO now performs at the newly renovated

**CHARLESTON**
ARTS AND CULTURE

Art Mecca is one of Charleston's many fine-art galleries.

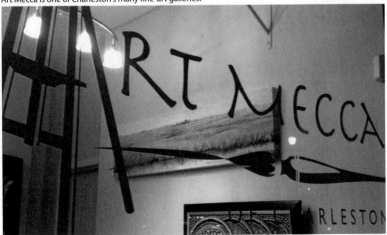

and reimagined Gaillard Center, modeled on European concert halls. Check the website for upcoming concerts.

**MAP 2:** Gaillard Center, 95 Calhoun St., 843/554-6060, www.charlestonsymphony.com

# FOLLY BEACH AND THE SOUTHWEST ISLANDS
## Cinema
### TERRACE THEATRE
The most interesting art house and indie venue in town is The Terrace, and not only because they offer beer and wine, which you can enjoy at your seat. Shows before 5pm are $7. It's west of Charleston on James Island; get there by taking U.S. 17 west from Charleston and go south on Highway 171, then take a right on Maybank Highway (Hwy. 700).

**MAP 5:** 1956D Maybank Hwy., 843/762-4247, www. terracetheater.com

# Shops

Shopping in Charleston centers on King Street, unique not only for the fact that so many national-name stores are lined up so close to each other, but also because there are so many great restaurants of so many different types scattered in and among the retail outlets, ideally positioned for when you need to take a break to rest and refuel.

King Street has three distinct areas with three distinct types of merchandise: **Lower King** is primarily top-of-the-line antiques stores (most are closed Sundays, so plan your trip accordingly); **Middle King** is where you'll find upscale name-brand outlets such as Banana Republic and American Apparel as well as some excellent shoe stores; and **Upper King,** north of Calhoun Street, is where you'll find funky housewares shops, generally locally owned.

King Street is Charleston's shopping mecca.

## WATERFRONT
### Home Goods
#### CHARLESTON COOKS!
Affiliated with the hip local restaurant chain Maverick Kitchens, Charleston Cooks! has an almost overwhelming array of gourmet items and kitchenware, and even offers cooking classes.

MAP 1: 194 E. Bay St., 843/722-1212, www.charlestoncooks.com; Mon.-Sat. 10am-9pm, Sun. 11am-6pm

#### INDIGO
Indigo, a favorite home accessories store, has plenty of one-of-a-kind pieces, many of them by regional artists and rustic in flavor, almost like outsider art.

MAP 1: 4 Vendue Range, 800/549-2513; Sun.-Thurs. 10am-6pm, Fri.-Sat. 10am-7pm

## FRENCH QUARTER
### Antiques and Vintage
#### CURIOSITY
A cute little shop tucked away in an alley, Curiosity is a find even by the standards of antiques/vintage crazy Charleston. A nice plus is the prices here are a bit lower than in the premier antiques shops on Lower King Street, which would never be accused of being bargain priced.

MAP 1: 56 1/2 Queen St., 843/647-7763, www.curiositycharleston.com

### Books and Music
#### SHOPS OF HISTORIC CHARLESTON FOUNDATION
Along the same lines as the Preservation Society is the great Shops of Historic Charleston Foundation, with plenty of tasteful Charleston-themed gift ideas, from books to kitchenware, housed in a beautiful building.

MAP 1: 108 Meeting St., 843/724-8484, www.historiccharleston.org

## NORTH OF BROAD
### Antiques
#### ALEXANDRA AD
A relatively new addition to Lower King's cluster of antiques shops, Alexandra AD features great chandeliers, lamps, and fabrics.

MAP 1: 156 King St., 843/722-4897; Mon.-Sat. 10am-5pm

#### GEORGE C. BIRLANT & CO.
Since 1929, George C. Birlant & Co. has been importing 18th- and 19th-century furniture, silver, china, and crystal, and deals in the famous "Charleston Battery Bench."

MAP 1: 191 King St., 843/722-3842; Mon.-Sat. 9am-5:30pm

### Books and Music
#### PAULINE BOOKS AND MEDIA
The charming Pauline Books and Media is run by the Daughters of Saint Paul and carries Christian books, Bibles, rosaries, and images from a Roman Catholic perspective.

MAP 1: 243 King St., 843/577-0175; Mon.-Sat. 10am-6pm

#### PRESERVATION SOCIETY OF CHARLESTON BOOK AND GIFT SHOP
It's easy to overlook at the far southern end of retail development on King, but the excellent Preservation Society of Charleston Book and Gift Shop is perhaps the best place in town to pick up books on Charleston lore and history as well as locally themed gift items.

MAP 1: 147 King St., 843/722-4630; Mon.-Sat. 10am-5pm

### Clothes
#### BERLINS MEN'S AND WOMEN'S
A charmingly old-school and notable locally owned clothing store on King Street is the classy Berlins Men's and Women's, dating from 1883. It has survived both the Great Charleston Earthquake of 1886 and Hurricane

Hugo in 1989. Despite the name, Berlins focuses on men's clothing, offering designs from Canali, Coppley, Jack Victor, and more.
**MAP 1**: 114-120 King St., 843/722-1665; Mon.-Sat. 9:30am-6pm

## OOPS!

Big companies' losses are your gain at Oops!, which buys factory mistakes and discontinued lines from major brands at a discount, passing along the savings to you. The range here tends toward colorful and preppy.
**MAP 1**: 326 King St., 843/722-7768; Mon.-Fri. 10am-6pm, Sat. 10am-7pm, Sun. noon-6pm

## THE TRUNK SHOW

Women come from throughout the region to shop at the incredible consignment store The Trunk Show. You can find one-of-a-kind vintage and designer wear and accessories. Some finds are bargains, some not so much, but there's no denying the quality and breadth of the offerings.
**MAP 1**: 281 Meeting St., 843/722-0442; Mon.-Sat. 10am-6pm

## WORTHWHILE

For a locally owned clothing shop, try the innovative Worthwhile, which has lots of organic fashions.
**MAP 1**: 268 King St., 843/723-4418, www. shopworthwhile.com; Mon.-Sat. 10am-6pm, Sun. noon-5pm

## Jewelry
### ART JEWELRY BY MIKHAIL SMOLKIN

Art Jewelry by Mikhail Smolkin features one-of-a-kind pieces by this St. Petersburg, Russia, native.
**MAP 1**: 312 King St., 843/722-3634, www. fineartjewelry.com; Mon.-Sat. 10am-5pm

## CROGHAN'S JEWEL BOX

Since 1919, Croghan's Jewel Box has offered amazing locally crafted diamonds, silver, and designer pieces to generations of Charlestonians. An expansion in the late 1990s tripled the size of the historic location.
**MAP 1**: 308 King St., 843/723-3594, www. croghansjewelbox.com; Mon.-Fri. 9:30am-5:30pm, Sat. 10am-5pm

## JOINT VENTURE ESTATE JEWELERS

Joint Venture Estate Jewelers specializes in antique, vintage, and modern estate jewelry as well as pre-owned watches, including Rolex, Patek Philippe, and Cartier, with a fairly unique consignment emphasis.
**MAP 1**: 185 King St., 843/722-6730, www.jventure. com; Mon.-Sat. 10am-5:30pm

## Shoes
### BOB ELLIS SHOE STORE

A famous locally owned place for footwear is Bob Ellis Shoe Store, which has served Charleston's elite with high-end shoes since 1950.
**MAP 1**: 332 King St., 843/722-2515, www. bobellisshoes.com; Mon.-Sat. 10am-6pm

## COPPER PENNY SHOOZ

Copper Penny Shooz combines hip and upscale footwear for women, "curated with a Southern eye," as this Charleston-based regional chain's motto goes.
**MAP 1**: 317 King St., 843/723-3838; Mon.-Sat. 10am-7pm, Sun. noon-6pm

## PHILLIPS SHOES

Funky and fun Phillips Shoes deals in Dansko for men, women, and kids (don't miss the awesome painting above the register of Elvis fitting a customer).
**MAP 1**: 320 King St., 843/965-5270; Mon.-Sat. 10am-6pm

## RANGONI OF FLORENCE

Rangoni of Florence imports the best women's shoes from Italy, with a few men's designs as well.
**MAP 1**: 270 King St., 843/577-9554; Mon.-Sat. 9:30am-6pm, Sun. 12:30pm-5:30pm

## Shopping Centers and Malls
### BELMOND CHARLESTON PLACE

Belmond Charleston Place, usually just called "Charleston Place," a combined retail-hotel development begun to much controversy in the late 1970s, was the first big downtown redevelopment project of Mayor Riley's tenure. While naysayers said people would never come downtown to shop for boutique items, Riley proved them wrong, and years later Belmond Charleston Place remains a big shopping draw for locals and visitors alike. Highlights inside the large, stylish space include Gucci, Talbots, Louis Vuitton, Yves Delorme, Everything But Water, and Godiva.

MAP 1: 205 Meeting St., 843/722-4900, www. charlestonplaceshops.com; Mon.-Wed. 10am-6pm, Thurs.-Sat. 10am-8pm, Sun. noon-5pm

### CITY MARKET

For years dominated by a flea market vibe, City Market was recently upgraded and is now chockablock with boutique retail all along its lengthy interior. The more humble crafts tables are toward the back. If you must have one of the handcrafted sweetgrass baskets, try out your haggling skills—the prices have wiggle room built in. In addition to the myriad of tourist-oriented shops in the City Market itself, there are a few gems in the surrounding area that also appeal to locals.

MAP 1: Meeting St. and Market St., 843/973-7236; daily 9:30am-10:30pm

## Sporting Goods
### HALF MOON OUTFITTERS

With retail locations in Charleston and throughout South Carolina and Georgia and a new cutting-edge, green-friendly warehouse in North Charleston, Half Moon Outfitters is something of a local legend. Here you can find not only top-of-the-line camping and outdoor gear and good tips on local recreation, but also some really stylish outdoorsy apparel as well.

MAP 1: 280 King St., 843/853-0990, www. halfmoonoutfitters.com; Mon.-Sat. 10am-7pm, Sun. noon-6pm

# UPPER KING
## Arts and Crafts
### ARTIST & CRAFTSMAN SUPPLY

Charleston's favorite art supply store is Artist & Craftsman Supply, part of a well-regarded Maine-based chain. They cater to the pro as well as the dabbler and have a fun children's art section as well.

MAP 2: 143 Calhoun St., 843/579-0077, www. artistcraftsman.com; Mon.-Fri. 9am-8pm, Sat.-Sun. 9am-6pm

## Books and Music
### BLUE BICYCLE BOOKS

Housed in an extremely long and narrow storefront on Upper King, Jonathan Sanchez's funky and friendly Blue Bicycle Books deals primarily in used books and has a particularly nice stock of local and regional books, art books, and fiction.

MAP 2: 420 King St., 843/722-2666, www. bluebicyclebooks.com; Mon.-Sat. 10am-7:30pm, Sun. 1pm-6pm

## Health and Beauty
### ALLURE SALON

For stylish haircuts and expert, cutting-edge color work, go to Allure on Upper King. They've styled some of Charleston's poshest weddings and are the founding hair care sponsor of Charleston Fashion Week.

MAP 2: 415 King St., 843/722-8689; Tues. and Thurs. 10am-7pm, Wed. and Fri. 9am-5pm, Sat. 10am-3pm

### SPA ADAGIO

Inside the Francis Marion Hotel near Marion Square is Spa Adagio, offering massage, waxing, and skin and nail care.

MAP 2: 387 King St., 843/577-2444; Mon.-Sat. 10am-7pm, Sun. by appointment only

## Home Goods
### HAUTE DESIGN STUDIO

Head to Haute Design Studio for upper-end furnishings with an edgy feel.

MAP 2: 489 King St., 843/577-9886, www. hautedesign.com; Mon.-Fri. 9am-5:30pm

# HAMPTON PARK
## Hats
### MAGAR HATWORKS
If hats are your thing, make sure you visit Magar Hatworks, where Leigh Magar makes and sells her whimsical, all-natural hats, some of which she designs for Barneys New York. MAP 2: 57 Cannon St., 843/577-7740, www.magarhatworks.com; by appointment

# WEST ASHLEY
## Home Goods
### ESD, ELIZABETH STUART DESIGN
Probably Charleston's best-regarded home goods store is the nationally recognized ESD, Elizabeth Stuart Design, with a wide range of antique and new furnishings, art, lighting, jewelry, and more. MAP 3: 422 Savannah Hwy./U.S. 17, 843/225-6282, www.esdcharleston.com; Mon.-Sat. 10am-6pm

## Music
### MONSTER MUSIC AND MOVIES
In an age when it's harder and harder to find brick and mortar music/movie stores, Monster is a great find. They have new and used vinyl and CDs, and of course host a great deal of sales and in-store performances on Record Store Day. MAP 3: 946 Orleans Rd., 843/571-4657; Mon.-Sat. 10am-9pm, Sun. noon-7pm

# NORTH CHARLESTON
## Health and Beauty
### STELLA NOVA
Inside this locally owned cosmetics store and studio you'll find a wide selection of high-end makeup and beauty products, with a staff of 30 beauty experts. There's also a West Ashley location (2048 Sam Rittenberg Blvd.). MAP 3: 1320 Theater Dr., 843/884-3838, www.stella-nova.com: Mon.-Fri. 9am-7pm, Sat. 9am-5pm, Sun. noon-5pm

## Music
### THE GUITAR CENTER
The biggest music store in the region is The Guitar Center in North Charleston across from Northwood Mall. With just about everything a musician might want or need, it's part of a chain that has been around since the late 1950s, but the Charleston location is relatively new. MAP 3: 7620 Rivers Ave., 843/572-9063; Mon.-Fri. 11am-7pm, Sat. 10am-7pm, Sun. noon-6pm

### FOX MUSIC HOUSE
Fox Music House in North Charleston is a neighborhood favorite, and has been locally owned since 1928. They specialize more in pianos and keyboards. MAP 3: 3005 W. Montague Ave., 843/740-7200; Mon.-Fri. 10am-6pm, Sat. 10am-5pm

## Shopping Centers
### TANGER OUTLET
North Charleston hosts the Tanger Outlet. Get factory-priced bargains from stores such as Adidas, Banana Republic, Brooks Brothers, CorningWare, Old Navy, Timberland, and more. MAP 3: 4840 Tanger Outlet Blvd., 843/529-3095, www.tangeroutlet.com; Mon.-Sat. 10am-9pm, Sun. 11am-6pm

# MOUNT PLEASANT AND EAST COOPER
## Antiques
### PAGE'S THIEVES MARKET
Mount Pleasant boasts a fun antiques and auction spot, Page's Thieves Market. Its rambling interior has hosted bargain and vintage shoppers for 50 years, and it's routinely voted Charleston's Best Antiques Store. MAP 4: 1460 Ben Sawyer Blvd., 843/884-9672, www.pagesthievesmarket.com; Mon.-Fri. 9am-5:30pm, Sat. 9am-5pm

## Shopping Centers
### MOUNT PLEASANT TOWNE CENTER
The most pleasant mall in the area is the retro-themed, pedestrian-friendly Mount Pleasant Towne Center, which opened in 1999 to serve the growing population of East Cooper residents tired of having to cross a bridge to get

to a big mall. In addition to national chains you'll find a few cool local stores in here, like Stella Nova spa and day salon, Copper Penny Shooz, and the men's store Jos. A. Bank.

MAP 4: 1600 Palmetto Grande Dr., 843/216-9900, www.mtpleasanttownecentre.com; Mon.-Sat. 10am-9pm, Sun. noon-6pm

**GWYNN'S OF MOUNT PLEASANT**
In a Harris Teeter grocery shopping center, Gwynn's is an old-fashioned department store specializing in women's clothing and shoes, with a distinct local and Southern sensibility.

MAP 4: 916 Houston Northcutt Blvd., 843/884-9518; Mon.-Sat 10am-7pm

# Sports and Activities

Because of the generally great weather in Charleston, encouraged by the steady, soft sea breeze, outdoor activities are always popular and available. Though it's not much of a spectator sports town, there are plenty of things to do on your own, such as play golf and tennis, walk, hike, boat, and fish.

Offshore diving centers on a network of **artificial reefs** (see www.dnr.sc.gov for a list and locations), particularly the "Charleston 60" sunken barge and the popular "Train Wreck," comprising 50 deliberately sunk New York City subway cars. In addition to being fun dive sites, these artificial reefs have proven to be important feeding and spawning grounds for marine life.

The country's first golf course was constructed in Charleston in 1786, so as you'd expect there's great golfing in the area, generally on the outlying islands. The folks at the nonprofit **Charleston Golf, Inc.** (423 King St., 843/958-3629, www.charlestongolfguide.com) are your best one-stop resource for tee times and packages.

Charleston-area beaches are perfect for a leisurely bike ride on the sand. Sullivan's Island is a particular favorite, and you might be surprised at how long you can ride in one direction on these beaches. Those desiring a more demanding use of their legs can walk or ride their bike in the dedicated pedestrian and bike lane on the massive **Arthur Ravenel Jr. Bridge** over the Cooper River, the longest cable-stayed bridge in the Western Hemisphere.

For casual fishing off a pier, try the well-equipped **Folly Beach Fishing Pier** (101 E. Arctic Ave., Folly Beach, 843/588-3474, daily dawn-dusk, $5-7 parking, $8 fishing fee, rod rentals available) on Folly Beach or the **North Charleston Riverfront Park** (843/745-1087, www.northcharleston.org, daily dawn-dusk) along the Cooper River on the grounds of the old Navy Yard. Get onto the Navy Yard grounds by taking I-26 north to exit 216B. Take a left onto Spruill Avenue and a right onto McMillan Avenue.

Key local marinas include **Shem Creek Marina** (526 Mill St., 843/884-3211, www.shemcreekmarina.com), **Charleston Harbor Marina** (24 Patriots Point Rd., 843/284-7062, www.charlestonharbormarina.com), **Charleston City Marina** (17 Lockwood Dr., 843/722-4968), **Charleston Maritime Center** (10 Wharfside St., 843/853-3625, www.cmcevents.com), and the **Cooper River Marina** (1010 Juneau Ave., 843/554-0790, www.ccprc.com).

Good fishing charter outfits include **Barrier Island Eco Tours** (50 41st Ave., 843/886-5000, www.nature-tours.com, about $80) out of Isle of Palms; **Bohicket Boat Adventure & Tour Co.** (2789 Cherry Point Rd., 843/559-3525, www.bohicketboat.com, $375/half-day for 1-2 passengers) out of the Edisto River; and **Reel Fish Finder Charters** (315 Yellow Jasmine Court, Moncks Corner, 843/697-2081, www.reelfishfinder.com, $400/half-day for 1-3 passengers). Captain James picks up clients at many different marinas in the area. For a list of all public landings in Charleston County, go to www.ccprc.com.

Many kayakers put in at the Shem Creek

Marina or the public Shem Creek Landing in Mount Pleasant. From here it's a safe, easy paddle—sometimes with appearances by dolphins or manatees—to the Intracoastal Waterway. Some kayakers like to go from Shem Creek straight out into Charleston Harbor to Crab Bank Heritage Preserve, a prime birding island. Another good place to put in is at **Isle of Palms Marina** (50 41st Ave., 843/886-0209) behind the Wild Dunes Resort on Morgan Creek, which empties into the Intracoastal Waterway. Behind Folly Beach is an extensive network of waterways, including lots of areas that are great for camping and fishing. The Folly River Landing is just over the bridge to the island.

# SOUTH OF BROAD
## Tours
### CHARLESTON ART TOURS

Art lovers should check out the offerings from Charleston Art Tours. Sandra and Teri offer a selection of visual art-themed packages, including a French Quarter Tour and a Charleston Renaissance Tour.

MAP 1: 53 Broad St., 843/860-3327, www. charlestonarttours.com; $48-55

# WATERFRONT
## Walking Tours
### ED GRIMBALL'S WALKING TOURS

Since 1996, Ed Grimball's Walking Tours has run twice-weekly historical tours that take you through the heart of Charleston, courtesy of the knowledgeable and sprightly Ed himself, a native Charlestonian. All of Ed's walks start from the big Pineapple Fountain in Waterfront Park, and reservations are a must.

MAP 1: Waterfront Park, Concord St., 843/813-4447, www.edgrimballtours.com; $22 adults, $8 children

## Water Tours
### SANDLAPPER WATER TOURS

Sandlapper Water Tours offers many types of evening and dolphin cruises on a 45-foot catamaran. The company also offers Charleston's only waterborne ghost tour. Most of the tours leave from the Maritime Center near East Bay and Calhoun Streets.

MAP 1: Charleston Maritime Center, 10 Wharfside St., 843/849-8687, www.sandlappertours.com; Mar.-Aug.; $20-27

### SPIRITLINE CRUISES

The best all-around tour of Charleston Harbor is the 90-minute ride offered by Spiritline Cruises, which leaves from either Aquarium Wharf or Patriots Point. Allow about 30 minutes for ticketing and boarding. They also have a three-hour dinner cruise in the evening leaving from Patriots Point (about $50 pp) and a cruise to Fort Sumter.

MAP 1: Charleston Harbor, 800/789-3678, www. spiritlinecruises.com; $22 adults, $12 ages 4-11

# NORTH OF BROAD
## Walking Tours
### BULLDOG TOURS

Ghost tours are very popular in Charleston. Bulldog Tours has exclusive access to the Old City Jail, which features prominently in most of its tours. The most popular tour, the Haunted Jail Tour ($22 adults, $10 children), leaves daily at 7pm, 8pm, 9pm, and 10pm; meet at the jail at 21 Magazine St. The Ghosts and Dungeons tour ($22) runs March-November Tuesday-Saturday at 7pm and 9pm and leaves from 18 Anson Street.

MAP 1: 18 Anson St., 843/722-8687, www. bulldogtours.com; $22

### CHARLESTON STROLLS

Charleston Strolls is another popular tour good for a historical overview and tidbits. The two-hour tours leave twice daily from the Mills House Hotel.

MAP 1: Mills House Hotel, 115 Meeting St., 843/722-8687, www.charlestonstrolls.com; daily 10am and 2pm; $25 adults, $10 children

### ORIGINAL CHARLESTON WALKS

Original Charleston Walks has received much national TV exposure. Its two-hour tours leave from the corner of Market and State

# Carriage Tours

Tours leave from the Palmetto Carriage Barn in Charleston.

The city of Charleston strictly regulates the treatment and upkeep of carriage horses and mules as well as the allowed amount of carriage traffic. Only 20 carriages are allowed out on the streets at any one time, so occasionally yours will have to wait until another one returns.

There's not a lot of difference in service or price among the carriage companies, and that's chiefly by design. The city divides the tours into three routes, or "zones." Which zone your driver explores is determined by lottery at the embarkation point—you don't get to decide the zone and neither does your driver. Typically, rides take 1-1.5 hours and hover around $25 per adult, about half that per child. They are, however, of uniformly high quality.

Tours sometimes book up early, so call ahead. The oldest and in my opinion best service in town is **Palmetto Carriage Works** (40 N. Market St., 843/723-8145, www.palmettocarriage. com), which offers free parking at its "red barn" base near City Market. Another popular tour is **Old South Carriage Company** (14 Anson St., 843/723-9712, www.oldsouthcarriage.com) with its Confederate-clad drivers. **Carolina Polo & Carriage Company** (16 Hayne St., 843/577-6767, www.cpcc.com) leaves from several spots, including the Doubletree Hotel and the company's Hayne Street stables.

Streets and cover a full slate, including a popular adults-only pub crawl.

**MAP 1**: Market St. and State St., 843/408-0010, www. charlestonwalks.com; times and prices vary

## UPPER KING
### African American History Tours
#### GULLAH TOURS

Alphonso Brown's Gullah Tours features stories told in the Gullah dialect. Tours run Monday-Saturday and leave from the African American Art Gallery, near the visitors center.

**MAP 2**: African American Art Gallery, 43 John St., 843/763-7551, www.gullahtours.com; Mon.-Fri. 11am and 1pm, Sat. 11am, 1pm, and 3pm; $18

### SITES & INSIGHTS TOURS

Charleston is rich in African American history. Al Miller's Sites & Insights Tours has several packages, including a Black History and Porgy & Bess Tour as well as a good combo city and island tour, all departing from the visitors center.

MAP 2: Charleston Visitor Reception and Transportation Center, 375 Meeting St., 843/552-9995, www.sitesandinsightstours.com; tour times vary; $13-18

## Motorized Tours

### ADVENTURE SIGHTSEEING

Leaving from the Charleston Visitor Reception and Transportation Center, Adventure Sightseeing offers several comfortable 1.5- to 2-hour rides, including the only motorized tour to the Citadel area, leaving at various times throughout the day.

MAP 2: Charleston Visitor Reception and Transportation Center, 375 Meeting St., 843/762-0088, www.adventuresightseeing.com; daily various times; $20 adults, $11 children

### CHARLESTON'S FINEST HISTORIC TOURS

You can make a day of it with Charleston's Finest Historic Tours, which has a basic two-hour city tour each day at 10:30am and offers some much longer tours to outlying plantations. The company offers free downtown pickup from most lodgings.

MAP 2: Charleston Visitor Reception and Transportation Center, 375 Meeting St., 843/577-3311, www.historictoursofcharleston.com; daily 10:30am; $21 adults, $10.50 children

### GRAY LINE OF CHARLESTON

The old faithful Gray Line of Charleston offers a 90-minute Historic Charleston Tour. Tours depart from the visitors center every 30 minutes. Hotel pickup is available by reservation. The last tour leaves at 2pm during the off-season.

MAP 2: Charleston Visitor Reception and Transportation Center, 375 Meeting St., 843/722-4444, www.graylineofcharleston.com; Mar.-Nov. daily 9:30am-3pm, Dec.-Feb daily 9:30am-2pm; $21-34 adults, $12-19 children

# HAMPTON PARK

## Spectator Sports

### CHARLESTON RIVER DOGS

A New York Yankees Class A affiliate in the South Atlantic League, the Charleston River Dogs play April-August at **Joseph P. Riley Jr. Park**, aka "The Joe." The park is great, and there are a lot of fun promotions to keep things interesting should the play on the field be less than stimulating. It's also another part of the civic legacy of longtime mayor Joe Riley, in partnership with the adjacent Citadel. Inspired by the retro design of Baltimore's Oriole Park at Camden Yards, The Joe opened in 1997 to rave reviews from locals and baseball connoisseurs all over the nation. There are no bad seats, so you might as well save a few bucks and go for the general admission ticket. From downtown, get to The Joe by taking Broad Street west until it turns into Lockwood Drive. Follow that north until you get to Brittlebank Park and The Joe, next to The Citadel. Expect to pay $5 for parking.

MAP 2: Joseph P. Riley Jr. Park, 360 Fishburne St., 843/577-3647, www.riverdogs.com; $8-11 general admission

### CITADEL BULLDOGS

The Citadel plays Southern Conference football home games at **Johnson Hagood Stadium,** next to the campus on the Ashley River near Hampton Park. The basketball team plays home games at **McAlister Field House** on campus. The school's hockey team skates home games at the **Carolina Ice Palace** (7665 Northwoods Blvd., North Charleston).

MAP 2: The Citadel, 171 Moultrie St., 843/953-3294, www.citadelsports.com; ticket prices vary

# WEST ASHLEY

## Diving

A network of artificial reefs (www.dnr.sc.gov) offer a selection of fun dives sites, especially the "Charleston 60" and the popular "Train

Wreck" (50 deliberately sunk New York City subway cars). In addition to Charleston Scuba, you also might want to check out **Cooper River Scuba** (843/572-0459, www.cooperriverdiving.com) and **Atlantic Coast Dive Center** (209 Scott St., 843/884-1500).

### CHARLESTON SCUBA

Probably Charleston's best-regarded outfitter and charter operator is Charleston Scuba in West Ashley. They offer training classes, charters, and offshore diving trips.
**MAP 3**: 335 Savannah Hwy., 843/763-3483, www.charlestonscuba.com

# Summer Fun

## WATER PARKS

During the summer months, Charleston County operates three water parks: **Splash Island Waterpark** (444 Needlerush Pkwy., Mount Pleasant, 843/884-0832); **Whirlin' Waters Adventure Waterpark** (University Blvd., North Charleston, 843/572-7275); and **Splash Zone Waterpark at James Island County Park** (871 Riverland Dr., 843/795-7275), on James Island west of town. Admission runs about $10 per person. Go to www.ccprc.com for more information.

## THE BEACH AT SULLIVAN'S ISLAND

For a totally go-it-alone type of beach day, go to the three-mile-long beach on the Atlantic Ocean at **Sullivan's Island.** There are no facilities, no lifeguards, strong offshore currents, and no parking lots on this residential island (park on the side of the street). There's also a lot of dog walking on this beach, since no leash is required November-February. Get there from downtown by crossing the Ravenel Bridge over the Cooper River and bearing right onto Coleman Boulevard, which turns into Ben Sawyer Boulevard. Take the Ben Sawyer Bridge onto Sullivan's Island. Beach access is plentiful and marked.

## Hiking and Biking
### WEST ASHLEY GREENWAY

The West Ashley Greenway is an urban walking and biking trail built on a former railbed. The 10-mile trail runs parallel to U.S. 17 and passes parks, schools, and the Clemson Experimental Farm, ending near Johns Island. To get to the trailhead from downtown, drive west on U.S. 17. About 0.5 mile after you cross the bridge, turn left onto Folly Road (Hwy. 171). At the second light, turn right into South Windermere Shopping Center; the trail is behind the center on the right.
**MAP 3**: South Windermere Shopping Center (80 Folly Rd.) to Johns Island, paralleling U.S. 17; dawn-dusk

# NORTH CHARLESTON
## Ice-Skating
### CAROLINA ICE PALACE

Ice-skating in South Carolina? Yep, 100,000 square feet of it, year-round at the two NHL-size rinks of the Carolina Ice Palace. This is also the practice facility for the local hockey team, the Stingrays, as well as where The Citadel's hockey team plays.
**MAP 3**: 7665 Northwoods Blvd., 843/572-2717, www.carolinaicepalace.com; daily public sessions; $7 adults, $6 children

## SPECTATOR SPORTS
### SOUTH CAROLINA STINGRAYS

An ECHL professional hockey team, the South Carolina Stingrays get a good crowd out to their rink at the North Charleston Coliseum, playing October-April.
**MAP 3**: North Charleston Coliseum, 5001 Coliseum Dr., 843/744-2248, www.stingrayshockey.com; $15

# MOUNT PLEASANT AND EAST COOPER
## Beaches
### ISLE OF PALMS COUNTY PARK

On Isle of Palms you'll find Isle of Palms County Park, which has restrooms, showers, a picnic area, a beach volleyball area, and beach chair and umbrella rentals. Get there by taking the Isle of Palms Connector (Hwy. 517) to the island, go through the light at Palm

Boulevard, and take the next left at the park gate. There's good public beach access near the Pavilion Shoppes on Ocean Boulevard, accessed via J. C. Long Boulevard.

**MAP 4:** 14th Ave., Isle of Palms, 843/886-3863, www.ccprc.com; fall-spring daily 10am-dark, summer daily 9am-dark; $5 per vehicle, free for pedestrians and cyclists

### Bird-Watching
#### CRAB BANK SEABIRD SANCTUARY

Right in Charleston Harbor is the little Crab Bank Seabird Sanctuary, where thousands of migratory birds can be seen, depending on the season. The sanctuary has been designated an "Important Bird Area." From mid-October through mid-March you can either kayak there yourself or take a charter with **Nature Adventures Outfitters** (1900 Iron Swamp Rd., Awendaw Island, 800/673-0679). During nesting season, mid-March to mid-October, the sanctuary is closed to the public.

**MAP 4:** Charleston Harbor, 803/734-3886, www.dnr.sc.gov; Oct. 16-Mar. 14 daily dawn-dusk

#### I'ON SWAMP TRAIL

Once part of a rice plantation, the I'on Swamp Trail is one of the premier bird-watching sites in South Carolina, particularly during spring and fall migrations. The rare Bachman's warbler, commonly considered one of the most elusive birds in North America, has been seen here. To get here, make the 10-minute drive to Mount Pleasant, then head north on U.S. 17 and take a left onto I'on Swamp Road (Forest Service Rd. 228). The parking area is 2.5 miles ahead on the left.

**MAP 4:** 15 miles northeast of Charleston, via U.S. 17, 843/928-3368, www.fs.fed.us; daily dawn-dusk; free

### Boating
#### BARRIER ISLAND ECO TOURS

Barrier Island Eco Tours can take you on a passenger boat ride up to the Cape Romain NWR out of Isle of Palms, with a focus on undeveloped Capers Island. Plan on seeing plenty of dolphins!

**MAP 4:** 50 41st Ave., 843/886-5000, www.nature-tours.com; $38 adults, $28 children

### Golf
#### PATRIOTS POINT LINKS

The 18-hole Patriots Point Links on the Charleston Harbor, right over the Ravenel Bridge, is one of the most convenient courses in the area, and it boasts some phenomenal views.

**MAP 4:** 1 Patriots Point Rd., Mount Pleasant, 843/881-0042, www.patriotspointlinks.com; $100/18 holes

#### RIVERTOWNE GOLF COURSE

On Mount Pleasant you will find perhaps the best course in the area for the money, the award-winning Rivertowne Golf Course at the Rivertowne Country Club. Opened in 2002, the course was designed by Arnold Palmer.

**MAP 4:** 1700 Rivertowne Country Club Dr., Mount Pleasant, 843/856-9808, www.rivertownecountryclub.com; $150/18 holes

#### WILD DUNES RESORT

Two excellent resort-style public courses are at Wild Dunes Resort on Isle of Palms. The resort has been named one of the state's best by *Golf Digest*.

**MAP 4:** 5757 Palm Blvd., Isle of Palms, 888/845-8932, www.wilddunes.com; $165/18 holes

### Hiking and Biking
#### AWENDAW PASSAGE

The most ambitious trail in South Carolina is the **Palmetto Trail**, begun in 1997 and eventually covering 425 miles from the Atlantic to the Appalachians. The coastal terminus of the Palmetto Trail, the 7-mile Awendaw Passage, winds through the Francis Marion National Forest. It begins at the trailhead at the Buck Hall Recreational Area, which has parking and restroom facilities. Get there by taking U.S. 17 north from Charleston about 20 miles and through the Francis Marion National Forest and then Awendaw. Take a right onto Buck Hall Landing Road.

**MAP 4:** Buck Hall Recreational Area, McClellanville, 843/887-3257, www.palmettoconservation.org; $5 vehicle fee

## Spectator Sports
### CHARLESTON BATTERY

The professional USL Pro soccer team Charleston Battery plays April-July at **MUSC Health Stadium** on Daniel Island, north of Charleston. To get here from downtown, take I-26 north and then I-526 to Mount Pleasant. Take exit 23A, Clements Ferry Road, and then a left on St. Thomas Island Drive. MUSC Health Stadium is about one mile along on the left.

**MAP 4**: MUSC Health Stadium, 1990 Daniel Island Dr., 843/971-4625, www.charlestonbattery.com; about $10

## Surfing
### SOL SURFERS SURF CAMP

Mount Pleasant is home to Sol Surfers Surf Camp, which offers surf camps during the summer and private and group lessons throughout the year. The surf camp shuttle picks up students at the Parrot Surf Shop (811 Coleman Blvd.). Surf camps take place on the eastern end of Folly Beach.

**MAP 4**: 1170 Lazy Ln., Mount Pleasant, 843/881-6700, www.solsurfers.net

## Tennis
### FAMILY CIRCLE TENNIS CENTER

Tennis fans are in for a treat at the Family Circle Tennis Center on Daniel Island. This multimillion-dollar facility is owned by the city of Charleston and was built in 2001 specifically to host the annual Family Circle Cup women's competition, which is now known as the Volvo Car Open. But it's also open to the public year-round (except when the Volvo Car Open is on) with 17 courts.

**MAP 4**: 161 Seven Farms Dr., 800/677-2293, www. volvocaropen.com; Mon.-Thurs. 8am-8pm, Fri. 8am-7pm, Sat. 8am-5pm, Sun. 9am-5pm; $15/hour

## Kayaking Tours
### COASTAL EXPEDITIONS

An excellent outfit for guided kayak tours is Coastal Expeditions, which also runs the only approved ferry service to the Cape Romain National Wildlife Refuge. They'll rent you a kayak for roughly $50 per day. Coastal Expeditions also sells an outstanding kayaking, boating, and fishing map of the area (about $12).

**MAP 4**: 654 Serotina Ct., 843/881-4582, www. coastalexpeditions.com

### NATURE ADVENTURES OUTFITTERS

The best tour operator close to downtown is Nature Adventures Outfitters, which puts in on Shem Creek in Mount Pleasant for most of its 2-, 2.5-, 3-, and 3.5-hour and full-day guided trips, with prices from $40 to $85. They also offer blackwater tours out of landings at other locations; see the website for specific directions for those tours.

**MAP 4**: Shrimp Boat Ln., 843/568-3222, www. kayakcharlestonsc.com

# FOLLY BEACH AND THE SOUTHWEST ISLANDS

Behind Folly Beach is an extensive network of waterways, including lots of areas that are great for camping and fishing. The Folly River Landing is just over the bridge to the island.

## Beaches
### FOLLY BEACH COUNTY PARK

In addition to the charming town of Folly Beach itself, there's the modest county-run

---

# Free Tennis, Anyone?

There are four free, public, city-funded facilities on the peninsula:

- **Moultrie Playground:** Broad St. and Ashley Ave., 843/769-8258, www.charlestoncity.info, six lighted hard courts

- **Jack Adams Tennis Center:** 290 Congress St., six lighted hard courts

- **Hazel Parker Playground:** 70 E. Bay St., on the Cooper River, one hard court

- **Corrine Jones Playground:** Marlowe St. and Peachtree St., two hard courts

Folly Beach County Park at the far west end of Folly Island. It has a picnic area, restrooms, outdoor showers, and beach chair and umbrella rentals. Get there by taking Highway 171 (Folly Rd.) until it turns into Center Street, and then take a right on West Ashley Avenue.

**MAP 5:** 1100 W. Ashley Ave., Folly Beach, 843/588-2426, www.ccprc.com; May-Feb. daily 10am-dark, Mar.-Apr. daily 9am-dark; $7 per vehicle, free for pedestrians and cyclists

### KIAWAH ISLAND BEACHWALKER PARK

On the west end of Kiawah Island to the south of Charleston is Kiawah Island Beachwalker Park, the only public facility on this mostly private resort island. It has restrooms, showers, a picnic area with grills, and beach chair and umbrella rentals. Get there from downtown by taking Lockwood Avenue onto the Highway 30 Connector bridge over the Ashley River. Turn right onto Folly Road, then take a left onto Maybank Highway. After about 20 minutes you'll take another left onto Bohicket Road, which leads you to Kiawah in 14 miles. Turn left from Bohicket Road onto the Kiawah Island Parkway. Just before the security gate, turn right on Beachwalker Drive and follow the signs to the park.

**MAP 5:** Kiawah Island, 843/768-2395, www.ccprc. com; Mar.-Apr. and Oct. Sat.-Sun. 10am-6pm, May-Aug. daily 9am-7pm, Sept. daily 10am-6pm; $7 per vehicle, free for pedestrians and cyclists

## Bird-Watching
### LEGARE FARMS

On Johns Island southwest of Charleston is Legare Farms, which holds migratory bird walks ($6 adults, $3 children) in the fall each Saturday at 8:30am.

**MAP 5:** 2620 Hanscombe Point Rd., Johns Island, 843/559-0788, www.legarefarms.com; farm hours vary

## Ecotours

This aspect of Charleston's tourism scene is very well represented. The best operators include: **Barrier Island Eco Tours** (50 41st Ave., 843/886-5000, www.nature-tours. com, from $40), taking you up to the Cape Romain Refuge out of Isle of Palms and **Coastal Expeditions** (514-B Mill St., 843/884-7684, www.coastalexpeditions. com, prices vary), with a base on Shem Creek in Mount Pleasant, offering several different-length sea kayak adventures.

## Golf
### CHARLESTON MUNICIPAL GOLF COURSE

The main public course is the 18-hole, renovated and upgraded City of Charleston Golf Course, affectionately referred to as The Muni. To get there from the peninsula, take U.S. 17 south over the Ashley River, take Highway 171 (Folly Rd.) south, and then take a right onto Maybank Highway.

**MAP 5:** 2110 Maybank Hwy., 843/795-6517, www. charleston-sc.gov/golf; $22-24/18 holes

### KIAWAH ISLAND GOLF RESORT

Probably the most renowned area facilities are at the acclaimed Kiawah Island Golf Resort, about 20 miles from Charleston. The resort has five courses in all, the best known of which is the **Kiawah Island Ocean Course,** site of the famous "War by the Shore" 1991 Ryder Cup. This 2.5-mile course, which is walking-only until noon each day, hosted the Senior PGA Championship in 2007 and the PGA Championship in 2012. The resort offers a golf academy and private lessons galore. These are public courses, but be aware that tee times are limited for golfers who aren't guests at the resort.

**MAP 5:** 12 Kiawah Beach Dr., Kiawah Island, 800/654-2924, www.kiawahresort.com/golf; $150-350/18 holes, 25 percent discount for resort guests

## Surfing and Kiteboarding

The surfing at the famous Washout area on the east side of Folly Beach isn't what it used to be due to storm activity and beach erosion. But diehards still gather at this area when the swell hits. Check out the conditions yourself from the three views of the **Folly Surfcam** (www.follysurfcam.com).

### FOLLY BEACH SHAKA SURF SCHOOL

Around since 2004, Folly Beach Shaka Surf School offers private and group surf lessons, including youth surf camps throughout summer, women-only weekend outings, and yoga classes geared toward surfers. Surf camps are located on the east end of Folly Beach.
**MAP 5**: 107 E. Indian Ave., Folly Beach, 843/607-9911, www.shakasurfschool.com

### MCKEVLIN'S SURF SHOP

The best local surf shop is undoubtedly the historic McKevlin's Surf Shop on Folly Beach, one of the first surf shops on the East Coast, dating to 1965.
**MAP 5**: 8 Center St., Folly Beach, 843/588-2247, www.mckevlins.com; spring-summer daily 10am-6pm, fall-winter daily 10am-5:30pm

## Tennis

### KIAWAH ISLAND GOLF RESORT

The best resort tennis activity is at the Kiawah Island Golf Resort. The resort's Roy Barth Tennis Center has nine clay and three hard courts, while the West Beach Tennis Club has 10 Har-Tru courts and 2 lighted hard courts.
**MAP 5**: 12 Kiawah Beach Dr., Kiawah Island, 800/654-2924, www.kiawahresort.com; $44/hour for nonguests

# Restaurants

Charleston's long history of good taste and livability combines with an affluent and sophisticated population to attract some of the brightest chefs and restaurateurs in the country. A long list of James Beard Award nominees each year confirms the city's role as perhaps the preeminent hub of culinary excellence in the American South.

Kitchens here eschew fickle trends, instead emphasizing quality, professionalism, and, most of all, freshness of ingredients. The farm-to-table movement is as strong here as anywhere in the country and drives the menus of most of the premier establishments.

If you come here in the first week or two of the New Year, keep in mind that is usually the time when Charleston's more popular restaurants might close briefly for renovations.

While almost all the foodie news out of Charleston is good, sadly Carolina's—one of Charleston's most fabled restaurants, and the only fine-dining spot south of Broad Street—closed permanently in 2015.

## WATERFRONT
### New Southern
### CYPRESS $$$

While not as flashy as some other local chefs, Craig Deihl has, over the past decade, brought Cypress—which shares ownership with Magnolias—to the forefront of the local foodie movement. From aged beef sourced at a local farm to sustainably caught wreckfish, the menu reflects a deep commitment to locavore sensibilities. Any meat or seafood entrée is a can't-lose proposition here.
**MAP 1**: 167 E. Bay St., 843/727-0111, www.magnoliasblossom-cypress.com; Sun.-Thurs. 5:30pm-10pm, Fri.-Sat. 5:30pm-11pm

### MAGNOLIAS $$$

Magnolias began life as one of Charleston's first serious eating spots. A warm wood interior highlights the renovation, and the menu remains as attractive as ever, with a delightful take on Southern classics like the lump crab cakes, the shellfish over grits, and a rainbow trout. The appetizers are particularly

# Best Restaurants

★ **Greatest Food Adventure:** Sean Brock's flagship restaurant, **McCrady's** combines old-school attention to service and detail with a daring approach to cuisine (page 104).

★ **Most Scrumptious Breakfast:** It's not fancy, but **Dixie Supply Bakery & Café** offers hearty Southern takes on breakfast classics (page 105).

★ **Most Delightful Date Night:** The award-winning **FIG** offers incredible fine dining with friendly service in a classy but relaxed atmosphere (page 107).

★ **Most Muscular Mussels:** The best bowl of mussels you'll have outside France is at the bistro **39 Rue de Jean** (page 110).

★ **Freshest Comfort Food:** Charleston is full of great farm-to-table spots, but **The Glass Onion** offers the most accessible Southern classics made from local produce (page 111).

★ **Most Ridiculous Ribs:** The smoky slabs at **Fiery Ron's Home Team BBQ** are so good you'll hardly be able to stand it, but try anyway (page 112).

★ **Best Bar for Burgers:** In West Ashley, **Gene's Haufbrau** combines an awesome beer selection with some of the best burgers in town (page 112).

★ **Best She-Crab Soup:** Just north of town on Highway 17 you'll find **See Wee Restaurant,** known for its seafood (page 114).

★ **Closest Intersection of France and South Carolina:** On Johns Island is **Fat Hen,** where the specialties are Southern in origin and French in execution (page 115).

strong—start with the famous fried green tomatoes or maybe the boiled peanut hummus. **MAP 1:** 185 E. Bay St., 843/577-7771, www.magnoliasblossom-cypress.com; Mon.-Sat. 11:30am-10pm, Sun. 3:45pm-10pm

### ★ MCCRADY'S $$$

Few restaurants in Charleston have inspired such impassioned advocates as legendary Chef Sean Brock's flagship restaurant, McCrady's. Brock's then-groundbreaking sous vide (or vacuum cooking technique) was spoken of in reverent tones by his clientele. In an expansion and reimagining, Brock has "relocated" the original McCrady's to a spot right next door, where it continues to offer the sophisticated, almost frighteningly delicious tasting-menu experience for which it is renowned. Brock has repurposed the former McCrady's space as **McCrady's Tavern,** a return to the original

use of the building as a watering hole and community gathering spot back in the 1770s. Former McCrady's sous chef John Sleasman runs the kitchen at the "new" McCrady's. In a nod to a more egalitarian dining experience, the tavern's casual, New Southern menu is overseen by Justin Cherry, former head chef at another Brock sensation, Husk. Either spot is a core stop of any Charleston foodie pilgrimage. **MAP 1:** 2 Unity Alley and 155 Bay St., www. mccradysrestaurant.com; Sun.-Thurs. 5:30pm-10pm, Fri.-Sat. 5:30pm-11pm

### SLIGHTLY NORTH OF BROAD $$$

Don't be put off by the initials of Slightly North of Broad. Its acronym, "SNOB," is an ironic play on the often pejorative reference to the insular South of Broad neighborhood. This hot spot, routinely voted best restaurant in town in such contests, is anything but snobby. Hopping with happy foodies for lunch and dinner, the fun is enhanced by the long, open kitchen with its own counter area. The dynamic but comforting menu here is practically a bible of the new wave of Lowcountry cuisine, with dishes like beef tenderloin, jumbo lump crab cakes, grilled barbecue tuna—and of course the pan-seared flounder. An interesting twist at SNOB is the selection of "medium plates," i.e., dishes a little more generous than an appetizer but with the same adventurous spirit.

**MAP 1**: 192 E. Bay St., 843/723-3424, www.snobcharleston.com; daily 11:30am-2:30pm and 5pm-10pm

## FRENCH QUARTER
### Breakfast and Brunch
### ★ DIXIE SUPPLY BAKERY & CAFÉ $

You can sit inside the crowded, noisy diner or outside literally in the parking lot of a strip mall; either way you're doing the right thing at Dixie Supply Bakery & Café. Dixie Supply has a certain amount of cachet after an appearance on *Diners, Drive-ins and Dives,* but don't let the trendiness keep you away. A case could be made that their signature tomato pie—melted cheese over a perfect tomato slice with a delicious crust on the bottom, served with a hunk of sweet potato corn bread—is the single best dish in Charleston. You place your order at the front counter; the cook's a few feet away. When your plate is ready, they call you, and you just come up and get your food and take it back to your table. It can get crowded, but just brave the lines and go. And while they do take plastic, they appreciate cash.

**MAP 1**: 62 State St., 843/722-5650, www.dixiecafecharleston.com; daily 8am-2:30pm

## NORTH OF BROAD
### Classic Southern
### HUSK $$$

Executive chef Sean Brock of McCrady's fame already has a healthy reputation as one of Charleston's—indeed, the country's—leading purveyors of the farm-to-table fine-dining aesthetic. He cemented that reputation with Husk, voted "Best New Restaurant in the U.S." by *Bon Appétit* magazine soon after its 2011 opening. The spare, focused menu—"If it doesn't come from the South, it's not coming through the door," Brock says of his ingredients—is constantly changing with the seasons. On a recent lunch visit my party enjoyed two types of catfish (a fried catfish BLT on Texas toast and a lightly cornmeal-dusted broiled catfish with local vegetables), Husk's signature cheeseburger, and—wait for it—lamb barbecue. Another visit brought a wonderful appetizer of teriyaki pig's ears in lettuce wraps! Husk is literally right next door to Poogan's Porch, and as with Poogan's, reservations are recommended.

**MAP 1**: 76 Queen St., 843/577-2500, www.huskrestaurant.com; Mon.-Thurs. 11:30am-2pm and 5:30pm-10pm, Fri.-Sat. 11:30am-2pm and 5:30pm-11pm, Sun. 10am-2:30pm and 5:30pm-10pm

the view from the top of Husk

## JESTINE'S KITCHEN $$

The long lines at Wentworth and Meeting Streets across from the fire station are waiting to follow Rachael Ray's lead and get into Jestine's Kitchen to enjoy a simple Southern take on such meat-and-three comfort food classics as meat loaf, pecan-fried fish, and fried green tomatoes. Most of the recipes are handed down from the restaurant's namesake, Jestine Matthews, the African American woman who raised owner Dana Berlin.
**MAP 1:** 251 Meeting St., 843/722-7224; Tues.-Thurs. 11am-9:30pm, Fri.-Sat. 11am-10pm

## PENINSULA GRILL $$$

Walk through the gaslit courtyard of the Planter's Inn at Market and Meeting Streets into the intimate dining room of the Peninsula Grill and begin an epicurean journey you'll not soon forget. Known far and wide for impeccable service, Peninsula Grill might be Charleston's quintessential purveyor of high-style Lowcountry cuisine. Longtime chef Robert Carter has moved on, but the kitchen is in able hands with new executive chef Graham Dailey. From the lobster skillet cake and crab cake appetizer to the bourbon-grilled jumbo shrimp to the benne-crusted rack of lamb to sides like wild mushroom grits and hoppin' John, the menu reads like a "greatest hits" of regional cooking. You'll almost certainly want to start with the sampler trio of soups and finish with the legendary coconut cake. Reservations are strongly recommended.
**MAP 1:** 112 N. Market St., 843/723-0700, www. peninsulagrill.com; daily from 5:30pm

## POOGAN'S PORCH $$

Named for a now-deceased beloved dog who once greeted guests, Poogan's Porch, in business over 40 years now, is the prototype of a classic Charleston restaurant: lovingly restored old home, professional but unpretentious service, great fried green tomatoes, and rich, calorie-laden Lowcountry classics. I can't decide which entrée I like best, the crab cakes or the shrimp and grits. Some swear that even the biscuits at Poogan's—flaky, freshbaked, and moist—are better than some entrées around town, although that's a stretch. Brunch is the big thing here, a bustling affair with big portions, Bloody Marys, mimosas, and soft sunlight.
**MAP 1:** 72 Queen St., 843/577-2337, www. poogansporch.com; Mon.-Fri. 11:30am-2:30pm and 5pm-9:30pm, Sat.-Sun. 9am-3pm and 5pm-9:30pm

# New Southern
## CHARLESTON GRILL $$$

Inside the plush Charleston Place Hotel you'll find Charleston Grill, one of the city's favorite (and priciest) fine-dining spots for locals and visitors alike. Veteran executive chef Bob Waggoner was recently replaced by his longtime sous chef Michelle Weaver, but the menu still specializes in French-influenced Lowcountry cuisine like a niçoise vegetable tart. There are a lot of great fusion dishes as well, such as the tuna and *hamachi* sashimi topped with pomegranate molasses and lemongrass oil. Reservations are a must.
**MAP 1:** 224 King St., 843/577-4522, www. charlestongrill.com; dinner daily from 6pm

## CIRCA 1886 $$$

Focusing on purely seasonal offerings that never stay on the menu longer than three months, Circa 1886 combines the best old-world tradition of Charleston with the vibrancy of its more adventurous kitchens. The restaurant—surprisingly little known despite its four-star Mobil rating—is located in the former carriage house of the grand Wentworth Mansion B&B just west of the main College of Charleston campus. It is now the playground of Chef Marc Collins, who delivers entrées like a robust beef au poivre and a shrimp-and-crab stuffed flounder, to name two recent offerings. Be sure to check the daily prix fixe offerings; those can be some great deals.
**MAP 1:** 149 Wentworth St., 843/853-7828, www. circa1886.com; Mon.-Sat. 5:30pm-9:30pm

Cru Café is a popular spot in a restored historic home downtown.

FIG is one of Charleston's great champions of the Sustainable Seafood Initiative, and the kitchen staff strives to work as closely as possible with local farmers and anglers in determining its seasonal menu.

**MAP 1:** 232 Meeting St., 843/805-5900, www.eatatfig. com; Mon.-Thurs. 6pm-11pm, Fri.-Sat. 6pm-midnight

## Coffee, Tea, and Sweets
### BLACK TAP COFFEE ⑤

Considered the best local coffeehouse in town, Black Tap features an array of Counter Culture beans roasted and served to perfection by skilled baristas. Cold brew and pour-over cups are specialties of the house, as is their signature Lavender Latte. A bit off the beaten King Street path but still well within walking distance of that shopping thoroughfare, this smallish but very well-equipped java joint can also be a destination in itself for an awesome cup and the requisite free Wi-Fi.

**MAP 1:** 70.5 Beaufain St., 843/793-4402; Mon.-Fri. 7am-7pm, Sat.-Sun. 8am-6pm

### CRU CAFÉ ⑤⑤⑤

Cru Café boasts an adventurous menu within a traditional-looking Charleston single house just around the corner from the main stable for the city's carriage tours, with a choice of interior or exterior seating. Sample entrées include poblano and mozzarella fried chicken and seared maple leaf duck breast.

**MAP 1:** 18 Pinckney St., 843/534-2434; Tues.-Thurs. 11am-3pm and 5pm-10pm, Fri.-Sat. 11am-3pm and 5pm-11pm

### ★ FIG ⑤⑤⑤

Just across the street from Hyman's Seafood is that establishment's diametrical opposite, the intimate bistro and stylish bar FIG—but the two do share one key thing: a passion for fresh, simple ingredients. While Hyman's packs in the tourists, FIG—short for "Food Is Good"—attracts young professional scenesters as well as the die-hard foodies. Chef Mike Lata won James Beard's Best Chef of the Southeast award in 2009.

### CITY LIGHTS COFFEEHOUSE ⑤

If you find yourself needing a quick pick-me-up while shopping on King Street, avoid the lines at the two Starbucks on the avenue and instead turn east on Market Street and duck inside City Lights Coffeehouse. The sweet goodies are delectable in this cozy little Euro-style place, and the Counter Culture organic coffee is to die for. If you're really lucky, they'll have some of their Ethiopian Sidamo brewed.

**MAP 1:** 141 Market St., 843/853-7067; Mon.-Thurs. 7am-9pm, Fri.-Sat. 7am-10pm, Sun. 8am-6pm

### KAMINSKY'S ⑤

Routinely voted as having the best desserts in the city, the cakes alone at Kaminsky's are worth the trip to the City Market area. The fresh fruit torte, the red velvet, and the "Mountain of Chocolate" are the three best sellers. There's also a Mount Pleasant location (1028 Johnnie Dodds Blvd., 843/971-7437).

**MAP 1:** 78 N. Market St., 843/853-8270; daily noon-2am

## French
### GAULART & MALICLET ⑤⑤

On the north side of Broad Street itself you'll find Gaulart & Maliclet, subtitled "Fast and French." This is a gourmet bistro with a strong takeout component. Prices are especially reasonable for this area of town, with great lunch specials under $10, Thursday night Fondue for Two specials at about $20, and breakfast all day.

MAP 1: 98 Broad St., 843/577-9797, www. fastandfrenchcharleston.com; Mon. 8am-4pm, Tues.-Thurs. 8am-10pm, Fri.-Sat. 8am-10:30pm

### QUEEN STREET GROCERY ⑤

If you find yourself in lodging near the Broad Street area—or if you just love crepes—you will want to acquaint yourself with the Queen Street Grocery. The kind of place frequented almost exclusively by locals, this corner store is where you can load up on some of the tastiest made-to-order crepes this side of France—as well as light groceries, beer, wine, and cigarettes.

MAP 1: 133 Queen St., 843/723-4121, www. queenstreetgrocerycafe.com; kitchen Mon.-Sat. 10am-5pm, Sun. 11am-3pm, store Mon.-Sat. 8am-8:30pm

## Mediterranean
### FULTON FIVE ⑤⑤⑤

The cuisine of northern Italy comes alive in this bustling, dimly lit room, from the *insalata de funghi* to the sublime risotto. It's not cheap, and the portions aren't necessarily the largest, but with these tasty, non-tomato-based dishes and this romantic, gusto-filled atmosphere, you'll be satiated with life itself.

MAP 1: 5 Fulton St., 843/853-5555, www.fultonfive. com; Mon.-Sat. 5:30pm-close

## Seafood
### HYMAN'S SEAFOOD ⑤⑤

Hyman's Seafood is thought by many locals to border on a tourist trap, and it's mostly tourists who line up for hours to get in. To keep things manageable, Hyman's offers the same menu and prices for both lunch and dinner. After asking for some complimentary fresh boiled peanuts in lieu of bread, start with the Carolina Delight, a delicious appetizer (also available as an entrée) involving a lightly fried cake of grits topped with your choice of delectable seafood, or maybe a half-dozen oysters from the Half Shell oyster bar. Definitely try the she-crab soup, some of the best you'll find anywhere. As for entrées, the ubiquitous Lowcountry crispy scored flounder is always a good bet.

MAP 1: 215 Meeting St., 843/723-6000, www. hymanseafood.com; Mon.-Thurs. 11am-9pm, Fri.-Sun. 11am-11pm

# UPPER KING
## Classic Southern
### VIRGINIA'S ON KING ⑤⑤

One of a comparatively few great Charleston restaurants with an equally expert focus on breakfast as on the other meals, Virginia's is a great place to enjoy Southern classics like fried green tomatoes, tomato pie, and their signature she-crab soup. I will say their Salmon BLT lunch dish (or in their old Southern parlance, "dinner," supper being the name of the last meal of the day) is one of the best seafood dishes I've had anywhere. As for that breakfast, the omelets are solid but most of their lunch menu is also available.

MAP 2: 412 King St., 912/735-5900, www. holycityhospitality.com; Mon.-Fri. 7am-10pm, Sat. 8am-10pm, Sun. 10am-3pm

### THE MACINTOSH ⑤⑤

Rapidly gaining a reputation as one of the best brunch scenes in town, the relatively new The Macintosh combines the best of Charleston's Classic/New South style with a gastropub sensibility, complete with an extensive craft beer menu. The chef is three-time James Beard semifinalist Jeremiah Bacon, which means you can't really go wrong. But for brunch I'd suggest the baked chorizo, and from the small but artfully curated dinner menu, any seafood dish is good. Happy hour (Mon.-Fri.

# Lowcountry Locavores

Charleston has merged its own indigenous and abiding culinary tradition with the "new" idea that you should grow your food as naturally as possible and purchase it as close to home as you can. From bacon and snapper to sweet potatoes, the typical Charleston dish of today harkens back to its soulful Southern roots, before the days of factory food.

Spurred in part by an influx of trained chefs after the establishment of the Spoleto Festival in the 1970s, the locavore movement in Charleston came from the efforts of epicureans committed to sustainability and the principles of community-supported agriculture (CSA). Spearheaded by visionaries like the James Beard Award-winning Mike Lata of the bistro FIG and Sean Brock of Mc-Crady's, sustainable food initiatives have sprung up in Charleston and the Lowcountry, such as the South Carolina Aquarium's Sustainable Seafood Initiative (http://scaquarium.org), partnering with local restaurants to assure a sustainable wild-caught harvest; Certified South Carolina (www.certifiedsc.com), guaranteeing that the food you eat was grown in the Palmetto State; a local chapter of the Slow Food Movement (http://slowfoodcharleston.org); and Cypress Artisan Meat Share (www.magnolias-blossom-cypress.com), in which a group of highly regarded restaurants makes their fine locally sourced meats available to the public.

The list of Holy City restaurants relying almost exclusively on local and sustainable sources is long, but here are a few notable examples:

- **Husk** (76 Queen St., 843/577-2500, www.huskrestaurant.com)

- **Cypress** (167 E. Bay St., 843/727-0111, www.magnolias-blossom-cypress.com)

- **Charleston Grill** (224 King St., 843/577-4522, www.charlestongrill.com)

- **FIG** (232 Meeting St., 843/805-5900, www.eatatfig.com)

- **Al Di La** (25 Magnolia Rd., 843/571-2321)

- **Queen Street Grocery** (133 Queen St., 843/723-4121)

- **Middleton Place Restaurant** (4300 Ashley River Rd., 843/556-6020, www.middletonplace.org)

- **Circa 1886** (149 Wentworth St., 843/853-7828, www.circa1886.com)

- **COAST Bar and Grill** (39D John St., 843/722-8838, www.coastbarandgrill.com)

- **Cru Café** (18 Pinckney St., 843/534-2434, www.crucafe.com)

- **Hominy Grill** (207 Rutledge Ave., 912/937-0930, www.hominygrill.com)

- **Peninsula Grill** (112 N. Market St., 843/723-0700, www.peninsulagrill.com)

---

5pm-7pm) is also a big draw here, with its own special $5 small plate bar food menu.
**MAP 2:** 479 King St., 843/789-4299, www.themacintoshcharleston.com; Mon.-Sat. 6:30am-7pm, Sun. 9am-6pm

## American
### EDMUND'S OAST ⑤

Charleston's fave rave is this boisterous beer garden/brewpub on the Upper Peninsula, boasting a 40-tap array, several brews made on-site, and perhaps surprisingly, an excellent cocktail menu as well. The small plates, though, might be what stay with you. Expressive, excellent charcuterie and pitch-perfect sliders are the highlights. If you sit at the bar, the $4 per plate happy hour items (4:30pm-6:30pm) are a must-try; I suggest the smoked wings.
**MAP 2:** 1081 Morrison Dr., 843/727-1145, www.edmundsoast.com; Mon.-Thurs. 5:30pm-10pm, Fri.-Sat. 5:30pm-11pm, Sun. 10am-2:30pm and 5:30pm-10pm

## Asian

### BASIL ⑤⑤

There's usually a long wait to get a table at the great Thai place Basil on Upper King, since they don't take reservations. But Basil also has one of the hippest, most happening bar scenes in the area, so you won't necessarily mind. Revelers enjoy fresh, succulent takes on Thai classics like cashew chicken and pad thai, all cooked by Asian chefs. The signature dish, as you might imagine, is the basil duck.
MAP 2: 460 King St., 843/724-3490, www.
basilthairestaurant.com; Mon.-Thurs. 11:30am-2:30pm and 5pm-10:30pm, Fri.-Sat. 5pm-11pm, Sun. 5pm-10pm

## Barbecue

### FIERY RON'S HOME TEAM ⑤

The new downtown/upper peninsula outpost of Charleston's favorite barbecue chain boasts a bit of an upscale feel from the original West Ashley location and the Sullivan's Island version. But don't be deceived by the excellent artisanal cocktail menu; the barbecue here is just as good.
MAP 2: 126 Williman St., 843/225-7427, www.
hometeambbq.com; daily 11am-10pm

## Coffee, Tea, and Sweets

### KUDU COFFEE ⑤

By common consensus, the best java joint in Charleston is Kudu Coffee in the Upper King area. A kudu is an African antelope, and the Africa theme extends to the beans, which all have an African pedigree. Poetry readings and occasional live music add to the mix. A lot of green-friendly, left-of-center community activism goes on here as well.
MAP 2: 4 Vanderhorst St., 843/853-7186; Mon.-Sat. 6:30am-7pm, Sun. 9am-6pm

## Italian

### INDACO ⑤⑤⑤

One of Upper King's newest "it" restaurants, Indaco features a small but well-curated menu of antipasti, custom wood-fired gourmet pizzas, and delicious Italian specialties like black pepper tagliatelle. Yes, there's brussels sprout pizza, and it's quite delicious! Indaco is set in a stylish, bustling restored warehouse environment that draws some of Charleston's most beautiful foodies.
MAP 2: 525 King St., 843/727-1218, www.
indacocharleston.com; Sun.-Thurs. 5pm-10pm, Fri.-Sat. 5pm-midnight

## Mexican

### JUANITA GREENBERG'S NACHO ROYALE ⑤

The quesadillas at Juanita Greenberg's Nacho Royale are perfectly packed with jack cheese but not overly so, full of spicy sausage, and finished with a delightful *pico de gallo*. This modest Mexican joint on Upper King caters primarily to a college crowd, as you can tell from the reasonable prices, the large patio out back, the extensive tequila list, and the bar that stays open until 2am on weekends.
MAP 2: 439 King St., 843/723-6224, www.
juanitagreenbergs.com; daily 11am-11pm

## Seafood

### COAST BAR AND GRILL ⑤⑤⑤

Near 39 Rue de Jean you'll find the affiliated COAST Bar and Grill makes the most of its loud, hip former warehouse setting. The raw bar is satisfying, with a particularly nice take on and selection of ceviche. COAST is a strong local advocate of the Sustainable Seafood Initiative, whereby restaurants work directly with the local fishing industry.
MAP 2: 39D John St., 843/722-8838, www.
coastbarandgrill.com; daily 5:30pm-close

### ★ 39 RUE DE JEAN ⑤⑤⑤

The best mussels I've ever had were at 39 Rue de Jean. But anything off the bistro-style menu is unbelievably tasty, from the foie gras to the comfit to the coq au vin to the steak frites. There are incredible Prohibition-style cocktails to go along with the extensive wine list.
MAP 2: 39 John St., 843/722-8881, www.
holycityhospitality.com; Mon.-Thurs. 11:30am-11pm, Fri.-Sat. 11:30am-1am, Sun. 10am-11pm

# HAMPTON PARK
## Classic Southern
### HOMINY GRILL 💲💲

With a motto like "Grits are good for you," you know what you're in store for at Hominy Grill, set in a renovated barbershop at Rutledge Avenue and Cannon Street near the Medical University of South Carolina. Primarily revered for his Sunday brunch, Chef Robert Stehling has fun—almost mischievously so—breathing new life into American and Southern classics. Because this is largely a locals' place, you can impress your friends back home by saying you had the rare pleasure of the Hominy's sautéed shad roe with bacon and mushrooms—when the shad are running, that is.

**MAP 2:** 207 Rutledge Ave., 912/937-0930; Mon.-Fri. 7:30am-8:30pm, Sat.-Sun. 9am-8:30pm

### MOE'S CROSSTOWN TAVERN 💲💲

Moe's Crosstown Tavern is not only one of the classic Southern dives, but also has one of the best kitchens on this side of town, known for hand-cut fries, great wings, and, most of all, excellent burgers. On Tuesdays, the burgers are half price at happy hour—one of Charleston's best deals.

**MAP 2:** 714 Rutledge Ave., 843/722-3287; Mon.-Sat. 11am-midnight, bar until 2am

## Italian
### TRATTORIA LUCCA 💲💲💲

A rave of Charleston foodies is the Tuscan-inspired fare of Chef Ken Vedrinski at Trattoria Lucca. The menu is simple but perfectly focused, featuring handmade pasta and signature items like the pork chop or the fresh cheese plate. You'll be surprised at how much food your money gets you here. Monday evenings see a family-style prix fixe communal dinner.

**MAP 2:** 41 Bogard St., 843/973-3323, www. luccacharleston.com; Mon.-Sat. 6pm-10pm

# WEST ASHLEY
## Classic Southern
### MIDDLETON PLACE RESTAURANT 💲💲

Tucked away on the grounds of the Middleton Place Plantation is the romantic Middleton Place Restaurant. Theirs is a respectful take on traditional plantation fare like hoppin' John, gumbo, she-crab soup, and collards. The special annual Thanksgiving buffet is a real treat. Reservations are required for dinner. A nice plus is being able to wander the gorgeous landscaped gardens before dusk if you arrive at 5:30pm or later with a dinner reservation.

**MAP 3:** 4300 Ashley River Rd., 843/556-6020, www. middletonplace.org; Tues.-Thurs. and Sun. 11am-3pm and 6pm-8pm, Fri.-Sat. 11am-3pm and 6pm-9pm

## New Southern
### ★ THE GLASS ONION 💲💲

One of the more unassuming advocates of farm-to-table dining, The Glass Onion is also in an unassuming location on U.S. 17 (Savannah Hwy.) on the western approach to town. That said, their food is right in the thick of the sustainable food movement and is incredibly tasty to boot (not to mention that there is more parking there than there is downtown). The interior says "diner," and indeed the emphasis here is on Southern soul and comfort food classics. A recent trip saw a duck leg with pork belly as a special entrée, and a chicken and andouille gumbo that was zesty without being overspiced, thick without being pasty. There are occasional "all-you-can-eat quail" nights, and every Tuesday is "fried chicken dinner" night, with what many insist is the best fried chicken in Charleston. The Glass Onion also boasts a good variety of specialty craft brews to wash it all down with. Another plus: In this town full of Sunday brunches, Glass Onion's specialty is a Saturday brunch!

**MAP 3:** 1219 Savannah Hwy., 843/225-1717, www. ilovetheglassonion.com; Mon.-Thurs. 11am-9pm, Fri. 11am-10pm, Sat. 10am-3pm and 4pm-10pm

## American

### ★ GENE'S HAUFBRAU

The kitchen at Gene's Haufbrau complements its fairly typical bar-food menu with some good wraps. Start with the "Drunken Trio" (beer-battered cheese sticks, mushrooms, and onion rings) and follow with a portobello wrap or a good old-fashioned crawfish po'boy. One of the best meals for the money in town is Gene's rotating $7.25 blue plate special, offered Monday-Friday 11:30am-4pm. The late-night kitchen hours, until 1am, are a big plus.

MAP 3: 17 Savannah Hwy., 843/225-4363, www. genes-haufbrau.com; daily 11:30am-2am

### BOXCAR BETTY'S ⓢ

If you're any kind of fan of fried chicken, whether good old-fashioned Southern fried or the type of sandwich you might get at Chick-fil-A, you will want to check out Boxcar Betty's. Be warned, these juicy, incredibly tasty flour-breaded fried chicken sandwiches are addictive.

MAP 3: 1922 Savannah Hwy., 843/225-7470, www. boxcarbetty.com; daily 11am-9pm

## Barbecue

### ★ FIERY RON'S HOME TEAM BBQ ⓢⓢ

My favorite barbecue joint anywhere, the rowdy and always hopping Fiery Ron's Home Team BBQ has pulled pork and ribs that rank with the best I've had anywhere in the country. Even the sides are amazing here, including perfect collards and tasty mac and cheese. Pitmaster Madison Ruckel provides an array of table-side sauces, including hot sauce, indigenous South Carolina mustard sauce, and his own "Alabama white," a light and delicious mayonnaise-based sauce. As if that weren't enough, the owners' close ties to the regional jam-band community mean there's great live blues and indie rock after 10pm most nights (Thursday is bluegrass night) to spice up the bar action, which goes until 2am.

MAP 3: 1205 Ashley River Rd., 843/225-7427, www. hometeambbq.com; Mon.-Sat. 11am-9pm, Sun. 11:30am-9pm

Fiery Ron's Home Team BBQ

# Farmers Markets

Charleston Farmers Market

A fun and favorite local fixture April–mid-December, the **Charleston Farmers Market** (843/724-7309, www.charlestoncity.info, Sat. 8am-2pm) rings beautiful Marion Square with stalls of local produce, street eats, local arts and crafts, and kids' activities.

Running April-October, East Cooper has its own version in the **Mount Pleasant Farmers Market** (843/884-8517, http://townofmountpleasant.com, Tues. 3pm-dark) at the Moultrie Middle School on Coleman Boulevard.

## Mediterranean
### AL DI LA $$

Anything on this northern Italian-themed menu is good, but the risotto—a legacy of original chef John Marshall—is the specialty dish at Al Di La, a very popular West Ashley fine-dining spot. Reservations are recommended.

MAP 3: 25 Magnolia Rd., 843/571-2321, www.aldilarestaurant.com; Tues.-Sat. 6pm-10pm

# NORTH CHARLESTON
## Pizza
### EVO PIZZERIA $$

If you have a hankering for pizza in North Charleston, don't miss EVO Pizzeria in the Olde North Charleston area at Park Circle. They specialize in a small but rich menu of unusual gourmet pizza toppings, like pistachio pesto.

MAP 3: 1075 E. Montague Ave., 843/225-1796, www.evopizza.com; Tues.-Fri. 11am-2:30pm and 5pm-10pm, Sat. 6pm-10pm

# SUMMERVILLE
## American
### ALEX'S RESTAURANT $

For a down-home-style pancakes-and-sandwich place that's popular with the locals at all hours of the day, try Alex's Restaurant.

MAP 3: 120 E. 5th N. St., 843/871-3202; daily 24 hours

### GUERIN'S PHARMACY $

A popular local landmark is Guerin's Pharmacy, which claims to be the state's oldest pharmacy. Complete with an old-fashioned soda fountain, they offer malted milkshakes and lemonade.

MAP 3: 140 S. Main St., 843/873-2531; Mon.-Fri. 9am-6pm, Sat. 9am-5pm

## MOUNT PLEASANT AND EAST COOPER

In Mount Pleasant, most of the restaurant action centers on the picturesque shrimping village of Shem Creek, which is dotted on both banks with bars and restaurants, most dealing in fresh local seafood. As with Murrells Inlet up the coast, some spots on Shem Creek border on tourist traps. Don't be afraid to go where the lines aren't.

### American
#### POE'S TAVERN $$

For a burger and an adult beverage or two, go straight to friendly Poe's Tavern, a nod to Edgar Allan Poe's stint at nearby Fort Moultrie.

MAP 4: 2210 Middle St., 843/883-0083, www. poestavern.com; daily 11am-2am, kitchen until 10pm

### Seafood
#### RED DRUM GASTROPUB $$

If you find yourself thirsty and hungry in Mount Pleasant after dark, you might want to stop in the Red Drum Gastropub, so named because the food here is just as important as the drink. While you're likely to need reservations for the dining room, where you can enjoy Lowcountry-Tex-Mex fusion-style cuisine with a typically Mount Pleasant-like emphasis on seafood, the bar scene is very hopping and fun, with live music every Wednesday-Thursday night.

MAP 4: 803 Coleman Blvd., 843/849-0313, www. reddrumrestaurant.com; daily 5:30pm-10pm, lunch/ brunch Sat.-Sun. 10:30am-2pm

#### ★ SEE WEE RESTAURANT $$

A must-stop roadside diner in the Awendaw area is See Wee Restaurant, about 20 minutes' drive north of Charleston in a humble former general store on the west side of U.S. 17 (the restrooms are still outside). Folks come from Charleston and as far away as Myrtle Beach to

enjoy signature menu items like the grouper and the unreal she-crab soup, considered by some epicures to be the best in the world; you can't miss with any of their seafood entrées. Occasionally the crowds can get thick, but rest assured it's worth any wait.

MAP 4: 4808 U.S. 17 N., 843/928-3609; Mon.-Thurs. 11am-8:30pm, Fri.-Sat. 11am-9:30pm, Sun. 11am-8pm

#### VICKERY'S SHEM CREEK BAR AND GRILL $$

A popular spot, especially for the younger crowd, is Vickery's Shem Creek Bar and Grill. With a similar menu to its partner location on the peninsula, this Vickery's has the pleasant added bonus of a beautiful view overlooking the creek. You'll get more of the Vickery's Cuban flair here, with a great black bean soup and an awesome Cuban sandwich.

MAP 4: 1313 Shrimp Boat Ln., 843/884-4440; daily 11:30am-1am

#### WATER'S EDGE $$$

A well-regarded spot on Shem Creek is Water's Edge, which consistently takes home a *Wine Spectator* Award of Excellence for its great selection of vintages. Native Charlestonian Jimmy Purcell concentrates on fresh seafood with a slightly more upscale flair than many Shem Creek places.

MAP 4: 1407 Shrimp Boat Ln., 843/884-4074; daily 11am-11pm

### Vegetarian
#### THE SPROUT CAFE $

For a real change of pace, try The Sprout Cafe on U.S. 17. Dealing totally in raw foods, the restaurant emphasizes healthy and fresh ingredients. You might be surprised at the inventiveness of their breakfast-through-dinner seasonal menu—memorably described by the staff as "grab and go"—which might include a tasty crepe topped with a pear-and-nut puree and maple syrup, or a raw squash and zucchini "pasta" dish topped with walnut "meatballs."

MAP 4: 629 Johnnie Dodds Blvd., 843/849-8554, www.thehealthysprout.com; Mon.-Fri. 6am-8pm, Sat. 9am-3pm, Sun. 11am-3pm

# FOLLY BEACH AND THE SOUTHWEST ISLANDS

## American

### TATTOOED MOOSE $

Three words: Duck fat fries. This dive bar sensation on Johns Island combines classic bar food with a typically Charlestonian touch of Old South culinary bravado. While the fries—served straight up with roasted garlic and blue cheese or with gravy—are the signature menu item, the sandwiches are simply fantastic. Try the duck comfit sandwich, or the "Lucky Number One," a pork belly sandwich. Brunch is becoming huge here and is well worth the drive, and live music is featured most nights.

MAP 5: 3328 Maybank Hwy., 843/277-2990, www. tattooedmoose.com; daily 11:30am-1am

## Barbecue

### JB'S SMOKESHACK $

If barbecue is your thing, head straight to JB's Smokeshack, considered one of the better 'cue joints in the Lowcountry. True connoisseurs will tell you it's their chicken that's really awesome, however. They offer a buffet for $8.88 pp ($5 under age 11), or you can opt for a barbecue plate, including hash, rice, and two sides. In a nice twist, the plates include a three-meat option: pork, chicken, ribs, or brisket.

MAP 5: 3406 Maybank Hwy., 843/557-0426, www. jbssmokeshack.com; Wed.-Sat. 11am-8:30pm

## Breakfast and Brunch

### LOST DOG CAFÉ $

The closest thing to a taste of old Folly is the Lost Dog Café, so named for its bulletin board stacked with alerts about lost pets, pets for adoption, and new pups and kittens for sale or giveaway. They open early, the better to offer a tasty, healthy breakfast to the surfing crowd. It's a great place to pick up a quick, inexpensive, and tasty meal while you're near the beach.

MAP 5: 106 W. Huron Ave., 843/588-9669; daily 6:30am-3pm

## SUNRISE BISTRO $

For a hearty and delicious breakfast, go to Sunrise Bistro, one of those unassuming diners that always seems to have an eager crowd. Everything, from the omelets to the pancakes down to the simplest bagel with coffee, is spot-on, and a great value to boot. The best offerings here are during the day.

MAP 5: 1797 Main Rd., 843/718-1858, www. sunrise-bistro.com; Tues.-Thurs. 7am-2:30pm, Fri.-Sat. 7am-2:30pm and 5pm-9pm, Sun. 9am-1pm

## French

### ★ FAT HEN $$

Fat Hen is a self-styled "country French bistro" begun by a couple of old Charleston restaurant hands. The fried oysters are a particular specialty. There's also a bar menu for late-night hours (10pm-2am).

MAP 5: 3140 Maybank Hwy., 843/559-9090; Tues.-Sat. 11:30am-3pm and 5:30pm-10pm, Sun. 10am-3pm

## Mexican

### TACO BOY $

Taco Boy is a fun place to get a fish taco, have a margarita, and take a walk on the nearby beach afterward. Though no one is under any illusions that this is an authentic Mexican restaurant, the fresh guacamole is particularly rave-worthy, and there's a good selection of tequilas and beers *hecho en México*, with the bar staying open until 2am on weekends.

MAP 5: 15 Center St., 843/588-9761; Sun.-Thurs. 11am-10pm, Fri.-Sat. 11am-11pm

## Seafood

### BLU $$

Set within the trendy Tides boutique hotel, Blu offers an equally high standard of food and décor, along with some amazing views of the ocean. The menu isn't particularly pretentious but offers high-quality Sustainable Seafood Initiative options, all of which are recommended.

MAP 5: 1 Center St., 843/588-6658, www. blufollybeach.com; breakfast daily 7am-11am, lunch daily 11am-5pm, dinner Sun.-Thu. 5pm-9pm, Fri.-Sat. 5pm-10pm

**BOWENS ISLAND RESTAURANT** $

Fans of the legendary Bowens Island Restaurant, on James Island just before you get to Folly, went into mourning when it burned to the ground in 2006. But you can't keep a good oysterman down, and owner Robert Barber rebuilt. A universe removed from the Lexus-and-khaki scene downtown, Bowens Island isn't the place for the uptight. This is the spot to go when you want shovels of oysters literally thrown onto your table, freshly steamed and delicious and all-you-can-eat. The fried shrimp, flounder, and hush puppies are incredible too. To get there from the peninsula, take Calhoun Street west onto the James Island Connector (Hwy. 30). Take exit 3 onto Highway 171 south and look for Bowens Island Road on the right. The restaurant will be on the left in a short while, after passing by several ritzy McMansions that in no way resemble the restaurant you're about to experience.

**MAP 5**: 1870 Bowens Island Rd., 843/795-2757; Tues.-Sat. 5-10pm; cash only

# Hotels

As one of the country's key national and international destination cities, Charleston has a very well-developed infrastructure for housing visitors. It's a task made much easier by the city's long-standing tradition of hospitality and the high standards it has set for itself over the decades.

Because the bar is set so high, few visitors experience a bad stay in town. Hotels and bed-and-breakfasts are well maintained and have a high level of service ranging from very good to excellent. There's a 12.5 percent tax on hotel rooms in Charleston. No one can say lodging is inexpensive near the tourist areas of the city, but you almost always get what you pay for—and then some.

The real issue for most visitors boils down to two questions: How much do you want to spend, and in which part of town do you want to stay? Because the price differential is not that much between the peninsula and the outskirts, I recommend staying on the peninsula. You'll pay more, but not *that* much more, with the bonus of being able to walk to most places you want to see—which is the best way to enjoy the city.

The farther south you go on the peninsula, the quieter and more affluent it tends to be. Folks looking for a more wild and woolly good time will be drawn to the Upper King area farther north.

Charleston County runs a family-friendly, fairly boisterous campground at **James Island County Park** (871 Riverland Dr., 843/795-7275, www.ccprc.com, $31 tent site, $37 pull-through site). A neat feature here is the $5-pp round-trip shuttle to the visitors center downtown, Folly Beach Pier, and Folly Beach County Park. The park also has 10 furnished cottages (843/795-4386, $138) for rent, sleeping up to eight people. Reservations are recommended. For more commercial camping in Mount Pleasant, try the **KOA of Mt. Pleasant** (3157 U.S. 17 N., 843/849-5177, www.koa.com, from $30 tent sites, from $50 pull-through sites).

## SOUTH OF BROAD

★ **GOVERNOR'S HOUSE INN** $$$

On the south side of Broad Street is a great old Charleston lodging, Governor's House Inn. This circa-1760 building, a National Historic Landmark, is associated with Edward Rutledge, signer of the Declaration of Independence. Though most of its 11 guest rooms—all with four-poster beds, period furnishings, and high ceilings—go for around $300, some of the smaller guest rooms can be had for closer to $200 in the off-season.

**MAP 1**: 117 Broad St., 843/720-2070, www.governorshouse.com

# Best Hotels

★ **Closest Brush with the Declaration of Independence:** Before purchasing what is now the **Governor's House Inn** and being elected chief executive of South Carolina, Edward Rutledge was the youngest signer of the Declaration (page 116).

★ **Most Romantic Getaway:** Local legend has it that as a young naval officer, John F. Kennedy met one of his many paramours, an alleged German spy, at **Two Meeting Street Inn** (page 117).

★ **Best Rooftop Bar:** Enjoy views of the French Quarter and the Waterfront from the famous Rooftop Bar on top of **The Vendue** (page 118).

★ **Cozy in the City:** Though close to the City Market area's tourist bustle, the classy **Andrew Pinckney Inn** is quiet and calming (page 118).

★ **Most Comfortable Lap of Luxury:** The **Belmond Charleston Place** is smack downtown and offers the city's premier lodging and spa facilities steps away from Charleston's prime shopping district (page 118).

★ **Closest Brush with the Constitution:** The only B&B in the United States that was once the home of a signer of the U.S. Constitution, the **John Rutledge House Inn** is one of the South's most sumptuous and highest-rated lodgings (page 119).

★ **Least Expensive Awesome Stay:** The charming **Not So Hostel** offers friendly and informal communal lodging a quick bike ride away from downtown (page 120).

★ **Most Calming Commune with Nature:** The sparsely modernist **The Inn at Middleton Place** offers a relaxing, state-of-the-art getaway in the scenic and peaceful heart of the old Middleton Place Plantation grounds (page 121).

★ **Best Outdoor Pool:** The **Kiawah Island Golf Resort** not only offers first-class golf and accommodations on a beautifully preserved barrier island, it also has a huge resort-style pool just off a windswept beach (page 122).

## ★ TWO MEETING STREET INN ⑤⑤

The nine guest rooms of Two Meeting Street Inn down by the Battery are individually appointed, with themes like "The Music Room" and the "The Spell Room." The decor in this 1892 Queen Anne bed-and-breakfast is very traditional, with lots of floral patterns and hunt club-style pieces and artwork. It's considered by many to be the most romantic lodging in town, and you won't soon forget the experience of sitting on the veranda enjoying the sights, sounds, and breezes. Three of the guest rooms—the Canton, Granite, and Roberts—can be had for not much over $200.

**MAP 1:** 2 Meeting St., 843/723-7322, www.twomeetingstreet.com

## WATERFRONT

### HARBOURVIEW INN ⑤⑤⑤

About as close to the Cooper River as a hotel gets, the Harbourview Inn comprises a "historic wing" and a larger, newer, but still tastefully done main building. For the best of those eponymous harbor views, try to get a room on the third floor or you might have some obstructions. It's the little touches that keep guests happy here, with wine, cheese, coffee, tea, and cookies galore and an emphasis on smiling, personalized service. The guest rooms are quite spacious, with big baths and 14-foot ceilings. You can take your complimentary breakfast—good but not great—in your room or eat it on the nice rooftop terrace. MAP 1: 2 Vendue Range, 843/853-8439, www. harbourviewcharleston.com

### ★ THE VENDUE ❸❸❸

The guest rooms and the thoroughly hospitable service are the focus at nearby The Vendue, just off a $5 million renovation and expansion. All guest rooms are sumptuously appointed in that boutique style, with lots of warm, rich fabrics, unique pieces, and high-end bath amenities. That said, the public spaces are cool as well, the renovation being particularly focused on featuring quality art and essentially creating one huge exhibition space. The inn gets a lot of traffic in the evenings because of the popular and hopping Rooftop Bar, which has amazing views. MAP 1: 19 Vendue Range, 800/845-7900, www. thevendue.com

## FRENCH QUARTER

### FRENCH QUARTER INN ❸❸❸

A great place in this part of town is the French Quarter Inn. The decor in the 50 surprisingly spacious guest rooms is suitably high-period French, with low-style noncanopied beds and crisp fresh linens. Many guest rooms feature fireplaces, whirlpool baths, and private balconies. One of Charleston's hottest restaurants, Tristan, is on the ground floor. You're treated to champagne on your arrival, and goodies are available all day, with wine and cheese served every night at 5pm. MAP 1: 166 Church St., 843/722-1900, www. fqicharleston.com

## NORTH OF BROAD

### ★ ANDREW PINCKNEY INN ❸❸

It calls itself a boutique hotel, perhaps because each room is totally different and sumptuously appointed. But the charming Andrew Pinckney Inn is very nearly in a class by itself in Charleston not only for its great rates but for its casual West Indies-style decor, charming courtyard, gorgeous three-story atrium, and rooftop terrace on which you can enjoy your complimentary (and delicious) breakfast. For the money and the amenities, it's possibly the single best lodging package in town. MAP 1: 199 Church St., 843/937-8800, www. andrewpinckneyinn.com

### ★ BELMOND CHARLESTON PLACE ❸❸❸

Considered Charleston's premier hotel, Charleston Place maintains a surprisingly high level of service and decor considering its massive 440-room size. Currently owned by the London-based Orient-Express Hotels, Belmond Charleston Place is routinely rated as one of the best hotels in North America by *Condé Nast Traveler* and other publications. The guest rooms aren't especially large, but they are well appointed, featuring Italian marble baths, high-speed Internet, and voice messaging—and, of course, there's a pool available. A series of suite offerings—Junior, Junior Executive, Parlor, and the 800-square-foot Senior—feature enlarged living areas and multiple TVs and phones. A Manager's Suite on the Private Club level up top comprises 1,200 square feet of total luxury that will set you back at least $1,600 per night. It's the additional offerings that make Charleston Place closer to a lifestyle decision than a lodging choice. The on-site **spa** (843/937-8522) offers all kinds of massages, including couples and "mommy to be" sessions. Diners and tipplers have three fine options to choose from: the famous **Charleston Grill** (843/577-4522, daily 6pm-close, $27-65) for fine dining; the breakfast, lunch, and brunch hot spot **Palmetto Cafe** (843/722-4900, daily 6:30am-3pm, $24-31); and the **Thoroughbred Club** (daily 11am-midnight) for cocktails and for groups of 10 or more, afternoon tea. MAP 1: 205 Meeting St., 843/722-4900, www. charlestonplace.com

## FULTON LANE INN $$$

Affiliated with the Kings Courtyard—and right next door, in fact—is the smaller, cozier Fulton Lane Inn, with its lobby entrance on tiny Fulton Lane between the two inns. Small, simple guest rooms—some with fireplaces—have comfortable beds and spacious baths. This is the kind of place for active people who plan to spend most of their days out and about but want a cozy place to come back to at night. You mark down your continental breakfast order at night, leave it on your doorknob, and it shows up at the *exact* time you requested the next morning. Then when you're ready to shop and walk, just go down the stairs and take the exit right out onto busy King Street. Also nice is the $12-per-day parking with free in-and-out privileges.

MAP 1: 202 King St., 866/720-2940, www. fultonlaneinn.com

## ★ JOHN RUTLEDGE HOUSE INN $$$

On the north side of Broad Street, the magnificent John Rutledge House Inn is very close to the old South of Broad neighborhood not only in geography but in feel. Known as "America's most historic inn," the Rutledge House boasts a fine old pedigree indeed: Built for Constitution signer John Rutledge in 1763, it's one of only 15 homes belonging to the original signers to survive. George Washington breakfasted here with Mrs. Rutledge in 1791. The interior is stunning: Italian marble fireplaces, original plaster moldings, and masterful ironwork abound in the public spaces. The inn's 19 guest rooms are divided among the original mansion and two carriage houses. A friendly and knowledgeable concierge will give you all kinds of tips and make reservations for you.

MAP 1: 116 Broad St., 843/723-7999, www. johnrutledgehouseinn.com

## KINGS COURTYARD INN $$$

If you plan on some serious shopping, you might want to stay right on the city's main shopping thoroughfare at the Kings Courtyard Inn. This 1853 Greek Revival building houses a lot more guest rooms—more than 40—than meets the eye, and it can get a little crowded at times. Still, its charming courtyard and awesome location on King Street are big bonuses, as is the convenient but cramped parking lot right next door (about $12 per day, a bargain for this part of town), with free in-and-out privileges.

MAP 1: 198 King St., 866/720-2949, www. kingscourtyardinn.com

## MILLS HOUSE HOTEL $$$

Although it is a newer building by Charleston standards, the Mills House Hotel boasts an important pedigree and still tries hard to maintain the old tradition of impeccable Southern service at this historic location. An extensive round of renovations in 2007 has been well received. Dating to 1853, the first incarnation was a grand edifice that hosted luminaries such as Robert E. Lee. Through the years, fire and restoration wrought their changes, and the modern version basically dates from an extensive renovation in the 1970s. Because of its healthy banquet and event schedule—much of it centering on the very good restaurant and lounge inside—the Mills House isn't the place to go for peace and quiet. Rather, this Wyndham-affiliated property is where you go to feel the bustle of downtown Charleston and to be conveniently close to its main sightseeing and shopping attractions. Some of the upper floors of this seven-story building offer spectacular views. A particular delight is the courtyard complete with fountain, where you can enjoy a cocktail or coffee.

MAP 1: 115 Meeting St., 843/577-2400, www. millshouse.com

# UPPER KING
## ASHLEY INN $

Stretching the bounds of the "Upper King" definition, we come to the Ashley Inn well northwest of Marion Square, almost in the Citadel area. Although it's too far to walk from here to most any historic attraction in Charleston, the Ashley Inn does provide free bikes to its guests as well as free off-street parking, a particularly nice touch. It also deserves a special mention not only because of the romantic, well-appointed nature of its six guest rooms, suite, and carriage house but for its outstanding breakfasts. You get to pick a main dish, such as Carolina sausage pie, stuffed waffles, or cheese blintzes.

**MAP 2:** 201 Ashley Ave., 843/723-1848, www. charleston-sc-inns.com

### FRANCIS MARION HOTEL $$

In a renovated 1924 building overlooking beautiful Marion Square, the Francis Marion Hotel offers quality accommodations in the hippest, most bustling area of the peninsula—but be aware that it's quite a walk down to the Battery from here. The guest rooms are plush and big, though the baths can be cramped. The hotel's parking garage costs a reasonable $12 per day, with valet parking available until about 8pm. A Starbucks in the lobby pleases many guests on their way out or in. Most rooms hover around $300, but some are a real steal.

**MAP 2:** 387 King St., 843/722-0600, www. francismarionhotel.com

## HAMPTON PARK
### ★ NOT SO HOSTEL $

Charleston's least-expensive lodging is also its most unique: the Not So Hostel. The already-reasonable prices also include a make-your-own bagel breakfast, off-street parking, bikes, high-speed Internet access in the common room, and even an airport, train, and bus shuttle. The inn actually comprises three 1840s Charleston single houses, all with the obligatory piazzas. (However, unlike some hostels, there's air-conditioning in all the rooms.) Because the free bike usage makes up for its off-the-beaten-path location, a stay at the Not So Hostel is a fantastic way to enjoy the Holy City on a budget. One caveat: While they offer private rooms in addition to dorm-style accommodation, keep in mind this is still a hostel, despite the Charleston-style hospitality and perks. In other words, if there's a problem at 3am, you may not be able to get anyone to help you in a hurry. They now have an annex at 33 Cannon Street with all-private rooms ($75-85).

**MAP 2:** 156 Spring St., 843/722-8383, www. notsohostel.com

Not So Hostel is conveniently located.

## WEST ASHLEY
### ★ THE INN AT MIDDLETON PLACE $$

Looking like Frank Lloyd Wright parachuted into a 300-year-old plantation and got to work, The Inn at Middleton Place is one of Charleston's unique lodgings—and not only because it's on the grounds of the historic and beautiful Middleton Place Plantation. The four connected buildings, comprising over 50 guest rooms, are modern yet deliberately blend in with the forested, neutral-colored surroundings. The spacious guest rooms have that same woodsy minimalism, with excellent fireplaces, spacious Euro-style baths, and huge floor-to-ceiling windows overlooking the grounds and the river. Guests also have full access to the rest of the gorgeous Middleton grounds. The only downside is that you're a lengthy drive from the peninsula and all its attractions, restaurants, and nightlife. But don't worry about food—the excellent Middleton Place Restaurant is open for lunch and dinner. There are nightly happy hours at the lodge, a great way to meet some of your fellow lodging mates and relax.

**MAP 3**: 4290 Ashley River Rd., 843/556-0500, www.theinnatmiddletonplace.com

## SUMMERVILLE
### WOODLANDS RESORT & INN $$$

The renowned Woodlands Resort & Inn is one of a handful of inns in United States with a five-star rating both for lodging and dining. Its 18 guest rooms within the 1906 great house are decorated in a mix of old-fashioned plantation high style and contemporary designer aesthetics, with modern, luxurious baths. There's also a freestanding guest cottage ($850) that seeks to replicate a hunting lodge type of vibe. As you'd expect, there's a full day spa on the premises; a one-hour massage, the most basic offering, will run you $110. The pool is outside, but it's heated for year-round enjoyment, at least theoretically. Woodlands is making a big play for the growing pet-friendly market and eagerly pampers your dog or cat while you stay. Within Woodlands is its award-winning world-class restaurant, simply called **The Dining Room** (Mon.-Sat. 11am-2pm and 6pm-9pm, brunch Sun. 11:30am-2pm, $25-40). It will come as no surprise to find out that the 900-entry wine list and sommelier are collectively awesome, as are the desserts. Jackets are required, and reservations are strongly advised.

**MAP 3**: 125 Parsons Rd., 843/875-2600, www.woodlandsmansion.com

The Inn at Middleton Place

## MOUNT PLEASANT AND EAST COOPER

### WILD DUNES RESORT ⑤⑤⑤

One of the more accessible and enjoyable resort-type stays in the Charleston area is on the Isle of Palms at Wild Dunes Resort. This is the place to go for relaxing, beach-oriented vacation fun in your choice of a traditional hotel room, a house, or a villa. Bustling Mount Pleasant is only a couple minutes away, and Charleston proper not much farther.

MAP 4: 5757 Palm Blvd., 888/778-1876, www.wilddunes.com

## FOLLY BEACH AND THE SOUTHWEST ISLANDS

### TIDES FOLLY BEACH ⑤⑤⑤

The upbeat but still cozy boutique hotel in the new mode has guests raving. It has a combination of attentive staff, great oceanfront views, and an excellent on-site restaurant, Blu. Prices are from $229 and up.

MAP 5: 1 Center St., 843/588-6464, www.tidesfollybeach.com

### ★ KIAWAH ISLAND GOLF RESORT ⑤⑤⑤

This beautiful island with a beautiful beach to match—about 45 minutes away from downtown Charleston—has as its main attraction the sumptuous Kiawah Island Golf Resort, a key location for PGA tournaments. But even if you don't play golf, the resort is an amazing stay. The main component is The Sanctuary, an upscale hotel featuring an opulent lobby complete with grand staircases, a large pool area overlooking the beach, tasteful Spanish Colonial-style architecture, and 255 smallish but excellently appointed guest rooms.

MAP 5: 1 Sanctuary Beach Dr., 800/654-2924, www.kiawahgolf.com

# Transportation and Services

## AIR

Way up in North Charleston is **Charleston International Airport** (CHS, 5500 International Blvd., 843/767-1100, www.chs-airport.com), served by American (www.aa.com), Delta (www.delta.com), JetBlue (www.jetblue.com), and Southwest (www.southwest.com).

It'll take about 20 minutes to make the 12-mile drive from the airport to downtown, and vice versa. The airport is conveniently located just off the I-526/Mark Clark Expressway perimeter highway off of I-26. As in most cities, taxi service from the airport is regulated. This translates to about $30 for two people from the airport to Charleston Place downtown.

## CAR

There are two main routes into Charleston, I-26 from the west-northwest (which dead-ends downtown) and U.S. 17 from the west (called Savannah Highway when it gets close to Charleston proper), which continues on over the Ravenel Bridge into Mount Pleasant and beyond. There's a fairly new perimeter highway, I-526 (Mark Clark Expressway), which loops around the city from West Ashley to North Charleston to Daniel Island and into Mount Pleasant. It's accessible both from I-26 and U.S. 17.

Keep in mind that I-95, while certainly a gateway to the region, is actually a good ways out of Charleston, about 30 miles west of the city. Charleston is almost exactly two hours from Savannah by car, and about an hour's drive from Beaufort and Hilton Head.

## Car Rentals

Charleston International Airport has rental kiosks for **Avis** (843/767-7031), **Budget** (843/767-7051), **Dollar** (843/767-1130), **Enterprise** (843/767-1109), **Hertz** (843/767-4550), **National** (843/767-3078), and **Thrifty** (843/647-4389). There are a couple of rental locations downtown: **Budget** (390 Meeting St., 843/577-5195) and **Enterprise** (398 Meeting St., 843/723-6215). **Hertz** has a location in West Ashley (3025 Ashley Town Center Dr., 843/573-2147), as does **Enterprise** (2004 Savannah Hwy., 843/556-7889).

## BUS

Public transportation by **Charleston Area Regional Transit Authority** (CARTA, 843/724-7420, www.ridecarta.com) is a convenient and inexpensive way to enjoy Charleston without the more structured nature of an organized tour. There's a wide variety of routes, but most visitors will limit their acquaintance to the free tidy, trolley-like **DASH** (Downtown Area Shuttle) buses run by CARTA primarily for visitors. Keep in mind that DASH only stops at designated places.

## TAXI

The South is generally not big on taxis, and Charleston is no exception. The best bet is simply to call rather than try to flag one down. Charleston's most fun service is **Charleston Black Cabs** (843/216-2627, www.charleston-blackcabcompany.com), using Americanized versions of the classic British taxi. A one-way ride anywhere on the peninsula below the bridges is about $10 pp, and rates go up from there. They're very popular, so call as far ahead as you can or try to get one at their stand at Charleston Place. Two other good services are **Safety Cab** (843/722-4066) and **Yellow Cab** (843/577-6565).

You can also try a human-powered taxi service from **Charleston Rickshaw** (843/723-5685). A cheerful (and energetic) young cyclist will pull you and a friend to most points on the lower peninsula for about $10-15. Call 'em or find one by City Market. They work late on Friday and Saturday nights too.

## PARKING

As you'll quickly see, parking is at a premium in downtown Charleston. An exception seems to be the large number of free spaces all along the Battery, but unless you're an exceptionally strong walker, that's too far south to use as a reliable base from which to explore the whole peninsula.

Metered spaces are enforced 8am-6pm Monday through Saturday. Most metered parking downtown is on and around Calhoun Street, Meeting Street, King Street, Market Street, and East Bay Street. That may not sound like a lot, but it constitutes the bulk of the area that most tourists visit. Most meters have three-hour limits, but you'll come across some as short as 30 minutes.

The city has several conveniently located and comparatively inexpensive parking garages. I strongly suggest that you make use of them. They're located at the aquarium, Camden and Exchange Streets, Charleston Place, Concord and Cumberland Streets, East Bay and Prioleau Streets, Marion Square, Gaillard Auditorium, Liberty and St. Philip Streets, Majestic Square, the Charleston Visitor Reception and Transportation Center, and Wentworth Street.

There are several private parking garages as well, primarily clustered in the City Market area. They're convenient, but many have parking spaces that are often too small for some vehicles. The city's website (www.charlestoncity.info) has a good interactive map of parking.

## TOURIST INFORMATION
### Visitors Centers

I highly recommend a stop at the **Charleston Visitor Reception and Transportation Center** (375 Meeting St., 800/774-0006, www.charlestoncvb.com, Mon.-Fri. 8:30am-5pm). Housed in a modern building with an inviting, open design, the center has several high-tech interactive exhibits, including an amazing model of the city under glass. Wall after wall of well-stocked, well-organized brochures will keep you informed on everything a visitor would ever want to know about or see in the city. A particularly welcoming touch is the inclusion of the work of local artists all around the center. I recommend using the attached parking garage not only for your stop at the center but also anytime you want to see the many sights this part of town has to offer, such as the Charleston Museum, the Manigault and Aiken-Rhett Houses, and the Children's Museum. The big selling point of the center is the friendliness of the smiling and courteous staff, who welcome you in true Charleston fashion and are there to book rooms and tours and find tickets for shows and attractions. Go to the center to take advantage of the great deal offered by the **Charleston Heritage Passport** (www. heritagefederation.org), which gives you 40 percent off admission to all of Charleston's key historic homes, the Charleston Museum, and the two awesome plantation sites on the Ashley River: Drayton Hall and Middleton Place. You can get the Heritage Passport *only* at the Charleston Visitor Reception and Transportation Center on Meeting Street.

Other area visitors centers include the **Mt. Pleasant-Isle of Palms Visitors Center** (99 Harry M. Hallman Jr. Blvd., 800/774-0006, daily 9am-5pm) and the new **North Charleston Visitors Center** (4975B Centre Pointe Dr., 843/853-8000, Mon.-Sat. 10am-5pm).

## Hospitals

If there's a silver lining in getting sick or injured in Charleston, it's that there are plenty of high-quality medical facilities available. The premier institution is the **Medical University of South Carolina** (171 Ashley Ave., 843/792-2300, www.muschealth.com) in the northwest part of the peninsula. Two notable facilities are near each other downtown: **Roper Hospital** (316 Calhoun St., 843/402-2273, www.roperhospital.com) and **Charleston Memorial Hospital** (326 Calhoun St., 843/792-2300). In Mount Pleasant there's **East Cooper Regional Medical Center** (1200 Johnnie Dodds Blvd., www.eastcoopermedctr.com). In West Ashley there's **Bon Secours St. Francis Hospital** (2095 Henry Tecklenburg Ave., 843/402-2273, www.ropersaintfrancis.com).

## Police

For nonemergencies in Charleston, West Ashley, and James Island, contact the **Charleston Police Department** (843/577-7434, www.charlestoncity.info). You can also contact the police department in Mount Pleasant (843/884-4176). North Charleston is a separate municipality with its own police department (843/308-4718, www.northcharleston.org). Of course, for emergencies always call **911.**

## Media

The daily newspaper of record is the *Post and Courier* (www.charleston.net). Its entertainment insert, *Preview,* comes out on Thursdays. The free alternative weekly is the *Charleston City Paper* (www.charlestoncitypaper.com), which comes out on Wednesdays and is the best place to find local music and arts listings. A particularly well-done and lively metro glossy is *Charleston* magazine (www.charlestonmag.com), which comes out once a month.

The National Public Radio affiliate is the South Carolina ETV radio station WSCI at 89.3 FM. South Carolina ETV is on television at WITV. The local NBC affiliate is WCBD, the CBS affiliate is WCSC, the ABC affiliate is WCIV, and the Fox affiliate is WTAT.

## Libraries

The main branch of the **Charleston County Public Library** (68 Calhoun St., 843/805-6801, www.ccpl.org, Mon.-Thurs. 9am-9pm, Fri.-Sat. 9am-6pm, Sun. 2pm-5pm) has been at its current site since 1998. Named for Sullivan's Island's most famous visitor, the **Edgar Allan Poe** (1921 I'on Ave., 843/883-3914, www.ccpl.org, Mon. and Fri. 2pm-6pm, Tues., Thurs., and Sat. 10am-2pm) has been housed in Battery Gadsden, a former Spanish-American War gun emplacement, since 1977.

The College of Charleston's main library is the **Marlene and Nathan Addlestone Library** (205 Calhoun St., 843/953-5530, www.cofc.edu), home to special collections, the Center for Student Learning, the main computer lab, the media collection, and even a café. The college's **Avery Research Center for African American History and Culture** (125 Bull St., 843/953-7609, www. cofc.edu/avery, Mon.-Fri. 10am-5pm, Sat. noon-5pm) houses documents relating to the history and culture of African Americans in the Lowcountry.

For other historical research on the area, check out the collections of the **South Carolina Historical Society** (100 Meeting St., 843/723-3225, www.southcarolinahistoricalsociety.org, Mon.-Fri. 9am-4pm, Sat. 9am-2pm). There's a $5 research fee for nonmembers.

## Gay and Lesbian Resources

Contrary to many media portrayals of the region, Charleston is quite open to gays and lesbians, who play a major role in arts, culture, and business. As with any other place in the South, however, it's generally expected that people—straights as well—will keep personal matters and politics to themselves in public settings. A key local advocacy group is the **Alliance for Full Acceptance** (29 Leinbach Dr., Suite D-3, 843/883-0343, www.affa-sc. org). The **Lowcountry Gay and Lesbian Alliance** (843/720-8088) holds a potluck the last Sunday of each month. For the most up-to-date happenings, try the *Charleston City Paper.*

# Beaufort and the Lowcountry

# For many people around the world, the Lowcountry is the first image that comes to mind when they think of the American South.

For the people that live here, the Lowcountry is altogether unique, but it does embody many of the region's most noteworthy qualities: an emphasis on manners, a constant look back into the past, and a slow and leisurely pace (embodied in the joking but largely accurate nickname "Slowcountry").

History hangs in the humid air where first the Spanish and French came to interrupt the native tribes' ancient reverie, followed by the English. Although time, erosion, and development have erased most traces of these various occupants, you can almost hear their ghosts in the rustle of the branches in a sudden sea breeze or in the piercing call of a heron over the marsh.

Artists and arts lovers the world over are drawn here to paint, photograph, or otherwise be inspired by some of the most gorgeous wetlands in the United States, so vast that human habitation appears fleeting and intermittent. Sprawling between Beaufort and Charleston is the huge ACE (Ashley, Combahee, Edisto) Basin, a beautiful and important estuary and

a national model for good conservation practices. In all, the defining characteristic of the Lowcountry is its liquid nature—not only literally, in the creeks and waterways that dominate every vista and the seafood cooked in all manner of ways, but figuratively too, in the slow but deep quality of life here. Once outside what passes for urban areas, you'll find yourself taking a look back through the decades to a time of roadside produce stands, shade-tree mechanics, and men fishing and crabbing on tidal creeks—not for sport but for the family dinner. Indeed, not so very long ago, before the influx of resort development, retirement subdivisions, and tourism, much of the Lowcountry was like a flatter, more humid Appalachia—poverty-stricken and desperately underserved. While the archetypal South has been marketed in any number of ways to the rest of the world, here you get a sense that this is the real thing—timeless, endlessly alluring, but somehow very familiar.

South of Beaufort is the historically significant Port Royal area and the East Coast

**Previous:** Hilton Head Island; a Lowcountry road. **Above:** the Hunting Island Light.

Look for ★ to find recommended
sights, activities, dining, and lodging.

# Highlights

**★ Henry C. Chambers Waterfront Park:** Walk the dog or while away the time on a porch swing at this clean and inviting gathering place on the serene Beaufort River (page 132).

**★ St. Helena's Episcopal Church:** To walk through this Beaufort sanctuary and its walled graveyard is to walk through Lowcountry history (page 134).

**★ Penn Center:** It's the center of modern Gullah culture and education, and a key site in the history of the civil rights movement as well (page 145).

**★ Hunting Island State Park:** One of the most peaceful natural getaways on the East Coast is only minutes away from the more civilized temptations of Beaufort (page 150).

**★ ACE Basin:** You can take a lifetime to learn your way around this massive, marshy estuary—or just a few hours to soak in its lush beauty (page 151).

**★ Edisto Beach State Park:** Relax at this quiet, friendly, and relatively undeveloped park on Sea Island, a mecca for shell collectors (page 154).

**★ Pinckney Island National Wildlife Refuge:** This well-maintained sanctuary is a major birding location and a great getaway from nearby Hilton Head (page 158).

**★ Coastal Discovery Museum at Honey Horn:** This beautifully repurposed plantation house and spacious grounds near the island's entrance are a great way to learn about Hilton Head history, both human and natural (page 158).

**★ Old Town Bluffton:** Gossipy and gorgeous by turns, the charming "Old Town" on the May River centers on a thriving artist colony (page 172).

**★ South Carolina Artisans Center:** Visual artists and fine craftspeople from all over the state contribute work to this high-quality collective in Walterboro (page 178).

# Beaufort and the Lowcountry

© AVALON TRAVEL

Marine Corps Recruit Depot of Parris Island. East of Beaufort is the center of Gullah culture, St. Helena Island, and the scenic gem of Hunting Island. To the south is the scenic but entirely developed golf and tennis mecca, Hilton Head Island, and Hilton Head's close neighbor but diametrical opposite in every other way, Daufuskie Island, another important Gullah center. Nestled between is the close-knit and gossipy little village of Bluffton on the gossamer May River.

## PLANNING YOUR TIME

A commonsense game plan is to use centrally located Beaufort as a home base and spend **three days** exploring the region. Take at least half a day of leisure to walk all over Beaufort, a delightfully walkable place. You can easily traverse the entire historic downtown leisurely in that time. Another full day should go to St. Helena's Penn Center and on to Hunting Island. If you're in the mood for a road trip, dedicate a full day to tour the surrounding area to the north and northeast, with a jaunt to the ACE Basin National Wildlife Refuge. While the New York accents fly fast and furious on Hilton Head Island, that's no reason for you to rush. Plan on at least half a day just to enjoy the fine broad beaches alone. I recommend another half day to tour the island itself, maybe including a stop in Sea Pines for a late lunch or dinner.

# Beaufort

Sandwiched halfway between the prouder, louder cities of Charleston and Savannah, Beaufort is in many ways a more authentic slice of life from the past than either of those two. If you want to party, stay in those two cities. If you want to relax in a similar environment, Beaufort's your ticket.

Long a staple of movie crews seeking to portray some archetypal aspect of the old South (*The Prince of Tides, The Great Santini, Forrest Gump*) or just to film beautiful scenery for its own sake (*Jungle Book, Last Dance*), Beaufort—pronounced "BYOO-fert," by the way, not "BO-fort"—features many

aerial view of Beaufort

# Beaufort

well-preserved examples of Southern architecture, most all of them in idyllic, family-friendly neighborhoods.

The pace in Beaufort is languid, slower even than the waving Spanish moss in the massive old live oak trees. The line between business and pleasure is a blurry one here. As you can tell from the signs you see on storefront doors saying things like "Back in an hour or so," time is an entirely negotiable commodity. The architecture combines the relaxed Caribbean flavor of Charleston with the Anglophilic dignity of Savannah. In fact, plenty of people prefer the individualistic old homes of Beaufort, seemingly tailor-made for the exact spot on which they sit, to the historic districts of either Charleston or Savannah in terms of sheer architectural delight.

While you'll run into plenty of charming and gracious locals during your time here, you might be surprised at the number of transplanted Northerners. That's due not only to the high volume of retirees who've moved to the area, but also to the active presence of three major U.S. Navy facilities: the Marine Corps Air Station Beaufort, the Marine Corps Recruit Depot on nearby Parris Island, and the Beaufort Naval Hospital.

The two main avenues to remember are Bay Street, along the Beaufort River and the real center of downtown; and Boundary Street, which becomes Carteret Street as you arrive into downtown proper.

## HISTORY

This was the site of the second landing by the Spanish on the North American continent, the expedition of Captain Pedro de Salazar in 1514 (Ponce de León's more famous landing at St. Augustine was but a year earlier).

A Spanish slaver made a brief stop in 1521, long enough to name the area Santa Elena. Port Royal Sound didn't get its modern name until the first serious attempt at a permanent settlement, Jean Ribault's exploration in 1562. Though ultimately disastrous, Ribault's base of Charlesfort was the first French settlement in America.

After the French faded, Spaniards returned and lasted two decades in Santa Elena. But Indian attacks and Francis Drake's attack on St. Augustine forced the Spanish to abandon the area in 1587. Within the next generation, British indigo planters had established a firm presence, chief among them John "Tuscarora Jack" Barnwell and Thomas Nairn. These men would go on to found the town of Beaufort, named for the Duke of Beaufort, and it was chartered in 1711 as part of the Carolina colony. In 1776, Beaufort planter Thomas Heyward Jr. signed the Declaration of Independence.

After independence, Lowcountry planters turned to cotton as the main cash crop, since England had been their prime customer for indigo. The gambit paid off, and Beaufort soon became one of the wealthiest towns in the new nation. In 1861, only seven months after secessionists fired on Fort Sumter in nearby Charleston, a Union fleet sailed into Port Royal and occupied the Lowcountry for the duration of the war.

Gradually developing their own distinct dialect and culture, much of it linked to their West African roots, isolated Lowcountry African Americans became known as the Gullah. Evolving from an effort by abolitionist missionaries early in the Civil War, in 1864 the Penn School was formed on St. Helena Island specifically to teach the children of the Gullah communities. Now known as the Penn Center, the facility has been a beacon for the study of this aspect of African American culture ever since.

## SIGHTS
### ★ Henry C. Chambers Waterfront Park

A tastefully designed, well-maintained, and user-friendly mix of walkways, bandstands, and patios, **Henry C. Chambers Waterfront Park** (843/525-7054, www.cityofbeaufort.org, daily 24 hours) is a favorite gathering place for locals and visitors alike, beckoning one and all with its open green space and wonderful marsh-front views. Kids will especially enjoy the park not only because there's so much room to run around in, but

Henry C. Chambers Waterfront Park

# Pat Conroy's Lowcountry

No other person was as closely associated with the South Carolina Lowcountry as beloved author Pat Conroy, who passed away in 2016. After moving around as a child in a military family, he began high school in Beaufort. His painful teen years there formed the basis of his first novel, a brutal portrait of his domineering Marine pilot father, Colonel Donald Conroy, aka Colonel Bull Meecham of *The Great Santini* (1976). Many scenes from the 1979 film adaptation were filmed at the famous Tidalholm, the Edgar Fripp House (1 Laurens St.) in Beaufort. (The house was also front and center in *The Big Chill*.)

Pat Conroy

Conroy's pattern of thinly veiled autobiography actually began with his first book, the self-published *The Boo*, a tribute to a teacher at The Citadel in Charleston while Conroy was still a student there. His second work, *The Water is Wide* (1972), is a chronicle of his experiences teaching in a one-room African American school on Daufuskie Island. Though ostensibly a straightforward first-person journalistic effort, Conroy changed the location to the fictional Yamacraw Island, supposedly to protect Daufuskie's fragile culture from curious outsiders. The 1974 film adaptation starring Jon Voight was titled *Conrack* after the way his students mispronounced his name. You can visit that same one-room school today on Daufuskie. Known as the Mary Field School, the building is now a local community center.

Conroy also wrote the foreword to the cookbook *Gullah Home Cooking the Daufuskie Way: Smokin' Joe Butter Beans, Ol' 'Fuskie Fried Crab Rice, Sticky-Bush Blackberry Dumpling, and Other Sea Island Favorites* by Daufuskie native and current Savannah resident Sallie Ann Robinson. Conroy would go on to publish in 1980 *The Lords of Discipline*, a reading of his real-life experience with the often-savage environment faced by cadets at The Citadel—though Conroy would change the name, calling it the Carolina Military Institute. Still, when it came time to make a film adaptation in 1983, The Citadel refused to allow it to be shot there, so the "Carolina Military Institute" was filmed in England instead.

For many of his fans, Conroy's *The Prince of Tides* is his ultimate homage to the Lowcountry. Surely, the 1991 film version starring Barbra Streisand and Nick Nolte—shot on location and awash in gorgeous shots of the Beaufort River marsh—did much to implant an idyllic image of the area with audiences around the world. According to local legend, Streisand originally didn't intend to make the film in Beaufort, but a behind-the-scenes lobbying effort allegedly coordinated by Conroy himself, and including a stay at the Rhett House Inn, convinced her.

The Bay Street Inn (601 Bay St.) in Beaufort was seen in the film, as was the football field at the old Beaufort High School. The beach scenes were shot on nearby Fripp Island. Interestingly, some scenes set in a Manhattan apartment were actually shot within the old Beaufort Arsenal (713 Craven St.), now a visitors center. Similarly, the Beaufort Naval Hospital doubled as New York's Bellevue.

Despite the many personal tribulations he faced in the area, to the end Conroy never gave up on the Lowcountry. He is interred in the old Gullah Cemetery on St. Helena Island, S.C., near the historic Penn Center, beside Civil Rights heroine Agnes Sherman. As for the "Great Santini" himself, you can visit the final resting place of Colonel Conroy in the Beaufort National Cemetery—Section 62, Grave 182.

also because of the charming playground at the east end near the bridge, complete with a jungle gym in the form of a Victorian home. The clean, well-appointed public restrooms are a particularly welcome feature.

## John Mark Verdier House Museum

A smallish but stately Federalist building on the busiest downtown corner, the **John Mark Verdier House Museum** (801 Bay St., 843/379-6335, www.historicbeaufort.org, tours on the half-hour Mon.-Sat. 10:30am-3:30pm, $5) is the only historic Beaufort planter's home open to regular tours. Built in 1805 for John Mark Verdier, its main claims to fame are acting as the Union headquarters during the long occupation of Beaufort during the Civil War and hosting Revolutionary War hero the Marquis de Lafayette, who stayed at the Verdier House on his 1825 U.S. tour. In 2011 the Verdier House was extensively and professionally restored, with exterior paint now reflecting the authentic 1863 look. There's a neat diorama inside portraying what Bay Street would have looked like at that time.

## Beaufort Arsenal Visitors Center and History Museum

The imposing yellow-gray tabby facade of the 1852 **Beaufort Arsenal** (713 Craven St.) houses the **Beaufort Visitors Center** (843/986-5400, www.beaufortsc.org, Mon.-Sat. 9am-5pm) and **Beaufort History Museum** (www.beauforthistorymuseum.com, Mon.-Sat. 10am-4pm, $5). The Visitors Center is a great place to purchase various tour tickets, and the adjacent museum is a small but informative stop to learn more about the area's long and important history. There are also public restrooms.

## ★ St. Helena's Episcopal Church

Nestled within a low brick wall surrounding this historic church and cemetery, **St. Helena's Episcopal Church** (505 Church St., 843/522-1712, Tues.-Fri. 10am-4pm, Sat. 10am-1pm) has witnessed some of Beaufort's most compelling tales. Built in 1724, this was the parish church of Thomas Heyward, one of South Carolina's signers of the Declaration of Independence. John "Tuscarora Jack"

the John Mark Verdier House Museum

Barnwell, one of Beaufort's founders, is buried on the grounds.

The balcony upstairs was intended for black parishioners; as was typical throughout the region before the Civil War, both races attended the same church services. After the entire congregation fled with the Union occupation, Federal troops decked over the second floor and used St. Helena's as a hospital—with surgeons using tombstones as operating tables. The wooden altar was carved by the crew of the USS *New Hampshire* while the warship was docked in the harbor during Reconstruction.

While the cemetery and sanctuary interior are likely to be your focus, take a close look at the church exterior—many of the bricks are actually ships' ballast stones. Also be aware that you're not looking at the church's original footprint; the building has been expanded several times since its construction (a hurricane in 1896 destroyed the entire east end). A nearly $3 million restoration, mostly for structural repairs, was completed in 2000.

## Tabernacle Baptist Church

Built in 1845, the handsome **Tabernacle Baptist Church** (911 Craven St., 843/524-0376) had a congregation of over 3,000 before the Civil War. Slaves made up most of the congregation, and during the war freed slaves purchased the church. A congregant was the war hero Robert Smalls, who seized the Confederate steamer he was forced to serve on and delivered it to Union forces. He is buried in the church cemetery and has a nice memorial dedicated to him facing the street.

## Beaufort National Cemetery

Begun by order of Abraham Lincoln in 1863, **Beaufort National Cemetery** (1601 Boundary St., daily 8am-sunset) is one of the few cemeteries containing the graves of both Union and Confederate troops. This national cemetery is where 19 soldiers of the all-black 54th and 55th Massachusetts Infantries were reinterred after being found on Folly Island near Charleston. Also buried here is "The

Great Santini" himself, novelist Pat Conroy's father, Donald.

## Santa Elena History Center

The actual historical site is on nearby Parris Island, but in downtown Beaufort you'll find the **Santa Elena History Center** (1501 Bay St., 843/379-1550, www.santa-elena.org, Tue.-Sat. 10am-4pm, Sun. 1-4pm, free), detailing the Spanish occupation of the area beginning 450 years ago, long before English-speaking settlers arrived. This is a new and growing venture, and exhibits and resources will be added as funds become more available.

## A Walking Tour of Beaufort Homes

Here's a walking tour of some of Beaufort's fine historic homes in private hands. You won't be taking any tours of the interiors, but these homes are part of the legacy of the area and are locally valued as such. Be sure to respect the privacy of the inhabitants by keeping the noise level down and not trespassing on private property to take photos.

- **Thomas Fuller House:** Begin at the corner of Harrington and Bay Streets and view the 1796 Thomas Fuller House (1211 Bay St.), one of the oldest in Beaufort and especially unique in that much of the building material is tabby (hence the home's other name, the Tabby Manse).

- **Milton Maxcy House:** Walk east on Bay Street one block and take a left on Church Street; walk up to the corner of Church and Craven Streets. Otherwise known as the Secession House (113 Craven St.), this 1813 home was built on a tabby foundation dating from 1743. In 1860, when it was the residence of attorney Edmund Rhett, the first Ordinance of Secession was signed here, and the rest, as they say, is history.

- **Lewis Reeve Sams House:** Resume the walking tour on the other side of the historic district at the foot of the bridge in the old neighborhood simply called "The Point." The beautiful Lewis Reeve Sams

House (601 Bay St.) at the corner of Bay and New Streets, with its double-decker veranda, dates from 1852 and like many Beaufort mansions served as a Union hospital during the Civil War.

- **Berners Barnwell Sams House:** Continue up New Street, where shortly ahead on the left you'll find the 1818 Berners Barnwell Sams House (310 New St.), which served as the African American hospital during the Union occupation. Harriet Tubman of Underground Railroad fame worked here for a time as a nurse.

- **Joseph Johnson House:** Continue up New Street and take a right on Craven Street. Cross East Street to find the 1850 Joseph Johnson House (411 Craven St.), with the massive live oak in the front yard. Legend has it that when the Yankees occupied Hilton Head, Mr. Johnson buried his valuables under an outhouse. After the war he returned to find his home for sale due to unpaid back taxes. He dug up his valuables, paid the taxes, and resumed living in the home. You might recognize the home from the film *Forces of Nature*.

- **Marshlands:** Backtrack to East Street, walk north to Federal Street, and go to its end. Built by James R. Verdier, Marshlands (501 Pinckney St.) was used as a hospital during the Civil War, as many Beaufort homes were, and is now a National Historic Landmark. It was the setting of Francis Griswold's 1931 novel *A Sea Island Lady*.

- **The Oaks:** Walk up to King Street and take a right. Soon after you pass a large open park on the left, King Street dead-ends at Short Street. The Oaks (100 Laurens St.) at this corner was owned by the Hamilton family, who lost a son who served with General Wade Hampton's cavalry in the Civil War. After the conflict, the family couldn't afford the back taxes; neighbors paid the debts and returned the deed to the Hamiltons.

- **Edgar Fripp House:** Continue east on Laurens Street toward the water to find this handsome Lowcountry mansion, sometimes called Tidalholm (1 Laurens St.). Built in 1856 by the wealthy planter for whom nearby Fripp Island is named, this house was a key setting in *The Big Chill* and *The Great Santini*.

- **Francis Hext House:** Go back to Short Street, walk north to Hancock Street, and take a left. A short way ahead on the right, the handsome red-roofed estate known as Riverview (207 Hancock St.) is one of the oldest structures in Beaufort; it was built in 1720.

the Lewis Reeve Sams House

- **Robert Smalls House:** Continue west on Hancock Street, take a short left on East Street, and then a quick right on Prince Street. The 1834 Robert Smalls House (511 Prince St.) was the birthplace of Robert Smalls, a former slave and Beaufort native who stole the Confederate ship *Planter* from Charleston Harbor while serving as helmsman and delivered it to Union troops in Hilton Head. Smalls and a few compatriots commandeered the ship while the officers were at a party at Fort Sumter. Smalls used the bounty he earned for the act of bravery to buy his boyhood home. After the war, Smalls was a longtime U.S. congressman.

# ENTERTAINMENT AND NIGHTLIFE
## Performing Arts

Beaufort's fine arts scene is small but professional in outlook. Most performances are based in the nice new Performing Arts Center on the oak-lined campus of the **University of South Carolina Beaufort** (USCB, 801 Carteret St., 843/521-4100, www.uscb.edu). A prime mover of the local performing arts scene is **Beaufort Performing Arts Inc.,** formed by a mayoral task force in 2003 specifically to encourage arts and cultural development within the area. Ticket prices typically range $12-40.

Perhaps surprising for such a small place, Beaufort boasts its own full orchestra, the **Beaufort Orchestra** (1106 Carteret St., 843/986-5400, www.beaufortorchestra.org), which plays in the Performing Arts Center.

**ArtWorks** (2127 Boundary St., 843/379-2787, www.beaufortartscouncil.org) is a 12,000-square-foot combined arts education/performance space run by the Arts Council of Beaufort.

## Cinema

One of only two functional drive-ins in the state, the **Highway 21 Drive In** (55 Parker Dr., 843/846-4500, www.hwy21drivein.com) has two screens, great sound, movies Friday through Sunday, and awesome concessions that include Angus beef hamburgers. All you need to provide is the car and the company.

# Festivals and Events

Surprising for a town so prominent in so many films, Beaufort didn't have its own film festival until 2007. The **Beaufort Film Festival** (843/986-5400, www.beaufortfilmfestival.com) is held in February. It's small in scale but growing steadily each year and boasts a diverse range of high-quality, cutting-edge entries, including shorts and animation. Most events are held at the University of South Carolina Beaufort campus.

Now over 20 years old, the **Gullah Festival of South Carolina** (www.theoriginalgullahfestival.org) celebrates Gullah history and culture on Memorial Day weekend at various locations throughout town, mostly focusing on Waterfront Park.

By far the biggest single event on the local festival calendar is the over 50-year-old **Beaufort Water Festival** (www.bftwaterfestival.com), held over two weeks in June or July each year, centering on the Waterfront Park area. One of the most eclectic and idiosyncratic events of its kind in a region already known for quirky hyperlocal festivals, the signature events are the Saturday-morning two-hour Grand Parade and a blessing and parade of the shrimp fleet on the closing Sunday.

Fall in the Lowcountry means shrimping season, and early October brings the **Beaufort Shrimp Festival** (www.beaufortsc.org). Highlights include an evening concert with specially lighted shrimp boats docked along the river, a 5K run over the Woods Memorial Bridge, and a more laid-back 5K walk through the historic district. Various cooking competitions are held, obviously centering on the versatile crustaceans that are the raison d'être of the shrimp fleet.

St. Helena Island hosts the three-day **Penn Center Heritage Days** (www.penncenter.com) each November, without a doubt the Beaufort area's second-biggest celebration after the Water Festival. Focusing on Gullah culture, history, and delicious food, Heritage Days does a great job of combining fun with education.

## SHOPS

While the sprawl outside town has every chain store you already have back home, the main downtown drag of Bay Street is where you'll find the vast bulk of Beaufort's independent shopping opportunities. Just a few short blocks long, it's a convenient and pleasurable experience.

The recently renovated Old Bay Marketplace, with a facade so bright red you can't miss it, hosts a few cute shops, most notably the stylish **Lulu Burgess** (917 Bay St., 843/524-5858, Mon.-Sat. 10am-6pm, Sun. noon-5pm), an eclectic store that brings a rich, quirky sense of humor to its otherwise tasteful assortment of gift items for the whole family.

Another great women's clothing store nearby is **Go Fish** (719 Bay St., 843/379-8448, www.shopgofish.com, Mon.-Fri. 10am-6pm, Fri.-Sat. 10am-8pm), a regional chain with particularly high-quality but affordable garments, jewelry, and shoes.

At the far end of Bay Street is **Bay Street Treasures** (1001 Bay St., 843/379-4488, Mon.-Sat. 10am-5pm), an eclectic home goods/furnishings store, strong with regional and Lowcountry appeal.

My favorite shop in Beaufort is **Nevermore Books** (201 Carteret St., 843/812-9460, www.nevermorebooks.com, Tues.-Fri. 10am-5pm, Sat. 11am-4pm), a very short walk off Bay Street around the corner on Carteret. While Edgar Allen Poe is the ostensible theme of this locally owned shop—check out the awesome window display!—they specialize in fiction of all types and have a range of regional books as well.

### Art Galleries

A complete art experience blending the traditional with the cutting edge is at the **I. Pinckney Simons Art Gallery** (711 Bay St., 843/379-4774, www.ipinckneysimonsgallery.com, Tues.-Fri. 11am-5pm, Sat. 11am-3pm), which is pronounced "Simmons" despite the spelling.

For a taste of Gullah-themed art, head to **LyBenson's Gallery & Studio** (211 Charles

Bay Street Treasures

St., 843/525-9006, www.lybensons.com). Not just a place to enjoy and purchase art, they have some small exhibits on local history and culture, including a room dedicated to local African American hero and one-time Congressman Robert Smalls.

Right on the water is a fun local favorite, the **Longo Gallery** (103 Charles St., 843/522-8933, Mon.-Sat. 11am-5pm). Owners Suzanne and Eric Longo provide a whimsical assortment of less traditional art than you might find in the more touristy waterfront area. Take Charles Street as it works its way toward the waterfront, and the gallery is right behind a storefront on the corner of Charles and Bay Streets.

You'll find perhaps the area's best-known gallery over the bridge on St. Helena Island. Known regionally as one of the best places to find Gullah folk art, **Red Piano Too** (870 Sea Island Parkway, 843/838-2241, www.red-pianotoo.com, Mon.-Sat. 10am-5pm) is on the corner before you turn onto the road to the historic Penn Center. Over 150 artists from a diverse range of traditions and styles are represented in this charming little 1940 building with the red tin awning.

# SPORTS AND ACTIVITIES

Beaufort County comprises over 60 islands, so it's no surprise that nearly all recreation in the area revolves around the water, which dominates so many aspects of life in the Lowcountry. The closer to the ocean you get, the more it's a salt marsh environment. But as you explore more inland, including the sprawling ACE Basin, you'll encounter primarily blackwater.

## Kayaking

The Lowcountry is tailor-made for kayaking. Most kayakers put in at the public landings in nearby **Port Royal** (1 Port Royal Landing Dr., 843/525-6664) or **Lady's Island** (73 Sea Island Pkwy., 843/522-0430), across the river from downtown Beaufort. If you don't feel comfortable with your navigation skills, it's a good idea to contact Kim and David at **Beaufort Kayak Tours** (843/525-0810, www.beaufortkayaktours.com), who rent kayaks and can guide you on a number of excellent tours of all three key areas. They charge about $40 for adults and $30 for children for a two-hour trip. A tour with Beaufort Kayak Tours is also the best (and nearly the only) way to access the historically significant ruins of the early British tabby Fort Frederick, now located on the grounds of the Beaufort Naval Hospital and inaccessible by car.

## Fishing and Boating

Key marinas in the area are the **Downtown Marina** (1006 Bay St., 843/524-4422) in Beaufort, the **Lady's Island Marina** (73 Sea Island Pkwy., 843/522-0430), and the **Port Royal Landing Marina** (1 Port Royal Landing Dr., 843/525-6664). Hunting Island has a popular 1,000-foot fishing pier at the south end. A good local fishing charter service is Captain Josh Utsey's **Lowcountry Guide Service** (843/812-4919, www.

beaufortscfishing.com). Captain Ed Hardee (843/441-6880) offers good inshore charters.

The ACE Basin is a very popular fishing, crabbing, and shrimping area. It has about two dozen public boat ramps, with colorful names like Cuckold's Creek and Steamboat Landing. There's a useful map of them all at www.acebasin.net, or look for the brown signs along the highway.

## Hiking and Biking

Despite the Lowcountry's, well, lowness, biking opportunities abound. It might not get your heart rate up like a ride in the Rockies, but the area lends itself to laid-back two-wheeled enjoyment. Many local B&Bs provide bikes free for guests, and you can rent your own just across the river from Beaufort in Lady's Island at **Lowcountry Bikes** (102 Sea Island Pkwy., 843/524-9585, Mon.-Tues. and Thurs.-Fri. 10am-6pm, Wed. 10am-1pm, Sat. 10am-3pm, about $5 per hour). They can also hook you up with some good routes around the area.

## Tours

Colorful character Jon Sharp has retired from his popular walking tours, but filling his shoes is Janet Matlock, who took over the venture and now runs the equally popular **Janet's Walking History Tour** (843/226-4412, www.janetswalkinghistory.com, $25). This highly recommended two-hour jaunt begins and ends at the Downtown Marina (1006 Bay St.) and takes you all through the downtown area. Tours leave at 12:30pm Monday and 11am Tuesday-Saturday; during the hot months of June-September they leave at 10am Monday-Saturday.

**The Spirit of Old Beaufort** (103 West St. Extension, 843/525-0459, www.thespiritofoldbeaufort.com, Mon.-Sat. 10:30am, 2pm, and 7pm, $18) runs a year-round series of good themed walking tours, roughly two hours long, with guides usually in period dress. If you don't want to walk, you can hire one of their guides to join you in your own vehicle (from $50).

As you might expect, few things could be more Lowcountry than an easygoing carriage ride through the historic neighborhoods. **Southurn Rose Buggy Tours** (843/524-2900, www.southurnrose.com, daily 10am-5pm, $18 adults, $7 children)—yes, that's how they spell it—offers 50-minute narrated carriage rides of the entire Old Point, including movie locations, embarking and disembarking near the Downtown Marina about every 40 minutes.

An important specialty bus tour in the area is **Gullah-N-Geechie Man Tours** (843/838-7516, www.gullahngeechietours.net, $20 adults, $18 children), focusing on the rich Gullah history and culture of the St. Helena Island area, including the historic Penn Center. Call for pickup information.

# RESTAURANTS

Because of Beaufort's small size and insular nature, many of its restaurants double as nightlife hotspots, with hopping bar scenes—or as hopping as it gets here, anyway—at dinner hours and beyond, often with a crowd of regulars. That said, those looking for a late-night rowdy time will be happier seeking it in the notorious party towns of Charleston or Savannah.

## New Southern

The stylishly appointed **Wren Bistro, Bar and Market** (210 Carteret St., 843/524-9463, www.wrenbistroandbar.com, Mon.-Sat. 11am-11pm, $15-25) is known for any of its chicken dishes. While the food is great, the interior is particularly well done, simultaneously warm and classy. As seems to be typical of Beaufort, the lunches are as good as the dinners, and the bar scene is quite active.

## Breakfast and Brunch

One of the best breakfasts I've had anywhere was a humble two-egg plate for five bucks at Beaufort's most popular morning hangout, ★ **Blackstone's Café** (205 Scott St., 843/524-4330, Mon.-Sat. 7:30am-2:30pm, Sun. 7:30am-2pm, under $10), complete with tasty

hash browns, a comparative rarity in this part of the country, where grits rule as the breakfast starch of choice.

## Burgers and Sandwiches

Another lunch favorite is **Magnolia Bakery Café** (703 Congress St., 843/524-1961, Mon.-Sat. 9am-5pm, under $10). Lump crab cakes are a specialty item, but you can't go wrong with any of the lunch sandwiches. Vegetarian diners are particularly well taken care of with a large selection of black bean burger plates. As the name indicates, the range of desserts here is tantalizing, with the added bonus of a serious espresso bar.

It's a 20-minute drive out of downtown, but **Maggie's Pub** (17 Market St., 843/379-1719, www.maggiespub.net, Tues.-Sat. 5pm-9pm, $12)—within a small shopping center in the new residential development of Habersham—is not only a happening neighborhood tavern, it also has the best grass-fed burgers in town and some excellent fish 'n' chips. While a very friendly place, be aware it's a heavily

Have breakfast at Blackstone's Café.

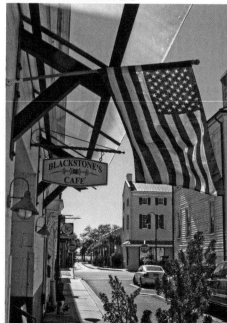

# Lowcountry Boil or Frogmore Stew?

Near Beaufort it's called Frogmore stew after the township (now named St. Helena) just over the river. Closer to Savannah it's simply called Lowcountry boil. Supposedly the first pot of this delectable, hearty concoction was made by Richard Gay of the Gay Fish Company. As with any vernacular dish, dozens of local and family variants abound. The key ingredient that makes Lowcountry boil/Frogmore stew what it is—a well-blended mélange with a character all its own rather than just a bunch of stuff thrown together in a pot of boiling water—is some type of crab-boil seasoning. You'll find Zatarain's seasoning suggested on a lot of websites, but Old Bay is far more common in the eponymous Lowcountry where the dish originated.

In any case, here's a simple six-serving recipe to get you started. The only downside is that it's pretty much impossible to make it for just a few people. The dish is intended for large gatherings, whether a football tailgate party on a Saturday or a family afternoon after church on Sunday. Note the typical ratio of one ear of corn and 0.5 pound each of meat and shrimp per person.

- 6 ears fresh corn on the cob, cut into 3-inch sections
- 3 pounds smoked pork sausage, cut into 3-inch sections
- 3 pounds fresh shrimp, shells on
- 5 pounds new potatoes, halved or quartered
- 3 ounces Old Bay Seasoning

Put the sausage and potato pieces, along with the Old Bay, in two gallons of boiling water. When the potatoes are about halfway done, about 15 minutes in, add the corn and boil for about half that time, seven minutes. Add the shrimp and boil for another three minutes, until they just turn pink. Do not overcook the shrimp. Take the pot off the heat and drain; serve immediately. If you cook the shrimp just right, the oil from the sausage will cause those shells to slip right off.

This is but one of dozens of recipes. Some cooks add some lemon juice and beer in the water as it's coming to a boil; others add onion, garlic, or green peppers.

local crowd. Get here by taking Boundary Street/Highway 21 west out of downtown, a left onto Parris Island Gateway/Highway 280, a right on Broad River Boulevard, and then a right on Joe Frazier Road. Veer onto Cherokee Farms Road and then left into the Habersham Marketplace area.

## Coffee, Tea, and Sweets

The closest thing to a hipster coffeehouse in Beaufort is **City Java and News** (301 Carteret St., 843/379-5282, Mon.-Sat. 6am-6:30pm, Sun. 7am-6:30pm), a sunny and well-kept little modernist space next to the similarly modernist City Loft Hotel. Their espresso is big-city quality, their periodicals are timely, and their pastries and sandwiches are good for tiding you over when you need some quick energy for more walking around town.

A few blocks across downtown is a great coffee place, **Common Ground Coffeehouse and Market Cafe** (102 West St., 843/524-2326, daily 7:30am-10pm). Located in a historic building facing the river, this is not just a serenely pleasant and convenient place to enjoy your coffee, but their cakes, cookies, light sandwiches, and fresh Italian gelatos are all delightfully delicious. Get here by strolling down Bay Street; it's at the end of an alley between two blocks, and is right on the Waterfront Park. There's an open mic every Friday night.

## Seafood

The hottest dinner table in town is at the ★ **Saltus River Grill** (802 Bay St., 843/379-3474, Sun.-Thurs. 5pm-9pm, Fri.-Sat. 5pm-10pm, $10-39), famous throughout the state for its raw bar menu. Other specialties include she-crab bisque, lump crab cakes, and the ubiquitous shrimp and grits. The Saltus River Grill is more upscale in feel and in price than most Lowcountry places, with a very see-and-be-seen attitude and a hopping bar. Reservations are recommended.

The short and focused menu at **Plum's** (904½ Bay St., 843/525-1946, lunch daily 11am-4pm, dinner daily 5pm-10pm, $15-25) keys in on entrées highlighting local ingredients, such as the shrimp penne *all'amatriciana* and fresh black mussel pasta. Because of the outstanding microbrew selection, Plum's is a big nightlife hangout as well; be aware that after 10pm, when food service ends but the bar remains open until 2am, it's no longer smoke-free.

An up-and-comer downtown is **Breakwater Restaurant & Bar** (203 Carteret St., 843/379-0052, www.breakwatersc.com, dinner Thurs.-Sat. 6pm-9:30pm, bar until 2am, $10-20). The concise menu makes up in good taste what it lacks in comprehensiveness, with an emphasis on seafood, of course.

### Steaks

★ **Luther's Rare & Well Done** (910 Bay St., 843/521-1888, daily 10am-midnight, from $8) on the waterfront is the kind of meat-lover's place where even the French onion soup has a morsel of rib eye in it. While the patented succulent rubbed steaks are a no-brainer here, the handcrafted specialty pizzas are also quite popular. Housed in a historic pharmacy building, Luther's is also a great place for late eats after many other places in this quiet town have rolled up the sidewalk. A limited menu of appetizers and bar food to nosh on at the inviting and popular bar is available after 10pm.

### Tapas

Right around the corner from Breakwater is **Emily's** (906 Port Republic St., 843/522-1866, www.emilysrestaurantandtapasbar.com, dinner Mon.-Sat. 4pm-10pm, bar until 2am, $10-20), a very popular fine-dining spot

Common Ground Coffeehouse and Market Cafe

that specializes in a more traditional brand of rich, tasty tapas and is known for its active bar scene.

For years the now-defunct Lowcountry Winery occupied this storefront, but now you'll find **Wined It Up** (705 Bay St., 843/379-5585, www.wineditup.net), a wine bar and deli. They offer at least 20 wines by the glass, with a neat small plate/tapas menu. Hear live music on Friday nights. If someone in your party isn't an oenophile, they have craft beer on tap as well.

## HOTELS

Beaufort's historic district is blessed with an abundance of high-quality accommodations that blend well with their surroundings. There are plenty of budget-minded chain places, some of them acceptable, in the sprawl of Boundary Street outside of downtown, but here are some suggestions within bicycling distance of the historic district. (That's not a hypothetical, as most inns offer free bicycles to use as you please during your stay.)

## Under $150

The **Best Western Sea Island Inn** (1015 Bay St., 843/522-2090, www.bestwestern. com, $135-170) is a good value for those for whom the B&B experience is not paramount. Anchoring the southern end of the historic district in a tasteful low brick building, the Best Western offers decent service, basic amenities, and surprisingly attractive rates for the location on Beaufort's busiest street.

## $150-300

Any list of upscale Beaufort lodging must highlight the ★ **Beaufort Inn** (809 Port Republic St., 843/379-4667, www.beaufor-tinn.com, $152-425), consistently voted one of the best B&Bs in the nation. It's sort of a hybrid in that it comprises not only the 1897 historic central home, but also a cluster of freestanding historic cottages, each with a charming little porch and rocking chairs. Within or outside the main building, each suite has a character all its own, whether it's the 1,500-square-foot loft apartment or one of the cozier choice rooms with a queen-size bed.

The 18-room circa-1820 **Rhett House Inn** (1009 Craven St., 843/524-9030, www. rhetthouseinn.com, $175-320) is the local vacation getaway for the stars. Such arts and entertainment luminaries as Robert Redford, Julia Roberts, Ben Affleck, Barbra Streisand, Dennis Quaid, and Demi Moore have all stayed here at one time or another.

There's nothing like enjoying the view of the Beaufort River from the expansive porches of the ★ **Cuthbert House Inn** (1203 Bay St., 843/521-1315, www.cuthberthouseinn.com, $205-250). This grand old circa-1790 Federal mansion was once the home of the wealthy Cuthbert family of rice and indigo planters. General Sherman spent a night here in 1865. Some of the king rooms have fireplaces and claw-foot tubs. Of course you get a full Southern breakfast in addition to sunset hors d'oeuvres on the veranda.

While a stay at a B&B is the classic way to enjoy Beaufort, many travelers swear by the new **City Loft Hotel** (301 Carteret St., 843/379-5638, www.citylofthotel.com, $200). Housed in a former motel, City Loft represents a total modernist makeover, gleaming from stem to stern with chrome and various art deco touches.

## TRANSPORTATION AND SERVICES

The **Beaufort Visitors Information Center** (713 Craven St., 843/986-5400,

the Beaufort Inn

www.beaufortsc.org, daily 9am-5:30pm), the headquarters of the Beaufort Chamber of Commerce and Convention and Visitors Bureau, has relocated from its old Carteret Street location and can now be found within the Beaufort Arsenal.

## Air

While the Marines can fly their F-18s directly into Beaufort Naval Air Station, you won't have that luxury. The closest major airport to Beaufort is the **Savannah/Hilton Head International Airport** (SAV, 400 Airways Ave., 912/964-0514, www.savannahairport.com) off I-95 outside Savannah. From there it's about an hour to Beaufort. If you're not going into Savannah for any reason, the easiest route to the Beaufort area from the airport is to take I-95's exit 8, and from there take U.S. 278 east to Highway 170.

Alternately, you could fly into **Charleston International Airport** (CHS, 5500 International Blvd., www.chs-airport.com), but because that facility is on the far north side of Charleston, it will take a bit longer (about an hour and 20 minutes) to get to Beaufort. From the Charleston Airport the best route south to Beaufort is U.S. 17 south, exiting onto U.S. 21 at Gardens Corner and then into Beaufort.

## Car

If you're coming into the region by car, I-95 will be your likely primary route, with your main point of entry being exit 8 off I-95 connecting to U.S. 278 east to Highway 170. Beaufort is a little over an hour from Charleston.

Don't be discouraged by the big-box sprawl that assaults you on the approaches to Beaufort on Boundary Street, lined with the usual discount megastores, fast-food outlets, and budget motels. After you make the big 90-degree bend where Boundary turns into Carteret Street—known locally as the "Bellamy Curve"—it's like entering a whole new world of slow-paced, Spanish moss-lined avenues, friendly people, gentle breezes, and inviting storefronts.

While you can make your way to downtown by taking Carteret Street all the way to Bay Street—don't continue over the big bridge unless you want to go straight to Lady's Island and St. Helena Island—I suggest availing yourself of one of the "Downtown Access" signs before you get that far. Because Carteret Street is the only way to that bridge, it can get backed up at rush hour. By taking a quick right and then a left all the way to Bay Street, you can come into town from the other, quieter end, with your first glimpse of downtown proper being its timelessly beguiling views of the Beaufort River.

## Getting Around

Unlike Charleston or Savannah, any visitor in reasonably good shape can walk the entire length and breadth of Beaufort's 300-acre downtown with little trouble. In fact, that's by far the best way to experience it.

There's no public transportation to speak of in Beaufort, but that's OK—the historic section is quite small and can be traversed in an afternoon. A favorite mode of transport is by bicycle, often complimentary to bed-and-breakfast guests. You can also rent one at **Lowcountry Bikes** (102 Sea Island Pkwy., 843/524-9585, Mon.-Tues. and Thurs.-Fri. 10am-6pm, Wed. 10am-1pm, Sat. 10am-3pm, about $5 per hour) in Lady's Island just over the bridge.

# Outside Beaufort

The areas outside tourist-traveled Beaufort can take you even further back into sepia-toned Americana, into a time of sharecropper homesteads, sturdy oystermen, and an altogether variable and subjective sense of time.

About 15 minutes east of Beaufort is the center of Gullah culture, St. Helena Island, and the scenic gem of Hunting Island. Just a few minutes south of Beaufort is the East Coast Marine Corps Recruit Depot of Parris Island. About 10 minutes away is the little community of Port Royal.

## SIGHTS
### ★ Penn Center

By going across the Richard V. Woods Memorial Bridge over the Beaufort River on the Sea Island Parkway (which turns into U.S. 21), you'll pass through Lady's Island and reach St. Helena Island. Known to old-timers as Frogmore, the area took back its old Spanish-derived place name in the 1980s. Today St. Helena Island is most famous for the **Penn Center** (16 Martin Luther King Jr. Dr., 843/838-2474, www.penncenter.com,

Mon.-Sat. 11am-4pm, $4 adults, $2 seniors and children), the spiritual home of Gullah culture and history. When you visit here among the live oaks and humble but well-preserved buildings, you'll instantly see why Martin Luther King Jr. chose this as one of his major retreat and planning sites during the civil rights era. The dream began as early as 1862, when a group of abolitionist Quakers from Philadelphia came during the Union occupation with the goal of teaching recently freed slave children. They were soon joined by African American educator Charlotte Forten. After Reconstruction, the Penn School continued its mission by offering teaching as well as agricultural and industrial trade curricula. In the late 1960s, the Southern Christian Leadership Conference used the school as a retreat and planning site, with both the Peace Corps and the Conscientious Objector Programs training here. The Penn Center continues to serve an important civil rights role by providing legal counsel to African American homeowners in St. Helena. Because clear title is difficult to acquire in the area due to the fact

the Penn Center on St. Helena Island

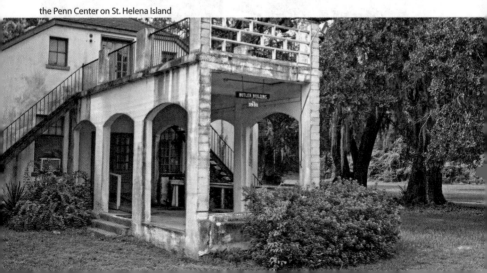

that so much of the land has stayed in the families of former slaves, developers are constantly making shady offers so that ancestral land can be opened up to upscale development.

The 50-acre campus is part of the Penn School Historic District, a National Historic Landmark comprising 19 buildings, most of key historical significance. The Retreat House was intended for Dr. King to continue his strategy meetings, but he was assassinated before being able to stay there. The museum and bookshop are housed in the Cope Building, now called the York W. Bailey Museum, situated right along MLK Jr. Drive.

To get to the Penn Center from Beaufort (about 10 miles), proceed over the bridge until you get to St. Helena Island. Take a right onto MLK Jr. Drive when you see the Red Piano Too Art Gallery. The Penn Center is a few hundred yards down on your right. If you drive past the Penn Center and continue a few hundred yards down MLK Jr. Drive, look for the ancient tabby ruins on the left side of the road. This is the **Chapel of Ease,** the remnant of a 1740 church destroyed by forest fire in the late 1800s.

## Fort Fremont Preserve

Military historians and sightseers of a particularly adventurous type will want to drive several miles past the Penn Center on St. Helena Island to visit **Fort Fremont Preserve** (Lands End Rd., www.fortfremont. org, daily 9am-dusk, free). Two artillery batteries remain of this Spanish-American War-era coastal defense fort (an adjacent private residence is actually the old army hospital). The fort was active until 1921, but now the big guns are long gone. Their heavy concrete emplacements, however—along with many very dark tunnels and small rooms—are still here and make for a very interesting visit. Guided docent tours happen the fourth Saturday of the month starting at 10:30am at the St. Helena Branch of the Beaufort County Library (6355 Jonathan Francis Senior Rd.). Tours are free, last two hours, and reservations aren't required.

## Old Sheidon Church

About 20 minutes north of Beaufort are the poignantly desolate ruins of the once-magnificent **Old Sheldon Church** (Old Sheldon

the Old Sheldon Church ruins

# The Lost Art of Tabby

Let's clear up a couple of misconceptions about tabby, that unique construction technique combining oyster shells, lime, water, and sand found along the South Carolina and Georgia coasts.

First, it did not originate with Native Americans. The confusion is due to the fact that the native population left behind many middens, or trash heaps, of oyster shells. While these middens indeed provided the bulk of the shells for tabby buildings to come, Native Americans had little else to do with it.

Second, although the Spanish were responsible for the first use of tabby in the Americas, contrary to lore almost all remaining tabby in the area dates from later English settlement. The British first fell in love with tabby after the siege of Spanish-held St. Augustine, Florida, and quickly began building with it in their colonies to the north.

Scholars are divided as to whether tabby was invented by West Africans or its use spread to Africa from Spain and Portugal, circuitously coming to the United States through the knowledge of imported slaves. The origin of the word itself is also unclear, as similar words exist in Spanish, Portuguese, Gullah, and Arabic to describe various types of wall.

the Chapel of Ease on St. Helena Island

We do know for sure how tabby is made: The primary technique was to burn alternating layers of oyster shells and logs in a deep hole in the ground, thus creating lime. The lime was then mixed with oyster shells, sand, and freshwater and poured into wooden molds, or "forms," to dry and then be used as building blocks, much like large bricks. Tabby walls were usually plastered with stucco. Tabby is remarkably strong and resilient, able to survive the hurricanes that often batter the area. It also stays cool in the summer and is insect-resistant, two enormous advantages down here.

Following are some great examples of true tabby you can see today on the South Carolina and Georgia coasts, from north to south:

- **Dorchester State Historic Site** in Summerville, north of Charleston, contains a well-preserved tabby fort.

- Several younger tabby buildings still exist in downtown Beaufort: the **Barnwell-Gough House** (705 Washington St.); the Thomas Fuller House, or **"Tabby Manse"** (1211 Bay St.); and the **Saltus House** (800 block of Bay St.), perhaps the tallest surviving tabby structure.

- The **Chapel of Ease** on St. Helena Island dates from the 1740s. If someone tells you Sherman burned it down, don't believe it; the culprit was a forest fire.

- The **Stoney-Baynard Ruins** in Sea Pines Plantation on Hilton Head are all that's left of the home of the old Braddock's Point Plantation. Foundations of a slave quarters are nearby.

- **Wormsloe Plantation** near Savannah has the remains of Noble Jones's fortification on the Skidaway Narrows.

- **St. Cyprian's Episcopal Church** in Darien is one of the largest tabby structures still in use.

- **Fort Frederica** on St. Simons Island has not only the remains of a tabby fort but many foundations of tabby houses in the surrounding settlement.

- The remarkably intact walls of the **Horton-DuBignon House** on Jekyll Island, Georgia, date from 1738, and the house was occupied into the 1850s.

Church Rd., off U.S. 17 just past Gardens Corner, daily dawn-dusk, free). One of the first Greek Revival structures in the United States, the house of worship held its first service in 1757. The sanctuary was first burned by the British in 1779. After being rebuilt in 1826, the sanctuary survived until General Sherman's arrival in 1865, whereupon Union troops razed it once more. Nothing remains now but these towering walls and columns made of red brick instead of the tabby often seen in similar ruins on the coast. It's now owned by the nearby St. Helena's Episcopal Church in Beaufort, which holds outdoor services here the second Sunday after Easter.

## Oyotunji Village

Continuing north of the Sheldon Church a short way, the more adventurous can find a quirky Lowcountry attraction, **Oyotunji Village** (56 Bryant Lane, 843/846-8900, www.oyotunji.org, daily 11am-dusk, $10). Built in 1970 by self-proclaimed "King" Ofuntola Oseijeman Adelabu Adefunmi I, a former used car dealer with an interesting past, Oyotunji claims to be North America's only authentic African village, and also claims to be a separate kingdom and not a part of the United States—though I'm sure the State Department begs to differ. Take U.S. 17 north out of Beaufort; about 25 minutes later Oyotunji Village will be on your right.

## Port Royal

This sleepy hamlet between Beaufort and Parris Island touts itself as a leader in "small-town New Urbanism," with an emphasis on livability, retro-themed shopping areas, and relaxing walking trails. However, **Port Royal** is still pretty sleepy—but not without very real charms, not the least of which is the fact that everything is within easy walking distance of everything else. The highlight of the year is the annual Softshell Crab Festival, held each April to mark the short-lived harvesting season for that favorite crustacean.

While much of the tiny historic district has a scrubbed, tidy feel, the main historic structure is the charming little **Union Church** (11th St., 843/524-4333, Mon.-Fri. 10am-4pm, donation), one of the oldest buildings in town, with guided docent tours.

Don't miss the boardwalk and observation tower at **The Sands** municipal beach and boat ramp. The 50-foot-tall structure provides a commanding view of Battery Creek. The little beach is artificial (made from dredged material) but still somewhat unusual in this area.

the view from the observation tower at The Sands

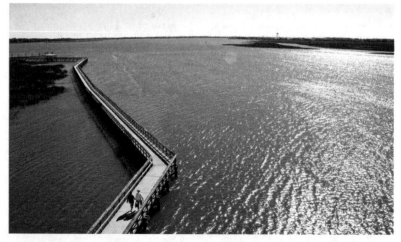

To get to The Sands, head east onto 7th Street off the main drag of Parris Avenue. Seventh Street turns into Sands Beach Road for a brief stretch and then merges with 6th Street, taking you directly to The Sands.

A must-stop for families is the **Port Royal Maritime Center** (310 Okatie Hwy., 843/645-7774, www.portroyalsoundfoundation.org, Tue.-Sat. 10am-5pm, free), a new venture that is a great resource for learning about the area's ecological history. They have a 3,000-gallon aquarium, a touch tank, and numerous exhibits about local habitat and marine life, including the prehistoric species that kids love. Overlooking the undeveloped Chechessee River, it's also scenic location in its own right.

Another environmentally oriented point of pride is the **Lowcountry Estuarium** (1402 Paris Ave., 843/524-6600, www.lowcountryestuarium.org, Wed.-Sat. 10am-5pm, feedings at 11:30am and 3pm, $5 adults, $3 children). The point of the facility is to give hands-on opportunities to learn more about the flora and fauna of the various ecosystems of the Lowcountry, such as salt marshes, beaches, and estuaries.

If you get hungry in Port Royal, try the waterfront seafood haven **11th Street Dockside** (1699 11th St., 843/524-7433, daily 4:30pm-10pm, $17-27). The Dockside Dinner is a great sampler plate with lobster tail, scallops, crab legs, and shrimp. The views of the waterfront and the adjoining shrimp-boat docks are relaxing and beautiful.

To get to Port Royal from Beaufort, take Ribault (pronounced "REE-bo") Road south, then a left onto Parris Avenue, which takes you directly into downtown Port Royal for a total drive of about 10 minutes.

## Parris Island

Though more commonly known as the home of the legendary **Marine Corps Recruit Depot Parris Island** (283 Blvd. de France, 843/228-3650, www.mcrdpi.marines.mil, free), the island is also of historic significance as the site of some of the earliest European presence in the New World. Today it's where all female U.S. Marine recruits and most all male recruits east of the Mississippi River go through the grueling 13-week boot camp. Almost every Friday during the year marks the graduation of a company of newly minted Marines. That's why you might notice an influx of visitors to the area each Thursday, aka "Family Day," with the requisite amount of celebration on Fridays after that morning's ceremony.

You don't have to be a Marine to enjoy Parris Island.

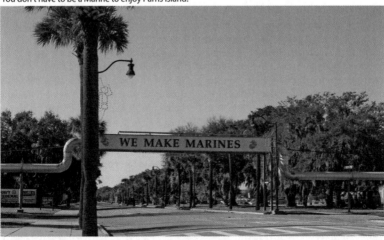

Unlike many military facilities in the post-9/11 era, Parris Island still hosts plenty of visitors. Just check in with the sentry at the gate and show your valid driver's license, registration, and proof of insurance. Rental car drivers must show a copy of the rental agreement. On your way to the depot proper, there are a couple of beautiful picnic areas. Once inside, stop first at the **Douglas Visitor Center** (Bldg. 283, Blvd. de France, 843/228-3650, Mon. 7:30am-noon, Tues.-Wed. 7:30am-4:30pm, Thurs. 6:30am-7pm, Fri. 7:30am-3pm), a great place to find maps and information. As you go by the big parade ground, or "deck," be sure to check out the beautiful sculpture re-creating the famous photo of Marines raising the flag on Iwo Jima. A short way ahead is the **Parris Island Museum** (Bldg. 111, 111 Panama St., 843/228-2951, www.mcrdpimuseum.com, daily 10am-4:30pm, free), detailing the proud history of the Corps with a particular focus on this Recruit Depot.

The Spanish built Santa Elena nearby the original French settlement, Charlesfort. They then built two other settlements, San Felipe and San Marcos. The Santa Elena site, now on the circa-1950s Parris Island Depot golf course, is a National Historic Landmark. So far, archaeologists have found a residence of a wealthy family in the town and have identified two of Santa Elena's five forts. Many artifacts are viewable at the nearby **clubhouse-interpretive center** (daily 7am-5pm, free). You can take a self-guided tour; to get to the site from the museum, continue on Panama Street and take a right on Cuba Street. Follow the signs to the golf course and continue through the main parking lot of the course.

To make the 15-minute drive to Parris Island from Beaufort, take Ribault Road south, which turns into U.S. 21. Continue through and out of Port Royal and follow the signs for the Parris Island Gateway.

## ★ Hunting Island State Park

Rumored to be a hideaway for Blackbeard himself, the aptly named Hunting Island was indeed for many years a notable

the lighthouse at Hunting Island State Park

hunting preserve, and its abundance of wildlife remains to this day. The island is one of the East Coast's best birding spots and also hosts dolphins, loggerheads, alligators, and deer. Thanks to preservation efforts by President Franklin Roosevelt and the Civilian Conservation Corps, however, the island is no longer for hunting but for sheer enjoyment. And enjoy it people do, to the tune of one million visitors per year. A true family-friendly outdoor adventure spot, **Hunting Island State Park** (2555 Sea Island Pkwy., 866/345-7275, www.huntingisland.com, winter daily 6am-6pm, during daylight saving time daily 6am-9pm, $5 adults, $3 children) has something for everyone—kids, parents, and newlyweds. Yet it still retains a certain sense of lush wildness—so much so that it doubled as Vietnam in the movie *Forrest Gump.*

At the north end past the campground is the island's main landmark, the historic **Hunting Island Light,** which dates from 1875. Although the lighthouse ceased operations in 1933, a rotating light—not strong enough to serve as an actual navigational aid—is turned on at night. While the 167-step trek to the top (donation $2 pp) is strenuous, the view is stunning. At the south end of the island is a marsh walk, nature trail, and a fishing pier complete with a cute little nature center. Hunting Island's three miles of beautiful beaches also serve as a major center of loggerhead turtle nesting and hatching, a process that begins around June as the mothers lay their eggs and culminates in late summer and early fall, when the hatchlings make their daring dash to the sea. At all phases the turtles are strictly protected, and while there are organized events to witness the hatching of the eggs, it is strictly forbidden to touch or otherwise disturb the turtles or their nests. Contact the park ranger for more detailed information. The tropical-looking inlet running through the park is a great place to kayak or canoe.

Getting to Hunting Island couldn't be easier—just take the Sea Island Parkway (U.S. 21 East) about 20 minutes beyond Beaufort and you'll run right into it.

### ★ ACE Basin

Occupying pretty much the entire area between Beaufort and Charleston, the **ACE Basin**—the acronym signifies its role as the collective estuary of the Ashepoo, Combahee, and Edisto Rivers—is one of the most enriching natural experiences the country has to offer. The ACE Basin's three core rivers, the Edisto being the largest, are the framework for a matrix of waterways crisscrossing its approximately 350,000 acres of salt marsh. It's the intimate relationship with the tides that makes the area so enjoyable, and also what attracted so many plantations throughout its history (canals and dikes from the old paddy fields are still visible throughout). Other uses have included tobacco, corn, and lumbering. While the ACE Basin can in no way be called "pristine," it's a testament to the power of nature that after 6,000 years of human presence and often intense cultivation, the basin manages to retain much of its untamed feel. The ACE Basin is so big that it is actually divided into several parts for management purposes under the umbrella of the ACE Basin Project (www.acebasin.net), a task force begun in 1988 by the state of South Carolina, the U.S. Fish and Wildlife Service, and various private firms and conservation groups. The project is now considered a model for responsible watershed preservation techniques in a time of often rampant coastal development. A host of species, both common and endangered, thrive

The Grove Plantation House is the main office for the Ernest F. Hollings ACE Basin NWR.

in the area, including wood storks, alligators, sturgeon, loggerheads, teals, and bald eagles.

About 12,000 acres of the ACE Basin Project comprise the **Ernest F. Hollings ACE Basin National Wildlife Refuge** (8675 Willtown Rd., 843/889-3084, www.fws.gov/acebasin, grounds year-round daily dawn-dusk, office Mon.-Fri. 7:30am-4pm, free), run by the U.S. Fish and Wildlife Service. The historic 1828 **Grove Plantation House** is in this portion of the basin and houses the refuge's headquarters. Sometimes featured on local tours of homes, it's one of only three antebellum homes left in the ACE Basin. Surrounded by lush, ancient oak trees, it's really a sight in and of itself.

This section of the refuge, the **Edisto Unit,** is about an hour's drive from Beaufort. It is almost entirely composed of paddies from the area's role as a rice plantation before the Civil War. To get to the Edisto Unit of the Hollings/ACE Basin National Wildlife Refuge, take U.S. 17 to Highway 174 (going all the way down this route takes you to Edisto Island) and turn right onto Willtown Road. The unpaved entrance road is about two miles ahead on the left. There are restrooms and a few picnic tables.

You can also visit the two parts of the **Combahee Unit** of the refuge, which offers a similar scene of trails among impounded wetlands along the Combahee River, with parking; it's farther west near Yemassee. The Combahee Unit is about 30 minutes from Beaufort. Get here by taking a left off U.S. 17 onto Highway 33. The larger portion of the Combahee Unit is soon after the turnoff, and the smaller, more northerly portion is about five miles up the road.

About 135,000 acres of the entire ACE Basin falls under the protection of the South Carolina Department of Natural Resources (DNR) as part of the **National Estuarine Research Reserve System** (www.nerrs.noaa.gov/acebasin). The DNR also runs two Wildlife Management Areas (WMAs), **Donnelly WMA** (843/844-8957, www.dnr.sc.gov, year-round Mon.-Sat. 8am-5pm) and

Bear Island WMA (843/844-8957, www.dnr.sc.gov, Feb. 1-Oct. 14 Mon.-Sat. dawn-dusk), both of which provide rich opportunities for birding and wildlife observation.

## KAYAKING

You can put in at the ramp at the **Lady's Island Marina** (73 Sea Island Pkwy., 843/522-0430) just across the bridge from Beaufort. **Hunting Island State Park** (2555 Sea Island Pkwy., 866/345-7275, www.huntingisland.com, winter daily 6am-6pm, during daylight saving time daily 6am-9pm, $5 adults, $3 children) has a wonderful inlet that is very popular with kayakers.

A good service for rentals and knowledgeable guided tours of the ACE Basin is **Outpost Moe's** (843/844-2514, www.geocities.ws/outpostmoe), where the basic 2.5-hour tour costs $40 pp, and an all-day extravaganza through the basin is $80. Moe's provides lunch for most of its tours. Another premier local outfitter for ACE Basin tours is **Carolina Heritage Outfitters** (U.S. 15 in Canadys, 843/563-5051, www.canoesc.com), which focuses on the Edisto River trail. In addition to guided tours ($30) and rentals, you can camp overnight in their cute tree houses ($125) along the kayak routes. They load you up with your gear and drive you 22 miles upriver; then you paddle downriver to the tree house for the evening. The next day, you paddle yourself the rest of the way downriver back to home base.

To have a drier experience of the ACE Basin from the deck of a larger vessel, try **ACE Basin Tours** (1 Coosaw River Dr., Beaufort, 843/521-3099, www.acebasintours.com, Mar.-Nov. Wed. and Sat. 10am, $35 adults, $15 children), which will take you on a three-hour tour in the 40-passenger *Dixie Lady.* To get to their dock from Beaufort, take Carteret Street over the bridge to St. Helena Island, and then take a left on Highway 802 east (Sam's Point Rd.). Continue until you cross Lucy Point Creek; the ACE Basin Tours marina is on your immediate left after you cross the bridge.

The state of South Carolina has conveniently

gathered some of the best self-guided kayak trips at www.acebasin.net/canoe.html.

## GOLF

Golf is much bigger in Hilton Head than in the Beaufort area, but there are some local highlights. The best-regarded public course in the area, and indeed one of the best military courses in the world, is **Legends at Parris Island** (Bldg. 299, Parris Island, 843/228-2240, www.mccssc.com, $30). Call in advance for a tee time.

Another popular public course is **South Carolina National Golf Club** (8 Waveland Ave., Cat Island, 843/524-0300, www.scnational.com, $70). Get to secluded Cat Island by taking the Sea Island Parkway onto Lady's Island and continuing south as it turns into Lady's Island Drive. Turn onto Island Causeway and continue for about three miles.

## CAMPING

**Hunting Island State Park** (2555 Sea Island Pkwy., 866/345-7275, www.huntingisland.com, winter daily 6am-6pm, during daylight saving time daily 6am-9pm, $5 adults, $3 children, $25 RV sites, $19 tent sites, $87-172 cabin) has 200 campsites with individual water and electric hookups on the north end of the island. There used to be plenty of cabins for rent, but beach erosion has sadly made the ones near the water uninhabitable. One cabin near the lighthouse is still available for rent, and it is in such high demand that the park encourages you to camp instead.

Another neat place to camp is **Tuck in the Wood** (22 Tuc In De Wood Lane, St. Helena, 843/838-2267, $25), a very well-maintained 74-site private campground just past the Penn Center on St. Helena Island.

# Edisto Island

One of the last truly unspoiled places in the Lowcountry, Edisto Island has been highly regarded as a getaway spot since the Edisto people first started coming here for shellfish. In fact, locals here swear that the island was settled by English-speaking colonists even before Charleston was settled in 1670.

Now this barrier island, for the moment unthreatened by the encroachment of planned communities and private resorts so endemic to the Carolina coast, is a nice getaway for area residents in addition to being a great—if a little isolated—place to live for its 800 or so full-time residents, who operate on "Edisto Time," with a *mañana* philosophy (i.e., it'll get done when it gets done) that results in a mellow pace of life out in these parts.

There are rental homes galore on Edisto Island. Because of the lack of hotels, this is the most popular option for most vacationers here—indeed, it's just about the only option. Contact **Edisto Sales and Rentals Realty**

(1405 Palmetto Blvd., 800/868-5398, www.edistorealty.com).

## SIGHTS

The **Edisto Museum** (8123 Chisolm Plantation Rd., 843/869-1954, www.edistomuseum.org, Tues.-Sat. noon-5pm, $4 adults, $2 children, free under age 10), a project of the Edisto Island Historic Preservation Society, has recently expanded and incorporated a nearby slave cabin. Its well-done exhibits of local lore and history are complemented by a gift shop. The Edisto Museum is before you get to the main part of the island, off Highway 174.

Opened in 1999 by local snake hunters the Clamp brothers, the **Edisto Island Serpentarium** (1374 Hwy. 174, 843/869-1171, www.edistoserpentarium.com, hours vary, $14.95 adults, $10.95 ages 4-12, free age 3 and younger) is educational and fun, taking you up close and personal with a variety of reptilian creatures native to the area. They usually close Labor Day-April 30.

The **Botany Bay Wildlife Management Area** (www.preserveedisto.org, Wed.-Mon. dawn-dusk, free) is a great way to enjoy the unspoiled nature of Edisto Island. On the grounds of two former rice and indigo plantations comprising 4,000 acres, Botany Bay features several historic remains of the old plantations and a small, wonderful beach. There are no facilities to speak of, so pack and plan accordingly. Botany Bay is closed on hunt days, which vary depending on the hunting season but are fairly rare.

## SPORTS AND ACTIVITIES

As the largest river of the ACE (Ashepoo, Combahee, Edisto) Basin complex, the Edisto River figures large in the lifestyle of residents and visitors. A good public landing is at Steamboat Creek off Highway 174 on the way down to the island. Take Steamboat Landing Road (Hwy. 968) from Highway 174 near the James Edwards School. Live Oak Landing is farther up Big Bay Creek near the Interpretive Center at the state park. The **Edisto Marina** (3702 Docksite Rd., 843/869-3504) is on the far west side of the island.

Captain Ron Elliott of **Edisto Island Tours** (843/869-1937) offers various eco-tours and fishing trips as well as canoe and kayak rentals for about $25 per day. A typical kayak tour runs about $35 pp for a 1.5-2-hour trip, and he offers a "beachcombing" trip for $15 pp. **Ugly Ducklin'** (843/869-1580) offers creek and inshore fishing charters. You can get gear as well as reserve boat and kayak tours of the entire area, including into the ACE Basin, at **Edisto Watersports & Tackle** (3731 Docksite Rd., 843/869-0663, www.edistowatersports.com). Their guided tours run about $30 pp, with a two-hour rental running about $20.

Riding a bike on Edisto Beach and all around the island is a great and relaxing way to get some exercise and enjoy its scenic, laid-back beauty. The best place to rent a bike—or a kayak or canoe, for that matter—is **Island Bikes and Outfitters** (140 Jungle Rd., 843/869-4444, Mon.-Sat. 9am-4pm). Bike rentals run about $16 per day; single kayaks are about $60 per day.

## ★ Edisto Beach State Park

**Edisto Beach State Park** (8377 State Cabin Rd., 843/869-2156, www.southcarolinaparks. com, Nov.-mid-Mar. daily 8am-6pm,

Edisto Island is a great place to relax.

mid-Mar.-Oct. daily 6am-10pm, $5 adults, $3 children, free under age 6) is one of the world's foremost destinations for shell collectors. Largely because of fresh loads of silt from the adjacent ACE Basin, there are always new specimens, many of them fossils, washing ashore. The park stretches almost three miles and features the state's longest system of fully accessible hiking and biking trails, including one leading to the 4,000-year-old shell midden, now much eroded from past millennia. The new and particularly well-done **interpretive center** (Tues.-Sat. 9am-4pm) has plenty of interesting exhibits about the nature and history of the park as well as the surrounding ACE Basin.

### CAMPING

A great thing about Edisto Island is the total absence of ugly chain lodging or beachfront condo development. My recommended option is staying at **Edisto Beach State Park** (843/869-2156, www.southcarolinaparks.com, $25 tent sites, $75-100 cabins) itself, either at a campsite on the Atlantic side or in a marshfront cabin on the northern edge. During high season (Apr.-Nov.), there's a minimum weeklong stay in the cabins; during the off-season, the minimum stay is two days. You can book cabins up to 11 months in advance.

## SHOPS

Not only a convenient place to pick up odds and ends, the **Edistonian Gift Shop & Gallery** (406 Hwy. 174, 843/869-4466, daily 9am-7pm) is also an important landmark as the primary supply point before you get into the main part of town. Think of a really nice convenience store with an attached gift shop and you'll get the picture.

For various ocean gear, try the **Edisto Surf Shop** (145 Jungle Rd., 843/869-9283, daily 9am-5pm). You can find whimsical Lowcountry-themed art for enjoyment or purchase at **Fish or Cut Bait Gallery** (142 Jungle Rd., 843/869-2511, www.fishorcutbaitgallery. com, Tues.-Sat. 10am-5pm).

For fresh seafood, try **Flowers Seafood**

**Company** (1914 Hwy. 174, 843/869-0033, Mon.-Sat. 9am-7pm, Sun. 9am-5pm).

## RESTAURANTS

One of the all-time great barbecue places in South Carolina is on Edisto: ★ **Po Pigs Bo-B-Q** (2410 Hwy. 174, 843/869-9003, Wed.-Sat. 11:30am-9pm, $4-10), on the way into town. This is the real thing, the full pig cooked in all its many ways: white meat, dark meat, cracklin's, and hash, served in the local style of "all you care to eat." Unlike many barbecue spots, they do serve beer and wine.

Another popular joint on the island is **Whaley's** (2801 Myrtle St., 843/869-2161, Tues.-Sat. 11:30am-2pm and 5pm-9pm, bar daily 5pm-2am, $5-15), a down-home place in an old gas station a few blocks off the beach. This is a good place for casual seafood like boiled shrimp, washed down with a lot of beer. The bar is open seven days a week.

The legendary ★ **Old Post Office** (1442 Hwy. 174, 843/869-2339, www.theoldpost-officerestaurant.com, Tues.-Sun. 5:30pm-10pm, $20), a Lowcountry-style fine-dining spot, served a devoted clientele for 20 years. It recently reopened with a bang and thankfully kept its old-school mystique intact. Specialties include fine crab cakes drizzled with mousseline sauce, the pecan-encrusted Veal Edistonian, and a Carolina rib eye topped with a pimiento cheese sauce.

## TRANSPORTATION

Edisto Island is basically halfway between Beaufort and Charleston. There's one main land route here, south on Highway 174 off U.S. 17. It's a long way down from U.S. 17 to Edisto, but the 20- to 30-minute drive is scenic and enjoyable. Most activity on the island centers on the township of Edisto Beach, which voted to align itself with Colleton County for its lower taxes (the rest of Edisto Island is part of Charleston County).

Once in town, there are two main routes to keep in mind. Palmetto Boulevard runs parallel to the beach and is noteworthy for the lack of high-rise development so common in other beach areas of South Carolina. Jungle Road runs parallel to Palmetto Boulevard several blocks inland and contains the tiny business district.

## Tours

Edisto has many beautiful plantation homes, relics of the island's longtime role as host to cotton plantations. While all are in private hands and therefore off limits to the public, an exception is offered through **Edisto Island Tours & T'ings** (843/869-9092, $20 adults, $10 under age 13). You'll take a van tour around Edisto's beautiful churches and old plantations.

# Hilton Head Island

Literally the prototype of the modern planned resort community, Hilton Head Island is also a case study in how a landscape can change when money is introduced. From Reconstruction until the post-World War II era, the island consisted almost entirely of African Americans with deep roots in the area. In the mid-1950s Hilton Head began its transformation into an almost all-white, up-scale golf, tennis, and shopping mecca populated largely by Northern transplants and retirees. As you can imagine, the flavor here is now quite different from surrounding areas of the Lowcountry, to say the least, with an emphasis on material excellence, top prices, get-it-done-yesterday punctuality, and the attendant aggressive traffic.

These days, Hilton Head gets the most national media attention for the RBC Heritage golf tournament each April, when the entire island is packed with golf fans for this extremely popular PGA event.

One of the unsung positive aspects of modern Hilton Head is its dedication to sustainable living. With the support of voters, the town routinely buys large tracts of land to preserve as open space. Hilton Head was the first municipality in the country to mandate the burying of all power lines, and one of the first to regularly use covenants and deed restrictions. All new development must conform to rigid guidelines on setbacks and tree canopy. It has one of the most comprehensive signage ordinances in the country as well, which means no garish commercial displays will disrupt your views of the night sky. If those are "elite" values, then certainly we might do well in making them more mainstream.

## HISTORY

The second-largest barrier island on the East Coast was named in 1663 by adventurer Sir William Hilton, who thoughtfully named the island—with its notable headland or "Head"—after himself. Later it gained fame as the first growing location of the legendary "Sea Island Cotton," a long-grain variety that, following its introduction in 1790 by William Elliott II of the Myrtle Bank Plantation, would soon be the dominant version of the cash crop.

Nearby Bluffton was settled by planters from Hilton Head Island and the surrounding area in the early 1800s as a summer retreat. Though Charleston likes to claim the label today, Bluffton was actually the genuine "cradle of secession." Indeed, locals still joke that the town motto is "Divided We Stand."

Though it seems unlikely given the island's modern demographics, Hilton Head was almost entirely African American through much of the 20th century. When Union troops occupied the island at the outbreak of the Civil War, freed and escaped slaves flocked to the island, and most of the dwindling number of African Americans on the island today are descendants of this original Gullah population.

In the 1950s the Fraser family bought 19,000 of the island's 25,000 acres with the intent to continue forestry on them. But in 1956—not at all coincidentally the same

# Hilton Head Island

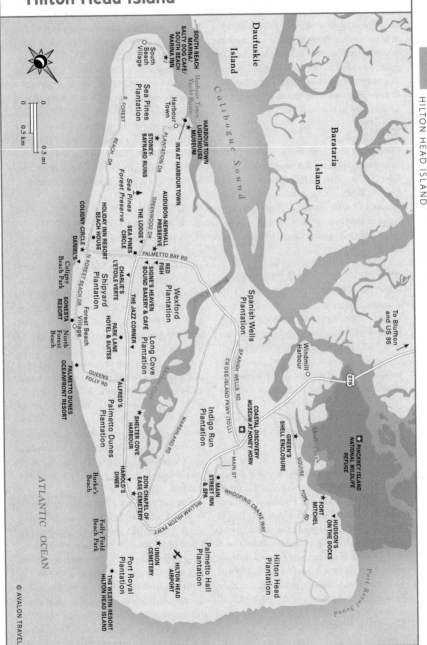

Daufuskie Island

Barataria Island

Calibogue Sound

Broad Creek

Port Royal Sound

Shell Creek

To Bluffton and US 95

278

SOUTH BEACH MARINA/
SALTY DOG CAFÉ/
SOUTH BEACH MARINA INN
South Beach Village
Harbour Town Yacht Basin
Harbour Town
HARBOUR TOWN LIGHTHOUSE MUSEUM
INN AT HARBOURTOWN
Sea Pines Plantation
STONEY-BAYNARD RUINS
AUDUBON-NEWHALL PRESERVE
Sea Pines Forest Preserve
PLANTATION DR
GREENWOOD DR
THE LODGE
SEA PINES CIRCLE
PALMETTO BAY RD
WEXFORD Plantation
RED FISH
CHARLIE'S L'ETOILE VERTE
SIGNE'S HEAVEN BOUND BAKERY & CAFÉ
Long Cove Plantation
Broad Creek
Spanish Wells Plantation
CROSS-ISLAND PKWY (TOLL)
SPANISH WELLS RD
Windmill Harbour
HOLIDAY INN RESORT BEACH HOUSE
COLIGNY CIRCLE
DANIEL'S
N FOREST BEACH DR
S FOREST BEACH DR
Coligny Beach Park
SONESTA RESORT
Shipyard Plantation
THE JAZZ CORNER
PARK LANE HOTEL & SUITES
Forest Beach Village
North Forest Beach
QUEENS FOLLY RD
ALFRED'S
Palmetto Dunes Plantation
SHELTER COVE HARBOUR
Indigo Run Plantation
COASTAL DISCOVERY MUSEUM AT HONEY HORN
GREEN'S SHELL ENCLOSURE
MARSHLAND RD
MAIN ST
MAIN STREET INN & SPA
HUDSON'S ON THE DOCKS
SQUIRE POPE RD
PINCKNEY ISLAND NATIONAL WILDLIFE REFUGE
FORT MITCHEL
PALMETTO DUNES OCEANFRONT RESORT
Burke's Beach
HAROLD'S DINER
ZION CHAPEL OF EASE CEMETERY
WILLIAM HILTON PKWY
WHOOPING CRANE WAY
Palmetto Hall Plantation
Hilton Head Plantation
Folly Field Beach Park
UNION CEMETERY
HILTON HEAD AIRPORT
Port Royal Plantation
THE WESTIN RESORT HILTON HEAD ISLAND
ATLANTIC OCEAN

S FOREST BEACH DR

© AVALON TRAVEL

0    0.5 km
0    0.5 mi

year the first bridge to the island was built—Charles Fraser convinced his father to sell him the southern tip. Fraser's brainchild and decades-long labor of love—some said his obsession—Sea Pines Plantation became the prototype for the golf-oriented resort communities so common today on both U.S. coasts. Fraser himself was killed in a boating accident in 2002 and is buried under the famous Liberty Oak in Harbour Town.

## SIGHTS

Contrary to what many think, there are things to do on Hilton Head that don't involve swinging a club at a little white ball or shopping for designer labels, but instead celebrate the area's history and natural setting. The following are some of those attractions, arranged in geographical order from where you first access the island.

### ★ Pinckney Island National Wildlife Refuge

Actually consisting of many islands and hammocks, **Pinckney Island National Wildlife Refuge** (912/652-4415, daily dawn-dusk, free) is the only part of this small but very well-managed 4,000-acre refuge that's open to the public. Almost 70 percent of the former rice plantation is salt marsh and tidal creeks, making it a perfect microcosm for the Lowcountry as a whole, as well as a great place to kayak or canoe. Native Americans liked the area as well, with a 10,000-year presence and over 100 archaeological sites being identified to date. Like many coastal refuges, it was a private game preserve for much of the 20th century. Some of the state's richest birding opportunities abound here, with observers able to spot gorgeous white ibis and rare wood storks, along with herons, egrets, eagles, and ospreys, with little trouble from the refuge's miles of trails. Getting here is easy: On U.S. 278 east to Hilton Head, the refuge entrance is right between the two bridges onto the island.

### Green's Shell Enclosure

Less known than the larger Native American shell ring farther south at Sea Pines, **Green's Shell Enclosure** (803/734-3886, daily dawn-dusk) is certainly easier to find, and you don't have to pay $5 to enter the area, as with Sea Pines. This three-acre heritage preserve dates back to at least the 1300s. The heart of the site comprises a low embankment, part of the original fortified village. To get here, take a left at the intersection of U.S. 278 and Squire Pope Road. Turn left into Green's Park, pass the office on the left, and park. The entrance to the shell enclosure is on the left behind a fence. You'll see a small community cemetery that has nothing to do with the shell ring; veer to your right to get to the short trail entrance.

### ★ Coastal Discovery Museum at Honey Horn

With the acquisition of Honey Horn's 70-acre spread of historic plantation land, Hilton Head finally has a full-fledged museum worthy of the name, and the magnificent **Coastal Discovery Museum** (70 Honey Horn Dr., 843/689-6767, www.coastaldiscovery.org, Mon.-Sat. 9am-4:30pm, Sun. 11am-3pm, free) is a must-see, even for those who came to the island mostly to golf and soak up sun.

The facility centers on the expertly restored Discovery House, the only antebellum house still existing on Hilton Head, with exhibits and displays devoted to the history of the island. The museum is also a great one-stop place to sign up for a variety of specialty on-site and off-site guided tours, such as birding and Gullah history tours. The cost for most on-site tours is a reasonable $10 adults and $5 children.

But the real draw is the 0.5-mile trail through the Honey Horn grounds, including several boardwalk viewpoints over the marsh, a neat little butterfly habitat, a few gardens, and a stable and pasture that host Honey Horn May and Tadpole, the museum's two Marsh Tackies—short, tough little ponies descended from Spanish horses and used to great effect by Francis "Swamp Fox" Marion and his freedom fighters in the American Revolution. The trail even features a replica of an ancient the Coastal Discovery Museum at Honey Horn

Native American shell ring of oyster shells, but do be aware that it is not a genuine shell ring (you can find the real thing at Green's Shell Enclosure a bit farther west on Highway 278 and in Sea Pines at the south end of the island).

While a glance at a map and area signage might convince you that you must pay the $1.25 toll on the Cross Island Parkway to get to Honey Horn, that isn't so. The exit to Honey Horn on the parkway is actually before you get to the toll plaza, therefore access is free.

## Union Cemetery

A modest but key aspect of African American history on Hilton Head is at **Union Cemetery** (Union Cemetery Rd.), a small burial ground featuring several graves of black Union Army troops (you can tell by the designation "USCI" on the tombstone, for "United States Colored Infantry"). Also of interest are the charming hand-carved cement tombstones of nonveterans. To get here, turn north off of William Hilton Parkway onto Union Cemetery Road. The cemetery is a short way ahead on the left. There is no signage or site interpretation.

## Zion Chapel of Ease Cemetery

More like one of the gloriously desolate scenes common to the rest of the Lowcountry, this little cemetery in full view of the William Hilton Parkway at Folly Field Road is all that remains of one of the "Chapels of Ease," a string of chapels set up in the 1700s. The **Zion Chapel of Ease Cemetery** (daily dawn-dusk, free) is said to be haunted by the ghost of William Baynard, whose final resting place is in a mausoleum on the site (the remains of his ancestral home are farther south at Sea Pines Plantation).

## Audubon-Newhall Preserve

Plant lovers shouldn't miss this small but very well-maintained 50-acre wooded tract in the south-central part of the island on Palmetto Bay Road between the Cross Island Parkway and the Sea Pines Circle. Almost all plant life, even that in the water, is helpfully marked and identified. The **Audubon-Newhall Preserve** (year-round dawn-dusk, free) is open to the public, but you can't camp here. For more information, call the **Hilton Head Audubon Society** (843/842-9246).

## Sea Pines Plantation

This private residential resort development at the extreme west end of the island—the first on Hilton Head and the prototype for every other such development in the country—hosts several attractions that collectively are well worth the $5 per vehicle "road use" fee, which you pay at the main entrance gate.

### HARBOUR TOWN

It's not particularly historic and not all that natural, but **Harbour Town** is still pretty cool. The dominant element is the squat, colorful **Harbour Town Lighthouse Museum** (149 Lighthouse Rd., 843/671-2810, www.harbourtownlighthouse.com, daily 10am-dusk, $3), which has never really helped a ship navigate its way near the island. The 90-foot structure was built in 1970 purely to give visitors a little atmosphere, and that it does, as kids especially love climbing the stairs to the top ($2 pp) and looking out over the island's expanse.

### STONEY-BAYNARD RUINS

The **Stoney-Baynard ruins** (Plantation Dr., dawn-dusk, free), tabby ruins in a residential neighborhood, are what remains of the circa-1790 central building of the old Braddock's Point Plantation, first owned by patriot and raconteur Captain "Saucy Jack" Stoney and later by the Baynard family. Active during the island's heyday as a cotton center, the plantation was destroyed after the Civil War. Two other foundations are nearby, one for slave quarters and one whose use is still unknown.

### SEA PINES FOREST PRESERVE

The **Sea Pines Forest Preserve** (175 Greenwood Dr., 843/363-4530, free) is set amid the Sea Pines Plantation golf resort development, but you don't need a bag of clubs to enjoy this 600-acre preserve, which is built on the site of an old rice plantation (dikes and logging trails are still visible). Here you can ride a horse, fish, or just take a walk on the eight miles of trails (dawn-dusk) and enjoy the natural beauty around you. No bike riding is allowed on the trails, however.

the Audubon-Newhall Preserve

In addition to the Native American shell ring farther north off Squire Pope Road, the Sea Pines Forest Preserve also boasts a shell ring set within a canopy of tall pines. Scientists date the ring itself to about 1450 BC, although human habitation on the island goes as far back as 8000 BC.

## Tours and Cruises

Most guided tours on Hilton Head focus on the water. **Harbour Town Cruises** (843/363-9023, www.vagabondcruise.com, $30-60) offers several sightseeing tours as well as excursions to Daufuskie and Savannah. They also offer a tour on a former America's Cup racing yacht.

"Dolphin tours" are extremely popular on Hilton Head, and there is no shortage of operators. **Dolphin Watch Nature Cruises** (843/785-4558, $25 adults, $10 children) departs from Shelter Cove, as does **Lowcountry Nature Tours** (843/683-0187, www.lowcountrynaturetours.com, $40 adults, $35 children, free under age 3). The *Gypsy* (843/363-2900, www.bitemybait.com, $15 adults, $7 children) sails out of South Beach Marina, taking you all around peaceful Calibogue Sound. Two dolphin tours are based on Broad Creek, the large body of water that almost bisects the island through the middle. "Captain Jim" runs **Island Explorer Tours** (843/785-2100, www.dolphintourshiltonhead.com, two-hour tour $45 pp) from a dock behind the old Oyster Factory on Marshland Road. Not to be outdone, "Captain Dave" leads tours at **Dolphin Discoveries** (843/681-1911, two-hour tour $40 adults, $30 under age 13), leaving out of Simmons Landing next to the Broad Creek Marina on Marshland Road. **Outside Hilton Head** (843/686-6996, www.outsidehiltonhead.com) runs a variety of water ecotours and dolphin tours as well as a guided day-trip excursion to Daufuskie, complete with golf cart rental.

There is a notable land-based tour by **Gullah Heritage Trail Tours** (leaves from Coastal Discovery Museum at Honey Horn, 843/681-7066, www.gullahheritage.com, $32 adults, $15 children) delving into the island's rich, if poorly preserved, African American history from slavery through the time of the freedmen.

## ENTERTAINMENT AND NIGHTLIFE
### Nightlife

The highest-quality live entertainment on the island is at **The Jazz Corner** (1000 William Hilton Pkwy., 843/842-8620, www.thejazzcorner.com, dinner daily 6pm-9pm, late-night menu after 9pm, dinner $15-20, cover varies), which brings in the best names in the country to perform in this space in the unlikely setting of a boutique mall, the Village at Wexford. The dinners are actually quite good, but the attraction is definitely the music. Reservations are recommended. Live music starts around 7pm.

For years islanders jokingly referred to the "Barmuda Triangle," an area named for the preponderance of bars within vague walking distance of Sea Pines Circle. While some of the names have changed over the years, the longtime anchor of the Barmuda Triangle is the **Tiki Hut** (1 S. Forest Beach Dr., 843/785-5126, Sun.-Thurs. 11am-8pm, Fri.-Sat. 11am-10pm, bar until 2am), actually part of The Beach House hotel at the entrance to Sea Pines. This popular watering hole is the only beachfront bar on the island, which technically makes it the only place you can legally drink alcohol on a Hilton Head beach. Another Barmuda Triangle staple is **Hilton Head Brewing Company** (7 Greenwood Dr., 843/785-3900, daily 11am-2am), the only brewpub on the island and indeed South Carolina's first microbrewery since Prohibition. They offer a wide range of handcrafted brews, from a Blueberry Wheat to a Mocha Porter. Another Triangle fave is **The Lodge** (7 Greenwood Dr., 843/842-8966, www.hiltonheadlodge.com, daily 11:30am-midnight). After the martini and cigar craze waned, this popular spot successfully remade itself into a beer-centric place with 36 rotating taps. They still mix a mean martini, though.

Despite its location in the upscale strip mall of the Village at Wexford, the **British Open Pub** (1000 William Hilton Pkwy./Hwy. 278, 843/686-6736, daily 11am-10pm) offers a fairly convincing English vibe with, as the name suggests, a heavy golf theme. The fish-and-chips and shepherd's pie are both magnificent.

Inside Sea Pines is the **Quarterdeck Lounge and Patio** (843/842-1999, www.seapines.com, Sun.-Thurs. 5:30pm-10pm, Fri.-Sat. 5:30pm-midnight) at the base of the Harbour Town Lighthouse. This is where the party's at after a long day on the fairways during the Heritage golf tournament. Within Sea Pines at the South Beach marina is also where you'll find **The Salty Dog Cafe** (232 S. Sea Pines Dr., 843/671-2233, www.saltydog.com, lunch daily 11am-3pm, dinner daily 5pm-10pm, bar daily until 2am), one of the area's most popular institutions (some might even call it a tourist trap) and something akin to an island empire, with popular T-shirts, a gift shop, books, and an ice cream shop, all overlooking the marina. My suggestion, however, is to make the short walk to the affiliated **Wreck of the Salty Dog** (843/671-7327, daily until 2am), where the marsh views are better and the atmosphere not quite so tacky.

A gay-friendly bar on Hilton Head is **Cool Cats Lounge** (32 Palmetto Bay Rd., Mon.-Fri. 8pm-3am, Sat. 8pm-2am), with a friendly dive-bar atmosphere and a small but lively dance floor.

## Performing Arts

Because so many residents migrated here from art-savvy metropolitan areas in the Northeast, Hilton Head maintains a very high standard of top-quality entertainment. Much of the activity centers on the multimillion-dollar **Arts Center of Coastal Carolina** (14 Shelter Cove Lane, 843/842-2787, www.artshhi.com), which hosts touring shows, resident companies, musical concerts, dance performances, and visual arts exhibits.

Under the direction of maestro John Morris Russell, the **Hilton Head Symphony Orchestra** (843/842-2055, www.hhso.org) performs a year-round season of masterworks and pops programs at various venues, primarily the First Presbyterian Church (540 William Hilton Pkwy./Hwy. 278). They also take their show on the road with several concerts in Bluffton and even perform several "Symphony Under the Stars" programs at Shelter Cove. **Chamber Music Hilton Head** (www.cmhh.org) performs throughout the year with selections ranging from Brahms to Smetana at All Saints Episcopal Church (3001 Meeting St.).

## Cinema

There's an art house on Hilton Head, the charming **Coligny Theatre** (843/686-3500, www.colignytheatre.com) in the Coligny Plaza shopping center before you get to Sea Pines. For years this was the only movie theater for miles around, but it has reincarnated as a primarily indie film venue. Look for the entertaining murals by local artist Ralph Sutton. Showtimes are Monday 11:30am and

4pm, Tuesday and Friday 11:30am, 4pm, and 7pm, Wednesday-Thursday and Saturday-Sunday 4pm and 7pm.

## Festivals and Events

Late February-early March brings the **Hilton Head Wine and Food Festival** (www.hiltonheadhospitality.org), culminating in what they call "The East Coast's Largest Outdoor Public Tasting and Auction," which is generally held at the Coastal Discovery Museum at Honey Horn. Some events charge admission.

Without question, Hilton Head's premier event is the **RBC Heritage Golf Tournament** (843/671-2248, http://theheritagegolfsc.com), held each April (usually the week after the Masters) at the Harbour Town Golf Links on Sea Pines Plantation. Formerly known as the Verizon Heritage Classic, the event is South Carolina's only PGA Tour event and brings thousands of visitors to town. The entire island gets *quite* crowded during this time, so be aware.

A fun and fondly anticipated yearly event is the **Kiwanis Club Chili Cookoff** (www.hiltonheadkiwanis.org), held each October at Honey Horn on the south end. A low admission price gets you all the chili you can eat plus free antacids. All funds go to charity, and all excess chili goes to a local food bank.

Every November brings Hilton Head's second-largest event, the **Hilton Head Concours d'Elegance & Motoring Festival** (www.hhiconcours.com), a multiday event bringing together vintage car clubs from throughout the nation and culminating in a prestigious "Best of Show" competition. It started as a fund-raiser for the Hilton Head Symphony, but now people come from all over the country to see these fine vintage cars in a beautiful setting.

## SHOPS

As you'd expect, Hilton Head is a shopper's delight, with an emphasis on upscale stores and prices to match. Keep in mind that hours may be shortened in the off-season (Nov.-Mar.). Here's a rundown of the main island shopping areas in the order you'll encounter them as you enter the island.

## Shelter Cove

**Shelter Cove Towne Centre** (40 Shelter Cove Lane, www.sheltercovetownecentre), a new and repurposed former mall space, centers around a Belk anchor store and a Kroger. New retail locations are steadily opening there. The nearby **Plaza at Shelter Cove** (50 Shelter Cove Lane, www.theplazaatsheltercove.com) features a Whole Foods and the flagship location of **Outside Hilton Head** (843/686-6996, www.outsidehiltonhead.com, Mon.-Sat. 10am-5:30pm, Sun. 11am-5:30pm), a complete outdoor outfitter with a knowledgeable staff.

## Village at Wexford

Easily my favorite place to shop on Hilton Head, this well-shaded shopping center on William Hilton Parkway (Hwy. 278) hosts plenty of well-tended shops, including the foodie equipment store **Le Cookery** (843/785-7171, Mon.-Sat. 10am-6pm), the Lily Pulitzer signature women's store **S. M. Bradford Co.** (843/686-6161, Mon.-Sat. 10am-6pm) and the aromatic **Scents of Hilton Head** (843/842-7866, Mon.-Fri. 10am-6pm, Sat. 10am-5pm).

My favorite shop on all Hilton Head is at Wexford, **The Oilerie** (843/681-2722, www.oilerie.com, Mon.-Sat. 10am-7pm, Sun. noon-5pm). This franchise provides free samples of all its high-quality Italian olive oils and vinegars. After you taste around awhile, you pick what you want and the friendly staff bottles it for you in souvenir-quality glassware. They also have a selection of spices, soaps, and other goodies.

## Coligny Circle

This is the closest Hilton Head comes to funkier beach towns like Tybee Island or Folly Beach, although it doesn't really come that close. You'll find dozens of delightful and somewhat quirky stores here, many keeping long hours in the summer, like the self-explanatory **Coligny Kite & Flag Co.**

(843/785-5483, Mon.-Sat. 10am-9pm, Sun. 11am-6pm), the comprehensive and stylish **Quiet Storm Surf Shop** (843/671-2551) and **Fresh Produce** (843/842-3410, www.freshproduceclothes.com), actually a very cute women's clothing store. Kids will love both **The Shell Shop** (843/785-4900, Mon.-Sat. 10am-9pm, Sun. noon-9pm) and **Black Market Minerals** (843/785-7090, Mon.-Sat. 10am-10pm, Sun. 11am-8pm).

## Harbour Town

The **Shoppes at Harbour Town** (www.seapines.com) are a collection of about 20 mostly boutique stores along Lighthouse Road in Sea Pines Plantation. At **Planet Hilton Head** (843/363-5177, www.planethiltonhead.com, daily 10am-9pm) you'll find some cute, eclectic gifts and home goods. Other clothing highlights include **Knickers Men's Store** (843/671-2291, daily 10am-9pm) and **Radiance** (843/363-5176, Mon.-Tues. 10am-5pm, Wed.-Sat. 10am.-9pm, Sun. 11am-9pm), a very cute and fashion-forward women's store.

The **Top of the Lighthouse Shoppe** (843/671-2810, www.harbourtownlighthouse.com, daily 10am-9pm) is where many a climbing visitor has been coaxed to part with some of their disposable income. And, of course, as you'd expect being near the legendary Harbour Town links, there's the **Harbour Town Pro Shop** (843/671-4485), routinely voted one of the best pro shops in the nation.

## South Beach Marina

On South Sea Pines Drive at the marina you'll find several worthwhile shops, including a good ship's store and all-around grocery dealer **South Beach General Store** (843/671-6784, daily 8am-10pm). I like to stop in **Blue Water Bait and Tackle** (843/671-3060, daily 7am-8pm) and check out the cool nautical stuff. They can also hook you up with a variety of kayak trips and fishing charters. And, of course, right on the water there's the ever-popular **Salty Dog Cafe** (843/671-2233, www.saltydog.com, lunch daily 11am-3pm, dinner daily 5pm-10pm), whose ubiquitous T-shirts seem to adorn every other person on the island.

## Art Galleries

Despite the abundant wealth apparent in some quarters here, there's no freestanding art museum in the area, that role being filled by independent galleries. A good representative example is **Morris & Whiteside Galleries** (220 Cordillo Pkwy., 843/842-4433, www.morris-whiteside.com, Mon.-Fri. 9am-5pm, Sat. 10am-4pm), located in the historic Red Piano Art Gallery building, which features a variety of paintings and sculpture, heavy on landscapes but also showing some fine figurative work. The nonprofit **Art League of Hilton Head** (14 Shelter Cove Lane, 843/681-5060, Mon.-Sat. 10am-6pm) is located in the Walter Greer Art Gallery within the Arts Center of Coastal Carolina and displays work by member artists in all media. The **Nash Gallery** (13 Harbourside Lane, 843/785-6424, Mon.-Fri. 10am-9pm, Sat. 10am-8pm, Sun. 11am-5pm) in Shelter Cove Harbour deals more in North American craft styles. Hilton Head art isn't exactly known for its avant-garde nature, but you can find some whimsical stuff at **Picture This** (78D Arrow Rd., 843/842-5299, Mon.-Fri. 9:30am-5:30pm, Sat. 9:30am-12:30pm), including a selection of Gullah craft items. A wide range of regional painters, sculptors, and glass artists is featured at **Endangered Arts** (841 William Hilton Pkwy., 843/785-5075, www.endangeredarts.com).

## SPORTS AND ACTIVITIES

### Beaches

First, the good news: Hilton Head Island has 12 miles of some of the most beautiful, safe beaches you'll find anywhere. The bad news is that there are only a few ways to gain access, generally at locations referred to as "beach parks." Don't just drive into a residential neighborhood and think you'll be able to park and find your way to the beach; for better or worse, Hilton Head is not set up for that kind of casual access.

Driessen Beach Park has 207 long-term parking spaces, costing $0.25 for 30 minutes. There's free parking but fewer spaces at the Coligny Beach Park entrance and at Fish Haul Creek Park. Also, there are 22 metered spaces at Alder Lane Beach Access, 51 at Folly Field Beach Park, and 13 at Burkes Beach Road. Most other beach parks have permit parking only. Clean, well-maintained public restrooms are available at all the beach parks. You can find **beach information** at 843/342-4580 and www.hiltonheadislandsc.gov. Beach park hours vary: Coligny Beach Park is open daily 24 hours; all other beach parks are open March-September daily 6am-8pm and October-February daily 6am-5pm.

Alcohol is strictly prohibited on Hilton Head's beaches. There are lifeguards on all the beaches during the summer, but be aware that the worst undertow is on the northern stretches. Also remember to leave the sand dollars where they are; their population is dwindling due to souvenir hunting.

### Kayaking

Kayakers will enjoy Hilton Head Island, which offers several gorgeous routes, including Calibogue Sound to the south and west and Port Royal Sound to the north. For particularly good views of life on the salt marsh, try Broad Creek, which nearly bisects Hilton Head Island, and Skull Creek, which separates Hilton Head from the natural beauty of Pinckney Island. Broad Creek Marina is a good place to put in. There are also two public landings, Haigh Landing and Buckingham Landing, on Mackay Creek at the entrance to the island, one on either side of the bridge.

If you want a guided tour, there are plenty of great kayak tour outfits to choose from in the area. Chief among them is **Outside Hilton Head** (32 Shelter Cove Lane, 800/686-6996, www.outsidehiltonhead.com). They offer a wide range of guided trips, including

"The Outback," in which you're first boated to a private island and then taken on a tour of tidal creeks, and five- or seven-hour "Ultimate Lowcountry Day" trips to Daufuskie, Bluffton, or Bull Creek. Other good places to book a tour or just rent a kayak are **Water-Dog Outfitters** (Broad Creek Marina, 843/686-3554) and **Kayak Hilton Head** (Broad Creek Marina, 843/684-1910). Leaving out of the Harbour Town Yacht Basin is **H2O Sports** (843/671-4386, www.h2osportsonline.com), which offers 90-minute guided kayak tours ($30) and rents kayaks for about $20 per hour. Within **Palmetto Dunes Oceanfront Resort** (4 Queens Folly Rd., 800/827-3006, www.palmettodunes.com) is **Palmetto Dunes Outfitters** (843/785-2449, www.pd-outfitters.com, daily 9am-5pm), which rents kayaks and canoes and offers lessons on the resort's 11-mile-long lagoon.

### Fishing and Boating

As you'd expect, anglers and boaters love the Hilton Head-Bluffton area, which offers all kinds of saltwater, freshwater, and fly-fishing opportunities. Captain Brian Vaughn runs **Off the Hook Charters** (68 Helmsman Way, 843/298-4376, www.offthehookcharters.com), which offers fully licensed half-day trips

($400). **Miss Carolina Sportfishing** (168 Palmetto Bay Rd., 843/298-2628, www.miss-carolinafishing.com) offers deep-sea action at a little over $100 per hour. Captain Dave Fleming of **Mighty Mako Sport Fishing Charters** (164 Palmetto Bay Rd., 843/785-6028, www.mightymako.com) can take you saltwater fishing, both backwater and near-shore, on the 25-foot *Mighty Mako* for about $400 for a half-day. If you're at the South Beach Marina area of Sea Pines Plantation, head into **Blue Water Bait and Tackle** (843/671-3060) and see if they can hook you up with a trip.

Public landings in the Hilton Head area include the Marshland Road Boat Landing and the Broad Creek Boat Ramp under the Charles Fraser Bridge, and the Haigh Landing on Mackay Creek.

### Hiking and Biking

Although the very flat terrain is not challenging, Hilton Head provides some scenic and relaxing cycling opportunities. Thanks to wise planning and foresight, the island has an extensive and award-winning 50-mile network of biking trails that does a great job of keeping cyclists out of traffic. A big plus is the long bike path paralleling the William

The beach at Hilton Head has one of the most bikeable paths in the Lowcountry.

Hilton Parkway, enabling cyclists to use that key artery without braving its traffic. There is even an underground bike path beneath the parkway to facilitate crossing that busy road. In addition, there are also routes along Pope Avenue as well as North and South Forest Beach Drive. Go to www.hiltonheadisland. org/biking to download a map of the island's entire bike path network.

**Palmetto Dunes Oceanfront Resort** (4 Queens Folly Rd., 800/827-3006, www. palmettodunes.com) has a particularly nice 25-mile network of bike paths that all link up to the island's larger framework. Within the resort is **Palmetto Dunes Outfitters** (843/785-2449, www.pdoutfitters.com, daily 9am-5pm), which will rent you any type of bike you might need. Sea Pines Plantation also has an extensive 17-mile network of bike trails; you can pick up a map at most information kiosks within the plantation.

But the best bike path on Hilton Head is the simplest of all, and where no one will ask you where you're staying that night: the beach. For a few hours before and after low tide, the beach effectively becomes a 12-mile bike path around most of the island, and a pleasant morning or afternoon ride may well prove to be the highlight of your trip.

There's a plethora of bike rental facilities on Hilton Head with competitive rates. Be sure to ask if they offer free pickup and delivery. Try **Hilton Head Bicycle Company** (112 Arrow Rd., 843/686-6888, daily 9am-5pm, $16/day).

Hikers will particularly enjoy Pinckney Island National Wildlife Refuge, which takes you through several key Lowcountry ecosystems, from maritime forest to salt marsh. Other peaceful, if nonchallenging, trails are at the Audubon-Newhall Preserve.

## Horseback Riding
Within the Sea Pines Forest Preserve is **Lawton Stables** (190 Greenwood Dr., 843/671-2586, www.lawtonstableshhi.com), which features pony rides, a small-animal

farm, and guided horseback rides through the preserve. You don't need any riding experience, but you do need reservations.

## Bird-Watching
The premier birding locale in the area is the **Pinckney Island National Wildlife Refuge** (U.S. 278 east, just before Hilton Head, 912/652-4415, www.fws.gov, free). You can see bald eagles, ibis, wood storks, painted buntings, and many more species. Birding is best in spring and fall. The refuge has several freshwater ponds that serve as wading bird rookeries. During migration season, so many beautiful birds make such a ruckus that you'll think you've wandered onto an Animal Planet shoot.

## Golf
Hilton Head is one of the world's great golf centers, with no fewer than 23 courses, and one could easily write a book about nothing but that. This, however, is not that book. Perhaps contrary to what you might expect, most courses on the island are public, and some are downright affordable. All courses are 18 holes unless otherwise described; greens fees are averages and vary with season and tee time.

The best-regarded course, with prices to match, is **Harbour Town Golf Links** (Sea Pines Plantation, 843/363-4485, www.seapines.com, $239). It's on the island's south end at Sea Pines and is the home of the annual RBC Heritage Classic, far and away the island's number-one tourist draw.

There are two Arthur Hills-designed courses on the island, **Arthur Hills at Palmetto Dunes Resort** (843/785-1140, www.palmettodunes.com, $125) and **Arthur Hills at Palmetto Hall** (Palmetto Hall Plantation, 843/689-4100, www.palmettohallgolf.com, $130), both of which now offer the use of Segway vehicles on the fairways. The reasonably priced **Barony Course** at Port Royal Plantation (843/686-8801, www. portroyalgolfclub.com, $98) also boasts some of the toughest greens on the island. Another challenging and affordable course is the **George Fazio** at Palmetto Dunes Resort (843/785-1130, www.palmettodunes.com, $105).

**Hilton Head National Golf Club** (60 Hilton Head National Dr., 843/842-5900, www.golfhiltonheadnational.com), which is actually on the mainland just before you cross the bridge to Hilton Head, is still highly rated for both condition and service, despite recently losing nine holes to a road widening project. *Golf Week* has named it one of the country's best golf courses. The 18-hole course is public and green fees are below $100.

It's a good idea to book tee times through the **Golf Island Call Center** (888/465-3475, www.golfisland.com), which can also hook you up with good packages.

### Tennis

One of the top tennis destinations in the country, Hilton Head has over 20 tennis clubs, some of which offer court time to the public (walk-on rates vary; call for information). They are: **Palmetto Dunes Tennis Center** (Palmetto Dunes Resort, 843/785-1152, www.palmettodunes.com, $30 per hour), **Port Royal Racquet Club** (Port Royal Plantation, 843/686-8803, www.portroyalgolfclub.com, $25 per hour), **Sea Pines Racquet Club** (Sea Pines Plantation, 843/363-4495, www.seapines.com, $25 per hour), **South Beach Racquet Club** (Sea Pines Plantation, 843/671-2215, www.seapines.com, $25 per hour), and **Shipyard Racquet Club** (Shipyard Plantation, 843/686-8804, $25 per hour).

Free, first-come-first-served play is available at the following public courts, maintained by the Island Recreation Association (www.islandreccenter.org): **Chaplin Community Park** (Singleton Beach Rd., four courts, lighted), **Cordillo Courts** (Cordillo Pkwy., four courts, lighted), **Fairfield Square** (Adrianna Lane, two courts), **Hilton Head High School** (School Rd., six courts), and **Hilton Head Middle School** (Wilborn Rd., four courts).

### Zip Line

Billing itself as the only zip line experience within 250 miles, the new **Zip Line Hilton Head** (33 Broad Creek Marina Way, 843/682-6000, www.ziplinehiltonhead.com) offers an extensive canopy tour making great use of the area's natural scenery and features. You generally "fly" in groups of about eight. Reservations strongly encouraged. The latest offering is "Aerial Adventure," a challenging two-hour trip ($50) with about 50 obstacles.

## RESTAURANTS

Because of the cosmopolitan nature of the population, with so many transplants from the northeastern United States and Europe, there is uniformly high quality in Hilton Head restaurants. And because of another demographic quirk of the area, its large percentage of senior citizens, you can also find some great deals by looking for some of the common "early bird" dinner specials, usually starting around 5pm. That said, Hilton Head has shed its reputation as a somewhat stodgy food town and does offer some fun, cutting-edge, big-city style spots to enjoy.

### Bistro

Combining rib-sticking comfort food with hearty European style cuisine is ★ **Lucky Rooster** (841 William Hilton Pkwy., 843/681-3474, www.luckyroosterhhi.com, daily 5pm-10pm, $15). This really is one of the most vibrant and satisfying menus on the island, from the fried green tomatoes to the pan-fried sweetbread starters, to the short rib and shrimp 'n' grits and mushroom lasagna entrees. A lively full bar complements the bistro-style scene.

An upgrade of a longtime island favorite called simply Daniel's, **Crave by Daniel's** (2 N. Forest Beach Dr., 843/341-9379, http://danielshhi.com, daily 4pm-2am, $25) is now an upscale steakhouse with a twist. In addition to offering gorgeous cuts of meat like a center-cut filet mignon, they specialize in what they call "big small plates." Try a sizzling cinnamon steak kebab or a gyro pizzetta.

## Breakfast and Brunch

There are a couple of great diner-style places on the island. Though known more for its hamburgers and Philly cheesesteaks, **Harold's Diner** (641 William Hilton Pkwy., 843/842-9292, Mon.-Sat. 7am-3pm, $4-6) has great pancakes as well as its trademark brand of sarcastic service. Unpretentious and authentic in a place where those two adjectives are rarely used, it has been said of Harold's that "the lack of atmosphere *is* the atmosphere." The place is small, popular, and does not take reservations.

If you need a bite in the Coligny Plaza area, go to **Skillets** (1 N. Forest Beach Dr., 843/785-3131, www.skilletscafe.com, breakfast daily 7am-5pm, dinner daily 5pm-9pm, $5-23) in Coligny Plaza. Their eponymous stock-in-trade is a layered breakfast dish of sautéed ingredients served in a porcelain skillet, like the "Kitchen Sink" (pancakes ringed with potatoes, sausage, and bacon, topped with two poached eggs).

A great all-day breakfast place with a twist is ★ **Signe's Heaven Bound Bakery & Café** (93 Arrow Rd., 843/785-9118, www. signesbakery.com, Mon.-Fri. 8am-4pm, Sat. 9am-2pm, $5-10). Breakfast is tasty dishes like frittatas and breakfast polenta, while the twist is the extensive artisanal bakery, with delicious specialties like the signature key lime pound cake. You'll be surprised at the quality of the food for the low prices. Expect a wait during peak periods.

## German

I'm pretty sure you didn't come all the way to South Carolina to eat traditional German food, but while you're here, check out ★ **Alfred's** (807 William Hilton Pkwy./ Hwy. 278, 843/341-3117, wwww.alfredshiltonhead.com, $20-30), one of the more unique spots on Hilton Head and a big favorite with the locals. Expect a wait. Bratwurst, veal cordon bleu, and of course Wiener schnitzel are all standouts. I recommend the German Mix Platter ($25), which features a brat, some sauerbraten, and a schnitzel.

## Seafood and Southern

Honest-to-goodness Southern cookin' isn't always that easy to come by on this island full of transplants from outside the South. But a great place to find it is **A Lowcountry Backyard** (32 Palmetto Bay Rd., #4A, www.hhbackyard. com, Mon.-Sat. 11am-3pm, 4:30pm-9pm, Sat. brunch 9am-noon, Sun. brunch 9 am-3pm, $15). As the name implies, this is regional cuisine served in a relaxed and casual atmosphere fitting for island life. As with many Hilton Head establishments, it's located within a strip mall setting, the Village Exchange. That said, once you're inside you won't notice at all.

Not to be confused with Charley's Crab House next door to Hudson's, seafood lovers will enjoy the experience down near Sea Pines at ★ **Charlie's L'Etoile Verte** (8 New Orleans Rd., 843/785-9277, http://charliesgreenstar.com, lunch Tues.-Sat. 11:30am-2pm, dinner Mon.-Sat. 5:30pm-10pm, $25-40), which is considered by many connoisseurs to be Hilton Head's single best restaurant. The emphasis here is on "French country kitchen" cuisine—think Provence, not Paris. In keeping with that theme, each day's menu is concocted from scratch and handwritten. Listen to these recent entrées and feel your mouth water: flounder sauté meunière, grilled wild coho salmon with basil pesto, and breast of duck in a raspberry demi-glace. Get the picture? Of course, you'll want to start with the escargot and leeks vol-au-vent, the house pâté, or even some pan-roasted Bluffton oysters. Reservations are essential.

A longtime Hilton Head favorite is **Red Fish** (8 Archer Rd., 843/686-3388, www. redfishofhiltonhead.com, lunch Mon.-Sat. 11:30am-2pm, dinner daily beginning with early-bird specials at 5pm, $20-37). Strongly Caribbean in decor as well as menu, with romanticism and panache to match, this is a great place for couples. The creative but accessible menu by executive chef Sean Walsh incorporates unique spices, fruits, and vegetables for a fresh, zesty palette. Reservations are essential.

Fresh seafood lovers will enjoy one of

Hilton Head's staples, the huge **Hudson's on the Docks** (1 Hudson Rd., 843/681-2772, www.hudsonsonthedocks.com, lunch daily 11am-4pm, dinner daily from 5pm, $14-23) on Skull Creek just off Squire Pope Road on the less-developed north side. Much of the catch—though not all of it, by any means—comes directly off the boats you'll see dockside. Try the stuffed shrimp filled with crabmeat. Leave room for one of the homemade desserts crafted by Ms. Bessie, a 30-year veteran employee of Hudson's.

## HOTELS

Generally speaking, accommodations on Hilton Head are often surprisingly affordable given their overall high quality and the breadth of their amenities.

### Under $150

You can't beat the price at **Park Lane Hotel and Suites** (12 Park Lane, 843/686-5700, www.hiltonheadparklanehotel.com, $130). This is your basic suite-type hotel (formerly a Residence Inn) with kitchens, laundry, a pool, and a tennis court. The allure here is the price, hard to find anywhere these days at a resort location. For a nonrefundable fee, you can bring your pet. The one drawback is that the beach is a good distance away. The hotel does offer a free shuttle, however, so it would be wise to take advantage of that and avoid the usual beach-parking hassles. As you'd expect given the price, rooms here tend to go quickly; reserve early.

### $150-300

A great place for the price is the **South Beach Inn** (232 S. Sea Pines Dr., 843/671-6498, www.sbinn.com, $186) in Sea Pines. Located near the famous Salty Dog Cafe and outfitted in a similar nautical theme, the inn not only has some pretty large guest rooms for the price, it offers a great view of the marina and has a very friendly feel. As with all Sea Pines accommodations, staying on the plantation means you don't have to wait in line with other visitors to pay the $5-per-day "road fee." Sea Pines also offers a free trolley to get around the plantation.

One of Hilton Head's favorite hotels for beach lovers is **The Beach House** (1 South Forest Beach Dr., 855/474-2882, www.beachhousehhi.com, $200), formerly the Holiday Inn Oceanfront and home of the famed Tiki Hut bar on the beach. Staff turnover is less frequent here than at other local accommodations, and while it's no Ritz-Carlton and

The Beach House boasts the only beachfront bar on Hilton Head.

occasionally shows signs of wear, it's a good value in a bustling area of the island.

One of the better resort-type places for those who prefer the putter and the racquet to the Frisbee and the surfboard is the **Inn and Club at Harbour Town** (7 Lighthouse Lane, 843/363-8100, www.seapines.com, $199) in Sea Pines. The big draw here is the impeccable service, delivered by a staff of "butlers" in kilts, mostly Europeans who take the venerable trade quite seriously. While it's not on the beach, you can take advantage of the free Sea Pines Trolley every 20 minutes.

Recently rated the number-one family resort in the United States by *Travel + Leisure,* the well-run ★ **Palmetto Dunes Oceanfront Resort** (4 Queens Folly Rd., 800/827-3006, www.palmettodunes.com, $150-300) offers something for everybody in terms of lodging. There are small, cozy condos by the beach or larger villas overlooking the golf course and pretty much everything in between. The prices are perhaps disarmingly affordable considering the relative luxury and copious recreational amenities, which include 25 miles of very well-done bike trails, 11 miles of kayak and canoe trails, and, of course, three signature links. As with most developments of this type on Hilton Head, most of the condos

are privately owned, and therefore each has its own particular set of guidelines and cleaning schedules.

A little farther down the island you'll find the **Sonesta Resort** (130 Shipyard Dr., 843/842-2400, www.sonesta.com/hiltonhead-island, $160-200), which styles itself as Hilton Head's only green-certified accommodations. The guest rooms are indeed state-of-the-art, and the expansive, shaded grounds near the beach are great for relaxation. No on-site golf here, but immediately adjacent is a well-regarded tennis facility with 20 courts.

Another good resort-style experience heavy on the golf is on the grounds of the Port Royal Plantation on the island's north side, **The Westin Resort Hilton Head Island** (2 Grasslawn Ave., 843/681-4000, www.westin.com/hiltonhead, from $200), which hosts three PGA-caliber links. The beach is also but a short walk away. This AAA four diamond-winning Westin offers a mix of suites and larger villas.

## Vacation Rentals

Many visitors to Hilton Head choose to rent a home or villa for an extended stay, and there is no scarcity of availability. Try **Resort Rentals of Hilton Head** (www.hhivacations.

Sonesta Resort

com) or **Destination Vacation** (www.destinationvacationhhi.com).

# TRANSPORTATION AND SERVICES

The best place to get information on Hilton Head, book a room, or secure a tee time is just as you come onto the island at the **Hilton Head Island Chamber of Commerce Welcome Center** (100 William Hilton Pkwy., 843/785-3673, www.hiltonheadisland.org, daily 9am-6pm).

## Air

A few years back, the **Savannah/Hilton Head International Airport** (SAV, 400 Airways Ave., Savannah, 912/964-0514, www.savannahairport.com) added Hilton Head to its name specifically to identify itself with that lucrative market. The move has been a success, and this facility remains the closest large airport to Hilton Head Island and Bluffton. However, it's not actually *that* close: Keep in mind that when your plane touches down in Savannah, you're still about a 45-minute drive to Hilton Head proper. From the airport, go north on I-95 into South Carolina, and take exit 8 onto U.S. 278 east.

There is a local regional airport as well, the **Hilton Head Island Airport** (HXD, 120 Beach City Rd., 843/689-5400, www.bcgov.net). While attractive and convenient, keep in mind that it only hosts propeller-driven commuter planes because of the runway length and concerns about noise.

## Car

Hilton Head is about 30 minutes from I-95. If you're entering the area by car, the best route is exit 8 off I-95 onto U.S. 278, which takes you by Bluffton and right into Hilton Head. Near Bluffton, U.S. 278 is called Fording Island Road, and on Hilton Head proper it becomes the William Hilton Parkway business route.

Hilton Head Islanders have long referred to their island as the "shoe" and speak of driving to the toe or going to the heel. If you take a look at a map, you'll see why: Hilton Head bears an uncanny resemblance to a running shoe pointed toward the southwest, with the aptly named Broad Creek forming a near facsimile of the Nike "swoosh" symbol.

Running the length and circumference of the shoe is the main drag, U.S. 278 Business (William Hilton Parkway), which crosses onto Hilton Head right at the "tongue" of the shoe, a relatively undeveloped area. The Cross Island Parkway toll route (U.S. 278), beginning up toward the ankle as you first get on the island, is a quicker route straight to the toe near Sea Pines.

While it is technically the business spur, when locals say "278" they're talking about the William Hilton Parkway. It takes you along the entire sole of the shoe, including the beaches, and on down to the toe, where you'll find a usually-crowded British-style roundabout called Sea Pines Circle. It's also the site of the Harbour Town Marina and the island's oldest planned development, Sea Pines Plantation.

## Getting Around

While making your way around the island, always keep in mind that the bulk of it consists of private developments, and local law enforcement frowns on people who aimlessly wander among the condos and villas.

Other than taxi services, there is no public transportation to speak of in Hilton Head, unless you want to count the free shuttle around Sea Pines Plantation. Taxi services include **Yellow Cab** (843/686-6666), **Island Taxi** (843/683-6363), and **Ferguson Transportation** (843/842-8088).

# Bluffton and Daufuskie Island

Just outside Hilton Head are two of the Lowcountry's true gems, Bluffton and Daufuskie Island. While Bluffton's outskirts have been taken over by the same gated community and upscale strip mall sprawl spreading throughout the coast, at its core is a delightfully charming little community on the quiet May River, now called Old Bluffton, where you'd swear you just entered a time warp.

Daufuskie Island still maintains much of its age-old isolated, timeless personality, and the island—still accessible only by boat—is still one of the spiritual centers of the Gullah culture and lifestyle.

## ★ OLD TOWN BLUFFTON

Similar to Beaufort, but even quieter and smaller, historic Bluffton is an idyllic village on the banks of the serene and well-preserved May River. Bluffton was the original hotbed of secession, with Charleston diarist Mary Chesnut famously referring to the town as "the center spot of the fire eaters." During their Civil War occupation, Union troops repaid the favor of those original Bluffton secessionists, which is why only nine homes in Bluffton are of antebellum vintage; the rest were torched in a search for Confederate guerrillas.

The center of tourist activity focuses on "Old Town," the **Old Bluffton Historic District,** several blocks of 1800s-vintage buildings clustered between the parallel Boundary and Calhoun Streets (old-timers sometimes call this "the original square mile"). Many of the buildings are private residences, but most have been converted into art studios and antiques stores.

There are two basic parts of Old Town: The area nearest the May River itself, with Calhoun Street as the main axis; and the area just north of May River Road, usually called "The Promenade." While a much newer development, The Promenade is still frequented by locals and has a lot of the same friendly feel

as the more historic area a few blocks to the south.

While its outskirts (so-called "Greater Bluffton") are now a haven for planned communities hoping to mimic some aspect of Bluffton's historic patina, the town itself remains an authentic look at old South Carolina. Development has officially discovered Bluffton, which is considered more and more to be part of the Hilton Head metro area. But Old Town is still a pocket of comparative relaxation. Enjoy it while you can.

### Heyward House Historic Center

The **Heyward House Historic Center** (70 Boundary St., 843/757-6293, www.heyward-house.org, Mon.-Fri. 10am-5pm, Sat. 10am-4pm, tours $5 adults, $2 students) is not only open to tours but also serves as Bluffton's visitors center. Built in 1840 as a summer home for the owner of Moreland Plantation, John Cole, the house was later owned by George Cuthbert Heyward, grandson of Declaration of Independence signer Thomas Heyward. (Remarkably, it stayed in the family until the 1990s.) Of note are the intact slave quarters on the grounds.

The Heyward House also sponsors walking tours of the historic district (843/757-6293, $15, by appointment only). Download your own walking tour map at www.heyward-house.org.

### Church of the Cross

Don't fail to go all the way to the end of Calhoun Street, as it dead-ends on a high bluff on the May River at the Bluffton Public Dock. Overlooking this peaceful marsh-front vista is the photogenic **Church of the Cross** (110 Calhoun St., 843/757-2661, www.the-churchofthecross.net, free tours Mon.-Sat. 10am-2pm). The current sanctuary was built in 1854 and is one of only two local churches

## Bluffton Oyster Company

You might want to get a gander at the state's last remaining working oyster house, the **Bluffton Oyster Company** (63 Wharf St., 843/757-4010, www.blufftonoyster.com, Mon.-Sat. 9am-5:30pm), and possibly purchase some of their maritime bounty. Larry and Tina Toomer continue to oversee the oyster-harvesting-and-shucking family enterprise, which has roots going back to the early 1900s.

## SHOPS

Bluffton's eccentric little art studios, most clustered in a two-block stretch on Calhoun Street, are by far its main shopping draw. Named for the Lowcountry phenomenon you find in the marsh at low tide among the fiddler crabs, Bluffton's **Pluff Mudd Art** (27 Calhoun St., 843/757-5551, Mon.-Sat. 10am-5:30pm) is a cooperative of 16 great young painters and photographers from throughout the area. The **Guild of Bluffton Artists** (20 Calhoun St., 843/757-5590, Mon.-Sat. 10am-4:30pm) features works from many local artists, as does the outstanding **Society of Bluffton Artists** (48 Boundary St., 843/757-6586, Mon.-Sat. 10am-5pm, Sun. 11:30am-3pm). For cool, custom handcrafted pottery, try **Preston Pottery**

the Church of the Cross in Bluffton

not burned in the Civil War. The parish itself began in 1767, with the first services on this spot held in the late 1830s. While the church looks as if it were made of cypress, it's actually constructed of heart pine.

Enjoy fresh May River oysters at Bluffton Oyster Company.

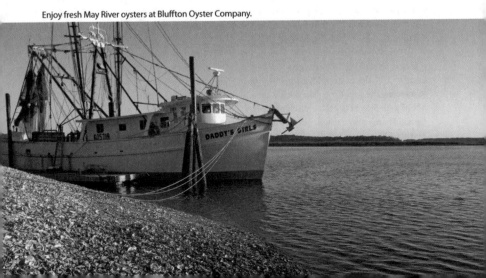

and Gallery (10 Church St., 843/757-3084, Tues.-Sat. 10am-5pm). Another great Bluffton place is the hard-to-define Eggs'n'tricities (71 Calhoun St., 843/757-3446, Mon.-Sat. 10am-5pm). The name pretty much says it all for this fun and eclectic vintage, junk, jewelry, and folk art store.

If you want to score some fresh local seafood for your own culinary adventure, the no-brainer choice is the Bluffton Oyster Company (63 Wharf St., 843/757-4010, Mon.-Sat. 9am-5:30pm), the state's only active oyster facility. They also have shrimp, crab, clams, and fish, nearly all of it from the nearly pristine May River on whose banks the facility sits.

For a much more commercially intense experience, head just outside of town on U.S. 278 on the way to Hilton Head to find the dual Tanger Outlet Centers (1414 Fording Island Rd., 843/837-4339, Mon.-Sat. 10am-9pm, Sun. 11am-6pm), an outlet-shopper's paradise with virtually every major brand represented.

## SPORTS AND ACTIVITIES

A key kayaking outfitter in Bluffton is Native Guide Kayak Tours (8 2nd St., 843/757-5411, www.nativeguidetours.com), which features tours of the May and New Rivers led by native Ben Turner. Another good outfit is Swamp Girls Kayak Tours (843/784-2249, www.swampgirls.com), the labor of love of Sue Chapman and Cheryl Longshore.

To put in your own kayak or canoe on the scenic, well-preserved May River, go to the Alljoy Landing at the eastern terminus of Alljoy Road along the river. Or try the dock at the end of Calhoun Street near the Church of the Holy Cross. There's also a rough put-in area at the Bluffton Oyster Company (63 Wharf St.), which has a public park adjacent to it. For fishing, public landings include the dock on Calhoun Street, Alljoy Landing, and Bluffton Oyster Company.

The closest public golf courses to Bluffton are the Arnold Palmer-designed Crescent Pointe Golf Club (1 Crescent Pointe Dr., 888/292-7778, www.crescentpointegolf.com, $90) and the nine-hole Old Carolina Golf Club (89 Old Carolina Rd., 888/785-7274, www.oldcarolinagolf.com, $26), certainly one of the best golf deals in the region.

## RESTAURANTS
### American

Probably the single most popular place in Bluffon is the friendly Old Town Dispensary (15 Captains Cove, 843/837-1893, daily 11am-2am, $15-25), just off the Calhoun Street center of activity. This is an outstanding place to go for some cut-above pub/bar food or casual drinks, with plenty of outdoor seating and usually some live music going on.

Another very popular casual spot in Old Town, and frequented by many locals, is Captain Woody's Bar & Grill (17 State of Mind St., 843/757-6222, $10-15). Unpretentious and friendly, this is a good place to enjoy a burger and a beer in a relaxed, patio-style environment with plenty going on around you.

### Breakfast and Brunch

No discussion of Bluffton cuisine is complete without the famous Squat 'n' Gobble (1231 May River Rd., 843/757-4242, daily 24 hours), a local phenomenon not to be confused with a similarly named chain of eateries in California. Long a site of gossiping and politicking as well as, um, squatting and gobbling, this humble diner on May River Road is an indelible part of the local consciousness.

### Coffee

If you're looking for a coffeehouse in Old Town, go no farther than ★ Corner Perk (1297 May River Rd., Fording Island Rd., 843/816-5674, Fri.-Sat. 7am-11pm, Tues.-Thurs. 7am-4pm., Sun. brunch 7am-4pm, $10-20) in The Promenade, just off the main drag. Their coffee is truly wonderful, and the sandwich-heavy lunch menu compares with anything else in town. Upstairs is The Roasting Room, a more upscale, full-service bourbon bar.

### French

Most dining in Bluffton is pretty casual, but you'll get the white tablecloth treatment at **Claude & Uli's Signature Bistro** (1533 Fording Island Rd., 843/837-3336, lunch Mon.-Fri. 11:30am-2:30pm, dinner Mon.-Sat. from 5pm, $18-25) just outside of town in Moss Village. Chef Claude does a great veal cordon bleu as well as a number of fine seafood entrées, such as an almond-crusted tilapia and an excellent seafood pasta. Don't miss their specialty soufflé for dessert; order it with dinner, as it takes almost half an hour to bake.

## Mexican

My favorite restaurant in Bluffton is ★ **Mi Tierra** (101 Mellichamp Center, 843/757-7200, lunch daily 11am-4pm, dinner Mon.-Fri. 4pm-9pm, Sat.-Sun. 4pm-10pm, $3-15). They serve very high-quality but unpretentious Tex-Mex-style food in a fun atmosphere at great prices.

## HOTELS
### Under $150

A quality bargain stay right between Bluffton and Hilton Head is the **Holiday Inn Express Bluffton** (35 Bluffton Rd., 843/757-2002, www.ichotelsgroup.com, $120), on U.S.

278 as you make the run onto Hilton Head proper. It's not close to the beach or to Old Town Bluffton, so you'll definitely be using your car, but its central location will appeal to those who want to keep their options open.

### Over $300

For an ultra-upscale spa and golf resort environment near Bluffton, the clear pick is the **Inn at Palmetto Bluff** (19 Village Park Square, 843/706-6500, www.palmettobluffresort.com, $650-900) just across the May River. This auberge property was picked recently as the number-two U.S. resort by *Condé Nast Traveler* magazine. Lodging is dispersed among a series of cottages and "village home" rentals. There are three top-flight dining options on the grounds: the fine-dining **River House Restaurant** (843/706-6542, breakfast daily 7am-11am, lunch or "porch" menu daily 11am-10pm, dinner daily 6pm-10pm, $30-40); the **May River Grill** (Tues.-Sat. 11am-4pm, $9-13) at the golf clubhouse; and the casual **Buffalo's** (843/706-6630, Sun.-Tues. 11:30am-5pm, Wed.-Sat. 11:30am-9pm, $10-15).

the famous Squat 'n' Gobble restaurant

## TRANSPORTATION

To make the 40-minute drive to Bluffton from Beaufort, take Highway 170 south to U.S. 278 east. Bluffton is a short 15 minutes away from Hilton Head, taking U.S. 278 west.

## DAUFUSKIE ISLAND

Sitting between Savannah and Hilton Head Island and accessible only by water, Daufuskie Island—pronounced "da-FUSK-ee"—has about 500 full-time residents, most of whom ride around on golf carts or bikes (there's only one paved road, Haig Point Road, and cars are a rare sight), and all of whom are very laid-back. Once the home of rice and indigo plantations and rich oyster beds—the latter destroyed by pollution and overharvesting—the two upscale residential resort communities on the island, begun in the 1980s, give a clue as to where the future might lie, although the recent global economic downturn, perhaps thankfully, slowed development to a standstill.

The area of prime interest to visitors is the unincorporated western portion, or **Historic District,** the old stomping grounds of Pat Conroy during his stint as a teacher of resident African American children. His old one-room schoolhouse of *The Water is Wide* fame, the **Mary Field School,** is still here, as is the adjacent 140-year-old **Union Baptist Church,** but Daufuskie students now have a surprisingly modern new facility (middle school students are still ferried to mainland schools every day). Farther north on Haig Point Road is the new **Billie Burn Museum,** housed in the old Mt. Carmel Church and named after the island's resident historian. On the southern end you'll find the **Bloody Point Lighthouse,** named for the vicious battle fought nearby during the Yamasee War of 1815 (the light was actually moved inland in the early 1900s). Other areas of interest throughout the island include Native American sites, tabby ruins, the old Baptist Church, and a couple cemeteries.

Download a very well-done, free self-guided tour of Daufuskie's historic sites at www.hiltonheadisland.org; look for the "Robert Kennedy Historic Trail Guide" (not a nod to the former attorney general and U.S. senator, but a longtime island resident and historian).

The **Melrose Beach Golf Club** (55 Avenue of the Oaks, 888/851-4971, www.melroseonthebeach.com) is an iteration of the long-troubled Melrose golf resort that recently went through an extended bankruptcy. As of this writing its future seemed in dire jeopardy and at some point it will likely become residences.

For overnight stays, you can rent a humble but cozy cabin at **Freeport Marina** (843/785-8242, $100-150, golf cart $60 extra per day), near the ferry dock and overlooking the water. There are vacation rental options island-wide as well; go to www.daufuskieislandrentals.com for info on a wide variety of offerings. Sorry, no camping available!

There are no grocery stores as commonly understood on Daufuskie, only a couple of general store-type places. So if you've booked a vacation rental, most grocery items will need to be brought in with you.

For the freshest island seafood, check out the **Old Daufuskie Crab Company** (Freeport Marina, 843/785-6652, daily 11:30am-9pm, $8-22). The deviled crab is the house specialty. The other place to dine out on the island is **Marshside Mama's** (15 Haig Pt. Rd., 843/785-4755, www.marshsidemamas.com, hours change frequently, $10-15), a laid-back spot to enjoy grouper, gumbo, and Lowcountry boil, and frequent live music. Reservations strongly encouraged.

For hand-crafted island art, go to **Iron Fish Gallery** (168 Benjies Point Rd., 843/842-9448, call ahead for hours), featuring the work of Chase Allen. His "coastal sculptures" include fanciful depictions of fish, stingrays, and even mermaids.

### Transportation and Services

The main public ferry between Daufuskie and Hilton Head is **Calibogue Cruises** (18 Simmons Rd., 843/342-8687, www.

# Who Are the Gullah?

A language, a culture, and a people with a shared history, Gullah is more than that—it's also a state of mind. Simply put, the Gullah are African Americans of the Sea Islands of South Carolina and Georgia. (In Georgia, the term *Geechee,* from the nearby Ogeechee River, is more or less interchangeable.) Protected from outside influence by the isolation of this coastal region after the Civil War, Gullah culture is the closest living cousin to the West African traditions of those imported to this country as slaves.

While you might hear that *Gullah* is a corruption of "Angola," some linguists think it simply means "people" in a West African language. In any case, the Gullah speak what is known as a creole language, meaning one derived from several sources. Gullah combines elements of Elizabethan English, Jamaican patois, and several West African dialects; for example "goober" (peanut) comes from the Congo *n'guba.* Another creole element is a word with multiple uses; for example, Gullah's *shum* could mean "see them," "see him," "see her," or "see it" in either past or present tense, depending on context. Several white writers in the 1900s published collections of Gullah folk tales, but it wasn't until later linguistic research was done that the Gullah tongue was recognized as something more than just broken English. Lorenzo Dow Turner's groundbreaking *Africanisms in the Gullah Dialect,* published in 1949, traced elements of the language to Sierra Leone in West Africa and more than 300 Gullah words directly to Africa.

Gullah is typically spoken very rapidly, which of course only adds to its impenetrability to the outsider. Gullah also relies on colorful turns of phrase. *"E tru mout"* ("He true mouth") means the speaker is referring to someone who doesn't lie. *"Ie een crack muh teet"* ("I didn't even crack my teeth") means "I kept quiet." A forgetful Gullah speaker might say, *"Mah head leab me"* ("My head left me").

Gullah music, as practiced by the world-famous Hallelujah Singers of St. Helena Island, also uses many distinctly African techniques, such as call-and-response (the folk hymn "Michael Row the Boat Ashore" is a good example). The most famous Americans with Gullah roots are boxer Joe Frazier (Beaufort), hip-hop star Jazzy Jay (Beaufort), NFL great Jim Brown (St. Simons Island, Georgia), and Supreme Court Justice Clarence Thomas (Pin Point, Georgia, near Savannah).

Upscale development continues to claim more and more traditional Gullah areas, generally by pricing the Gullah out through rapidly increasing property values. Today, the major pockets of living Gullah culture in South Carolina are in Beaufort, St. Helena Island, Daufuskie Island, Edisto Island, and a northern section of Hilton Head Island.

The old ways are not as prevalent as they were, but several key institutions are keeping alive the spirit of Gullah: the **Penn Center** (16 Martin Luther King Dr., St. Helena, 843/838-2474, www.penncenter.com, Mon.-Sat. 11am-4pm, $4 adults, $2 seniors and children) on St. Helena Island near Beaufort; the **Avery Research Center** (66 George St., Charleston, 843/953-7609, www.cofc.edu/avery, Mon.-Fri. 10am-5pm, Sat. noon-5pm) at the College of Charleston; and **Geechee Kunda** (622 Ways Temple Rd., Riceboro, Georgia, 912/884-4440, www.geecheekunda.com) near Midway off U.S. 17.

daufuskiefreeport.com). Taking off from Broad Creek Marina on Hilton Head, the pleasant short ride—a half hour each way—brings you in on the landward side of the island. Cost is $33 per person round trip, or $64 per person round trip including a meal at the Old Daufuskie Crab Company and a golf cart rental. Ferries run three times a day Mondays, Wednesdays, and Fridays, and twice a day Tuesdays, Thursdays, Saturdays, and Sundays. Ferry reservations are essential!

While the ferry trip and many vacation rentals include the rental of a golf cart, for *a la carte* service—get it?—rent one near Freeport Marina by calling 843/342-8687 (rates vary but hover around $30 per person per day). As the amount of golf carts is limited, I strongly recommend reserving yours in advance. All standard rules of the road apply, including needing a valid driver's license.

# Points Inland

It's likely that at some point you'll find yourself traveling inland from Beaufort, given that area's proximity to I-95. While this area is generally more known for offering interstate drivers a bite to eat and a place to rest their heads, there are several spots worth checking out in their own right, especially Walterboro and the Savannah National Wildlife Refuge.

## WALTERBORO

The very picture of the slow, moss-drenched Lowcountry town—indeed, the municipal logo is the silhouette of a live oak tree—Walterboro is a delightful, artsy oasis. Right off I-95, Walterboro serves as a gateway of sorts to the Lowcountry, and the cheap commercial sprawl on the interstate shows it. But don't be put off by this ugliness—once you get into town it's as charming as they come, with roots dating back to 1783.

Walterboro is chiefly known to the world at large for being one of the best antiquing locales on the East Coast. Indeed, many of the high-dollar antique shops on Charleston's King Street actually do their picking right here in the local stores, selling their finds at a significant markup in Charleston! (Another advantage Walterboro antiques shopping has over Charleston: plenty of free parking.)

Convenient and walkable, the two-block **Arts and Antiques District** on Washington Street centers on more than a dozen antiques and collectible stores, interspersed with a few gift shops and eateries. The best shop, though by no means the only one you should check out, is **Bachelor Hill Antiques** (255 E. Washington St., 843/549-1300, Mon.-Sat. 9am-6pm, Sun. 9am-4pm), which has several rooms packed with interesting and unique items, from collectibles to furniture to most everything in between.

Walterboro is about a 45-minute drive from Beaufort. Take U.S. 21 north to I-95, then take exit 53 or 57. Walterboro is about an hour's drive from Charleston or Savannah.

## Sights

### ★ SOUTH CAROLINA ARTISANS CENTER

If you're in town, don't miss the **South Carolina Artisans Center** (334 Wichman St., 843/549-0011, www.scartisanscenter.com, Mon.-Sat. 9am-5pm, Sun. 1pm-5pm, free), an expansive and vibrant collection of the best work of local and regional painters, sculptors, jewelers, and other craftspeople, for sale and for enjoyment. Imagine a big-city folk art gallery, except without the pretension, and you get the idea. You can find most any genre represented here, including jewelry, watercolors, shawls, photography, and sweetgrass baskets. The Artisans Center hosts numerous receptions, and every third Saturday of the month they hold live artist demonstrations 11am-3pm.

### MUSEUMS

Walterboro boasts three small museums. The relocated and upgraded **Colleton Museum** (506 E. Washington St., 843/549-2303, www.cm-fm.org, Tues. noon-6pm, Wed.-Fri. 10am-5pm, Sat. 10am-2pm, free) is one of the best examples of a small-town museum you're likely to find anywhere. It has a lot of surprisingly well-curated exhibits about local history, from Native American days through the colonial and Civil War periods through the present day. Adjacent is the Farmers Market, open from May until the end of October on Tuesdays 2pm-6pm and on Saturdays 10am-2pm.

The **Bedon-Lucas House Museum** (205 Church St., 843/549-9633, Thurs.-Sat. 1pm-4pm, $3 adults, free under age 8) was built by a local planter in 1820. An example of the local style of "high house," built off the ground to escape mosquitoes and catch the breeze, the house today is a nice mix of period furnishings and unadorned simplicity.

The **Slave Relic Museum** (208 Carn St., 843/549-9130, www.slaverelics.org, by appointment, $6 adults, $5 children) houses the Center for Research and Preservation of the African American Culture. It features artifacts, photos, and documents detailing the Atlantic passage, slave life, and the Underground Railroad.

### TUSKEGEE AIRMEN MEMORIAL

Yes, the Tuskegee Airmen of World War II fame were from Alabama, not South Carolina. But a contingent trained in Walterboro, at the site of the present-day **Lowcountry Regional Airport** (537 Aviation Way, 843/549-2549) a short ways south of downtown on U.S. 17. Today, on a publicly accessible, low-security area of the airport stands the **Tuskegee Airmen Memorial,** an outdoor monument to these brave flyers. There's a bronze statue and several interpretive exhibits.

### GREAT SWAMP SANCTUARY

A short way out of town in the other direction is the **Great Swamp Sanctuary** (www.thegreatswamp.org, daily dawn-dusk, free), a still-developing ecotourism project focusing on the Lowcountry environment. Located in one of the few braided-creek habitats accessible to the public, the 842-acre sanctuary has three miles of walking and biking trails, some along the path of the old Charleston-Savannah stagecoach route. Kayakers and canoeists can paddle more than two miles of winding creeks. There are three entry points to the Great Swamp Sanctuary, all off Jefferies Boulevard. In west-to-east order from I-95: north onto Beach Road, north onto Detreville Street (this is considered the main entrance), and west onto Washington Street.

## Festivals and Events

In keeping with South Carolina's tradition of towns hosting annual events to celebrate signature crops and products, Walterboro's **Colleton County Rice Festival** (http://thericefestival.org, free) happens every April. There's a parade, live music, a 5K run, and the crowning of the year's "Rice Queen," and you just might find yourself learning something about the unique coastal lifestyle built around this ultimate cash crop of the early South.

## Restaurants

The story of food in Walterboro revolves around ★ **Duke's Barbecue** (949 Robertson Blvd., 843/549-1446, $7), one of the best-regarded barbecue spots in the Lowcountry and one of the top two joints named "Duke's" in the state (the other, by common consensus, is in Orangeburg). The pulled pork is delectable, cooked with the

Walterboro's downtown is an antique shopper's treat.

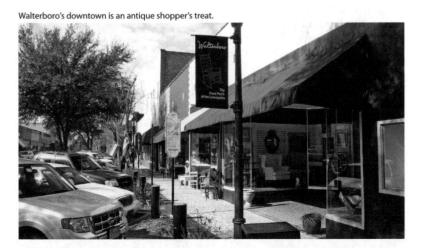

# Tuskegee Airmen in Walterboro

In a state where all too often African American history is studied in the context of slavery, a refreshing change is the tale of the Tuskegee Airmen, one of the most lauded American military units of World War II. Though named for their origins at Alabama's Tuskegee Institute, the pilots of the famed 332nd Fighter Group actually completed their final training in South Carolina at Walterboro Army Airfield, where the regional airport now sits.

The U.S. military was segregated during World War II, with African Americans mostly relegated to support roles. An interesting exception was the case of the 332nd, formed in 1941 as the 99th Pursuit Squadron by an act of Congress and the only all-black flying unit in the American military at the time. For the most part flying P-47 Thunderbolts and P-51 Mustangs, the pilots of the 332nd had one of the toughest missions of the war: escorting bombers over the skies of Germany and protecting them from Luftwaffe fighters. Though initially viewed with skepticism, the Tuskegee Airmen wasted no time in proving their mettle.

In fact, it wasn't long before U.S. bomber crews—who were, needless to say, all white—specifically requested that they be escorted by the airmen, who were given the nickname "Red-tail Angels" because of the distinctive markings of their aircraft. While legend has it that the 332nd never lost a bomber, this claim has been debunked. But as Tuskegee Airman Bill Holloman said, "The Tuskegee story is about pilots who rose above adversity and discrimination and opened a door once closed to black America, not about whether their record is perfect." The 332nd's reputation for aggressiveness in air combat was so widely known that the Germans also had a nickname for them—*Schwartze Vogelmenschen*, or "Black Birdmen."

Today Walterboro honors the Airmen with a monument on the grounds of the Lowcountry Regional Airport, on U.S. 17 just northeast of town. In an easily accessible part of the airport grounds, the monument features a bronze statue and several interpretive exhibits. Another place to catch up on Tuskegee Airmen history is at the **Colleton Museum** (506 E. Washington St., 843/549-2303, www.colletonmuseum.com, Tues. noon-6pm, Wed.-Fri. 10am-5pm, Sat. 10am-2pm, free), which has a permanent exhibit on the pilots and their history in the Walterboro area.

Walterboro Army Airfield's contribution to the war effort was not limited to the Tuskegee Airmen. Seven of the famed Doolittle Raiders were trained here, there was a compound for holding German prisoners of war, and it was also the site of the U.S. military's largest camouflage school.

indigenous South Carolina mustard-based sauce. Unlike most area barbecue restaurants, some attention is devoted to the veggies, such as collard greens, green beans, and black-eyed peas with rice.

## Hotels

If you're looking for big-box lodging, the section of Walterboro close to I-95 is chockablock with it. The quality is surprisingly good, perhaps because they tend to cater to Northerners on their way to and from Florida. A good choice is **Holiday Inn Express & Suites** (1834 Sniders Hwy., 843/538-2700, www.hi-express.com, $85), or try the **Comfort Inn & Suites** (97 Downs Lane, 843/538-5911, www.choicehotels.com, $95).

If you'd like something with a bit more character, there are two B&Bs on Hampton Street downtown. **Old Academy Bed & Breakfast** (904 Hampton St., 843/549-3232, www.oldacademybandb.com, $80-115) has four guest rooms housed in Walterboro's first school building. They offer a full continental breakfast. Note that credit cards are not accepted. Although built recently (by local standards), the 1912 **Hampton House Bed and Breakfast** (500 Hampton St., 843/542-9498, www.hamptonhousebandb.com, $125-145) has three well-appointed guest rooms and offers a full country breakfast. By appointment only, you can see the Forde Doll and Dollhouse Collection, with over 50 dollhouses and oodles of antique dolls.

## HARDEEVILLE

For most travelers, Hardeeville is known for its plethora of low-budget lodging and garish fireworks stores at the intersection of I-95 and U.S. 17. Truth be told, that's about all that's here. However, train buffs will enjoy getting a gander at the rare and excellently restored **Narrow Gauge Locomotive** near the intersection of U.S. 17 and Highway 46. Donated by the Argent Lumber Company in 1960, Engine No. 7 memorializes the role of the timber industry in the area.

Hardeeville is about a half-hour drive from both Beaufort and Savannah, at the intersection of I-95 and U.S. 17.

### Restaurants

If you're hungry in Hardeeville, go straight to ★ **Mi Tierrita** (U.S. 17 and I-95, 843/784-5011, $5), an excellent, authentic Mexican restaurant near the confluence of I-95 and U.S. 17. It's pretty beat-up on the inside, but the food is delicious and many steps above the typical watered-down Tex-Mex you find in the Southeast.

If barbecue is your thing, go on Highway 170A on the "backside" of Hardeeville in the hamlet of Levy to **The Pink Pig** (3508 S. Okatie Hwy., 843/784-3635, www.the-pink-pig.com, Tues.-Wed. and Sat. 11am-3pm, Thurs.-Fri. 11am-3pm and 5pm-7pm, $5-15).

They offer three sauces: honey mustard, spicy, and "Gullah." The place is surprisingly hip, with good music piped in and a suitably cutesy, kid-friendly decor with plenty of the eponymous rosy porcine figures.

## SAVANNAH NATIONAL WILDLIFE REFUGE

Roughly equally divided between Georgia and South Carolina, the sprawling, 30,000-acre **Savannah National Wildlife Refuge** (912/652-4415, www.fws.gov/savannah, daily dawn-dusk, free) is one of the premier bird-watching and nature-observing locales in the Southeast. The system of dikes and paddy fields once used to grow rice now helps make this an attractive stopover for migrating birds. Bird-watching is best October-April. While you can kayak on your own on miles of creeks, you can also call **Swamp Girls Kayak Tours** (843/784-2249, www.swampgirls.com), who work out of nearby Hardeeville, for a guided tour. The wildlife refuge is about 20 minutes from Savannah, two hours from Charleston, and an hour from Beaufort. To get here, take exit 5 off I-95 onto U.S. 17. Go south to U.S. 170 and look for Laurel Hill Wildlife Drive. Be sure to stop by the brand-new **visitors center** (off U.S. 170 at Laurel Hill Wildlife Drive, Mon.-Sat. 9am-4:30pm).

a resident of the Savannah National Wildlife Refuge

# Savannah

# Rarely has a city owed so much to the vision of one person than Savannah owes to General James Edward Oglethorpe.

Given the mission by King George II of England to buffer Charleston from the Spanish, this reformer had a far more sweeping vision in mind. After befriending the local Creek people, Oglethorpe laid out his settlement in a deceptively simple plan that is still studied the world over as a model of nearly perfect urban design. Many of his other progressive ideas—such as prohibiting slavery and hard liquor, to name two—soon went by the wayside. But the legacy of his original plan lives on.

Savannah was built as a series of rectangular "wards," each constructed around a central square. As the city grew, each square took on its own characteristics, depending on who lived on the square and how they made their livelihood. Sounds simple—and it is. That's why its effectiveness has lasted so long.

It is this individuality that is so well documented in John Berendt's *Midnight in the Garden of Good and Evil*. The squares of Savannah's downtown—since 1965 a National Landmark Historic District—are also responsible for the city's walkability, another defining characteristic. Just as cars entering a square must yield to traffic already within, pedestrians are obliged to slow down and interact with the surrounding environment, both constructed and natural. You become participant and audience simultaneously, a feat made easier by the local penchant for easy conversation.

In an increasingly homogenized society, Savannah is one of the last places left where eccentricity is celebrated and even encouraged. This outspoken, often stubborn determination to make one's own way in the world is personified by the old Georgia joke about Savannah being the capital of "the state of Chatham," a reference to the county in which it resides. In typical contrarian fashion, Savannahians take this nickname as a compliment.

This spirit of independence extends to Savannah's growing hipster culture, helped along by the steady expansion of the Savannah College of Art and Design (SCAD), which

**Previous:** Savannah's skyline; springtime azaleas in downtown Savannah. **Above:** detail of St. John's Cathedral.

# Highlights

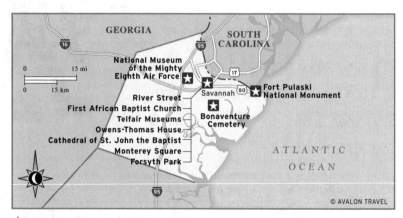

★ **River Street:** Despite River Street's tourist tackiness, there's nothing like strolling the cobblestones amid the old cotton warehouses, enjoying the cool breeze off the river, and watching the huge ships on their way to the bustling port (page 198).

★ **First African Baptist Church:** The oldest black congregation in the United States still meets in this historic sanctuary, a key stop on the Underground Railroad (page 201).

★ **Telfair Museums:** Old school meets new school in this museum complex that comprises the traditional **Telfair Academy of Arts and Sciences** (page 209) and the ultramodern **Jepson Center for the Arts** (page 208).

★ **Owens-Thomas House:** One of the country's best examples of Regency architecture and an example of state-of-the-art historic preservation, this is Savannah's single greatest historic home (page 210).

★ **Cathedral of St. John the Baptist:** This soaring Gothic Revival edifice is complemented by its ornate interior and its matchless location on verdant Lafayette Square, stomping ground of the young Flannery O'Connor (page 215).

★ **Monterey Square:** Perhaps Savannah's quintessential square, with some of the best examples of local architecture and world-class ironwork all around its periphery (page 218).

★ **Forsyth Park:** This verdant expanse ringed by old live oaks is the true center of downtown life; it's Savannah's backyard (page 222).

★ **Bonaventure Cemetery:** This historic burial ground is the final resting place for some of Savannah's favorite citizens, including the great Johnny Mercer (page 227).

★ **Fort Pulaski National Monument:** This well-run site, built with the help of a young Robert E. Lee, is not only historically significant, its beautiful setting makes it a great place for the entire family (page 230).

★ **National Museum of the Mighty Eighth Air Force:** This museum tells the story of the U.S. Eighth Air Force, who executed American bombing missions over Nazi Germany, and includes restored WWII and Cold War-era aircraft (page 237).

boasts much of downtown Savannah as its campus.

That said, Savannah's larger share of the tourism and development spotlight in recent years also means it is struggling with the same balancing act as many burgeoning destination cities: The balance between retaining historic character and authenticity with economic development, which often takes the form of corporate chains.

Savannah is also known for being able to show you a rowdy good time, and not only during its massive, world-famous St. Patrick's Day celebration. Savannahians, like New Orleanians, will use any excuse for a party, and any excuse to drink in the full flavor of natural beauty here—whether in the heady glory of a spring day with all the flowers blooming, or the sweet release of the long-awaited autumn, brisk and bracing but not so crisp that you can't wear shorts.

And like New Orleans, Savannah also has a very liberal open-container law—adults can walk with alcoholic beverages around downtown—which no doubt adds to the generally merry atmosphere.

## HISTORY

To understand the inferiority complex that Savannah occasionally feels with regards to Charleston, you have to remember that literally from day one Savannah was intended to play second fiddle to its older, richer neighbor to the north. By the early 1700s, the land south of Charleston was a staging area for attacks by the Spanish and Native Americans. So in 1732, King George II granted a charter to the Trustees of Georgia, a proprietary venture that was the brainchild of a 36-year-old general and member of parliament, General James Edward Oglethorpe.

On February 12, 1733, the *Anne* landed with 114 passengers along the high bluff on the south bank of the Savannah River. Oglethorpe bonded with Tomochichi, the local Creek Indian chief, and the colony prospered. (Contrary to what locals might tell you, Savannah did not get its name because it resembles a grassy savanna. The city is named for the Savannah River, which itself is named for a wandering, warring offshoot of a local Shawnee people.)

Ever the idealist, Oglethorpe had a plan for the new "classless society" in Savannah that prohibited slavery, rum, and—wait for it—lawyers! But as the settlers enviously eyed the dominance of Charleston's slave-based rice economy, the Trustees bowed to public pressure and relaxed restrictions on slavery and rum.

By 1753, the crown reclaimed the charter, making Georgia England's 13th American colony. Though part of the new United States in 1776, Savannah was captured by British forces in 1778, who held the city against a combined assault a year later. After the Revolution, Savannah became the first capital of Georgia, a role it had until 1786.

Despite hurricanes and yellow fever epidemics, Savannah's heyday was the antebellum period from 1800 to 1860, when for a time it outstripped Charleston as a center of commerce. By 1860, Savannah's population doubled after an influx of European immigrants, chief among them Irish workers coming to lay track on the new Central of Georgia line.

Blockaded for most of the Civil War, Savannah didn't see much action other than the fall of Fort Pulaski in April 1862, when a Union force successfully laid siege using rifled artillery, a revolutionary new technology that instantly rendered the world's masonry forts obsolete. War came to Savannah's doorstep when General William T. Sherman's March to the Sea concluded with his capture of the town in December 1864. On December 22, Sherman sent a now-legendary telegram to President Lincoln bearing these words: "I beg to present you as a Christmas gift, the City of Savannah with 150 heavy guns and plenty of ammunition and also about 25,000 bales of cotton."

After a lengthy Reconstruction period, Savannah began reaching out to the outside world. From 1908 to 1911 it was a national center of road racing. In the Roaring '20s, native son Johnny Mercer rose to prominence, and the

# Map 1: Downtown Savannah

## SIGHTS

| | | | |
|---|---|---|---|
| 7 | World War II Memorial | 55 | Trustees Garden |
| 13 | City Hall | 72 | Trustees Theater |
| 14 | Chatham Artillery Guns | 73 | Jen Library |
| 20 | Savannah Cotton Exchange | 77 | Telfair Academy of Arts and Sciences |
| 21 | Rousakis Plaza | 78 | Trinity United Methodist Church |
| 25 | Factor's Walk | 79 | Federal Courthouse and Post Office |
| 28 | Emmet Park | 81 | Evangelical Lutheran Church of the Ascension |
| 30 | The Brice | 83 | Owens-Thomas House |
| 32 | The Waving Girl | 84 | Isaiah Davenport House Museum |
| 34 | First African Baptist Church | 85 | Kehoe House |
| 36 | Haitian Monument | 89 | Second African Baptist Church |
| 37 | Ships of the Sea Maritime Museum | 90 | Cunningham House |
| 43 | U.S. Custom House | 92 | Jepson Center for the Arts |
| 47 | Christ Episcopal Church | 93 | Juliette Gordon Low Birthplace |
| 48 | Olde Pink House | | |
| 50 | Oliver Sturgis House | | |
| 51 | Lucas Theatre for the Arts | | |
| 54 | Hampton Lillibridge House and Charles Oddingsells House | | |

## RESTAURANTS

| | | | |
|---|---|---|---|
| 16 | Olympia Café | 49 | Olde Pink House |
| 19 | Vic's on the River | 56 | The Grey |
| 22 | Treylor Park | 59 | The Coffee Fox |
| 29 | B. Matthew's Eatery | 67 | Kayak Kafe |
| 35 | Vinnie VanGoGo's | 71 | Leopold's Ice Cream |
| 38 | Lulu's Chocolate Bar | 76 | Tequila's Town |
| 42 | Co Savannah | 80 | Wright Square Cafe |
| 44 | Sapphire Grill | 82 | Zunzi's |
| 45 | The Lady & Sons | 87 | 17Hundred90 Inn |

## NIGHTLIFE

| | | | |
|---|---|---|---|
| 2 | Chuck's Bar | 40 | 22 Square |
| 5 | Club One Jefferson | 46 | The Jinx |
| 8 | Kevin Barry's Irish Pub | 53 | Abe's on Lincoln |
| 9 | Rocks on the Roof | 60 | Circa 1875 |
| 12 | Moon River Brewing Company | 63 | Chive Sea Bar and Lounge |
| 24 | Bayou Café | 70 | O'Connell's |
| 39 | Rail Pub | | |

## ARTS AND CULTURE

| | | | |
|---|---|---|---|
| 52 | Lucas Theatre for the Arts | 62 | Savannah Philharmonic |

© AVALON TRAVEL

SEE MAP 2

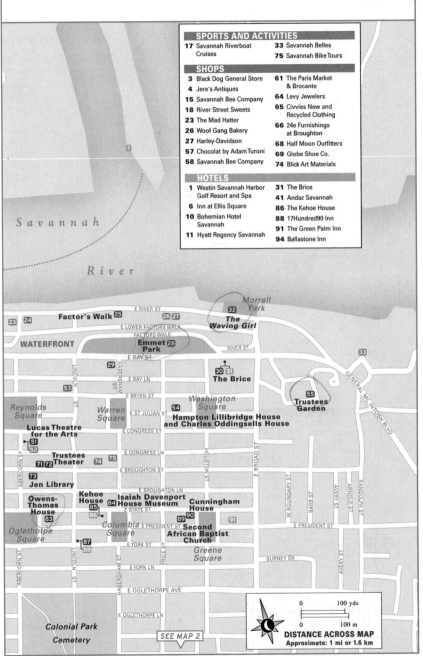

## SPORTS AND ACTIVITIES

17 Savannah Riverboat Cruises
33 Savannah Belles
75 Savannah Bike Tours

## SHOPS

3 Black Dog General Store
4 Jere's Antiques
15 Savannah Bee Company
18 River Street Sweets
23 The Mad Hatter
26 Woof Gang Bakery
27 Harley-Davidson
57 Chocolat by Adam Turoni
58 Savannah Bee Company
61 The Paris Market & Brocante
64 Levy Jewelers
65 Civvies New and Recycled Clothing
66 24e Furnishings at Broughton
68 Half Moon Outfitters
69 Globe Shoe Co.
74 Blick Art Materials

## HOTELS

1 Westin Savannah Harbor Golf Resort and Spa
6 Inn at Ellis Square
10 Bohemian Hotel Savannah
11 Hyatt Regency Savannah
31 The Brice
41 Andaz Savannah
86 The Kehoe House
88 17Hundred90 Inn
91 The Green Palm Inn
94 Ballastone Inn

Savannah

River

Morrell Park

E RIVER ST

Factor's Walk 25

The Waving Girl 32

E LOWER FACTORS WALK

FACTORS WALK

WATERFRONT

Emmet Park 28

RIVER ST

E BAY ST

29

HABERSHAM ST

LINCOLN ST

53

GENERAL MCINTOSH BLVD

33

E BAY LN

30 31

The Brice

E BRYAN ST

Washington Square

54

Trustees Garden 55

Reynolds Square

Warren Square

E ST JULIAN ST

Hampton Lillibridge House and Charles Oddingsells House

Lucas Theatre for the Arts

E CONGRESS ST

51
52

Trustees Theater

71 72 74 75

E CONGRESS LN

HOUSTON ST

E BROAD ST

73

Jen Library

E BROUGHTON ST

E BROUGHTON LN

Owens-Thomas House 83

Kehoe House

85

84

Isaiah Davenport House Museum

Cunningham House

89 90

91

W BOUNDARY ST

BARR ST

AVERY ST

ARNOLD ST

RANDOLPH ST

86

E STATE ST

Oglethorpe Square

Columbia Square

E PRESIDENT ST

Second African Baptist Church

E PRESIDENT ST

87
88

E YORK ST

Greene Square

BURNEY DR

ABERCORN ST

LINCOLN ST

E YORK LN

HABERSHAM ST

PRICE ST

AVERY ST

E OGLETHORPE AVE

E OGLETHORPE LN

Colonial Park Cemetery

SEE MAP 2

0        100 yds

0        100 m

DISTANCE ACROSS MAP
Approximate: 1 mi or 1.6 km

# Map 2: Historic District South

0   100 yds
0   100 m

**DISTANCE ACROSS MAP**
Approximate: 1.1 mi or 1.7 km

SEE MAP 1

Orleans Square

SCAD Museum of Art

To 3 Muse Arts Warehouse

Savannah History Museum

Battlefield Park

Pulaski Square

Georgia State Railroad Museum

Savannah Children's Museum

Chatham Square

Ralph Mark Gilbert Civil Rights Museum

SEE MAP 3

## SIGHTS

**2** SCAD Museum of Art
**4** Savannah History Museum
**7** Battlefield Park
**8** Georgia State Railroad Museum
**9** Savannah Children's Museum
**10** Independent Presbyterian Church
**13** First Baptist Church
**14** Historic Savannah Theatre
**17** Colonial Cemetery
**20** Hilton Savannah DeSoto
**22** Cathedral of St. John the Baptist
**23** Beach Institute
**24** Green-Meldrim House
**26** Unitarian Universalist Church of Savannah
**27** Andrew Low House Museum
**28** Hamilton-Turner Inn
**29** Flannery O'Connor Childhood Home
**30** Scottish Rite Temple
**32** Poetter Hall
**34** Jones Street
**45** Ralph Mark Gilbert Civil Rights Museum
**46** Mercer-Williams House Museum
**49** Temple Mickve Israel
**50** Wesley Monumental United Methodist Church
**51** Massie Heritage Center

## RESTAURANTS

**11** Angel's BBQ
**33** Crystal Beer Parlor
**36** Mrs. Wilkes' Dining Room

© AVALON TRAVEL

Independent Presbyterian Church ⑩

⑪

⑫

Historic Savannah Theatre ⑭ ⑮

⑬
First Baptist Church

Chippewa Square

⑯

E PERRY ST

E PERRY LN

**HISTORIC DISTRICT**

⑱

⑰ Colonial Cemetery

E OGLETHORPE AVE

W HULL ST

E HULL ST

W MC DONOUGH ST

E MC DONOUGH ST

E PERRY ST

E PERRY LN

E LIBERTY

⑲

⑳
Hilton Savannah DeSoto

Green-Meldrim House

㉔

Madison Square

㉕

E HARRIS ST

E MACON ST

㉑

E LIBERTY LN

㉒
Cathedral of St. John the Baptist

㉖
Unitarian Universalist Church of Savannah

Beach Institute ㉓

Lafayette Square

㉗

Andrew Low House Museum

Scottish Rite ㉚ ㉛ Temple
㉜ Poetter Hall

E CHARLTON LN

㉘ Hamilton-Turner Inn

W CHARLTON ST

E CHARLTON ST

㉙
Flannery O'Connor Childhood Home

**Jones Street** ㉟

�34
㊱ ㊲
㊳
㉝34

E JONES ST

E JONES LN

㊴

㊵

㊶

㊷

E TAYLOR ST

㊸

Monterey Square

㊻
Mercer-Williams House Museum

㊼ ㊽

E WAYNE ST

㊾
Temple Mickve Israel

E GORDON LN

**Wesley Monumental United Methodist Church**

㊿
Calhoun Square

E GORDON ST

Whitefield Square

�51

Massie Heritage Center

�52

E GASTON ST

MARINE MEMORIAL

**VICTORIAN DISTRICT**

Forsyth Fountain

Forsyth Park

CONFEDERATE MEMORIAL

### NIGHTLIFE
6 The Distillery
16 McDonough's
21 The Original
53 The Chromatic Dragon

### ARTS AND CULTURE
3 Muse Arts Warehouse
15 Historic Savannah Theatre

### SPORTS AND ACTIVITIES
1 Savannah Derby Devils
5 Savannah Movie Tour
39 Sixth Sense Savannah Ghost Tour
35 Old City Walks
52 Savannah Tours by Foot

### SHOPS
18 The Book Lady
19 Saints and Shamrocks
25 E. Shaver Bookseller
31 shopSCAD
37 One Fish Two Fish
40 Small Pleasures
41 The Corner Door
42 V&J Duncan
43 Madame Chrysanthemum
44 Custard Boutique
47 Alex Raskin Antiques
48 Folklorico

### HOTELS
12 Foley House Inn
38 Eliza Thompson House

# Map 3: Victorian District and SoFo District

SAVANNAH

**SIGHTS**
4 Forsyth Park
8 Carnegie Branch Library
9 Laurel Grove Cemetery

**RESTAURANTS**
6 The Sentient Bean
10 Cotton & Rye
11 Butterhead Greens
12 Foxy Loxy
13 Elizabeth on 37th
14 Back in the Day Bakery
17 Green Truck Neighborhood Pub
18 The Florence

**NIGHTLIFE**
7 American Legion Bar

**SPORTS AND ACTIVITIES**
5 Forsyth Park
19 Wilderness Southeast

**SHOPS**
15 Graveface Records & Curiosities
16 Gypsy World

**HOTELS**
1 Gastonian Inn
2 Dresser-Palmer House
3 Mansion on Forsyth Park

SEE MAP 2

W WAYNE ST
W GWINNETT ST
EMERALD DR
GWINNETT CT
W ANDERSON ST
W 31ST ST
W 32ND ST
W 35TH ST
W 36TH ST
W 37TH ST
W 38TH ST
W 39TH ST
W 40TH ST
W 41ST ST
W 42ND ST
W VICTORY DR
W 44TH ST
W 45TH ST
W 46TH ST
W 47TH ST

MONTGOMERY ST
MARTIN LUTHER KING JR BLVD
MAY ST
STILES AVE
OGEECHEE RD RD
HOPKINS ST
STEVENS ST
BULLOCH ST
FLORENCE ST
BURROUGHS ST
MARTIN LUTHER KING JR BLVD
MONTGOMERY ST

Laurel Grove Cemetery 9
Laurel Grove Cemetery 9

16
404
25
204
80

0        250 yds
0        250 m
**DISTANCE ACROSS MAP**
Approximate: 2.2 mi or 3.5 km

SAVANNAH

# Map 4: Southside and Eastside

**SAVANNAH**

## SIGHTS
- **1** Old Fort Jackson
- **3** Oatland Island Wildlife Center
- **4** Bonaventure Cemetery
- **7** Daffin Park
- **9** Thunderbolt Museum
- **11** Savannah State University
- **14** University of Georgia Marine Educational Center and Aquarium
- **17** Wormsloe State Historic Site
- **18** Isle of Hope
- **20** Pin Point Heritage Museum
- **23** Skidaway Island State Park

## RESTAURANTS
- **6** Desposito's
- **16** Sandfly BBQ

## ARTS AND CULTURE
- **19** Armstrong State University Masquers

## SPORTS AND ACTIVITIES
- **2** Savannah Fly Fishing Charters
- **5** Savannah Canoe & Kayak
- **8** Daffin Park
- **10** Telecaster Charters
- **12** Miss Judy Charters
- **13** Wilmington Island Club
- **15** Bacon Park
- **21** Moon River Kayak Tours
- **22** Skidaway Narrows
- **24** Skidaway Island State Park

DISTANCE ACROSS MAP
Approximate: 6.3 mi or 10.1 km

© AVALON TRAVEL

# Map 5: Tybee Island

SOUTH CAROLINA

GEORGIA

Savannah River

Fort Pulaski
National Monument

Tybee Island
Light Station
and
Museum

SOLOMON AVE.

VAN HORNE ST.

Cockspur
Island

80

Lazaretto

Tybee Post
Theater

1ST ST.

Creek

DAVIS ISLAND RD.

3RD ST.

8TH ST.

BUTLER AVE.

SEE
DETAIL

### SIGHTS
| | |
|---|---|
| **1** Fort Pulaski National Monument | **14** Tybee Post Theater |
| **11** Tybee Island Light Station and Museum | **19** South End |
| | **23** Tybee Island Marine Science Center |

### RESTAURANTS
| | |
|---|---|
| **7** The Crab Shack | **12** North Beach Grill |
| **8** Huc-a-Poo's Bites & Booze | **20** Tybee Island Social Club |
| | **22** The Breakfast Club |

### SPORTS AND ACTIVITIES
| | |
|---|---|
| **2** Fort Pulaski National Monument | **9** Sea Kayak Georgia |
| **3** McQueen's Island Trail | **15** High Tides Surf Shop |
| **4** Lazaretto Creek | **16** Tybee Island Memorial Park |
| **5** Amick's Deep Sea Fishing | **17** Little Tybee Island |
| **6** North Island Surf and Kayak | **18** North Beach |

### HOTELS
| | |
|---|---|
| **10** River's End Campground | **24** Atlantis Inn |
| **13** Lighthouse Inn | **25** Beachview Bed & Breakfast |
| **21** The Georgianne Inn | |

Little Tybee
Island

2ND AVE.

LOVELL AVE.

9TH ST.

10TH ST.

11TH ST.

JONES AVE.

12TH ST.

BUTLER AVE.

13TH ST.

14TH ST.

15TH ST.

TABRISA ST.

17TH ST.

0    750 yds

0    750 m

**DISTANCE ACROSS MAP**
Approximate: 3.8 mi or 6.1 km

SAVANNAH

# Map 6: Greater Savannah

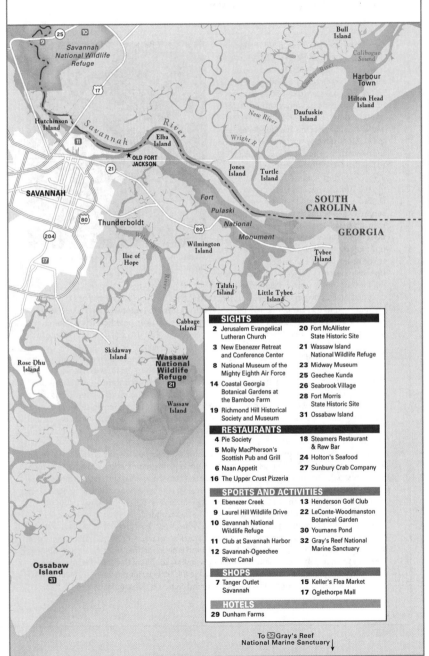

## SIGHTS

**2** Jerusalem Evangelical Lutheran Church
**3** New Ebenezer Retreat and Conference Center
**8** National Museum of the Mighty Eighth Air Force
**14** Coastal Georgia Botanical Gardens at the Bamboo Farm
**19** Richmond Hill Historical Society and Museum
**20** Fort McAllister State Historic Site
**21** Wassaw Island National Wildlife Refuge
**23** Midway Museum
**25** Geechee Kunda
**26** Seabrook Village
**28** Fort Morris State Historic Site
**31** Ossabaw Island

## RESTAURANTS

**4** Pie Society
**5** Molly MacPherson's Scottish Pub and Grill
**6** Naan Appetit
**16** The Upper Crust Pizzeria
**18** Steamers Restaurant & Raw Bar
**24** Holton's Seafood
**27** Sunbury Crab Company

## SPORTS AND ACTIVITIES

**1** Ebenezer Creek
**9** Laurel Hill Wildlife Drive
**10** Savannah National Wildlife Refuge
**11** Club at Savannah Harbor
**12** Savannah-Ogeechee River Canal
**13** Henderson Golf Club
**22** LeConte-Woodmanston Botanical Garden
**30** Youmans Pond
**32** Gray's Reef National Marine Sanctuary

## SHOPS

**7** Tanger Outlet Savannah
**15** Keller's Flea Market
**17** Oglethorpe Mall

## HOTELS

**29** Dunham Farms

To 32 Gray's Reef National Marine Sanctuary ↓

# A Visionary Aristocrat

One of the greatest products of the Enlightenment, **James Edward Oglethorpe** was a study in contrasts, embodying all the vitality, contradiction, and ambiguity of that turbulent age. A stern moralist yet an avowed liberal, an aristocrat with a populist streak, an abolitionist and an anti-Catholic, a man of war who sought peace—the founder of Georgia would put his own inimitable stamp on the new nation to follow, a legacy personified to this day in the city he designed.

After making a name for himself fighting the Turks, the young London native and Oxford graduate would return home only to serve a two-year prison sentence for killing a man in a brawl. The experience was a formative one for Oglethorpe, scion of a large and upwardly mobile family, as he was now forced to see how England's underbelly really lived. Upon his release, the 25-year-old Oglethorpe ran for the "family" House of Commons seat

a monument to General James Edward Oglethorpe

once occupied by his father and two brothers, and won. He distinguished himself as a campaigner for human rights and an opponent of slavery. Another jail-related epiphany came when Oglethorpe saw a friend die of smallpox in debtors prison. More than ever, Oglethorpe was determined to right what he saw as a colossal wrong in the draconian English justice system. His crusade took the form of establishing a sanctuary for debtors in North America.

To that end, he and his friend Lord Perceval established the Trustees, a 21-member group who lobbied King George for permission to establish such a colony. The grant from the king—who was more interested in containing the Spanish than in any humanitarian concerns—would include all land between the Altamaha and Savannah Rivers and from the headwaters of these rivers to the "south seas." Ironically, there were no debtors among Savannah's original colonists. Nonetheless, the new settlement was indeed a reflection of its founder's core values, banning rum as a bad influence (though beer and wine were allowed), prohibiting slavery, and eschewing lawyers on the theory that a gentleman should always be able to defend himself.

Nearing 40 and distracted by war with the Spanish, Oglethorpe's agenda gradually eroded in the face of opposition from settlers, who craved not only the more hedonistic lifestyle of their neighbors to the north in Charleston but the economic advantage that city enjoyed through the use of slave labor. In nearly the same hour as his greatest military victory, crushing the Spanish at the Battle of Bloody Marsh on St. Simons Island, Oglethorpe also suffered an ignominious defeat: being replaced as head of the 13th colony, which he had founded.

He went back to England, never to see the New World again. But his heart was always with the colonists. After successfully fending off a political attack and a court-martial, Oglethorpe married and commenced a healthy retirement. He supported independence for the American colonies, making a point to enthusiastically receive the new ambassador from the United States, one John Adams. The old general died on June 30, 1785, at age 88. Fittingly for this lifelong philanthropist and humanitarian, his childhood home in Godalming, Surrey, is now a nursing home.

great Flannery O'Connor was born in downtown Savannah. World War II provided an economic lift, but the city was still known as the "pretty woman with a dirty face," as Britain's Lady Astor famously described it in 1946.

Almost in answer to Astor's quip, city leaders in the 1950s began a misguided program to retrofit the city's infrastructure for the automobile era. Savannah's preservation movement had its seed in the fight by seven Savannah women to save the Davenport House and other buildings from demolition.

Savannah played a pioneering, though largely unsung, role in the civil rights movement. Ralph Mark Gilbert, pastor of the historic First African Baptist Church, launched one of the first black voter registration drives in the South. Gilbert's efforts were kept alive in the 1950s and 1960s by the beloved W. W. Law, a letter carrier who was head of the local chapter of the NAACP for many years.

Savannah's longstanding diversity was further proved in 1970, when Greek American John P. Rousakis began his 21-year stint as mayor. During Rousakis's tenure, the first African American city alderman was elected, the movie industry discovered the area, and Atlanta was awarded the 1996 Summer Olympics, which brought several events venues to Savannah. The opening of the Savannah College of Art and Design in 1979 ushered another important chapter in Savannah's renaissance, which is ongoing to this day.

After the publication of John Berendt's *Midnight in the Garden of Good and Evil* in 1994, nothing would ever be the same in Savannah. Old-money families cringed as idiosyncrasies and hypocrisies were laid bare in "The Book." Local merchants and politicians, however, delighted in the influx of tourists.

A more recent driver of tourism to the area was the arrival of Paula Deen, whose once-ubiquitous presence on the Food Network convinced many thousands of visitors to come eat at her world-famous, if perhaps overrated, The Lady and Sons restaurant.

Today, Savannah has emerged from the recession of '08 with style and continued emphasis—some locals say too much emphasis—on developing the tourist sector.

## PLANNING YOUR TIME

It's hard to imagine fully enjoying Savannah in a single day. Plan on **two nights** at an absolute minimum—not only to enjoy all the sights, but to fully soak in the local color and attitude. Like Charleston, you don't need a car to have a great time and see most sights worth enjoying. A strong walker can easily traverse the length and breadth of downtown in a day, although less energetic travelers should consider a central location or make use of the free downtown shuttle. To fully enjoy Savannah, however, you'll need access to a vehicle so you can go east to Tybee Island and south to various historic sites with spottier public transportation. You'll appreciate downtown all the more when you can get away and smell the salt air.

Much more than just a parade, St. Patrick's Day in Savannah—an event generally expanded to include several days before and after the holiday itself—is also a time of immense crowds, with the city's usual population of about 150,000 doubling with the influx of partying visitors. Be aware that lodging on and around March 17 fills up well in advance. Unless you know someone who lives here, it's best not to just spontaneously show up in Savannah on St. Patrick's weekend.

## ORIENTATION

It's tempting for newcomers to assume that Savannah jumps across the river into South Carolina. But Savannah emanates strictly southward from the river and never crosses the state line. (Don't be confused by the spit of land you see across the main channel of the Savannah River, the one bearing the squat Trade and Convention Center and the towering Westin Savannah Harbor hotel. That's not South Carolina—it's Hutchinson Island, Georgia, annexed by the city of Savannah for development. South Carolina begins farther north, after you cross the river's Back Channel.)

The downtown area is bounded on the east by East Broad Street and on the west by Martin Luther King Jr. Boulevard (formerly West Broad St.). Technically, Gwinnett Street is the southern boundary of the National Historic Landmark District, though in practice locals extend the boundary several blocks southward. The Eastside includes many areas that are technically islands, but their boundaries are so blurred by infill of the marsh and by well-constructed roads that you'll sense little difference from the mainland. To most locals, "Southside" refers to the generic strip mall sprawl below Derenne Avenue, but for our purposes here the term also includes some outlying islands. I include them in the southern part of town because of the general direction and length of travel.

# Sights

It's best to introduce yourself to the sights of Savannah by traveling from the river southward. It's no small task to navigate the nation's largest contiguous Historic District, but when in doubt it's best to follow James Oglethorpe's original plan of using the five "monumental" squares on Bull Street (Johnson, Wright, Chippewa, Madison, and Monterey) as focal points.

## WATERFRONT
### ★ River Street

It's much tamer than it was 30 years ago—when muscle cars cruised its cobblestones and a volatile mix of local teenagers, sailors on shore leave, and soldiers on liberty made things less than family-friendly after dark—but River Street still has more than enough edginess to keep things interesting. Families are safe and welcome here, but energetic pub crawling remains a favorite pastime for locals and visitors alike.

If you have a car, park it somewhere else and walk. The cobblestones—actually old ballast stones from some of the innumerable ships that docked here over the years—are tough on the suspension, and much of River Street is dedicated to pedestrian traffic anyway. If you do find yourself driving here, keep in mind that the north-south "ramps" leading up and off River Street are all extensions of major downtown streets, so you can easily drive or walk up them and find yourself in the middle of bustling Bay Street and on to points beyond.

### FACTOR'S WALK

One level up from River Street, Factor's Walk has nothing to do with math, though a lot of money has been counted here. In arcane usage, a "factor" was a broker, i.e., a middleman for the sale of cotton, Savannah's chief export during most of the 1800s. Factors mostly worked in Factor's Row, the traditional phrase for the actual buildings on River Street, most all of which were used in various import-export activities before their current transformation into a mélange of shops, hotels, restaurants, and taverns. Factor's Walk is divided into Lower Factor's Walk, comprising the alleys and back entrances behind Factor's Row, and Upper Factor's Walk, the system of crosswalks at the upper levels of Factor's Row that lead directly to Bay Street.
MAP 1: E. River St.

### ROUSAKIS PLAZA

Rousakis Plaza is a focal point for local festivals. It's a great place to sit, feed the pigeons, and watch the huge container ships go back and forth from the Georgia Ports Authority's sprawling complex farther upriver (you can see the huge Panamax cranes in the distance). The African American Monument at the edge of Rousakis Plaza was erected in 2002 to controversy for its stark tableau of a dazed-looking African American family with broken shackles around their feet. Adding to the controversy was the graphic content of the inscription at the base of the 12-foot statue, written especially for the monument by famed poet Maya Angelou. It reads:

> We were stolen, sold and bought to-
> gether from the African continent. We got
> on the slave ships together. We lay back
> to belly in the holds of the slave ships
> in each other's excrement and urine to-
> gether, sometimes died together, and
> our lifeless bodies thrown overboard
> together. Today, we are standing up to-
> gether, with faith and even some joy.

Nearby you can't miss the huge, vaguely cubist Hyatt Regency Savannah, another controversial local landmark. The modern architecture of the Hyatt caused quite a stir when it was first built in 1981, not only because it's so contrary to the area's historic architecture but because its superstructure effectively cuts off one end of River Street from the other. "Underneath" the Hyatt—actually still River Street—you'll find elevators to the hotel lobby, the best way to get up off the waterfront if you're not up for a walk up the cobblestones. Immediately outside the west side of the Hyatt up toward Bay Street is another exit and entry point, a steep and solid set of antebellum stairs that, despite its decidedly pre-Americans with Disabilities Act aspect, is nonetheless one of the quicker ways to leave River Street for those with strong legs and good knees.

MAP 1: E. River St., behind City Hall

### THE WAVING GIRL

At the east end of River Street is the statue of Florence Martus, aka *The Waving Girl,* set in the emerald-green expanse of little Morrell Park. Beginning in 1887 at the age of 19, Martus—who actually lived several miles downriver on Elba Island—took to greeting every passing ship with a wave of a handkerchief by day and a lantern at night, without fail for the next 40 years. Ship captains returned the greeting with a salute of their own on the ship's whistle, and word spread all over the world of the beguiling woman who waited on the balcony of that lonely house. Was she looking for a sign of a long-lost love who went to sea and never returned? Was she trying to get a handsome sea captain to sweep her off her feet and take her off that little island? No one knows for sure, but the truth is probably more prosaic. Martus was a lifelong spinster who lived with her brother, the lighthouse keeper, and was by most accounts an eccentric, if delightful, person—which of course makes her an ideal Savannah character. After her brother died, Martus moved into a house on the Wilmington River, whiling away the hours by—you guessed it—waving at passing cars. Martus became such an enduring symbol of the personality and spirit of Savannah that a U.S. Liberty ship was named for her in 1943. She died at the age of 75, a few months after the ship's christening.

MAP 1: Morrell Park, E. River St. and E. Broad St.

### WORLD WAR II MEMORIAL

Near the foot of the Bohemian Hotel Savannah Riverfront on River Street is a 21st-century addition to Savannah's public monuments. Installed in 2010, the World War II Memorial—fairly modernist by local standards—features a copper-and-bronze globe torn in half to represent the European and Pacific theaters of the war. The more than 500 local people who gave their lives in that conflict are memorialized by name.

MAP 1: W. River St., near Bohemian Hotel Savannah Riverfront, 102 W. Bay St.

## Bay Street

Because so few downtown streets can accommodate 18-wheelers, Bay Street unfortunately has become the default route for industrial traffic in the area on its way to and from the industrial west side of town. In front of the Hyatt Regency Savannah is a concrete bench marking the spot on which Oglethorpe pitched his first tent.

### CHATHAM ARTILLERY GUNS

Directly adjacent to City Hall on the east is a small canopy sheltering two cannons, which together compose the oldest monument in the World War II Memorial by sculptor Kim Brandell

Savannah. These are the Chatham Artillery Guns, presented to the local militia group of the same name by President George Washington during his one and only visit to town in 1791. Today, locals use the phrase "Chatham Artillery" differently, to refer to a particularly potent local punch recipe that mixes several hard liquors.

**MAP 1:** Adjacent to City Hall, 2 E. Bay St.

### CITY HALL

Dominating Bay Street is City Hall, with its gold-leaf dome. The 1907 building was designed by acclaimed architect Hyman Witcover and erected on the site of Savannah's first town hall.

**MAP 1:** 2 E. Bay St.

### SAVANNAH COTTON EXCHANGE

Directly behind the Chatham Artillery Guns is the ornate Savannah Cotton Exchange, built in 1886 to facilitate the city's huge cotton export business. Once nicknamed "King Cotton's Palace" but now a Masonic lodge, this delightful building by William Gibbons Preston is one of Savannah's many great examples of the Romanesque style. You'll become well acquainted with Preston's handiwork during your stay in Savannah, as the Boston architect built many of Savannah's finest buildings. The fanciful lion figure in front—sometimes mistakenly referred to as a griffin—represents Mark the Evangelist. However, it isn't original—the first lion was destroyed in 2009 in a bizarre traffic accident.

**MAP 1:** 100 E. Bay St.

### U.S. CUSTOM HOUSE

The large gray Greek Revival building directly across from City Hall is the U.S. Custom House (not "customs," regardless of what the tour guides may say). Built on the spot of Georgia's first public building in 1852, the Custom House was also Georgia's first federal building and was the first local commission for renowned New York architect John Norris, who went on to design 22 other buildings in Savannah. Within its walls was held

# The Rebirth of Ellis Square

Ellis Square has been completely reimagined.

Ellis Square's history as Savannah's main open-air marketplace goes back to 1755, when there was a single City Market building in the square itself. The fourth City Market was built in 1872, an ornate Romanesque affair with a 50-foot roofline. In 1954, the city decided to build a parking garage in the square. So the magnificent City Market building—and Ellis Square—simply ceased to exist.

Several large warehouses surrounding City Market survived. Now a hub of tourism, City Market encompasses working art studios, hip bars, cute cafés, live music in the east end of the courtyard, cutting-edge art galleries, gift shops, and restaurants.

The eyesore that was the Ellis Square parking garage is gone, and the square has been rebuilt as a pedestrian hangout, complete with a fountain, all atop a huge underground parking garage. Be sure to check out the smallish bronze of native Savannahian and Oscar-winning lyricist Johnny Mercer on the square's western edge.

the trial of the captain and crew of the notorious slave ship *Wanderer,* which illegally plied its trade after a national ban on the importation of slaves. Local newspaper publisher and educator John H. DeVeaux worked here after his appointment as the first African American U.S. Collector of Customs.

**MAP 1:** 1 E. Bay St.

## CITY MARKET
### Franklin Square

Just west of City Market is Franklin Square, once known simply as "Water Tank Square" because that's where the city reservoir was back in the day. Don't be alarmed by the numbers of men hanging out in the square. Scruffy heirs to an old Savannah tradition, most of them are day laborers for hire. Until recently, Franklin Square was, like Ellis Square, a victim of "progress," this time in the form of a highway going right through the middle of it. But as part of the city's effort to reclaim its history, Franklin Square was returned to its original state in the mid-1980s.

### ★ FIRST AFRICAN BAPTIST CHURCH

Without a doubt the premier historic attraction on Franklin Square—and indeed one of the most significant historic sites in Savannah—is the First African Baptist Church. It's the oldest black congregation in North America, dating from 1777. The church also hosted the first African American Sunday school, begun in 1826. The church's founding pastor, George Liele, was the first black Baptist in Georgia and perhaps the first black missionary in the country. He baptized his successor, Andrew Bryan, a slave who opted to stay in Savannah and preach instead of leave with many other blacks after the British vacated the city in 1782. Third pastor Andrew Marshall was an ardent supporter of American independence and purchased his freedom shortly after the end of the Revolution. He served as George Washington's personal servant during his visit here. This founding trio is immortalized in stained glass windows in the sanctuary.

The present building dates from 1859 and was built almost entirely by members of the congregation themselves, some of whom redirected savings intended to purchase their freedom toward the building of the church. It houses the oldest church organ in Georgia. A key staging area for the fabled Underground Railroad, First African Baptist still bears the scars of that turbulent time. In the floor of the fellowship hall—where many civil rights meetings were held, because it was safer for white citizens to go there instead of black activists going outside the church—you'll see breathing holes, drilled for use by escaped slaves hiding in a cramped crawlspace.

**MAP 1:** 23 Montgomery St., 912/233-2244, http://firstafricanbc.com; tours Tues.-Sat. 11am and 2pm, Sun. 1pm; $7 adults, $6 students/seniors

### HAITIAN MONUMENT

The Haitian Monument in the center of the square commemorates the sacrifice and service of "Les Chasseurs Volontaires de Saint-Domingue," the 750 Haitian volunteers who fought for American independence and lost many of their number during the unsuccessful attempt to wrest Savannah back from the British in 1779.

**MAP 1:** Franklin Square

the First African Baptist Church, home of the oldest black congregation in America

## HISTORIC DISTRICT NORTH
### Johnson Square

Due east of City Market, Johnson Square, Oglethorpe's very first square, is named for Robert Johnson, governor of South Carolina at the time of Georgia's founding. It was here that one of Georgia's first "liberty poles" was erected to urge citizens to rally for independence. And it was here that a gathering in 1861 celebrated Georgia's secession, ironically with a huge banner draped over the Greene Monument bearing the words "Don't Tread on Me"—a slogan used in the founding of the very union the secessionists sought to dissolve.

The roomy, shaded square, ringed with major bank branches and insurance firms, is dominated by the Nathanael Greene Monument in honor of George Washington's second-in-command, who was granted nearby Mulberry Grove plantation for his efforts. Marquis de Lafayette dedicated the towering obelisk during his one and only visit to Savannah in 1825. At the time it did not honor any one person. Its dedication to Greene came in 1886, followed by the reinterment of Greene's remains directly underneath the monument in 1901. In typically maddening Savannah fashion, there is a separate square named for Greene, and which has no monument to him at all.

### CHRIST EPISCOPAL CHURCH

The southeast corner of Johnson Square is dominated by Christ Episcopal Church, aka Christ Church, a historic house of worship also known as the "Mother Church of Georgia" because its congregation traces its roots to that first Anglican service in Savannah, held the same day Oglethorpe landed. While this spot on Johnson Square was reserved for the congregation from the very beginning, this is actually the third building on the site, dating from 1838. Much of the interior is more recent than that, however, since a fire gutted the inside of the church in 1895. In the northeast bell tower is a bell forged in 1919 by Revere and Sons of Boston.

MAP 1: 28 Bull St., 912/236-2500, www. christchurchsavannah.org

## Reynolds Square

Walk directly east of Johnson Square to find yourself at Reynolds Square, named for John Reynolds, the first (and exceedingly unpopular) royal governor of Georgia. First called "Lower New Square," Reynolds Square originally served as site of the filature, or cocoon storage warehouse, during the fledgling colony's ill-fated flirtation with the silk industry (a federal building now occupies the site). As with Johnson Square, the monument in Reynolds Square has nothing to do with its namesake, but is instead a likeness of John Wesley dedicated in 1969 near the spot believed to have been his home. On the northeast corner of the square is the parish house of Christ Church, Wesley's congregation during his stay in Savannah.

### LUCAS THEATRE FOR THE ARTS

The other major Savannah landmark on Reynolds Square is the Lucas Theatre for the Arts. Built in 1921 as part of Arthur Lucas's regional chain of movie houses, the Lucas also featured a stage for road shows. Ornate and stately but with cozy warmth to spare, the venue was a hit with Savannahians for four decades, until the advent of TV and residential flight from downtown led to financial disaster. In 1976, the Lucas closed after a screening of *The Exorcist*. When the building faced demolition in 1986, a group of citizens created a nonprofit to save it. Despite numerous starts and stops, the 14-year campaign finally paid off in a grand reopening in 2000, an event helped immeasurably by timely donations from *Midnight* star Kevin Spacey and the cast and crew of the locally shot *Forrest Gump*. The theater's schedule stays pretty busy, so it should be easy to check out a show while you're in town. MAP 1: 32 Abercorn St., 912/525-5040, www. lucastheatre.com

### OLDE PINK HOUSE

A Reynolds Square landmark, the Olde Pink House is not only one of Savannah's most romantic restaurants but quite a historic site as well. It's the oldest Savannah mansion from the 18th century still standing as well as the first place in Savannah where the Declaration of Independence was read aloud. Pink inside as well as out, the Georgian mansion was built in 1771 for rice planter James Habersham Jr., one of America's richest men at the time and a member of the notorious "Liberty Boys" who plotted revolution. The building's pink exterior was a matter of serendipity, resulting from its core redbrick seeping through the formerly white stucco outer covering. MAP 1: 23 Abercorn St.

### OLIVER STURGIS HOUSE

At the southwest corner of Reynolds Square is the understated Oliver Sturgis House, former home of the partner with William Scarbrough in the launching of the SS *Savannah*. This is one of the few Savannah buildings to feature the stabilizing earthquake rods that are much more common in Charleston. Don't miss the dolphin downpour spouts at ground level. MAP 1: 27 Abercorn St.

the Olde Pink House on Reynolds Square

## Columbia Square

Named for the mythical patroness of America, Columbia Square features at its center not an expected portrait of that female warrior figure but the original fountain from Noble Jones's Wormsloe Plantation, placed there in 1970.

### ISAIAH DAVENPORT HOUSE MUSEUM

Columbia Square is primarily known as the home of the Isaiah Davenport House Museum. The house museum is a delightful stop in and of itself because of its elegant simplicity, sweeping double staircase, and near-perfect representation of the Federalist style. But the Davenport House occupies an exalted place in Savannah history as well, because the fight to save it began the preservation movement in Savannah. In 1955 the Davenport House, then a tenement, was to be demolished for a parking lot. But Emma Adler and six other Savannah women, angered by the recent destruction of Ellis Square, refused to let it go down quietly. Together they formed the Historic Savannah Foundation in order to raise the $22,500 needed to purchase the Davenport House. By 1963 the Davenport House—built in 1820 for his own family by master builder Isaiah Davenport—was open to the public as a museum.

Most Octobers, the Davenport House hosts living history dramatizations based on Savannah's yellow fever plague of the 1820s. Despite the grim subject matter, the little playlets are usually quite entertaining. Other special seasonal tours include a Madeira wine tour and "Tea with Mrs. Davenport."

**MAP 1:** 324 E. State St., 912/236-8097, www. davenporthousemuseum.org; Mon.-Sat. 10am-4pm, Sun. 1pm-4pm; $9 adults, $5 children

### KEHOE HOUSE

Across the corner from the Davenport House is the Classical Revival masterpiece Kehoe House, designed for local ironworks owner William Kehoe in 1892 by DeWitt Bruyn. Sadly, the proof of Kehoe's self-described "weakness for cupolas" no longer exists, the cupola having rotted away. Once a funeral home, the Kehoe House is now one of Savannah's premier bed-and-breakfasts. It's unique not only in its exuberantly Victorian architecture but in its twin fireplaces and ubiquitous rococo ironwork, courtesy of the irrepressible Kehoe himself.

**MAP 1:** 123 Habersham St.

## Warren and Washington Squares

Warren Square and its neighbor Washington Square formed the first extension of Oglethorpe's original four and still boast some of the oldest houses in the historic district. Both squares are lovely little garden spots, ideal for a picnic in the shade.

### THE BRICE

Now a hotel, The Brice on Washington Square was once a cotton warehouse and subsequently one of the nation's first Coca-Cola bottling plants.

**MAP 1:** 601 E. Bay St.

### HAMPTON LILLIBRIDGE HOUSE AND CHARLES ODDINGSELLS HOUSE

Two houses near Washington Square were restored by the late Jim Williams of *Midnight* fame: the Hampton Lillibridge House, which once hosted an Episcopal exorcism, and the Charles Oddingsells House.

**MAP 1:** 507 E. St. Julian St. and 510 E. St. Julian St.

## Greene Square

Named for Revolutionary War hero Nathanael Greene, but bearing no monument to him whatsoever, Greene Square is of particular importance to local African American history. In 1818, the residence at 542 East State Street was constructed for free blacks Charlotte and William Wall. The property at 513 East York Street was built for the estate of Catherine DeVeaux, part of a prominent African American family.

### CUNNINGHAM HOUSE

At the corner of Houston (pronounced "HOUSE-ton") and East State Streets is the 1810 Cunningham House, built for Henry Cunningham, former slave and founding pastor of the Second African Baptist Church.

**MAP 1:** Houston St. and State St.

### SECOND AFRICAN BAPTIST CHURCH

The Second African Baptist Church, on the west side of the square, is where General Sherman made his famous promise of "40 acres and a mule." The founding pastor of the church was Henry Cunningham, whose home, the Cunningham House, is also on Green Square.

**MAP 1:** 124 Houston St., 912/233-6163, www. secondafrican.org

## Old Fort

One of the lesser-known aspects of Savannah history is this well-trod neighborhood at the east end of Bay Street, once the site of groundbreaking experiments and piratical intrigue, and then a diverse melting pot of Savannah citizenry.

### EMMET PARK

Just north of Reynolds Square on the north side of Bay Street you'll come to Emmet Park, first a Native American burial ground and then known as "the Strand" or "Irish Green" because of its proximity to the Irish slums of the Old Fort. In 1902 the park was named for Robert Emmet, an Irish patriot of the early 1800s, who was executed by the British for treason. Within it is the eight-foot **Celtic Cross**, erected in 1983 and carved of Irish limestone. The Celtic Cross is at the center of a key ceremony for local Irish Catholics during the week prior to St. Patrick's Day.

Close by is one of Savannah's more recent monuments, the **Vietnam War Memorial** at East Bay Street and Rossiter Lane. The reflecting pool is in the shape of Vietnam itself, and the names of all 106 Savannahians killed in the conflict are carved into an adjacent marble tablet.

Walk a little farther east and you'll find my favorite little chapter of Bay Street history, the **Beacon Range Light,** tucked into a shady corner. Few visitors bother to check out this masterfully crafted 1858 navigation aid, intended to warn approaching ships of the old wrecks sunk in the river as a defense during the Revolutionary War.

MAP 1: E. Bay St. west of E. Broad St.

### TRUSTEES' GARDEN

At the east end of Bay Street where it meets East Broad Street rises a bluff behind a masonry wall—at 40 feet off the river, still the highest point in Chatham County. This is Trustees' Garden, the nation's first experimental garden. Modeled on the Chelsea Botanical Garden in London, it was intended to be the epicenter of Savannah's silk industry. Alas, the colonists had little knowledge of native soils or climate—they thought the winters would be milder—and the experiment was not as successful as hoped. Soon Trustees' Garden became the site of Fort Wayne, named after General "Mad Anthony" Wayne of Revolutionary War fame, who retired to a plantation near Savannah. The Fort Wayne area—still called the "Old Fort" neighborhood by old-timers—fell from grace and became associated with the "lowest elements" of Savannah society, which in the 19th and early 20th centuries were Irish and African Americans. It also became known for its illegal activity and as the haunt of sea salts such as the ones who frequented what is now the delightfully schlocky **Pirates' House** restaurant. That building began life in 1753 as a seamen's inn and was later chronicled by Robert Louis Stevenson in *Treasure Island* as a rogue's gallery of pirates and nautical ne'er-do-wells.

Find the **Herb House** on East Broad Street, the older-looking clapboard structure next to the Pirates' House entrance. You're looking at what is considered the single oldest building in Georgia and one of the oldest in the United States. Constructed in 1734, it was originally the home of Trustees' Garden's chief gardener.

To the rear of Trustees' Garden is the 1881 Hillyer building, now the **Charles H. Morris Center,** a mixed-use performing arts and meeting space that is heavily used during the springtime Savannah Music Festival.

MAP 1: 10 E. Broad St., 912/443-3277, http://trusteesgarden.com

## Broughton Street

Downtown's main shopping district for most of the 20th century, Broughton Street once dazzled shoppers with decorated gaslights, ornate window displays, and fine examples of terrazzo, a form of mosaic that still adorns many shop entrances. Postwar suburbs and white flight brought neglect to the area by the 1960s, and many thought Broughton was gone for good. But with the downtown renaissance brought about largely by the Savannah College of Art and Design (SCAD), Broughton was able not only to get back on its feet, but also to thrive as a commercial center once again.

### JEN LIBRARY

The Savannah College of Art and Design's Jen Library is a state-of-the-art facility set in the circa-1890 Levy and Maas Brothers department stores. An important piece of Broughton Street history happened farther west at its intersection with Whitaker Street. Tondee's Tavern was where the infamous "Liberty Boys" met over ale and planned Savannah's role in the American Revolution. Only a plaque marks the site's contribution to Savannah's colonial history.

MAP 1: 201 E. Broughton St.

### TRUSTEES THEATER

Around the corner from the Lucas Theatre on Reynolds Square is the art moderne Trustees Theater, a Savannah College of Art and Design (SCAD) operation that seats 1,200 and hosts concerts, film screenings, and the school's much-anticipated spring fashion show. It began life in the postwar boom of 1946 as the Weis Theatre, another one of those ornate Southern movie houses that took full commercial advantage of being the only buildings at the time to have air-conditioning. But by the end of the 1970s it had followed the fate of Broughton Street, lying dormant and neglected until its purchase and renovation by SCAD in 1989.

This block of Broughton in front of Trustees Theater is usually blocked off to mark the gala opening of the Savannah Film

# A Southern St. Paddy's Day

Savannah's St. Patrick's Day Parade

Savannah hosts the second-largest St. Patrick's Day celebration in the world, second only to New York City's. With its fine spring weather and walkability—not to mention its liberal rules allowing you to carry an adult beverage on the street—Savannah is tailor-made for a boisterous outdoor celebration.

Ironically, given St. Patrick's Day's current close association with the Catholic faith, the first parade in Savannah was organized by Irish Protestants. Thirteen members of the local Hibernian Society—the country's oldest Irish society—took part in a private procession to Independent Presbyterian Church in 1813. The first public procession was in 1824, when the Hibernians invited all local Irishmen to parade through the streets. The first recognizably modern parade, with bands and a "grand marshal," happened in 1870.

Organized by a "committee" of about 700 local Irishmen—with but a tiny sprinkling of women—today's three-hour procession includes marchers from all the local Irish organizations, in addition to marching bands and floats representing many local groups. The assembled clans wear kelly green blazers, brandishing their walking canes and to-go cups, some pushing future committee members in strollers.

Festival each fall. Searchlights crisscross the sky, limos idle in wait, and Hollywood guests strike poses for the photographers.

**MAP 1:** 216 E. Broughton St., 912/525-5051, www.trusteestheater.com

## Wright Square

The big monument in Wright Square, Oglethorpe's second square, has nothing to do with James Wright, royal governor of Georgia before the Revolution, for whom it's named. Instead the monument honors William Gordon, former mayor and founder of the Central of Georgia Railway, which upon completion of the Savannah-Macon run was the longest railroad in the world. Gordon is in fact the only native Savannahian honored in a city square. But more importantly, Wright Square is the final resting place for the great Yamacraw chief Tomochichi, buried in 1737 in an elaborate state funeral at James Oglethorpe's insistence. A huge boulder of north Georgia granite honoring the chief was placed in a corner of the square in 1899 under the auspices of William Gordon's daughter-in-law. However, Tomochichi is not buried under the boulder but rather somewhere underneath the Gordon monument. So why not rename it Tomochichi Square? Old ways die hard down here, my friend.

### EVANGELICAL LUTHERAN CHURCH OF THE ASCENSION

Next to the old courthouse is the historic Evangelical Lutheran Church of the Ascension, built in the 1870s for a congregation that traced its roots to some of the first Austrian Salzburgers to come to Savannah in 1734.
**MAP 1:** 120 Bull St., 912/232-4151, www.elcota.org

### FEDERAL COURTHOUSE AND POST OFFICE

On the west side of Wright Square is the Federal Courthouse and Post Office, built in 1898 out of Georgia marble. The building's stately facade makes an appearance in several films, including the original *Cape Fear* and *Midnight in the Garden of Good and Evil*.
**MAP 1:** 125-127 Bull St.

## Telfair Square

One of the few Savannah squares to show consistency in nomenclature, Telfair Square was indeed named for Mary Telfair, last heir of a family that was one of the most important in Savannah history. Mary bequeathed the family mansion to the Georgia Historical Society upon her death in 1875 to serve as a museum. Originally called St. James Square after a similar square in London, Telfair was the last of Oglethorpe's original four squares.

Telfair Square hosts two of the three buildings operated by **Telfair Museums,** an umbrella organization that relies on a combination of private and public funding and has driven much of the arts agenda in Savannah for the last 125 years. The third component of Telfair Museums is the **Owens-Thomas House** on Oglethorpe Square.

Get a triple site pass to the Jepson Center, the Telfair Academy, and the Owens-Thomas House for $20 per person.

### ★ JEPSON CENTER FOR THE ARTS

The proudest addition to the Telfair Museums group is the striking, 64,000-square-foot Jepson Center for the Arts, whose ultramodern exterior sits catty-corner from the Telfair Academy of Arts and Sciences. Promoting a massive, daringly designed new facility devoted to nothing but modern art was a hard

the monument to Yamacraw Chief Tomochichi in Wright Square

sell in this traditional town, especially when renowned architect Moshe Safdie insisted on building a glassed-in flyover across a lane between two buildings. After a few delays in construction, the Jepson opened its doors in 2006 and has since wowed locals and visitors alike with its cutting-edge traveling exhibits and rotating assortment of late-20th-century and 21st-century modern art. If you get hungry, you can enjoy lunch in the expansive atrium café, and, of course, there's a nice gift shop.

Each late January-early February the Jepson Center hosts most events of the unique Pulse Art + Technology Festival, a celebration of the intersection of cutting-edge technology and performing and visual arts.

MAP 1: 207 W. York Ln., 912/790-8800, www.telfair. org; Tues.-Sat. 10am-5pm, Sun.-Mon. noon-5pm; $12 adults, $5 students

### ★ TELFAIR ACADEMY OF ARTS AND SCIENCES

The oldest public art museum in the South, the Telfair Academy of Arts and Sciences was built in 1821 by the great William Jay for Alexander Telfair, scion of that famous Georgia family. The five statues in front are of Phidias, Raphael, Rubens, Michelangelo, and Rembrandt. As well as displaying Sylvia Judson Shaw's now-famous *Bird Girl* sculpture, which originally stood in Bonaventure Cemetery (actually the third of four casts by the sculptor), the Telfair Academy features an outstanding collection of primarily 18th- and 20th-century works, most notably the largest public collection of visual art by Khalil Gibran. Major paintings include works by Childe Hassam, Frederick Frieseke, Gari Melchers, and the massive *Black Prince of Crécy* by Julian Story.

MAP 1: 121 Barnard St., 912/790-8800, www.telfair. org; Tues.-Sat. 10am-5pm, Sun.-Mon. noon-5pm; $12 adults, $5 students

### TRINITY UNITED METHODIST CHURCH

Directly between the Telfair and the Jepson stands Trinity United Methodist Church, Savannah's first Methodist church. Built in 1848 on the site of the Telfair family garden, its masonry walls are of famous "Savannah Gray" bricks—a lighter, more porous and elegant variety—under stucco. Virgin longleaf pine was used for most of the interior, fully restored in 1969. Call ahead for a tour.

MAP 1: 225 W. President St., 912/233-4766, www. trinitychurch1848.org; sanctuary daily 9am-5pm, services Sun. 8:45am and 11am

Jepson Center for the Arts

## Oglethorpe Square

Don't look for a monument to Georgia's founder in the square named for him. That would be way too easy, so of course his monument is in Chippewa Square. Originally called "Upper New Square," Oglethorpe Square was created in 1742.

### JULIETTE GORDON LOW BIRTHPLACE

Around the corner from Wright Square at Oglethorpe and Bull is the Juliette Gordon Low Birthplace, declared the city's very first National Historic Landmark in 1965, and fresh off a significant restoration effort. The founder of the Girl Scouts of the USA lived here from her birth in 1860 until her marriage. The house was completed in 1821 for Mayor James Moore Wayne, future Supreme Court justice, but the current furnishings, many original, are intended to reflect the home during the 1880s.

Also called the Girl Scout National Center, the Low birthplace is probably Savannah's most festive historic site because of the heavy traffic of Girl Scout troops from across the United States. They flock here year-round to take part in programs and learn more about their organization's founder, whose family sold the house to the Girl Scouts in 1953. You don't have to be affiliated with the Girl Scouts to tour the home. Tours are given every 15 minutes, and tickets are available at the Oglethorpe Avenue entrance. Be aware the site is closed most holidays, sometimes for extended periods; be sure to check the website for details.

**MAP 1:** 10 E. Oglethorpe Ave., 912/233-4501, www. juliettegordonlowbirthplace.org; Mar.-Oct. Mon.-Sat. 10am-4pm; $15 adults, $12 children, $10 Girl Scouts

### ★ OWENS-THOMAS HOUSE

The square's main claim to fame, the Owens-Thomas House, lies on the northeast corner. Widely known as the finest example of Regency architecture in the United States, the Owens-Thomas House was designed by brilliant young English architect William Jay. One of the first professionally trained architects in the United States, Jay was only 24 when he designed the home for cotton merchant or "factor" Richard Richardson, who lost the house in the depression of 1820 (all that remains of Richardson's tenure are three marble-top tables). The house's current name is derived from Savannah mayor George Owens, who bought the house in 1830. It remained in his family until 1951, when his granddaughter

Telfair Academy of Arts and Sciences

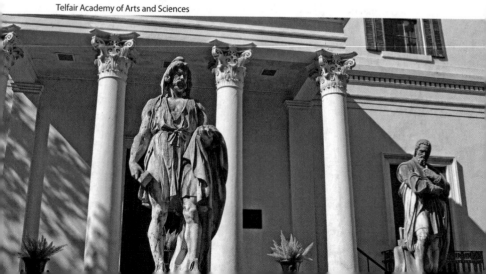

# Scout's Honor

Known as "Daisy" to family and friends, **Juliette Magill Kinzie** Gordon was born to be a pioneer. Her father's family took part in the original settlement of Georgia, and her mother's kin were among the founders of Chicago. Mostly known as the founder of the **Girl Scouts of the USA,** Daisy was also an artist, adventurer, and healer. Born and raised in the house on Oglethorpe Avenue in Savannah known to Girl Scouts across the nation as simply "The Birthplace," she was an animal lover with an early penchant for theater, drawing, and poetry.

In 1911 while in England, Daisy met Robert Baden-Powell, founder of the Boy Scouts and Girl Guides in Britain. Struck by the simplicity and usefulness of his project, she carried the seeds of a similar idea back with her to the United States. "I've got something for the girls of Savannah, and all of America, and all the world, and we're going to start it tonight," were her famous words in a phone call to a cousin after meeting Baden-Powell. So on March 12, 1912, Daisy gathered 18 girls to register the first troop of American Girl Guides, later the Girl Scouts of the USA.

Juliette "Daisy" Gordon Low died of breast cancer in her bed in the Andrew Low House on January 17, 1927. She was buried in Laurel Grove Cemetery. Girl Scout troops from all over the United States visit her birthplace, the Andrew Low House, and her gravesite to this day, often leaving flowers and small personal objects near her tombstone as tokens of respect and gratitude.

Margaret Thomas bequeathed it to the Telfair Academy of Arts and Sciences, which currently operates the site.

Several things about the Owens-Thomas House stand out. First, it's constructed mostly of tabby, a mixture of lime, oyster shells, and sand. Its exterior is English stucco while the front garden balustrade is a type of artificial stone called Coade stone. Perhaps most interestingly, a complex plumbing system features rain-fed cisterns, flushing toilets, sinks, bathtubs, and a shower. When built, the Owens-Thomas House in fact had the first indoor plumbing in Savannah.

While inside the house, notice the little touches like the unusual curved walls, with doors bowed to match, and the recessed skylights. While many Owens family furnishings are part of the collection, much of it is representative of American and European work from 1750 to 1830. On the south facade is a beautiful cast-iron veranda from which Revolutionary War hero Marquis de Lafayette addressed a crowd of starstruck Savannahians during his visit in 1825. The 1990s marked the most intensive phase of restoration for the home, which began with a careful renovation of the carriage house and the associated slave quarters—discovered in a surprisingly intact

state, including the original "haint blue" paint. The carriage house, where all tours begin, is now the home's gift shop.

The Owens-Thomas House is owned and operated by the Telfair Museums. Get a combination pass to all Telfair sites—the Jepson Center for the Arts, the Telfair Academy of Arts and Sciences, and the Owens-Thomas House—for $20 per person.

**MAP 1:** 124 Abercorn St., 912/233-9743, www.telfair. org; Tues.-Sat. 10am-5pm, Sun.-Mon. noon-5pm, last tour 4:30pm; $20 adults, $15 students, ticket includes Jepson Center and Telfair Academy

## Martin Luther King Jr. Boulevard
### SHIPS OF THE SEA MARITIME MUSEUM

One of Savannah's more unique museums is the quirky Ships of the Sea Maritime Museum. The stunning Greek Revival building in which it resides is known as the Scarbrough House because it was initially built in 1819 by the great William Jay for local shipping merchant William Scarbrough, co-owner of the SS *Savannah*, the first steamship to cross the Atlantic. After the Scarbroughs sold the property, it became the West Broad School for African Americans from Reconstruction through integration.

One of the Historic Savannah Foundation's key restoration projects in the 1970s, the museum got another major facelift in 1998, including a roof based on the original Jay design, an outdoor performance space, and a delightful enlargement of the mansion's garden out back. Inside, children, maritime buffs, and crafts connoisseurs can find intricate and detailed scale models of various historic vessels, such as Oglethorpe's *Anne,* the SS *Savannah,* and the NS *Savannah,* the world's first nuclear-powered surface vessel. There's even a model of the *Titanic.*

**MAP 1:** 41 MLK Jr. Blvd., 912/232-1511, http://shipsofthesea.org; Tues.-Sun. 10am-5pm; $9 adults, $7 students

## HISTORIC DISTRICT SOUTH
### Chippewa Square

Named for a battle in the War of 1812, Chippewa Square has a large monument not to the battle, natch, but to James Oglethorpe, clad in full soldier's regalia. Notice the general is still facing south, toward the Spanish.

Yes, the bench on the square's north side is in the same location as the one Tom Hanks occupied in *Forrest Gump,* but it's not the same bench that hosted the two-time Oscar winner's backside—that one was donated by Paramount Pictures to be displayed in the Savannah History Museum on MLK Jr. Boulevard.

From Chippewa Square look south for the huge rectangular steel-and-glass structure dominating the skyline along Liberty Street. That's the infamous **Drayton Tower,** an outstanding, nearly pure example of the internationalist architecture style nonetheless loathed by traditionalists since its construction in 1955. Until recently it served as low-cost housing for students and seniors. They've since been kicked out, as now the building is subdivided into high-end condos with retail on the ground floor.

### COLONIAL CEMETERY

Just north of Chippewa Square is Oglethorpe Avenue, originally called South Broad and the southern boundary of the original colony. At Oglethorpe and Abercorn Streets is Colonial Cemetery, first active in 1750. You'd be forgiven for assuming it's the "DAR" cemetery; the Daughters of the American Revolution contributed the ornate iron entranceway in 1913, thoughtfully dedicating it to themselves instead of the cemetery itself.

Unlike the picturesque beauty of

Chippewa Square

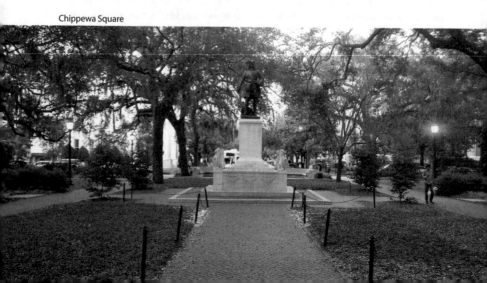

Bonaventure and Laurel Grove Cemeteries, Colonial Cemetery has a morbid feel. The fact that burials stopped here in 1853 plays into that desolation, but maybe another reason is because it's the final resting ground of many of Savannah's yellow fever victims. Famous people buried here include Button Gwinnett, one of Georgia's three signers of the Declaration of Independence. The man who reluctantly killed Gwinnett in a duel, General Lachlan McIntosh, is also buried here. The original burial vault of Nathanael Greene is in the cemetery, although the Revolutionary War hero's remains were moved to Johnson Square over a century ago.

Vandalism through the years, mostly by Union troops, took a toll on the old gravestones. Many line the east wall of the cemetery, with no one alive able to remember where they originally stood.

**MAP 2:** Oglethorpe St. and Abercorn St., www.savannahga.gov; daily 8am-dusk

### FIRST BAPTIST CHURCH

The nearby First Baptist Church—not to be confused with the more famous First African Baptist Church on Franklin Square—claims to be the oldest original church building in Savannah, with a cornerstone dating from 1830. Services were held here throughout the Civil War, with Union troops attending during the occupation. The church was renovated by renowned local architect Henrik Wallin in 1922. Call ahead for a tour.

**MAP 2:** 223 Bull St., 912/234-2671; service Sun. 11am

### HISTORIC SAVANNAH THEATRE

At the square's northeast corner is the Historic Savannah Theatre, which claims to be the oldest continuously operating theater in the United States. Designed by William Jay, it opened in 1818 with a production of *The Soldier's Daughter*. In the glory days of gaslight theater in the 1800s, some of the nation's best actors, including Edwin Booth, brother to Lincoln's assassin, regularly trod the boards of its stage. Other notable visitors were Sarah Bernhardt, W. C. Fields, and Oscar Wilde.

Due to a fire in 1948, little remains of Jay's original design except a small section of exterior wall. The building is currently home to a semiprofessional revue company specializing in oldies shows.

**MAP 2:** 222 Bull St., 912/233-7764, www.savannahtheatre.com

### INDEPENDENT PRESBYTERIAN CHURCH

Built in 1818, possibly by William Jay—scholars are unsure of the scope of his involvement—Independent Presbyterian Church is called the "mother of Georgia Presbyterianism." A fire destroyed most of Independent Presbyterian's original structure in 1889, but the subsequent rebuilding was a very faithful rendering of the original design, based on London's St. Martin-in-the-Fields. The marble baptism font survived the fire and is still used today. Note also the huge mahogany pulpit, another original feature. The church's steeple made a cameo appearance in *Forrest Gump* as a white feather floated by.

Lowell Mason, composer of the hymn "Nearer My God to Thee," was organist at Independent Presbyterian. In 1885 President Woodrow Wilson married local parishioner Ellen Louise Axson in the manse to the rear of the church. Presiding was her grandfather, minister at the time. During the Great Awakening in 1896, almost 3,000 people jammed the sanctuary to hear famous evangelist D. L. Moody preach. Call ahead for a tour.

**MAP 2:** 207 Bull St., 912/236-3346, www.ipcsav.org; services Sun. 11am, Wed. noon

## Madison Square

Named for the nation's fourth president, Madison Square memorializes a local hero who gave his life for his city during the American Revolution. Irish immigrant Sergeant William Jasper, hero of the Battle of Fort Moultrie in Charleston three years earlier, was killed leading the American charge during the 1779 Siege of Savannah, when an allied army failed to retake the city from the British. The monument in the square honors

Jasper, but he isn't buried here; his body was interred in a mass grave near the battlefield along with other colonists and soldier-immigrants killed in the one-sided battle.

The two small, suitably warlike cannons in the square have nothing to do with the Siege of Savannah. They commemorate the first two highways in Georgia, today known as Augusta Road and Ogeechee Road.

### GREEN-MELDRIM HOUSE

Given the house's beauty and history, visitors will be forgiven for not immediately realizing that the Green-Meldrim House is also the rectory of the adjacent St. John's Episcopal Church, which acquired it in 1892. Though it's known primarily for serving as General William T. Sherman's headquarters during his occupation of Savannah, visitors find the Green-Meldrim House a remarkably calming, serene location in and of itself, quite apart from its role as the place where Sherman formulated his ill-fated "40 acres and a mule" Field Order No. 15, giving most of the Sea Islands of Georgia and South Carolina to freed blacks. A tasteful example of Gothic Revival architecture, this 1850 design by John Norris features a beautiful external gallery of filigree ironwork. The interior is decorated with a keen and rare eye for elegant minimalism in this sometimes rococo-minded town.

**MAP 2:** 1 W. Macon St., 912/232-1251, www.stjohnssav.org; tours every 30 minutes Tues. and Thurs.-Fri. 10am-4pm, Sat. 10am-1pm; $8 adults, $5 students and children

### HILTON SAVANNAH DESOTO

At the north side of Madison Square is the Hilton Savannah DeSoto. Imagine occupying that same space the most glorious, opulent, regal building you can think of, a paradise of brick, mortar, and buff-colored terra-cotta. That would have been the old DeSoto Hotel, which from its opening in 1890 was known as one of the world's most beautiful hotels and the clear masterpiece in Boston architect William Gibbons Preston's already-impressive

Savannah portfolio. Alas, it didn't have air-conditioning, so the Hilton chain demolished it in 1968 to build the current nondescript box.

**MAP 2:** 15 E. Liberty St., 912/232-9000, www.desotohilton.com

### POETTER HALL

The Savannah College of Art and Design's first building, Poetter Hall, known to old-timers as the Savannah Volunteer Guards Armory, is directly across from the Scottish Rite Temple. With its imposing but somewhat whimsical facade right out of a Harry Potter movie, this brick and terra-cotta gem of a Romanesque Revival building was built in 1893 by William Gibbons Preston. It housed National Guard units (as well as a high school) until World War II, when the USO occupied the building during its tenant unit's service in Europe.

**MAP 2:** 342 Bull St., www.scad.edu

### SCOTTISH RITE TEMPLE

The old Scottish Rite Temple at Charlton and Bull Streets was designed by Hyman Witcover, who also designed City Hall. A popular drugstore with a soda fountain for many years, it currently houses the **Gryphon Tea Room,** run by the Savannah College of Art and Design.

**MAP 2:** Charlton St. and Bull St., 912/525-5880; Mon.-Sat. 11am-6pm, Sun. 11am-3pm

## Lafayette Square

Truly one of Savannah's favorite squares, especially on St. Patrick's Day, verdant Lafayette Square boasts a number of important sights and attractions.

### ANDREW LOW HOUSE MUSEUM

A major landmark on Lafayette Square is the Andrew Low House Museum, once the home of Juliette "Daisy" Gordon Low, the founder of the Girl Scouts of the USA, who was married to cotton heir William "Billow" Low, Andrew Low's son. Despite their happy-go-lucky nicknames, the union of Daisy and

Billow was a notably unhappy one. Still, divorce was out of the question, so the couple lived separate lives until William's death in 1905. The one good thing that came out of the marriage was the germ for the idea for the Girl Scouts, which Juliette got from England's "Girl Guides" while living there with her husband, Savannah being the couple's winter residence.

Designed by the great New York architect John Norris, the Low House is a magnificent example of the Italianate style. Check out the cast-iron balconies on the long porch, a fairly rare feature in historic Savannah homes. Antiques junkies will go nuts over the furnishings, especially the massive secretary in the parlor, one of only four of this type in existence (a sibling is in the Metropolitan Museum of Art). Author William Makepeace Thackeray ate in the dining room, now sporting full French porcelain service, and slept in an upstairs room; he also wrote at the desk by the bed. Also on the second floor you'll see the room where Robert E. Lee stayed during his visit and the bed where Juliette Gordon Low died.

MAP 2: 329 Abercorn St., 912/233-6854, www.andrewlowhouse.com; Mon.-Sat. 10am-4pm, Sun. noon-4pm; $10 adults, $8 children

## ★ CATHEDRAL OF ST. JOHN THE BAPTIST

Spiritual home to Savannah's Irish community and the oldest Catholic church in Georgia, the Cathedral of St. John the Baptist was initially known as Our Lady of Perpetual Help. It's the place to be for mass the morning of March 17 at 8am, as the clans gather in their green jackets and white dresses to take a sip of communion wine before moving on to harder stuff in honor of St. Patrick.

Despite its overt Celtic character today, the parish was originally founded by French émigrés from Haiti who arrived after the successful overthrow of the colonial government by a slave uprising on the island in the late 1700s. They were joined by other Gallic Catholics when some nobles fled from the French Revolution. The first sanctuary on the site was built in 1873, after the diocese traded a lot at Taylor and Lincoln Streets to the Sisters of Mercy in exchange for this locale.

the Cathedral of St. John the Baptist

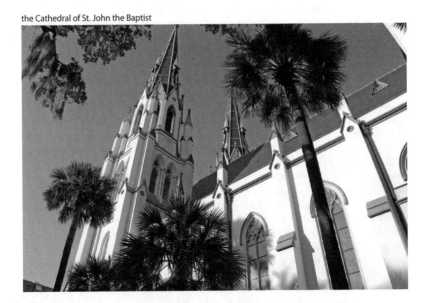

# The Story of "Jingle Bells"

Boston and Savannah vie over bragging rights as to where the classic Christmas song "Jingle Bells" was written. The song's composer, James L. Pierpont, led a life at times as carefree as the song itself. Born in Boston, Pierpont ventured from his wife and young children in 1849 to follow the gold rush to San Francisco. When his brother John was named minister of the new Unitarian congregation in Savannah 1853, Pierpont followed him, becoming music director and organist, again leaving behind his wife and children in Boston. During this time Pierpont became a prolific composer of secular tunes, including polkas, ballads, and minstrel songs.

In August 1857, a Boston-based publisher, Oliver Ditson and Co., published Pierpont's song "One Horse Open Sleigh." Two years later it was rereleased with the current title, "Jingle Bells." At neither time, however, was the song a popular hit. It took action by his son Juriah in 1880 to renew the copyright to what would become one of the most famous songs of all time.

In Massachusetts, they swear Pierpont wrote the song while at the home of one Mrs. Otis Waterman. In Georgia, scholars assure us a homesick Pierpont wrote the tune during a winter at a house at Oglethorpe and Whitaker Streets, long since demolished. The Savannah contingent's ace in the hole is the fact that "Jingle Bells" was first performed in public at a Thanksgiving program at the local Unitarian Universalist Church in 1857. And despite persistent claims in Massachusetts that he wrote the song there in 1850, Southern scholars point out that Pierpont was actually in California in 1850.

In a distressingly common event back then in Savannah, fire swept through the edifice in 1898, leaving only two spires and the external walls. In an amazing story of determination and skill, the cathedral was completely rebuilt within a year and a half. In the years since, many renovations have been undertaken, including an interior renovation following the Second Vatican Council to incorporate some of that body's sweeping reforms (for example, a new altar allowing the celebrant to face the congregation). The most recent renovation, from 1998 to 2000, involved the intricate removal, cleaning, and releading of more than 50 of the cathedral's stained glass windows, a roof replacement, and an interior makeover.

When inside the magnificent interior, look for the new 9,000-pound altar and the 8,000-pound baptismal font, both made of Italian marble.

In 2003 an armed man entered the cathedral and set the pulpit and bishop's chair on fire, resulting in nearly $400,000 of damage. The pulpit you see now is an exact replica carved in Italy. The arsonist claimed he did it as a statement against organized religion. **MAP 2:** 222. E. Harris St., 912/233-4709, www. savannahcathedral.org; daily 9am-noon and 12:30pm-5pm, mass Sun. 8am, 10am, 11:30am, Mon.-Sat. noon, Latin mass Sun. 1pm

## FLANNERY O'CONNOR CHILDHOOD HOME

On a corner of Lafayette Square stands the rather Spartan facade of the Flannery O'Connor Childhood Home. The Savannah-born novelist lived in this three-story townhome from her birth in 1925 until 1938 and attended church at the cathedral across the square. Once a fairly nondescript attraction for so favorite a native daughter, a recent round of renovations has returned the two main floors to the state Flannery would have known, including an extensive library. A nonprofit association sponsors O'Connor-related readings and signings. While the current backyard garden dates to 1993, it's the place where five-year-old Flannery is said to have taught a chicken to walk backward, foreshadowing the eccentric, Gothic flavor of her writing. **MAP 2:** 207 E. Charlton St., 912/233-6014, www. flanneryoconnorhome.org; Fri.-Wed.1pm-4pm; $6 adults, $5 students, free under age 15

## HAMILTON-TURNER INN

Across from the O'Connor house is the Hamilton-Turner Inn. Now a privately owned bed-and-breakfast, this 1873 Second Empire mansion is best known for the showmanship of its over-the-top Victorian appointments and its role in *Midnight in the Garden of Good and Evil* as the home of Joe Odom's girlfriend "Mandy Nichols" (real name Nancy Hillis). In 1883 it was reportedly the first house in Savannah to have electricity.

**MAP 2:** 330 Abercorn St., 912/233-1833, www. hamilton-turnerinn.com

## Troup Square

Low-key Troup Square boasts the most modern-looking monument downtown, the **Armillary Sphere.** Essentially an elaborate sundial, the sphere is a series of astrologically themed rings with an arrow that marks the time by shadow. It is supported by six tortoises.

## BEACH INSTITUTE

Just east of Troup Square, near the intersection of Harris and Price Streets, is the Beach Institute. Built as a school by the Freedmen's Bureau soon after the Civil War, it was named after its prime benefactor, Alfred Beach, editor of *Scientific American*. It served as an African American school through 1919. Restored by SCAD and given back to the city to serve as a museum, the Beach Institute houses the permanent Ulysses Davis collection and a rotating calendar of art events with a connection to black history.

**MAP 2:** 502 E. Harris St., 912/234-8000; Tues.-Sun. noon-5pm; $4

## JONES STREET

There aren't a lot of individual attractions on Jones Street, the east-west avenue between Taylor and Charlton Streets just north of Monterey Square. Rather, it's the small-scale, throwback feel of the place and its tasteful, dignified homes, including the former home of **Joe Odom** (16 E. Jones St.), that are the attraction. The **Eliza Thompson House** (5 W. Jones St.), now a bed-and-breakfast, was the first home on Jones Street. Cotton factor Joseph Thompson built the house for his wife, Eliza, in 1847. The carriage house is not original to the structure, having been built almost from scratch in 1980.

**MAP 2:** Jones St. between Taylor St. and Charlton St.

Troup Square

## UNITARIAN UNIVERSALIST CHURCH OF SAVANNAH

Troup Square is the home of the historic Unitarian Universalist Church of Savannah. This original home of Savannah's Unitarians, who sold the church when the Civil War came, was recently reacquired by the congregation. It is where James L. Pierpont first performed his immortal tune "Jingle Bells." When he did so, however, the church was actually on Oglethorpe Square. The entire building was moved to Troup Square in the mid-1800s.

**MAP 2:** 313 E. Harris St., 912/234-0980, www.jinglebellschurch.org; service Sun. 11am

## ★ Monterey Square

Originally named "Monterrey Square" to commemorate the local Irish Jasper Greens' participation in a victorious Mexican-American War battle in 1846, the spelling morphed into its current version somewhere along the way. But Monterey Square remains one of the most visually beautiful and serene spots in all of Savannah. At the center of the square is a monument not to the victory for which it is named but to Count Casimir Pulaski, killed while attempting to retake the city from the British, and whose remains supposedly lie under the 55-foot monument.

As early as 1912, people began noticing the disintegration of the monument due to substandard marble used in some key parts, but it wasn't until the 1990s that a full restoration was accomplished. The restoration company discovered that one of the monument's 34 sections had been accidentally installed upside down. In the true spirit of preservation, they dutifully put the section back—upside down. The *Goddess of Liberty* atop the monument, however, is not original; you can see her in the Savannah History Museum. Fans of ironwork will enjoy the ornate masterpieces in wrought iron featured at many houses on the periphery of the square.

## MERCER-WILLIAMS HOUSE MUSEUM

Many visitors come to see the Mercer-Williams House Museum. While locals never begrudge the business Savannah has enjoyed since the publishing of "The Book," *Midnight in the Garden of Good and Evil*, it's a shame that this grand John Norris building is now primarily known as a crime scene involving antiques dealer Jim Williams and his lover. Therefore it might come as no surprise that if you take a tour of the home, you might hear less about "The Book" than you

the Mercer-Williams House

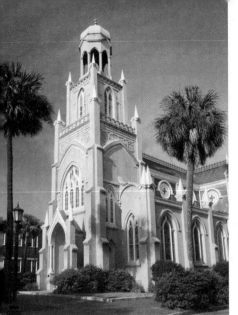

Temple Mickve Israel

completion in 1868. Just so you know, and despite what any tour guide might tell you, the great Johnny Mercer himself never lived in the house. Technically, no member of his family ever did either.

Tours of the home's four main rooms begin in the carriage house to the rear of the mansion. They're worth it for art aficionados even though the upstairs, Dr. Kingery's residence, is off-limits. Be forewarned that if you're coming just to see things about the book or movie, you might be disappointed. **MAP 2:** 429 Bull St., 912-236-6352, www. mercerhouse.com; Mon.-Sat. 10:30am-4pm, Sun. noon-4pm; $12.50 adults, $8 students

### TEMPLE MICKVE ISRAEL

Directly across Monterey Square from the Mercer House is Temple Mickve Israel, a notable structure for many reasons: It's Georgia's first synagogue; it's the only Gothic synagogue in the country; and it's the third-oldest Jewish congregation in North America (following those in New York and Newport, Rhode Island). Notable congregants have included Dr. Samuel Nunes Ribeiro, who helped stop an epidemic in 1733, and his descendant Raphael Moses, considered the father of the peach industry in the Peach State.

Mickve Israel offers 30- to 45-minute tours of the sanctuary and museum. No reservations are necessary for tours. **MAP 2:** 20 E. Gordon St., 912-233-1547, www. mickveisrael.org; Mon.-Fri. 10am-1pm and 2pm-4pm, closed Jewish holidays; $4 suggested donation

## Calhoun Square

The last of the 24 squares in Savannah's original grid, Calhoun Square is also the only square with all its original buildings intact—a rarity indeed in a city ravaged by fire so many times in its history.

### MASSIE HERITAGE CENTER

Dominating the south side of Calhoun Square is Savannah's first public elementary school and the spiritual home of Savannah educators, the Massie Heritage Center. In 1841, Peter

may have expected. Now proudly owned by Jim Williams's sister Dorothy Kingery, an established academic in her own right, the Mercer-Williams House deliberately concentrates on the early history of the home and Jim Williams's prodigious talent as a collector and conservator of fine art and antiques. That said, Dr. Kingery's mama didn't raise no fool, as we say down here. The house was known to generations of Savannahians as simply the Mercer House until *Midnight in the Garden of Good and Evil* took off, at which time the eponymous nod to the late Mr. Williams was added.

The house was built for General Hugh W. Mercer, Johnny Mercer's great-grandfather, in 1860, but the war interrupted construction. General Mercer—descendant of the Revolutionary War general and George Washington's close friend Hugh Mercer—survived the war, in which he was charged with the defense of Savannah. But he soon fell on hard times and was forced to sell the house to John Wilder, who moved in after

# Family Fun in Savannah

Savannah is more than historic mansions and to-go cup pub crawls. There's plenty for tykes to see and do. Here are a few spots:

- **Ellis Square:** This square's modernist renovation includes a large wading fountain area—a great spot to cool off when it gets hot.

- **Georgia State Railroad Museum:** Climb aboard these big machines, which feature frequent short train rides along a short length of track complete with old-fashioned steam whistle. As a bonus, located within the Railroad Museum complex is the small but growing **Savannah Children's Museum.**

- **Jepson Center for the Arts:** In addition to being that rarity—a shiny new modernist building in this very historic old city—there is a neat children's section inside this arts center, the **Artzeum.**

- **Massie School Heritage Center:** This restored historic schoolhouse was the first school for emancipated African Americans in Savannah, and indeed was a public school in the 1970s. Not only is this a charming slice of nostalgia, a recent upgrade and renovation makes it possibly the single best stop for an all-around Savannah history lesson.

- **Oatland Island Educational Center:** To view wildlife up close and personal, head a few minutes east of town to this facility, which houses cougars and an entire wolf pack, in addition to many other animals along its winding marsh-side nature trail.

Massie, a Scots planter with a populist streak, endowed the school to give poor children as good an education as the children of rich families, like Massie's own, received. Another of Savannah's masterpieces by John Norris—whose impressive oeuvre includes the Andrew Low House, the Mercer-Williams House, and the Green-Meldrim House—the central portion of the trifold building was completed in 1856. After the Civil War, the "Massie School," as it's known locally, was designated as the area's African American public school. Classes ceased in 1974, and it now operates as a living-history museum, centering on the period-appointed one-room "heritage classroom" but with several other exhibit spaces of note.

A million-dollar renovation in 2012 added an interactive model of Oglethorpe's urban design and several interesting exhibits on aspects of Savannah architecture and history. In all, Massie provides possibly the best one-stop tour for an all-encompassing look at Savannah history and culture. You can either do a self-guided tour or take the very informative guided tour at 11am or 2pm for the same admission price. Call ahead to double-check tour availability; lots of school groups come through here and sometimes the schedule is shifted.

**MAP 2:** 207 E. Gordon St., 912/201-5070, www.massieschool.com; Mon.-Sat. 10am-4pm, Sun. noon-4pm; $8 adults, $5 youth

## WESLEY MONUMENTAL UNITED METHODIST CHURCH

Catty-corner to the Massie School is the Wesley Monumental United Methodist Church. This home of Savannah's first Methodist parish was named not only for movement founder John Wesley but also for his musical younger brother Charles. Built in 1875 on the model of Queen's Kirk in Amsterdam and the fourth incarnation of the parish home, this is another great example of Savannah's Gothic churches. Its acoustically wonderful sanctuary features a magnificent Noack organ, which would no doubt please the picky ears of Charles Wesley himself, author of the lyrics to "Hark! The Herald Angels Sing."

**MAP 2:** 429 Abercorn St., 912/232-0191, www.
wesleymonumental.org; sanctuary daily 9am-5pm,
services Sun. 8:45am and 11am

## Martin Luther King Jr. Boulevard
### BATTLEFIELD PARK

Right off MLK Jr. Boulevard is Battlefield Park, aka the Spring Hill Redoubt, a reconstruction of the British fortifications at the Siege of Savannah with an interpretive site. Note that the redoubt is not at the actual location of the original fort; that lies underneath the nearby Sons of the Revolution marker. Eight hundred granite markers signify the battle's casualties, most of whom were buried in mass graves soon afterward. Sadly, most of the remains of these brave men were simply bulldozed up and discarded without ceremony during later construction projects.

**MAP 2:** Corner of MLK Jr. Blvd. and Louisville Rd.;
dawn-dusk; free

### GEORGIA STATE RAILROAD MUSEUM

The Georgia State Railroad Museum, aka "The Roundhouse," is an ongoing homage to the deep and strangely underreported influence of the railroad industry on Savannah. Constructed in 1830 for the brand-new Central of Georgia line, the Roundhouse's design was cutting-edge for the time, the first building to put all the railroad's key facilities in one place. Spared by Sherman, the site saw its real heyday after the Civil War. But as technology changed, so did the Roundhouse, which gradually fell further into neglect until the 1960s, when preservation-minded buffs banded together to raise enough money to save it. The real highlight of the Roundhouse is the thing in the middle that gave the structure its name, a huge central turntable for positioning rolling stock for repair and maintenance. Frequent demonstrations occur with an actual steam

locomotive firing up and taking a spin on the turntable.

**MAP 2:** 601 W. Harris St., 912/651-6823, www.
chsgeorgia.org; daily 9am-5pm; $10 adults, $6 students

### SAVANNAH CHILDREN'S MUSEUM

Next to the Railroad Museum is the Savannah Children's Museum, open since 2012. The children's museum is a work in progress that currently has an outdoor "Exploration Station" and a pending larger facility.

**MAP 2:** 655 Louisville Rd., 912/651-6823, www.
savannahchildrensmuseum.org; Tues.-Sat. 10am-4pm,
Sun. 11am-4pm; $7.50

### RALPH MARK GILBERT CIVIL RIGHTS MUSEUM

One of the former black-owned bank buildings on MLK Jr. Boulevard is now home to the Ralph Mark Gilbert Civil Rights Museum. Named for a pastor of the First African Baptist Church and a key early civil rights organizer, the building was also the local NAACP headquarters for a time. Three floors of exhibits here include photos and interactive displays, the highlight for historians being a fiber-optic map of nearly 100 significant civil rights sites. The first floor features a re-creation of the Azalea Room of the local Levy's department store, an early boycott diner where blacks were not allowed to eat, though they could buy goods from the store. The second floor is more for hands-on education, with classrooms, a computer room, and a video and reading room. A film chronicles mass meetings, voter registration drives, boycotts, sit-ins, kneel-ins (the integration of churches), and wade-ins (the integration of beaches).

**MAP 2:** 460 MLK Jr. Blvd., 912/231-8900; Tues.-Sat.
10am-4pm; $10

### SAVANNAH HISTORY MUSEUM

The Savannah History Museum, first stop for many a visitor to town because it's in the same restored Central of Georgia passenger shed as the visitors center, contains many interesting exhibits on local history, concentrating mostly on colonial times. Toward the rear of the museum is a room for rotating exhibits, as well as one of Johnny Mercer's four Oscars, and, of course, the historic "*Forrest Gump* bench" that Tom Hanks sat on during his scenes in Chippewa Square.

MAP 2: 303 MLK Jr. Blvd., 912/651-6825, www. chsgeorgia.org; daily 9am-5:30pm; $7 adults, $4 children

## SCAD MUSEUM OF ART

In 2011, the Savannah College of Art and Design (SCAD) expanded this handsome building into an old railroad facility immediately behind it, more than doubling exhibition space and adding the impressive Walter O. Evans Collection of African American Art. The SCAD Museum of Art now hosts a rotating series of exhibits, from standard painting to video installations, many of them commissioned by the school itself.

MAP 2: 601 Turner Blvd., 912/525-5220, www. scadmoa.org; Tues.-Wed. and Fri. 10am-5pm, Thurs. 10am-8pm, Sat. 10am-5pm, Sun. noon-5pm; $10 adults, $5 students

# VICTORIAN DISTRICT
## CARNEGIE BRANCH LIBRARY

The Carnegie Branch Library is the only example of prairie architecture in town, designed by Savannah architect Julian de Bruyn Kops and built, as the name implies, with funding from tycoon-philanthropist Andrew Carnegie in 1914. But more importantly, the Carnegie Library was for decades the only public library for African Americans in Savannah. One of its patrons was a young Clarence Thomas, who would of course grow up to be a U.S. Supreme Court justice.

MAP 3: 537 E. Henry St., 912/652-3600, www. liveoakpl.org; Mon. 10am-8pm, Tues.-Thurs. 10am-6pm, Fri. 2pm-6pm, Sat. 10am-6pm

## ★ FORSYTH PARK

A favorite with locals and visitors alike, the vast, lush expanse of Forsyth Park is a center of local life, abuzz with activity and events year-round. The park owes its existence to

the Forsyth Fountain

William B. Hodgson, who donated its core 10 acres to the city for use as a park. Deeply influenced by the then-trendy design of green-space areas in France, Forsyth Park's landscape design by William Bischoff dates to 1851. Named for Georgia governor John Forsyth, the park covers 30 acres, and its perimeter is about a mile.

Near the center of the park is the "fort," actually a revitalized version of an old dummy fort used for military drills in the early 20th century. Now managed by the nearby Mansion on Forsyth hotel, it's a good place to stop in and get a snack or use the public restroom.

The park is a center of activities all year long, from free festivals to concerts to Ultimate Frisbee games to the constant circuit around the periphery of walkers, joggers, dog owners, and bicyclists. The only time you shouldn't venture into the park is after midnight; otherwise, enjoy.

MAP 3: Bordered by Drayton St., Gaston St., Whitaker St., and Park Ave., 912/351-3850; daily 8am-dusk

# A Walking Tour of Forsyth Park

As you approach the park, don't miss the ornate ironwork on the west side of Bull Street marking the **Armstrong House,** designed by Henrik Wallin. Featured in the 1962 film *Cape Fear* as well as 1997's *Midnight in the Garden of Good and Evil*, this Italianate mansion was once home to Armstrong Junior College before its move to the south side. Directly across Bull Street is another site of *Midnight* fame, the **Oglethorpe Club,** one of the many brick and terra-cotta designs by local architect Alfred Eichberg.

It's easy to miss, but as you enter the park's north side, you encounter the **Marine Memorial,** erected in 1947 to honor the 24 Chatham County Marines killed in World War II. Subsequently, the names of Marines killed in Korea and Vietnam were added. Look west at the corner of Whitaker and Gaston Streets; that's **Hodgson Hall,** home of the Georgia Historical Society. This 1876 building was commissioned by Margaret Telfair to honor her late husband, William Hodgson.

Looking east at the corner of Drayton and Gaston Streets, you'll see the old **Poor House and Hospital,** in use until 1854, when it was converted to serve as the headquarters for the Medical College of Georgia. During the Civil War, General Sherman used the hospital to treat Federal soldiers. From 1930 to 1980 the building was the site of Candler Hospital. Behind the old hospital's cast-iron fence is Savannah's most famous tree, the 300-year-old **Candler Oak.** During Sherman's occupation, wounded Confederate prisoners were treated within a barricade around the oak. The tree is in the National Register of Historic Trees and was the maiden preservation project of the Savannah Tree Foundation, which secured the country's first-ever conservation easement on a single tree.

Walking south into the park proper, you can't miss the world-famous **Forsyth Fountain,** an iconic Savannah sight. Cast in iron on a French model, the fountain was dedicated in 1858. Two other versions of this fountain exist—one in Poughkeepsie, New York, and the other in, of all places, the central plaza in Cusco, Peru.

Continuing south, you'll encounter two low buildings in the center of the park. The one on the east side is the so-called "Dummy Fort," circa 1909, formerly a training ground for local militia. Now it's the **Forsyth Park Café** (daily 7am-dusk). To the west is the charming **Fragrant Garden for the Blind.** One of those precious little Savannah gems that is too often overlooked, the Fragrant Garden was initially sponsored by the local Garden Club and based on others of its type throughout the United States.

The tall monument dominating Forsyth Park's central mall is the **Confederate Memorial.** Dedicated in 1875, it wasn't finished until several years later. A New York sculptor carved the Confederate soldier atop the monument.

My favorite Forsyth Park landmark is at the extreme southern end. It's the Memorial to Georgia Veterans of the Spanish-American War, more commonly known as *The Hiker* because of the subject's casual demeanor and confident stride. Savannah was a major staging area for the 1898 conflict, and many troops were bivouacked in the park. Sculpted in 1902 by Alice Ruggles Kitson, more than 50 replicas of *The Hiker* were made and put up all over the United States.

# SOFO DISTRICT

## LAUREL GROVE CEMETERY

Its natural vista isn't as alluring as Bonaventure Cemetery's, but Laurel Grove Cemetery boasts its own exquisitely carved memorials and a distinctly Victorian type of surreal beauty that not even Bonaventure can match. In keeping with the racial apartheid of Savannah's early days, there are actually two cemeteries: **Laurel Grove North** (802 W. Anderson St.) for whites, and **Laurel Grove South** (2101 Kollock St.) for blacks. Both are well worth visiting.

By far the most high-profile plot in the North Cemetery is that of Juliette Gordon Low, founder of the Girl Scouts of the USA. Other historically significant sites there include the graves of 8th Air Force founder Frank O. Hunter, Central of Georgia Railway founder William Gordon, and "Jingle Bells" composer James Pierpont. But it's the graves of the anonymous and near-anonymous that are the most poignant sights. The various sections for infants, known as "babylands," cannot fail to move. "Mr. Bones," a former Savannah police dog, is the only animal buried at Laurel Grove. There's an entire site reserved for victims of the great yellow fever epidemic. And don't blink or you'll miss the small rock pile, or cairn, near Governor James Jackson's tomb, the origin and purpose of which remains a mystery. Make sure to view the otherworldly display of Victorian statuary, originally from the grand Greenwich Plantation, which burned in the early 20th century. As with Bonaventure, throughout Laurel Grove you'll find examples of so-called "slave tiles," actually Victorian garden tiles, lining gravesites.

Laurel Grove South features the graves of Savannah's early black Baptist ministers, such as Andrew Bryan and Andrew Cox Marshall. Some of the most evocative gravesites are those of African Americans who obtained their freedom and built prosperous lives for themselves and their families. The vast majority of local firefighters in the 1800s were African Americans, and their simple graves are among the most touching, such as the headstone for one known simply as "August," who died fighting a fire.

To get to Laurel Grove North, take MLK Jr. Boulevard to Anderson Street and turn west. To get to Laurel Grove South, take Victory Drive (U.S. 80) west to Ogeechee Road. Take a right onto Ogeechee, then a right onto West 36th Street. Continue on to Kollock Street.

MAP 3: 802 W. Anderson St. and 2101 Kollock St.; daily 8am-5pm; free

# SOUTHSIDE

## ISLE OF HOPE

A charming, friendly seaside community and National Historic District, Isle of Hope is one of a dwindling number of places where parents still let their kids ride around all day on bikes, calling them in at dinnertime. It doesn't boast many shops or restaurants—indeed, the marina is the only real business—but the row of waterfront cottages on Bluff Drive should not be missed. You might recognize some of them from movies such as *Forrest Gump* and *Glory*. Built from 1880 to 1920, they reflect Isle of Hope's reputation as a healing area and serene Wilmington River getaway from Savannah's capitalist hustle.

To get to Isle of Hope, take Victory Drive (U.S. 80) east and take a right on Skidaway Road. Continue south on Skidaway Road and take a left on Laroche Avenue. Continue until you hit Bluff Drive.

MAP 4: 10 miles south of Savannah

## WORMSLOE STATE HISTORIC SITE

The one-of-a-kind Wormsloe State Historic Site was first settled by Noble Jones, who landed with Oglethorpe on the *Anne* and fought beside him in the War of Jenkins' Ear. One of the great renaissance men of history, this soldier was also an accomplished carpenter, surveyor, forester, botanist, and physician. Wormsloe became famous for its bountiful gardens, so much so that the famed naturalist William Bartram mentioned them in his diary after a visit in 1765 with father John Bartram. After his death, Noble Jones was originally buried in the family plot on the waterfront, but now his remains are at Bonaventure Cemetery. Jones's descendants donated 822 acres of Wormsloe to The Nature Conservancy, which transferred the property to the state. The house, dating from 1828, and 65.5 acres of land are still owned by his family, and no, you can't visit them.

The stunning entrance canopy of 400 live oaks, Spanish moss dripping down the entire length, is one of those iconic images of Savannah that will stay with you forever. A small interpretive museum, a one-mile nature walk, and occasional living-history demonstrations make this a great site for the entire family. Walk all the way to the Jones Narrows to see the ruins of the site's original 1739 fortification, one of the oldest and finest examples of tabby construction in the United States. No doubt the area's abundance of Native American shell middens, where early inhabitants discarded their oyster shells, came in handy for its construction. You can see one nearby.

To get to Wormsloe, take Victory Drive (U.S. 80) to Skidaway Road. Go south on Skidaway Road for about 10 miles and follow the signs; you'll see the grand entrance on the right.

**MAP 4:** 7601 Skidaway Rd., 912/353-3023, www.gastateparks.org/info/wormsloe; Tues.-Sun. 9am-5pm; $10 adults, $4.50 children

## Pin Point

Off Whitfield Avenue (Diamond Causeway) on the route to Skidaway Island is tiny Pin Point, a predominantly African American township better known as the boyhood home of Supreme Court Justice Clarence Thomas. Pin Point traces its roots to a community of former slaves on Ossabaw Island. Displaced by a hurricane, they settled at this idyllic site overlooking the Moon River, itself a former plantation.

### PIN POINT HERITAGE MUSEUM

Many Pin Point residents made their living by shucking oysters at the Varn Oyster Company, the central shed of which still remains and forms the basis of the Pin Point Heritage Museum, opened in 2012. The museum tells the story of the Pin Point community through exhibits, a

the iconic live oak entrance at Wormsloe

the Pin Point Heritage Museum

film, and demonstrations of some of the maritime activities at the Varn Oyster Company through the decades, such as crabbing, canning, shucking, and shrimp-net making. **MAP 4:** 9924 Pin Point Ave., http://chsgeorgia.org/PHM; Thurs.-Sat. 9am-5pm; $8 adults, $4 children

## Skidaway Island

Skidaway Island is notable for two beautiful and educational nature-oriented sites.

### SKIDAWAY ISLAND STATE PARK

A site of interest to visitors is Skidaway Island State Park. Yeah, you can camp here ($25-28), but the awesome nature trails leading out to the marsh—featuring an ancient Native American shell midden and an old whiskey still—are worth a trip just on their own, especially when combined with the Marine Educational Center and Aquarium. To get here, take Victory Drive (U.S. 80) until you get to Waters Avenue and continue south as it turns into Whitefield Avenue and then the Diamond Causeway. The park is on your left after the drawbridge. An alternative route from downtown is to take the Truman Parkway all the way to its dead end at Whitefield Avenue, take a left and continue as it turns into Diamond Causeway as it enters Skidaway.
**MAP 4:** 52 Diamond Causeway, 912/598-2300, www.gastateparks.org/info/skidaway; daily 7am-10pm; parking $5

### UNIVERSITY OF GEORGIA MARINE EDUCATIONAL CENTER AND AQUARIUM

The University of Georgia Marine Educational Center and Aquarium shares a picturesque 700-acre campus on the scenic Skidaway River with the research-oriented **Skidaway Institute of Oceanography,** also University of Georgia (UGA) affiliated. It hosts scientists and grad students from around the nation, often for trips on its research vessel, the RV *Sea Dawg.* The main attraction of the Marine Center is the small but well-done and recently upgraded aquarium featuring 14 tanks with 200 live animals.
**MAP 4:** 30 Ocean Science Circle, 912/598-3474, www.marex.uga.edu; Mon.-Fri. 9am-4pm, Sat. 10am-5pm; $6 adults, $3 children, cash only

# Pin Point on the Moon River

On Ossabaw Island, former slaves had settled into freedom as subsistence farmers after the Civil War. But when a massive hurricane devastated the island in 1893, many moved to the mainland, south of Savannah along what would later be known as Moon River, to a place called Pin Point. While many continued farming, plenty gained employment at local factories, where crabs and oysters were packed and sold. The largest and longest-lived of those factories was A. S. Varn & Son, which employed nearly 100 Pin Point residents—about half of the adult population.

Because so many local people worked at the same place, Pin Point developed a strong community bond, one that was instrumental in forging the life and career of future Supreme Court Justice Clarence Thomas, who was born at Pin Point in 1948. Until he was seven, Thomas lived in a tiny house there with his parents, one without plumbing and insulated with newspapers. After a house fire, Thomas moved to Savannah with his grandparents.

While times have certainly changed here—paved roads finally came in the 1970s, and most of the old shotgun shacks have been replaced with mobile homes—Pin Point remains a small, close-knit community of about 300 people, with most property still owned by descendants of the freedmen who bought it after Reconstruction. The Varn factory remained the economic heart of Pin Point until it shut down in 1985. Today, the old factory forms the heart of an ambitious new project, the **Pin Point Heritage Museum** (www.pinpointheritagemuseum.com), which conveys the spirit and history of that community, including its most famous native son, through a series of exhibits and demonstrations.

## EASTSIDE

### ★ BONAVENTURE CEMETERY

On the banks of the Wilmington River just east of town lies one of Savannah's most unique sights, Bonaventure Cemetery. John Muir, who went on to found the Sierra Club, wrote of Bonaventure's Spanish moss-bedecked beauty in his 1867 book *A Thousand-mile Walk to the Gulf,* marveling at the screaming bald eagles that then frequented the area. The bald eagles are long gone, but, like Muir, Savannahians to this day reserve a special place in their hearts for Bonaventure. While its pedigree as Savannah's premier public cemetery goes back 100 years, it was used as a burial ground as early as 1794. In the years since, this achingly poignant vista of live oaks and azaleas has been the final resting place of such local and national luminaries as Johnny Mercer, Conrad Aiken, Wormsloe Historic Site founder Noble Jones, and, of course, the Trosdal plot, former home of the famous *Bird Girl* statue (the original is now in the Telfair Academy of Arts and Sciences). Fittingly, the late, great Jack Leigh, who took the *Bird Girl*

photo for the cover of *Midnight in the Garden of Good and Evil,* is interred here as well.

Go to Section K to see the Greek cemetery, a veritable stone chronicle of that local community's history from the late 1800s. Section K also holds many memorials to Spanish-American War veterans, commemorated by a special cross. Close by is the Jewish section, established by congregants of Temple Mickve Israel, with many evocative inscriptions on the tombs of the numerous Holocaust survivors buried here. Closer to the river is an interesting plot set aside for railroad conductors.

Several local tour companies offer options that include a visit to Bonaventure. If you're doing a self-guided tour, go by the small visitors center at the entrance and pick up one of the free guides to the cemetery, assembled by the local volunteer Bonaventure Historical Society. By all means, do the tourist thing and pay your respects at Johnny Mercer's final resting place, and go visit beautiful little "Gracie" in Section E, Lot 99. But I also suggest doing as the locals do: Bring a picnic lunch and a blanket and set yourself beside the

# Johnny Mercer's Black Magic

The great Johnny Mercer is not only without a doubt Savannah's most noteworthy progeny, he is also one of the greatest lyricists music has ever known. Born in 1909, he grew up in southside Savannah on a small river then called the Back River but since renamed Moon River in honor of his best-known song.

Armed with an innate talent for rhythm and a curious ear for dialogue—both qualities honed by his frequent boyhood contact with Savannah African American culture and musicians during the Jazz Age, Mercer wrote what is arguably his greatest song, "Moon River," in 1961. The song, debuted by Audrey Hepburn in the film *Breakfast at Tiffany's*, won an Academy Award for Best Original Song. In addition to "Moon River," Mercer won three other Oscars, for "On the Atchinson, Topeka and the Santa Fe" (1946), "In the Cool, Cool, Cool of the Evening" (1951), and "Days of Wine and Roses" (1962).

Today you can pay your respects to Mercer in three places: his boyhood home (509 E. Gwinnett St., look for the historical marker in front of this private residence); the bronze sculpture of Mercer in the newly revitalized Ellis Square near City Market; and at his gravesite in beautiful Bonaventure Cemetery. And regardless of what anyone tells you, neither Johnny Mercer nor any member of his family ever lived in the Mercer-Williams House on Monterey Square, of *Midnight in the Garden of Good and Evil* fame. Although it was built for his great-grandfather, the home was sold to someone else before it was completed.

breezy banks of the Wilmington River, taking in all the lazy beauty and evocative bygone history surrounding you.

To get here from downtown, take the President Street Extension east and take a right on Pennsylvania Avenue, then a left on Bonaventure Road. Alternatively, go east on Victory Drive (U.S. 80) and take a left on Whatley Road in the town of Thunderbolt. Veer left onto Bonaventure Road. The cemetery is one mile ahead on the right.

**MAP 4:** 330 Bonaventure Rd., 912/651-6843; daily 8am-5pm; free

## DAFFIN PARK

A century spent in Forsyth Park's more genteel shadow doesn't diminish the importance of Daffin Park as Savannah's second major green space. Daffin not only hosts a large variety of local athletes on its fields and courts, but the park's east end is the setting for Historic Grayson Stadium, home of the minor league Savannah Sand Gnats. One of the great old ballparks of America, this venue dates from 1941 and has hosted greats such as Babe Ruth, Jackie Robinson, and Mickey Mantle.

Most picturesque for the visitor, however,

is the massive fountain set in the middle of the expansive central pond on the park's west side. Originally built in the shape of the continental United States, the pond was the backdrop for a presidential visit by Franklin D. Roosevelt in 1933 that included a speech to an African American crowd. On the far west end of Daffin Park along Waters Avenue is a marker commemorating the site of the grandstand for the Great Savannah Races of 1911.

**MAP 4:** 1500 E. Victory Dr.; daily dawn-dusk

## OATLAND ISLAND WILDLIFE CENTER

The closest thing Savannah has to a zoo is the vast, multipurpose Oatland Island Wildlife Center. Set on a former Centers for Disease Control site, it has undergone an extensive environmental cleanup and is now owned by the local school system, although supported purely by donations. Families by the hundreds come here for a number of special Saturdays throughout the year, including an old-fashioned cane grinding in November and a day of sheep shearing in April.

The main attractions here are the critters, located at various points along a meandering two-mile nature trail through the woods and along the marsh. All animals at Oatland are there because they're somehow unable to return to the wild. Highlights include a tight-knit pack of eastern wolves, a pair of bison, cougars (once indigenous to the region), some really cute foxes, and an extensive raptor aviary. Kids will love the petting zoo of farm animals, some of which are free to roam the grounds at will.

The massive central building was designed by noted local architect Henrik Wallin as a retirement home for railroad conductors. Inside, check out the display of a huge set of whalebones, the remains of a 50-foot-long endangered fin whale that washed ashore on Tybee Island in 1989.

To get here from downtown, take the President Street Extension (Islands Expressway) about five miles. Begin looking for the Oatland Island sign on the right. You'll go through part of a residential neighborhood until you take a bend to the right; Oatland's gate is then on the left. To get here from Bonaventure Cemetery, go straight out the gate on Bonaventure Road and take a right on Pennsylvania Avenue. As you dead-end on Islands Expressway, take a right and look for the entrance farther along on the right.
**MAP 4:** 711 Sandtown Rd., 912/898-3980, www.oatlandisland.org; daily 10am-5pm; $5 adults, $3 children

### OLD FORT JACKSON

The oldest standing brick fort in Georgia, Old Fort Jackson, named for Georgia governor James Jackson, is also one of eight remaining examples of the so-called Second System of American forts built prior to the War of 1812. Its main claim to fame is its supporting role in the saga of the CSS *Georgia,* a Confederate ironclad now resting under 40 feet of water directly in front of the fort. Built with $115,000 in funds raised by the Ladies Gunboat Society, the *Georgia*—wrapped in an armor girdle of rails—proved too heavy for its engine. So it was simply anchored in the channel opposite Fort Jackson as a floating battery. With General Sherman's arrival in 1864, Confederate forces evacuating to South Carolina scuttled the vessel where it lay to keep it out of Yankee hands.

Operated by the nonprofit Coastal Heritage Society, Fort Jackson is in an excellent state of preservation and provides loads of information for history buffs as well as for kids, who will enjoy climbing the parapets and running on the large parade ground (this area was once a rice field). Inside the fort's casemates underneath the ramparts you'll find well-organized exhibits on the fort's construction and history. Most visitors especially love the daily cannon firings during the summer. If you're really lucky, you'll be around when Fort Jackson fires a salute to passing military vessels on the river—the only historic fort in the United States that does so.

To get to Fort Jackson, take the President Street Extension (Islands Expressway) east out of downtown. The entrance is several miles down on the left.
**MAP 4:** Fort Jackson Rd., 912/232-3945, http://chsgeorgia.org; daily 9am-5pm; $7 adults, $4 children

## Thunderbolt

Near the Bonaventure Cemetery is the little fishing village of Thunderbolt, almost as old as Savannah itself. According to Oglethorpe, the town was named for "a rock which was here shattered by a thunderbolt, causing a spring to gush from the ground, which continued ever afterward to emit the odor of brimstone."

### SAVANNAH STATE UNIVERSITY

Continue on River Road and you'll soon be at the entrance to Savannah State University. This historically black university began life in 1890 as the Georgia State Industrial College for Colored Youth. Famous graduates include NFL great Shannon Sharpe. The main landmark is the newly restored Hill Hall, a 1901 building featured in the film *The General's Daughter.*
**MAP 4:** 3219 College St., 912/356-2186, www.savstate.edu

## THUNDERBOLT MUSEUM

Just off Victory Drive is the Thunderbolt Museum, housed in the humble former town hall. Cross Victory Drive onto River Road and notice how the road is built around the live oak tree in the middle of it. Most of the nice views of the river have been obscured by high-rise condos, but there's a cute public fishing pier.

**MAP 4:** Victory Dr. and Mechanics Ave., 912/351-0836, http://thunderboltmuseum.org; Wed.-Thurs. 9:30am-2:30pm, Sat. 1pm-5pm; free

## TYBEE ISLAND

Its name means "salt" in the old Euchee tongue, indicative of the island's chief export in those days. And Tybee Island—"Tybee" to locals—is indeed one of the essential seasonings of life in Savannah. First incorporated as Ocean City and then Savannah Beach, the island has since reclaimed its original name. Eighteen miles and about a half-hour drive from Savannah, in truth Tybee is part and parcel of the city's social and cultural fabric. Many of the island's 3,000 full-time residents,

known for their boozy bonhomie and quirky personal style, commute to work in the city.

Its wide, beautiful beaches are lined with rare sea oats waving in the Atlantic breeze. The entire island has become a focal point of Georgia's booming film industry. The recent reboot of *Baywatch* with Dwayne "The Rock" Johnson was filmed on Tybee's beach, as was the Miley Cyrus film *The Last Song*.

## ★ FORT PULASKI NATIONAL MONUMENT

There's one must-see before you get to Tybee Island proper. On Cockspur Island you'll find Fort Pulaski National Monument. Not only a delight for any history buff, the fort's also a fantastic place to take the kids. They can climb on the parapets, earthworks, and cannons, and burn off calories on the great nature trail nearby. Along the way they'll no doubt learn a few things as well.

By all means, stop by the visitors center, a few hundred yards from the fort itself— but the palpable pleasure starts when you cross the drawbridge over the moat and see

## The Tybee Bomb

On a dark night in 1958 at the height of the Cold War, a USAF B-47 Stratojet bomber made a simulated nuclear bombing run over southeast Georgia. A Charleston-based F-86 fighter on a mock intercept came too close, clipping the bomber's wing. Before bringing down the wounded B-47 at Savannah's Hunter Airfield, Commander Howard Richardson decided to jettison his lethal cargo: a 7,000-pound Mark 15 hydrogen bomb, serial number 47782. Richardson, who won the Distinguished Flying Cross for his efforts that night, jettisoned the bomb over water. What no one knows is exactly where. And thus began the legend of "the Tybee Bomb." Speculation ran wild, with some locals fearing a nuclear explosion, radioactive contamination, or even that a team of scuba-diving terrorists would secretly retrieve the ancient weapon.

Former Army colonel Derek Duke has taken it as his personal mission to find the bomb. Duke claims to have found a radiation-emitting object off Little Tybee Island during a search in 2004.

Commander Richardson, now retired, says the bomb wasn't armed when he jettisoned it. Environmentalists say that doesn't matter, because the enriched uranium the Air Force admits was in the bomb is toxic whether or not there's the risk of a nuclear detonation. People who work in the fishing industry on Tybee say the fact that the bomb also had 400 pounds of high explosive "nuclear trigger" is reason enough to get it out of the waterways.

And what of the Air Force? In 2000 they sent a team to Savannah to find the bomb, concluding it was buried somewhere off the coast in 5-15 feet of mud. In 2005, in another attempt to find the weapon, they sent another team of experts down to look one last time. Their verdict: The bomb's still lost.

# The Siege of Fort Pulaski

Fort Pulaski National Monument

Fort Pulaski's construction was part of a broader initiative by President James Madison in the wake of the disastrous War of 1812, which dramatically revealed the shortcomings of U.S. coastal defense. Based on state-of-the-art European design forged in the cauldron of the Napoleonic Wars, Fort Pulaski's thick masonry construction used 25 million bricks, many of them of the famous "Savannah Gray" variety handmade at the nearby Hermitage Plantation.

When Georgia seceded from the Union in January 1861, a small force of Confederates immediately took control of Fort Pulaski and Fort Jackson. In early 1862 a Union sea-land force came to covertly lay the groundwork for a siege of Fort Pulaski. The siege would rely on several batteries secretly set up across the Savannah River. Some of the Union guns utilized new rifled-chamber technology, which dramatically increased the accuracy, muzzle velocity, and penetrating power of their shells. The Union barrage began at 8:15am on April 10, 1862, and Fort Pulaski's walls crumbled under the withering fire. At least one shell struck a powder magazine, igniting an enormous explosion. After 30 hours, Confederate general Charles Olmstead surrendered the fortress.

It was not only Fort Pulaski that was rendered obsolete—it was the whole concept of masonry fortification. From that point forward, military forts would rely on earthwork rather than brick. The section of earthwork you see as you enter Fort Pulaski, the "demilune," was added after the Civil War.

a cannon pointed at you from a narrow gun port. Enter the inside of the fort and take in just how big it is—Union occupiers regularly played baseball on the huge, grassy parade ground. Take a walk around the perimeter, underneath the ramparts. This is where the soldiers lived and worked, and you'll see recreations of officers' quarters, meeting areas, sick rooms, and prisoners' bunks among the cannons, where Confederate prisoners of war were held after the fort's surrender. Cannon firings happen most Saturdays.

And now for the pièce de résistance:

Take the steep corkscrew staircase up to the ramparts themselves and take in the jaw-dropping view of the lush marsh, with the Savannah River and Tybee Island spreading out in the distance. Stop and sit near one of the several remaining cannons and contemplate what went on here a century and a half ago. (Warning: There's no railing of any kind on the inboard side of the ramparts. Keep the kids well back from the edge, because it's a lethal fall to the fort interior.) Afterward, take a stroll all the way around the walls and see the power of those Yankee guns. Though much of the devastation was soon repaired, some sections of the wall remain in their damaged state. You can even pick out a few cannonballs still stuck in the masonry, like blueberries in a pie.

Save some time and energy for the extensive palmetto-lined nature trail through the sandy upland of Cockspur Island on which the fort is located. There are informative markers, a picnic area, and, as a bonus, a coastal defense facility from the Spanish-American War, Battery Hambright.

Continue east on U.S. 80, passing over Lazaretto Creek, named for the quarantine, or "lazaretto," built in the late 1700s to make sure newcomers, mostly slaves, were free of disease. As you cross, look to your left over the river's wide south channel. On a tiny oyster shell islet, find the little **Cockspur Beacon** lighthouse, in use from 1848 to 1909, when major shipping was routed through the deeper north channel of the river. The site is now preserved by the National Park Service and is accessible only by boat or kayak. You have to time your arrival with the right tide; check with a local rental place for advice.

**MAP 5:** U.S. 80 E., 912/786-5787, www.nps.gov/fopu; daily 9am-5pm; $7, free under age 16

### SOUTH END

Butler Avenue is Tybee's main drag, the beach fully public and accessible from any of the numbered side streets on the left. Go all the way down to **Tybrisa Street** (formerly 16th St.) to get a flavor of old Tybee. Here's where you'll find the old five-and-dimes like T. S. Chu's, still a staple of local life, and little diners, ice cream spots, and taverns. The new pride of the island is the large, long pier structure called the **Tybrisa Pavilion II,** built in 1996 in an attempt to re-create the lost glory of the Tybrisa Pavilion, social and spiritual center of the island's gregarious resort days. Built in 1891 by the Central of Georgia Railway, the Tybrisa hosted name entertainers and big bands on its expansive dance floor. Sadly, fire destroyed it in 1967, an enormous blow to area morale.

**MAP 5:** Butler Ave.

### TYBEE ISLAND MARINE SCIENCE CENTER

Literally at the foot of the Tybrisa Pavilion you'll find the little Tybee Island Marine Science Center, with nine aquariums and a touch tank featuring native species. Here is the nerve center for the Tybee Island Sea Turtle Project, an ongoing effort to document and preserve the local comings and goings of the island's most beloved inhabitant and unofficial mascot, the endangered sea turtle.

**MAP 5:** 1510 Strand Ave., 912/786-5917, www. tybeemarinescience.org; daily 10am-5pm; $4 adults, $3 children

### TYBEE ISLAND LIGHT STATION AND MUSEUM

At North Campbell Avenue is the entrance to the less-populated, more historically significant north end of Tybee Island, once almost entirely taken up by Fort Screven, a coastal defense fortification of the early 1900s. Rebuilt several times in its history, the Tybee Island Light Station traces its construction to the first year of the colony, based on a design by the multitalented Noble Jones. At its completion in 1736, it was the tallest structure in the United States. One of a handful of working 18th-century lighthouses today, the facility has been restored to its 1916-1964 incarnation, featuring a nine-foot-tall first-order Fresnel lens installed in 1867.

The entrance fee gives you admission to the lighthouse, the lighthouse museum, and the nearby Tybee Island Museum. All the outbuildings on the lighthouse grounds are original, including the residence of the lighthouse keeper, also the oldest building on the island. If you've got the legs and the lungs, definitely take all 178 steps up to the top of the lighthouse for a stunning view of Tybee, the Atlantic, and Hilton Head Island.

To get to the lighthouse, take a left onto North Campbell Avenue then left again on Van Horne Street. Take an immediate right onto Meddin Drive. Continue until you see a lighthouse on the left and a parking lot on the right.

the Tybee Island Light Station and Museum

All around the area of the north end around the lighthouse complex you'll see low-lying concrete bunkers. These are remains of Fort Screven's coastal defense batteries, and many are in private hands. Battery Garland is open to tours, and also houses the **Tybee Island Museum** (30 Meddin Ave., 912/786-5801, Wed.-Mon. 9am-5:30pm, last ticket sold 4:30pm, $9 adults, $7 children, includes admission to lighthouse and lighthouse museum), a charming, almost whimsical little collection of exhibits from various eras of local history.

**MAP 5:** 30 Meddin Ave., 912/786-5801, www.tybeelighthouse.org; Wed.-Mon. 9am-5:30pm, last ticket sold 4:30pm; $9 adults, $7 children

### TYBEE POST THEATER

The new pride of the north end is the Tybee Post Theater, a recently fully restored performing arts venue that was once, as the name implies, the theater for the Ft. Screven

the restored Tybee Post Theater

military facility. The small but cozy 200-seat space now offers a range of programming from live music to live theatre to film screenings, the latter its original purpose when built in 1930. Indeed, the theater was one of the first in Georgia to host the new "talkie" films.

**MAP 5:** 10 Van Horne Ave., 912/472-4790, www.tybeeposttheater.org; prices vary

## GREATER SAVANNAH
### Midway and Liberty County

Locals will tell you that Midway is named because it's equidistant from the Savannah and Altamaha Rivers on Oglethorpe's old "river road," which it certainly is, but others say the small but very historic town is actually named after the Medway River in England. In seeking to pacify the local Creek people, the Council of Georgia in 1752 granted a group of Massachusetts Puritans then residing in Dorchester, South Carolina, a 32,000-acre land grant as incentive to move south. After moving into Georgia and establishing New Dorchester, they soon founded a nearby settlement that would later take on the modern spelling of Midway. Midway's citizens were very aggressive early on in the cause for American independence, which is why the area's three original parishes were combined and named Liberty County in 1777—the only Georgia county named for a concept rather than a person. Two of Georgia's three signers of the Declaration of Independence, Lyman Hall and Button Gwinnett, resided primarily in Midway, and both attended the historic Midway Church. A key part of Liberty County history is no more: The once-thriving seaport of Sunbury, which formerly challenged Savannah for economic supremacy in the region, no longer exists.

Tourism in this area has been made much more user-friendly by the liberal addition of signage for the "Liberty Trail," a collection of key attractions. When in doubt, follow the signs. The main highways in Midway are I-95, U.S. 17, and U.S. 84, also called Oglethorpe Highway, which becomes Highway 38 (Islands Hwy.) east of I-95.

### FORT MORRIS STATE HISTORIC SITE

Built to defend the once-proud port of Sunbury, Fort Morris State Historic Site was reconstructed during the War of 1812 and was an encampment during the Civil War. It was here that Colonel John McIntosh gave his famous reply to the British demand for his surrender: "Come and take it." The museum has displays of military and everyday life of the era. Reenactments and cannon firings are highlights. There's a visitors center and a nature trail. The site is about 50 minutes from Savannah. To get here, take exit 76 off I-95 south. Go east on Islands Highway and take a left on Fort Morris Road; the site is two miles down.

**MAP 6:** 2559 Ft. Morris Rd., 912/884-5999, www.gastateparks.org/info/ftmorris; Thurs.-Sat. 9am-5pm; $4.50 adults, $3 children

### GEECHEE KUNDA

A little way south of Midway on the Liberty Trail in tiny Riceboro is Geechee Kunda, a combination museum-outreach center on the site of the former Retreat rice and indigo plantation. It's now dedicated to explaining and exploring the culture of Sea Island African Americans on the Georgia coast. (Don't be confused: *Geechee* is the Georgia word for the Gullah people. Both groups share similar folkways and history, and the terms are virtually interchangeable.) There are artifacts from slavery and Reconstruction, including authentic Geechee/Gullah relics. Geechee Kunda is about 40 minutes from Savannah. Take exit 67 off I-95 and head north about two miles on U.S. 17.

**MAP 6:** 622 Ways Temple Rd., Riceboro, 912/884-4440, www.geecheekunda.com; Tues.-Sat. 11am-5pm

### MIDWAY MUSEUM

In Midway proper is the charming Midway Museum and the adjacent **Midway Church,** sometimes called the Midway Meetinghouse. The museum contains a variety of artifacts, most from the 18th and 19th centuries,

# Sunbury: Gone But Not Forgotten

If you spend much time in Liberty County, you'll probably hear someone mention that a certain place or person is "over near Sunbury." Such is the legacy of this long-gone piece of Georgia history that locals still refer to it in the present tense, though the old town itself is no more.

Founded soon after Midway in 1758, Sunbury rivaled Savannah as Georgia's main commercial port by 1761, with a thriving trade in lumber, rice, indigo, corn, and, unfortunately, slaves. At one time, seven square-rigged vessels called on the port in a single day.

At various times, all three of Georgia's signers of the Declaration of Independence—Button Gwinnett, Lyman Hall, and George Walton—had connections to Sunbury. The beginning of the end came with those heady days of revolution, however, when Sunbury was the scene of much fighting between colonists and the British army. A British siege in 1778 culminated in this immortal reply from the colonial commander, Colonel John McIntosh, to a redcoat demand for surrender: "Come and take it." By the beginning of 1779, a separate British assault did so.

After U.S. independence, Sunbury remained the Liberty County seat until 1797, but it was never the same, beset by decay, hurricanes, and yellow fever outbreaks. By 1848, nothing of the town remained but the old cemetery, which you can find a short drive from the Fort Morris State Historic Site; ask a park employee for directions.

and an extensive genealogy collection. The Midway Church, built in 1756, was burned during the Revolution but rebuilt in 1792. Both Button Gwinnett and Lyman Hall attended services here, and during the Civil War some of Sherman's cavalry set up camp on the grounds. The cemetery across the street is wonderfully poignant and is the final resting place of two Revolutionary War generals; Union cavalry kept horses within its walls. The museum, church, and cemetery are 30 miles from Savannah and easy to find: take exit 76 from I-95 south, and take a right on U.S. 84 (Oglethorpe Hwy.). Turn right on U.S. 17, and they're just ahead on the right.

MAP 6: 491 N. Coastal Hwy., 912/884-5837, www. themidwaymuseum.org; Tues.-Sat. 10am-4pm; $3

### SEABROOK VILLAGE

West off Islands Highway is Seabrook Village, a unique living-history museum chronicling the everyday life of Liberty County's African Americans, with a direct link to Sherman's famous "40 acres and a mule" Field Order No. 15. There are eight restored vernacular buildings on the 100-acre site, including the simple but sublime one-room Seabrook School. From Savannah, take exit 76 off I-95, and then a left

onto U.S. 84. After about two miles, take a left onto Trade Hill Road.

MAP 6: 660 Trade Hill Rd., 912/884-7008; Tues.-Sat. 10am-4pm; $3

## Ossabaw Island
OSSABAW ISLAND

Owned and operated by Georgia as a heritage and wildlife preserve, the island was a gift to the state in 1978 from Eleanor Torrey-West and family, who still retain some property on the island. All public use of the island is managed by the Ossabaw Island Foundation (www.ossabawisland.org).

The 12,000-acre island is much older than Wassaw Island to its north and so has traces of human habitation back to 2000 BC. The island's name comes from an old Muskogean word referring to yaupon holly, found in abundance on the island and used by Native Americans in purification rituals to induce vomiting. There are several tabby ruins on the island, along with many miles of walking trails. Unlike the much-younger Wassaw, Ossabaw Island was not only timbered extensively but hosted several rice and cotton plantations.

Descendants of the island's slaves moved to the Savannah area after the Civil War, founding the community of Pin Point. Similarly to Jekyll Island to the south, Ossabaw was a hunting preserve for wealthy families in the Roaring '20s. Even today, hunting is an important activity on the island, with lotteries choosing who gets a chance to pursue its overly large populations of deer and wild hogs, the latter of which are descended from pigs brought by the Spanish.

Now reserved exclusively for educational and scientific purposes, the island is accessible only by boat. Georgia law ensures public access to all beaches up to the high-tide mark—which simply means that the public can ride out to Ossabaw and go on the beach for day use, but any travel to the interior is restricted and you must have permission first. Contact the Ossabaw Island Foundation for information. Boat trips take about 1.5 hours and vary in price. Day trips can be arranged with charter operators at the marinas in Savannah.

MAP 6: Ossabaw Island, www.ossabawisland.org

## Wassaw Island
### WASSAW ISLAND NATIONAL WILDLIFE REFUGE

Unique in that it's the only Georgia barrier island never cleared for agriculture or development, the 10,000-acre Wassaw Island National Wildlife Refuge is accessible only by boat. There are striking driftwood-strewn beaches, and the interior of the island has some beautiful old-growth stands of longleaf pine and live oak. Wassaw is a veritable paradise for nature lovers and bird-watchers, with migratory activity in the spring and fall, waterfowl in abundance in the summer, and manatee and loggerhead turtle activity (about 10 percent of Georgia's transient loggerhead population makes use of Wassaw for nesting). There are also about 20 miles of trails and a decaying Spanish-American War-era battery, Fort Morgan, on the north end. National Wildlife Refuge Week is celebrated in October.

Because of its comparatively young status—it was formed only about 1,600 years ago—Wassaw Island also has some unique geographical features. You can still make out the parallel ridge features, vestiges of successive ancient shorelines. A central ridge forms the backbone of the island, reaching an amazing (for this area) elevation of 45 feet above sea level at the south end. Native Americans first settled the island, whose name comes from an ancient word for sassafras, which was found in abundance here. During the Civil War, both Confederate and Union troops occupied the island successively. In 1866 the wealthy New England businessman George Parsons bought the island, which stayed in that family's hands until it was sold to the Nature Conservancy in 1969 for $1 million. The Conservancy in turn sold Wassaw to the U.S. government for $1 to be managed as a wildlife refuge.

It's easiest to get to Wassaw Island from Savannah. Boat rides take roughly 30 minutes and cost around $50 round-trip. Charters and scheduled trips are available from **Captain Walt's Charters** (Thunderbolt Marina, 3124 River Dr., 912/507-3811, www.waltsadventure.com/charters), the **Bull River Marina** (8005 E. U.S. 80, 912/897-7300), **Delegal Marina** (1 Marina Dr., 912/598-0023), **Captain Joe Dobbs** (Delegal Marina, 1 Marina Dr., 912/598-0090, www.captjdobbs.com), and **Isle of Hope Marina** (50 Bluff Dr., 912/354-8187, www.isleofhopemarina.com). Most docking is either at the beaches on the north and south ends or in Wassaw Creek, where the U.S. Fish and Wildlife Service dock is also located (temporary mooring only). There's no camping allowed on Wassaw Island; it's for day use only.

MAP 6: Wassaw Island, www.fws.gov/wassaw; daily dawn-dusk

## West Chatham
### COASTAL GEORGIA BOTANICAL GARDENS AT THE HISTORIC BAMBOO FARM

A joint project of the University of Georgia and Chatham County, this farm is an education and demonstration center featuring a wide array of native species in addition to the garden's eponymous Asian "wonder weed," which has its roots in a private collection

# The Salzburgers of New Ebenezer

Perhaps the most unsung chapter in Europe's great spiritual diaspora of the 1700s, the Salzburgers of New Ebenezer—a thrifty, peaceful, and hard-working people—were Georgia's first religious refugees and perhaps the most progressive as well. The year after Oglethorpe's arrival, a contingent of devout Lutherans from Salzburg in present-day Austria arrived after being expelled from their home country for their beliefs. Oglethorpe, mindful of Georgia's mission to provide sanctuary for persecuted Protestants and wishing for a military buffer to the west, eagerly welcomed them. Given land about 25 miles west of Savannah, the Salzburgers named their first settlement Ebenezer ("stone of help" in Hebrew). They later moved the site to better land nearer to the river and called it New Ebenezer, and so it remains to this day.

Because the settlers spoke German instead of English, the upriver colony maintained its isolation. Still, the Salzburgers were among Oglethorpe's most ardent and loyal supporters. Their pastor and de facto political leader, Johann Martin Boltzius, seeking to build an enlightened agrarian utopia, was an outspoken foe of slavery and the exploitative plantation system. The fragile silk industry thrived in New Ebenezer while it had failed miserably in Savannah, and the nation's first rice mill was built here.

The Trustees' turnover of Georgia to the crown in 1750 signaled the final victory of pro-slavery forces—even Pastor Boltzius acquired a couple of slaves as domestic servants. New Ebenezer's influence began a decline that accelerated when British forces pillaged much of the town in the Revolution. Fifty years later, nothing at all remained except the old Jerusalem Church, now the **Jerusalem Evangelical Lutheran Church.**

Although New Ebenezer is often called a "ghost town," this is a misnomer. Extensive archaeological work continues in the area, and the Georgia Salzburger Society works hard to maintain several historic buildings and keep the legacy alive through special events.

dating from the late 1800s. Many of the mature trees were planted in the 1930s. The garden also periodically holds you-pick-'em harvest days for berries. To get here, take exit 94 off of I-95 and take Highway 204 east toward Savannah. Turn right on East Gateway Boulevard, then left on Canebrake Road. Enter at the Canebrake gate. Note: No pets allowed on-site, even on a leash.
MAP 6: 2 Canebrake Rd., 912/921-5460, www. coastalgeorgiabg.org; Mon.-Fri. 8am-5pm, Sat. 10am-5pm, Sun. noon-5pm; $5 adult, $3 children

## Pooler
### ★ NATIONAL MUSEUM OF THE MIGHTY EIGHTH AIR FORCE
Military and aviation buffs mustn't miss the National Museum of the Mighty Eighth Air Force in Pooler, Georgia, right off I-95. The 8th Air Force was born at Hunter Field in Savannah as the 8th Bomber Command in 1942, becoming the 8th Air Force in 1944; it is now based in Louisiana.

A moving testament to the men and machines who conducted those strategic bombing campaigns over Europe in World War II, the museum also features later 8th Air Force history such as the Korean War, the Linebacker II bombing campaigns over North Vietnam, and the Persian Gulf. Inside you'll find airplanes like the P-51 Mustang and the German ME-109. The centerpiece, however, is the restored B-17 bomber "The City of Savannah," the newest jewel of the collection, acquired from the National Air and Space Museum in Washington DC.

Outside are several more aircraft, including a MiG-17, an F-4 Phantom, and a B-47 Stratojet bomber like the one that dropped the fabled "Tybee Bomb" in 1958. The nearby Chapel of the Fallen Eagles is a fully functioning sanctuary that honors the more than 26,000 members of the Mighty Eighth that died during World War II.

To get to the Mighty Eighth Museum from downtown, take I-16 west until it intersects

I-95. Take I-95 north, take exit 102, and follow the signs.

MAP 6: 175 Bourne Ave., Pooler, 912/748-8888, www.mightyeighth.org; daily 9am-5pm; $10 adults, $6 children and active-duty military

## Richmond Hill and Bryan County

Known as the "town that Henry Ford built," Richmond Hill is a growing bedroom community of Savannah in adjacent Bryan County. Sherman's March to the Sea ended here with much destruction, so little history before that time is left. Most of what remains is due to Ford's philanthropic influence, still felt in many place-names around the area, including the main drag, Highway 144, known as Ford Avenue. After the auto magnate and his wife Clara made the area, then called Ways Station, a summer home, they were struck by the area's incredible poverty and determined to help improve living conditions, building hospitals, schools, churches, and homes. The Fords eventually acquired over 85,000 acres in Bryan County, including the former Richmond plantation. What is now known as Ford Plantation—currently a private luxury resort—was built in the 1930s and centered on the main house, once the central building of the famous Hermitage Plantation on the Savannah River, purchased and moved by Ford south to Bryan County.

### FORT MCALLISTER STATE HISTORIC SITE

Perhaps the main attraction in Richmond Hill, especially for Civil War buffs, is Fort McAllister State Historic Site. Unlike the masonry forts of Savannah, Fort McAllister is an all-earthwork fortification on the Ogeechee River, the site of a short but savage assault by Sherman's troops in December 1864 in which 5,000 Union soldiers quickly overwhelmed the skeleton garrison of 230 Confederate defenders. After the war, the site fell into disrepair until Henry Ford funded and spearheaded restoration in the 1930s, as he did with so many historic sites

in Bryan County. The fort, which features many reenactments throughout the year, has a **Civil War Museum** (Mon.-Sat. 9am-5pm, Sun. 2pm-5pm, $5). An adjacent recreational site features a beautiful oak-lined picnic ground, a nature trail, and the nearby 65-site Savage Island Campground. Bryan County is just 15 minutes from Savannah. Take I-95 south and then exit 90. From there, head east about six miles on Highway 144/Ford Drive.

MAP 6: 3894 Ft. McAllister Rd., Richmond Hill, 912/727-2339, www.gastateparks.org/info/ftmcallister; daily 7am-10pm; $7.50 adults, $4.50 children

### RICHMOND HILL HISTORICAL SOCIETY AND MUSEUM

The little Richmond Hill Historical Society and Museum is housed in a former kindergarten built by Henry Ford.

MAP 6: Ford Ave. and Timber Trail Rd., Richmond Hill, 912/756-3697; daily 10am-4pm; donations accepted

## New Ebenezer
### JERUSALEM EVANGELICAL LUTHERAN CHURCH

Few people visit New Ebenezer today, west of Savannah in Effingham County. Truth is there's not much there anymore except for one old church. But, oh, what a church. The Jerusalem Evangelical Lutheran Church hosts the oldest continuous congregation in the United States. Built of local clay brick in 1769, its walls are 21 inches thick. Some original panes of glass remain, and its European bells are still rung before each service. Several surrounding structures are also heirs to New Ebenezer's Salzburg legacy.

MAP 6: 2966 Ebenezer Rd., Rincon, 912/754-3915, http://jerusalematebenezer.org; service Sun. 11am

### NEW EBENEZER RETREAT AND CONFERENCE CENTER

Around the corner from the Jerusalem Evangelical Lutheran Church is a much newer spiritually themed site, the New Ebenezer Retreat and Conference Center. Built in 1977, the retreat provides acres of calm surroundings, lodging, and meals in an ecumenical Christian setting.

The New Ebenezer Retreat and Conference Center offers a range of very reasonably priced lodgings, most including meals, in a beautiful setting. The extremely fast-growing town of Rincon, through which you will most likely drive on your way to New Ebenezer, offers an assortment of the usual chain food and lodging establishments.

While most facilities are for guests of the retreat, you can tour the grounds on your own. It's scenic and peaceful, and the cottages are charming.

MAP 6: 2887 Ebenezer Rd., Rincon, 912/754-9242, www.newebenezer.org

# Entertainment and Nightlife

Savannah is known for its copious watering holes hosting a diverse range of local residents and adventurous visitors. Savannah is a hard-drinking town, and not just on St. Patrick's Day. The ability to legally walk downtown streets with beer, wine, or a cocktail in hand definitely contributes to the overall joie de vivre. Bars close in Savannah at 3am, a full hour later than in Charleston. A citywide indoor smoking ban is in effect and you may not smoke cigarettes in any bar in Savannah. Recent state legislation finally allows Savannah bars that don't serve food to open on Sundays, but not all have made the switch; call ahead.

## WATERFRONT
### Bars and Pubs
#### BAYOU CAFE

One of Savannah's favorite and most raucous historic taverns is possibly the River Street bar most visited by actual locals. The Bayou Cafe, overlooking River Street but situated on one of the cobblestone "ramps" going down from Bay Street to the waterfront, offers a convivial dive-bar type atmosphere and a solid Cajun-style pub food menu. The main floor is the traditional tavern, where the best local blues musicians play frequent gigs. The second floor is more of a game room and general younger folks' party area.

MAP 1: 4 N. Abercorn Ramp, 912/233-6411, daily 11am-3am

#### KEVIN BARRY'S IRISH PUB

The main landmark on the west end of River Street is the famous (or infamous, depending on which side of "The Troubles" you're on) Kevin Barry's Irish Pub, one of Savannah's most beloved establishments. KB's is open seven days a week, with evenings seeing performances by a number of Irish troubadours, all veterans of the East Coast trad circuit.

MAP 1: 117 W. River St., 912/233-9626, www. kevinbarrys.com; daily 11am-3am

#### ROCKS ON THE ROOF

Uncharacteristically, Savannah now sports several good hotel bars, and one of the best is Rocks on the Roof, atop the Bohemian Hotel Savannah Riverfront on the waterfront. In good weather the exterior walls are opened up to reveal a large wraparound seating area with stunning views of downtown on one side and of the Savannah River on the other.

MAP 1: 102 W. Bay St., 912/721-3800; daily 11am-3pm

### Gay and Lesbian
#### CHUCK'S BAR

A friendly, kitschy little tavern at the far west end of River Street near the Jefferson Street ramp, Chuck's Bar is a great place to relax and see some interesting local characters. Karaoke at Chuck's is especially a hoot, and they keep the Christmas lights up all year.

MAP 1: 301 W. River St., 912/232-1005; Mon.-Wed. 8pm-3am, Thurs.-Sat. 7pm-3am

### CLUB ONE JEFFERSON

Any examination of gay and lesbian nightlife in Savannah must, of course, begin with Club One Jefferson of *Midnight in the Garden of Good and Evil* fame, with its famous drag shows, including the notorious Lady Chablis, upstairs in the cabaret, and its rockin' 1,000-square-foot dance floor downstairs. Cabaret show times are Thursday-Saturday 10:30pm and 12:30am, Sunday 10:30pm, and Monday 11:30pm. Call for Lady Chablis's show times. As at all local gay nightclubs, straights are more than welcome.

MAP 1: 1 Jefferson St., 912/232-0200, www.clubone-online.com; Mon.-Sat. 5pm-3am, Sun. 5pm-2am

## CITY MARKET
### Bars and Pubs
#### MOON RIVER BREWING COMPANY

Moon River Brewing Company is directly across from the Hyatt Regency Savannah and offers half a dozen handcrafted beers in a rambling old space that housed Savannah's premier hotel back in antebellum days. The particular highlight these days, however, is the dog-friendly enclosed beer garden on the busy corner of Bay and Whitaker, with frequent live music and a congenial al fresco atmosphere, with access to the full menu.

MAP 1: 21 W. Bay St., 912/447-0943, www.moonriverbrewing.com; Mon.-Thurs. 11am-11pm, Fri.-Sat. 11am-midnight, Sun. 11am-10pm

### THE RAIL PUB

In the City Market area, your best bet is The Rail Pub, one of Savannah's oldest and most beloved taverns and a great place to get a pint or a shot or do karaoke in a quite boisterous but still cozy and friendly environment spread over two floors. They give you roasted peanuts with your drink; just let the shells fall on the floor like everyone else does.

MAP 1: 405 W. Congress St., 912/238-1311, www.therailpub.com; Mon.-Sat. 3pm-3am

### 22 SQUARE

In the modernist Andaz Savannah hotel overlooking bustling Ellis Square, 22 Square is a great place for an upscale cocktail and for meeting interesting people from all over. Try the refreshing Savannah Fizz or one of their mean Sazeracs.

MAP 1: 14 Barnard St., 912/233-2116, www.savannah.andaz.hyatt.com; Mon.-Thurs. 4pm-10pm, Fri.-Sat. 2pm-midnight, Sun. 4pm-10pm

## The To-Go Cup Tradition

Arguably the single most civilized trait of Savannah, and certainly one of the things that most sets it apart, is the glorious old tradition of the "to-go cup." True to its history of hard partying and general open-mindedness, Savannah, like New Orleans, legally allows you to walk the streets downtown with an open container of your favorite adult beverage. Of course, you have to be 21 or over, and the cup must be Styrofoam or plastic, never glass or metal, and no more than 16 ounces. While there are boundaries to where to-go cups are legal, in practice this includes almost all areas of the historic district frequented by visitors. The quick and easy rule of thumb is to keep your to-go cups north of Jones Street.

Every other election year, some local politician tries to get the church folk all riled up and proposes doing away with to-go cups in the interest of public safety, and he or she is inevitably shouted down by the outcry from the tourism-conscious chamber of commerce and from patriotic Savannahians defending their way of life. Every downtown watering hole has stacks of cups at the bar for patrons to use. You can either ask the bartender for a to-go cup—aka a "go cup"—or just reach out and grab one yourself. Don't be shy; it's the Savannah way.

# Craft Breweries

Savannah is finally catching up to the craft brewery trend, and **Southbound Brewing Company's** (107 E. Lathrop Ave., 912/335-7716, southboundbrewingco.com, tours 5:30pm Wed.-Fri. 2pm Sat., $15) tasting events are getting rave reviews. Tours include 36 ounces of beer served on-site and your choice of a 22-ounce bomber, a 32-ounce growler fill, a six-pack, or a pint glass. The tastings attract a large crowd, so don't dilly-dally. As is the case with many up-and-coming breweries, the large, restored warehouse space isn't in the most scenic neighborhood. But Southbound's offerings include a rotating series of special event beers and the occasional rock concert.

Savannah's other key craft brewery is **Service Brewing** (574 Indian St., servicebrewing.com, 5:30pm-7:30pm Thurs.-Fri., 2pm-4pm Sat., $12 per person), so named because its founders are ex-military; they donate a portion of all profits to veteran service organizations. Basic tastings include either a 36-ounce flight of six ounces per pour or three 12-ounce pours. Service is a wee bit closer to downtown than Southbound, and within walking distance of the River Street/City Market area.

## Live Music and Karaoke

### THE JINX

Despite its high-volume offerings, The Jinx is a friendly watering hole and the closest thing Savannah has to a full-on Athens, Georgia, music club, with a very active calendar of rock and metal shows. Shows start late here, never before 11pm and often later than that. If you're here for the music and have sensitive ears, bring earplugs. The beer offerings are good, but this is the kind of place where many regular patrons opt for tallboy PBRs.

**MAP 1:** 127 W. Congress St., 912/236-2281, www. thejinx.net; Mon.-Sat. 4pm-3am

## HISTORIC DISTRICT NORTH

### Bars and Pubs

#### ABE'S ON LINCOLN

No, Lincoln Street in Savannah isn't named for Abraham Lincoln. But dark, fun little Abe's is on Lincoln Street and it's also the oldest bar in town, with a very eclectic clientele.

**MAP 1:** 17 Lincoln St., 912/349-0525, http://abesonlincoln.com; Mon.-Sat. 4pm-3am

#### CHIVE SEA BAR AND LOUNGE

For swank partying on Broughton Street, head to Chive Sea Bar and Lounge, which backs up its tasty menu with a high-end bar in a wonderful, modernist space.

**MAP 1:** 4 W. Broughton St., 912/233-1748, www. chivelounge.com; Mon.-Fri. 11am-10pm, Sat. noon-midnight, Sun. 5pm-10pm

#### CIRCA 1875

On Whitaker Street is a hip hangout with an excellent menu, Circa 1875, where the burgers are as good as the martinis. The vintage vibe takes you back to the days of the Parisian salons.

**MAP 1:** 48 Whitaker St., 912/443-1875, www.circa1875. com; Mon.-Thurs. 6pm-10pm, Fri.-Sat. 6pm-11pm

#### O'CONNELL'S

Without question, the place in Savannah that comes closest to replicating an actual, authentic Irish pub environment is tiny, cozy O'Connell's, where they know how to pour a Guinness, feature Magner's cider on tap, and the house specialty is the "pickleback"—a shot of Jameson's followed by a shot of, yes, pickle brine. In classic Emerald Isle tradition, most seating is bench-style, to encourage conversation.

**MAP 1:** 42 Drayton St., 912/231-2298; daily 3pm-3am

# HISTORIC DISTRICT SOUTH
## Bars and Pubs
### THE DISTILLERY

The Distillery is located in, yes, a former distillery. As such, the atmosphere isn't exactly dark and romantic—it's sort of one big open room—but the excellent location at the corner of MLK Jr. Boulevard and Liberty Street, the long vintage bar, and the great selection of beers on tap combine to make this a happening spot. The fish-and-chips are also great.

MAP 2: 416 W. Liberty St., 912/236-1772, www.distillerysavannah.com; Mon.-Sat. 11am-close, Sun. noon-close

### THE CHROMATIC DRAGON

And now for something completely different: Gamers and geeks alike will enjoy video and board game action—as well as the food and drink—at the Chromatic Dragon. While you can get a meal and a brew here, the focus is on the gaming, so much so that you are asked "analog or digital?" as you walk in, in other words board games or video consoles, the latter mainly Xbox360 and PS3. They offer a vast array of both, or you can bring your own.

MAP 3: 514 MLK Jr Blvd., 912/289-0350, www.chromaticdragon.com; Thurs.-Sat. 11am-2am, Sun.-Wed. 11am-11pm

### THE ORIGINAL

For 65 years, perhaps Savannah's most beloved dive bar/watering hole was **Pinkie Master's,** at 318 Drayton Street downtown. Once the hub of local old-school Democratic Party political gossip, Pinkie's had become a symbol of the best of Savannah: locals and visitors socializing in a relaxed and fun vintage-themed atmosphere.

While you will no doubt still see Pinkie's featured prominently in guidebooks and websites, it's very important to know that as of December 2015, Pinkie Masters is no more—at least the way it was. However, the original Pinkie's space is still a bar and is still quite friendly and unpretentious. In fact, it's called simply "The Original"—a nod to the retro Pabst Blue Ribbon sign outside.

MAP 2: 318 Drayton St., 912/999-7106, www.theoriginalsavannah.com; Mon.-Thurs. 3pm-3am, Fri.-Sat. noon-3am

## Live Music and Karaoke
### MCDONOUGH'S

Savannah's undisputed karaoke champion is McDonough's, an advantage compounded by the fact that a lot more goes on here than karaoke. The kitchen at McDonough's is quite capable, and many locals swear you can get the best burger in town here. Despite the sports bar atmosphere, the emphasis is on the karaoke, which ramps up every night at 9:30pm.

MAP 2: 21 E. McDonough St., 912/233-6136, www.mcdonoughsofsavannah.com; Mon.-Sat. 8pm-3am, Sun. 8pm-2am

# SOFO DISTRICT
## Bars and Pubs
### AMERICAN LEGION BAR

The real hipsters hang out in ironic fashion drinking PBRs at the American Legion Bar, located in, yes, an actual American Legion post. While the Legionnaires themselves are a straitlaced patriotic bunch, the patrons of "the Legion," as the bar is colloquially known, tend toward the counterculture. Here is where you'll find Savannah's movers and shakers in the grassroots arts and cultural community.

Fun historical fact: The building housing the Legion was the birthplace of the U.S. 8th Air Force during World War II.

MAP 3: 1108 Bull St., 912/233-9277, http://alpost135.com; Mon.-Sat. 4pm-2am

# FESTIVALS AND EVENTS

Savannah's calendar fairly bursts with festivals, many outdoors. Dates shift from year to year, so it's best to consult the listed websites for details.

## January

Floats and bands take part in the **Martin Luther King Jr. Day Parade** downtown to commemorate the civil rights leader and Georgia native. The bulk of the route is on historic MLK Jr. Boulevard, formerly West Broad Street.

Straddling January and February is the weeklong **PULSE Art + Technology Festival** (www.telfair.org), an adventurous event that brings video artists and offbeat electronic performance art into the modern Jepson Center for the Arts.

## February

Definitely not to be confused with St. Patrick's Day, the **Savannah Irish Festival** (912/232-3448, www.savannahirish.org) focuses on Celtic music.

Hosted by the historically black Savannah State University at various venues around town, the monthlong **Black Heritage Festival** (912/691-6847) is tied into Black History Month and boasts name entertainers like the Alvin Ailey Dance Theatre (performing free!). This event also usually features plenty of historical lectures devoted to the very interesting and rich history of African Americans in Savannah.

Also in February is the quickly growing **Savannah Book Festival** (www.savannahbookfestival.org), modeled after a similar event in Washington DC and featuring many national and regional authors at various venues downtown.

## March

One of the most anticipated events for house-proud Savannahians, the **Tour of Homes and Gardens** (912/234-8054, www.savannahtourofhomes.org) offers guests the opportunity to visit six beautiful sites off the usual tourist-trod path. This is a great way to expand your understanding of local architecture and hospitality beyond the usual house museums.

One of Savannah's most unique festivals is the multiday indie rock festival **Savannah Stopover** (www.savannahstopover.com) in early mid-March. The idea is simple: Book bands that are already driving down to Austin, Texas, for the following week's South By Southwest so they can "stop over" and play at various venues in downtown Savannah. Get it? This is a great way to see up-and-coming bands before they blow up big; previous headliners have included St. Paul & The Broken Bones, Grimes, and Reptar. Admission is generally by ticketed wristband, and most venues are for ages 21 and over.

More than just a day, the citywide **St. Patrick's Day** (www.savannahsaintpatricksday.com) celebration generally lasts at least half a week and temporarily triples the population. The nearly three-hour parade—second-biggest in the United States—always begins at 10am on St. Patrick's Day (unless that falls on a Sunday, in which case it's generally on the previous Saturday) and includes an interesting mix of marching bands, wacky floats, and sauntering local Irishmen in kelly green jackets. The appeal comes not only from the festive atmosphere and generally beautiful spring weather, but also from Savannah's unique law allowing partiers to walk the streets with a cup filled with the adult beverage of their choice. While the parade itself is very family-friendly, afterward hardcore partiers generally head en masse to River Street, which is blocked off for the occasion and definitely not where you want to take small children. If you want to hear traditional Celtic music on St. Patrick's Day in Savannah, River Street also isn't the place to go, with the exception of Kevin Barry's on the west end. For authentic Irish music on St. Paddy's Day, wander around the pubs on the periphery of City Market.

The three-week **Savannah Music Festival** (912/234-3378, www.savannahmusicfestival.org) is held at various historic venues around town and begins right after St. Patrick's Day. Past festivals have featured Wynton Marsalis, Dianne Reeves, and the Avett Brothers. The jazz portion is locked down tight, thanks to the efforts of festival director Rob Gibson, a Georgia native who cut his teeth as the founding director of Jazz at Lincoln Center. The classical side is helmed by one of the world's great young violinists, Daniel Hope, acting as associate director. Other genres are featured in abundance as well, including gospel, bluegrass, zydeco, world music, and the always-popular American Traditions vocal competition. The most economical way to enjoy the Savannah Music Festival is to purchase tickets online before December of the previous year at a 10 percent discount. However, if you just want to take in a few events, individual tickets are available at a tiered pricing system. You can buy tickets to individual events in town at the walk-up box office beside the Trustees Theater on Broughton Street.

## April

Short for "North of Gaston Street," the **NOGS Tour of Hidden Gardens** (912/961-4805, www.gcofsavnogstour.org, $30) is available two days in April and focuses on a selection of Savannah's amazing private gardens chosen for excellence of design, historical interest, and beauty.

Everyone loves the annual free **Sidewalk Arts Festival** (912/525-5865, www.scad.edu) presented by the Savannah College of Art and Design in Forsyth Park. Contestants claim a rectangular section of sidewalk on which to display their chalk art talent. There's a non-contest section with chalk provided.

## May

The SCAD-sponsored **Sand Arts Festival** (www.scad.edu) on Tybee Island's North Beach centers on a competition of sand castle design, sand sculpture, sand relief, and wind sculpture. You might be amazed at the level of artistry lavished on the sometimes-wondrous creations, only for them to wash away with the tide.

If you don't want to get wet, don't show up at the **Tybee Beach Bum Parade,** an uproarious event held the weekend prior to Memorial Day weekend. With a distinctly boozy overtone, this unique 20-year-old event features homemade floats filled with partiers who squirt the assembled crowds with various water pistols. The crowds, of course, pack their own heat and squirt back.

## July

Two key events happen around **Fourth of July,** primarily the large fireworks show on River Street on July 4 but also an impressive fireworks display from the Tybee pier and pavilion on July 3. A nice bonus of the Tybee event is that sometimes you can look out over the Atlantic and see a similar fireworks display on nearby Hilton Head Island, South Carolina, a few minutes away by boat (but nearly an hour by car).

## September

The second-largest gay and lesbian event in Georgia (only Atlanta's version is larger), the **Savannah Pride Festival** (www.savannah-pride.org, various venues, free) happens every September. Crowds get pretty big for this festive, fun event, which usually features lots of dance acts and political booths.

Over Labor Day weekend you can check out the Savannah Craft Brew Festival (International Trade & Convention Center, 1 International Dr., www.savannahcraftbrewfest.com, $50). This day-long tasting event features a healthy range of breweries from around the nation, not only from Georgia's own burgeoning craft brew industry.

## October

The Savannah Philharmonic Orchestra plays a free concert in Forsyth Park that draws thousands of noshers. Arrive early to check out the ostentatious, whimsical picnic displays, which compete for prizes. Then set out your blanket, pop open a bottle of wine, and enjoy the sweet sounds.

The combined aroma of beer, sauerkraut, and sausage that you smell coming from the waterfront is the annual **Oktoberfest on the River** (www.riverstreetsavannah.com), which has evolved to be Savannah's second-largest celebration (behind only St. Patrick's Day). Live entertainment of varying quality is featured, though the attraction, of course, is the aforementioned beer and German food. A highlight is the Saturday morning "Weiner Dog Races" involving, you guessed it, competing dachshunds.

It's a fairly new festival, but the **Tybee Island Pirate Festival** (http://tybeepiratefest.com) is a fun and typically rollicking Tybee event in October featuring, well, everybody dressing up like pirates, saying "Arr" a lot, eating, drinking, and listening to cover bands. It may not sound like much, and it's really not, but it's typically very well attended.

Sponsored by St. Paul's Greek Orthodox Church, the popular **Savannah Greek Festival** (www.stpaulsgreekorthodox.org) features food, music, and Greek souvenirs. The weekend event is held across the street from the church at the parish center—in the gym, to be exact, right on the basketball court. Despite the pedestrian location, the food is authentic and delicious, and the atmosphere convivial and friendly.

Hosted by the Savannah College of Art and Design, the weeklong **Savannah Film Festival** (www.scad.edu) beginning in late October is rapidly growing not only in size

but in prestige as well. Lots of older, more established Hollywood names appear as honored guests for the evening events, while buzz-worthy up-and-coming actors, directors, producers, writers, and animators give excellent workshops during the day. Many of these usually jaded showbiz types really let their hair down for this festival, because, as you'll see, Savannah is the real star. The best way to enjoy this excellent event is to buy a pass, which enables you to walk from event to event. Most importantly, the passes gain you admission to what many locals consider the best part of the festival: the after-parties, where you'll often find yourself face to face with some famous star or director. But whatever you do, don't ask for an autograph. The thing at these parties is to be cool—and if you can't *be* cool, at least act that way.

One of Savannah's most unique events is late October's **"Shalom Y'all" Jewish Food Festival** (912/233-1547, www.mickveisrael. org), held in Forsyth Park and sponsored by the historic Temple Mickve Israel. Latkes, matzo, and other nibbles are all featured along with entertainment.

# Arts and Culture

There are more art galleries per capita in Savannah than in New York City—one gallery for every 2,191 residents, to be exact. Savannah College of Art & Design (SCAD) galleries are in abundance all over town, displaying the handiwork of students, faculty, alumni, and important regional and national artists. Savannah's arts scene also shines a spotlight on theater, classical music, and cool movie houses.

## HISTORIC DISTRICT NORTH
### Cinema
#### LUCAS THEATRE FOR THE ARTS
The ornate, beautifully restored historic Lucas Theatre for the Arts downtown is a classic

Southern movie house. The Savannah Film Society and Savannah College of Art and Design host screenings there throughout the year. Check the website for scheduling. **MAP 1:** 32 Abercorn St., 912/525-5040, www. lucastheatre.com; most screenings under $10

### Music
#### SAVANNAH PHILHARMONIC
The Savannah Philharmonic is a professional symphony orchestra that performs concertos and sonatas at various venues around town and is always worth checking out. **MAP 1:** 216 E. Broughton St. (box office), 912/525-5050, www.savannahphilharmonic.org; Mon.-Fri 10am-5pm

# A City of Art

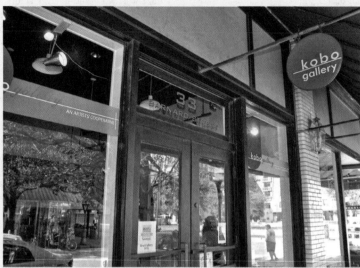

Kobo Gallery is just off Ellis Square.

For art lovers, the no-brainer package experience for the visitor is the combo of the **Telfair Academy of Arts and Sciences** (121 Barnard St., 912/790-8800, www.telfair.org) and the **Jepson Center for the Arts** (207 W. York St., 912/790-8800, www.telfair.org). These two arms of the Telfair Museums run the gamut of art, from old-school portraiture to cutting-edge contemporary art.

**SCAD galleries** (912/525-5225, www.scad.edu) are abundant. Outposts with consistently impressive exhibits are the **Gutstein Gallery** (201 E. Broughton St.) and **Pinnacle Gallery** (320 E. Liberty St.). The college also runs its own museum, the **SCAD Museum of Art** (227 MLK Jr. Blvd., 912/525-7191, www.scad.edu), which recently doubled in size to accommodate a new wing devoted to the Walter O. Evans Collection of African American Art.

The small and avant-garde **ArtRise Savannah** (2427 DeSoto Ave., 912/335-8204, www.artrisesavannah.org) helps coordinate "Art March" gallery crawls in the SoFo (South of Forsyth) district the first Friday of the month. **Non-Fiction Gallery** (1522 Bull St., 912/662-5152), also in SoFo, exhibits work by many of Savannah's up-and-coming talents. Nearby is **Sulfur Studios** (2301 Bull St., sulfurstudios.org), which not only hosts rotating exhibits, but also coordinates many community forums and events of a cutting-edge nature.

Overlooking Ellis Square downtown is well-regarded **Kobo Gallery** (33 Barnard St., 912/201-0304, www.kobogallery.com), a local artist co-op featuring some of Savannah's best contemporary artists who frequently put on group shows. One of the featured artists is always on duty, so stopping in can be a very informative experience.

There are several good galleries in the beach town of Tybee Island as well, chief among them **Dragonfly Studio** (1204 Hwy 80, 912/786-4431, www.dragonflystudioarts.com), which hosts work by the very best coastal artists in a cute little roadside shack.

## HISTORIC DISTRICT SOUTH
### Performing Arts
#### HISTORIC SAVANNAH THEATRE

The semipro troupe at the Historic Savannah Theatre performs a busy rotating schedule of oldies revues (a typical title: *Return to the '50s*), but they make up for their lack of originality with the tightness and energy of their talented young cast of regulars.

MAP 2: 222 Bull St., 912/233-7764, www. savannahtheatre.com

#### MUSE ARTS WAREHOUSE

The multiuse venue Muse Arts Warehouse hosts community-based plays and performances within a well-restored historic train depot, converted into a black box setting. Get there by taking Liberty Street west from downtown, where it turns into Louisville Road.

MAP 2: 703D Louisville Rd., 912/713-1137, www. musesavannah.org

## SOUTHSIDE
### Performing Arts
#### ARMSTRONG STATE UNIVERSITY MASQUERS

There are few things to recommend Savannah's south side to the visitor, but one of them is the Armstrong State University Masquers, the second-oldest college theater group in the country (only Harvard's Hasty Pudding Theatricals is older). The Masquers boast a performance space at the Jenkins Theatre, and might surprise you with the high quality of their performances despite being a student program. Parking is never a problem.

MAP 4: 11935 Abercorn St., 912/927-5381, www. finearts.armstrong.edu

# Shops

Savannah has also perfected the fine art of shopping, with a focus on antiques and independent home goods stores, with some unique boutiques sprinkled throughout the city. Downtown Savannah's main shopping district is **Broughton Street**. The historic center of downtown shopping has recently seen a major renaissance and is once again home to the most vibrant shopping scene in Savannah, just like it was in the 1940s and 1950s. Many national chain stores have made inroads onto the avenue, including Anthropologie, Banana Republic, H&M, J. Crew, Kate Spade, Michael Kors, Urban Outfitters, Goorin Bros. Hats, Free People, and The Gap, among others.

A bit south of downtown proper, but still a short drive away, is the **Starland District**. This up-and-coming mixed-use area is home to a growing variety of more hipster-oriented shops.

Focusing on upscale art and home goods, the small but chic and friendly **Downtown Design District** runs three blocks on Whitaker Street, a short walk from beautiful Forsyth Park.

## WATERFRONT
### Antiques
#### JERE'S ANTIQUES

One of the coolest antiques shops in town is Jere's Antiques. It's in a huge historic warehouse on Factor's Walk and has a concentration on fine European pieces.

MAP 1: 9 N. Jefferson St., 912/236-2815, www. jeresantiques.com; Mon.-Sat. 9:30am-5pm

### Clothes
#### HARLEY-DAVIDSON

You won't be buying a Softail Deluxe at this retail merchandise store, but you can certainly clothe your inner biker here.

MAP 1: 503 E. River St., 912/231-8000, www. savannahhd.com; Mon.-Sat. 10am-6pm, Sun. noon-6pm

### THE MAD HATTER

Probably the closest thing to a unique shop on River Street proper is The Mad Hatter, which as the name suggests, offers a wide variety of headwear.

**MAP 1:** 123 E. River St., 912/232-7566

## Gourmet Treats
### SAVANNAH BEE COMPANY

While the flagship location of this very popular locally based, regional chain is actually just a few blocks north on Broughton Street, this River Street location on the ground floor of the Hyatt Regency hotel offers a similar range of honey-based goods from lip balm to lotion to, yes, honey.

**MAP 1:** 1 W. River St., 912/234-7088, www. savannahbee.com; Mon.-Sat. 10am-7pm, Sun. 11am-8pm

### RIVER STREET SWEETS

Cater to your sweet tooth—and bring some goodies back with you—at River Street Sweets, where you can witness Southern delicacies

the Savannah Bee Company on Broughton

like pralines being made as you shop. And of course there are free samples.

**MAP 1:** 13 E. River St., 912/234-4608, www. riverstreetsweets.com; daily 9am-11pm

## Pet Goods
### BLACK DOG GENERAL STORE

The first Southern location of this national boutique chain offers upscale doggie treats and gear.

**MAP 1:** 211 W. River St., 912/335-7472, www. theblackdog.com; daily 10am-9pm

### WOOF GANG BAKERY

On the opposite end of River Street from the Black Dog General store is Woof Gang Bakery, specializing in gourmet treats and food for your canine companion.

**MAP 1:** 425A E. River St., 912/999-6409, www. woofgangbakery.com; Fri.-Sat. 9am-9pm, Sun.-Thurs. 9am-8pm

# HISTORIC DISTRICT NORTH
## Art Supply
### BLICK ART MATERIALS

A great art town needs a great art supply store, and in Savannah that would be Blick Art Materials, which has all the equipment and tools for the serious artist—priced to be affordable for students. But casual shoppers will enjoy it as well for its collection of offbeat gift items.

**MAP 1:** 318 E. Broughton St., 912/234-0456, www. dickblick.com; Mon.-Fri. 8am-8pm, Sat. 10am-7pm, Sun. 11am-6pm

## Clothes and Fashion
### GLOBE SHOE CO.

Perhaps Broughton Street's most beloved old shop is Globe Shoe Co., a Savannah institution and a real throwback to a time of personalized retail service. They have no website and no Facebook page—they're all about simple one-to-one service, like in the old days.

**MAP 1:** 17 E. Broughton St., 912/232-8161; Mon.-Sat. 10am-6pm

## CIVVIES NEW AND RECYCLED CLOTHING

Inhabiting a well-restored upstairs space, Civvie's is perhaps Savannah's most well-regarded vintage store, with a variety of retro clothes and shoes and a strong local following. They also have a nifty section of campy, kitschy gift items.

**MAP 1:** 14 E. Broughton St., 912/236-1551; Mon.-Sat. 11am-7pm, Sun. 11am-5pm

## LEVY JEWELERS

Now recently moved to what's considered Savannah's prime downtown corner, at Bull and Broughton, is century-old family-owned Levy Jewelers. They have a complete showcase of necklaces, watches, and rings from two dozen internationally recognized designers.

**MAP 1:** 2 E. Broughton St., 912/233-1163; Mon.-Sat. 10am-9pm, Sun. noon-6pm

## Gourmet Treats
### CHOCOLAT BY ADAM TURONI

Chocolate lovers need to head straight to Chocolat by Adam Turoni, a tiny space with a big taste. Adam's handcrafted, high-quality chocolates are miniature works of art—and delicious ones at that. Be prepared to be overwhelmed.

**MAP 1:** 323 W. Broughton St., 912/335-2914, www. chocolatat.com; daily 11am-6pm

## SAVANNAH BEE COMPANY

One of the more unique Savannah retail shops is the Savannah Bee Company, which carries an extensive line of honey and honey-based merchandise, from foot lotion to lip balm. All the honey comes from area hives owned by company founder and owner Ted Dennard. The flagship Broughton location provides plenty of sampling opportunities at the little café area and even boasts a small theater space for instructional films.

**MAP 1:** 104 W. Broughton St., 912/233-7873, www. savannahbee.com; Mon.-Sat. 10am-7pm, Sun. 11am-5pm

## Home Goods
### THE PARIS MARKET & BROCANTE

While Savannah is an Anglophile's dream, Francophiles will enjoy The Paris Market & Brocante on a beautifully restored corner of Broughton Street. Home and garden goods, bed and bath accoutrements, and a great selection of antique and vintage items combine for a rather opulent shopping experience. Plus there's an old-school Euro café inside, where you can enjoy a coffee, tea, or hot chocolate.

Chocolat by Adam Turoni

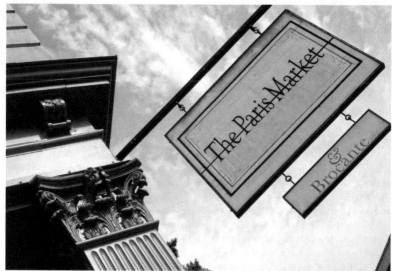

The Paris Market & Brocante is a unique shop on Broughton Street.

**MAP 1:** 36 W. Broughton St., 912/232-1500, www.
theparismarket.com; Mon.-Sat. 10am-6pm, Sun.
11am-4pm

### 24E FURNISHINGS AT BROUGHTON

Those looking for great home decorating ideas with inspiration from both global and Southern aesthetics, traditional as well as sleekly modern, should check out 24e Furnishings at Broughton, located in an excellently restored 1921 storefront. Be sure to check out the expansive second-floor showroom.

**MAP 1:** 24 E. Broughton St., 912/233-2274, www.
twentyfoure.com; Mon.-Thurs. 10am-6pm, Fri.-Sat.
10am-7pm, Sun. noon-5pm

## Outdoor Outfitters
### HALF MOON OUTFITTERS

Outdoors lovers should make themselves acquainted with Half Moon Outfitters, a full-service camping, hiking, skiing, and kayaking store. Half Moon is part of a regional chain.

**MAP 1:** 15 E. Broughton St., 912/201-9313, www.
halfmoonoutfitters.com; Mon.-Sat. 10am-7pm, Sun.
noon-6pm

## HISTORIC DISTRICT SOUTH
### Antiques
#### ALEX RASKIN ANTIQUES

Possibly the most beloved antiques store in town is Alex Raskin Antiques in Monterey Square, catty-corner from the Mercer-Williams House Museum, set in the historic Hardee Mansion. A visit is worth it just to explore the home. But the goods Alex lovingly curates are among the best and most tasteful in the region.

**MAP 2:** 441 Bull St., 912/232-8205, www.
alexraskinantiques.com; Mon.-Sat. 10am-5pm

#### THE CORNER DOOR

For a European take on antiques and collectibles, try The Corner Door, set in a unique building in the Downtown Design District and staffed by very friendly and knowledgeable antiques experts.

**MAP 2:** 417 Whitaker St., 912/238-5869; Tues.-Sat.
10am-5pm

#### SMALL PLEASURES

Small Pleasures is one of Savannah's hidden gems. They deal in a tasteful range of vintage

Alex Raskin Antiques is on beautiful Monterey Square.

MAP 2: 326 Bull St., 912/234-7257; Mon.-Sat. 9am-6pm

## V&J DUNCAN

The beautiful Monterey Square location and a mention in *Midnight in the Garden of Good and Evil* combine to make V&J Duncan a Savannah "must-shop." Owner John Duncan and his wife Virginia ("Ginger" to friends) have collected an impressive array of prints, books, and maps over the past quarter century, and are themselves a treasure trove of information.

MAP 2: 12 E. Taylor St., 912/232-0338, www.vjduncan. com; Mon.-Sat. 10:30am-4:30pm

## Clothes
### CUSTARD BOUTIQUE

Custard Boutique in the Downtown Design District has a cute, cutting-edge selection of women's clothes in a range of styles and is easily the match of any other women's clothing store in town.

MAP 2: 414 Whitaker St., 912/232-4733; Mon.-Sat. 10:30am-6pm, Sun. noon-5pm

and estate jewelry, in a suitably small but delightfully appointed space in the Downtown Design District.

MAP 2: 412 Whitaker St., 912/234-0277; Mon.-Sat. 10:30am-5pm

## Books and Music
### THE BOOK LADY

Specializing in "gently used" books in good condition, The Book Lady on Liberty Street features many rare first editions. Enjoy a gourmet coffee while you browse the stacks.

MAP 2: 6 E. Liberty St., 912/233-3628; Mon.-Sat. 10am-5:30pm

### E. SHAVER BOOKSELLER

The fact that E. Shaver Bookseller is one of the few locally owned independent bookstores left in town should not diminish the fact that it is also one of the best bookstores in town. The friendly, well-read staff can help you around the rambling old interior of their ground-level store and its generous stock of regionally themed books.

## Gifts and Souvenirs
### FOLKLORICO

Set in a stunningly restored multilevel Victorian within a block of Forsyth Park, the globally conscious Folklorico brings in a fascinating and diverse collection of sustainably made jewelry, gifts, and home goods from around the world, focusing on Central and South America and Asia.

MAP 2: 440 Bull St., 912/232-9300; Mon.-Sat. 10am-5pm, Sun. 1pm-5pm

### SAINTS AND SHAMROCKS

In this town so enamored of all things Irish, a great little locally owned shop is Saints and Shamrocks, across the intersection from The Book Lady. Pick up your St. Patrick's-themed gear and gifts to celebrate Savannah's highest holiday along with high-quality Irish imports.

MAP 2: 309 Bull St., 912/233-8858, www. saintsandshamrocks.org; Mon.-Sat. 9:30am-5:30pm, Sun. 11am-4pm

## SHOPSCAD

Not only a valuable outlet for SCAD students and faculty to sell their artistic wares, shopSCAD is also one of Savannah's most unique boutiques. You never really know what you'll find, but whatever it is, it will be one-of-a-kind. The jewelry in particular is always cutting edge in design and high quality in craftsmanship. The designer T-shirts are a hoot too.

**MAP 2:** 340 Bull St., 912/525-5180, www. shopscadonline.com; Mon.-Wed. 9am-5:30pm, Thurs.-Fri. 9am-8pm, Sat. 10am-8pm, Sun. noon-5pm

### Home Goods
#### MADAME CHRYSANTHEMUM

Madame Chrysanthemum, set in a charming, cozy corner spot in the Downtown Design District, deals in fun home items and gift ideas with a hip and enjoyable Savannah style.

**MAP 2:** 101 W. Taylor St., 912/238-3355; Mon.-Sat. 10am-5pm

#### ONE FISH TWO FISH

An eclectic European-style home goods store is One Fish Two Fish. Owner Jennifer Beaufait Grayson, a St. Simons Island native, came to town a decade ago to set up shop in this delightfully restored old dairy building in the Downtown Design District.

**MAP 2:** 401 Whitaker St., 912/484-4600; Mon.-Sat. 10am-5:30pm, Sun. noon-5pm

## SOFO DISTRICT
### Books and Music
#### GRAVEFACE RECORDS & CURIOSITIES

For the latest in vinyl, from new releases to vintage retro releases to locally released albums to Record Store Day specials, check out Graveface in the Starland District. This is also a great place to get offbeat, kitschy gifts and unusual DVDs.

**MAP 3:** 5 W. 40th St., 912/335-8018; Mon.-Sat. 11am-7pm, Sun. noon-6pm

### Clothes
#### GYPSY WORLD

Easily one of the best vintage stores in town, Gypsy World in the Starland District has a remarkable range of tasteful retro styles, including vintage furs, usually well within a reasonable budget.

**MAP 3:** 2405 Bull St., 912/704-2347; Tues.-Sat. 9:30am-5pm

## GREATER SAVANNAH
### Malls
#### KELLER'S FLEA MARKET

A local tradition for 20 years, Keller's Flea Market packs in about 10,000 shoppers over the course of a typical weekend. It offers a range of bargains in antiques, home goods, produce, and general kitsch, and there are concessions on-site.

**MAP 6:** 5901 Ogeechee Rd., I-95 exit 94, Southside, 912/927-4848, www.ilovefleas.com, Sat.-Sun. 8am-6pm

#### OGLETHORPE MALL

The mall closest to downtown—though not that close, at about 10 miles south—is Oglethorpe Mall in Southside. Its anchor stores are Sears, Belk, J. C. Penney, and Macy's.

**MAP 6:** 7804 Abercorn St., Southside, 912/354-7038, www.oglethorpemall.com; Mon.-Sat. 10am-9pm, Sun. noon-6pm

#### TANGER OUTLETS SAVANNAH

This outlet mall—actually in the adjacent city of Pooler, not Savannah—is marketed as a destination in itself, and it boasts a large number of stores even by the standards of outlet malls. Brands include American Eagle, Banana Republic, Chico's, Columbia, Gap, J. Crew, Cole Haan, Crocs, Oakley, Nike, and Under Armour.

**MAP 6:** 200 Tanger Outlet Blvd., Pooler, 912/348-3125, www.tangeroutlet.com; Mon.-Sat. 9am-9pm, Sun. 10am-7pm

# Sports and Activities

Savannah offers copious outdoor options that take full advantage of the city's temperate climate and the natural beauty of its marshy environment next to the Atlantic Ocean.

Savannah is a saltwater angler's paradise, rich in trout, flounder, and king and Spanish mackerel. Offshore there's a fair amount of deep-sea action, including large grouper, white and blue marlin, wahoo, snapper, sea bass, and big amberjack near some of the many offshore wrecks.

Diving is a challenge off the Georgia coast because of the silty nature of the water and its mercurial currents. Though not particularly friendly to the novice, plenty of great offshore opportunities abound around the many artificial reefs created by the Georgia Department of Natural Resources (www.coastalgadnr.org).

Other than some action around the pier, the surfing is poor on Tybee Island, with its broad shelf, tepid wave action, and lethal rip currents. But board surfers and kiteboarders have a lot of fun on the south end of Tybee beginning at about 17th Street. The craziest surf is past the rock jetty, but be advised that the rip currents are especially treacherous there.

Hiking in Savannah and the Lowcountry is largely a 2-D experience given the flatness of the terrain, but there are plenty of good nature trails from which to observe the area's rich flora and fauna up close, in beautiful settings.

The best guided water tour in the area is Capt. Rene Heidt's **Sundial Nature Tours** (912/786-9470, www.sundialcharters.com). Rene is an expert in local marine life and offers a variety of tours, including dolphin watches, fossil hunts, and trips to various barrier islands. Rates start at about $160 for two people.

Bicycling is fun all around the Savannah area. Plenty of folks ride their bikes downtown, and it is particularly enriching and fun to pedal around the squares. Legally, however, you're not allowed to ride through the squares; you're supposed to stay on the street around them. And always yield to traffic already within the square as you enter. Other good cycling opportunities are at Fort Pulaski and Tybee Island.

Savannah was the first city in Georgia to unveil a public **bike-share program** (http://catchacat.org, $2 per half hour, daily 5:30am-11pm), and you can now be the beneficiary. Head to Ellis Square adjacent to City Market; the rack is on the south side of the square.

## WATERFRONT
### Water Tours
### SAVANNAH BELLES

If you've just *got* to get out on the river for a short time, by far the best bargain is to take one of the four little Savannah Belles water ferries, named after famous women in Savannah history, which shuttle passengers from River Street to Hutchinson Island and back every 15-20 minutes. Pick one up on River Street in front of City Hall or at the Waving Girl landing a few blocks east.

**MAP 1:** River St. at City Hall and Waving Girl Landing, www.catchacat.org; daily 7:30am-10:30pm; free

### SAVANNAH RIVERBOAT CRUISES

The heavy industrial buildup on the Savannah River means that the main river tours, all departing from the docks in front of the Hyatt Regency Savannah, tend to be disappointing in their unrelenting views of cranes, docks, storage tanks, and smokestacks. Still, for those into that kind of thing, narrated trips up and down the river on the *Georgia Queen* and the *Savannah River Queen* are offered by Savannah Riverboat Cruises. You can opt for just sightseeing, or an added dinner cruise.

**MAP 1:** 9 E. River St., 800/786-6404, www.savannahriverboat.com; starts at $22.95 adults, $13.95 ages 4-12

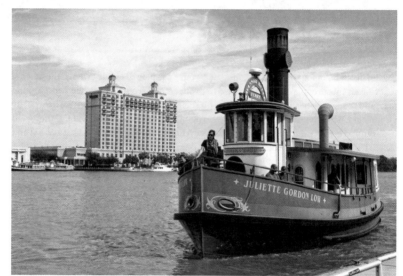

The free Savannah Belles ferries run between downtown and Hutchinson Island.

## HISTORIC DISTRICT NORTH
### Biking
### SAVANNAH BIKE TOURS

To see downtown Savannah by bicycle—quite a refreshing experience—try Savannah Bike Tours for a two-hour trip through all 19 squares and Forsyth Park with your "rolling concierge." Pedaling around the squares and stopping to explore certain sights is a unique pleasure. Tours leave daily at 9:30am, 12:30pm, and 4pm. Rent bikes from them or ride your own.

**MAP 1:** 41 Habersham St., 912/704-4043, www.savannahbiketours.com; $15 adults, $10 under age 12

## HISTORIC DISTRICT SOUTH
### Spectator Sports
### SAVANNAH DERBY DEVILS

For sports action that's a good bit more hard-hitting and comes with a certain hipster kitsch quotient, check out the bruising bouts of the women of the Savannah Derby Devils, who bring the roller derby thunder against other regional teams. They skate downtown at the Savannah Civic Center, and the matches are usually quite well attended.

**MAP 2:** Savannah Civic Center, 301 W. Oglethorpe Ave., 912/651-6556, www.savannahderby.com

### Specialty Tours
### SAVANNAH TASTE EXPERIENCE

Consistently one of the highest-quality tours in town, Savannah Taste Experience takes you on several foodie stops to taste, sip, and learn about Savannah's culinary scene. The basic tour is "First Squares" ($49 adults, $37 children), which focuses on spots within easy walking distance of the waterfront; it meets on River Street outside the Bohemian Hotel. The "Famous and Secret East Side Tour" ($57 adults, $47 children) takes you to more off-the-beaten-path spots; it meets at the Pirate's House. Food and drink is of course included, so come hungry and thirsty!

**MAP 2:** Meeting point River Street outside Bohemian Hotel., 912/221-4439, www.savannahtasteexperience.com; $49 adults, $37 children

### SAVANNAH MOVIE TOUR

To learn about Savannah's history of filmmaking and to enjoy the best of local cuisine,

# Sightseeing in Savannah

Savannah's tourist boom has resulted in a similar explosion of well over 50 separate tour services, ranging from simple guided trolley journeys to horse-drawn carriage rides to specialty tours to ecotourism adventures. Fair warning: Although local tour guides technically must pass a competency test demonstrating their knowledge of Savannah history, in practice whatever they learned is often thrown out the window in favor of whatever sounds good to them at the time. I've heard the craziest, most untrue things said from passing trolleys and horse carriages. By all means go on a tour, but do so with the knowledge that some of what you're likely to hear won't be true at all.

## WALKING TOURS

Storyteller and author Ted Eldridge leads **A Walk Through Savannah Tours** (meeting point at various locations in the historic district, 912/921-4455, www.awalkthroughsavannah. bravehost.com; $15 adults, $5 6-12, free under age 6) and offers all kinds of specialty walking tours, such as a garden tour, a ghost tour, a historic churches tour, and of course, a *Midnight in the Garden of Good and Evil* tour.

## WHEELED TOURS

For a unique tour experience, take a seat on the **Savannah Slow Ride** (various meeting points, 912/414-5634, www.savannahslowride.com, $25), a sort of combination bar, bicycle, and carriage ride. You get on with a group and everyone helps pedal around the squares on about a two-hour ride at five miles per hour or less. You can even bring your to-go cup with you. Pickup points depend on the tour; call for details.

## GHOST TOURS

The copious ghost tours, offered by all the companies, can be fun for the casual visitor who wants entertainment rather than actual history. Students of the paranormal are likely to be disappointed by the cartoonish, Halloween aspect of some of the tours. A standout in the ghost field is **Hearse Ghost Tours** (various pick-up locations, 912/695-1578, www.hearseghosttours.com, $15), a unique company that also operates tours in New Orleans and St. Augustine, Florida. Up to eight guests at a time ride around in the open top of a converted hearse, painted all black, of course, and get a 90-minute, suitably over-the-top narration from the driver-guide. It's still pretty cheesy, but a hip kind of cheesy.

## HORSE AND CARRIAGE TOURS

Ah, yes—what could be more romantic and more traditional than enjoying downtown Savannah the way it was originally intended to be traveled, by horse-drawn carriage? Indeed, this is one of the most fun ways to see the city, for couples as well as for those with horse-enamored children. Yes, the horses sometimes look tired, but the tour operators generally take great care to keep the horses hydrated and out of the worst of the heat. There are three main purveyors of equine tourism in town: **Carriage Tours of Savannah** (912/236-6756, www.carriagetoursofsavannah. com), **Historic Savannah Carriage Tours** (888/837-1011, www.savannahcarriage.com), and **Plantation Carriage Company** (912/201-0001). The length of the basic tour and the price are about the same for all—45-60 minutes, about $25 adults and $15 children. All offer specialty tours as well, from ghost tours to evening romantic rides with champagne. Embarkation points vary; check company websites for pickup points. Some will pick you up at your hotel.

try a Savannah Movie Tour, taking you to various film locations in town. The company also offers the Foody Tour ($48) featuring six to nine local eateries.

**MAP 2:** Meeting point Savannah Visitors Center, 301 MLK Jr. Blvd., 912/234-3440, www. savannahmovietours.com; $25 adults, $15 children

### OLD CITY WALKS

The premium tour option is Old City Walks, explorations of well-known and of little-known Savannah attractions, guided by long-time local expert Phil Sellers. These aren't budget tours but they are the state of the art locally. There are several tours and many times; Sellers also offers privately scheduled tours.

**MAP 2:** E. Jones Lane, 912/358-0700, www. oldcitywalks.com; $48

### SAVANNAH TOURS BY FOOT

Longtime tour guide and raconteur Greg Proffit and his staff offer fun walking "pub crawls," Savannah Tours by Foot, wherein the point is to meet your guide at some local tavern, ramble around, learn a little bit, and imbibe a lot, though not necessarily in that order. The adult tour is the "Creepy Crawl" ($25), whereas the tour suitable for kids and Girl Scouts is the "Creepy Stroll" ($16 adults, $10 children). You may not want to believe everything you hear, but you're sure to have a lot of fun. The tours book up early, so make arrangements in advance.

**MAP 2:** 527 E. Gordon St., 912/238-3843, www. savannahtours.com; $10-18 adults

### SIXTH SENSE SAVANNAH GHOST TOUR

For those who take their paranormal activity *very* seriously, there's Shannon Scott's Sixth Sense Savannah Ghost Tour, an uncensored, straightforward look at Savannah's poltergeist population.

**MAP 2:** Meeting point Clary's Cafe, 404 Abercorn St., 866/666-3323, www.sixthsensesavannah.com; $20, midnight tour $38.50

## SOFO DISTRICT
### Ecotours
### WILDERNESS SOUTHEAST

The 35-year-old nonprofit Wilderness Southeast offers guided trips, including paddles to historic Mulberry Grove, birding trips, and beach explorations. Regularly scheduled "Walks on the Wild Side" run the gamut from "Alligators to Anhingas" to the "Urban Forest" to "Explore the Night Sky" to the "Blackwater River Float." Custom tours are also available.

**MAP 3:** 3025 Bull St., 912/897-5108, www. naturesavannah.org; $10-35

## VICTORIAN DISTRICT
### Tennis
### FORSYTH PARK

The closest public courts to the downtown area are at the south end of Forsyth Park, which features four free lighted courts. They are first-come, first-served and unstaffed, and as you might expect, they get serious use.

**MAP 3:** Bordered by Drayton St., Gaston St., Whitaker St., and Park Ave., 912/351-3850; daily 8am-dusk; free

## SOUTHSIDE
### Bird-Watching
### SKIDAWAY ISLAND STATE PARK

Skidaway Island State Park is part of the **Colonial Coast Birding Trail** (http://georgiawildlife.dnr.state.ga.us). Spring and fall bring a lot of the usual warbler action, while spring and summer feature nesting ospreys and painted buntings, always a delight.

**MAP 4:** 52 Diamond Causeway, 912/598-2300, www. gastateparks.org; daily 7am-10pm; parking $5 per vehicle per day

### Fishing
### MISS JUDY CHARTERS

Perhaps the best-known local angler is Captain Judy Helmey, aka "Miss Judy." In addition to her frequent and entertaining newspaper columns, she runs a variety of well-regarded charters out of Miss Judy Charters. Four-hour trips start at $500. To get there, go west on U.S. 80, take a right onto Bryan Woods Road, a left onto Johnny Mercer

# Trolley Tours

an Old Town Trolley Tour

The vehicles of choice for the bulk of the masses visiting Savannah, trolleys allow you to sit back and enjoy the views in reasonable comfort. As in other cities, the guides provide commentary while attempting, with various degrees of success, to navigate the cramped downtown traffic environment. The main trolley companies in town are **Old Savannah Tours** (912/234-8128, www.oldsavannahtours.com, basic on-off tour $27 adults, $12 children), **Old Town Trolley Tours** (800/213-2474, www.trolleytours.com, basic on-off tour $27.99 adults, $10 children), and **Oglethorpe Trolley Tours** (912/233-8380, www.oglethorpetours.com, basic on-off tour $22.50 adults, $10 children). All embark from the Savannah Visitors Center on Martin Luther King Jr. Boulevard about every 20-30 minutes on the same schedule, daily 9am-4:30pm.

Frankly there's not much difference between them, as they all offer a very similar range of services for similar prices, with most offering pickup at your downtown hotel. While the common "on-off privileges" allow trolley riders to disembark for a while and pick up another of the same company's trolleys at marked stops, be aware there's no guarantee the next trolley—or the one after that—will have enough room to take you on board.

Boulevard, a right onto Wilmington Island Way, and a right down the dirt lane at her sign. **MAP 4:** 124 Palmetto Dr., 912/897-2478, www.missjudycharters.com; from $500

### TELECASTER CHARTERS

A great inshore charter service is offered by Telecaster Charters, with 4-, 6-, and 8-hour inshore trips priced from $300 for two anglers. **MAP 4:** 2812 River Dr., Thunderbolt, 912/308-4622, www.telecastercharters.com; from $300

## Golf
### WILMINGTON ISLAND CLUB

The Wilmington Island Club has arguably the quickest greens in town and is unarguably the most beautiful local course, set close by the Wilmington River amid lots of mature pines and live oaks. **MAP 4:** 501 Wilmington Island Rd., 912/897-1612; greens fees about $70

## Hiking
### SKIDAWAY ISLAND STATE PARK

My favorite trails are at Skidaway Island State Park. The three-mile Big Ferry Trail is the best overall experience, taking you out to a wooden viewing tower from which you can see the vast expanse of the Skidaway Narrows. A detour takes you past a Native American shell midden, Confederate earthworks, and even a rusty old still—a nod to Skidaway Island's former notoriety as a bootlegger's sanctuary. The shorter but still fun Sandpiper Trail is wheelchair accessible.

MAP 4: 52 Diamond Causeway, 912/598-2300, www.gastateparks.org; daily 7am-10pm; parking $5 per vehicle per day

## Kayaking and Canoeing
### MOON RIVER KAYAK TOURS

Run by Captain Mike Neal, an experienced local boatman and conservationist, Moon River Kayak Tours focuses on 2.5-hour tours of the Skidaway Narrows and scenic Moon River, departing from the public boat ramp at the foot of the bridge to Skidaway Island. No kayaking experience is required.

MAP 4: 45 Diamond Causeway, 912/898-1800, www.moonriverkayak.com; $50

### SKIDAWAY NARROWS

A pleasant kayaking route is the Skidaway Narrows. Begin this paddle at the public boat ramp, which you find by taking Waters Avenue all the way until it turns to Whitefield Avenue and then Diamond Causeway. Continue all the way over the Moon River to a drawbridge; park at the foot of the bridge. Once in the water, paddle northeast. Look for the osprey nests on top of the navigational markers in the narrows as you approach Skidaway Island State Park. Continuing on, you'll find scenic Isle of Hope high on a bluff to your left, with nearly guaranteed dolphin sightings around marker 62.

MAP 4: Intersection of Moon River and Diamond Causeway

## Tennis
### BACON PARK

On the south side, Bacon Park has 16 lighted hard courts. It's the city's best tennis facility, but it's the farthest from downtown. It's the most heavily trafficked of the city's courts, and a destination for local expert players.

MAP 4: 6262 Skidaway Rd., 912/351-3850; daily 8am-dusk; $3

# EASTSIDE
## Fishing
### SAVANNAH FLY FISHING CHARTERS

Shallow-water fly-fishers might want to contact Savannah Fly Fishing Charters. Captain Scott Wagner takes half- and full-day charters both day and night from Savannah all the way down to St. Simons Island. Half-day rate starts at $300. Book early.

MAP 4: 56 Sassafras Trail, 912/308-3700, www.savannahfly.com; from $300

## Kayaking and Canoeing
### SAVANNAH CANOE & KAYAK

The most highly regarded local canoe and kayak tour operator and rental house is Savannah Canoe & Kayak, run by the husband-wife team of Nigel and Kristin Law. They offer several kayak trips, including a short jaunt to Little Tybee Island.

MAP 4: 414 Bonaventure Rd., 912/341-9502, www.savannahcanoeandkayak.com; half-day tour $55

## Tennis
### DAFFIN PARK

South of Highway 80 is Daffin Park, where there are six clay courts and three lighted hard courts. This is mostly a locals-frequented spot, but the park is nice to visit.

MAP 4: 1001 E. Victory Dr., 912/351-3850; daily 8am-dusk; $3

# TYBEE ISLAND
## Biking
### FORT PULASKI NATIONAL MONUMENT

Many locals like to load up their bikes and go to Fort Pulaski. From the grounds you can ride all over scenic and historic Cockspur Island.

**MAP 5:** 912/786-5787, www.nps.gov; daily 9am-5pm; $7 pp, free under age 16

### MCQUEEN'S ISLAND TRAIL

Outside of town, much biking activity centers on Tybee Island, with the six-mile McQueen's Island Trail being a popular and simple ride. The trail started as a rail route for Central of Georgia Railway and was converted to a multiuse trail in the 1990s. Over half of the trail was closed in late 2013 for safety reasons; water has eroded portions of the trail over the years. In 2014, erosion repair work began.

**MAP 5:** U.S. 80 near Fort Pulaski National Monument

## Bird-Watching
### NORTH BEACH

An excellent birding spot on the **Colonial Coast Birding Trail** (http://georgiawildlife.dnr.state.ga.us) is Tybee Island's North Beach area. You'll see a wide variety of shorebirds and gulls, as well as piping plover, northern gannets, and purple sandpipers (winter).

**MAP 5:** Savannah River to 1st St., Tybee Island; parking $5 per day, meters available

## Fishing
### AMICK'S DEEP SEA FISHING

A highly regarded local fishing charter is Tybee-based Amick's Deep Sea Fishing. Captain Steve Amick and crew run offshore charters daily starting at $120 per person. Go east on U.S. 80 and turn right just past the Lazaretto Creek Bridge.

**MAP 5:** 1 Old Hwy. 80, Tybee Island, 912/897-6759, www.amicksdeepseafishing.com; from $120 pp

## Kayaking and Canoeing
### LAZARETTO CREEK

Lazaretto Creek, on the western edge of the island, is a great place to explore Tybee and environs. From here you can meander several miles through the marsh, or go the other way and actually head into a channel of the Savannah River. If you're into ocean kayaking, you can even head into the Atlantic from here. Put in at the Lazaretto Creek landing, at the foot of the Lazaretto Creek bridge on the south side of U.S. 80 on the way to Tybee Island. This is a peaceful, pretty paddle for novice and experienced kayakers alike. You can also put in at the nearby **Tybee Marina** (4 Old Tybee Rd., 912/786-5554, www.tybee-islandmarina.com), also on Lazaretto Creek.

**MAP 5:** Intersection of U.S. 80 and Tybee Island

### LITTLE TYBEE ISLAND

Maybe the single best kayak or canoe adventure in Savannah is the run across the Back River from Tybee to Little Tybee Island, an undeveloped state heritage site that despite its name is actually twice as big as Tybee, albeit mostly marsh. Many kayakers opt to camp on the island. You can even follow the shoreline out into the Atlantic, but be aware that wave action can get intense offshore. Begin the paddle at the public boat ramp on the Back River. To get here, take Butler Avenue all the way to 18th Street and take a right, then another quick right onto Chatham Avenue. The parking lot for the landing is a short way up Chatham Avenue on your left. Warning: Do not attempt to swim to Little Tybee, no matter how strong a swimmer you think you are—the currents are exceptionally vicious. Also, do not be tempted to walk far out onto the Back River beach at low tide. The tide comes in very quickly and often strands people on the sandbar.

**MAP 5:** South of Tybee Island

### NORTH ISLAND SURF AND KAYAK

To rent an ocean-worthy kayak on Lazaretto Creek, stop by North Island Surf and Kayak, located at Tybee Marina. Reservations are recommended.

MAP 5: 1C Old Hwy. 80, 912/786-4000, www. northislandkayak.com; Mon.-Fri. 10am-5pm, Sat.-Sun. 9am-6pm; $45

### SEA KAYAK GEORGIA

On U.S. 80 just as you get on Tybee is a quality tour service, Sea Kayak Georgia. Run by locals Marsha Henson and Ronnie Kemp, Sea Kayak offers many different types of kayak tours.

MAP 5: 1102 U.S. 80, 888/529-2542, www. seakayakgeorgia.com; half-day tour $55

## SURFING AND BOARDING
### HIGH TIDES SURF SHOP

The best—and pretty much only—surf shop in town is High Tides Surf Shop. You can get a good local surf report and forecasts at their website.

MAP 5: 405 U.S. 80, 912/786-6556, www. hightidesurfshop.com

### Tennis
### TYBEE ISLAND MEMORIAL PARK

If you get the tennis jones on Tybee, there are two free hard courts at Tybee Island Memorial Park that are lighted.

MAP 5: Butler Ave. and 4th St., 912/786-4573, www. cityoftybee.org; daily 8am-dusk; free

## GREATER SAVANNAH
### Bird-Watching
### LAUREL HILL WILDLIFE DRIVE

Wading birds in particular are in wide abundance at the **Savannah National Wildlife Refuge.** The views are excellent all along the Laurel Hill Wildlife Drive, which takes you through the heart of the old paddy fields that once crisscrossed the entire area. To get here, take U.S. 17 north over the big Talmadge Bridge, over the Savannah River into South Carolina. Turn left on Highway 170 south and look for the entrance to Laurel Hill Wildlife Drive on the left.

MAP 6: Two miles east of Port Wentworth, 843/784-2468, www.fws.gov/savannah; daily dawn-dusk; free

### LECONTE-WOODMANSTON BOTANICAL GARDEN

LeConte-Woodmanston Botanical Garden is a bit hard to find. Part of William Bartram's historic nature trail, this was the home of Dr. Louis LeConte, renowned 19th-century botanist, and his sons John LeConte, first president of the University of California, Berkeley, and Joseph LeConte, who founded the Sierra Club with John Muir. The highlight here is the rare tidally influenced freshwater wetland, featuring the blackwater Bulltown Swamp. This visit is best done in a four-wheel-drive vehicle. The garden is about 40 minutes from Savannah. Take I-95 south to exit 76. Turn right on U.S. 84, then left on U.S. 17. Turn right on Barrington Ferry Road until the pavement ends at Sandy Run Road. Continue until you see the historical markers. Turn left onto the dirt road, then drive another mile.

MAP 6: 4918 Barrington Ferry Rd., Riceboro, 912/884-6500, www.leconte-woodmanston.org; daily 9am-5pm; $5

### YOUMANS POND

Youmans Pond is a prime stop for migratory fowl. Its main claim to fame is that it was visited in 1773 by the great naturalist William Bartram on one of his treks across the Southeast. Youmans Pond has changed little since then, with its tree-studded pond and oodles of owls, ospreys, herons, egrets, wood storks, and many more. Youmans Pond is about 40 minutes from Savannah. To get here, take I-95 south to exit 76. Take a left onto Highway 38 (Islands Hwy.) and then a left onto Camp Viking Road. About one mile ahead, take a right onto Lake Pamona Drive. About 0.75 mile ahead, look for the pond on the right. It's unmarked, but there's a wooden boardwalk.

MAP 6: Lake Pamona Dr., Midway; daily; free

## Diving

### GRAY'S REEF NATIONAL MARINE SANCTUARY

Certainly no underwater adventure in the area would be complete without a dive at Gray's Reef National Marine Sanctuary. Administered by the National Oceanic and Atmospheric Administration, this fully protected marine sanctuary 17 miles offshore is in deep enough water to provide divers good visibility of its live-bottom habitat. Not a classic living coral reef but rather one built by sedimentary deposits, Gray's Reef provides a look at a truly unique ecosystem. Some key dive charter operators that can take you to Gray's Reef are Captain Walter Rhame's **Mako Dive Charter** (600 Priest Landing Dr., 912/604-6256), which leaves from the Landings Harbor Marina; **Georgia Offshore** (1191 Lake Dr., Midway, 912/658-3884); and **Fantasia Scuba** (3 E. Montgomery Cross Rd., 912/921-8933).

The best all-around dive shop in town is **Diving Locker and Ski Chalet** (74 W. Montgomery Cross Rd., 912/927-6603, www.divinglockerskichalet.com, Mon.-Fri. 10am-6pm, Sat. 10am-5pm) on the south side.

MAP 6: 16 miles east of Sapelo Island, 912/598-2345, www.graysreef.noaa.gov

## Golf

### CLUB AT SAVANNAH HARBOR

A relatively new course but not one you'd call a bargain is the Club at Savannah Harbor, across the Savannah River on Hutchinson Island, adjacent to the Westin Savannah Harbor Resort. Home to the Liberty Mutual Legends of Golf Tournament each spring, the club's tee times are 7:30am-3pm.

MAP 6: 2 Resort Dr., 912/201-2007, www.theclubatsavannahharbor.com; greens fees $135, $70 for twilight

### HENDERSON GOLF CLUB

There are a couple of strong public courses in Savannah that are also very good bargains. Chief among these has to be the Henderson Golf Club, an excellent municipal course with very reasonable greens fees that include a half cart.

MAP 6: 1 Al Henderson Blvd., 912/920-4653, www.hendersongolfclub.com; greens fees Mon.-Fri. $28, Sat.-Sun. $33

## Hiking

### SAVANNAH-OGEECHEE RIVER CANAL

A relic of the pre-railroad days, the Savannah-Ogeechee River Canal is a 17-mile barge route joining the two rivers. Finished in 1830, it saw three decades of prosperous trade in cotton, rice, bricks, guano, naval stores, and food crops before the coming of the railroads finished it off. You can walk some of its length today near the Ogeechee River terminus, admiring the impressive engineering of its multiple locks used to stabilize the water level. Back in the day, the canal would continue through four lift locks as it traversed 16 miles before reaching the Savannah River. Naturalists will enjoy the built-in nature trail that walking along the canal provides. Be sure to check out the unique sand hills on a nearby trail, a vestige of a bygone geological era when this area was an offshore sandbar. Kids will enjoy the impromptu menagerie of gopher turtles near the site's entrance. Do bring mosquito repellent, although often there's a community spray can at the front door of the little visitors center/museum where you pay your fee.

To get here, get on I-95 south, take exit 94, and go west on Fort Argyle Road (Hwy. 204). The canal is a little over two miles from the exit.

MAP 6: 681 Ft. Argyle Rd., 912/748-8068, www.savannahogeecheecanal.com; daily 9am-5pm; $2 adults, $1 students

## Kayaking and Canoeing

### EBENEZER CREEK

About 18 miles north of town, but worth the trip for any kayaker, is the beautiful blackwater Ebenezer Creek, near the tiny township of New Ebenezer in Effingham County. Cypress trees lining this nationally designated Wild and Scenic River hang overhead, and wildlife abounds on this peaceful paddle. Look for old wooden sluice gates, vestiges of the area's rice plantation past. To get here, take exit 109 off I-95. Go north on Highway 21 to Rincon, Georgia, then east on Highway 275 (Ebenezer Rd.). Put in at the private Ebenezer Landing.

**MAP 6:** Intersection of Ebenezer Rd. and Savannah River, New Ebenezer; $5 put-in fee

### SAVANNAH NATIONAL WILDLIFE REFUGE

One of the great overall natural experiences in the area is the massive Savannah National Wildlife Refuge. This 30,000-acre reserve—half in Georgia, half in South Carolina—is on the Atlantic Flyway, so you'll be able to see birdlife in abundance, in addition to alligators and manatees. Earthen dikes crisscrossing the refuge are vestigial remnants of paddy fields from plantation days.

You can kayak on your own, but many opt to take guided tours offered by **Wilderness Southeast** (912/897-5108, www.wildernesssoutheast.org, two-hour trips from $37.50 for two people), **Sea Kayak Georgia** (888/529-2542, www.seakayakgeorgia.com, $55 pp), and **Swamp Girls Kayak Tours** (843/784-2249, www.swampgirls.com, $45). To get here, take U.S. 17 north over the big Talmadge Bridge, over the Savannah River into South Carolina. Turn left on Highway 170 south and look for the entrance to Laurel Hill Wildlife Drive on the left.

**MAP 6:** 694 Beech Hill Lane, Hardeeville, SC (visitors center), 843/784-2468, www.fws.gov/refuge/savannah; daily dawn-dusk; free

## Restaurants

Savannah is a fun food town, with a selection of cuisine concocted by a cast of executive chefs who despite their many personal idiosyncrasies tend to go with what works rather than experiment for the sake of experimentation. Here's a breakdown of the most notable offerings by area and by type of cuisine.

You'll note there's rarely a separate *Seafood* section listed; that's because seafood is an intrinsic part of most restaurant fare in Savannah, whether through regular menu offerings or through specials. For the freshest seafood, consider a trip to Tybee Island or Thunderbolt (which is on the way to Tybee). As the downtown area continues to focus more and more on tourism, locals are tending to popularize more humble, often culturally diverse restaurants outside of the historic district that are well worth a stop.

### WATERFRONT
#### Classic Southern
##### TREYLOR PARK $$$

The bustling, friendly interior of this popular Bay Street spot plays up the shabby chic undertone of Savannah life, with tasty gourmet takes on downmarket Southern classics like the chicken biscuit, pot pie, and sloppy joe. Don't miss their signature starter dish, the PB&J Wings. A particularly tasteful cocktail menu and a well-curated craft beer list round out the experience.

**MAP 1:** 115 E. Bay St., 912/495-5557, www.treylorpark. com; Mon.-Fri. noon-1am, Sat. 10am-2am, Sun. 10am-1am

##### VIC'S ON THE RIVER $$$

Very few restaurants on River Street rise above tourist schlock, but a standout is Vic's on the River. With dishes like wild Georgia shrimp, stone-ground grits, and blue crab cakes with a three-pepper relish, Vic's combines a romantic old Savannah atmosphere with an adventurous take on Lowcountry cuisine. Note the entrance to the dining room is not on River Street but on the Bay Street level on Upper Factor's Walk.

**MAP 1:** 16 E. River St., 912/721-1000, www. vicsontheriver.com; Sun.-Thurs. 11am-10pm, Fri.-Sat. 11am-11pm

# Best Restaurants

★ **Best Breakfast Downtown:** Hands down, it's **B. Matthew's Eatery** on Bay Street, where you can't go wrong with the omelets or the pancakes (page 263).

★ **Closest Thing to a Charleston Restaurant in Savannah:** Find amazing takes on savory Southern classics at **Sapphire Grill,** where chef Chris Nason brings the expertise he acquired running world-class restaurants in nearby Charleston, South Carolina (page 264).

★ **Best for Chocoholics:** From chocolate-chip cheesecake to specialty martinis, **Lulu's Chocolate Bar** can satisfy your sweet tooth (page 264).

★ **Best Repurpose:** Dine on James Beard Award-winning soul food in a former bus depot at **The Grey** (page 265).

★ **Most Luscious Lunch:** The dishes at **Kayak Kafe** are light and adventurous and make for a perfect pit stop during a day of shopping on Broughton Street (page 265).

★ **Best South of the Border:** The best Mexican spot downtown is **Tequila's Town** (page 266).

★ **Tastiest Brush with Hollywood:** Movie producer and Savannah native Stratton Leopold is often seen behind the counter at **Leopold's Ice Cream,** helping dish out scoops of his old family recipe ice cream flavors among Hollywood memorabilia (page 266).

★ **Most Authentic Southern Experience:** Eat around a communal table in a convivial atmosphere at **Mrs. Wilkes' Dining Room** and enjoy what many consider the finest fried chicken in the South, among other classic dishes (page 266).

★ **Most Romantic Date Night:** One of Savannah's original fine-dining restaurants, **Elizabeth on 37th** remains the local gold standard for a wonderful evening with wonderful food and service (page 267).

★ **Best Celebrity Chef's Place:** Nope, it's not Paula Deen's—regional foodie guru Hugh Acheson brings unique takes on Northern Italian cuisine to **The Florence** (page 268).

★ **Best Memphis BBQ: Sandfly BBQ** serves the best Memphis-style brisket in Georgia (page 268).

## Breakfast

### ★ B. MATTHEW'S EATERY ⑤⑤

If you're downtown and need something more than your hotel breakfast—and you will!—go to B. Matthew's Eatery, widely considered the best breakfast in the entire Savannah Historic District. The omelets—most under $10—are uniformly wonderful, and the sausage and bacon are excellent and not greasy. There are more healthful selections as well, and you can actually get a decent bowl of oatmeal—but I

suggest something more decadent. Sunday brunch is incredible. And they don't do just breakfast—lunch sandwiches and salads are of similarly high quality, and dinner entrées (from $17) include killer osso buco, lamb, and seafood. A recent renovation has upped the already high ambience level.

**MAP 1:** 325 E. Bay St., 912/233-1319, www. bmatthewseatery.com; Mon.-Thurs. 8am-9pm, Fri.-Sat. 8am-10pm, Sun. 9am-3pm

## Asian
### CO SAVANNAH ⑤⑤

The newest and most widely regarded as best Asian fusion cuisine in town is at CO Savannah, a block off the waterfront. This regional chain has a menu particularly strong in bánh mì and specialty sushi rolls, with a cocktail and beer menu superior to most similar places in town. It's a fun place to get plates to share. Speaking of beverages, upstairs you'll find the affiliated **Savannah Cocktail Co.** (www.savannahcocktailco. com, daily 5pm-1am), which offers a great Sunday brunch.

**MAP 1:** 10 Whitaker St., 912/234-5375, www.eatatco. com, Sun.-Thurs. 11am-10pm, Fri.-Sat. 11am-11pm

## Greek
### OLYMPIA CAFÉ ⑤⑤

A worthwhile place to stop for a relaxing and tasty meal on River Street is Olympia Café, which serves a variety of Greek dishes such as dolmas, spanokopita, seafood, and lemon chicken in a friendly atmosphere. The standard menu items aren't particularly cheap, but the daily specials often offer a surprisingly good deal for your money.

**MAP 1:** 5 E. River St., 912/233-3131, www.olympiacafe. net; daily 11am-10pm

# CITY MARKET
## Classic Southern
### THE LADY & SONS ⑤⑤

Every year, thousands of visitors come to Savannah for the privilege of waiting for hours outside in all weather, the line stretching a full city block, for a chance to eat at The Lady & Sons and sample some of local celebrity Paula Deen's "home" cooking—actually a fairly typical Southern buffet with some decent fried chicken, collard greens, and mac and cheese. For the privilege, you must begin waiting in line as early as 9:30am for lunch and as early as 3:30pm for dinner in order to be assigned a dining time. You almost assuredly will never see Paula, who has precious little to do with the restaurant these days.

**MAP 1:** 102 W. Congress St., 912/233-2600, www. ladyandsons.com; Mon.-Sat. 11am-3pm and 5pm-close, Sun. 11am-5pm

## New Southern
### ★ SAPPHIRE GRILL ⑤⑤⑤

Accomplishing the difficult task of being achingly hip while also offering some of the best food in town, Sapphire Grill comes closer than any other Savannah restaurant to replicating a high-class trendy Manhattan eatery—at prices to match. With its bare stone walls, lean ambience, and romantically dark interior, you'd be tempted to think it's all sizzle and no steak. But executive chef Chris Nason, former exec at Charleston's Anson Restaurant, has a way with coastal cuisine, relying on the freshest local seafood. His classic meat dishes like lamb, filet mignon, and veal are equally skillful. The lobster bisque is a must-have.

**MAP 1:** 110 W. Congress St., 912/443-9962, www. sapphiregrill.com; Fri.-Sat. 5:30pm-11:30pm, Sun.-Thurs. 6pm-10:30pm

## Coffee, Tea, and Sweets
### ★ LULU'S CHOCOLATE BAR ⑤

Combine a hip bar with outrageously tasty dessert items and you get Lulu's Chocolate Bar. While the whole family is welcome before 10pm to enjoy chocolate-chip cheesecake and the like, after that it's 21-and-over. The late crowd is younger and trendier and comes mostly for the unique specialty martinis, including the pineapple upside-down martini. The prices are quite reasonable all around and this remains one of the most fun places in town.

**MAP 1:** 42 MLK Jr. Blvd., 912/238-2012, www. luluschocolatebar.net; Fri.-Sat. 2pm-2am, Sun.-Thurs. noon-midnight

## Italian
### VINNIE VANGOGO'S ⑤

One would never call Savannah a great pizza town, but the best pizza here is Vinnie VanGoGo's at the west end of City Market on Franklin Square. Their pizza is a thin-crust

Neapolitan style—although the menu claims it to be New York style—with a delightful tangy sauce and fresh cheese. Individual slices are huge, so don't feel obliged to order a whole pie. The waiting list for a table can get pretty long. It's cash only.

MAP 1: 317 W. Bryan St., 912/233-6394, www. vinnievangogos.com; Mon.-Thurs. 4pm-11:30pm, Fri. 4pm-1am, Sat. noon-1am, Sun. noon-11:30pm; cash only

# HISTORIC DISTRICT NORTH
## Classic Southern
### ★ THE GREY ⑤⑤⑤

Savannah's most dramatic restaurant success story is The Grey, located in a stunningly restored former bus depot and taking the national foodie world by storm with beloved regional vernacular and Soul Food cuisine classics like seafood boudin, veal sweetbreads, roasted yardbird, fisherman's stew, and more, depending on seasonal whim and sourcing availabilities. A James Beard Award finalist in 2015, The Grey features the talents of standout executive chef Mashama Bailey, who though New York-trained, grew up in Savannah and has a close eye on what makes the South tick food wise. You can keep a close eye too; the open kitchen dominating the middle of the place provides a perfect view. The wonderfully nostalgic yet tasteful dining area mimics the retro art deco look of the old depot; you can sit at a table but you can also enjoy the full menu at the wraparound bar, which I recommend. Up front, at the entrance, is the "Diner Bar," a smaller offset bar area offering a punchy bar food menu strong on sandwiches.

MAP 1: 109 MLK Jr. Blvd., 912/662-5999, www. thegreyrestaurant.com; Sun., Tues.-Thurs. 5:30pm-10pm, Fri.-Sat. 5:30pm-11pm, supper every third Sunday of the month

### ★ KAYAK KAFE ⑤⑤

The best lunch on Broughton Street is at Kayak Kafe, where you can get a killer fresh salad or a fish taco to refresh your energy level during a busy day of shopping or sightseeing. Vegetarians, vegans, and those on a gluten-free diet will be especially pleased by the available options. As one of the very few Broughton Street places with outdoor sidewalk tables, this is also a great people-watching spot.

MAP 1: 1 E. Broughton St., 912/233-6044, www. eatkayak.com; Mon.-Thurs. 11am-10pm, Fri.-Sat. 11am-11pm, Sun. 11am-5pm

### OLDE PINK HOUSE ⑤⑤

Once the home of General James Habersham and the first place the Declaration of Independence was read aloud in Savannah, the Olde Pink House is still a hub of activity in Savannah, as visitors and locals alike frequent the classic interior of the dining room and the downstairs Planter's Tavern. Olde Pink House is known for its savvy (and often sassy) service and the uniquely regional flair it adds to traditional dishes, with liberal doses of pecans, Vidalia onions, shrimp, and crab. The she-crab soup and lamb chops in particular are crowd-pleasers, and the scored crispy flounder stacks up to similar versions of this dish at several other spots in town. Reservations are recommended.

MAP 1: 23 Abercorn St., 912/232-4286; Sun.-Thurs. 5:30pm-10:30pm, Fri.-Sat. 5:30pm-11pm

### 17HUNDRED90 ⑤⑤

One of Savannah's oldest continuously operating culinary institutions and lodgings, 17Hundred90 Inn and Restaurant, has recently vaulted itself into the upper echelon of Savannah cuisine with the addition of a dynamic menu by new executive chef Jim Deja. Expect strong showings on the usual Southern classics—the crab stew is a must-have starter—but some unique takes, which you won't find anywhere else in town, such as a mouthwatering brisket ciabatta. Even the honey butter rolls brought to each table are delectable. The dining room is nostalgically no-frills and straight out of the historic namesake era; there's live piano accompaniment in the main dining room in the evenings. The attached bar area is a popular local watering hole; you can order from the full menu at the bar if you prefer.

MAP 1: 307 E. President St., 912/236-7122, www.17hundred90.com

### Coffee, Tea, and Sweets
#### THE COFFEE FOX $

There's a Starbucks on Broughton Street, but the best coffee on that busy thoroughfare is at The Coffee Fox, a locally owned joint that expertly treads the fine line between hipster hangout and accessible hot spot. The freshly baked goodies are nearly as good as the freshly brewed java, which includes cold-brew and pour-over offerings.

MAP 1: 102 W. Broughton St., 912/401-0399, www. thecoffeefox.com; Mon.-Sat. 7am-11pm, Sun. 8am-4pm

#### ★ LEOPOLD'S ICE CREAM $

He helped produce *Mission Impossible III* and other movies, but Savannah native Stratton Leopold's other claim to fame is running the 100-year-old family business at Leopold's Ice Cream. Now in a new location but with the same delicious family ice cream recipe, Leopold's also offers soup and sandwiches to go with its delicious sweet treats. Memorabilia from Stratton's various movies is all around the shop, which stays open after every evening performance at the Lucas Theatre around the corner. You can occasionally find Stratton himself behind the counter doling out scoops.

MAP 1: 212 E. Broughton St., 912/234-4442, www. leopoldsicecream.com; Sun.-Thurs. 11am-10pm, Fri.-Sat. 11am-11pm

#### WRIGHT SQUARE CAFE $

For a more upscale take on sweets, check out the chocolate goodies at Wright Square Cafe. While they do offer tasty wraps and sandwiches, let's not kid ourselves; the draw here is the outrageous assortment of high-quality European-style brownies, cookies, cakes, and other sweet treats.

MAP 1: 21 W. York St., 912/238-1150, www. wrightsquarecafe.com; Mon.-Fri. 7:30am-5:30pm, Sat. 9am-5:30pm

### Mexican
#### ★ TEQUILA'S TOWN $$

The best Mexican spot downtown is Tequila's Town, a relatively new place that fills an oft-noted void in the Savannah foodie scene. Their menu is comprehensive and authentic, a clear step above the usual gringo-oriented fat-fest. Highlights include the chiles rellenos and the seafood, not to mention the guacamole prepared tableside!

MAP 1: 109 Whitaker St., 912/236-3222, www. tequilastown.com; Mon.-Thurs. 11am-10pm, Fri.-Sat. 11am-11pm, Sun. noon-10pm

### South African
#### ZUNZI'S $

Look for the long lunchtime line outside the tiny storefront that is Zunzi's. This takeout joint is one of Savannah's favorite lunch spots, the labor of love of South African expatriates Gabby and Johnny DeBeer, who've gotten a lot of national attention for their robust, rich dishes like the exquisite South African-style sausage.

MAP 1: 108 E. York St., 912/443-9555, http://zunzis. com; Mon.-Sat. 11am-6pm

## HISTORIC DISTRICT SOUTH
### Classic Southern
#### CRYSTAL BEER PARLOR $

A very popular spot with locals and tourists alike, the Crystal Beer Parlor offers one of the best burgers downtown. With a history going back to the 1930s, this has been a friendly family tradition for generations of Savannahians. The lively bar area has a very wide range of craft brews, and there are plenty of snug booths to sit in and enjoy their solid American menu.

MAP 2: 301 W. Jones St., 912/349-1000, www. crystalbeerparlor.com; daily 11am-10pm

#### ★ MRS. WILKES' DINING ROOM $$

The rise of Paula Deen and her Lady & Sons restaurant has only made local epicures even more exuberant in their praise for Mrs.

Wilkes' Dining Room, Savannah's original comfort food mecca. The delightful Sema Wilkes herself has passed on, but nothing has changed—not the communal dining room, the cheerful service, the care taken with takeout customers, nor, most of all, the food, a succulent mélange of the South's greatest hits, including the best fried chicken in town, snap beans, black-eyed peas, and collard greens. While each day boasts a different set menu, almost all of the classics are on the table at each meal. Be prepared for a long wait, however; lines begin forming early in the morning.

MAP 2: 107 W. Jones St., 912/232-5997, www.mrswilkes.com; Mon.-Fri. 11am-2pm

## Barbecue
### ANGEL'S BBQ ⑤

A great local barbecue joint tucked away in a lane is Angel's BBQ, which was featured on the Travel Channel's *Man v. Food*. Get there by finding Independent Presbyterian Church at the northwest corner of Chippewa Square and walking down the lane next to the church. Angel's offers a particularly Memphis-style take on barbecue, but you might try the unique house specialty, the barbecued bologna. Don't miss the peanuts-and-greens on the side. Vegetarians can opt for the Faux-Q, barbecue-flavored tofu.

MAP 2: 21 W. Oglethorpe Lane, 912/495-0902, www.angels-bbq.com; Tues. 11:30am-3pm, Wed.-Sat. 11:30am-6pm

# SOFO DISTRICT
## New Southern
### BUTTERHEAD GREENS ⑤

A down-to-earth experience is at the farm-to-table diner Butterhead Greens, a favorite student and hipster hangout known for its sandwiches and fresh vegetarian dishes. Service is on the slow side and the vibe is very casual, but the eats are delicious and worth the wait.

MAP 3: 1813 Bull St., 912/201-1808, www.butterheadgreens.com; Mon.-Thurs. 7am-8pm, Fri.-Sat. 8am-5pm

★ **ELIZABETH ON 37TH** ⑤⑤⑤

Before there was Paula Deen, there was Elizabeth Terry, Savannah's first high-profile chef and founder of this most elegant of all Savannah restaurants, Elizabeth on 37th. Terry has since sold the place to two of her former waiters, Greg and Gary Butch, but this restaurant has continued to maintain her high standards. Executive chef Kelly Yambor uses eclectic, seasonally shifting ingredients that blend the South with the south of France. Along with generally attentive service, it makes for a wonderfully old-school fine-dining experience. Reservations are recommended.

MAP 3: 105 E. 37th St., 912/236-5547; daily 6pm-10pm

### COTTON & RYE ⑤⑤

One of the newer and more buzzworthy eat-and-drink spots in town is Cotton & Rye, which while off the usual tourist-beaten path is certainly well worth the trip if you want to go where the locals go. Set in a smallish, restored old bank building, the atmosphere is both upscale and invitingly cozy. The menu is strong on fresh artisanal meats in the Southern style; try the hanger steak or the fried chicken. In a neat twist, the entire wine and beer menu is all-American.

MAP 3: 1801 Habersham St., 912/777-6286, www.cottonandrye.com, Fri.-Sat. 5pm-10:30pm, Mon.-Thurs. 5pm-10pm

## Burgers
### GREEN TRUCK
### NEIGHBORHOOD PUB ⑤

Cozy Green Truck Neighborhood Pub earns its raves on the basis of delicious regionally sourced meat and produce offered at reasonable prices. (The large selection of craft beers on tap is a big draw too). The marquee item is the signature five-ounce grass-fed burger. A basic burger is $7, but several other increasingly more dressed-up versions are offered, none over $12.50. Burgers are also offered with chicken or veggie patties. It's a small room that often has a big line, and they don't take reservations, so be prepared.

MAP 3: 2430 Habersham St., 912/234-5885, http://greentruckpub.com; Tues.-Sat. 11am-11pm

## Coffee, Tea, and Sweets
### BACK IN THE DAY BAKERY ⑤⑤

Primarily known for its sublime sweet treats, James Beard Award-nominated Back in the Day Bakery also offers a small but delightfully tasty (and tasteful) range of lunch soups, salads, and sandwiches (11am-2pm). Lunch highlights include the baguette with camembert, roasted red peppers, and lettuce, as well as the caprese, the classic tomato, mozzarella, and basil trifecta on a perfect ciabatta. But whatever you do, save room for dessert, which runs the full sugar spectrum: red velvet cupcakes, lemon bars, macaroons, carrot cake, and many others.

MAP 3: 2403 Bull St., 912/495-9292, www.backinthedaybakery.com; Tues.-Fri. 9am-5pm, Sat. 8am-3pm

### FOXY LOXY ⑤

Foxy Loxy is a classic coffeehouse set within a cozy multistory Victorian on Bull Street. Added pluses include the authentic Tex-Mex menu, wine and beer offerings, and freshly baked sweet treats.

MAP 3: 1919 Bull St., 912/401-0543, www.foxyloxycafe.com; Mon.-Sat. 7am-11pm

### THE SENTIENT BEAN ⑤

The coffee at The Sentient Bean is all fair trade and organic, and the all-vegetarian fare is a major upgrade above the usual coffeehouse offerings. But "The Bean" is more than a coffeehouse—it's a community. Probably the best indie film venue in town, the Bean regularly hosts screenings of cutting-edge left-of-center documentary and kitsch films, as well as rotating art exhibits.

MAP 3: 13 E. Park Ave., 912/232-4447, www.sentientbean.com; daily 7:30am-10pm

## Italian
### ★ THE FLORENCE ⑤⑤⑤

Regionally famous chef Hugh Acheson is known for several high-profile restaurants in Atlanta and Athens, but The Florence is his first effort in Savannah. Inspired by Italian cuisine but influenced by a more modern and subtle spice palate, the entrées at The Florence are served in cast-iron skillets, reflecting the generally rustic ambience in this tastefully restored former warehouse literally alongside railroad tracks. Try one of the meatball appetizers and the ricotta cavatelli—scrumptious ricotta cheese dumplings with pork shoulder.

MAP 3: 1 W. Victory Dr., 912/234-5522, www.theflorencesavannah.com; Tues.-Wed. and Sun. 5pm-10pm, Thurs.-Sat. 5pm-11pm

# EASTSIDE
## Classic Southern
### DESPOSITO'S ⑤⑤

Located just across the Wilmington River from the fishing village of Thunderbolt, Desposito's is a big hit with locals and visitors alike, although it's not in all the guidebooks. The focus here is on crab, shrimp, and oysters, and lots of them, all caught wild in local waters and served humbly on tables covered with newspapers.

MAP 4: 187 Old Tybee Rd., 912/897-9963, www.despositosseafood.com; Tues.-Fri. 5pm-10pm, Sat. noon-10pm

## Barbecue
### ★ SANDFLY BBQ ⑤

If you're out this way visiting Wormsloe or Skidaway Island State Park, or if you're just crazy about good barbecue, definitely make a point to hit little Sandfly BBQ, unique in the area for its dedication to real Memphis-style barbecue. Anything is great—this is the best brisket in the area—but for the best overall experience try the Hog Wild platter. Service is friendly, the price is right, and everything on the menu is superb.

MAP 4: 8413 Ferguson Ave. 912/356-5463, www.sandflybbq.com; Mon.-Sat. 11am-8pm

# TYBEE ISLAND
## Breakfast and Brunch
### THE BREAKFAST CLUB $

Considered the best breakfast in the Savannah area for 30 years and counting, The Breakfast Club, with its brisk diner atmosphere and hearty Polish sausage-filled omelets, is like a little bit of Chicago in the South. Lines start early for a chance to enjoy such house specialties as Helen's Solidarity, the Athena Omelet, and the Chicago Bear Burger, but don't worry—you'll inevitably strike up a conversation with someone interesting while you wait.

**MAP 5:** 1500 Butler Ave., 912/786-5984, http://tybeeisland.com/breakfast-club; daily 6:30am-1pm

## Casual Dining
### THE CRAB SHACK $$

Set in a large former fishing camp overlooking Chimney Creek, The Crab Shack is a favorite local seafood place and something of an attraction in itself. Don't expect gourmet fare or quiet seaside dining; the emphasis is on mounds of fresh, tasty seafood, heavy on the raw-bar action. Getting there is a little tricky: Take U.S. 80 to Tybee, cross the bridge over Lazaretto Creek, and begin looking for Estill Hammock Road to Chimney Creek on the right. Take Estill Hammock Road and veer right. After that, it's hard to miss.

**MAP 5:** 40 Estill Hammock Rd., 912/786-9857, www.thecrabshack.com; Mon.-Thurs. 11:30am-10pm, Fri.-Sun. 11:30am-11pm

### HUC-A-POO'S BITES & BOOZE $

Known far and wide for its sublime pizza is Huc-a-Poo's Bites & Booze. Individual slices run about four bucks, can easily feed two, and are quite delicious. Out of the tourist ruckus and tucked away within a small shopping center just as you arrive onto Tybee proper, Huc-a-Poo's also has a very lively bar scene.

**MAP 5:** 1213 E. Hwy. 80, 912/786-5900, http://hucapoos.com; daily 11am-11pm

### NORTH BEACH GRILL $$

One of Tybee's more cherished restaurants is on the north end in the shadow of the Tybee Light Station. Like a little slice of Jamaica near the dunes, the laid-back North Beach Grill deals in tasty Caribbean fare, such as its signature jerk chicken, fish sandwiches, and, of course, delicious fried plantains, all overseen by chef-owner "Big George" Spriggs. Frequent live music adds to the island vibe.

**MAP 5:** 33 Meddin Ave., 912/786-4442; daily 11:30am-10pm

Sandfly BBQ

## TYBEE ISLAND SOCIAL CLUB ❸❸

For a leisurely and tasty dinner, try Tybee Island Social Club. Their menu is somewhat unusual for this seafood-heavy island: It's primarily an assortment of gourmet-ish tacos, including fish, duck, and lime- and tequila-marinated steak, all under $10 each. The beer and wine list is accomplished, and the live entertainment is usually very good—which is fortunate, since the service here is on the slow side.

**MAP 5:** 1311 Butler Ave., 912/472-4044, http://tybeeislandsocialclub.com; Tues. 5pm-9:30pm, Wed.-Fri. noon-9:30pm, Sat.-Sun. 11:30am-10pm

# GREATER SAVANNAH

The Pooler/West Chatham area is the fastest growing in the Savannah metro area. It is also dominated by new chain restaurants. Here are a couple of tasty departures from the mass-market trend for you to seek if you find yourself out that way.

## Pooler/West Chatham
### PIE SOCIETY ❸

Get some incredibly tasty little pasties and meat pies, old English style, at this charming little family spot run by British expats. Everything is all homemade and usually fresh out of the oven. Note the early opening hours, all the better to get your piping hot, fresh breakfast baked items.

**MAP 6:** 115 Canal St., 912/856-4785, www.thebritishpiecompany.com; Mon.-Fri. 7am-6:30pm, Sat. 7am-5pm

### MOLLY MACPHERSON'S SCOTTISH PUB AND GRILL ❸❸

A mirror image of the one on Congress Street in Savannah, this edition of Molly's delivers the same high-quality pub items like Shepherd's Pie and Fish-and-Chips, along with an outstanding selection of beers on tap and of course, Scotch.

**MAP 6:** 110 Towne Center Dr., 912/348-3200, www.macphersonspub.com; Mon.-Sat. 11am-2am, Sun. 11am-11pm

## To Market, To Market

Savannah's first and still premier health-food market, **Brighter Day Natural Foods** (1102 Bull St., 912/236-4703, www.brighterdayfoods.com, Mon.-Sat. 9am-7pm, Sun. noon-5:30pm) has been the labor of love of Janie and Peter Brodhead for 30 years, all of them in the same location at the southern tip of Forsyth Park. Boasting organic groceries, regional produce, a sandwich and smoothie bar with a takeout window, and an extensive vitamin, supplement, and herb section, Brighter Day is an oasis in Savannah's sea of chain supermarkets.

Just opened in 2013, **Whole Foods Market** (1815 E. Victory Dr., www.wholefoodsmarket.com, daily 8am-9pm) offers the chain's usual assortment of organic produce, with a very good fresh meat and seafood selection.

Fairly new but already thriving, the **Forsyth Park Farmers Market** (www.forsythfarmersmarket.org, Sat. 9am-1pm) happens in the south end of scenic and wooded Forsyth Park. You'll find very fresh fruit and produce from a variety of fun and friendly regional farmers. If you have access to a real kitchen while you're in town, you might be glad to know there's usually a very good selection of organic, sustainably grown meat and poultry products as well—not always a given at farmers markets.

If you need some good-quality groceries downtown—especially after hours—try **Parker's Market** (222 E. Drayton St., 912/231-1001, daily 24 hours). In addition to a pretty wide array of gourmet-style grab 'n' go victuals inside, there are gas pumps outside to fuel your vehicle.

There's one 24-hour full-service supermarket in downtown Savannah: **Kroger** (311 E. Gwinnett St., 912/231-2260, daily 24 hours).

### NAAN APPETIT $

This is unpretentious but tasty Indian food at a good price. Try the lamb masala curry or the chili paneer.

MAP 6: 1024 U.S. Hwy 80, 912/348-2446, www. naanappetit.com; Tues.-Fri. 11am-3pm, 5pm-9:30pm, Sat.-Sun. noon-3pm, 5pm-10:30pm

## Midway and Liberty County
### HOLTON'S SEAFOOD $$

Many locals eat at least once a week at Holton's Seafood, an unpretentious and fairly typical family-run fried seafood place just off I-95 at the Midway exit.

MAP 6: 13711 E. Oglethorpe Hwy., Midway, 912/884-9151, daily lunch and dinner

### SUNBURY CRAB COMPANY $$

A restaurant of note in Midway is the Sunbury Crab Company, providing, you guessed it, great crab cakes in a casual atmosphere on the Midway River. Get here by taking Highway 38 east of Midway and then a left onto Fort Morris Road.

MAP 6: 541 Brigantine Dunmore Rd., Midway, 912/884-8640; Wed.-Fri. dinner, Sat.-Sun. lunch and dinner

## Richmond Hill
### STEAMERS RESTAURANT & RAW BAR $$

A popular place on U.S. 17 is Steamers Restaurant & Raw Bar, home of some good Lowcountry boil in a relaxed, homey atmosphere.

MAP 6: 4040 U.S. 17, Richmond Hill, 912/756-3979; daily 5pm-10pm

### THE UPPER CRUST PIZZERIA $

There's no end to the chain food offerings in Richmond Hill, but one of the better restaurants in town is The Upper Crust, a casual American place with great pizza in addition to soups, salads, and hot sandwiches.

MAP 6: 1702 U.S. 17, Richmond Hill, 912/756-6990; Mon.-Sat. lunch and dinner, Sun. dinner

# Hotels

The hotel scene in Savannah, once notorious for its absurdly high price-to-service ratio, has improved a great deal. Perhaps ironically, several stylish new downtown hotels opened concurrently with the recent economic downturn. Their appearance means increased competition, and therefore marginally lower prices, across the board.

The other good news for visitors is that there are now many comparatively new hotels of note directly in the downtown area within walking distance of most sites. Some of them are the more widely recognized chains, and others represent more boutique companies and provide a commensurately higher level of service. The less-good news, especially for locals, is that the ominously rising skyline the newer, bigger hotels represent is a change from the friendly small-scale historical footprint Savannah is known for in the first place.

Savannah's many historic bed-and-breakfasts are competitive with the hotels on price, and often outperform them on service and ambience. If you don't need a swimming pool and don't mind climbing some stairs every now and then, a B&B is usually your best bet. And the breakfasts, of course, are great too.

The best campground in town is at the well-managed and rarely crowded **Skidaway Island State Park** (52 Diamond Causeway, 912/598-2300, www.gastateparks.org; parking $5 per vehicle per day, tent and RV sites $26-40). There are 88 sites with 30-amp electric hookups. A two-night minimum stay is

# Best Hotels

★ **Best Rooftop Bar:** The boutique **Bohemian Hotel Savannah Riverfront** isn't only a swank stay on the waterfront, its Rocks on the Roof bar offers stunning wraparound alfresco views of the river and surrounding downtown area (page 272).

★ **Expertly Repurposed Coca-Cola Bottling Plant:** The historic building housing **The Brice** hasn't bottled soft drinks for decades, but it now hosts this tastefully modernist boutique hotel, complete with an upscale in-house Italian restaurant, Pacci. The Brice is in a comparatively quiet corner of downtown but still well within walking distance of most downtown attractions (page 273).

★ **Most Excellent View of Ellis Square:** A major part of the dramatic reclamation of Ellis Square was the building of the modernist **Andaz Savannah.** From its windows you get a great view of downtown, and the bar/restaurant combo is top-notch (page 274).

★ **Closest B&B to the Squares:** Probably the friendliest downtown B&B, **Foley House Inn** is also among the closest in walking distance to most of the downtown action (page 275).

★ **Classiest B&B near Forsyth Park:** It's not as close to the downtown squares as other places, but **The Gastonian** inn is a world-class stay just steps away from vast, green Forsyth Park and its iconic fountain (page 275).

★ **Best Stay on The Beach:** The lodging scene on Tybee Island is hit or miss. If you can get a room at the delightful and charming **The Georgianne Inn,** circa 1910, you'll enjoy a peaceful stay that's still close to the entertainment on the south end of the island (page 275).

required on weekends, and there's a three-night minimum for Memorial Day, Labor Day, Independence Day, and Thanksgiving. Despite these restrictions and the comparatively high rates, the natural beauty of the park and its easy access to some great nature trails make it worth the price.

There's one campground on Tybee Island, the **River's End Campground and RV Park** (915 Polk St., 912/786-5518, www.cityoftybee. org; water-and-electric sites $34, 50-amp full-hookup sites $45, cabins $150) on the north side. River's End offers 100 full-service sites plus some primitive tent sites. The highlight, however, are the incredibly cute little cabins; book well in advance. While During Tybee's sometimes-chilly off-season (Nov.-Mar.), you can relax and get warm inside the common River Room. River's End also offers a swimming pool and laundry facilities.

Totally wilderness camping can be done on state-owned Little Tybee, accessible across the Back River by boat only; there are no facilities. The best camping and wilderness resource locally is **Half Moon Outfitters** (15 E. Broughton St., 912/201-9393, www.half-moonoutfitters.com).

## WATERFRONT

### ★ BOHEMIAN HOTEL SAVANNAH RIVERFRONT ⑤⑤⑤

The Bohemian Hotel Savannah Riverfront is gaining a reputation as one of Savannah's premier hotels, both for the casual visitor as well as visiting celebrities. Located between busy River Street and bustling City Market, this isn't the place for peace and quiet, but its combination of boutique-style retro-hip decor and happening rooftop bar scene makes it a great place to go for a fun stay that's as much Manhattan as Savannah. Valet parking is available, which you will come to appreciate.

MAP 1: 102 W. Bay St., 912/721-3800, www. bohemianhotelsavannah.com

## ★ THE BRICE ⑤⑤⑤

It's not exactly brand-new—it occupies the space formerly occupied by the well-regarded Mulberry Inn—but The Brice features a complete boutique-style upgrade to this historic building, which formerly housed Savannah's first Coca-Cola bottling plant, on the eastern edge of the historic district. With great service and 145 rooms, most complete with a modernized four-poster bed, The Brice also features **Pacci Italian Kitchen + Bar** (breakfast daily 7am-10am, lunch daily 11am-3pm, brunch 10am-3pm Sat.-Sun., dinner 5pm-10pm Mon.-Thurs. and Sun., 5pm-10:30pm Sat., $15-25), one of the better hotel restaurant/bar combos in town.

MAP 1: 601 E. Bay St., 912/238-1200, www. thebricehotel.com

## HYATT REGENCY SAVANNAH ⑤⑤⑤

For years critics have called it an insult to architecture and to history. The modernist Hyatt Regency Savannah is more than three decades old, but a competent renovation means that the Hyatt—a sort of exercise in cubism straddling an entire block of River Street—has avoided the neglect of many older chain properties downtown. Three sides of the hotel offer views of the bustling Savannah waterfront, with its massive ships coming in from all over the world.

MAP 1: 2 E. Bay St., 912/238-1234, www.savannah. hyatt.com

## WESTIN SAVANNAH HARBOR GOLF RESORT AND SPA ⑤⑤

If you require a swank pool, look no further than the Westin Savannah Harbor Golf Resort and Spa, which has a beautiful resort-style pool across the Savannah River from downtown and overlooking the old city. Accessing the hotel—located on a cross-channel island—is a bit of a process, but one made easier by charming river ferries that run regularly and free of charge. The attached golf course is a good one, and packages are available.

MAP 1: 1 Resort Dr., 912/201-2000, www. westinsavannah.com

the Westin Savannah Harbor Golf Resort and Spa

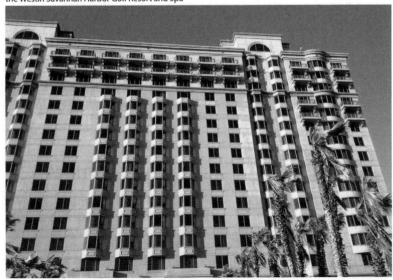

# CITY MARKET

### ★ ANDAZ SAVANNAH $$$

Providing a suitably modernist decor to go with its somewhat atypical architecture for Savannah, the Andaz Savannah overlooks restored Ellis Square and abuts City Market with its shopping, restaurants, and nightlife. A boutique offering from Hyatt, the Andaz's guest rooms and suites feature top-of-the-line linens, extra-large and well-equipped baths, in-room snack bars, and technological features such as MP3 docking stations, free Wi-Fi, and, of course, the ubiquitous flat-screen TV. Customer service is a particular strong suit. Just off the lobby is a very hip lounge-wine bar that attracts locals as well as hotel guests. Keep in mind things can get a little noisy in this area at night on weekends.
MAP 1: 14 Barnard St., 912/233-2116, www.savannah.andaz.hyatt.com

### INN AT ELLIS SQUARE $$

A Days Inn property, the Inn at Ellis Square is smack-dab between City Market and Bay Street—in other words, the heart of the tourist action. Set in the renovated 1851 Guckenheimer Building, the inn is one of the better-appointed chain hotels in town.
MAP 1: 201 W. Bay St., 912/236-4440, www.innatellissquare.com

# HISTORIC DISTRICT NORTH

### BALLASTONE INN $$$

Once a bordello, the 1838 mansion that is home to the 16-room Ballastone Inn is one of Savannah's favorite inns. Highlights include an afternoon tea service and one of the better full breakfasts in town. Note that some guest rooms are at what Savannah calls the "garden level," meaning sunken basement-level rooms with what amounts to a worm's-eye view.
MAP 1: 14 E. Oglethorpe Ave., 912/236-1484, www.ballastone.com

### THE GREEN PALM INN $$

Easily the best bed-and-breakfast for the price in Savannah is The Green Palm Inn, a folksy and romantic little Victorian number with some neat gingerbread exterior stylings and four cute guest rooms, each named after a species of palm tree. It's situated on the very easternmost edge of the Savannah Historic District—hence its reasonable rates. Delightful innkeeper Diane McCray provides a very good and generous breakfast plus a pretty much constant dessert bar.
MAP 1: 546 E. President St., 912/447-8901, www.greenpalminn.com

### 17HUNDRED90 INN $$

Famous for its host of resident ghosts—which many employees do swear aren't just tourist tales—17hundred90 offers 14 cozy rooms within the historic building that dates from, yep, 1790. The addition of several nearby guest houses, booked through the Inn, has expanded the footprint of this great old Savannah name. The great plus here—in addition to the ghost stories of course—is the excellent on-site restaurant and bar, popular with both locals and tourists alike.
MAP 1: 307 E. President St., 912/236-7122, www.17hundred90.com

### THE KEHOE HOUSE $$

One of Savannah's favorite bed-and-breakfasts, The Kehoe House is a great choice for its charm and attention to guests. Its historic location, on quiet little Columbia Square catty-corner to the Isaiah Davenport House, is within walking distance to all the downtown action, but far enough from the bustle to get some peace out on one of the rocking chairs on the veranda.
MAP 1: 123 Habersham St., 912/232-1020, www.kehoehouse.com

# HISTORIC DISTRICT SOUTH

### ELIZA THOMPSON HOUSE $$

One of Savannah's original historic B&Bs, the Eliza Thompson House is a bit out of the bustle on serene, beautiful Jones Street but still close enough to get involved whenever you feel the urge. You can enjoy the various culinary offerings—breakfast, wine and cheese, night-time munchies—either in the parlor or on the patio overlooking the house's classic Savannah garden.

**MAP 2:** 5 W. Jones St., 912/236-3620, www. elizathompsonhouse.com

### ★ FOLEY HOUSE INN ⑤⑤

The circa-1896 Foley House Inn is a four-diamond B&B with some rooms available at a three-diamond price. Its 19 individualized Victorian-decor guest rooms, in two town houses, range from the smaller Newport overlooking the "grotto courtyard" to the four-poster, bay-windowed Essex room, complete with a fireplace and a whirlpool bath. The location on Chippewa Square is pretty much perfect: well off the busy east-west thoroughfares but in the heart of Savannah's active theater district and within walking distance of anywhere.

**MAP 2:** 14 W. Hull St., 912/232-6622, www.foleyinn. com

## VICTORIAN DISTRICT
### DRESSER-PALMER HOUSE ⑤⑤

A short walk from Forsyth Park, the Dresser-Palmer House features 15 guest rooms in two wings but still manages to make things feel pretty cozy. Garden-level rooms go for a song (under $200).

**MAP 3:** 211 E. Gaston St., 912/238-3294, www. dresserpalmerhouse.com

### ★ THE GASTONIAN ⑤⑤⑤

The 1868 Gastonian inn got a major renovation in 2005 and remains a favorite choice for travelers to Savannah, mostly for its 17 sumptuously decorated guest rooms and suites, all with working fireplaces, and the always outstanding full breakfast. They pile on the epicurean delights with teatime, evening nightcaps, and complimentary wine. This is one of the six properties owned by the local firm HLC, which seems to have consistently higher standards than most out-of-town chains.

**MAP 3:** 220 E. Gaston St., 912/232-2869, www. gastonian.com

### MANSION ON FORSYTH PARK ⑤⑤⑤

How ironic that a hotel built in a former mortuary would be one of the few Savannah hotels not to have a resident ghost story. But that's the case with Mansion on Forsyth Park, which dominates an entire block alongside Forsyth Park, including partially within the high-Victorian former Fox & Weeks Mortuary building. Its sumptuous guest rooms, equipped with big beds, big baths, and big-screen TVs, scream "boutique hotel," as does the swank little bar and the alfresco patio area.

**MAP 3:** 700 Drayton St., 912/238-5158, www. mansiononforsythpark.com

## TYBEE ISLAND

Most of the hotels on Tybee Island are what we describe in the South as "rode hard and put away wet," meaning that they see a lot of wear and tear from eager vacationers. I encourage a B&B stay. Also be aware that places on Butler Avenue, even the substandard ones, charge a premium during the high season (Mar.-Oct.).

### ATLANTIS INN ⑤

For those looking for the offbeat, try the Atlantis Inn. Its reasonably priced, whimsically themed rooms are a hoot, and you're a short walk from the ocean and a very easy jaunt around the corner from busy Tybrisa Street. The downside, however, is no dedicated parking.

**MAP 5:** 20 Silver Ave., 912/786-8558, www. atlantisinntybee.com

### ★ THE GEORGIANNE INN ⑤⑤

The best B&B-style experience on Tybee can be found at The Georgianne Inn, a short walk off the beach and close to most of the island's action, yet not so close that you can't get away when you want to. The complimentary bikes to use while you're there are a nice plus.

**MAP 5:** 1312 Butler Ave., 912/786-8710, www. georgianneinn.com

# Stay the Week

For long-term stays on Tybee Island, weekly rentals are the name of the game. Though not cheap—expect to pay roughly $1,000 per week in the summer—they provide a higher level of accommodations than some hotels on the island. For weekly rentals, try **Oceanfront Cottage Rentals** (800/786-5889, www.oceanfrontcottage.com), **Tybee Island Rentals** (912/786-4034, www.tybeeislandrentals.com), or **Tybee Vacation Rentals** (866/359-0297, www.tybeevacationrentals.com).

### BEACHVIEW BED & BREAKFAST ⑤⑤

For a classic B&B stay very close to the Tybrisa/South end action, Beachview is where to go. The food is great and the views from the extensive wraparound porches are wonderful, especially on a breezy Tybee night.
MAP 5: 1701 Butler Ave., 912/348-5202, www.beachviewbbtybee.com

### LIGHTHOUSE INN ⑤⑤

Tucked away on the north end near the Lighthouse, hence the name, the Lighthouse Inn offers a lot of privacy in a very cozy and lush corner lot. This is more the place for a quiet, secluded getaway.
MAP 5: 16 Meddin Dr., 912/786-0901, www.tybeebb.com

### RIVER'S END CAMPGROUND ⑤

RV campers and more adventurous trekkers have a great treat in store at River's End Campground, on Tybee's somewhat less-developed north end. There are plenty of full-hookup sites ($70-90), some limited service/tent sites ($60-70), and a set of adorable little cabins that sleep six ($125-160, two-night minimum).
MAP 5: 5 Fort Ave., 800/786-1016, www.riversendcampground.com

## GREATER SAVANNAH
### Midway and Liberty County
### DUNHAM FARMS ⑤⑤

While industry is coming quickly to Liberty County, it's still a small self-contained community with not much in the way of tourist amenities (many would say that is part of its charm). A great choice for a stay is Dunham Farms. The B&B ($165-205) is in the converted 1940s Palmyra Barn, and the self-catered circa-1840 Palmyra Cottage ($300) nearby is right on the river, with plenty of kayaking and hiking opportunities. Your hosts, Laura and Meredith Devendorf, couldn't be more charming or informed about the area, and the breakfasts are absurdly rich and filling in that hearty and deeply comforting Southern tradition.
MAP 6: 5836 Islands Hwy., Midway, 912/880-4500, www.dunhamfarms.com

# Transportation and Services

## AIR

Savannah is served by the fairly efficient **Savannah/Hilton Head International Airport** (SAV, 400 Airways Ave., 912/964-0514, www.savannahairport.com), directly off I-95 at exit 104. The airport is about 20 minutes from downtown Savannah and 45 minutes from Hilton Head Island. Airlines with routes to SAV include American Airlines (www.aa.com), Allegiant (www.allegiant.com), Delta (www.delta.com), JetBlue (www.jetblue.com), Sun Country (www.suncountry.com) and United (www.ual.com).

Taxi stands and Uber provide

transportation into Savannah. The maximum cab fare for destinations in the Historic District is $28.

## CAR

Savannah is the eastern terminus of I-16, and that interstate is the most common entrance to the city. However, most travelers get to I-16 via I-95, taking the exit for downtown Savannah (Historic District). Once on I-16, the most common entry points into Savannah proper are via the Gwinnett Street exit, which puts you near the southern edge of the Historic District near Forsyth Park, or, more commonly, the Montgomery Street exit farther into the heart of downtown.

Paralleling I-95 is the old coastal highway, now U.S. 17, which goes through Savannah. U.S. 80 is Victory Drive for most of its length through town; after you pass through Thunderbolt on your way to the islands area, however, it reverts to U.S. 80, the only route to and from Tybee Island.

In Savannah, for quick access to the south, take the one-way streets Price (on the east side of downtown) or Whitaker (on the west side of downtown). Conversely, if you want to make a quick trip north into downtown, three one-way streets taking you there are East Broad, Lincoln, and Drayton.

When you're driving downtown and come to a square, the law says traffic within the square *always* has the right of way. In other words, if you haven't yet entered the square, you must yield to any vehicles already in the square.

### Car Rentals

The majority of rental car facilities are at the Savannah/Hilton Head International Airport, including **Avis** (800/831-2847), **Budget** (800/527-0700), **Dollar** (912/964-9001), **Enterprise** (800/736-8222), **Hertz** (800/654-3131), **National** (800/227-7368), and **Thrifty** (800/367-2277). Rental locations away from the airport are **Avis** (7810 Abercorn St., 912/354-4718), **Budget** (7070 Abercorn St., 912/355-0805), and **Enterprise** (3028 Skidaway Rd., 912/352-1424; 9505 Abercorn St., 912/925-0060; 11506-A Abercorn Expressway, 912/920-1093; 7510 White Bluff Rd., 912/355-6622).

## TRAIN

Savannah is on the New York-Miami *Silver Service* of **Amtrak** (2611 Seaboard Coastline Dr., 912/234-2611, www.amtrak.com). To get to the station on the west side of town, take I-16 west and then I-516 north. Immediately take the Gwinnett Street-Railroad Station exit and follow the Amtrak signs.

## BUS

**Chatham Area Transit** (www.catchacat. org, Mon.-Sat. 5:30am-11:30pm, Sun. 7am-9pm, $1.25, includes one transfer, free for children under 41 inches tall, exact change only), Savannah's publicly supported bus system, is quite thorough and efficient considering Savannah's relatively small size. Plenty of routes crisscross the entire area.

Of primary interest to visitors is the free **Dot Express Shuttle** (daily 7am-9pm), which travels a continuous circuit route through the Historic District with 11 stops at hotels, historic sites, and the Savannah Visitors Center. The shuttle is wheelchair accessible.

If you're on River Street, a neat experience is to jump on the free **River Street Trolley** (www.catchacat.org, Thurs.-Sun.). This restored historic trolley moves on the old trolley lines on River Street, and while it only goes a short distance, serving six stops, it's certainly fun.

## TAXI

Taxi services in Georgia tend to be less regulated than in other states, but service is plentiful in Savannah and is generally reasonable. The chief local provider is **Yellow Cab** (866/319-9646, www.savannahyellowcab.com). For wheelchair accessibility, request cab number 14. Other providers include **Adam Cab** (912/927-7466), **Magikal Taxi Service** (912/897-8294), and **Sunshine Cab** (912/272-0971).

If you're not in a big hurry, it's always fun to take a **Savannah Pedicab** (912/232-7900, www.savannahpedicab.com) for quick trips around downtown, or with the competing company **Royal Bike Taxi** (912/341-3944, www.royalbiketaxi.com). In both cases your friendly driver will pedal one or two passengers anywhere within the Historic District, and you essentially pay what you think is fair (I recommend $5 per person minimum).

## PARKING

Parking is at a premium in downtown Savannah. Traditional coin-operated meter parking is available throughout the city, but more and more the city is going to self-pay kiosks, which accept debit/credit cards. Bottom line: Be sure to pay for all parking weekdays 8:30am-5pm.

As of this writing, one big plus is there is *no* enforcement of parking meters at all on weekends or any day after 5pm. However, there is a very unpopular political move afoot to expand paid parking to Saturdays and evenings, so check the meters on arrival.

The city operates several parking garages at various rates and hours: the **Bryan Street Garage** (100 E. Bryan St.), the **Robinson Garage** (132 Montgomery St.), the **State Street Garage** (100 E. State St.), the **Liberty Street Garage** (401 W. Liberty St.), and the new **Whitaker Street Garage** underneath revitalized Ellis Square.

Tybee Island has paid parking daily, year-round, from 8am-8pm.

## TOURIST INFORMATION
### Visitors Centers

The main clearinghouse for visitor information is the downtown **Savannah Visitors Center** (301 MLK Jr. Blvd., 912/944-0455, Mon.-Fri. 8:30am-5pm, Sat.-Sun. and holidays 9am-5pm). The newly revitalized Ellis Square features a small visitors kiosk (Mon.-Fri. 8am-6pm) at the northwest corner of the square, with public restrooms and elevators to the underground parking garage beneath the square.

Other visitors centers in the area include the **River Street Hospitality Center** (1 River St., 912/651-6662, daily 10am-10pm), the **Tybee Island Visitor Center** (S. Campbell Ave. and U.S. 80, 912/786-5444, daily 9am-5:30pm), and the **Savannah Airport Visitor Center** (464 Airways Ave., 912/964-1109, daily 10am-6pm).

**Visit Savannah** (101 E. Bay St., 877/728-2662, www.savannahvisit.com), the local convention and visitors bureau, maintains a list of lodgings on its website.

### Hospitals

Savannah has two very good hospital systems. Centrally located near midtown, **Memorial Health University Hospital** (4700 Waters Ave., 912/350-8000, www.memorialhealth.com) is the region's only Level-I Trauma Center and is one of the best in the nation. The St. Joseph's-Candler Hospital System (www.sjchs.org) has two units, **St. Joseph's Hospital** (11705 Mercy Blvd., 912/819-4100) on the extreme south side and **Candler Hospital** (5401 Paulsen St., 912/819-6000), closer to midtown.

### Police

The Savannah-Chatham County Metropolitan Police Department has jurisdiction throughout the city of Savannah and unincorporated Chatham County. For non-emergencies, call 912/651-6675; for emergencies, call 911.

### Media

The daily newspaper of record is the *Savannah Morning News* (912/525-0796, www.savannahnow.com). It puts out an entertainment insert, called "Do," on Thursdays. The free weekly newspaper in town is *Connect Savannah* (912/721-4350, www.connectsavannah.com), hitting stands each Wednesday. Look to it for culture and music coverage as well as an alternative take on local politics and issues.

Two glossy magazines compete: the hipper *The South* magazine (912/236-5501, www.

thesouthmag.com) and the more establishment *Savannah* magazine (912/652-0293, www.savannahmagazine.com).

The National Public Radio affiliate is the Georgia Public Broadcasting station WSVH (91.1 FM). Savannah State University offers jazz, reggae, and Latin music on WHCJ (90.3 FM). Georgia Public Broadcasting is on WVAN. The local NBC affiliate is WSAV, the CBS affiliate is WTOC, the ABC affiliate is WJCL, and the Fox affiliate is WTGS.

## Libraries

The **Live Oak Public Library** (www.liveoakpl.org) is the umbrella organization for the libraries of Chatham, Effingham, and Liberty Counties. By far the largest branch is south of downtown Savannah, the **Bull Street Branch** (222 Bull St., 912/652-3600, Mon.-Tues. 9am-8pm, Wed.-Fri. 9am-6pm, Sun. 2pm-6pm). Farthest downtown and tucked away on Upper Factor's Walk is the charming little **Ola Wyeth Branch** (4 E. Bay St., 912/232-5488, Mon.-Fri. noon-3pm). In midtown Savannah is the historic **Carnegie Branch** (537 E. Henry St., 912/231-9921, Mon. 10am-8pm, Tues.-Thurs. 10am-6pm, Fri. 2pm-6pm, Sat. 10am-6am).

The **Georgia Historical Society** (501 Whitaker St., 912/651-2128, www.georgiahistory.com, Tues.-Sat. 10am-5pm) has an extensive collection of clippings, photos, maps, and other archival material at its headquarters at the corner of Forsyth Park in Hodgson Hall. Their website has been extensively revamped and is now one of the Southeast's best online resources for Georgia history information.

The **Jen Library** (201 E. Broughton St., 912/525-4700, www.scad.edu, Mon.-Fri. 7:30am-1am, Sat. 10am-1am, Sun. 11am-1am, shorter hours during school breaks), run by the Savannah College of Art and Design, features 3,000 Internet connections in its cavernous 85,000-square-foot space. Its main claim to fame is the remarkable variety of art periodicals to which it subscribes, nearly 1,000 at last count. It was built for the school's 7,000-plus art students, but the public can enter and use it as well with photo ID (you just can't check anything out).

## Post Offices

There are two post offices of note for most visitors to Savannah. The largest with the longest hours is the **Main Branch** (2 N. Fahm St., Mon.-Fri. 8am-5:30pm, Sat. 9am-1pm). It's off Bay Street just past the western edge of the Historic District. A smaller but more convenient branch downtown is the **Telfair Square Station** (118 Barnard St., Mon.-Fri. 8am-5pm).

## Gay and Lesbian Resources

Visitors often find Savannah to be surprisingly cosmopolitan and diverse for a Deep South city, and nowhere is this truer than in its sizeable and influential gay and lesbian community. In line with typical Southern protocol, the community is largely apolitical and more concerned with integration than provocation. But they're still very much aware of their growing impact on the local economy and are major players in art and commerce.

The **Savannah Pride Festival** is held every September at various venues in town. Top-flight dance-oriented musical acts perform, restaurants show off their creativity, and activists staff information booths. The chief resource for local gay and lesbian information and concerns is the **First City Network,** whose main website (www.firstcitynetwork.net) features many useful links. Another great Internet networking resource is **Gay Savannah** (www.gaysavannah.com).

# The Golden Isles

**T**he Georgia coast retains a timeless mystique evocative of an era before the coming of Europeans, even before humankind itself.

Often called the Golden Isles because of the play of the afternoon sun on the vistas of marsh grass, its other nickname, "the Debatable Land," is a nod to its centuries-long role as a constantly shifting battleground of European powers.

On the map it looks relatively short, but Georgia's coastline is the longest contiguous salt marsh environment in the world—a third of the country's remaining salt marsh. Abundant with wildlife, vibrant with exotic, earthy aromas, constantly refreshed by a steady, salty sea breeze, it's a place with no real match anywhere else. Filled with rich sediments from rivers upstream and replenished with nutrients from the twice-daily ocean tide, Georgia's marshes from the mainland to the barrier islands are an amazing engine of natural production. Generating more food energy than any estuary on the East Coast, each acre of marsh produces about 20 tons of biomass—making it four times more productive than an acre of corn.

Ancient Native Americans held the area in special regard, intoxicated not only by the easy sustenance it offered but also by its spiritual solace. Their shell middens, many still in existence, are a sign of well-fed people thankful for nature's bounty. Avaricious for gold as they were, the Spanish also admired the almost monastic enchantment of Georgia's coast, choosing it as the site of their first colony in North America. Their subsequent chain of Roman Catholic missions are now long gone but certainly testified to their own quest here. While the American tycoons who used these barrier islands as personal playgrounds had avarice of their own, we must give credit where it's due: Their self-interest kept these places largely untouched by the kind of development that has plagued many of South Carolina's barrier islands to the north. Though isolated even today, the Golden Isles played an irreplaceable role in the defense of the young United States. It was here that massive live oaks were forested and used in the construction of the bulked-up superfast frigates of the fledgling U.S. Navy. The USS *Constitution* got its nickname, "Old

---

**Previous:** a kayaker photographs an alligator in the Okefenokee Swamp; shrimping boats in Darien. **Above:** a visitor on Cumberland Island.

# Highlights

★ **Jekyll Island Historic District:** Relax and soak in the salty breeze at this onetime playground of the country's richest people (page 295).

★ **The Village:** The center of social life on St. Simons Island has shops, restaurants, a pier, and a beachside playground (page 304).

★ **Fort Frederica National Monument:** An excellently preserved tabby fortress from the first days of English settlement in Georgia (page 306).

★ **Harris Neck National Wildlife Refuge:** This former wartime airfield is now one of the East Coast's best birding locations (page 313).

★ **Cumberland Island National Seashore:** Wild horses—such as the ones that live here—might not be able to drag you off this evocative, undeveloped island paradise (page 322).

★ **Okefenokee National Wildlife Refuge:** More than just a swamp, the Okefenokee is a natural wonderland that takes you back into the mists of prehistory (page 326).

# The Golden Isles

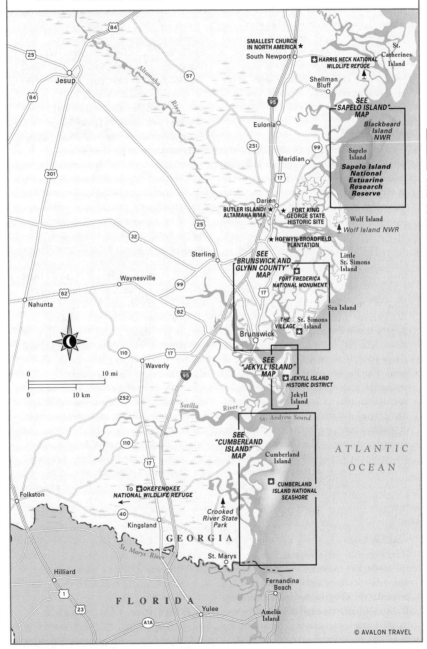

SMALLEST CHURCH IN NORTH AMERICA ★
South Newport ○

★ HARRIS NECK NATIONAL WILDLIFE REFUGE

St. Catherines Island

Jesup

Altamaha River

Shellman Bluff

Eulonia

*SEE "SAPELO ISLAND" MAP*

Blackbeard Island NWR

Meridian

Sapelo Island

*Sapelo Island National Estuarine Research Reserve*

Darien

BUTLER ISLAND/ ★
ALTAMAHA WMA

★ FORT KING GEORGE STATE HISTORIC SITE

Wolf Island

Sterling

★ HOFWYN-BROADFIELD PLANTATION

↑ Wolf Island NWR

*SEE "BRUNSWICK AND GLYNN COUNTY" MAP*

Little St. Simons Island

Waynesville

✦ FORT FREDERICA NATIONAL MONUMENT

Nahunta

Sea Island

THE VILLAGE

St. Simons Island

Brunswick

*SEE "JEKYLL ISLAND" MAP*

Waverly

✦ JEKYLL ISLAND HISTORIC DISTRICT

Jekyll Island

0      10 mi

0      10 km

Satilla River

St. Andrew Sound

*SEE "CUMBERLAND ISLAND" MAP*

Cumberland Island

ATLANTIC OCEAN

To ✦ OKEFENOKEE NATIONAL WILDLIFE REFUGE

✦ CUMBERLAND ISLAND NATIONAL SEASHORE

Folkston

↑ Crooked River State Park

GEORGIA

Kingsland

St. Marys River

Hilliard

FLORIDA

St. Marys

Fernandina Beach

Yulee

Amelia Island

© AVALON TRAVEL

Ironsides," from the strength of these pieces of Georgia oak, so resilient as to literally repel British cannonballs during the War of 1812. Although the South Carolina Sea Islands are generally seen as the center of Gullah culture, the African American communities of the Golden Isles, Georgia's Sea Islands, also boast a long and fascinating history of survival, resourcefulness, and proud cultural integrity that carries on to this day.

## HISTORY

For over 5,000 years, the Golden Isles of what would become Georgia were an abundant food and game source for Native Americans. In those days, long before erosion and channel dredging had taken their toll, each barrier island was an easy canoe ride away from the next one—a sort of early Intracoastal Waterway—and there was bounty for everyone. But all that changed in 1526 when the Golden Isles became the site of the first European settlement in what is now the continental United States, the fabled San Miguel de Gualdape, founded nearly a century before the first English settlements in Virginia. Historians remain unsure where expedition leader Lucas de Ayllón actually set up camp with his 600 colonists and slaves, but recent research breakthroughs have put it somewhere around St. Catherine's Sound. San Miguel disintegrated within a couple of months, but it set the stage for a lengthy Spanish presence on the Georgia coast that culminated in the mission period (1580-1684). With cooperation from the coastal chiefdoms of Guale and Mocama, almost all of Georgia's barrier islands and many interior spots hosted Catholic missions, each with an accompanying contingent of Spanish regulars. The missions began retreating with the English incursion into the American Southeast in the 1600s, and the coast was largely free of European presence until an early English outpost, Fort King George near modern-day Darien, Georgia, was established decades later in 1721. Isolated and hard to provision, the small fort was abandoned seven years later.

The next English project was Fort Frederica on St. Simons Island, commissioned by General James Edward Oglethorpe following his establishment of Savannah to the north. Oglethorpe's settlement of Brunswick and Jekyll Island came soon afterward. With the final vanquishing of the Spanish at the Battle of Bloody Marsh near Fort Frederica, the Georgia coast quickly emulated the profitable rice-based plantation culture of the South Carolina Lowcountry, and indeed many notable Carolina planters expanded their holdings with marshland on the Georgia coast.

During the Civil War the southern reaches of Sherman's March to the Sea came down as far as Darien, a once-vital trading port that was burned to the ground by Union troops. With slavery gone and the plantation system in disarray, the coast's African American population was largely left to its own devices. Although the famous "40 acres and a mule" land and wealth redistribution plan for freed slaves would not fruition, the black population of Georgia's Sea Islands, like that of South Carolina's, developed an inward-looking culture that persists to this day. The generic term for this culture is Gullah, but in Georgia you'll also hear it referred to as Geechee, local dialect for the nearby Ogeechee River.

As with much of the South after the Civil War, business carried on, with the area becoming a center for lumber, the turpentine trade, and an increasing emphasis on fishing and shrimping. But by the start of the 20th century, the Golden Isles had become firmly established as a playground for the rich, who hunted and dined on the sumptuous grounds of exclusive retreats such as the Jekyll Island Club.

As it did elsewhere, World War II brought new economic growth in the form of military bases, even as German U-boats ranged off the coast. Today the federal presence is most obvious in the massive Trident submarine base at Kings Bay toward the Florida border.

## PLANNING YOUR TIME

Generally speaking, the peak season in the Golden Isles (www.goldenisles.com) is

March-Labor Day. With the exception of some resort accommodations on St. Simons Island, Little St. Simons Island, and Sea Island, lodging is generally far more affordable than up the coast in either Savannah or Charleston.

Many travelers take I-95 south from Savannah to the Golden Isles, but **U.S. 17** roughly parallels the interstate—in some cases so closely that drivers on the two roads can see each other—and is a far more scenic and enriching drive for those with a little extra time to spend. Indeed, U.S. 17 is an intrinsic part of the life and lore of the region, and you are likely to spend a fair amount of time on it regardless.

Geographically, Brunswick is similar to Charleston in that it lies on a peninsula laid out roughly north-south. And like Charleston, it's separated from the Atlantic by barrier islands, in Brunswick's case St. Simons Island and Jekyll Island. Once you get within city limits, however, Brunswick has more in common with Savannah due to its Oglethorpe-designed grid layout. **Brunswick** itself can easily be fully experienced in a **single afternoon**. But really—as its nickname "Gateway to the Golden Isles"

indicates—Brunswick's main role is as an economic and governmental center for Glynn County, to which Jekyll Island and St. Simons Island, the real attractions in this area, belong.

Both Jekyll Island and St. Simons Island are well worth visiting, and have their own separate pleasures—Jekyll more contemplative, St. Simons more upscale. Give an **entire day to Jekyll** so you can take full advantage of its relaxing, open feel. A **half-day** can suffice for **St. Simons** because most of its attractions are clustered in the Village area near the pier, and there's little beach recreation to speak of.

Getting to the undeveloped barrier islands, Sapelo and Cumberland, takes planning in advance because there is no bridge to either. Both require a ferry booking and hence a more substantial commitment of time. There are no real stores and few facilities on these islands, so pack along whatever you think you'll need, including food, water, medicine, suntan lotion, insect repellent, and so on. **Sapelo Island** is limited to **day use** unless you have prior reservations, with the town of Darien in McIntosh County as the gateway. The same is true for Cumberland Island National Seashore, with the town of St. Marys in Camden County as the gateway.

# Brunswick and Glynn County

Consider Brunswick sort of a junior Savannah, sharing with that larger city to the north a heavily English flavor, great manners, a city plan with squares courtesy of General James Oglethorpe, a thriving but environmentally intrusive seaport, and a busy shrimping fleet. While Brunswick never became the dominant commercial center, à la Savannah, that it was envisioned to be, it has followed the Savannah model in modern times, both in terms of downtown revitalization and an increasing emphasis on port activity. Sadly, unlike Savannah, Brunswick has not seen fit to preserve the integrity of its six existing squares; all but one (Hanover Square) have been bisected by streets or built on.

The first real English-speaking settler in the area, Mark Carr, began cultivating land near Brunswick in 1738, but the city wasn't laid out until 1771, in a grid design similar to Savannah's. Originally comprising nearly 400 acres, Brunswick was named for Braunschweig, the seat of the House of Hanover in Germany and also for the Duke of Brunswick, a brother of King George III. The Brunswick area hosted a number of profitable plantations and a burgeoning lumber industry, but a series of financial panics in the late 1830s hit particularly hard. When the Civil War started, most white citizens fled to nearby Waynesville, Georgia, and wharves

# Brunswick and Glynn County

Brunswick Island

To Jekyll
Island

Brunswick River

4TH AVE

GLYNN AVE

Mary Ross Waterfront Park

BAY ST

ALBEMARLE ST

GLOUCESTER ST

MLK JR BLVD

NEWCASTLE ST

EGMONT ST

4TH ST

Brunswick

I ST

OCEAN HWY

ALTAMA AVE

27

17

SEE "BRUNSWICK" MAP

Overlook Park

Marshes of Glynn Park

F. J. TORRAS CAUSEWAY

To Hofwyl-Broadfield Plantation and Darien

Buck River

ST. SIMONS CAUSEWAY

Mackay River

Frederica River

Lanier Island

St. Simons Island

St. Simons Sound

Jekyll Island

VISITORS CENTER

THE VILLAGE

QUEENS COURT

PALMER'S

PIER

J. MAC'S

EPWORTH BY THE SEA

KINGS WAY

FREDERICA RD

DEMERE RD

SEA ISLAND RD

Dunbar Creek

ST. SIMONS' INN BY THE LIGHTHOUSE

ST. SIMONS LIGHTHOUSE MUSEUM/ MARITIME CENTER

VILLAGE INN AND PUB

MALCOLM MCKINNON AIRPORT

BLOODY MARSH BATTLEFIELD

DEMERE RD

KING AND PRINCE BEACH AND GOLF RESORT

Massengale Park

East Beach

OCEAN BLVD

FREDERICA RD

CHRIST CHURCH

To FORT FREDERICA NATIONAL MONUMENT and Lodge on Little St. Simons Island

Sea Island

THE SEA ISLAND RESORT/ THE CLOISTER

SEA ISLAND DR

ATLANTIC OCEAN

0
0   1 km
    1 mi

© AVALON TRAVEL

# Brunswick

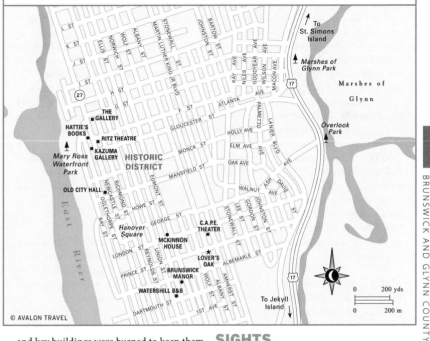

and key buildings were burned to keep them out of Union hands. Brunswick saw a boom in population during World War II as a home of wartime industry such as the J. A. Jones Construction Company, which in a two-year span built 99 massive Liberty ships and at its peak employed 16,000 workers (they managed to build seven ships in a single month in 1944).

Since the war, the shrimping industry has played a big role in Brunswick's economy, so much so that the city calls itself the "Shrimp Capital of the World." But lately the local shrimping industry has been in steep decline, both from depleted coastal stocks and increased competition from Asian shrimp farms. Hit hard by the recent economic downturn, Brunswick has seen better days. Despite an admirable effort at downtown revitalization centering on Newcastle Street, most visitors to the area seem content to employ Brunswick, as its nickname implies, as a "Gateway to the Golden Isles" rather than as a destination in itself.

# SIGHTS
## Brunswick Historic District

Technically, Brunswick has an "Old Town" district on the National Register of Historic Places as well as an adjacent district called "Historic Brunswick" centering on the storefronts of Newcastle Street. Since it's all pretty close together, we'll consider it all one nice package. Unlike Savannah, which renamed many of its streets in a fit of patriotism after the American Revolution, Brunswick's streets bear their original Anglophilic names, like Gloucester, Albemarle, and Norwich. You'd be forgiven for thinking that Brunswick's Union Street is a post-Civil War statement of national unity, but the name actually commemorates the union of Scotland and England in 1707. Most of the visitor-friendly activity centers on **Newcastle Street,** where you'll find the bulk of the galleries, shops, and restored buildings. Adjacent in the more historic areas are some nice residential homes.

The new pride of downtown is **Old City Hall** (1212 Newcastle St., 912/265-4032, www.brunswickgeorgia.net/och2.html), an amazing circa-1889 Richardsonian Romanesque edifice designed by noted regional architect Alfred Eichberg, who also planned many similarly imposing buildings in Savannah. Today it doubles as a rental event facility as well as a part-time courthouse; call ahead to take a gander inside.

Another active restored building is the charming **Ritz Theatre** (1530 Newcastle St., 912/262-6934, www.goldenislearts.org), built in 1898 to house the Grand Opera House and the offices of the Brunswick and Birmingham Railroad. This ornate three-story Victorian transitioned with the times, becoming a vaudeville venue, then a movie house. Under the management of the Golden Isles Arts and Humanities Association since 1989, the Ritz now hosts performances, studios, an art gallery, and classes.

## Mary Ross Waterfront Park

**Mary Ross Waterfront Park,** a downtown gathering place at Bay and Gloucester Streets, also has economic importance as a center of local industry—it's here where Brunswick's shrimp fleet is moored and the town's large port facilities begin. Unfortunately, nearby is a huge factory, dispensing its unpleasant odor over the waterfront 24-7. In 1989 the park was dedicated to Mary Ross, member of a longtime Brunswick shrimping family and author of the popular Georgia history book *The Debatable Land.* While the book is still a great read, sadly Ms. Ross was wrong when she wrote that the tabby ruins in the area were of Spanish origin. Devastated by the discovery that they actually dated from later and were of English construction, she vowed never to publish another word again.

At the entrance to the park is a well-done model of a Liberty ship, similar to the thousands that were built in Brunswick during World War II.

## Lover's Oak

At the intersection of Prince and Albany Streets, you'll find the **Lover's Oak**, a nearly 1,000-year-old tree. Local lore tells us that it has been a secret meeting place for young lovers for centuries (though one does wonder how much of a secret it actually could have been). It's about 13 feet in diameter and has 10 sprawling limbs.

Amid the light industrial sprawl of this area

Mary Ross Waterfront Park in Brunswick

of the Golden Isles Parkway is the interesting little **Overlook Park,** just south of the visitors center on U.S. 17—a good, if loud, place for a picnic. From the park's picnic grounds or overlook you can see the fabled Marshes of Glynn, which inspired Georgia poet Sidney Lanier to write his famous poem of the same title under the **Lanier Oak,** located a little farther up the road in the median.

## Hofwyl-Broadfield Plantation

South Carolina doesn't own the patent on well-preserved old rice plantations, as the **Hofwyl-Broadfield Plantation** (5556 U.S. 17, 912/264-7333, www.gastateparks. org, Wed.-Sun. 9am-5pm, last main house tour 4pm, $8 adults, $5 children), a short drive north of Brunswick, proves. With its old paddy fields along the gorgeous and relatively undeveloped Altamaha River estuary, the plantation's main home is an antebellum wonder, with an expansive porch and a nice house museum that includes silver, a model of a rice plantation, and a slide show. There's also a pleasant nature trail.

William Brailsford of Charleston finished the plantation in 1807, and it soon passed into the hands of the Troup family, who expanded the holdings to over 7,000 acres. Rice finally became financially unfeasible in the early 20th century, and the plantation turned to dairy farming, a pursuit that lasted until World War II. Ophelia Troup Dent would ultimately will the site to the state of Georgia in 1973.

The best way to get here is by taking U.S. 17 north of Brunswick for about 10 miles until you see the signs; the plantation entrance is on the east side of the road.

# ENTERTAINMENT AND NIGHTLIFE

The **Golden Isles Arts and Humanities Association** (1530 Newcastle St., 912/262-6934, www.goldenislesarts.org) is an umbrella organization for many arts activities in the Brunswick, Jekyll, and St. Simons area. They also manage the historic **Ritz Theatre** (1530 Newcastle St., 912/262-6934) in downtown Brunswick, which offers a yearly performance season that's worth checking out if you have a free weekend night.

## Nightlife

Brunswick is a conservative place with little bar scene to speak of. But a few miles offshore is quite a different story when the **Emerald**

the Ritz Theatre in Brunswick

# In the Footsteps of Bartram

The West has its stirring tale of Lewis and Clark, but the Southeast has its own fascinating—if somewhat less dramatic—tale of discovery, in the odyssey of William Bartram. In March 1773, the 33-year-old Bartram—son of royal botanist John Bartram and definitely a chip off the old block—arrived in Savannah to begin what would become a four-year journey through eight colonies. As Lewis and Clark would do in the following century, Bartram not only exhaustively documented his encounters with nature and with Native Americans, he also made discoveries whose impact has stayed with us to this day.

Young "Willie," born near Philadelphia in 1739, had a talent for drawing and for plants, which, of course, thrilled his father, who wrote to a friend that "Botany and drawing is his darling delight." A failure at business, Bartram was happy to settle on a traveling lifestyle that mixed both his loves: art and flora. After accompanying his father on several early trips, Bartram set out on his own at the request of an old friend of his father's in England, Dr. John Fothergill, who paid Bartram 50 pounds per year plus expenses to send back specimens and drawings.

Though Bartram's quest would eventually move farther inland and encompass much of the modern American South, most of its first year was spent in coastal Georgia. After arriving in Savannah he moved southward, roughly paralleling modern U.S. 17, to the now-dead town of Sunbury, through Midway, and on to Darien, where he stayed at the plantation of Lachlan McIntosh on the great Altamaha River, which inspired Bartram to pen some of his most beautiful writing. Bartram also journeyed to Sapelo Island, Brunswick, St. Marys, and even into the great Okefenokee Swamp. Using Savannah and Charleston as bases, Bartram mostly traveled alone, either by horse, by boat, or on foot. Word of his trip preceded him, and he was usually greeted warmly by local traders and Indian chiefs (except for one encounter with a hostile Native American near the St. Marys River). In many places, he was the first European seen since De Soto and the Spanish. His epic journey ended in late 1776, when Bartram gazed on his beloved Altamaha for the last time. Heading north and crossing the Savannah River south of Ebenezer, he proceeded to Charleston and from there to his hometown of Philadelphia—where he would remain for the rest of his days.

At its publication, his 1791 chronicle, *Travels Through North and South Carolina, Georgia, East and West Florida*, was hailed as "the most astounding verbal artifact of the early republic." In that unassuming yet timeless work, Bartram cemented his reputation as the country's first native-born naturalist and practically invented the modern travelogue. Thanks to the establishment of the William Bartram Trail in 1976, you can walk in his footsteps—or close to them, anyway, since historians are not sure of his route. The trail uses a rather liberal interpretation, including memorials, trails, and gardens, but many specific "heritage sites" in coastal Georgia have their own markers, as follows:

- River and Barnard Streets in Savannah to mark the beginning of Bartram's trek

- LeConte-Woodmanston Plantation in Liberty County (Barrington Ferry Rd. south of Sandy Run Rd. near Riceboro)

- 1.5 miles south of the South Newport River off U.S. 17

- St. Simon's Island on Frederica Road near the Fort Frederica entrance

- Off Highway 275 at Old Ebenezer Cemetery in Effingham County

Among the indigenous species Bartram was the first to record are: Fraser magnolia, Gopher tortoise, Florida sandhill crane, Flame azalea, and Oakleaf hydrangea.

**Princess Dinner and Casino Cruises** (Gisco Point, 912/265-3558, www.emerald-princesscasino.com, Mon.-Thurs. 7pm-midnight, Fri.-Sat. 11am-4pm and 7pm-1am, Sun. 1pm-6pm, $10) is operating. This is the classic gambling and party boat experience, with the action starting when the *Emerald Princess* slips into international waters and out of domestic gambling regulations. The 10 bucks for the cruise gets you a light dinner. Drinks and chips, of course, are on you. No one under age 21 is allowed, and minimum and maximum bets vary by table. Reservations are required. To get to the dock, take U.S. 17 over the massive Sidney Lanier Bridge. Take a left onto the Jekyll Island Causeway and then an immediate left onto Gisco Point Drive. Follow signs into the parking lot.

## Performing Arts

Based in St. Simons Island, the **Coastal Symphony of Georgia** (912/634-2006, www.coastalsymphonyofgeorgia.org), under the baton of Vernon Humbert, plays concerts in Brunswick during its season at different venues; most recently at the Brunswick High School auditorium. Check the website for details. The **Brunswick Community Concert Association** (912/638-5616, www.brunswickcommunityconcert.org, $25 adults, $10 students) brings an eclectic variety of high-quality national and regional vocal acts to various venues.

## Festivals and Events

Each Mother's Day at noon, parishioners of the local St. Francis Xavier Church hold the **Our Lady of Fatima Processional and Blessing of the Fleet** (www.brunswick.net), begun in 1938 by the local Portuguese fishing community. After the procession, at about 3pm at Mary Ross Waterfront Park, comes the actual blessing of the shrimping fleet.

Foodies will enjoy the **Brunswick Stewbilee** ($9 adults, $4 children), held on the second Saturday in October 11:30am-3pm. Pro and amateur chefs showcase their skills in creating the local signature dish and vying for

the title of "Brunswick Stewmaster." There are also car shows, contests, displays, and much live music.

## SHOPS

Right in the heart of the bustle on Newcastle is a good indie bookstore, **Hattie's Books** (1531 Newcastle St., 912/554-8677, www.hattiesbooks.com, Mon.-Fri. 10am-5:30pm, Sat. 10am-4pm). Not only do they have a good selection of local and regional authors, you can also get a good cup of coffee.

Like Beaufort, South Carolina, Brunswick has made the art gallery a central component of its downtown revitalization, with nearly all of them on Newcastle Street. Near Hattie's you'll find the **Ritz Theatre** (1530 Newcastle St., 912/262-6934, Tues.-Fri. 9am-5pm, Sat. 10am-2pm), which has its own art gallery inside. Farther down is **The Gallery on Newcastle Street** (1626 Newcastle St., 912/554-0056, www.thegalleryonnewcastle.com, Thurs.-Sat. 11am-5pm), showcasing the original oils of owner Janet Powers.

## SPORTS AND ACTIVITIES
### Hiking, Biking, and Bird-Watching

As one of the Colonial Coast Birding Trail sites, **Hofwyl-Broadfield Plantation** (5556 U.S. 17, 912/264-7333, www.gastateparks.org, Wed.-Sat. 9am-5pm) offers a great nature trail along the marsh. Clapper rails, marsh wrens, and a wide variety of warblers come through the site regularly.

Birders and hikers will also enjoy the **Earth Day Nature Trail** (1 Conservation Way, 912/264-7218), a self-guided, fully accessible walk where you can see such comparative rarities as the magnificent wood stork and other indigenous and migratory waterfowl. The trail includes observation towers. Binoculars are available for checkout. To get here, take U.S. 17 south through Brunswick. Just north of the big Sidney Lanier Bridge, turn left on Conservation Way (you'll see signage) to reach the parking lot.

Just across the Brunswick River from town is **Blythe Island Regional Park** (6616 Blythe Island Hwy., 912/261-3805), a 1,100-acre public park with a campground, picnic area, and boat landing. The views are great, and it's big enough to do some decent biking and hiking. The best way to get here is to get back on I-95 and head south. Take exit 29, head north for 0.5 mile on U.S. 82, then take a right onto Highway 303.

Another scenic park with a campground is **Altamaha Park of Glynn County** (1605 Altamaha Park Rd., 912/264-2342), northwest of Brunswick off U.S. 341, with 30 campsites and a boat ramp.

### Kayaking and Boating

Most recreational adventurers in the area prefer to launch from St. Simons Island. The key public landing in Brunswick, however, is **Brunswick Landing Marina** (2429 Newcastle St., 912/262-9264). You can also put in at the public boat ramps at **Blythe Island Regional Park** (6616 Blythe Island Hwy., 912/261-3805), which is on the Brunswick River, or the **Altamaha Park of Glynn County** (1605 Altamaha Park Rd., 912/264-2342), on the Altamaha River slightly north.

For expert guided tours at a reasonable price, check out **South East Adventures** (1200 Glynn Ave./U.S. 17, 912/265-5292, www.southeastadventure.com), which has a dock right on the fabled "Marshes of Glynn."

## RESTAURANTS

Brunswick isn't known for its breadth of cuisine options, and, frankly, most discriminating diners make the short drive over the causeway to St. Simons Island. One exception in Brunswick that really stands out, however, is **Indigo Coastal Shanty** (1402 Reynolds St., 912/265-2007, www.indigocoastal-shanty.com, Tues.-Fri. 11am-3pm, Fri.-Sat. also open 5pm-10pm, $12). This friendly, smallish place specializes in creative coastal themes, with dishes like the Charleston Sauté (shrimp and ham with peppers), Fisherman's Bowl (shrimp and fish in a nice broth), and even that old Southern favorite, a pimento cheeseburger.

## HOTELS

In addition to the usual variety of chain hotels—most of which you should stay far away from—there are some nice places to stay in Brunswick at very reasonable prices if you want to make the city a base of operations. In the heart of Old Town in a gorgeous Victorian is the ★ **McKinnon House** (1001 Egmont St., 912/261-9100, www.mckinnonhousebandb.com, $125), which had a cameo role in the 1974 film *Conrack*. Today, this bed-and-breakfast is Jo Miller's labor of love, a three-suite affair with some plush interiors and an exterior that is one of Brunswick's most photographed spots. Surprisingly affordable for its elegance, the **WatersHill Bed & Breakfast** (728 Union St., 912/264-4262, www.watershill.com, $100) serves a full breakfast and offers a choice of five themed suites, such as the French country Elliot Wynell Room or the large Mariana Mahlaney Room way up in the restored attic. Another good B&B is the **Brunswick Manor** (825 Egmont St., 912/265-6889, www.brunswickmanor.com, $130), offering four suites in a classic Victorian and a tasty meal each day.

The most unique lodging in the area is the ★ **Hostel in the Forest** (Hwy. 82, 912/264-9738, www.foresthostel.com, $25, cash only), essentially a group of geodesic domes and whimsical tree houses a little way off the highway. Formed more than 30 years ago as an International Youth Hostel, the place initially gives off a hippie vibe, with an evening communal meal (included in the rates) and a near-total ban on cell phones. But don't expect a wild time: No pets are allowed, the hostel discourages young children, and quiet time is strictly enforced beginning at 11pm. It's an adventurous, peaceful, and very inexpensive place to stay, but be warned that there is no heating or cooling. To reach the hostel, take I-95 exit 29 and go west for two miles. Make a U-turn at the intersection at mile marker 11. Continue east on Highway 82 for 0.5

# Brunswick Stew

Of course, Virginians being Virginians, they'll insist that the distinctive Southern dish known as Brunswick stew was named for Brunswick County, Virginia, in 1828, where a political rally featured stew made from squirrel meat. But all real Southern foodies know the dish is named for Brunswick, Georgia. Hey, there's a plaque to prove it in downtown Brunswick—although it says the first pot was cooked on July 2, 1898, on St. Simons Island, not in Brunswick at all. However, I think we can all agree that "Brunswick stew" rolls off the tongue much more easily than "St. Simons stew."

In any case, it seems likely that what we now know as Brunswick stew is based on an old colonial recipe, adapted from Native Americans, that relied on the meat of small game—originally squirrel or rabbit but nowadays mostly chicken or pork—along with vegetables like corn, onions, and okra simmered over an open fire. Today, this tangy, thick, tomato-based delight is a typical accompaniment to barbecue throughout the Lowcountry and the Georgia coast, as well as a freestanding entrée on its own. Done traditionally and correctly, a proper pot of Brunswick stew is an involved kitchen project taking most of a day, but it's worth it. Here's a typical recipe from Glynn County, home of the famous Brunswick Stewbilee festival held the second Saturday of October:

## SAUCE

Melt ¼ cup butter over low heat, then add:
1¾ cups ketchup
¼ cup yellow mustard
¼ cup white vinegar

Blend until smooth, then add:
½ tablespoon chopped garlic
1 teaspoon ground black pepper
½ teaspoon crushed red pepper
½ ounce Liquid Smoke
1 ounce Worcestershire sauce
1 ounce hot sauce
½ tablespoon fresh lemon juice

Blend until smooth, then add:
¼ cup dark brown sugar
Stir constantly and simmer for 10 minutes, being careful not to boil. Set aside.

## STEW

Melt ¼ pound butter in a two-gallon pot, then add:
3 cups diced small potatoes
1 cup diced small onion
2 14½-ounce cans chicken broth
1 pound baked chicken
8-10 ounces smoked pork

Bring to a boil, stirring until potatoes are nearly done, then add:
1 8½-ounce can early peas
2 14½-ounce cans stewed tomatoes
1 16-ounce can baby lima beans
¼ cup Liquid Smoke
1 14½-ounce can creamed corn

Stir in sauce. Simmer slowly for two hours. Makes one gallon of Brunswick stew.

mile. Look for a dirt road on the right with a gate and signage. This is now a "membership" organization so you'll need to join before booking.

## TRANSPORTATION AND SERVICES

Brunswick is directly off I-95. Take exit 38 to the Golden Isles Parkway, and take a right on U.S. 17. The quickest way to the historic district is to make a right onto Gloucester Street. Plans and funding for a citywide public transit system are pending, but currently Brunswick has no public transportation.

The **Brunswick-Golden Isles Visitor Center** (2000 Glynn Ave., 912/264-5337, daily 9am-5pm) is at the intersection of U.S. 17 and the Torras Causeway to St. Simons Island. It features the famous pot in which the first batch of Brunswick stew was cooked across the bridge on St. Simons. A downtown **information station** is in the Ritz Theatre (1530 Newcastle St., 912/262-6934, Tues.-Fri. 9am-5pm, Sat. 10am-2pm).

The newspaper of record in town is the *Brunswick News* (www.thebrunswicknews. com). The main **post office** (805 Gloucester St., 912/280-1250) is downtown.

# Jekyll Island

Few places in the United States have as paradoxical a story as Jekyll Island (www.jekyllisland.com). Once the playground of the world's richest people—whose indulgence allowed it to escape the overdevelopment that plagues nearby St. Simons—Jekyll then became a dedicated vacation area for Georgians of modest means, by order of the state legislature. Today, it's somewhere in the middle—a great place for a relaxing nature-oriented vacation that retains some of the perks of luxury of its Gilded Age pedigree.

## HISTORY

In prehistoric times, Jekyll was mainly a seasonal getaway for Native Americans. Indigenous people visited the area during the winter to enjoy its temperate weather and abundant shellfish. The Spanish also knew it well, calling it Isla de Las Ballenas (Island of the Whales) for the annual gathering of calving right whale families directly off the coast every winter—a mystical event that happens to this day. After securing safe access to the island from the Creeks in 1733, Georgia's founder, General James Oglethorpe, gave the island its modern name, after his friend Sir Joseph Jekyll. The first English settler was Major William Horton in 1735, recipient of

a land grant from the general, and the tabby ruins of one of Horton's homes remain today. A Frenchman, Christophe Du Bignon, purchased the island in 1800 and remained a leading figure. A mysterious event happened in 1858, when Jekyll Island was the final port of entry for the infamous voyage of *The Wanderer,* the last American slave ship. After intercepting the ship and its contraband manifest of 409 African slaves—the importation of slaves having been banned in 1808—its owners and crew were put on trial in Savannah.

As a home away from home for the country's richest industrialists—including J. P. Morgan, William Rockefeller, and William Vanderbilt—in the late 1800s and early 1900s, Jekyll Island was the unlikely seat of some of the most crucial events in modern American history. It was at the Jekyll Island Club in 1910 that the Federal Reserve banking system was set up, the result of a secret convocation of investors and tycoons. Five years later on the grounds of the club, AT&T president Theodore Vail would listen in on the first transcontinental phone call.

Jekyll's unspoiled beauty prompted the state legislature in 1947 to purchase the island and—ironically, considering the island's

# Jekyll Island

Driftwood
Beach

CLAM CREEK
PICNIC AREA

Brunswick River

North Beach

JEKYLL
ISLAND ⛺

HORTON HOUSE
TABBY RUINS ★

MAJOR HORTON RD

N BEACHVIEW DR

N RIVERVIEW DR

CAPTAIN WYLLY RD

To
Brunswick

Jekyll River

STABLE RD

JEKYLL ISLAND
GOLF RESORT ★

GEORGIA SEA
TURTLE CENTER ★

WELCOME
CENTER ■

LATITUDE 31 ▼ ● PIER RD

JEKYLL ISLAND CLUB/
COURTYARD AT CRANE

JEKYLL ISLAND ■
MINI GOLF

SHELL RD

JEKYLL ISLAND CAUSEWAY

JEKYLL ISLAND ✚
HISTORIC DISTRICT

TOLL
STATION

TIDELANDS 4-H NATURE CENTER ■

SUMMER WAVES ■

Jekyll

Sound

Intracoastal Waterway

HAMPTON INN
& SUITES JEKYLL
ISLAND

St.
Andrews
Park ⬇

S RIVERVIEW DR

S BEACHVIEW DR

South Dunes

ATLANTIC

OCEAN

0                1 mi

0        1 km

© AVALON TRAVEL

former history—declare it a totally accessible "playground" for Georgians of low to middle income (a causeway wasn't completed until the mid-1950s). This stated public mission is why prices on the island—currently administered on behalf of the state by the Jekyll Island Authority—have stayed so low and development has been so well managed. Every so often a controversial redevelopment plan is proposed, with the potential to introduce high-dollar resort-style development to parts of Jekyll for the first time since the days of J. P. Morgan and company. Residents and conservationists alike continue to work together to protect this magical barrier island known as "Georgia's Jewel."

## ORIENTATION

You'll have to stop at the entrance gate and pay a $6 "parking fee" to gain daily access to this state-owned island; a week-long pass is $28. (Bicyclists and pedestrians don't need to pay.) A friendly attendant will give you a map and a newsletter, and from there you're free to enjoy the whole island at your leisure.

As you dead-end into Beachview Drive, you're faced with a decision to turn either left or right. Most scenic and social activity is to the north, a left turn. For more peaceful beach-oriented activity with few services, turn right and head south. One historical reason for the lesser development at the south end is due to the fact that segregation laws were still in effect after the state's purchase of Jekyll in 1947. African American facilities were centered on the south end, while white activities were in the north.

## SIGHTS
### ★ Jekyll Island
### Historic District

A living link to one of the most glamorous eras of American history, the **Jekyll Island Historic District** is also one of the largest ongoing restoration projects in the southeastern United States. A visit to this 240-acre riverfront area is like stepping back in time to the Gilded Age, with croquet grounds, manicured

# Jekyll Island's Millionaire's Club

After the Civil War, as the Industrial Revolution gathered momentum seemingly everywhere but Georgia's Golden Isles, a couple of men decided to do something to break the foggy miasma of Reconstruction that had settled into the area and make some money in the process. In the late 1870s, John Eugene DuBignon and his brother-in-law Newton Finney came up with a plan to combine DuBignon's long family ties to Jekyll with Finney's extensive Wall Street connections in order to turn Jekyll into an exclusive winter hunting club. Their targeted clientele was a no-brainer: the newly minted American mega-tycoons of the Industrial Age. Finney found 53 such elite millionaires willing to pony up to become charter members of the venture, dubbed the Jekyll Island Club. Among them were William Vanderbilt, J. P. Morgan, and Joseph Pulitzer. As part of the original business model, in 1886 Finney purchased the island from DuBignon for $125,000.

With the formal opening two years later began Jekyll Island's half-century as a premier playground for the country's richest citizens, centered on the Victorian winter homes, called "cottages," built by each member and preserved today in the Historic District. While it was formed as a hunt club, the Jekyll Island Club welcomed the millionaires' families. In the 1920s, the focus began shifting to golf, and you can still play a portion of the historic course at the club today. By 1900 the club's membership represented one-sixth of the world's wealth. And the word *exclusive* has never been more appropriate: Nonmembers were not allowed to enjoy the facilities, regardless of social stature. Winston Churchill and even President William McKinley were refused admission.

As the mega-rich are wont to do even today, these influential men often mixed business with pleasure. In 1910, secret meetings of the so-called "First Name Club" led to the development of the Aldrich Plan, which laid the groundwork for the modern Federal Reserve System. Under assumed names, Senator Nelson Aldrich, Assistant Treasury Secretary A. Piatt Andrew, Banker's Trust vice president Benjamin Strong, National City Bank president Frank Vanderlip, investment banker Paul Warburg, and J. P. Morgan partner Henry P. Davison visited the club with the cover story of participating in a duck hunt. After they arrived by train at Brunswick, the stationmaster told them the cat was out of the bag and a gaggle of reporters had already gathered. But Davison took the stationmaster aside, saying, "Come out, old man, I will tell you a story." Returning a few minutes later, Davison told his colleagues, "That's all right. They won't give us away." What Davison's "story" was remains a mystery, but it must have been a pretty compelling one.

A few years later, AT&T president Theodore Vail, nursing a broken leg at his Mound Cottage on Jekyll, participated in the first transcontinental telephone call on January 25, 1915, among New York City, San Francisco, and the special line strung down the coast from New York and across Jekyll Sound to the club grounds. Also on the line were the telephone's inventor, Alexander

gardens, and even ferry boats with names like the *Rockefeller* and the *J. P. Morgan*. The Historic District essentially comprises the buildings and grounds of the old **Jekyll Island Club,** not only a full-service resort complex—consisting of the main building and several amazing "cottages" that are mansions themselves—but a sort of living history exhibit chronicling that time when Jekyll was a gathering place for the world's richest and most influential people.

The Queen Anne-style main clubhouse, with its iconic turret, dates from 1886. Within a couple of years the club had already outgrown it, and the millionaires began building the ornate cottages on the grounds surrounding it. The Chicora Cottage is gone, demolished after the supposedly accidental gunfire death of Edwin Gould in 1917, with only a hole in the ground remaining. But most of the others have been fully restored as lodgings. In 2000 renovations were done on the most magnificent outbuilding, the 24-bedroom Crane Cottage, a Mediterranean villa that also hosts a fine restaurant. The most recent renovation was the 2010 reopening of the Indian Mound Cottage, once William Rockefeller's vacation getaway, to tours.

the Jekyll Island Club

Graham Bell, his assistant Thomas Watson, the mayors of New York and San Francisco, and President Woodrow Wilson.

The millionaires continued to frolic on Jekyll through the Great Depression, but worsening international economic conditions reduced membership, even though the cost of membership was lowered in 1933. The outbreak of World War II and the resulting drain of labor into the armed forces put a further cramp in the club's workings, and it finally closed for good in 1942. By the time prowling German U-boats began appearing off the Georgia coast, prompting island-wide blackouts, the Jekyll Island Club era already seemed like ancient history. The state would acquire the island after the war in 1947, turning the once-exclusive playground of millionaires into a playground for all the people.

The **Jekyll Island Museum** (100 Stable Rd., 912/635-4036, www.jekyllisland.com, daily 9am-5pm, free), in the Historic District at the old club stables, houses some good history exhibits. The museum also provides a number of guided themed tours from $10 pp focusing on the Historic District, including the popular "Passport to the Century" (which includes entrance to two restored cottages) and "In the Service of Others" (focusing on the support staff of the golden age of the Jekyll Island Club). You can also purchase a guidebook for self-guided tours of the Historic District.

## Georgia Sea Turtle Center

Within the grounds of the Historic District in a whimsically renovated historic 1903 building is the **Georgia Sea Turtle Center** (214 Stable Rd., 912/635-4444, www.georgiaseaturtlecenter.org, daily 9am-5pm, $7 adults, $5 children), which features interactive exhibits on these important marine creatures, for whom Jekyll Island is a major nesting ground. Don't miss the attached rehabilitation building, where you can see the center's turtles in various states of treatment and rehabilitation before they are released into the wild. Children and adults alike will enjoy this unique opportunity to see these creatures up close and learn about the latest efforts to protect them.

In an effort to raise awareness about the need to protect the nesting areas of the big loggerheads that lay eggs on Jekyll each summer, the Sea Turtle Center also guides **nighttime tours** (early June-Aug. daily 8:30pm and 9:30pm) on the beach in order to explain about the animals and their habitat and hopefully to see some loggerheads in action. These tours fill up fast, so make reservations in advance.

## Driftwood Beach

Barrier islands like Jekyll are in a constant state of southward flux as currents erode the north end and push sand down the beach to the south end. This phenomenon has created **Driftwood Beach,** as the soil has eroded from under the large trees, causing them to fall and settle into the sand. In addition to being a naturalist's wonderland, it's also a starkly beautiful and strangely romantic spot. The newsletter you get as you enter the island has a map with Driftwood Beach on it, but here's a tip: Drive north on Beachview Drive until you see a pullover on your right

immediately after the Villas by the Sea (there's no signage). Park and take the short trail through the maritime forest, and you'll find yourself right there among the fallen trees and sand.

## Horton House Tabby Ruins

Round the curve and go south on Riverview Drive, and you'll see the large frame of a two-story house on the left (east) side of the road. That is the ruins of the old **Horton House,** built by Jekyll's original English-speaking settler, William Horton. Horton's house has survived two wars, a couple hurricanes, and a clumsy restoration in 1898. Its current state of preservation is thanks to the hands of the Jekyll Island Authority and various federal, state, and local partners. Horton's first house, also made of tabby, was burned by the Spanish during their retreat after losing the Battle of Bloody Marsh on nearby St. Simons Island. But the intrepid major rebuilt on the same spot in 1742, continuing to farm barley and indigo plants on the surrounding grounds as well as hosting Georgia's first brewery, the ruins of which are nearby.

Frenchman Christophe Poulain du Bignon would live in the Horton House for a while

Driftwood Beach

the tabby ruins of the Horton House

after purchasing the island in the 1790s. Across the street from the house is the poignant little **Du Bignon Cemetery,** around which winds a nicely done pedestrian and bike path overlooking one of the most beautiful areas of marsh you'll see in all the Golden Isles.

## ENTERTAINMENT AND NIGHTLIFE

There's no real nightlife to speak of on Jekyll, it being intended for quiet, affordable daytime relaxation. The focus instead is on several annual events held at the **Jekyll Island Convention Center** (1 N. Beachview Dr., 912/635-3400), which has undergone a massive restoration to bring it in line with modern convention standards.

At the beginning of the New Year comes one of the area's most beloved and well-attended events, the **Jekyll Island Bluegrass Festival** (www.adamsbluegrass.com). Many of the genre's biggest traditional names come to play at this casual multiday gathering. The focus here is on the music, not the trappings, so come prepared to enjoy wall-to-wall bluegrass played by the best in the business. Keep in mind that during this weekend the island is awash in RVs from all over the country, so if you're camping, you'd better make reservations.

In September as the harvest comes in off the boats, the **Wild Georgia Shrimp and Grits Festival** (www.jekyllisland.com, free admission) seeks to promote the value of the Georgia shrimping industry by focusing on how good the little critters taste in various regional recipes.

## SPORTS AND ACTIVITIES
### Hiking and Biking

Quite simply, Jekyll Island is a paradise for bicyclists and walkers, with a well-developed and very safe system of paths totaling about 20 miles and running the entire circumference of the island. The paths go by all major sights, including the Jekyll Island Club in the Historic District. In addition, walkers and bicyclists can enjoy much of the seven miles of beachfront at low tide.

Rent your bikes at **Jekyll Island Miniature Golf** (100 James Rd., 912/635-2648, daily 9am-8pm, $5.25 per hour, $11.50 per day). Take a left when you dead-end after the entrance gate, then another left.

### Bird-Watching

The **Clam Creek Picnic Area** on the island's north end is on the Colonial Coast Birding Trail, and without even trying you will see a wide variety of wading birds and shorebirds. Shell collectors will also have a blast, as will those with a horticultural bent, who will marvel at the variety of species presented in the various ecosystems on the island, from beach to marsh hammock to maritime forest.

## Golf and Tennis

True to Jekyll Island's intended role as a playground for Georgians of low to medium income, its golf and tennis facilities—all centrally located at the middle of the island—are quite reasonably priced. The **Jekyll Island Golf Resort** (322 Captain Wylly Rd., 912/635-2368, www.jekyllisland.com, greens fees $40-60) comprises the largest public golf resort in Georgia. A total of 63 holes on four courses—Pine Lakes, Indian Mound, Oleander, and Ocean Dunes (nine holes)—await. Check the resort's website for "golf passport" packages that include local lodging.

The adjacent **Jekyll Island Tennis Center** (400 Captain Wylly Rd., 912/635-3154, www.gate.net/~jitc, $25 per hour) boasts 13 courts, 7 of them lighted, as well as a pro shop (daily 9am-6pm).

If a different kind of golf is your thing, try **Jekyll Island Miniature Golf** (100 James Rd., 912/635-2648, Sun.-Thurs. 9am-8pm, Fri.-Sat. 9am-10pm, $6).

## Fishing

Continuing north on Beachview Drive, at the very top of the island is the well-done **Clam Creek Picnic Area** (daily dawn-dusk, free). This facility on the Colonial Coast Birding Trail has a spacious fishing pier over the Jekyll River and a trailhead through the woods and out onto the beach. About a 20-minute walk on the sand gets you to Driftwood Beach from the other side.

A good local fishing charter company is Captain Vernon Reynolds's **Coastal Expeditions** (3202 E. 3rd St., 912/265-0392, www.coastalcharterfishing.com), departing from the Jekyll Harbor Marina. Half-day and full-day trips are available; call for rates.

## Kayaking and Boating

Most kayaking activity in the area centers on St. Simons across the sound. But **Tidelands 4-H Nature Center** (100 Riverview Dr., 912/635-5032, www.tidelands4h.org) offers a variety of Jekyll-oriented guided kayak tours and also rents kayaks and canoes March-October.

## Water Parks

**Summer Waves** (210 S. Riverview Dr., 912/635-2074, www.jekyllisland.com, Memorial Day-Labor Day, $20 adults, $16 children under 48 inches tall) is just what the doctor ordered for kids with a surplus of energy. The 11-acre facility has a separate section for toddlers to splash around in, with the requisite more daring rides for hard-charging preteens. Hours vary, so call ahead.

## Horseback Riding and Tours

**Victoria's Carriages and Trail** (100 Stable Rd., 912/635-9500, Mon.-Sat. 11am-4pm) offers numerous options, both on horseback as well as in a horse-drawn carriage, including carriage tours of the island (Mon.-Sat. every hour 11am-4pm, $15 adults, $7 children). There's a 6pm-8pm night ride ($38 per couple). Horseback rides include a one-hour beach ride ($55) that leaves at 11am, 1pm, and 3pm and a sunset ride (6:30pm, $65) that lasts a little over an hour. Victoria's is at the entrance to the Clam Creek Picnic Area on the north end of the island directly across the street from the Jekyll Island Campground.

The **Tidelands 4-H Center** (912/635-5032) gives 1.5-2-hour Marsh Walks (Mon. 9am, $5 adults, $3 children) leaving from Clam Creek Picnic Area, and Beach Walks ($5 adults, $3 children) leaving Wednesdays at 9am from the St. Andrews Picnic area and Fridays at 9am from South Dunes Picnic Area.

Captain Eric Moody's **Coastal Expeditions** (3202 E. 3rd St., 912/265-0392, www.coastalcharterfishing.com, $24 adults, $10 children) provides dolphin tours March-May Tuesday-Saturday at 1:30pm, and three trips daily June-August.

# RESTAURANTS

Cuisine offerings are few and far between on Jekyll. I'd suggest you patronize one of the three dining facilities at the **Jekyll Island Club** (371 Riverview Dr.), which are all open to nonguests. They're not only delicious but pretty reasonable as well, considering the swank setting. My favorite is the ★ **Courtyard at Crane** (912/635-2400, lunch Sun.-Fri. 11am-4pm, Sat. 11am-2pm, dinner Sun.-Thurs. 5:30pm-9pm, $27-38). Located in the circa-1917 beautifully restored Crane Cottage, one of the old tycoon villas, the Courtyard offers romantic evening dining (call for reservations) as well as tasty and stylish lunch dining in the alfresco courtyard area or inside. The lunch menu—a great deal for the quality—is Mediterranean heavy, with wraps, sandwiches, and soups. The dinner menu moves more toward wine-country casual chic, with a lot of pork, veal, and beef dishes to go with the requisite fresh seafood. As a plus, the coffee is great—not at all a given in Southern restaurants. Casual dress is acceptable.

For a real and figurative taste of history, make a reservation at the **Grand Dining Room** (912/635-2400, breakfast Mon.-Sat. 7am-11am, Sun. 7am-10am, lunch Mon.-Sat. 11:30am-2pm, brunch Sun. 10:45am-2pm, dinner daily 6pm-10pm, dinner $26-35), the club's full-service restaurant. Focusing on continental cuisine—ordered either à la carte or as a prix fixe "sunset dinner"—the Dining Room features a pianist each evening and for Sunday brunch. Jackets or collared shirts are required for men.

For a tasty breakfast, lunch, or dinner on the go or at odd hours, check out **Café Solterra** (912/635-2600, daily 7am-10pm), great for deli-type food and equipped with Starbucks coffee. There are two places for seaside dining and cocktails at the historic Jekyll Island Club Wharf. **Latitude 31** (1 Pier Rd., 912/635-3800, www.crossoverjekyll.com, Tues.-Sun. 5:30pm-10pm, $15-25, no reservations) is an upscale seafood-oriented fine-dining place, while the attached **Rah Bar** (Tues.-Sat. 11am-close, Sun. 1pm-close, depending on weather) serves up oysters and shellfish in a very casual setting; try the Lowcountry boil or the crab legs.

## HOTELS
### Under $150

While most bargain lodging on Jekyll is sadly subpar, the old **Days Inn** (60 S. Beachview Dr., 912/635-9800, www.daysinnjekyll.com,

The Courtyard at Crane is a great place to get lunch or dinner.

$100) has undergone remodeling lately and is the best choice if budget is a concern (and you don't want to camp, that is). It has a good location on the south side of the island with nice ocean views.

### $150-300

Any discussion of lodging on Jekyll Island begins with the legendary ★ **Jekyll Island Club** (371 Riverview Dr., 800/535-9547, www. jekyllclub.com, $199-490), which is reasonably priced considering its history, postcard-perfect setting, and delightful guest rooms. Some of its 157 guest rooms in the club and annex areas are available for under $200, and even the finest, the Presidential Suite, tops out at less than $500 in high season (Mar.-Oct.). There are 60 guest rooms in the main club building, and several outlying cottages, chief among them the Crane, Cherokee, and Sans Souci Cottages, are also available. All rates include use of the big outdoor pool overlooking the river, and a neat amenity is a choice of meal plans for an extra daily fee.

Despite its auspicious beginnings, the club has not been a total success story. The state tried to run it as a resort in the 1950s and 1960s but gave up in 1971. With Historic Landmark District status coming in 1978, restoration wasn't far behind, and the club was reopened as a Radisson. Now operated by Landmark, the club is one of the "Historic Hotels of America" as ranked by the National Trust for Historic Preservation. Keep in mind that not all the fixtures are original and the present interior design scheme was done with an eye to current commercial taste (those crusty old millionaires would never have gone for pastels).

The first hotel built on the island in 35 years, the ★ **Hampton Inn & Suites Jekyll Island** (200 S. Beachview Dr., 912/635-3733, www.hamptoninn.com, $180-210) was built according to an exacting set of conservation guidelines, conserving much of the original tree canopy and employing various low-impact design and building techniques. Quite simply, it's one of the best eco-friendly hotel designs I've experienced. An elevated wooden walkway to the beach preserves as much of the natural dune-scape as possible, though keep in mind that the tradeoff is that you can't see the ocean from the hotel. The beach isn't far away, and the walk-in saltwater pool is particularly enjoyable and relaxing.

### Camping

One of the niftiest campgrounds in the entire area is the **Jekyll Island Campground** (197 Riverview Dr., 912/635-3021, tent sites $25, RV sites $32). It's a friendly place with an excellent location at the north end of the island—a short drive or bike ride from just about anywhere and directly across the street from the Clam Creek Picnic Area, with easy beach access. There are more than 200 sites from tent to full-service pull-through RV sites. There's a two-night minimum on weekends and a three-night minimum on holiday and special event weekends; reservations are recommended.

## TRANSPORTATION AND SERVICES

Jekyll Island is immediately south of Brunswick. Take I-95 exit 38 to the Golden Isles Parkway. Take a right onto U.S. 17 and keep going until you cross the huge Sidney Lanier Bridge over the Brunswick River. Take an immediate left at the foot of the bridge onto the Downing Musgrove Causeway (Jekyll Island Rd.). This long, scenic route over the beautiful marshes eventually takes you directly onto Jekyll, where you'll have to pay a $6 per vehicle fee to get onto the island. Once on the island, most sites are on the north end (a left as you reach the dead-end at Beachview Dr.). The main circuit route around the island is Beachview Drive, which suitably enough changes into Riverview Drive as it rounds the bend to landward at the north end.

Many visitors choose to bicycle around the island once they're here, which is certainly the best way to experience both the sights and the beach itself at low tide.

The **Jekyll Island Visitor Center** (901 Downing Musgrove Causeway, 912/635-3636, daily 9am-5pm) is on the long causeway along the marsh before you get to the island. Set in a charming little cottage it shares with the Georgia State Patrol, the center has a nice gift shop and loads of brochures on the entire Golden Isles region. Don't hesitate to ask questions of the person taking your $5 entrance fee when you get to the island itself.

The **U.S. Postal Service** keeps an outpost at 18 South Beachview Drive (912/635-2625).

# St. Simons Island

Despite a certain reputation for aloof affluence, the truth is that St. Simons Island is also very visitor friendly and there's more to do here than meets the eye. Think of St. Simons—with a year-round population of about 13,000—as a smaller, less-hurried Hilton Head and you've got the right idea. For those looking for island-style relaxation with no high-rise cookie-cutter development—but still all the modern amenities and luxuries—St. Simons fits the bill perfectly. A major difference from Hilton Head is that St. Simons respects much of its history, and a lot of it is still left to enjoy, particularly the expansive and archaeologically significant Fort Frederica National Monument.

## HISTORY

St. Simons Island and its much smaller, symbiotic neighbor Sea Island (originally Long Island) were well known to Native Americans as hunting and fishing grounds. Eventually the Spanish would establish two missions on St. Simons, one at the south end and one at the north end, as well as a town for nonconverted native peoples called San Simon, which would eventually give the island its modern name. A lasting European influence didn't come until 1736 with General James Oglethorpe's construction of Fort Frederica. The fort and surrounding town was a key base of operations for the British struggle to evict the Spanish from Georgia—which culminated in 1742 in the decisive Battle of Bloody Marsh south of the fort—but fell into decline after the Spanish threat subsided.

In the years after American independence, St. Simons woke up from its slumber as acre after acre of virgin live oak was felled to make the massive timbers of new warships for the U.S. Navy, including the USS *Constitution*. In their place was planted a new crop—cotton. The island's antebellum plantations boomed to world-class heights of profit and prestige when the superior strain of the crop known as Sea Island cotton came in the 1820s.

On St. Simons in 1803, one of the most poignant chapters in the dark history of American slavery was written. In one of the first documented slave uprisings in North America, a group of slaves from the Igbo

the beach at St. Simons Island

region of West Africa escaped custody and took over the ship that was transporting them to St. Simons from Savannah. But rather than do any further violence, immediately upon reaching shore on the west side of St. Simons, the slaves essentially committed mass suicide by walking into the swampy waters nearby, which forever after would be known as Ebo Landing (a corruption of the original Igbo).

The Civil War came to St. Simons in late 1861 with a Union blockade and invasion, leading Confederate troops to dynamite the island's lighthouse. Initially St. Simons was a sanctuary for freed slaves from the island's 14 plantations, and by late 1862 over 500 former slaves lived on St. Simons, including Susie King Taylor, who began a school for African American children. But in November of that year all former slaves were dispersed to Hilton Head and Fernandina, Florida. St. Simons was chosen as one of the implementation sites for General William Sherman's Special Field Order No. 15, the famous "40 acres and a mule" order. The order granted the Sea Islands of South Carolina and Georgia to freed slaves. However, Sherman's order was quickly rescinded by President Andrew Johnson.

The next landmark development for St. Simons didn't come until the building of the first causeway in 1924, which led directly to the island's resort development by the megarich industrialist Howard Coffin of Hudson Motors fame, who also owned nearby Sapelo Island to the north. By 1928, Coffin had completed the Sea Island Golf Club on the grounds of the old Retreat Plantation on the south end of St. Simons Island. He would move on to develop the famous Cloisters resort on Long Island (later Sea Island) itself.

## ORIENTATION

Because it's only a short drive from downtown Brunswick on the Torras Causeway, St. Simons has much less of a remote feel than most other Georgia barrier islands and is much more densely populated than any other Georgia island except for Tybee. Most

visitor-oriented activity on this 12-mile-long, heavily residential island about the size of Manhattan is clustered at the south end, where St. Simons Sound meets the Atlantic. The main reasons to travel north on the island are to golf or visit the historic site of Fort Frederica on the landward side.

## SIGHTS
### ★ The Village

Think of "The Village" at the extreme south end of St. Simons as a mix of Tybee's downscale accessibility and Hilton Head's upscale exclusivity. This compact, bustling area only a few blocks long offers not only boutique shops and stylish cafés, but also vintage stores and busking musicians. While visitors and residents here tend toward the affluent, they also tend not to be as flashy about it as in some other locales. You'll find the vast majority of quality eating spots here, along with most worthwhile lodging. It's fun to meander down Mallory Drive, casually shopping or noshing, and then make your way out onto the short but fun St. Simons Pier to enjoy the breeze and occasional spray coming off the sound. The long, low, sprawling building immediately to the north overlooking the expanse of Massengale Park is the old Casino building, now used for local government offices and community meetings.

## St. Simons Lighthouse Museum

Unlike many East Coast lighthouses, which tend to be in hard-to-reach places, anyone can walk right up to the St. Simons Lighthouse Museum (101 12th St., 912/638-4666, www. saintsimonslighthouse.org, Mon.-Sat. 10am-5pm, Sun. 1:30pm-5pm, $12 adults, $5 children). Once inside, you can enjoy the museum's exhibit and take the 129 steps up to the top of the 104-foot beacon—which is, unusually, still active—for a gorgeous view of the island and the ocean beyond.

The first lighthouse on the spot came about after planter John Couper sold this land, known as Couper's Point, to the government

# Golden Isles on the Page

And now from the Vast of the Lord will the waters of sleep
Roll in on the souls of men,
But who will reveal to our waking ken
The forms that swim and the shapes that creep
Under the waters of sleep?
And I would I could know what swimmeth below when the tide comes in
On the length and the breadth of the marvelous marshes of Glynn.

Sidney Lanier

Many authors have been inspired by their time in the Golden Isles, whether to pen flights of poetic fancy, page-turning novels, or politically oriented chronicles. Here are a few of the most notable names:

- **Sidney Lanier:** Born in Macon, Georgia, Lanier was a renowned linguist, mathematician, and legal scholar. Fighting as a Confederate during the Civil War, he was captured while commanding a blockade runner and taken to a POW camp in Maryland, where he came down with tuberculosis. After the war, he stayed at his brother-in-law's house in Brunswick to recuperate, and it was during that time that he took up poetry, writing the famous "Marshes of Glynn," quoted above.

- **Eugenia Price:** Although not originally from St. Simons, Price remains the best-known local cultural figure, setting her *St. Simons Trilogy* here. After relocating to the island in 1965, she stayed here until her death in 1996. She's buried in the Christ Church cemetery on Frederica Road.

- **Tina McElroy Ansa:** Probably the most notable literary figure currently living on St. Simons Island is award-winning African American author Tina McElroy Ansa. Few of her books deal with the Golden Isles region, but they all deal with life in the South, and Ansa is an ardent devotee of St. Simons and its relaxed, friendly ways.

- **Fanny Kemble:** In 1834, this renowned English actress married Georgia plantation heir Pierce Butler, who would become one of the largest slave owners in the United States. Horrified by the treatment of Butler's slaves at Butler Island, just south of Darien, Georgia, Kemble penned one of the earliest antislavery chronicles, *Journal of a Residence on a Georgian Plantation in 1838-1839*. Kemble's disagreement with her husband over slavery hastened their divorce in 1849.

in 1804 for $1. This original beacon was destroyed by retreating Confederate troops in 1862 to hinder Union navigation on the coast. Traces of its foundations are near the current facility. The existing lighthouse dates from 1872, built by Irishman Charles Cluskey, who was responsible for a lot of Greek Revival architecture up and down the Georgia coast. Attached to the lighthouse is the oldest brick structure in Glynn County, the 1872 lighthouse keeper's cottage, now a museum and gift shop run by the Coastal Georgia Historical Society.

## Maritime Center

A short walk from the lighthouse and also administered by the Coastal Georgia Historical Society, the **Maritime Center** (4201 1st St., 912/638-4666, www.saintsimonslighthouse.org, Mon.-Sat. 10am-5pm, Sun. 1:30pm-5pm, $12 adults, $5 children) is at the historic East Beach Coast Guard Station. Authorized by President Franklin Roosevelt in 1933 and completed in 1937 by the Works Progress Administration, the East Beach Station took part in military action in World War II, an episode chronicled in exhibits at the Maritime

Center. On April 8, 1942, the German U-boat U-123 torpedoed and sank two cargo ships off the coast of St. Simons Island. The Coast Guardsmen of East Beach station mounted a full rescue effort, saving many crewmen of the merchant ships, including one ship's canine mascot. The Coast Guard's tenure on East Beach ended after a 1993 fire burned down their boathouse. Two years later the station was decommissioned, and the Coasties moved to a new station in Brunswick.

### ★ Fort Frederica National Monument

The expansive and well-researched **Fort Frederica National Monument** (Frederica Rd., 912/638-3639, www.nps.gov/fofr, daily 9am-5pm, free) lies on the landward side of the island. Established by General James Oglethorpe in 1736 to protect Georgia's southern flank from the Spanish, the fort (as well as the village that sprang up around it, in which the Wesley brothers preached for a short time) was named for Frederick Louis, the Prince of Wales. The feminine suffix -*a* was added to distinguish it from the older Fort Frederick in South Carolina.

You don't just get to see a military fort here (actually the remains of the old powder magazine; most of the fort itself eroded into the river long ago); this is an entire colonial town site a mile in circumference, originally modeled after a typical English village. A self-guided walking tour through the beautiful grounds—the oak trees here have the longest, most luxurious Spanish moss I've ever seen—shows foundations of building sites that have been uncovered, including taverns, shops, and the private homes of influential citizens. Closer to the river is the large tabby structure of the garrison barracks.

As for the actual fort itself, from its location astride a bend in the Frederica River you can instantly see why this was such a strategic location, guarding the approach to the great Altamaha River. The Frederica garrison took part in an unsuccessful attack on St. Augustine, Florida, in 1740 and was also the force that sallied out of the fort and southward to repulse the Spanish at Bloody Marsh two years later.

Take in the accompanying exhibits in the visitors center, including a 23-minute film shown every half hour 9am-4pm that is actually quite good. A park ranger also gives informative talks throughout the day, and there are occasional reenactments by uniformed colonial "soldiers."

Fort Frederica National Monument

## Bloody Marsh Battlefield

There's not a lot to see at the site of the **Battle of Bloody Marsh** (Frederica Rd., 912/638-3639, www.nps.gov/fofr, daily 8am-4pm, free), but—as with the similarly stirring site of Custer's Last Stand at the Little Bighorn—your imagination fills in the gaps, giving it perhaps more emotional impact than other, more substantial historic sites.

Essentially just a few interpretive signs overlooking a beautiful piece of salt marsh, the site is believed to be near the place where British soldiers from nearby Fort Frederica ambushed a force of Spanish regulars on their way to besiege the fort. Frederica's garrison, the 42nd Regiment of Foot, was augmented by a company of tough Scottish Highlanders from Darien, Georgia, who legend says attacked to the tune of bagpipes. The battle wasn't actually that bloody—some accounts say the Spanish lost only seven men—but the stout British presence convinced the Spanish to leave St. Simons a few days later, never again to project their once-potent military power that far north in the New World.

While the Battle of Bloody Marsh site is part of the National Park Service's Fort Frederica unit, it's not at the same location. Get to the battlefield from the fort by taking Frederica Road south, and then a left (east) on Demere Road. The site is on your left as Demere Road veers right, in the 1800 block.

## Christ Church

Just down the road from Fort Frederica is historic **Christ Church** (6329 Frederica Rd., 912/638-8683, www.christchurchfrederica.org, daily 2pm-5pm). The first sanctuary dates from 1820, but the original congregation at the now-defunct town of Frederica held services under the oaks at the site as early as 1736. The founder of Methodism, John Wesley, and his brother Charles both ministered to island residents during 1736-37.

The original church was rendered unusable by Union occupation during the Civil War. A handsome new church, the one you see today, was funded and built in 1883 by a local mill owner, Anson Dodge, as a memorial to his first wife. But Christ Church's claim to fame in modern culture is as the setting of local novelist Eugenia Price's *The Beloved Invader*, the first work in her Georgia trilogy. The late Price, who died in 1996, is buried in the church cemetery.

## Tours

**St. Simons Island Trolley Tours** (912/638-8954, www.stsimonstours.com, daily 11am, $22 adults, $10 ages 4-12, free under age 4) offers just that, a ride around the island in comparative comfort, leaving from the pier.

# ENTERTAINMENT AND NIGHTLIFE
## Nightlife

St. Simons is far from Charleston's or Savannah's league when it comes to partying, but there is a fairly active nightlife scene, with a strong dose of island casual. Unlike some areas this far south on the Georgia coast, there's usually a sizeable contingent of young people out looking for a good time. The island's premier club, **Rafters Blues and Raw Bar** (315½ Mallory St., 912/634-9755, www.raftersblues.com, Mon.-Sat. 4:30pm-2am), known simply as "Rafters," brings in live music most every Thursday-Saturday night, focusing on the best acts on the regional rock circuit.

My favorite spot on St. Simons for a drink or an espresso—or a panini for that matter—is **Palm Coast Coffee, Cafe, and Pub** (316 Mallory St., 912/634-7517, www.palmcoastssi.com, daily 8am-10pm). This handy little spot, combining a hip, relaxing coffeehouse with a hearty menu of brunchy items, is in the heart of the village. The kicker, though, is the cute little bar the size of a large walk-in closet right off the side of the main room—a little bit of Key West on St. Simons. Mondays are open mic nights.

Inside the Village Inn is the popular nightspot the **Village Pub** (500 Mallory St., 912/634-6056, www.villageinnandpub.com, Mon.-Sat. 5pm-midnight, Sun. 5pm-10pm).

Palm Coast Coffee, Cafe, and Pub

Slightly more upscale than most watering holes on the island, this is the best place for a quality martini or other premium cocktail.

## Performing Arts

Because of its close proximity to Brunswick, a short drive over the bridge, St. Simons has a symbiotic relationship with that larger city in areas of art and culture. Each summer, beginning Memorial Day weekend and continuing into September, there are several **Jazz in the Park** concerts by regional artists. The shows are usually Sunday 7pm-9pm on the lawn of the St. Simons Lighthouse, and the beautiful setting and calming breeze is a delight. Admission is charged; bring a chair or blanket if you like.

## Cinema

The island has its own multiplex, the **Island Cinemas 7** (44 Cinema Lane, 912/634-9100, www.georgiatheatrecompany.com).

## SHOPS

Most shopping on St. Simons is centered in the Village and is a typical beach town mix of hardware and tackle, casual clothing, and souvenir stores. A funky highlight is **Beachview Books** (215 Mallory St., 912/638-7282, Mon.-Sat. 10:30am-5:30pm, Sun. 11:30am-3pm), a rambling used bookstore with lots of regional and local goodies, including books by the late great local author Eugenia Price. Probably the best antiques shop in this part of town is **Village Mews** (504 Beachview Dr., 912/634-1235, Mon.-Sat. 10am-5pm).

The closest thing to a mall is farther north on St. Simons at **Redfern Village,** with some cute indie stores like **Beach Cottage Linens** (912/634-2000, Mon.-Fri. 10am-5:30pm, Sat. 10am-5pm), **Thomas P. Dent Clothiers** (912/638-3118, Mon.-Sat. 9:30am-6pm), and the craftsy **Rarebbits and Pieces** (912/638-2866, Mon.-Sat. 10am-5:30pm). Redfern Village is on Frederica Road, one traffic light past the corner of Frederica Road and Demere Road.

## SPORTS AND ACTIVITIES

### Beaches

Keep going from the pier past the lighthouse to find **Massengale Park** (daily dawn-dusk),

SouthEast Adventure Outfitters

with a playground, picnic tables, and restrooms right off the beach on the Atlantic side. The beach itself on St. Simons is underwhelming compared to some in these parts, but nonetheless it's easily accessible from the pier area and good for a romantic stroll if it's not high tide. There's a great playground, Neptune Park, right next to the pier overlooking the waterfront.

## Kayaking and Boating

With its relatively sheltered landward side nestled in the marsh and an abundance of wildlife, St. Simons Island is an outstanding kayaking site, attracting connoisseurs from all over. A good spot to put in on the Frederica River is the **Golden Isles Marina** (206 Marina Dr., 912/634-1128, www.gimarina.com), which is actually on little Lanier Island on the Torras Causeway right before you enter St. Simons proper. For a real adventure, put in at the ramp at the end of South Harrington Street off Frederica Road, which

will take you out Village Creek on the seaward side of the island.

Undoubtedly the best kayaking outfitter and tour operator in this part of the Golden Isles is **SouthEast Adventure Outfitters** (313 Mallory St., 912/638-6732, www.southeastadventure.com, daily 10am-6pm), which also has a location in nearby Brunswick. Michael Gowen and company offer an extensive range of guided tours all over the St. Simons marsh and sound area as well as trips to undeveloped Little St. Simons Island to the north. Prices vary, so call or go to the website for information.

### Hiking and Biking

Like Jekyll Island, St. Simons is a great place for bicyclists. Bike paths go all over the island, and a special kick is riding on the beach almost the whole length of the island (but only at low tide). There are plenty of bike rental spots, with rates generally $15-20 per day depending on the season. The best place to rent bikes is **Monkey Wrench Bicycles** (1700 Frederica Rd., 912/634-5551). You can rent another kind of pedal-power at **Wheel Fun Rentals** (532 Ocean Blvd., 912/634-0606), which deals in four-seat pedaled carts with steering wheels.

### Golf and Tennis

A popular place for both sports is the **Sea Palms Golf and Tennis Resort** (5445 Frederica Rd., 800/841-6268, www.seapalms.com, greens fees $70-80) in the middle of the island, with three 9-hole public courses and three clay courts. The **Sea Island Golf Club** (100 Retreat Rd., 800/732-4752, www.seaisland.com, greens fees $185-260) on the old Retreat Plantation as you first come onto the island has two award-winning 18-hole courses, the Seaside and the Plantation. Another public course is the 18-hole **Hampton Club** (100 Tabbystone Rd., 912/634-0255, www.hamptonclub.com, greens fees $95) on the north side of the island, part of the King and Prince Beach and Golf Resort.

# RESTAURANTS

While the ambience at St. Simons has an upscale feel, don't feel like you have to dress up to get a bite to eat—the emphasis is on relaxation and having a good time.

## Breakfast and Brunch

★ **Palmer's Village Cafe** (223 Mallory St., 912/634-5515, www.palmersvillagecafe.com, Tues.-Sun. 7:30am-2pm, $10-15), formerly called Dressner's, is right in the middle of the Village's bustle. It's one of the island's most popular places but still has enough seats that you usually don't have to wait. Sandwiches and burgers are great, but breakfast all day is the real attraction and includes lovingly crafted omelets, hearty pancakes, and a "build your own biscuit" menu.

## Seafood

Despite its somewhat unappetizing name, **Mullet Bay** (512 Ocean Blvd., 912/634-9977, daily 11:30am-10pm, $7-18) in the Village is a favorite good old-fashioned Southern seafood place, the kind where you get a big fried platter with two sides and hush puppies. A popular seafood place right in the action in the Village is **Barbara Jean's** (214 Mallory St., 912/634-6500, www.barbarajeans.com, Sun.-Thurs. 11am-9pm, Fri.-Sat. 11am-10pm, $7-20), which also has a great variety of imaginative veggie dishes to go along with their formidable seafood menu, including some excellent she-crab soup and crab cakes. They also have plenty of good landlubber treats for those not inclined to eat the marine critters.

## Fine Dining

★ **Nancy** (26 Market St., 912/634-0885, www.nancyssi.com, lunch Tues.-Sat. 11:30am-2pm, dinner Thurs.-Sat. 6pm-10pm, $30) is an interesting concept: An upscale fine-dining spot with an affiliated boutique women's clothing shop. Nancy Herdlinger and Chef Abney Harper run this enterprise in a newer area a short drive outside The Village. It's now one of the premier fine dining spots on the Georgia coast south of Savannah. Any seafood dish is great, but I do suggest the short ribs if they're on the tightly curated menu.

Inside the King and Prince Resort, you'll find the old-school glory of the **Blue Dolphin** (201 Arnold Rd., 800/342-0212, lunch daily 11am-4pm, dinner daily 5pm-10pm, $15-30), redolent of the *Great Gatsby* era. The Blue Dolphin claims to be the only oceanfront dining on the island, and the views are certainly magnificent.

# HOTELS
## Under $150

A charming and reasonable place a stone's throw from the Village is ★ **Queens Court** (437 Kings Way, 912/638-8459, $85-135), a traditional roadside motel from the late 1940s, with modern upgrades that include a nice outdoor pool in the central courtyard area. Despite its convenient location, you'll feel fairly secluded.

One of the most interesting lodgings in the Lowcountry and Georgia coast is **Epworth by the Sea** (100 Arthur J. Moore Dr., 912/638-8688, www.epworthbythesea. org, $90-100). This Methodist retreat in the center of the island boasts an entire complex of freestanding motels and lodges on its grounds in various styles and configurations. Cafeteria-style meals are the order of the day, and there are plenty of recreational activities on-site, including tennis, volleyball, baseball, football, soccer, and basketball. They also rent bikes, which is always a great way to get around St. Simons. Everyone loves the **Lovely Lane Chapel,** a picturesque sanctuary that is a favorite spot for weddings and holds services Sunday at 8:45am (casual dress OK). Researchers can utilize the resources of the **Arthur J. Moore Methodist Museum and Library** (Tues.-Sat. 9am-4pm).

You couldn't ask for a better location than the **St. Simons' Inn by the Lighthouse** (609 Beachview Dr., 912/638-1101, www.saintsimonsinn.com, $120-300), which is indeed in the shadow of the historic lighthouse and right next to the hopping Village area. A so-called "condo-hotel," each of the standard and deluxe suites at the inn are individually owned by off-site owners—however, each guest gets full maid service and a complimentary breakfast.

## $150-300

The best-known lodging on St. Simons Island is the ★ **King and Prince Beach and Golf Resort** (201 Arnold Rd., 800/342-0212, $249-320). Originally opened as a dance club in 1935, the King and Prince brings a swank old-school glamour similar to the Jekyll Island Club (though less imposing). And like the Jekyll Island Club, the King and Prince is also designated as one of the Historic Hotels of America. Its nearly 200 guest rooms are spread over a complex that includes several buildings, including the historic main building, beach villas, and freestanding guesthouses. Some standard rooms can go for under $200 even in the spring high season. Winter rates for all guest rooms are appreciably lower and represent a great bargain. For a dining spot overlooking the sea, try the **Blue Dolphin** (lunch daily 11am-4pm, dinner daily 5pm-10pm, $15-30). The Resort's Hampton Club provides golf for guests and the public.

An interesting B&B on the island that's also within walking distance of most of the action on the south end is the 28-room **Village Inn & Pub** (500 Mallory St., 912/634-6056, www.villageinnandpub.com, $160-245), nestled among shady palm trees and live oaks. The pub, a popular local hangout in a renovated 1930 cottage, is a nice plus.

## Over $300

Affiliated with the Sea Island Resort, the **Lodge at Sea Island** (100 Retreat Ave., 912/638-3611, $650-2,500) is actually on the south end of St. Simons Island on the old Retreat Plantation. Its 40 grand guest rooms and suites all have great views of the Atlantic Ocean, the associated Plantation Course links, or both. Full butler service makes this an especially pampered and aristocratic stay.

# TRANSPORTATION AND SERVICES

Get to St. Simons through the gateway city of Brunswick. Take I-95 exit 38 for Golden Isles, which will take you to the Golden Isles Parkway. Take a right onto U.S. 17 and look for the intersection with the Torras Causeway, a toll-free road that takes you the short distance onto St. Simons.

Immediately as you cross the Frederica River onto the island, look for a quick right onto Kings Way to take you directly to the Village area. You can also take a quick left onto Demere Road to reach Frederica Road and the more northerly portion of the island, where you'll find Fort Frederica and Christ Church.

The main roads to remember are Kings Way, which turns into Ocean Boulevard as it nears the active south end of the island called "The Village"; Demere ("DEM-er-ee") Road, which loops west-to-east around the little island airport and then south, joining up with Ocean Boulevard down near the lighthouse; Frederica Road, the dominant north-south artery; and Mallory Street, which runs north-south through the Village area and dead-ends at the pier on St. Simons Sound. (You'll notice that Mallory Street is sometimes spelled "Mallery," which is actually the correct spelling of the avenue's namesake: Mallery King, child of Thomas King, owner of the historic Retreat Plantation.)

The **St. Simons Visitors Center** (530-B Beachview Dr., 912/638-9014, www.bgivb.com, daily 9am-5pm) is in the St. Simons Casino Building near Neptune Park and the Village. The main newspaper in St. Simons is the *Brunswick News* (www.thebrunswicknews.com). The **U.S. Postal Service** (800/275-8777) has an office at 620 Beachview Drive.

# LITTLE ST. SIMONS ISLAND

This 10,000-acre privately owned island, accessible only by water, is almost totally undeveloped—thanks to its salt-stressed trees, which discouraged timbering—and boasts seven miles of beautiful beaches. All activity centers on the circa-1917 ★ **Lodge on Little St. Simons Island** (1000 Hampton Point Dr., 888/733-5774, www.littlestsimonsisland.com, from $625), named by *Condé Nast Traveler* as the top U.S. mainland resort in 2007. Within it lies the famed Hunting Lodge, where meals and cocktails are served. With 15 ultra-plush guest rooms and suites in an assortment of historic buildings, all set amid gorgeous natural beauty—there are five full-time naturalists on staff—the Lodge is a reminder of what St. Simons proper used to look like. The guest count is limited to 30 people.

## Transportation

Unless you enlist the aid of a local kayaking charter company, you have to be a guest of the Lodge to have access to Little St. Simons. The ferry, a 15-minute ride, leaves from a landing at the northern end of St. Simons at the end of Lawrence Road. Guests have full use of bicycles once on the island and can also request shuttle transportation just about anywhere.

## SEA ISLAND

The only way to enjoy Sea Island—basically a tiny appendage of St. Simons facing the Atlantic Ocean—is to be a guest at ★ **The Sea Island Resort** (888/732-4752, www. seaisland.com, from $700). And guests visiting now are truly lucky; the legendary facility, routinely ranked as one of the best resorts on the planet, completed extensive renovations in 2008. The economic downturn combined with financial mismanagement sent the institution into bankruptcy followed by a sale in 2010. Guests won't notice, however. The rooms at the Resort's premier lodging institution, **The Cloister,** nearly defy description—enveloped in Old World luxury, they also boast 21st-century technology. And the service at The Cloister is equally world-class, featuring 24-hour butler service in the European tradition. There are cottages for rent on Sea Island as well, all of which grant temporary membership in the Sea Island Club and full use of its many amenities and services.

## Transportation

Get to Sea Island by taking Torras Causeway onto the island and then making a left onto Sea Island Causeway, which takes you all the way to the gate marking the only land entrance to Sea Island.

# Darien and McIntosh County

It doesn't get near the attention or the number of visitors as Savannah to the north or the St. Simons-Jekyll area to the south, but the small fishing and shrimping village of Darien in McIntosh County has an interesting and historic pedigree of its own. It is centrally located near some of the best treasures the Georgia coast has to offer, including the Harris Neck National Wildlife Refuge, the beautiful Altamaha River, and the sea island of Sapelo, and it also boasts what many believe to be the best traditional seafood restaurants in the state.

## HISTORY

Unlike Anglophilic Savannah to the north, the Darien area has had a distinctly Scottish flavor from the beginning. In 1736, Scottish Highlanders established a settlement at the mouth of the Altamaha River at the bequest of General James Oglethorpe, who wanted the tough Scots protecting his southern border from the Spanish. The colony was at the site of an earlier English effort, the abandoned Fort King George, but the Scots came up with a new name, Darien, honoring a failed 1697 settlement in Panama. Leading them was John McIntosh Mohr, who would go on to father several sons who would become famous in their own right and eventually lend his surname to the county. The Scots brought a singularly populist sentiment to the New World. When Georgia planters lobbied to legalize slavery, which was outlawed by Oglethorpe, the Scots of Darien signed a petition against them in 1739—believed to be the first organized protest against slavery in America. The Darien settlers were also known for keeping more cordial relations with the Native Americans than the area's English settlements did. Of course, they were a frugal bunch too.

Darien's heyday was unquestionably in that antebellum period, when for a brief time the town was the world's largest exporter of cotton, floated down the Altamaha on barges and shipped out through the town's port. The Bank of Darien was the largest bank south of Philadelphia in the early 1800s. A prosperous rice culture grew up around the Altamaha estuary as well, relying on the tidal flow of the area's acres and acres of marsh. Almost nothing from this period remains, however, because on June 11, 1863, a force of mostly African American Union troops under the command of Colonel Robert G. Shaw (portrayed in the movie *Glory*) burned Darien to the ground, with all its homes and warehouses going up in smoke.

After the Civil War, lumber became the new cash crop, and Darien once again became a thriving seaport and mill headquarters. The late 1800s saw a new reliance on shrimping and oystering, industries that survive to this day. A different kind of industry prospered in the years after World War II. In those pre-interstate highway days, U.S. 17 was the main route south to booming Florida. McIntosh County got a bad reputation for "clip joints," which would fleece gullible travelers with a variety of illegal schemes. This period is recounted in the best-seller *Praying for Sheetrock* by Melissa Fay Greene.

# SIGHTS
## Smallest Church in North America

While several other churches claim that title, fans of the devout and of roadside kitsch alike will enjoy the tiny and charming little **Memory Park Christ Chapel** (U.S. 17, daily 24 hours). The original 12-seat chapel was built in 1949 by local grocer Agnes Harper, when the church was intended as a round-the-clock travelers' sanctuary on what was then the main coastal road, U.S. 17. Upon her death, Harper simply willed the church to Jesus Christ. Sadly, in late 2015 a suspicious fire burned Mrs. Harper's church to the ground. A community effort, however, rebuilt it as close as they could. Get there by taking I-95 exit 67 and going south a short way on U.S. 17; the church is on the east side of the road.

## ★ Harris Neck National Wildlife Refuge

Literally a stone's throw away from the "Smallest Church" is the turnoff east onto the seven-mile Harris Neck Road leading to the **Harris Neck National Wildlife Refuge** (912/832-4608, www.fws.gov/harris-neck, daily dawn-dusk, free). In addition to being one of the single best sites in the South from which to view wading birds and waterfowl in their natural habitat, Harris Neck also has something of a poignant backstory. For generations after the Civil War, an African American community descended from the area's original slaves quietly struggled to eke out a living here by fishing and farming.

The settlers' land was taken by the federal government during World War II to build a U.S. Army Air Force base, primarily to train pilots on the P-40 Tomahawk fighter, the same plane used by the famed Flying Tigers. After the war, the base was decommissioned and given to McIntosh County as a municipal airport. But the notoriously corrupt local government so mismanaged the facility that the feds once again took it over, eventually transferring it to the forerunner of the U.S. Fish and Wildlife Service.

Now a nearly 3,000-acre nationally protected refuge, Harris Neck gets about 50,000 visitors a year to experience its mix of marsh, woods, and grassland ecosystems and for its nearly matchless bird-watching. Its former life as a military base has the plus of leaving behind a decent system of roads, many of them based on old runways. Most visitors use the four-mile "wildlife drive" to travel through the refuge, stopping occasionally for hiking or bird-watching. In the summer, look for egrets, herons, and wood storks nesting in rookeries. In the winter, waterfowl like mallards and teal flock to the brackish and freshwater pools. You can see painted buntings late April-late September.

Kayaks and canoes can put in at the public boat ramp on the Barbour River. Near the landing is the Gould Cemetery, an old African American cemetery that is publicly accessible. Charming handmade tombstones evoke the post-Civil War era of Harris Neck before the displacement of local citizens to build the airfield.

To get here, take I-95 exit 67 and go south on U.S. 17 about one mile, then east on Harris Neck Road (Hwy. 131) for seven miles to the entrance gate on the left.

## Shellman Bluff

Just northeast of Darien is the old oystering community of Shellman Bluff. It's notable not only for the stunning views from the high bluff, but also for fresh seafood. Go to Shellman's Fish Camp (1058 River Rd., 912/832-4331, call ahead) to put in for a kayak or canoe ride. Save room for some food; there are some great seafood places here.

To get to Shellman Bluff, take I-95 exit 67 for South Newport and get on U.S. 17 south. There are two easy ways to get to Shellman Bluff from U.S. 17: east on Minton Road and then left onto Shellman Bluff Road, or east on Pine Harbor Road followed by an immediate left onto Shellman Bluff Road. In either case, take Shellman Bluff Road until it dead-ends, then a right onto Sutherland Bluff Drive.

## Darien Waterfront Park

Right where U.S. 17 crosses the Darien River, you'll find the Darien Welcome Center (U.S. 17 and Fort King George Dr., 912/437-6684, daily 9am-5pm). From there it's a short walk down some steps to the newly refurbished little Darien Waterfront Park. This small but charming area on a beautiful bend of the Darien River—a tributary of the mighty Altamaha River just to the south—features

the old African American cemetery at Harris Neck

some old tabby warehouse ruins, some of the only remnants of Darien's glory days as a major seaport and old enough to have century-old live oaks growing around them. To the east are the picturesque docks where the town shrimp boat fleet docks.

## McIntosh Old Jail Art Center

Within Darien proper is the McIntosh Old Jail Art Center (404 North Way, 912/437-7711, www.visitdarien.com, Tues.-Sat. 10am-4pm), which also hosts several small art galleries and the McIntosh County History Museum.

## Vernon Square

Right around the corner from the welcome center on Washington Street is Vernon Square, a charming little nook of live oaks and Spanish moss that was the social center of Darien in the town's antebellum heyday. The Darien Methodist Church on the square was built in 1843, damaged during the Civil War, and then rebuilt in 1884 using materials from the first church. The nearby St. Andrews Episcopal Church, built in 1878, was once the site of the powerful Bank of Darien. Nearby is the affiliated and equally historic St. Cyprian's Episcopal Church (Fort King George Rd. and Rittenouse St.) built by an African American congregation and one of the largest tabby structures still in use anywhere.

## Fort King George State Historic Site

The oldest English settlement in what would become Georgia, Fort King George State Historic Site (1600 Wayne St., 912/437-4770, www.gastateparks.org/fortkinggeorge, Tues.-Sun. 9am-5pm, $7.50 adults, $4.50 children) for a short time protected the Carolinas from attack, from its establishment in 1721 to its abandonment in 1727. Walking onto the site, with its restored 40-foot-tall cypress blockhouse fort, instantly reveals why this place was so important: It guards a key bend in the wide Altamaha River, vital to any attempt to establish transportation and trade in the area. In addition to chronicling the ill-fated English occupation of the area—plagued by insects, sickness, danger, and boredom—the site also has exhibits about other aspects of local history, including the Guale Indians, the Spanish missionary presence, and the era of the great sawmills. Nature lovers will enjoy the site as well, as it offers gorgeous vistas of the marsh. Fort King George holds regular reenactments, living history demonstrations, and cannon firings; go to the website for details.

To get here, take U.S. 17 to the Darien River Bridge, and then go east on Fort King George Drive. There's a bike route to the fort if you want to park in town and pedal here.

## Butler Island

South of Darien is the Altamaha River, Georgia's largest watershed and only undammed river as well as one of the country's great estuarine habitats, with the second-largest watershed on the East Coast. It's a paradise for outdoors enthusiasts, one that amazed and delighted famed naturalist William Bartram on his journey here in the late 1700s. Over 30,000 ducks visit each year mid-October-mid-April on this key stop on the Colonial Coast Birding Trail.

A great place to enjoy the river ecosystem is the Altamaha Waterfowl Management Area (912/262-3173, http://georgiawildlife. dnr.state.ga.us). This was the site of Butler Island Plantation, one of the largest and most successful tidewater plantations in the antebellum era. (The 75-foot brick chimney just off U.S. 17 is part of an old rice mill belonging to the plantation.) In 1834, planter Pierce Butler II married English actress Fanny Kemble, who would go on to write one of the earliest antislavery chronicles, *Journal of a Residence on a Georgian Plantation in 1838-39*, about what she saw during her short stay at Butler Island. Just past the chimney is a large plantation house, which now contains offices of the Nature Conservancy. There's a picnic ground nearby. The dominance of the plantation culture in this area is proved by the dikes and gates throughout the marsh, still plainly visible from the road. Many are still used by the Georgia Department of Natural Resources to maintain bird habitat. Birds you can see throughout the area include endangered wood storks, painted bunting, white ibis, all types of ducks, and even bald eagles.

Some of the best hiking and birding in the area is just south of the chimney on U.S. 17. Park on the east side of the road at an old dairy barn, and from there you'll find the trailhead for a four-mile round-trip hike on the Billy Cullen Memorial Trail, which offers great bird-watching opportunities and interpretive signage. On the other side of U.S. 17 is the entrance to the Ansley Hodges Memorial, where a 0.25-mile hike takes you to an observation tower. Be aware that hunting goes on near this area on some Saturdays during the year.

Kayaks and canoes can easily put in at the state-run landing at **Champney River Park** right where U.S. 17 crosses the Champney River. There are a variety of fish camps up and down this entire riverine system, providing fairly easy launching and recovery.

## Tours

**Altamaha Coastal Tours** (229 Ft. King George Rd., 912/437-6010, www.altamaha. com) is your best bet for taking a guided kayak tour (from $50) or renting a kayak (from $20 per day) to explore the beautiful Altamaha River.

## RESTAURANTS

McIntosh County is a powerhouse in the food department, and as you might expect, fresh and delicious seafood in a casual atmosphere is the order of the day here.

**The Old School Diner** (1080 Jesse Grant Rd. NE, Townsend, 912/832-2136, http://old-schooldiner.com, Wed.-Fri. 5:30pm-9:30pm, Sat.-Sun. noon-9:30pm, $15-30, cash only) is located in a whimsical semirural compound seven miles off U.S. 17 just off Harris Neck Road on the way to the wildlife refuge. Run by the gregarious comfort-food culinary genius Jerome Brown, the restaurant is a reflection of the man himself—warm, inviting, eccentric, and full of life. The draw here is succulent fresh seafood in the coastal Georgia tradition—delicately fried and imbued with the subtle, inviting flavors of soul food. Old School's prices aren't so old school, but keep in mind that the portions are huge, rich, and filling.

Even farther off the main roads than the Old School Diner, the community of Shellman Bluff is well worth the drive. Find ★ **Hunters Café** (Shellman Bluff, 912/832-5771, lunch Mon.-Fri. 11am-2pm, dinner Mon.-Fri. 5pm-10pm, Sat.-Sun. 7am-10pm, $10-20) and get anything that floats your boat—it's all fresh and local. Wild Georgia shrimp are a particular specialty, as is the hearty cream-based crab stew. Take a right off Shellman Bluff Road onto Sutherland Bluff Drive, then a left onto New Shellman Road. Take a right onto the unpaved River Road and you can't miss it.

Another Shellman Bluff favorite is ★ **Speed's Kitchen** (Shellman Bluff, 912/832-4763, Thurs.-Sat. 5pm-close, Sun. noon-close, $10-20), where people move anything but fast, and the fried fish and crab-stuffed flounder are out of this world. Take a right off of Shellman Bluff Road onto Sutherland Bluff Drive. Take a right onto Speed's Kitchen Road.

On the Darien waterfront, you'll find **Skipper's Fish Camp** (85 Screven St., Darien, 912/437-3579, www.skippersfish-camp.com, daily 11am-9pm, $15-25), which, as is typical for this area, also hosts a marina. Try the fried wild Georgia shrimp, fresh from local waters. South of Darien just off U.S. 17 on the Altamaha River, try **Mudcat Charlie's** (250 Ricefield Way, 912/261-0055, daily 8am-2pm, $10-20), where fresh seafood is served in a friendly and very casual atmosphere, yes, right in the middle of a busy fish camp.

## HOTELS

If you want to stay in McIntosh County, I strongly recommend booking one of the five charming guest rooms at ★ **Open Gates**

**Bed and Breakfast** (301 Franklin St., Darien, 912/437-6985, www.opengatesbnb. com, $125-140). This lovingly restored and reasonably priced inn is on historic and relaxing Vernon Square in downtown Darien. Owners Zach Rath (the chef) and Carry May Aston are attentive innkeepers who rustle up a mean breakfast and have lots of pointers on how to enjoy the area.

## TRANSPORTATION AND SERVICES

U.S. 17 goes directly through Darien. The closest I-95 exit is exit 49. Once you get off U.S. 17, Darien is a pretty bike-friendly place; you can park the car downtown and ride your bike east on Fort King George Drive to visit Fort King George.

The **Darien Welcome Center** (1111 Magnolia Bluff Way, www.visitdarien.com, Mon.-Sat. 10am-8pm, Sun. 11am-6pm) is located within the Preferred Outlets mall just off I-95 at exit 49.

The closest hospital is the Brunswick campus of **Southeast Georgia Health System** (2415 Parkwood Dr., Brunswick, 912/466-7000, http://sghs.org).

## SAPELO ISLAND

One of those amazing, undeveloped Georgia barrier islands that can only be reached by boat, Sapelo also shares with some of those islands a link to the Gilded Age.

### History

The Spanish established a Franciscan mission on the north end of the island in the 1500s. Sapelo didn't become fully integrated into the Lowcountry plantation culture until its purchase by Thomas Spalding in the early 1800s. After the Civil War, many of the nearly 500 former slaves on the island remained, with a partnership of freedmen buying land as early as 1871.

Hudson Motors mogul Howard Coffin bought all of Sapelo, except for the African American communities, in 1912, building a palatial home and introducing a modern

infrastructure. Among Coffin's visitors were two presidents, Calvin Coolidge and Herbert Hoover, and aviator Charles Lindbergh. Coffin hit hard times in the Great Depression and in 1934 sold Sapelo to tobacco heir R. J. Reynolds, who consolidated the island's African Americans into the single Hog Hammock community. By the mid-1970s the Reynolds family had sold the island to the state, again with the exception of the 430 acres of Hog Hammock, which at the time had slightly more than 100 residents. Today most of the island is administered for marine research purposes under the designation of **Sapelo Island National Estuarine Research Reserve** (www.sapelonerr.org).

### Sights

Once on the island, you can take guided tours under the auspices of the Georgia Department of Natural Resources. Wednesday 8:30am-12:30pm is a tour of the island that includes the R. J. Reynolds Mansion (www.reynoldsonsapelo.com) on the south end as well as Hog Hammock and the Long Tabby ruins. Saturday 9am-1pm is a tour of the historic Sapelo Lighthouse on the north end along with the rest of the island. June-Labor Day there's an extra lighthouse and island tour Friday 8:30am-12:30pm. March-October on the last Tuesday of the month they do an extra-long day trip, 8:30am-3pm. Tours cost $10 adults, $6 children, free under age 6. Call 912/437-3224 for reservations. You can also arrange private tours.

Another key sight on Sapelo is a 4,500-year-old Native American shell ring on the north end, one of the oldest and best preserved anywhere. Beach lovers will especially enjoy the unspoiled strands on Sapelo, including the famous Nannygoat Beach.

## Hotels

While it's theoretically possible to stay overnight at the R. J. Reynolds Mansion (www.reynoldsonsapelo.com), it is limited to groups of at least 16 people. Realistically, to stay overnight on Sapelo you need a reservation with one of the locally owned guesthouses. One recommendation is Cornelia Bailey's six-room The Wallow (912/485-2206, call for rates) in historic Hog Hammock. The Baileys also run a small campground, Comyam's Campground (912/485-2206, $10 pp). Another option is The Weekender (912/485-2277, call for rates).

## Transportation and Services

Visitors to Sapelo must embark on the ferry at the Sapelo Island Visitors Center (912/437-3224, www.sapelonerr.org, Tues.-Fri. 7:30am-5:30pm, Sat. 8am-5:30pm, Sun. 1:30pm-5pm, $10 adults, $6 ages 6-18) in little Meridian, Georgia, on Highway 99 north of Darien. The visitors center actually has a nice nature hike of its own as well as an auditorium where you can see an informative video. From here it's a half-hour trip to Sapelo over the Doboy Sound. Keep in mind you must call in advance for reservations before showing up at the visitors center. April-October it's recommended to call at least a week in advance.

# ST. CATHERINE'S ISLAND

The interior of this beautiful island off the coast of Midway, Georgia, is off-limits to the public, but you can visit the beach up to the high-water mark by boat, enjoy its beautiful unspoiled beaches, and spy on local wildlife. While that's about all you can do, it's important to know a little of the interesting background of this island. Owned and administered by the St. Catherine's Island Foundation, it's unusual in that it has a 25-foot-high bluff on the northern end, an extraordinarily high geographic feature for a barrier island in this part of the world.

Once central to the Spanish missionary effort on the Georgia coast, St. Catherine's was found to be home to over 400 graves of Christianized Native Americans (a large shell ring also exists on the island). Declaration of Independence signer Button Gwinnett made a home here for a while until his death from a gunshot wound suffered in a duel in Savannah in 1777. After General Sherman's famous "40 acres and a mule" order, a freed slave named Tunis Campbell was governor of the island, living in Gwinnett's home. But when the order was rescinded, all former slaves had to leave for the mainland. In 1986, American Museum of Natural History archaeologist David Hurst Thomas began extensive research on Spanish artifacts left behind from the Santa Catalina de Guale mission, including foundations of living quarters, a kitchen, and a church—possibly the first church in what is now the United States. Today, however, the island, a National Historic Landmark, is better known as host to a New York Zoological Society project to recover injured or sick animals of endangered species and nurse them back to health for a possible return to the wild.

The closest marinas for the trip to the island's peaceful beaches are Shellman Fish Camp (1058 River Rd. NE, Townsend, 912/832-4331) in McIntosh County and

Halfmoon Marina (171 Azalea Rd., Midway, 912/884-5819) in Liberty County.

## BLACKBEARD ISLAND

While no one is positive if the namesake of Blackbeard Island actually landed here, the legends tell us he used it as a layover—even leaving some treasure here. Now federally administered as **Blackbeard Island National Wildlife Refuge** (912/652-4415, www.fws. gov/blackbeardisland), the island is accessible to the public by boat and gets about 10,000 visitors a year. Plenty of hiking trails exist, and the bird-watching is fantastic. It's also a major nesting ground for the endangered loggerhead turtle. Cycling is permitted, but overnight camping is not. For charters to Blackbeard, I recommend **SouthEast Adventures** (313 Mallory St., St. Simons, 912/638-6732) on St. Simons Island.

# Cumberland Island and St. Marys

Actually two islands—Great Cumberland and Little Cumberland—Cumberland Island National Seashore is the largest and one of the oldest of Georgia's barrier islands, and also one of its most remote and least developed. Currently administered by the National Park Service, it's accessible only by ferry or private boat. Most visitors to Cumberland get here from the gateway town of St. Marys, Georgia, a nifty little fishing village.

## ST. MARYS

Much like Brunswick to the north, the fishing town of St. Marys plays mostly a gateway role, in this case to the Cumberland Island National Seashore. That being said, it's a very friendly little waterfront community with undeniable charms of its own and a historic pedigree going back to the very beginnings of the nation.

### History

As early as 1767, once the Spanish threat subsided, plans were made to establish a town, then known as Buttermilk Bluff, in the area near the Florida border. But it wasn't until 20 years later that a meeting was held on Cumberland Island to close the deal with Jacob Weed to purchase the tract—acquired by confiscation from two loyalist landowners—for the grand sum of $38. The first influx of immigration to the area came as French Canadian refugees from Acadia (who would become known as Cajuns in Louisiana) came to St. Marys after being deported by the British. Another group of French speakers followed, fleeing Toussaint Louverture's slave rebellion in Haiti.

During the colonial period, St. Marys was the southernmost U.S. city and enjoyed not only importance as a seaport but military significance as well. Ironically, this strategic importance came into play more during the conflict with Great Britain than with anything to do with the Spanish. In 1812 a British force took over Cumberland Island and St. Marys, with a contingent embarking up the St. Marys River to track down the customs collector. However, in a bloody skirmish they were ambushed by American troops firing from the riverbanks. They vowed to avenge their loss by burning every building between the St. Marys and the Altamaha Rivers, but the ensuing peace treaty ending the War of 1812 brought a ceasefire.

Unlike towns such as Darien, which was put to the torch by Union troops, St. Marys was saved from destruction in the Civil War. The lumber industry boomed after that conflict as well as the local fishing and shrimping industries. A hotel was built in 1916 (and hosted Marjorie Kinnan Rawlings, author of *The Yearling*), but tourists didn't discover the area until the 1970s. It was also then that the U.S. Navy built the huge nuclear submarine base at Kings Bay, currently the area's largest employer

# Cumberland Island

ATLANTIC OCEAN

Little Cumberland Island

Intracoastal Waterway

Cumberland River

FIRST AFRICAN BAPTIST CHURCH

Whitney Lake

Brickhill River

MAIN RD

Cumberland Island

PLUM ORCHARD ★

CUMBERLAND ISLAND NATIONAL SEASHORE

MAIN RD

ATLANTIC OCEAN

Cumberland Sound

GREYFIELD INN

SEA CAMP DOCKS
SEA CAMP ▲

DUNGENESS DOCK
ICE HOUSE MUSEUM ★

To St. Marys

South End Ponds

Intracoastal Waterway

0    1 mi
0    1 km

© AVALON TRAVEL

with almost 10,000 workers. Development has increased in the area, with suburban sprawl beginning to cover the area like mushrooms after a heavy rain. Indeed, there's so much growth in the St. Marys-Camden County area that it's increasingly considered an outpost of the huge Jacksonville, Florida, metropolitan area to the south.

## Orientation

As in Brunswick, the waterfront faces opposite the ocean and is instead oriented west, toward a river, in this case the St. Marys River. Most activity in downtown St. Marys happens up and down Osborne Street, which perhaps not coincidentally is also how you get to the **Cumberland Island Visitor Center** (113 St. Marys St., 912/882-4335, daily 8am-4:30pm) and from there board the *Cumberland Queen* for the trip to the island. (Note: The Cumberland Island Visitor Center and the Cumberland Island Museum are in two different places, about a block apart.)

## Sights and Events

Tying the past to the present, it's only fitting that the home of the Kings Bay Submarine Base (which is not open to the public) has a museum dedicated to the "Silent Service." The **St. Marys Submarine Museum** (102 St. Marys St., 912/882-2782, www.stmaryswelcome.com, Tues.-Sat. 10am-4pm, Sun. 1pm-5pm, $5 adults, $3 children) on the riverfront has a variety of exhibits honoring the contribution of American submariners, including a bunch of cool models. There's a neat interactive exhibit where you can look through the genuine sub periscope that sticks out of the roof of the museum. Interpretation isn't a strong point—those without some previous knowledge won't find much help—but for military and nautical buffs the sheer amount of artifacts is amazing.

A block down Osborne Street from the waterfront—and *not* at the actual Cumberland Island Visitor Center or the actual ferry dock—is the handsome little **Cumberland Island National Seashore Museum** (129

Osborne St., 912/882-4336, www.stmaryswelcome.com, Wed.-Sun. 1pm-4pm, free). It has several very informative exhibits on the natural and human history of Cumberland, as well as a room devoted to the short but fascinating role the island played in the War of 1812.

The most notable historic home in St. Marys is the **Orange Hall House Museum** (311 Osborne St., 912/576-3644, www.orangehall.org, Tues.-Sat. 9am-4pm, Sun. 1pm-4pm, $3 adults, $1 children). This beautiful Greek Revival home, circa 1830, survived the Civil War and was the center of town social life during the Roaring '20s, when it was owned by a succession of socialites from up north. The home is gorgeous inside and out, particularly during the holidays when it gets the full decorative treatment.

As a nod to its Cajun history, St. Marys hosts a heck of a **Mardi Gras Festival** each February, closing down six blocks of the riverfront for a parade. There's also live entertainment, vendors, and a costume ball.

## Sports and Activities

For outdoor recreation near St. Marys, go to **Crooked River State Park** (6222 Charlie Smith Sr. Hwy., 912/882-5256, www.gastateparks.org, office Fri.-Wed. 8am-10pm, Thurs. 8am-5pm), which is not only a great place to put in for kayaking trips, including jaunts to Cumberland Island, but also has a wide range of lodging options as well. A key stop on the Colonial Coast Birding Trail, Crooked River features its own nature center and is near a historic site just upriver, the tabby ruins of the McIntosh Sugar Works—actually a lumber mill from the early 1800s. The easiest way to get here is to take I-95 exit 3 and go about eight miles east. To rent kayaks or book kayak and ecotours, try **Up the Creek Xpeditions** (111 Osborne St., 912/882-0911, www.upthecreekx.com), which can take you all around the area, including out to Cumberland Island.

## Restaurants

St. Marys cannot compete in culinary sophistication with Charleston or Savannah, but it does have some of the freshest seafood around. One of the best places to eat seafood on the waterfront in St. Marys is at **Lang's Marina Restaurant** (307 W. St. Marys St., 912/882-4432, lunch Tues.-Fri. 11am-2pm, dinner Wed.-Sat. 5pm-9pm, $15-20). Another pair of good waterfront spots, right next to each other, are **The Shark Bite** (104 W. St. Marys St., 912/576-6993, Tues.-Sat. 11am-9pm, $12-20), which has great burgers and live music, and **Riverside Café** (106 W. St. Marys St., 912/882-3466, Tues.-Sat. 11am-9pm, $15-20), which specializes in Greek favorites.

## Hotels

Don't even think about staying at a chain hotel when you're in St. Marys. Stay at one of these cute historic inns, all within easy walking distance of the waterfront, for a song.

The most notable lodging for historic as well as economic value is the 18-room **Riverview Hotel** (105 Osborne St., 912/882-3242, www.riverviewhotelstmarys.com, under $100). The waterfront locale, like many old hotels in this area, has a great retro feel. It was built in the 1920s and has hosted such notables as author Marjorie Rawlings, John Rockefeller, poet Sidney Lanier, and Andrew Carnegie. ★ **Emma's Bed and Breakfast** (300 West Conyers St., 912/882-4199, www.emmasbedandbreakfast.com, under $200) is situated on four beautiful acres in downtown St. Marys in a grand Southern-style mansion with all the trappings and hospitality you'd expect. You can also hang out on the stunning veranda at the historic ★ **Goodbread House** (209 Osborne St., 912/882-7490, www.goodbreadhouse.com, under $200), which offers rates below $100 in the off-season. The 1870 house features sumptuous interiors, including a classic dining room in which awesome breakfasts are served.

More outdoorsy visitors can stay at cottage, tent, or RV sites at **Crooked River State Park** (6222 Charlie Smith Sr. Hwy., 912/882-5256, www.gastateparks.org). There are 62 tent and RV sites (about $22) and 11 cottages ($85-110) as well as primitive camping ($25).

## Transportation and Services

Take I-95 exit 3 for Kingsland-St. Marys Road (Hwy. 40). This becomes Osborne Road, the main drag of St. Marys, as it gets closer to town. The road by the waterfront is St. Marys Street.

The **St. Marys Convention and Visitors Bureau** (406 Osborne St., 912/882-4000, www.stmaryswelcome.com) is a good source of information not only for the town but for Cumberland Island, but keep in mind that this is not actually where you catch the ferry to the island.

## ★ CUMBERLAND ISLAND NATIONAL SEASHORE

Not only one of the richest estuarine and maritime forest environments in the world, **Cumberland Island National Seashore** (912/882-4335, reservations 877/860-6787, www.nps.gov/cuis) is quite simply one of the most beautiful and romantic places on the planet, as everyone learned when the "it" couple of their day, John F. Kennedy Jr. and Carolyn Bessette, were wed on the island in 1996. With more than 16 miles of gorgeous beach and an area of over 17,000 acres, there's no shortage of beauty either, and the island's already remote feel is further enhanced by the efforts that have been taken to protect it from development.

Cumberland is far from pristine: It has been used for timbering and cotton, is dotted with evocative abandoned ruins, and hosts a band of beautiful but voracious wild horses. But it is still a remarkable island paradise in a world where those kinds of locations are getting harder and harder to find.

There are two ways to enjoy Cumberland: day trip or overnight stay. An early arrival and departure on the late ferry, combined with bike rental and a tour, still leaves plenty of time for daytrippers to relax. Camping overnight on Cumberland is quite enjoyable, but it's a bit rustic and probably isn't for novices.

Important note: Distances on the map can be deceiving. Cumberland is very narrow but also very long—about 18 miles tip to tip. You can walk the width of the island in minutes, but you will not be able to hike its length even in a day.

You can have a perfectly enjoyable time on Cumberland just hanging out on the more populated south end, but those who want to explore the island fully should consider renting a bike or booking seats on the new National Park Service van tour around the island.

## History

Like modern-day Americans, the Timucuan Indians also revered this site, visiting it often for shellfish and for sassafras, a medicinal herb common on the island. Cumberland's size and great natural harbor made it a perfect base for Spanish friars, who established the first mission on the island, San Pedro Mocama, in 1587. In fact, the first Christian martyr in Georgia was created on Cumberland, when Father Pedro Martinez was killed by the Indians.

As part of his effort to push the Spanish back into Florida for good, General James Oglethorpe established Fort William at the south end of Cumberland—the remains of which are now underwater—and a hunting lodge named Dungeness, an island placename that persists today. While land grants were made in the 1760s, they saw little follow-through, and by the time of naturalist William Bartram's visit in 1774, Cumberland Island was almost uninhabited. But inevitably, the Lowcountry planters' culture made its way down to Cumberland, which was soon the site of 15 thriving plantations and small farms. After the Revolution, the heirs of one of its heroes, General Nathanael Greene, established Dungeness Plantation in 1802, its central building a now-gone tabby structure built on top of an ancient shell mound.

Actual military action wouldn't come to Cumberland until the War of 1812, when the British came in force and occupied the island for two months, using Dungeness as their headquarters. In the process they freed 1,500 slaves, who would then emigrate to various British colonies. In 1818, Revolutionary War hero General "Light-Horse" Harry Lee—father of Robert E. Lee—arrived on Cumberland's shore, in failing health and determined to see the home of his old friend General Greene one last time. He died a month later and was buried here, his son returning later to erect a gravestone. Light-Horse Harry remained on Cumberland until 1913, when his remains were taken to Lexington, Virginia, to rest beside those of his son. His gravestone on Cumberland remains.

The Civil War—and another freeing of slaves—came again in the 1860s, when Union troops occupied the island. At war's end Cumberland was set aside as a home for freed African Americans—part of the famous and ill-fated "40 acres and a mule" proposal—but politics intervened: Most of Cumberland's slaves were rounded up and taken to Amelia Island, Florida, although some remained and settled at Cumberland's north end (the "Settlement" area today).

As elsewhere on the Georgia coast, the Industrial Revolution came to Cumberland in the form of a vacation getaway for a mega-tycoon, in this case Thomas Carnegie, industrialist and brother of the better-known Andrew Carnegie of Carnegie Library fame. Carnegie built a new, even grander Dungeness, which suffered the same fate as its predecessor in a 1959 fire.

Cumberland Island narrowly avoided becoming the next Hilton Head—literally—in 1969 when Hilton Head developer Charles Fraser bought the northern tip of the island and began bulldozing a runway. The dwindling but still influential Carnegies joined with the Georgia Conservancy to broker an agreement that resulted in dubbing Cumberland a National Seashore in 1972, saving it from further development. A $7.5 million gift from the Mellon Foundation enabled the purchase of Fraser's tract and the eventual incorporation of the island within the National Park system.

To learn more about Cumberland's fascinating history, visit the **Cumberland Island National Seashore Museum** (129 Osborne St., 912/882-4336, www.stmaryswelcome.com, Wed.-Sun. 1pm-4pm, free) while you're in St. Marys, a block away from the actual ferry docks.

## Sights

The ferry typically stops at two docks a short distance from each other, the Sea Camp dock and the Dungeness dock. At 4pm, rangers offer a "dockside" interpretive program at the Sea Camp. A short way farther north at the Dungeness Dock, rangers lead a highly-recommended "Dungeness Footsteps Tour" at 10am and 12:45pm, concentrating on the historic sites at the southern end of the island. Also at the Dungeness dock is the little **Ice House Museum** (912/882-4336, daily 9am-5pm, free), containing a range of exhibits on the island's history from Native American times to the present day.

Down near the docks are also where you'll find the stirring, almost spooky **Dungeness Ruins** and the nearby grave marker of Light-Horse Harry Lee. (You're very likely to see some wild horses around this area too.) The cause of the 1866 fire that destroyed the old Dungeness home is still unknown. Another even grander home was built on the same site during the Victorian era, but also fell victim to fire in the 1950s while uninhabited (the Rangers say it's the result of a dispute with locals over hunting rights). It's these Victorian ruins you see today.

A very nice addition to the National Park Service offering is a daily "Lands and Legacies" van tour (reservations 877/860-6787, $15 adults, $12 seniors and children) that takes you all around the island, eliminating the need for lengthy hikes. It's ideal for daytrippers—if a bit long at six hours—but anyone can take the ride. It leaves from the Sea Camp Ranger Station soon after the first morning ferry arrives. Reservations are strongly recommended.

Moving north on the Main Road (Grand Ave.)—a dirt path and the only route for motor vehicles—you come to the **Greyfield Inn** (904/261-6408, www.greyfieldinn.com). Because it is a privately owned hotel, don't trespass through the grounds. A good way farther north, just off the main road, you'll find the restored, rambling 20-room mansion **Plum Orchard,** another Carnegie

Plum Orchard can be toured on the second and fourth Sunday of the month.

legacy. Guided tours of Plum Orchard are available on the second and fourth Sunday of the month ($6 plus ferry fare); reserve a space at 912/882-4335.

At the very north end of the island, accessible only by foot or by bicycle, is the former freedmen's community simply known as **The Settlement,** featuring a small cemetery and the now-famous **First African Baptist Church** (daily dawn-dusk)—a 1937 version of the 1893 original—a humble and rustic one-room church made of whitewashed logs and in which the 1996 Kennedy-Bessette wedding took place.

## Sports and Activities

There are more than 50 miles of hiking trails all over Cumberland, about 15 miles of nearly isolated beach to comb, and acres of maritime forest to explore—the latter an artifact of Cumberland's unusually old age for a barrier island. Upon arrival, you might want to rent a bicycle at the **Sea Camp docks** (no reservations, arrange rentals on the ferry, adult bikes $16 per day, youth bikes $10, $20 overnight). The only catch with the bikes is that you shouldn't plan on taking them to the upcountry campsites.

Shell-and-sharks-teeth collectors might want to explore south of Dungeness Beach as well as between the docks. Unlike some parks, you are allowed to take shells and fossils off the island.

Wildlife enthusiasts will be in heaven. More than 300 species of birds have been recorded on the island, which is also a favorite nesting ground for female loggerhead turtles in the late summer. Of course, the most iconic image of Cumberland Island is its famous **wild horses,** a free-roaming band of feral equines who traverse the island year-round, grazing as they please.

The Rangers warn you about it, and I will too: Cumberland Island is home to some creepy-crawlies, including mosquitoes, gnats, and, yes, ticks, the latter of which are especially prevalent throughout the maritime forest as you work your way north. Bring high-strength insect repellant with you, or buy some at the camp store. Rangers recommend you do a frequent "tick check" on yourself and your companions.

## Hotels

The only "civilized" lodging on Cumberland is the 13-room ★ **Greyfield Inn** (Grand

# Wild Horses of Cumberland

the wild horses of Cumberland Island

Contrary to popular opinion, Cumberland Island's famous wild horses are not actually direct descendants of the first horses brought to the island by Spanish and English settlers, although feral horses have certainly ranged the island for most of recorded history. The current population of about 140 or so is actually descended from horses brought to the island by the Carnegie family in the 1920s. Responding to overwhelming public opinion, the National Park Service leaves the herd virtually untended and unsupervised. The horses eat, live, fight, grow up, give birth, and pass away largely without human influence, other than euthanizing animals who are clearly suffering and have no hope of recovery.

You're not guaranteed to see wild horses on Cumberland, but the odds are very heavily in your favor. They often congregate to graze around the Dungeness ruins, and indeed any open space. Over the years they've made trails through the forest and sand dunes, and can often be seen cavorting on the windy beach in the late afternoon and early evening.

Each stallion usually acquires a "harem" of dependent mares, and occasionally you might even witness spirited competition between stallions for mares and/or territory.

Gorgeous and evocative though these magnificent animals are, they have a big appetite for vegetation and frankly are not the best thing for this sensitive barrier island ecosystem. But their beauty and visceral impact on the visitor is undeniable, which means the horses are likely to stay as long as nature will have them.

And yes, these really are *wild* horses, meaning you should never try to feed or pet them, and you certainly won't be riding them.

Ave., 904/261-6408, www.greyfieldinn.com, $475), ranked by the American Inn Association as one of the country's "Ten Most Romantic Inns." Opened in 1962 as a hotel, the Greyfield was originally built in 1900 as the home of the Carnegies. The room rates include meals, transportation, tours, and bicycle usage.

Many visitors opt to camp on Cumberland (reservations 877/860-6787, limit of seven nights, $4) in one of three basic ways: at the **Sea Camp,** which has restrooms and shower facilities and allows fires; the remote but pleasant **Stafford Beach,** a vigorous three-mile hike from the docks and with a basic restroom and shower; and pure wilderness camping farther north at **Hickory Hill,** **Yankee Paradise,** and **Brickman Bluff,** all of which are a several-mile hike away, do not permit fires, and have no facilities of any kind. Reservations are required for camping. All trash must be packed out on departure, as there are no refuse facilities on the island. Responsible alcohol consumption is limited to those 21 and over.

Insect life is abundant. Bring heavy-duty repellant or purchase some at the camp store.

### Transportation and Services

The most vital information about Cumberland is how to get ashore in the first place. Most visitors do this by purchasing a ticket on the *Cumberland Queen* at the **Cumberland Island Visitor Center** (113 St. Marys St., St. Marys, 877/860-6787, daily 8am-4:30pm, $20 adults, $18 seniors, $12 under age 13) on the waterfront in St. Marys. I strongly suggest calling or faxing ahead. Be aware that there are often very long hold times by phone.

The ferry ride is 45 minutes each way. You can call for reservations Monday-Friday 10am-4pm. The ferry does not transport pets, bicycles, kayaks, or cars. However, you can rent bicycles at the Sea Camp docks once

you're there. Every visitor to Cumberland over age 16 must pay a $4 entry fee, including campers.

March 1-November 30, the ferry leaves St. Marys at 9am and 11:45am, returning from Cumberland at 10:15am and 4:45pm. March 1-September 30 Wednesday-Saturday, there's an additional 2:45pm departure from Cumberland back to St. Marys. December 1-February 28 the ferry operates only Thursday-Monday. Make sure you arrive and check in at least 30 minutes before your ferry leaves.

One of the quirks of Cumberland, resulting from the unusual way in which it passed into federal hands, is the existence of some private property on which you mustn't trespass, except where trails specifically allow it. Also, unlike the general public, these private landowners are allowed to use vehicles. For these reasons, it's best to make sure you have a map of the island, which you can get before you board the ferry at St. Marys or at the Ranger station at the Sea Camp dock.

There are no real stores and very few facilities on Cumberland. *Bring whatever you think you'll need,* whether it be food, water, medicine, suntan lotion, insect repellent, toilet paper, or otherwise.

# The Okefenokee Swamp

Scientists often refer to Okefenokee as an "analogue," an accurate representation of a totally different epoch in the earth's history. In this case it's the Carboniferous Period, about 350 million years ago, when the living plants were lush and green and the dead plants simmered in a slow-decaying peat that would one day end up as the oil that powers our civilization.

But for the casual visitor, Okefenokee might also be simply a wonderful place to get almost completely away from human influence and witness firsthand some of the country's most interesting wildlife in its natural habitat. Despite the enormous wildfires of the spring of 2007 and the summer of 2011—some

of the largest the Southeast has seen in half a century, so large they were visible from space—the swamp has bounced back, for the most part, and is once again hosting visitors who wish to experience its timeless beauty.

### ★ OKEFENOKEE NATIONAL WILDLIFE REFUGE

It's nearly the size of Rhode Island and just a short drive off I-95, but the massive and endlessly fascinating **Okefenokee National Wildlife Refuge** (912/496-7836, www.fws. gov/okefenokee, Mar.-Oct. daily dawn-7:30pm, Nov.-Feb. daily dawn-5:30pm, $5 per vehicle) is

# The Okefenokee Swamp

0    6 mi
0    6 km

Waycross

To Valdosta

Laura S Walker
State Park

OKEFENOKEE
SWAMP PARK
(NORTH ENTRANCE)

Cowhouse
Island

MAUL
HAMMOCK

Big Water
Lake

KINGFISHER
LANDING
(LAUNCH)

OKEFENOKEE
NATIONAL WILDLIFE
REFUGE

BIG WATER

Territory
Prairie

Big Water
Prairie

Floyd's
Prairie

CRAVEN'S
HAMMOCK

Minnie's
Island

BLUFF
LAKE

Pine
Island

Floyd's
Island

FOLKSTON INN B&B

Stephen C Foster
State Park

CEDAR
HAMMOCK

Folkston

SUWANNEE
RIVER SILL

(WEST ENTRANCE)

ROUND
TOP

Christie
Prairie

TRADER'S HILL
RECREATION AREA

Billy's
Island

CANAL
RUN

CHESSER
ISLAND
OBSERVATION
TOWER

To I-95

SUWANNEE CANAL
RECREATION AREA
(EAST ENTRANCE)

Bugaboo
Island

Buck
Prairie

Honey
Island

REFUGE
OFFICE

Okefenokee
National Wildlife
Refuge

Chesser
Prairie

FL

John's Negro
Island

WILDLIFE
DRIVE

SUWANNEE RIVER
VISITOR CENTER

CHESSER
HOMESTEAD

Fargo

Blackjack
Island

Grand
Prairie

Soldier's Camp
Island

FLORIDA

St. George

Moniac

To I-10

© AVALON TRAVEL

one of the lesser-visited national public lands. Is it that very name "swamp" that keeps people away, with its connotations of fetid misery and lurking danger? Or simply its location, out of sight and out of mind in south Georgia?

In any case, while it long ago entered the collective subconscious as a metaphor for the most untamed, darkly dangerous aspects of the American South—as well as the place where Pogo the Possum lived—the Okefenokee remains one of the most intriguing natural areas on the planet. The nearby old rail town of Folkston is the gateway to the swamp for most visitors off I-95, which is to say most of them. In true Georgia fashion, the town is insular but friendly, slow but sincere.

Several miles away, the state has also opened the **Suwanee River Visitor Center** (912/637-5274, www.gastateparks.org, Wed.-Sun. 9am-5pm), a "green" building featuring an orientation video and exhibits.

## History

The Okefenokee Swamp was created by an accident of geology. About 250,000 years ago, the Atlantic Ocean washed ashore about 70 miles farther inland from where it does today. Over time, a massive barrier island formed off this primeval Georgia coastline, running from

what is now Jesup, Georgia, south to Starke, Florida. When the ocean level dropped during the Pleistocene Era, this sandy island became a topographical feature known today as the Trail Ridge, its height effectively creating a basin to its west. Approximately 90 percent of the Okefenokee's water comes from rainfall into that basin, which drains slowly via the Suwannee and St. Marys Rivers.

Ordinarily, what the summer heat evaporates from the Okefenokee is more than replenished by rain, unless there's a severe drought like the one that caused the recent wildfires. But even the fires can't hold the swamp back. In fact, the Okefenokee is a fire ecosystem, meaning some plant species, like the cypress, depend on heat generated by wildfires to open their seed cones and perpetuate their lifecycle. Indeed, the particularly combustible peat that forms most of the swamp takes a long time to burn and sometimes remains smoldering under the surface, meaning that fire is never far away—sometimes it's right under your feet!

The massive Honey Prairie Fire of 2011 in the swamp's southwestern area, caused by a lightning strike, left scars that are visible to this day. Because of constant rejuvenation by water and fire, biologists estimate that the

Okefenokee Swamp Park is at the swamp's North Entrance.

oldest portion of this supposedly "ancient" swamp is actually no older than 7,000 years—the faintest blink of an eye in geological terms. Unlike Florida's Everglades, which are actually a single large and very slow-moving river, the Okefenokee is a true swamp.

Native Americans used the swamp as a hunting ground and gave us its current name, which means "Land of the Trembling Earth," a reference to the floating peat islands, called "houses," that dominate the landscape. The Spanish arrived about 1600, calling the swamp Laguna de Oconi (Lake Oconi) and establishing at least two missions in the area near two Timucuan villages. During the Seminole Wars of the 1830s, the Timucua took refuge within the swamp for a time before continuing south into Florida. While trade had occurred on the swamp's outskirts for nearly a century prior, it wasn't until the 1850s that the first nonnative settlers set up camp inside the swamp itself.

It's a common mistake to call the Okefenokee "pristine," because like much of the heavily timbered and farmed southeastern coast, it is anything but. The swamp's ancient cypress stands and primordial longleaf pine forests were heavily harvested in the early 20th century. About 200 miles of old railbed through the swamp remain as a silent testament to the scope of that logging operation. In 1918 the Okefenokee Society, the first organized attempt to protect the habitat, was formed in nearby Waycross, Georgia. In 1937, President Franklin Roosevelt brought the area within the federal wildlife refuge system.

## Sights

The Okefenokee features a wide variety of ecosystems, including peat bogs, sand hills, and black gum and bay forests. Perhaps most surprising are the wide-open vistas of the swamp's many prairies or extended grasslands, 22 in all, which besides being stirring to the eye are also great places to see birds. So you see, not all of the Okefenokee is wet. There is water aplenty here, though, with over 60 named lakes and 120 miles of boating trails.

And as you kayak or canoe on one of the water trails or on the old **Suwanee Canal** (a relic of the logging era), you'll notice the water is all very dark. This blackwater is not due to dirt or silt but to natural tannic acid released into the water from the decaying vegetation that gave the swamp its name. While I don't recommend that you drink the water, it's actually very clean despite its color.

As you'd expect in a national wildlife refuge, the Okefenokee hosts a huge variety of animal

You never know when you'll come across an alligator in the Okefenokee.

life—more than 400 species of vertebrates, including over 200 varieties of birds and more than 60 types of reptiles. Birders get a special treat in late November-early December when sandhill cranes come south to winter in the swamp. In January their colonies are at their peak, and the swamp echoes with their loud cries. Other common bird species you'll see are herons, egrets, and endangered wood storks and red-cockaded woodpeckers. The white ibis has seen a big spike in population in the refuge recently, as has the bald eagle.

A great way to see the sandhill cranes and other birds of the Okefenokee is to hike the 0.75-mile boardwalk out to the 50-foot **Chesser Island Observation Tower** on the eastern end of the swamp. This boardwalk is brand-new, a byproduct of the huge 2011 fire; you can see the charred piers of the old boardwalk as you stroll.

You can get to the tower by driving or biking the eight-mile round-trip **Wildlife Drive,** which also takes you by the old **Chesser Homestead,** the remnants of one of the oldest settlements in the swamp and a very interesting look back into early-20th-century rural homestead life. You can also hike out to Chesser; indeed, there are many miles of hiking trails through the upland areas of the swamp near the East Entrance.

Probably the first creature one thinks of

when one thinks of a swamp is the alligator. Certainly Okefenokee has plenty of them, and no one who has heard the roar of a male alligator break the quiet of the night will ever forget the experience. Most of the time, though, alligators are quite shy, and spotting them is an acquired skill. They often look like floating logs. Conversely, in warm weather you might see them out in the open sunning themselves. While no one can remember an incident of a gator attacking a human in the refuge, whatever you do, don't feed alligators in the wild.

As a Fish and Wildlife ranger in Okefenokee once told me: "If a gator attacks a human, at some point in the past someone has fed that gator. Gators get used to being fed. Unfortunately, they can't tell the difference between the person and the food."

Believe it or not, the alligator is not even the top predator in the Okefenokee; that title belongs to the black bear. Biologists estimate that as many as 90 percent of alligator eggs laid in the refuge are eaten by the local black bear population. And as with the gators, don't feed the bears.

## Touring the Refuge

For most visitors, the best way to enjoy the Okefenokee is to book a guided tour through **Okefenokee Adventures** (866/843-7926,

the view of Chesser Prairie from the observation tower

www.okefenokeeadventures.com), the designated concessionaire of the refuge. They offer a 90-minute guided boat tour ($18.50 adults, $11.25 children) that leaves each hour, and a 2.5-hour reservation-only sunset tour ($25 adults, $17 children) that takes you to see the gorgeous sunset over Chesser Prairie. Extended or custom tours, including multiday wilderness excursions, are also available. They also rent bikes, canoes, and camping gear, and even run a decent little café where you can either sit down and have a meal or take it to go out on the trail.

Privately owned canoes and boats with motors under 10 hp may put in with no launch fee, but you must sign in and out. No ATVs are allowed on the refuge, and bicycles are allowed only on designated bike trails. Keep in mind that some hunting goes on in the refuge at designated times. Pets must be leashed at all times.

## Camping

If fire and water levels permit, it's possible to stay the night in the swamp, canoeing to one of the primitive camping "islands" in the middle of the refuge. You need to make reservations up to two months in advance, however, by calling U.S. Fish and Wildlife (912/496-3331, Mon.-Fri. 7am-10am). A nonrefundable fee of $10 pp (which also covers your entrance fee) must be received 16 days before you arrive (mailing address: Okefenokee National Wildlife Refuge, Route 2, Box 3330, Folkston, GA 31537). Campfires are allowed only at Canal Run and Floyds Island. A camp stove is required for cooking at all other shelters. (Keep in mind that in times of extreme drought or fire threat, boat trips may not be allowed. Always check the website for the latest announcements.)

At Stephen Foster State Park (17515 Hwy. 177, 912/637-5274, fall-winter daily 7am-7pm, spring-summer daily 6:30am-8:30pm), aka the West Entrance, near Fargo, Georgia, there are 66 tent sites ($24) and nine cottages ($100). This part of the Okefenokee is widely considered the best way to get that "true swamp" experience.

## Transportation and Services

For anyone using this guide as a travel resource, the best way to access the Okefenokee—and the one I recommend—is the East Entrance (912/496-7836, www.fws.gov/okefenokee, Mar.-Oct. daily dawn-7:30pm, Nov.-Feb. daily dawn-5:30pm, $5 per vehicle), otherwise known as the Suwanee Canal Recreation Area. This is the main U.S. Fish and Wildlife Service entrance and the most convenient way to hike, rent boating and camping gear, and observe nature. The Richard S. Bolt Visitor Center (912/496-7836) has some cool nature exhibits and a surround-sound orientation video. Get to the East Entrance by taking I-95 exit 3 for Kingsland onto Highway 40 west. Go through Kingsland and into Folkston until Highway 40 dead-ends. Take a right, and then an immediate left onto Main Street. At the third light, make a left onto Okefenokee Drive (Hwy. 121) south.

Families with kids may want to hit the North Entrance at the privately run Okefenokee Swamp Park (U.S. 1, 912/283-0583, www.okeswamp.com, daily 9am-5:30pm, $12 adults, $11 ages 3-11) near Waycross, Georgia. (Fans of the old Pogo will recall Waycross from the comic strip; and yes, there's a real "Fort Mudge" nearby.) Here you will find a more touristy vibe, with a reconstructed pioneer village, a serpentarium, and animals in captivity. From here you can take various guided tours for an additional fee.

There's camping at the nearby but unaffiliated Laura S. Walker State Park (5653 Laura Walker Rd., 800/864-7275, www.gastateparks.org). Be aware the state park is not in the swamp and isn't very swampy, but it does have a nice humanmade lake where you can rent canoes. Get to the North Entrance by taking I-95 exit 29 and going west on U.S. 82 about 45 miles to Highway 177 (Laura Walker Rd.). Go south through Laura S. Walker State Park; the Swamp Park is several miles farther.

If you really want that cypress-festooned, classic swamp look, take the long way around the Okefenokee to Stephen Foster State

Park (17515 Hwy. 177, 912/637-5274, fall-winter daily 7am-7pm, spring-summer daily 6:30am-8:30pm), aka the **West Entrance,** near Fargo, Georgia. Guided tours are available. Get to Stephen Foster State Park by taking I-95 exit 3 and following the signs to Folkston. Get on Highway 121 south to St. George, and then go west on Highway 94.

# FOLKSTON

The chief attraction in Folkston and its main claim to fame is the viewing depot for the **Folkston Funnel** (912/496-2536, www.folkston.com), a veritable train-watcher's paradise. This is the spot where the big CSX double-track rail line—following the top of the ancient Trail Ridge—hosts 60 or more trains a day. They say 90 percent of all freight trains to and from Florida use this track.

Railroad buffs from all over the South congregate here, anticipating the next train by listening to their scanners. The first Saturday each April brings buffs together for the all-day Folkston RailWatch.

The old Atlantic Coast Line depot across the track from the viewing platform has been converted into the very interesting **Folkston Railroad Transportation Museum** (3795 Main St., 912/496-2536, www.

charltoncountyga.us, Mon.-Fri. 9am-5pm, Sat. 10am-3pm, free), with lots of history, maps, and technical stuff for the hardcore rail buff and novice alike.

## Restaurants

To fuel up in Folkston for your trek in the swamp, go no further than the friendly ★ **Okefenokee Restaurant** (1507 Third St., 912/496-3263, daily 11am-8pm, $10-20) across from the handsome county courthouse. Their huge buffet is a steal at under $10; come on Friday nights for a massive seafood buffet (mostly fried) for under $20 pp. In any case don't miss the fried catfish, featured at both buffets. It's some of the best I've had anywhere in the South.

## Hotels

For a bit of luxury in town, right outside the refuge's East Entrance is the excellent ★ **Inn at Folkston Bed and Breakfast** (509 W. Main St., 888/509-6246, www.innatfolkston.com, $120-170). There is nothing like coming back to its cozy Victorian charms after a long day out in the swamp. The four-room inn boasts an absolutely outstanding breakfast, an extensive reading library, and a whirlpool tub.

the Folkston Railroad Transportation Museum

# Background

# The Landscape

## GEOGRAPHY

The area covered by this guide falls within the Coastal Plain region of the southeastern United States, which contains some of the most unique ecosystems in North America. It's a place where water is never far away and features large in the daily lives, economy, and folkways of the region's people.

Although it's hundreds of miles away, the Appalachian mountain chain has a major influence on the southeastern coast. It's in Appalachia where so much of the coast's freshwater—in the form of rain—comes together and flows southeast—in the form of rivers—to the Atlantic Ocean. Moving east, the next level down from the Appalachians is the hilly Piedmont region, the eroded remains of an ancient mountain chain.

At the Piedmont's eastern edge is the fall line, so named because it's where rivers make a drop toward the sea, generally becoming navigable. Around the fall line zone in the Upper Coastal Plain you can sometimes spot sand hills, usually only a few feet in elevation, generally thought to be the vestigial remains of primordial sand dunes and offshore sandbars. Well beyond the fall line and the sometimes nearly invisible sand hills lies the Lower Coastal Plain, gradually built up over a 150-million-year span by sedimentary runoff from the Appalachian Mountains, which at that time were as high or even higher than the modern-day Himalayas.

The Coastal Plain was sea bottom for much of the earth's history, and in some eroded areas you can see dramatic proof of this in the form of prehistoric shells, shark's teeth, and fossilized whale bones and oyster beds, often many miles inland. Sea level has fluctuated wildly with climate and geological changes through the eons. At various times over the last 50 million years, the Coastal Plain has submerged, surfaced, and submerged again. At the height of the last major ice age, when global sea levels were very low, the east coast of North America extended out nearly 100 miles farther than the present shoreline. (We now call this former coastal region the continental shelf.) The Coastal Plain has been roughly in its current form for about the last 15,000 years.

### Rivers

Visitors from drier climates are sometimes shocked to see how huge the rivers can get in coastal Georgia and South Carolina. Wide and voluminous as they saunter to the sea, their seemingly slow speed belies the massive power they contain. Georgia and South Carolina's big alluvial, or sediment-bearing, rivers originate in the region of the Appalachian mountain chain.

The headwaters of the Savannah River, for example, are near Tallulah Gorge in extreme north Georgia. Some rivers form out of the confluence of smaller rivers, such as Georgia's mighty Altamaha River, actually the child of the Ocmulgee and Oconee Rivers in the middle of the state. Others, like the Ashley and Cooper Rivers in South Carolina, originate much closer to the coast in the Piedmont.

The blackwater river is a particularly interesting Southern phenomenon, duplicated only in South America and in one example each in New York and Michigan. While alluvial rivers generally originate in highlands and carry with them a large amount of sediment, blackwater rivers originate in low-lying areas and move slowly toward the sea, carrying with them very little sediment. Rather,

---

**Previous:** reenactors at Fort Frederica on St. Simons Island; the Old Exchange in Charleston their dark tea color comes from the tannic acid of decaying vegetation all along their banks, washed out by the slow, inexorable movement of the river toward the sea.

Blackwater courses featured prominently in this guide are the Edisto River (the longest blackwater river in the world), Ebenezer Creek near Savannah, and Georgia's Suwannee River, which originates in the Okefenokee Swamp and empties into the Gulf of Mexico. Georgia's Altamaha River is a hybrid of sorts because it is partially fed by the blackwater Ohoopee River.

## The Intracoastal Waterway

You'll often see its acronym, ICW, on signs—and sadly you'll probably hear the locals mispronounce it "intercoastal"—but the casual visitor might actually find the Intracoastal Waterway difficult to spot. Relying on a natural network of interconnected estuaries and channels, combined with artificial **cuts,** the ICW often blends in rather subtly with the region's already extensive network of creeks and rivers.

Mandated by Congress in 1919 and maintained by the U.S. Army Corps of Engineers, the Atlantic portion of the ICW runs from Key West, Florida, to Boston and carries recreational and barge traffic away from the perils of offshore currents and weather. Even if they don't use it specifically, kayakers and boaters often find themselves on it at some point during their nautical adventures.

## Estuaries

Most biologists will tell you that the Coastal Plain is where things get interesting. The place where a river interfaces with the ocean is called an estuary, and it's perhaps the most interesting place of all. Estuaries are heavily tidal in nature (indeed, the word derives from *aestus,* Latin for "tide"), and feature brackish water and heavy silt content. This portion of the U.S. coast typically has about a six- to eight-foot tidal range, and the coastal ecosystem depends on this steady ebb and flow for life. At high tide, shellfish open and feed. At

low tide, they literally clam up, keeping saltwater inside their shells until the next tide comes. Waterbirds and small mammals feed on shellfish and other animals at low tide, when their prey is exposed. High tide brings an influx of fish and nutrients from the sea, in turn drawing predators like dolphins, who often come into tidal creeks to feed. In the region covered by this guide, key estuaries from north to south are Cape Romain, Charleston Harbor, the ACE (Ashepoo, Combahee, Edisto) Basin, Beaufort River, May River, Calibogue Sound, Savannah River, Wilmington River, Midway River, Altamaha River, and the Brunswick River.

## Salt Marshes

All this water action in both directions—freshwater coming from inland, saltwater encroaching from the Atlantic—results in the phenomenon of the salt marsh, the single most recognizable and iconic geographic feature of the Georgia and South Carolina coast, also known simply as "wetlands." (Freshwater marshes are rarer, Florida's Everglades being perhaps the premier example.) Far more than just a transitional zone between land and water, marshes are also nature's nursery. Plant and animal life in marshes tend not only to be diverse, but to encompass multitudes as well.

You may not see its denizens easily, but on close inspection you'll find a marsh absolutely teeming with creatures. Visually, the main identifying feature of a salt marsh is its distinctive, reedlike marsh grasses, adapted to survive in brackish water. Like estuaries, marshes and all life in them are heavily influenced by the tides, which bring in nutrients.

The marsh has also played a key role in human history, for it was here that the massive rice and indigo plantations grew their signature crops, aided by the natural ebb and flow of the tides. While most marshes you see will look quite undisturbed, very little of them could be called pristine. In the heyday of the rice plantations, much of the coastal salt marsh was crisscrossed by the canal-and-dike system of the paddy fields.

You can still see evidence almost everywhere in this area if you look hard enough (the best time to look is right after takeoff or before landing in an airplane, since many approaches to regional airports take you over wetlands). Anytime you see a low, straight ridge running through a marsh, that's likely the eroded, overgrown remnant of an old paddy field dike. Kayakers occasionally find old wooden sluice gates on their paddles.

In the Lowcountry, you'll often hear the term **pluff mud.** This refers to the area's distinctive variety of soft, dark mud in the salt marsh, which often has an equally distinctive odor that locals love but some visitors have a hard time getting used to. Extraordinarily rich in nutrients, pluff mud helped make rice such a successful crop in the marshes of the Lowcountry.

In addition to their vital role as wildlife incubators and sanctuaries, wetlands are also one of the most important natural protectors of the health of the coastal region. They serve as natural filters, cleansing runoff from the land of toxins and pollutants before it hits the ocean. They also help humans by serving as natural hurricane barriers, their porous nature helping to ease the brunt of the damaging storm surge.

## Beaches and Barrier Islands

The beautiful, broad beaches of Georgia and South Carolina are almost all situated on barrier islands, long islands parallel to the shoreline and separated from the mainland by a sheltered body of water. Because they're formed from the deposit of sediment by offshore currents, they change shape over the years, with the general pattern of deposit going from north to south (meaning the northern end will begin eroding first). Most of the barrier islands are geologically quite young, only having formed within the last 25,000 years or so. Natural erosion by currents and by storms, combined with the accelerating effects of dredging for local port activity, has quickened the decline of many barrier islands. Many beaches in the area

are subject to a mitigation of erosion called **beach renourishment,** which generally involves redistributing dredged material closely offshore so that it will wash up on and around the beach.

As the name indicates, barrier islands are another of nature's safeguards against hurricane damage. Historically, the barrier islands have borne the vast bulk of the damage done by hurricanes in the region. Tybee Island near Savannah was completely under water in the hurricane of 1898. More recently, Sullivan's Island near Charleston was submerged by 1989's Hurricane Hugo. Like the marshes, barrier islands also help protect the mainland by absorbing the brunt of the storm's wind and surging water.

Though barrier islands are ephemeral by nature, they have played an important role in the area's geography from the beginning of time. In fact, nearly every major settlement on the Georgia coast today—including Savannah, Darien, and Brunswick—is built on the vestiges of massive barrier islands that once guarded a primordial shoreline many miles inland from the present one. By far the largest of these ancient barrier islands, now on dry land, is the fabled **Trail Ridge,** which runs from Jesup, Georgia, to Starke, Florida. The Trail Ridge's height all along its distance made it a favorite route first for Native Americans and then for railroads, which still run along its crest today. The Trail Ridge is such a dominant geographical feature even today that it's actually responsible for the formation of the Okefenokee Swamp. The ridge effectively acts as a levee on the swamp's eastern side, preventing its drainage to the sea.

## CLIMATE

One word comes to mind when one thinks about Southern climate: *hot.* That's the first word that occurs to Southerners as well, but virtually every survey of why residents are attracted to the area puts the climate at the top of the list. Go figure. How hot is hot? The average high for July, the region's hottest month, in Savannah is about 92°F, in Charleston about 89°F. While that's nothing compared to Tucson or Death Valley, when coupled with the region's notoriously high **humidity** it can have an altogether miserable effect.

Heat aside, there's no doubt that one of the most difficult things for an outsider to adjust to in the South is the humidity. The average annual humidity in Charleston and Savannah is about 55 percent in the afternoons and a whopping 85 percent in the mornings. The most humid months are August and September. There is no real antidote to humidity—other than air conditioning, that is—although many film crews and other outside workers swear by the use of Sea Breeze astringent. If you and your traveling companions can deal with the strong minty odor, dampen a hand towel with the astringent, drape it across the back of your neck, and go about your business.

Don't assume that because it's humid you shouldn't drink fluids. Just as in any hot climate, you should drink lots of water if you're going to be out in the Southern heat.

August and September are by far the wettest months in terms of rainfall, with averages well over six inches for each of those months. July is also quite wet, coming in at over five inches on average.

Winters here are pretty mild but can seem much colder than they actually are because of the dampness in the air. The coldest month is January, with a high of about 58°F for the month and 42°F the average low. You're highly unlikely to encounter snow in the area, but if you do, it will likely be only skimpy flurries that a resident of the Great Lakes region wouldn't even notice as snow. But don't let this lull you into a false sense of security.

If such a tiny flurry were to hit, be aware that most people down here have no clue how to drive in rough weather and will not be prepared for even such a small amount of snowfall. Visitors from snow country are often surprised, sometimes bordering on shock, by how completely a Southern city will shut down when that once-in-a-decade few tenths of an inch of snow finally hits.

## Hurricanes

The major weather phenomenon of concern for residents and visitors alike is the mighty hurricane. These massive storms, with counterclockwise-rotating bands of clouds and winds that can push 200 mph, are an ever-present danger to the southeast coast June-November each year. While the South Carolina coast has had its share of hurricane strikes, historically the Georgia coast has been relatively safe, if not immune, from major hurricane activity. In fact, as of this writing the last major storm to hit the Georgia coast directly was in 1898.

Meteorologists chalk this up to the Georgia coast's relatively sheltered, concave position relative to the rest of the southeastern coastline, as well as prevailing pressure and wind patterns that tend to deflect the oncoming storms. In any case, as most everyone is aware of now from the horrific, well-documented damage from such killer storms as Hugo, Andrew, and Katrina, hurricanes are not to be trifled with. Old-fashioned drunken "hurricane parties" are a thing of the past for the most part, the images of cataclysmic destruction everyone has seen on TV having long since eliminated any lingering romanticism about riding out the storm.

**Tornadoes**—especially those that come in the "back door" through the Gulf of Mexico and overland to the Georgia or Carolina coast—are a very present danger with hurricanes. As hurricanes die out over land, they can spawn dozens of tornadoes, which in many cases prove more destructive than the hurricanes that produced them.

Local TV, websites, and print media can be counted on to give more than ample warning in the event a hurricane is approaching the area during your visit. Whatever you do, do not discount the warnings; it's not worth it. If the locals are preparing to leave, you should too. Typically when a storm is likely to hit the area, there will first be a suggested evacuation. But if authorities determine there's an overwhelming likelihood of imminent hurricane damage, they will issue a **mandatory** evacuation order. What this means in practice is that if you do choose to stay behind, you cannot count on any type of emergency services or help whatsoever.

Generally speaking, the most lethal element of a hurricane is not the wind but the **storm surge,** the wall of ocean water that the winds drive before them onto the coast. During 1989's Hurricane Hugo, Charleston's Battery was inundated with a storm surge of over 12 feet, with an amazing 20 feet reported farther north at Cape Romain.

In the wake of such devastation, local governments have dramatically improved their once tepid disaster-response plans. For example, the large red traffic barriers you see stowed in their ready positions at many exits along I-16 in Georgia are a direct result of the chaos of the botched evacuation during Hurricane Floyd in 1999. Learning from that lesson, Georgia officials decided to make all four lanes of I-16 westbound in the event of a major evacuation, and those red barriers are there today to reroute traffic should they ever be needed.

## ENVIRONMENTAL ISSUES

The coast of Georgia and South Carolina is currently experiencing a double whammy, environmentally speaking: Not only are its distinctive wetlands extraordinarily sensitive to human interference, this is one of the most rapidly developing parts of the country. New and often poorly planned subdivisions and resort communities are popping up all over the place. Vastly increased port activity is also taking a devastating toll on the salt marsh and surrounding barrier islands. Combine all that with the South's often skeptical attitude toward environmental activism and you have a recipe for potential ecological disaster.

Thankfully, there are some bright spots. More and more communities are seeing the value of responsible planning and not greenlighting every new development sight unseen. Land trusts and other conservation organizations are growing in size, number, funding, and influence. The large number of marine biologists in these areas at various research and educational institutions means there's a wealth of education and talent available to advise local governments and citizens on how best to conserve the area's natural beauty.

Here's a closer look at some of the most urgent environmental issues facing the region today:

### Marsh Dieback

The dominant species of marsh grass, *Spartina alterniflora* (pronounced spar-TINE-uh) and *Juncus roemerianus,* thrive in the typically brackish water of the coastal marsh estuaries, their structural presence helping to stem erosion of banks and dunes. While drought and blight have taken their toll on the grass, increased coastal development and continued channel deepening have also led to a steady creep of ocean saltwater farther and farther into remaining marsh stands.

### Effects of Dredging

When Oglethorpe first sailed up the Savannah River, it was less than 20 feet deep. Today the Savannah River has been dredged to an average depth of 42 feet—and another deepening is planned, to nearly 50 feet.

Port activity is economically vital—and becoming more so—to the coastal cities of Charleston, Savannah, and Brunswick. The downside of such large-scale industrial dredging is threefold:

- The deeper the channel, the farther upstream salty ocean water is able to infiltrate. This destroys freshwater and brackish habitats such as the salt marsh.

- Deepening the channel increases both the volume and the velocity of the river, quickening erosion of the riverbanks.

- Too much dredging risks the intrusion of ocean saltwater into underground freshwater aquifers that provide drinking water to millions of people in the area.

Currently the debate over harbor deepening has hit home in both Charleston and

Savannah, two of the country's busiest ports. As of this writing the states of South Carolina and Georgia are both pursuing deepening at each city's port, much to the consternation of local environmentalists.

## The Paper Industry

Early in the 20th century, the Southeast's abundance of cheap undeveloped land and plentiful free water led to the establishment of massive pine tree farms to feed coastal pulp and paper mills. Chances are, if you used a paper grocery bag recently, it was made in a paper mill in the South.

But in addition to making a whole lot of paper bags and providing lots of employment for residents through the decades, the paper industry also gave the area lots of air and water pollution, stressed local rivers (it takes a lot of freshwater to make paper from trees), and took away natural species diversity from the area by devoting so much acreage to a single crop, pine trees.

When driving near rivers in this region, anytime you see a large industrial facility on the riverside it's probably a paper mill. The rotten egg smell that comes next is from the sulfurous discharge from its smokestacks.

## Aquifers

Unlike parts of the western United States, where individuals can enforce private property rights to water, the South has generally held that the region's water is a publicly held resource. The upside of this is that everybody has equal claim to drinking water without regard to status or income or how long they've lived here. The downside is that industry also has the same free claim to the water that citizens do—and they use a heck of a lot more of it.

Currently most of the Georgia and South

Carolina coasts get their water from aquifers, which are basically huge underground caverns made of limestone. Receiving **groundwater** drip by drip, century after century, from rainfall farther inland, the aquifers essentially act as massive sterile warehouses for freshwater, accessible through wells.

The aquifers have human benefit only if their water remains fresh. Once saltwater from the ocean begins intruding into an aquifer, it doesn't take much to render all of it unfit for human consumption—forever. What keeps that freshwater fresh is natural water pressure, keeping the ocean at bay.

But nearly a century ago, paper mills began pumping millions and millions of gallons of water out of coastal aquifers. Combined with the dramatic rise in coastal residential development and a continuing push to deepen existing shipping channels, the natural water pressure of the aquifers has decreased, leading to measurable saltwater intrusion at several points under the coast.

Currently, local and state governments in both states are increasing their reliance on **surface water** (treated water from rivers and creeks) to relieve the strain on the underground aquifer system. But it's too soon to tell if that has contained the threat from saltwater intrusion.

## Air Pollution

Despite growing awareness of the issue, air pollution is still a big problem in the coastal region. Paper mills still operate, putting out their distinctive rotten-eggs odor, and auto emissions standards are notoriously lax in both Georgia and South Carolina. The biggest culprits, though, are coal-powered electric plants, which are the norm throughout the region and which continue to pour large amounts of toxins into the atmosphere.

# Plants and Animals

## PLANTS

Probably the most iconic plant life of the coastal region is the **Southern live oak** (*Quercus virginiana*) the official state tree of Georgia. Named because of its evergreen nature, a live oak is technically any of a number of evergreens in the *Quercus* genus, many of which reside on the Georgia and South Carolina coast, but in local practice almost always refers to the Southern live oak.

Capable of living over 1,000 years and possessing wood of legendary resilience, the Southern live oak is one of nature's most magnificent creations. The timber value of live oaks has been well known since the earliest days of the American shipbuilding industry—when the oak dominated the entire coast inland of the marsh—but their value as a canopy tree has finally been widely recognized by local and state governments.

Fittingly, the other iconic plant life of the coastal region grows on the branches of the live oak. Contrary to popular opinion, **Spanish moss** (*Tillandsia usneoides*) is neither Spanish nor moss. It's an air plant, a wholly indigenous cousin to the pineapple. Also contrary to folklore, Spanish moss is not a parasite nor does it harbor parasites while living on an oak tree—although it can after it has already fallen to the ground.

Also growing on the bark of a live oak, especially right after a rain shower, is the **resurrection fern** (*Polypodium polypodioides*), which can stay dormant for amazingly long periods of time, only to spring back to life with the introduction of a little water. You can find live oak, Spanish moss, and resurrection fern anywhere in the **maritime forest** ecosystem of coastal Georgia and South Carolina, a zone generally behind the **interdune meadows,** which is right behind the beach zone.

The oak may be Georgia's state tree, but far and away its most important commercial

a live oak tree on Cumberland Island

tree is the pine, used for paper, lumber, and turpentine. Rarely seen in the wild today due to tree farming, which has covered most of southern Georgia, the dominant species is now the **slash pine** (*Pinus elliottii*), often seen in long rows on either side of rural highways. Before the introduction of large-scale monoculture tree farming, however, a rich variety of native pines flourished in the **upland forest** inland from the maritime forest, including **longleaf** (*Pinus palustris*) and **loblolly** (*Pinus taeda*) pines.

Right up there with live oaks and Spanish moss in terms of instant recognition would have to be the colorful, ubiquitous **azalea**, a flowering shrub of the *Rhododendron* genus. Over 10,000 varieties have been cultivated through the centuries, with quite a wide range of them on display during blooming season, March-April, on the Georgia and South Carolina coast (slightly earlier farther south, slightly later farther north).

The area's other great floral display comes from the **camellia** (*Camellia japonica*), a large, cold-hardy evergreen shrub that generally blooms in late winter (Jan.-Mar.). An import from Asia, the southeastern coast's camellias are close cousins to *Camellia sinensis*, also an import and the plant from which tea is made.

Other colorful ornamentals of the area include the ancient and beautiful **Southern magnolia** (*Magnolia grandiflora*), a native plant with distinctive large white flowers that evolved before the advent of bees; and the **flowering dogwood** (*Cornus florida*), which, despite its very hard wood—great for daggers, hence its original name "dagwood"—is actually quite fragile. An ornamental imported from Asia that has now become quite obnoxious in its aggressive invasiveness is the **mimosa** (*Albizia julibrissin*), which blooms March-August.

Moving into watery areas, you'll find the remarkable **bald cypress** (*Taxodium distichum*), a flood-resistant conifer recognizable by its tufted top, its great height (up to 130 feet), and its distinctive "knees," parts of

the root that project above the waterline and which are believed to help stabilize the tree in lowland areas. Much prized for its beautiful pest-resistant wood, great stands of ancient cypress once dominated the marsh along the coast; sadly, overharvesting and destruction of wetlands has made the magnificent sight of this ancient, dignified species much less common. The acres of **smooth cordgrass** for which the Golden Isles are named are plants of the *Spartina alterniflora* species. (A cultivated cousin, *Spartina anglica,* is considered invasive.) Besides its simple natural beauty, *Spartina* is also a key food source for marsh denizens. Playing a key environmental role on the coast are **sea oats** (*Uniola paniculata*). This wispy, fast-growing perennial grass anchors sand dunes and hence is a protected species on the Georgia coast (it's a misdemeanor to pick them).

South Carolina isn't called the "Palmetto State" for nothing. Palm varieties are not as common up here as in Florida, but you'll definitely encounter several types along the Georgia and South Carolina coast. The **cabbage palm** (*Sabal palmetto*), for which South Carolina is nicknamed, is the largest variety, up to 50-60 feet tall. Its "heart of palm" is an edible delicacy, which coastal Native Americans boiled in bear fat to make porridge. In dunes and sand hills you'll find clumps of the low-lying **saw palmetto** (*Serenoa repens*). The **bush palmetto** (*Sabal minor*) has distinctive fan-shaped branches. The common **Spanish bayonet** (*Yucca aloifolia*) looks like a palm, but it's actually a member of the agave family.

## ANIMALS
### On the Land

Perhaps the most iconic land animal—or semi-land animal, anyway—of the Georgia and South Carolina coast is the legendary **American alligator** (*Alligator mississippiensis*), the only species of crocodilian native to the area. Contrary to their fierce reputation, locals know these massive reptiles, 6-12 feet long as adults, to be quite shy. If you come in the colder months, you won't see them at all, since alligators require an outdoor temperature over 70°F to become active and feed (indeed, the appearance of alligators was once a well-known symbol of spring in the area).

Often all you'll see is a couple of eyebrow ridges sticking out of the water, and a gator lying still in a shallow creek can easily be mistaken for a floating log. But should you see one or more gators basking in the sun—a favorite activity on warm days for these cold-blooded creatures—it's best to admire them from afar. A mother alligator, in particular, will destroy anything that comes near her nest. Despite the alligator's short, stubby legs, it can run amazingly fast on land—faster than you, in fact.

If you're driving on a country road at night, be on the lookout for **white-tailed deer** (*Odocoileus virginianus*), which, besides being quite beautiful, also pose a serious road hazard. Because coastal development has dramatically reduced the habitat—and therefore the numbers—of their natural predators, deer are very plentiful throughout the area, and as you read this they are hard at work devouring vast tracts of valuable vegetation. No one wants to hurt poor little Bambi, but the truth is that area hunters perform a valuable service by culling the local deer population, which is in no danger of extinction anytime soon.

The coast hosts fairly large populations of playful **river otters** (*Lontra canadensis*). Not to be confused with the larger sea otters of the West Coast, these fast-swimming members of the weasel family inhabit inland waterways and marshy areas, with dominant males sometimes ranging as much as 50 miles within a single waterway. While you're unlikely to encounter an otter, if you're camping, you might easily run into the **raccoon** (*Procyon lotor*), an exceedingly intelligent and crafty relative of the bear, sharing that larger animal's resourcefulness in stealing your food. Though nocturnal, raccoons will feed whenever food is available. Rabies is prevalent in the raccoon population, and you should always, always keep your distance.

Another common campsite nuisance, the

a river otter on the Suwannee River

**opossum** (*Didelphis virginiana*) is a shy, primitive creature that is much more easily discouraged. North America's only marsupial, an opossum's usual "defense" against predators is to play dead. That said, however, they have an immunity to snake venom and often feed on the reptiles, even the most poisonous ones.

While you're unlikely to actually see a **red fox** (*Vulpes vulpes*), you might very well see their distinctive footprints in the mud of a marsh at low tide. These nocturnal hunters, a nonnative species introduced by European settlers, range the coast seeking mice, squirrels, and rabbits.

Once fairly common in Georgia and South Carolina, the **black bear** (*Ursus americanus*) has suffered from hunting and habitat destruction. Of the regions in this guide, the Okefenokee Swamp area is the only place in which you'll be close to one.

## In the Water

Without a doubt the most magnificent

denizen—if only part-time—of the southeastern coast is the **North Atlantic right whale** (*Eubalaena glacialis*), which can approach 60 feet in length. Each year December-March the mothers give birth to their calves and nurse them in the warm waters off the Georgia coast in an eons-old ritual. (In the summers they like to hang around the rich fishing grounds off the New England coast, although biologists still can't account for their whereabouts at other times of the year.) Their numbers were so abundant in past centuries that the Spanish name for Jekyll Island, Georgia, was Isla de las Ballenas (Island of the Whales). Whaling and encounters with ship propellers have taken their toll, and numbers of this endangered species are dwindling fast now, with fewer than 500 estimated left in the world.

Another of humankind's aquatic cousins, the **bottlenose dolphin** (*Tursiops truncatus*) is a well-known and frequent visitor to the coast, coming far upstream into creeks and rivers to feed. Children, adults, and experienced sailors alike all delight in encounters with the mammals, sociable creatures who travel in family units. They will gather near boats, surfacing often with the distinctive chuffing sound of air coming from their blowholes. Occasionally they'll even lift their heads out of the water to have a look at you; consider yourself lucky indeed to have such a close encounter. Don't be fooled by their cuteness, however. Dolphins live life with gusto and aren't scared of much. They're voracious eaters of fish, energetic lovers, and will take on an encroaching shark in a heartbeat.

Another beloved part-time marine creature of the barrier islands of the Georgia and South Carolina coast is the **loggerhead turtle** (*Caretta caretta*). Though the species prefers to stay well offshore most of the year, females weighing up to 300 pounds come out of the sea each May-July to dig a shallow hole in the dunes and lay over 100 leathery eggs, returning to the ocean and leaving the eggs to hatch on their own after two months.

Interestingly, the mothers prefer to nest at the same spot on the same island year after year. After hatching, the baby turtles then make a dramatic, extremely dangerous (and extremely slow) trek to the safety of the waves, at the mercy of various predators. A series of dedicated research and conservation efforts, like the Caretta Project based on Wassaw Island, Georgia, are working hard to protect the loggerheads' traditional nursery grounds to ensure survival of this fascinating, loveable, and threatened species.

Of course, the coastal waters and rivers are chockablock with fish. The most abundant and sought-after recreational species in the area is the **spotted sea trout** (*Cynoscion nebulosus*), followed by the **red drum** (*Sciaenops ocellatus*). Local anglers also pursue many varieties of **bass, bream, sheepshead,** and **crappie.** It may sound strange to some accustomed to considering it a "trash" fish, but many types of **catfish** are not only plentiful here but are a common and well-regarded food source. Many species of **flounder** inhabit the silty bottoms of estuaries all along the coast. Farther offshore are game and sport fish like **marlin, swordfish, shark, grouper,** and **tuna.**

Each March, anglers jockey for position on coastal rivers for the yearly running of the **American shad** (*Alosa sapidissima*) upstream to spawn. This large (up to eight pounds) catfish-like species is a regional delicacy as a seasonal entrée as well as for its tasty roe. There's a catch limit of eight shad per person per season. One of the more interesting fish species in the area is the endangered **shortnose sturgeon** (*Acipenser brevirostrum*). A fantastically ancient species that has evolved little in hundreds of millions of years, this small freshwater fish is known to exist in the Altamaha, Savannah, and Ogeechee Rivers of Georgia and the estuaries of the ACE Basin in South Carolina. Traveling upriver to spawn in the winter, the sturgeons remain around the mouths of waterways the rest of the year, venturing near the ocean only sparingly.

Crustaceans and shellfish have been a key food staple in the area for thousands of years, with the massive shell middens of the coast being testament to Native Americans' healthy appetite for them. The beds of the local variant, the **eastern oyster** (*Crassostrea virginica*), aren't what they used to be due to overharvesting, water pollution, and disruption of habitat. In truth, these days most local restaurants import the little filter feeders from the Gulf of Mexico. Oysters spawn May-August, hence the old folk wisdom about eating oysters only in months with the letter *r* so as not to disrupt the breeding cycle.

Each year April-January, shrimp boats up and down the southeastern coast trawl for **shrimp,** most commercially viable in two local species, the white shrimp (*Litopenaeus setiferus*) and the brown shrimp (*Farfantepenaeus aztecus*). Shrimp are the most popular seafood item in the United States and account for bringing hundreds of millions of dollars in revenue into the coastal economy. While consumption won't slow down anytime soon, the Georgia and South Carolina shrimping industries are facing serious threats, both from species decline due to pollution and overfishing as well as from competition from shrimp farms and the Asian shrimp industry.

Another important commercial crop is the **blue crab** (*Callinectes sapidus*), the species used in such Lowcountry delicacies as crab cakes. You'll often see floating markers bobbing up and down in rivers throughout the region. These signal the presence directly below of a crab trap, often of an amateur crabber.

A true living link to primordial times, the alien-looking **horseshoe crab** (*Limulus polyphemus*) is frequently found on beaches of the coast during the spring mating season (it lives in deeper water the rest of the year). More closely related to scorpions and spiders than crabs, the horseshoe has evolved hardly a lick in hundreds of millions of years.

Any trip to a local salt marsh at low tide will likely uncover hundreds of **fiddler crabs** (*Uca pugilator* and *Uca pugnax*), so-named for the way the males wave their single enlarged claw in the air to attract mates. (Their other,

smaller claw is the one they actually eat with.) The fiddlers make distinctive burrows in the pluff mud for sanctuary during high tide, recognizable by the little balls of sediment at the entrances (the crabs spit out the balls after sifting through the sand for food).

One charming beach inhabitant, the **sand dollar** (*Mellita quinquiesperforata*), has seen its numbers decline drastically due to being entirely too charming for its own good. Beachcombers are now asked to enjoy these flat little cousins to the sea urchin in their natural habitat and to refrain from taking them home. Besides, they start to smell bad when they dry out.

The **sea nettle** (*Chrysaora quinquecirrha*), a less-than-charming beach inhabitant, is a jellyfish that stings thousands of people on the coast each year (although only for those with severe allergies are the stings potentially life threatening). Stinging their prey before transporting it into their waiting mouths, the jellyfish also sting when disturbed or frightened. Most often, people are stung by stepping on the bodies of jellyfish washed up on the sand. If you're stung by a jellyfish, don't panic. You'll probably experience a stinging rash for about half an hour. Locals say applying a little baking soda or vinegar helps cut the sting. (Some also swear fresh urine will do the trick, and I pass that tip along to you purely in the interest of thoroughness.)

## In the Air

When enjoying the marshlands of the coast, consider yourself fortunate to see a **wood stork** (*Mycteria americana*), very recently taken off the endangered species list. The only storks to breed in North America, these graceful long-lived birds (routinely living over 10 years) are usually seen on a low flight path across the marsh, although at some birding spots beginning in late summer you can find them at a **roost,** sometimes numbering over 100 birds. Resting at high tide, they fan out over the marsh to feed at low tide on foot. Old-timers sometimes call them "Spanish buzzards" or simply "the preacher."

Often confused with the wood stork is the gorgeous **white ibis** (*Eudocimus albus*), distinguishable by its orange bill and black wingtips. Like the wood stork, the ibis is a communal bird that roosts in colonies.

Other similar-looking coastal denizens are the white-feathered **great egret** (*Ardea alba*) and **snowy egret** (*Egretta thula*), the former distinguishable by its yellow bill and the latter by its black bill and the tuft of plumes on the back of its head. Egrets are in the same family as herons.

The most magnificent in that family is the **great blue heron** (*Ardea herodias*). Despite their imposing height—up to four feet tall—these waders are shy. Often you hear them rather than see them, a loud shriek of alarm that echoes over the marsh.

So how to tell the difference between all these wading birds at a glance? It's actually easiest when they're in flight. Egrets and herons fly with their necks tucked in, while storks and ibis fly with their necks extended.

Dozens of species of shorebirds comb the beaches, including **sandpipers, plovers,** and the wonderful and rare **American oystercatcher** (*Haematopus palliatus*), instantly recognizable for its prancing walk, dark-brown back, stark white underside, and long bright-orange bill. **Gulls** and **terns** also hang out wherever there's water. They can frequently be seen swarming around incoming shrimp boats, attracted by the catch of little crustaceans.

The chief raptor of the salt marsh is the fish-eating **osprey** (*Pandion haliaetus*). These large grayish birds of prey are similar to eagles but are adapted to a maritime environment, with a reversible outer toe on each talon (the better for catching wriggly fish) and closable nostrils so they can dive into the water after prey. Very common all along the coast, they like to build big nests on top of buoys and channel markers in addition to trees.

The **bald eagle** (*Haliaeetus leucocephalus*) is making a comeback in the area thanks to increased federal regulation and better education of trigger-happy locals. Apparently not as all-American as their bumper stickers might sometimes indicate, local farmers would often regard the national symbol as more of a nuisance and fire away anytime they saw one. Of course, as we all should have learned in school, the bald eagle is not actually bald but has a head adorned with white feathers. Like the osprey, bald eagles prefer fish, but unlike the osprey will settle for rodents and rabbits.

Inland among the pines you'll find the most common area woodpecker, the huge **pileated woodpecker** (*Dryocopus pileatus*) with its large crest. Less common is the smaller, more subtly marked **red-cockaded woodpecker** (*Picoides borealis*). Once common in the vast primordial pine forests of the Southeast, the species is now endangered, its last real refuge being the big tracts of relatively undisturbed land on military bases.

## Insects

Down here they say that God invented bugs to keep the Yankees from completely taking over the South. And insects are probably the most unpleasant fact of life in the southeastern coastal region. The list of annoying indigenous insects must begin with the infamous **sand gnat** (*Culicoides furens*). This tiny and persistent nuisance, a member of the midge family, lacks the precision of the mosquito with its long proboscis. No, the sand gnat is more torture master than surgeon, brutally gouging and digging away its victim's skin until it hits a source of blood. Most prevalent in the spring and fall, the sand gnat is drawn to its prey by the carbon dioxide trail of its breath. While long sleeves and long pants are one way to keep gnats at bay, the only real antidote to the sand gnat's assault—other than never breathing—is the Avon skin-care product Skin So Soft, which has taken on a new and wholly unplanned life as the South's favorite anti-gnat lotion. In calmer moments, grow to appreciate the great contribution sand gnats make to the salt marsh ecosystem—as food for birds and bats.

Running a close second to the sand gnat are the over three dozen species of highly aggressive **mosquito,** which breeds anywhere a few drops of water lie stagnant. Not surprisingly, massive populations blossom in the rainiest months, in late spring and late summer, feeding in the morning and late afternoon. Like the gnat, the mosquito—the biters are always female—homes in on its victim by trailing the plume of carbon dioxide exhaled in the breath. More than just a biting nuisance, mosquitoes are now carrying West Nile disease to the Lowcountry and Georgia coast, signaling a possibly dire threat to public health. Alas, Skin So Soft has little effect on the mosquito. Try over-the-counter sprays, anything smelling of citronella, and wearing long sleeves and long pants when weather permits.

But undoubtedly the most viscerally loathed of all pests on the Lowcountry and Georgia coasts is the so-called "palmetto bug," or **American cockroach** (*Periplaneta americana*). These black, shiny, and sometimes grotesquely massive insects—up to two inches long—are living fossils, virtually unchanged over hundreds of millions of years. And perfectly adapted as they are to life in and among wet, decaying vegetation, they're unlikely to change a bit in 100 million more years. While they spend most of their time crawling around, usually under rotting leaves and tree bark, American cockroaches can indeed

fly—sort of. There are few more hilarious sights than a room full of people frantically trying to dodge a palmetto bug that has just clumsily launched itself off a high point on the wall. Because the cockroach doesn't know any better than you do where it's going, it can be a particularly bracing event—though the insect does not bite and poses few real health hazards.

Popular regional use of the term *palmetto bug* undoubtedly has its roots in a desire for polite Southern society to avoid using the ugly word *roach* and its connotations of filth and unclean environments. But the colloquialism actually has a basis in reality. Contrary to what anyone tells you, the natural habitat of the American cockroach—unlike its kitchen-dwelling, much-smaller cousin the German cockroach—is outdoors, often up in trees. They only come inside human dwellings when it's especially hot, especially cold, or especially dry outside. Like you, the palmetto bug is easily driven indoors by extreme temperatures and by thirst.

Other than visiting the Southeast during the winter, when the roaches go dormant, there's no convenient antidote for their presence. The best way to keep them out of your life is to stay away from decaying vegetation and keep doors and windows closed on especially hot nights.

# History

## BEFORE THE EUROPEANS

Based on artifacts found throughout the state, anthropologists know the first humans arrived on the coasts of South Carolina and Georgia at least 13,000 years ago, at the tail end of the last ice age. During this **Paleo-Indian Period,** sea levels were over 200 feet lower than present levels, and large mammals such as woolly mammoths, horses, and camels were hunted for food and skins. However, rapidly increasing temperatures, rising sea levels,

and efficient hunting techniques combined to quickly kill off these large mammals, relics of the Pleistocene Era, ushering in the **Archaic Period.** Still hunter-gatherers, Archaic Period Indians began turning to small game such as deer, bears, and turkeys, supplemented with fruit and nuts. The latter part of the Archaic era saw more habitation on the coasts, with an increasing reliance on fish and shellfish. It's to this time that the great **shell middens** of the Georgia and South Carolina coasts trace their origins. Basically serving as trash heaps for discarded oyster shells, as the middens grew in size they also took on a ceremonial status, often being used as sites for important rituals and meetings. Such sites are often called **shell rings,** and the largest yet found was over nine feet high and 300 feet in diameter.

The introduction of agriculture and improved pottery techniques about 3,000 years ago led to the **Woodland Period** of Native American settlement. Extended clan groups were much less migratory, establishing year-round communities of up to 50 people, who began the practice of clearing land to grow crops. The ancient shell middens of their ancestors were not abandoned, however, and were continually added onto. Native Americans had been cremating or burying their dead for years, a practice that eventually gave rise to the construction of the first **mounds** during the Woodland Period. Essentially built-up earthworks sometimes marked with spiritual symbols, often in the form of animal shapes, mounds not only contained the remains of the deceased but items like pottery to accompany the deceased into the afterlife.

Increased agriculture led to increased population, and with that population growth came competition over resources and a more formal notion of warfare. This period, about AD 800-1600, is termed the **Mississippian Period.** It was the Mississippians who would be the first Native Americans in what's now the continental United States to encounter European explorers and settlers after Columbus. The Native Americans who would later be called **Creek Indians** were the direct descendants of the Mississippians in lineage, language, and lifestyle. Native American social structure north of Mexico reached its apex with the Mississippians, who were not only prodigious mound builders but constructed elaborate wooden villages and evolved a top-down class system. The defensive palisades surrounding some of the villages attest to the increasingly martial nature of the groups and their chieftains, or *micos*.

Described by later European accounts as a tall, proud people, the Mississippians often wore elaborate body art and, like the indigenous inhabitants of Central and South America, used the practice of **head shaping,** whereby an infant's skull was deliberately deformed into an elongated shape by tying the baby's head to a board for about a year.

## THE SPANISH ARRIVE

The first known contact by Europeans on the southeastern coast came in 1521, roughly concurrent with Cortés's conquest of Mexico. A party of Spanish slavers ventured into what's now Port Royal Sound, South Carolina, from Santo Domingo in the Caribbean. Naming the area Santa Elena, they kidnapped a few Indian slaves and left, ranging as far north as the Cape Fear River in present-day North Carolina.

The first serious exploration of the coast came in 1526, when Lucas Vázquez de Ayllón and about 600 colonists made landfall at Winyah Bay in South Carolina, near present-day Georgetown. They didn't stay long, however, immediately moving down the coast and trying to set down roots in the St. Catherine's Sound area of modern-day Liberty County, Georgia.

That colony—called San Miguel de Gualdape—was the first European settlement in North America since the Vikings (the continent's oldest continuously occupied settlement, St. Augustine, Florida, wasn't founded until 1565). The colony also brought with it the seed of a future nation's dissolution: slaves from Africa. While San Miguel lasted only six weeks due to political tension and a slave uprising, artifacts from its brief life have been discovered in the area.

Hernando de Soto's ill-fated trek of 1539-1543 from Florida through Georgia to Alabama (where De Soto died of a fever) did not find the gold he anticipated, nor did it enter the coastal region covered in this guide. But De Soto's legacy was indeed soon felt there and throughout the Southeast in the form of various diseases for which the Mississippian people had no immunity whatsoever:

smallpox, typhus, influenza, measles, yellow fever, whooping cough, diphtheria, tuberculosis, and bubonic plague.

While the cruelties of the Spanish certainly took their toll, these deadly diseases were far more damaging to a population totally unprepared for them. Within a few years, the Mississippian people—already in a state of internal decline—were losing huge percentages of their population to disease, echoing what had already happened on a massive scale to the indigenous people of the Caribbean after Christopher Columbus's expeditions. As the viruses they introduced ran rampant, the Europeans themselves stayed away for a couple of decades after the ignominious end of De Soto's fruitless quest.

During that quarter-century, the once-proud Mississippian culture continued to disintegrate, dwindling into a shadow of its former greatness. In all, disease would claim the lives of at least 80 percent of all indigenous inhabitants of the Western Hemisphere.

## THE FRENCH MISADVENTURE

The next European presence on the Georgia and South Carolina coast was another ill-fated attempt, the establishment of Charlesfort in 1562 by French Huguenots under Jean Ribault on present-day Parris Island, South Carolina. Part of a covert effort by the Protestant French admiral Gaspard II de Coligny to send Huguenot colonists around the globe, Ribault's crew of 150 first explored the mouth of the St. Johns River near present-day Jacksonville, Florida, before heading north.

After establishing Charlesfort, Ribault returned to France for supplies. In his absence, religious war had broken out in his home country. Ribault sought sanctuary in England but was clapped in irons anyway. Meanwhile, most of Charlesfort's colonists grew so demoralized they joined another French expedition led by René Laudonnière at Fort Caroline on the St. Johns River. The remaining 27 built a ship to sail from Charlesfort back to France; 20 of them survived the journey, which was cut short in the English Channel when they had to be rescued.

Ribault himself was dispatched to reinforce Fort Caroline, but was headed off by a contingent from the new Spanish settlement at St. Augustine. The fate of the French presence on the southeast coast was sealed when not only did the Spanish take Fort Caroline but a storm destroyed Ribault's reinforcing fleet; Ribault and all survivors were killed as soon as they came ashore. To keep the French away for good and cement Spain's hold on this northernmost part of their province of La Florida, the Spanish built the fort of Santa Elena directly on top of Charlesfort. Both layers are currently being excavated and studied.

## THE MISSION ERA

With Spanish dominance of the region ensured for the near future, the lengthy mission era began. It's rarely mentioned as a key part of U.S. history, but the Spanish missionary presence on the Georgia coast was longer and more comprehensive than its much more widely known counterpart in California. St. Augustine's governor Pedro Menéndez de Avilés—sharing "biscuits with honey" on the beach at St. Catherine's Island with a local *mico*—negotiated for the right to establish a system of Jesuit missions in two coastal chiefdoms: the Mocama on and around Cumberland Island, and the Guale (pronounced "wallie") to the north. Those early missions, the first north of Mexico, were largely unsuccessful. But a renewed, organized effort by the Franciscan Order came to fruition during the 1580s. Starting with Santa Catalina de Guale on St. Catherine's Island, missions were established all along the Georgia coast.

The looming invasion threat to St. Augustine from English adventurer and privateer Sir Francis Drake was a harbinger of trouble to come, as was a Guale uprising in 1597. The Spanish consolidated their positions near St. Augustine, and Santa Elena was abandoned. As Spanish power waned, in 1629 Charles I of England laid formal claim to what is now the Carolinas, Georgia, and much of Florida, but made no effort to colonize the area. Largely left to their own devices and facing an indigenous population dying from disease, the missions in the Georgia interior nonetheless carried on. A devastating Indian raid in 1661 on a mission at the mouth of the Altamaha River, possibly aided by the English, persuaded the Spanish to pull the mission effort to the barrier islands. But even as late as 1667, right before the founding of Charles Towne far to the north, there were 70 missions still extant in the old Guale kingdom.

Pirate raids and slave uprisings finished off the Georgia missions for good by 1684. By 1706 the Spanish mission effort in the Southeast had fully retreated to St. Augustine. In an interesting postscript, 89 Native Americans—the only surviving descendants of Spain's Georgia missions—evacuated to Cuba with the final Spanish exodus from Florida in 1763.

## ENTER THE ENGLISH

With the native populations in steep decline due to disease and a wholesale retrenchment by European powers, a sort of vacuum came to the southeastern coast. Into the vacuum came the first English-speaking settlers of South Carolina. The first attempt was an expedition by a Barbadian colonist, William Hilton, in 1663. While he didn't establish a new colony, he did leave his name on the most notable geographic feature he saw—Hilton Head Island.

In 1665 King Charles II gave a charter to eight **Lords Proprietors** to establish a colony, generously to be named Carolina after the monarch himself. (One of the Proprietors, Lord Ashley Cooper, would see not one but both rivers in the Charleston area named after him.) Remarkably, none of the Proprietors ever set foot in the colony they established for their own profit. Before their colony was even set up, the Proprietors themselves set the stage for the vast human disaster that would eventually befall it. They encouraged slavery by promising that each colonist would receive 20 acres of land for every black male slave and

10 acres for every black female slave brought to the colony within the first year.

In 1666 explorer Robert Sandford officially claimed Carolina for the king. The Proprietors then sent out a fleet of three ships from England, only one of which, the *Carolina,* would make it the whole way. After stops in the thriving English colonies of Barbados and Bermuda, the ship landed in Port Royal. The settlers were greeted without violence, but the fact that the local indigenous people spoke Spanish led the colonists to conclude that perhaps the site was too close for comfort to Spain's sphere of influence.

A Kiawah chief, eager for allies against the fierce, slave-trading Westo people, invited the colonists north to settle instead. So the colonists—148 of them, including three African slaves—moved 80 miles up the coast and in 1670 pitched camp on the Ashley River at a place they dubbed Albemarle Point after one of their lost ships. Living within the palisades of the camp—you can visit it today at the Charles Towne Landing State Historic Site just outside Charleston—the colonists farmed 10-acre plots outside the walls.

A few years later some colonists from Barbados, which was beginning to suffer the effects of overpopulation, joined the Carolinians. The Barbadian influence, with an emphasis on large-scale slave labor and a caste system, would have an indelible imprint on the colony. Indeed, within a generation a majority of settlers in the new colony would be African slaves.

By 1680, however, Albemarle Point was feeling growing pains as well, and the Proprietors ordered the site moved to Oyster Point at the confluence of the Ashley and Cooper Rivers (the present-day Battery). Within a year Albemarle Point was abandoned, and the walls of Charles Towne were built a few hundred yards up from Oyster Point on the banks of the Cooper River.

The original Anglican settlers were quickly joined by various **Dissenters,** among them French Huguenots, Quakers, Congregationalists, and Jews. A group of

# Henry Woodward, Colonial Indiana Jones

He's virtually unsung in the history books, and there are no movies made about him, but Dr. Henry Woodward, the first English settler in South Carolina, lived a life that is the stuff of novels and screenplays. Educated in medicine in London, Woodward first tried his hand in the colony of Barbados. But Barbados, crowded and run by the elite planters, was no place for a young man with a sense of adventure but no contacts in the sugar industry. Still in his teens, Woodward left Barbados in Captain Robert Sandford's 1664 expedition to Carolina. Landing in the Cape Fear region, Sandford's cohort made its way down to Port Royal Sound to contact the Cusabo Indians. In 1666, in what is perhaps the New World's first "cultural exchange program," Woodward volunteered to stay behind while the rest of the expedition returned to England with a Native American named Shadoo.

Woodward learned the local language and established political relations with surrounding Native Americans, actions for which the Lords Proprietors granted him temporary "formall possession of the whole Country to hold as Tennant att Will." The Spanish had different plans, however. They came and kidnapped the young Englishman, taking him to what turned out to be a very permissive state of house arrest at the Spanish stronghold of St. Augustine in Florida. Surprising the Spanish with his request—in Latin, no less—to convert to Catholicism, Woodward was popular and treated well. An excellent student of the Catechism, Woodward became a favorite of the Spanish governor and was even promoted to official surgeon. During that time, he studied Spanish government, commerce, and culture, with the same diligence with which he had studied the Indians a year earlier. In 1668, Woodward was "rescued" by English privateers—pirates, really—under the command of Robert Searle, who'd come to sack St. Augustine. Woodward's sojourn with the pirates would last two years, during which he was kept on board as ship's surgeon. Was the pirate raid a coincidence? Or, as some scholars suggest, was Woodward really one of history's greatest spies? We will probably never know.

Incredibly, the plot thickens. In another coincidence, in 1670 Woodward was rescued when the pirates shipwrecked on the Caribbean island of Nevis. His rescuers were none other than the settlers on their way to found Charles Towne. Upon landfall, Woodward asserted his previous experience in the area to direct the colonists away from Port Royal to an area of less Spanish influence. That same year he began a series of expeditions to contact Native Americans in the Carolina interior—the first non-Spanish European to set foot in the area. Using economic espionage gained from the Spanish, Woodward's goal was to jump-start the trade in deerskins that would be the bulwark of the Charles Towne colony. Woodward's unlikely 1674 alliance with the aggressive Westo people was instrumental in this burgeoning trade. As if all this weren't enough, in 1680 Woodward, now with property of his own on Johns Island, would introduce local farmers to a certain strange crop recently imported from Madagascar: rice.

Woodward made enemies, however, of settlers who were envious of his growing affluence and suspicious of his friendship with the Westo. His outspoken disgust with the spread of Indian slavery brought a charge against him of undermining the interests of the crown. But Woodward, by now a celebrity of sorts, returned to England to plead his case directly to the Lords Proprietors. They not only pardoned him but made him their official Indian agent—with a 20 percent share of the profits. Woodward would never again see the land of his birth. He returned to the American colonies to trek inland, making alliances with groups of Creek Indians in Spanish-held territory. Hounded by Spanish troops, Woodward fell ill of a fever somewhere in the Savannah River valley. He made it to Charleston and safety but never fully recovered and died around 1690—after living the kind of life you usually only see in the movies.

Scottish Presbyterians established the short-lived Stuart Town near Port Royal in 1684. Recognizing this diversity, the colony in 1697 granted religious liberty to all "except Papists," meaning Catholics. The Anglicans attempted a crackdown on Dissenters in 1704, but two years later Queen Anne stepped in and ensured religious freedom for all Carolinians (again with the exception of Catholics, who wouldn't be a factor in the colony until after the American Revolution).

## THE YAMASEE WAR

Within 20 years the English presence had expanded throughout the Lowcountry to include Port Royal and Beaufort. Charles Towne became a thriving commercial center, dealing in deerskins with traders in the interior and with foreign concerns from England to South America. Its success was not without a backlash, as the local Yamasee people became increasingly disgruntled at the settlers' growing monopolies on deerskin and the trade in Native American slaves.

As rumors of war spread, on Good Friday, 1715, a delegation of six Carolinians went to the Yamasee village of Pocataligo to address some of the Native Americans' grievances in the hopes of forestalling violence. Their effort was in vain, however, as warriors murdered four of them in their sleep, the remaining two escaping to sound the alarm.

The treacherous attack signaled the beginning of the two-year Yamasee War, which would claim the lives of nearly 10 percent of the colony's population and an unknown number of Native Americans—making it one of the bloodiest conflicts fought on American soil.

Energized and ready for war, the Yamasee attacked Charles Towne itself and killed almost all the white traders in the interior, effectively ending commerce in the area. As Charles Towne began to swell with refugees from the hinterland, water and supplies ran low, and the colony's very existence was in peril.

After an initially poor performance by the Carolina militia, a professional army—including armed African slaves—was raised. Well trained and well led, the new army more than held its own despite being outnumbered. A key alliance with local Cherokees was all the advantage the colonists needed to turn the tide. While the Cherokee never received the overt military backing from the settlers that they sought, they did garner enough supplies and influence to convince their Creek rivals, the Yamasee, to begin the peace process. The war-weary settlers, eager to get back to life and to business, were eager to negotiate with them, offering goods as a sign of their earnest intent. By 1717 the Yamasee threat had subsided and trade in the region began flourishing anew.

No sooner had the Yamasee War ended, however, that a new threat emerged: the dreaded pirate Edward Teach, aka Blackbeard. Entering Charleston harbor in May 1718 with his flagship *Queen Anne's Revenge* and three other vessels, he promptly plundered five ships and began a full-scale blockade of the entire settlement. He took a number of prominent citizens hostage before finally departing northward.

## SLAVERY

For the colonists, the Blackbeard episode was the final straw. Already disgusted by the lack of support from the Lords Proprietors during the Yamasee War, the humiliation of the pirate blockade was too much to take. To almost universal agreement in the colony, the settlers threw off the rule of the Proprietors and lobbied in 1719 to become a crown colony, an effort that came to final fruition in 1729.

While this outward-looking and energetic Charleston was originally built on the backs of merchants, with the introduction of the rice and indigo crops in the early 1700s it would increasingly be built on the backs of slaves. For all the wealth gained through the planting of rice and cotton seeds, another seed was sown by the Lowcountry plantation culture. The area's total dependence on slave labor would ultimately lead to a disastrous war, a conflict signaled for decades to those smart enough to read the signs.

By the early 18th century Charleston and

# Pirates of the Atlantic

Pirates, along with their close cousins, slavers, were among the earliest explorers of the Atlantic seaboard of North America, and other than Native American chiefs, were the only real authority in the area for decades. The creeks and barrier islands of the Georgia and Carolina coast provided important, hard-to-find sanctuaries away from the regular pirate circuit in the booty-laden Spanish Caribbean.

For most of us, pirate stories and movies are a form of escapism, in which the most unlikely scenarios happen with ease. But a real-life pirate story from the earliest days of the Charleston seems almost too unbelievable, even for Hollywood. The encounter was at the hands of the infamous Edward Teach, aka Blackbeard. A tall, terrifying bully of a man, the legendary pirate also had a flair for the dramatic, as all proper pirates should. Given to twisting flaming wads of cloth into his beard when he attacked his prey, Blackbeard was also quite eccentric, as his Charleston escapade shows. In May 1718, Blackbeard, driven north from his usual hunting grounds in the Bahamas by a concerted effort of the British Navy, approached Charleston Harbor in his flagship *Queen Anne's Revenge,* accompanied by three smaller vessels. He immediately seized several ships and kidnapped several leading citizens, including Councilman Samuel Wragg and his four-year-old son. He sent one captive ashore with the message that unless his demand was met, the heads of Wragg and son would soon be delivered to the colonial governor's doorstep. Blackbeard's demand? A chest of medicine. For what purpose, we still aren't sure, but apparently it really was all he wanted. The medicines were delivered in short order, and Blackbeard released his hostages and sailed north to Ocracoke Island, North Carolina, to enjoy a royal pardon he'd just received.

One of the pirates serving under Blackbeard during the Charleston escapade was Stede Bonnet, quite a contrasting figure in his debonair nature and posh finery. When Charleston's Colonel William Rhett—his house at 54 Hasell Street, the city's oldest, is still standing—got wind that Bonnet and crew were still a-pirating off Cape Fear, North Carolina, he set out with a fleet to bring him to justice. And that he did, bringing pirate and crew back to Charleston for a trial that almost didn't happen after Bonnet escaped from custody dressed as a woman (he was captured on Sullivan's Island). The dashing Bonnet actually garnered quite a bit of public sympathy—especially when he begged not to be hanged—but it wasn't enough to forestall the grim fate of the pirate and his crew: public execution at White Point, the bodies left to dangle as a warning to other buccaneers. Another coastal menace, Richard Worley, was also hanged in Charleston. He was supposedly buried in a marshy creek downtown, where Meeting and Water Streets intersect today.

Though Savannah is home to the famous Pirate's House restaurant and got a major shout-out in Robert Louis Stevenson's *Treasure Island,* actual pirate history there is hard to nail down. There seems little doubt that a host of ne'er-do-wells made their way onto the rowdy Savannah waterfront, but the port's location nearly 20 miles upriver would have made it less-than-ideal territory for a true buccaneer, who always needed a fast getaway handy.

As for Blackbeard, his retirement plans were interrupted by a contingent of Virginians who tracked him down and killed him near Ocracoke. However, his legend lives to this day on Blackbeard Island, Georgia, a gorgeous, undeveloped barrier island that has changed little since the days when Teach himself allegedly stopped over between pirate raids. The legends even say he left some treasure there, but don't try to look for it—Blackbeard Island is now a National Wildlife Refuge.

Savannah were firmly established as the key American ports for the importation of African slaves, with about 40 percent of the trade centered in Charleston alone. As a result, the black population of the coast outnumbered the white population by more than three to one, and much more than that in some areas. The fear of violent slave uprisings had great influence over not only politics but day-to-day affairs.

These fears were eventually realized in the **Stono Rebellion** on September 9, 1739.

Twenty African American slaves led by an Angolan known only as Jemmy met near the Stono River near Charleston. Marching with a banner that read "Liberty," they seized guns with the plan of marching all the way to Spanish Florida and finding sanctuary in the wilderness. On the way they burned seven plantations and killed 20 more whites. A militia eventually caught up with them, killing 44 escaped slaves while losing 20 of their own. The prisoners were decapitated and had their heads spiked on every milepost between the spot of that final battle and Charleston. Inspired by the rebellion, at least two other uprisings would take place over the next two years in South Carolina and Georgia.

## OGLETHORPE'S VISION

In 1729, Carolina was divided into north and south. In 1731, a colony to be known as Georgia, after the new English king, was carved out of the southern part of the Carolina land grant. A young general, aristocrat, and humanitarian named James Edward Oglethorpe gathered together a group of Trustees—similar to Carolina's Lords Proprietors—to take advantage.

While Oglethorpe would go on to found Georgia, his wasn't the first English presence in the area. A garrison built Fort King George in modern-day Darien, Georgia, in 1721, which you can visit today. A cypress blockhouse surrounded by palisaded earthworks, the fort defended the southern reaches of England's claim for seven years before being abandoned in 1728.

On February 12, 1733, after stops in Beaufort and Charleston, the ship *Anne* with its 114 passengers made its way to the highest bluff on the Savannah River. The area was controlled by the peaceful Yamacraw people, who had been encouraged by the powers-that-be in Charleston to settle on this vacant land 12 miles up the Savannah River to serve as a buffer for the Spanish. Led by an elderly chief, or *mico*, named Tomochichi, the Yamacraw enjoyed the area's natural bounty of shellfish, fruit, nuts, and small game.

A deft politician, Oglethorpe struck up a treaty and eventually a genuine friendship with Tomochichi. To the Yamacraw, Oglethorpe was a rare bird—a white man who behaved with honor and was true to his word. The Native Americans reciprocated by helping the settlers and pledging fealty to the crown. Oglethorpe reported to the Trustees that Tomochichi personally requested "that we would Love and Protect their little Families."

In negotiations with local tribes using Mary Musgrove, a Creek-English settler in the area, as translator, the persuasive Oglethorpe convinced the coastal Creek to cede to the crown all Georgia land to the Altamaha River. Oglethorpe's impact was soon felt farther down the Georgia coast, as St. Simons Island, Jekyll Island, Darien, and Brunswick were settled in rapid succession and with them the entrenchment of the plantation system and slave labor.

While the Trustees' utopian vision was largely economic in nature, like Carolina the Georgia colony also emphasized religious freedom. While to modern ears Charleston's antipathy toward "papists" and Oglethorpe's original ban of Catholics from Georgia might seem incompatible with this goal, the reason was a coldly pragmatic one for the time: England's two main global rivals, France and Spain, were both staunchly Catholic countries.

## SPAIN VANQUISHED

Things heated up on the coast in 1739 with the so-called War of Jenkins' Ear, which despite its seemingly trivial beginnings over the humiliation of a British captain by Spanish privateers was actually a proxy struggle emblematic of changes in the European balance of power. A year later Oglethorpe cobbled together a force of settlers, Indian allies, and Carolinians to reduce the Spanish fortress at St. Augustine, Florida. The siege failed, and Oglethorpe retreated to St. Simons Island to await the inevitable counterattack. In 1742, a Spanish force invaded the island but was eventually turned back for good at the Battle of

**Bloody Marsh.** That clash marked the end of Spanish overtures on England's colonies in what is now the United States.

Though Oglethorpe returned to England a national hero, things fell apart in Savannah. The settlers became envious of the success of Charleston's slave-based rice economy and began wondering aloud why they couldn't also make use of free labor. With Oglethorpe otherwise occupied in England, the Trustees of Georgia—distant in more ways than just geographically from the new colony—bowed to public pressure and relaxed the restrictions on slavery and rum. By 1753 the Trustees voted to return their charter to the crown, officially making Georgia the 13th and final colony of England in America. With first the French and then the Spanish effectively shut off from the American East Coast, the stage was set for an internal battle between England and its burgeoning colonies across the Atlantic.

## REVOLUTION AND INDEPENDENCE

The population of the colonies swelled in the mid-1700s, not only from an influx of slaves, but also from a corresponding flood of European immigrants. The interior began filling up with Germans, Swiss, Scottish, and Irish settlers. Their subsequent demands for political representation led to tension between them and the coastal inhabitants, typically depicted through the years as an Upcountry versus Lowcountry competition. It is a persistent but inaccurate myth that the affluent elite on the southeastern coast were reluctant to break ties with England. While the Lowcountry's cultural and economic ties to England were certainly strong, the **Stamp Act** and the **Townshend Acts** combined to turn public sentiment against the mother country here as elsewhere in the colonies.

South Carolinian planters like Christopher Gadsden, Henry Laurens, John Rutledge, and Arthur Middleton were early leaders in the movement for independence. Planters in what would be called Liberty County, Georgia, also strongly agitated for the cause. War broke out

between the colonists and the British in New England, and soon made its way southward. The British failed to take Charleston—the fourth-largest city in the colonies—in June 1776, an episode that gave South Carolina its "Palmetto State" moniker when redcoat cannonballs bounced off the palm tree-lined walls of Fort Moultrie. The British under General Sir Henry Clinton successfully took the city in 1780, however, occupying it until 1782.

The British, under General Archibald Campbell, took Savannah in 1778. Royal Governor Sir James Wright returned from exile to Georgia to reclaim it for the crown, the only one of the colonies to be subsumed again into the British Empire. A polyglot force of colonists, Haitians, and Hessians attacked the British fortifications on the west side of Savannah in 1779 but were repulsed with heavy losses. Although the area's two major cities had fallen to the British, the war raged on throughout the surrounding area.

Indeed, throughout the Lowcountry, fighting was as vicious as anything yet seen on the North American continent. With over 130 known military engagements occurring here, South Carolina sacrificed more men during the war than any other colony—including Massachusetts, the "Cradle of the Revolution."

The struggle became a guerrilla war of colonists versus the British as well as a civil war between patriots and loyalists, or **Tories.** Committing what would today undoubtedly be called war crimes, the British routinely burned homes, churches, and fields and massacred civilians. Using Daufuskie Island as a base, British soldiers staged raids on Hilton Head plantations.

In response, patriots of the Lowcountry bred a group of deadly guerrilla soldiers under legendary leaders such as Francis Marion, "the Swamp Fox," and Thomas Sumter, "the Gamecock," who attacked the British in daring hit-and-run raids staged from swamps and marshes. A covert group of patriots called the **Sons of Liberty** met clandestinely throughout the Lowcountry, plotting revolution over

# Nathanael Greene and Mulberry Grove

Like John Wesley, Nathanael Greene's time in Savannah was short and mostly unfortunate. Unlike Wesley, however, Greene never got a chance to leave and start anew. One of the American Revolution's greatest heroes, Greene rose from the rank of private in the Continental Army to become George Washington's right-hand man. Ironically, this skillful soldier was born into a family of pacifist Quakers in Rhode Island in 1742. As a brigadier general in the Rhode Island militia, Greene's innate military prowess caught Washington's eye during the siege of Boston, whereupon the future president gave Greene command of the entire Southern theater of the fight for independence. While Greene never attempted the suicidal aim of taking on Lord Cornwallis's large and well-trained Southern contingent of British veterans, his guerrilla tactics did force the English contingent to divide and hence weaken itself. It was Greene who sent General "Mad Anthony" Wayne in 1782 to finally free Savannah from the British, who had resisted an earlier attempt to retake the city in 1779. Perhaps in a nod to his Quaker roots, Greene insisted that no revenge be taken on Savannah's loyalists, instead welcoming them into the new nation as partners. As a reward for his service, Washington granted Greene a large estate on the banks of the Savannah River known as Mulberry Grove, primarily known to history as the place where Eli Whitney would later invent the cotton gin while serving as tutor to the Greene children. (Wayne was awarded nearby Richmond Plantation.)

Mulberry Grove was less productive for Greene himself, however, who as a lifelong abolitionist refused to use slave labor on the plantation, and hence paid a steep financial price. The 44-year-old Greene spent less than a year at Mulberry Grove, mostly worrying about finances, when he caught sunstroke on a particularly brutal June day in 1786 and died shortly thereafter.

And there's where the real mystery begins. At some point Greene's remains were said to have been lost after a family vault in Colonial Cemetery was vandalized by Union troops. Almost a century passed until in 1900 the Society of the Cincinnati of Rhode Island appointed a search committee to find and properly inter the general's long-lost remains. The remains were indeed found—right in the vault in Colonial Cemetery where they were supposed to have been, which you can see to this day. However, they were underneath someone else: After removing the coffin of one Robert Scott, excavators found "a mass of rotten wood and human bones mixed with sand," along with a rusty coffin plate reading:

Nathanael Greene,
Obit June 19, 1786
Age, 41 Years

So it was that in 1902, Greene's remains were finally put to rest under his monument in Johnson Square—dedicated to him by the Marquis de Lafayette 76 years earlier in 1825.

Sadly, all buildings at Mulberry Grove were razed by Sherman's troops in 1864, with only a few brick stairs and portions of foundation remaining. The area—visited not once but twice by George Washington after his friend's untimely death—entered industrial use in 1975 and is currently occupied by the Georgia Ports Authority. No full-scale archaeological dig has ever been done at the site, although the nonprofit Mulberry Grove Foundation (www.mulberrygrove.org) is working toward that as well as a plan to make part of the 2,200-acre parcel a wildlife preserve.

Greene's widow, Catherine, would go on to remarry and build another mostly vanished plantation, the famed Dungeness on Cumberland Island.

pints of ale. Sometimes their efforts transcended talk, however, and atrocities were committed against area loyalists.

In all, four South Carolinians signed the Declaration of Independence (Thomas Heyward Jr., Thomas Lynch Jr., Arthur Middleton, and Edward Rutledge), as did three Georgians (Button Gwinnett, Lyman Hall, and George Walton).

## HIGH COTTON

True to form, the new nation wasted no time in asserting its economic strength. Rice planters from Georgetown north of Charleston on down to the Altamaha River in Georgia built on their already impressive wealth, becoming the new nation's richest men by far—with fortunes built on the backs of the slaves working in their fields.

In 1786, a new crop was introduced that would only enhance the financial clout of the coastal region: cotton. A former loyalist colonel, Roger Kelsal, sent some seed from the West Indies to his friend James Spaulding, owner of a plantation on St. Simons Island, Georgia. This crop, soon to be known as **Sea Island cotton** and considered the best in the world, would supplant rice as the crop of choice for coastal plantations. At the height of the Southern cotton boom in the early 1800s, a single Sea Island cotton harvest on a single plantation might go for $100,000— in 1820 dollars. While Charleston was still by far the largest, most powerful, and most influential city on the southeastern coast of the United States, at the peak of the cotton craze Savannah was actually doing more business—a fact that grated to no end on the Holy City's elite. Unlike Charleston, where the planters themselves dominated city life, in Savannah it was cotton brokers called **factors** who were the city's leading class. During this time most of the grand homes of downtown Savannah's historic district were built. This boom period, fueled largely by cotton exports, was perhaps most iconically represented by the historic sailing of the SS *Savannah* from Savannah to Liverpool in 29 days, the first transatlantic voyage by a steamship.

During the prosperous antebellum period, the economy of Charleston, Savannah, and surrounding areas was completely dependent on slave labor, but the cities themselves boasted large numbers of African Americans who were active in business and agriculture. For example, the vending stalls at the City Markets of both Charleston and Savannah were predominantly staffed by African American workers, some of them free.

## SECESSION

Much of the lead-in to the Civil War focused on whether slavery would be allowed in the newest U.S. territories in the West, but there's no doubt that all figurative roads eventually led to South Carolina. During Andrew Jackson's presidency in the 1820s, his vice president, South Carolina's John C. Calhoun, became a thorn in Jackson's side with his aggressive advocacy for **nullification.** In a nutshell, Calhoun said that if a state decided the federal government wasn't treating it fairly— in this case with regard to tariffs that were hurting the cotton trade in the Palmetto State—it could simply nullify the federal law, superseding it with law of its own.

As the abolition movement gained steam and tensions over slavery rose, South Carolina congressman Preston Brooks took things to the next level. On May 22, 1856, he beat fellow senator Charles Sumner of Massachusetts nearly to death with his walking cane on the Senate floor. Sumner had just given a speech criticizing pro-slavery forces—including a relative of Brooks—and called slavery "a harlot." (In a show of support, South Carolinians sent Brooks dozens of new canes to replace the one he broke over Sumner's head.)

In 1860, the national convention of the Democratic Party, then the dominant force in U.S. politics, was held in—where else?— Charleston. Rancor over slavery and state's rights was so high that they couldn't agree on a single candidate to run to replace President James Buchanan. Reconvening in Maryland,

# Robert E. Lee and Savannah

*That spot of spots! That place of places!! That city of cities!!!*

Robert E. Lee on Savannah, in a letter to John Mackay

Before reluctantly surrendering his commission to serve the Confederacy, Robert E. Lee was a bright young up-and-comer with the U.S. Army Corps of Engineers. As a 22-year-old lieutenant, the multitalented Virginian spent a year and a half in and around Savannah overseeing the construction of Fort Pulaski, named for the brave Polish count who lost his life in 1779's Siege of Savannah. On Lee's arrival in Savannah, construction was on hiatus due to the stifling summer heat. The handsome and dashing young man made the most of his time off, making significant inroads into downtown Savannah's high society. He was heartily welcomed into the home of his old West Point roommate John Mackay, whose three daughters adored him. The same was true of the two Minis daughters who lived nearby and also frequently had the young lieutenant over (and all this while Lee was conducting a long-distance courtship with his future wife back home in Virginia).

Construction of the fort on Cockspur Island began in 1829 under Major Samuel Babcock, whose health problems soon forced Lee to take over. Most of Lee's work focused on draining and diking the marshy island and its blue clay soil, and much of his handiwork remains functional today. After Lee was reassigned in 1831, Lieutenant Joseph Mansfield completed construction of the fort in 1847. A mix of slave labor and paid artisans lived in a sprawling construction camp. Today only Fort Pulaski's brick structures remain, the wooden ones not surviving a series of hurricanes in subsequent years.

Five years after the war, Robert E. Lee paid a final visit to Savannah at age 63, accompanied by his daughter Agnes, to see his old comrade-in-arms General Joseph E. Johnston, who lived at 105 East Oglethorpe Avenue. During his stay in town, Lee slept at the Andrew Low House (Andrew's wife, Mary, was Jack Mackay's niece). Lee died six months later.

Fort Pulaski is currently administered by the National Park Service, which maintains an excellent website (www.nps.gov) detailing the rich history and fascinating archaeology of this, one of Savannah's great must-see sights.

the party split along sectional lines, with the Northern wing backing Stephen A. Douglas. The Southern wing, fervently desiring secession, deliberately chose its own candidate, John Breckinridge, in order to split the Democratic vote and throw the election to Republican Abraham Lincoln, an outspoken opponent of the expansion of slavery. During that so-called **Secession Winter** before Lincoln took office, seven states seceded from the union, first among them the Palmetto State, followed by Mississippi, Florida, Alabama, Georgia, Louisiana, and Texas.

## CIVIL WAR

Five days after South Carolina's secession on December 21, 1860, U.S. Army major Robert Anderson moved his garrison from Fort Moultrie on Sullivan's Island to nearby Fort Sumter in Charleston Harbor. Over the next few months and into the spring, Anderson would ignore many calls to surrender, and Confederate forces would prevent any Union resupply or reinforcement. The stalemate was broken and the Confederates finally got their *casus belli* when a Union supply ship successfully ran the blockade and docked at Fort Sumter. Shortly before dawn on April 12, 1861, Confederate batteries around Charleston—ironically none of which were at the famous Battery itself—opened fire on Fort Sumter for 34 straight hours, until Anderson surrendered on April 13.

In a classic example of why you should always be careful what you wish for, the secessionists had been too clever by half in pushing for Lincoln. Far from prodding the North to sue for peace, the fall of Fort Sumter instead caused the remaining states in the Union to rally around the previously unpopular tall man from Illinois. Lincoln's skillful management of the Fort Sumter standoff meant that from then on, the South would bear history's blame for initiating the conflict that would claim over half a million American lives.

After Fort Sumter, four more Southern states—Virginia, Arkansas, North Carolina, and Tennessee—seceded to join the Confederacy. The Old Dominion was the real prize for the secessionists, as Virginia had the South's only ironworks and by far the largest manufacturing base.

In November 1861, a massive Union invasion armada landed in Port Royal Sound in South Carolina, effectively taking the entire Lowcountry out of the war. Hilton Head was a Union encampment, and Beaufort became a major hospital center for the U.S. Army. The coast of Georgia was also blockaded, with Union forces using new rifled cannons in 1862 to quickly reduce Fort Pulaski at the mouth of the Savannah River. Charleston, however, did host two battles in the conflict. The **Battle of Secessionville** came in June 1862, when a Union force attempting to take Charleston was repulsed on James Island with heavy casualties.

The next battle, an unsuccessful Union landing on Morris Island in July 1863, was immortalized by the movie *Glory*. The 54th Massachusetts Regiment, an African American unit with white commanders, performed so gallantly in its failed assault on the Confederate **Battery Wagner** that it inspired the North and was cited by abolitionists as further proof that African Americans should be given freedom and full citizenship rights. Another invasion attempt on Charleston would not come, but the city was besieged and bombarded for nearly two more years (devastation made even worse by a massive fire, unrelated to the shelling, that destroyed much of the city in 1861).

Otherwise, the coast grew quiet. From Charleston to Brunswick, white Southerners evacuated the coastal cities and plantations for the hinterland, leaving behind only slaves to fend for themselves. In many coastal areas, African Americans and Union garrison troops settled into an awkward but peaceful coexistence. Many islands under Union control, such as Cockspur Island, where Fort Pulaski sat, became endpoints in the Underground Railroad.

In Savannah, General William Sherman concluded his **March to the Sea** in Savannah in 1864, famously giving the city to Lincoln as a Christmas present. While staunch Confederates, city fathers were wise enough to know what would happen to their accumulated wealth and fine homes should they be foolhardy enough to resist Sherman's army of war-hardened veterans.

The only military uncertainty left was in how badly Charleston, the "cradle of secession," would suffer for its sins. Historians and local wags have long debated why Sherman spared Charleston, the hated epicenter of the Civil War. Did he fall in love with the city during his brief posting there as a young lieutenant? Did he literally fall in love there, with one of the city's legendarily beautiful and delicate local belles? We may never know for sure, but it's likely that the Lowcountry's marshy, mucky terrain simply made it too difficult to move large numbers of men and supplies. So Sherman turned his army inland toward the state capital, Columbia, which would not be so lucky.

For the African American population of Charleston and Savannah, however, it was not a time of sadness but the great Day of Jubilee. Soon after the Confederate surrender, black Charlestonians held one of the largest parades the city has ever seen, with one of the floats being a coffin bearing the sign, "Slavery is dead."

As for the place where it all began, a plucky Confederate garrison remained underground at Fort Sumter throughout the war, as the walls above them were literally pounded into dust by the long Union siege. The garrison quietly left the fort under cover of night on February 17, 1865. Major Robert Anderson, who surrendered the fort at war's beginning, returned to Sumter in April 1865 to raise the same flag he'd lowered exactly four years earlier. Three thousand African Americans attended the ceremonies. Later that same night, Abraham Lincoln was assassinated in Washington DC.

## RECONSTRUCTION

A case could be made that slavery need not have led the United States into Civil War. The U.S. government had banned the importation of slaves long before, in 1808. The great powers of Europe would soon ban slavery altogether (Spain in 1811, France in 1826, and Britain in 1833). Visiting foreign dignitaries in the mid-1800s were often shocked to find the practice in full swing in the American South. Even Brazil, the world center of slavery, where four out of every 10 slaves taken from Africa were brought (less than 5 percent came to the United States), would ban slavery in 1888, suggesting that slavery in the United States would have died a natural death. Still, the die was cast, the war was fought, and everyone had to deal with the aftermath.

For a brief time, Sherman's benevolent dictatorship on the coast held promise for an orderly postwar future. In 1865 he issued his sweeping "40 acres and a mule" order seeking dramatic economic restitution for coastal Georgia's free blacks. Politics reared its ugly head in the wake of Lincoln's assassination, however, and the order was rescinded, ushering in the chaotic Reconstruction era, echoes of which linger to this day.

Even as the trade in cotton and naval stores resumed to even greater heights than before, urban life and racial tension became more and more problematic. Urban populations swelled as freed blacks from all over the depressed countryside rushed into the cities. As one of them, his name lost to history, famously said: "Freedom was freer in Charleston."

## RECONCILIATION

The opening of the exclusive Jekyll Island Club in 1886 marked the coming of the effects of the Industrial Revolution to the Deep South and the rejuvenation of regional economies. In Savannah, the Telfair Academy of Arts and Sciences, the South's first art museum, opened that same year. The cotton trade built back up to antebellum levels, and the South was on the long road to recovery.

The Spanish-American War of 1898 was a major turning point for the South, the first time since the Civil War that Americans were joined in patriotic unity. The southeastern coast felt this in particular, as it was a staging area for the invasion of Cuba. President William McKinley addressed the troops bivouacked in Savannah's Daffin Park, and Charlestonians cheered the exploits of their namesake heavy cruiser the USS *Charleston,* which played a key role in forcing the Spanish surrender of Guam.

Charleston would elect its first Irish American mayor, John Grace, in 1911, who would serve until 1923 (with a break 1915-1919). Although it wouldn't open until 1929, the first Cooper River Bridge joining Charleston with Mount Pleasant was the child of the Grace administration, credited today for modernizing the Holy City's infrastructure.

The arrival of the tiny but devastating boll weevil all but wiped out the cotton trade on the coast after the turn of the century, forcing the economy to diversify. Naval stores and lumbering were the order of the day at the advent of World War I, the combined patriotic effort for which did wonders in repairing the wounds of the Civil War, still vivid in many local memories. A major legacy of World War I that still greatly influences life in the Lowcountry is the Marine Corps Recruit Depot Parris Island, which began life as a small Marine camp in 1919.

## RENAISSANCE AND DEPRESSION

In the Roaring '20s, that boom period following World War I, both Charleston and Savannah entered the world stage and made some of their most significant cultural contributions to American life. It was also the era of Prohibition. Savannah became notorious as a major import center for illegal rum from the Bahamas.

As elsewhere in the country, Prohibition ironically brought out a new appreciation for the arts and just plain having fun. The "Charleston" dance, originated on the streets of the Holy City and popularized in New York, would sweep the world. The Jenkins Orphanage Band, credited with the dance, traveled the world, even playing at President William Howard Taft's inauguration.

In the visual arts, the "Charleston Renaissance" took off, specifically intended to introduce the Holy City to a wider audience. Key work included the Asian-influenced art of self-taught painter Alice Ravenel Huger Smith and the etchings of Elizabeth O'Neill Verner. Edward Hopper was a visitor to Charleston during that time and produced several noted watercolors. The Gibbes Art Gallery, now the Gibbes Museum of Art, opened in 1905. Recognizing the cultural importance of the city and its history, in 1920 socialite Susan Pringle Frost and other concerned Charlestonians formed the Preservation Society of Charleston, the oldest community-based historic preservation organization in the country.

In 1924, lauded Charleston author DuBose Heyward wrote the locally set novel *Porgy.* With Heyward's cooperation, the book would soon be turned into the first American opera, *Porgy and Bess,* by George Gershwin, who labored over the composition in a cottage on Folly Beach. Ironically, *Porgy and Bess,* which premiered with an African American cast in New York in 1935, wouldn't be performed in its actual setting until 1970 because of segregation laws.

In Savannah, the Roaring '20s coincided with the rise of Johnny Mercer, who began his theater career locally in the Town Theater Group. In 1925, Flannery O'Connor was born in Savannah, and the quirky, Gothic nature of the city would mark her later writing indelibly. The Depression hit the South hard, but since wages and industry were already behind the national average, the economic damage wasn't as bad as elsewhere in the country. As elsewhere in the South, the public works programs of President Franklin D. Roosevelt's New Deal helped not only to keep locals employed but contributed greatly to the cultural and archaeological record of the region. The Civilian Conservation Corps built much of the modern state park system in the area.

## WORLD WAR II AND THE POSTWAR BOOM

With the attack on Pearl Harbor and the coming of World War II, life on the Georgia and South Carolina coast would never be the same. Military funding and facilities swarmed into the area, and populations and long-depressed living standards rose as a result. In many outlying Sea Islands of Georgia and South Carolina, electricity came for the first time.

The Charleston Navy Yard became the city's largest employer, and the city's population soared as workers swarmed in. The "Mighty Eighth" Air Force was founded and based in Savannah, and Camp Stewart, later Fort Stewart, was built in nearby Hinesville. In shipyards in Savannah and Brunswick, hundreds of Liberty ships were built to transport cargo to the citizens and allied armies of Europe.

The postwar U.S. infatuation with the automobile—and its troublesome child, the suburb—brought exponential growth to the great cities of the coast. The first bridge to Hilton Head Island was built in 1956, leading to the first of many resort developments, Sea Pines, in 1961. With rising coastal populations came pressure to demolish more and more fine old buildings to put parking lots and high-rises in their place. A backlash grew among the cities' elites, aghast at the destruction of so much history.

The immediate postwar era brought about the formation of both the Historic Charleston Foundation and the Historic Savannah Foundation, which began the financially and politically difficult work of protecting historic districts from the wrecking ball. They weren't always successful, but the work of these organizations—mostly older women from the upper crust—laid the foundation for the successful coastal tourist industry to come, as well as preserved important American history for the ages.

## CIVIL RIGHTS

The ugly racial violence that plagued much of the country during the civil rights era rarely visited the Georgia and South Carolina coast. Whether due to the laid-back ambience or the fact that African Americans were simply too numerous there to be denied, cities like Charleston and Savannah experienced little real unrest during that time.

Contrary to popular opinion, the civil rights era wasn't just a blip in the 1960s. The gains of that decade were the fruits of efforts begun decades earlier. Many of the exertions involved efforts to expand black suffrage. Though African Americans had secured the nominal right to vote years before, primary contests were not under the jurisdiction of federal law. As a result, Democratic Party primary elections—the de facto general elections because of that party's total dominance in the South at the time—were effectively closed to African American voters.

Savannah was at the forefront of expanding black suffrage, and Ralph Mark Gilbert, pastor of the historic First African Baptist Church, launched one of the first black voter registration drives in the South. In Charleston, the Democratic primary was opened to African Americans for the first time in 1947. In 1955, a successful black realtor, J. Arthur Brown, became head of the Charleston chapter of the NAACP and membership soared, bringing an increase in activism. In 1960, the Charleston Municipal Golf Course voluntarily integrated to avoid a court battle.

Martin Luther King Jr. visited South Carolina in the late 1960s, speaking in Charleston in 1967 and helping reestablish the Penn Center on St. Helena Island as not only a cultural center but a center of political activism as well. The hundred-day strike of hospital workers at the Medical University of South Carolina in 1969—right after King's assassination—got national attention and was the culmination of Charleston's struggle for civil rights. By the end of the 1960s, the city councils of Charleston and Savannah had elected their first black aldermen, and the next phase in local history began.

## A COAST REBORN

The decade of the 1970s brought the seeds of the future success of the South Carolina and Georgia coasts. In Charleston, the historic tenure of Mayor Joe Riley began, and in Savannah came the election of a similarly influential and long-serving mayor, John P. Rousakis. The Irish American and the Greek American would break precedents and forge key alliances in both municipalities, reviving local economies.

In the years 1970-1976, tourism in Charleston would increase by 60 percent. The resort industry, already established on Hilton Head, would hit Kiawah Island, Seabrook Island, and Isle of Palms with a vengeance. In Savannah, Rousakis renovated the then-seedy riverfront district, making it the centerpiece of the city's burgeoning tourist trade. The Savannah College of Art and Design (SCAD) opened in 1979 and began the process of renovating dozens of the city's historic buildings, a process that continues today.

The coast's combination of beautiful scenery and cheap labor proved irresistible to the movie and TV industry, which would begin filming many series and films in the area in the 1970s and continuing to this day. Beaufort, South Carolina, in particular would emerge from its stately slumber as the star of several popular films, including *The Great Santini* and *The Big Chill*.

Charleston received its first major challenge since the Civil War in 1989 when Hurricane Hugo—originally headed directly for Savannah—changed course at the last minute and slammed into the South Carolina coast just north of Charleston. The Holy City, including many of its most historic locations, was massively damaged, with hardly a tree left standing. In a testament to the toughness just beneath Charleston's genteel veneer, the city not only rebounded but came back stronger.

The economic boom of the 1990s was particularly good to Charleston and Savannah, whose ports saw a huge dividend from increasing globalization. Also in the 1990s came the *Midnight in the Garden of Good and Evil* phenomenon, which would put Savannah—already on the upswing—on the tourist map for good. Although not a Savannah native,

the iconic Paula Deen brought a new national focus on the city through her long presence on the Food Network and through her local restaurant, The Lady and Sons, which continues to pack in visitors.

Today Savannah's tourism business is healthier than ever, and Charleston is perennially ranked as one of the top U.S. cities for visitors as well as for residents. Attracted by the coastal region, artists, writers, and entrepreneurs continue to flock, increasing the economic and social diversity of the area and taking it to new heights of livability.

# Government and Economy

## GOVERNMENT

Charleston is run by the **strong mayor** form of municipal government, which means that the elected mayor has extensive powers, including the ability to veto a measure approved by the city council. In practice this means that a mayor, for better or worse, is able to stamp the city with his or her own vision—Riley's influence can be seen in everything from the chichi Charleston Place to new low-income housing developments.

Savannah, however, is run by the **council-manager** form of municipal government, in which the mayor is but one vote of many on the city council. Day-to-day operations are in the hands of an appointed city manager who answers to the council. In practice this means a generally more professional and objective approach to the nuts-and-bolts of government but an often-frustrating lack of accountability at the top.

Because of both states' strong rural roots, county governments are also very important, but becoming less so as urbanization continues and more areas consider city and county consolidation. In particular, county governments in Georgia hold great sway, in large part because there are so many of them. Visitors to the Peach State are often amazed by how

small the counties are, and how many there are—159 in total. In practice this means that county governments hold a greater proportion of political power than in states where the counties are much larger in land area, like South Carolina.

### Political Parties

For many decades, the South was dominated by the Democratic Party. Originally the party of slavery, segregation, and Jim Crow, the Democratic Party began attracting Southern African American voters in the 1930s with the election of Franklin D. Roosevelt. The allegiance of black voters was further cemented in the Truman, Kennedy, and Johnson administrations. The region would remain solidly Democratic until a backlash against the civil rights movement of the 1960s drove many white Southerners, ironically enough, into the party of Lincoln. This added racial element, so confounding to Americans from other parts of the country, remains just as potent today. The default mode in the South is that white voters are massively Republican, and black voters massively Democratic. Since South Carolina is 69 percent white and Georgia 67 percent white, doing the math translates to an overwhelming Republican dominance.

However, the coastal areas covered in this guide, with their large, predominantly Democratic African American populations, function somewhat separately from this realignment. But don't make the mistake of assuming that local African Americans are particularly liberal because of their voting habits. Deeply religious and traditional in background and upbringing, African Americans in the area covered by this guide are among the most socially conservative people in the region, even if their choice of political party does not always reflect that.

## Intrastate Relations

A few years back a sociologist proposed, partially tongue-in-cheek, that since the coastal regions of the Southeast have more in common with each other than with residents of other parts of their own states, the borders should be realigned to reflect this demographic, cultural, and historic affiliation. Anyone who has spent time in the inland areas of South Carolina and Georgia will immediately recognize the basic truth in this proposal, however unlikely it is to actually happen.

The simple, easily observable fact is that Charleston, Beaufort, Savannah, and Brunswick have far more in common with each other than Charleston has with, say, Spartanburg, South Carolina, or Savannah has with Macon, Georgia. I don't know what you would name the state that resulted from the union of the coastal cities and towns, but I do know that the food would be awesome.

Georgia's largest city and capital is Atlanta, which is even farther removed—both physically and metaphysically—from Savannah than Columbia is from Charleston. Indeed, Savannah and Chatham County are considered so different from the rest of Georgia that old-timers still call Savannah the capital of the "State of Chatham."

## ECONOMY

The coastal areas of South Carolina and Georgia are currently experiencing profound changes in economy and business. The rice crop moved offshore in the late 1800s, and the center of the cotton trade moved to the Gulf States in the early 1900s. That left timber as the main cash crop all up and down the coast, specifically huge pine tree farms to feed the pulp and paper business. For most of the 20th century, the largest employers along the coast were massive, sulfur-smelling paper mills, which had as big an effect on the local environment as on its economy. But even that is changing as Asian competition is driving paper companies to sell off their tracts for real estate development—not necessarily a more welcome scenario.

Since World War II, the U.S. Department of Defense has been a major employer and economic driver in the entire South, and the Georgia and South Carolina coast is no exception. Of the services, the U.S. Navy (which includes the Marines) is the dominant military presence in coastal South Carolina, employing over 16,000 military and civilian workers. Coastal Georgia tends to be more Army-dominated. Despite the closing of the Charleston Naval Yard in the mid-1990s, the grounds now host the East Coast headquarters of the Space and Naval Warfare Systems Center (SPAWAR), which provides high-tech engineering solutions for the Navy. Charleston also retains a large military presence in the Charleston Air Force Base near North Charleston, which hosts two airlift wings and employs about 6,000. Farther down the coast, Beaufort is home to the Naval Hospital Beaufort and the Marine Corps Air Station Beaufort and its six squadrons of FA-18 Hornets. On nearby Parris Island is the legendary Marine Corps Recruit Depot Parris Island, which puts all new Marine recruits from east of the Mississippi River through rigorous basic training.

In the middle of south-side Savannah sits Hunter Army Airfield, host to a battalion of U.S. Army Rangers. In nearby and largely rural Liberty County, Georgia, is the sprawling Fort Stewart, home base of the 3rd Infantry Division. Near the Florida border in

Savannah's shipping industry is vital to the local economy.

St. Marys is the Naval Submarine Base Kings Bay, home port of eight Trident subs.

Of course, tourism is also an important factor in the local economies of the area. The Holy City in particular has a well-honed tourist infrastructure, bringing at least $5 billion a year into the local economy. Savannah's tourism industry, though growing very rapidly, is still behind Charleston's at less than $2 billion a year.

But, despite all other trends, manufacturing and industry remain the largest sectors of the economy in both Charleston and Savannah—due in no small part to the fact that both South Carolina and Georgia are "right to work" states with exceedingly low unionization rates. Increasingly, however, higher education is more and more important to local economies and will only continue to be so.

# People and Culture

Contrary to how the region is portrayed in the media, the coast from Charleston down to the Georgia-Florida border is hardly exclusive to natives with thick, flowery accents who still obsess over the Civil War and eat grits three meals a day. As you will quickly discover, the entire coastal area is heavily populated with transplants from other parts of the country, and in some areas you can actually go quite a long time without hearing even one of those Scarlett O'Hara accents. Some of this is due to the region's increasing attractiveness to professionals and artists, drawn by the temperate climate, natural beauty, and business-friendly

environment. Part of it is due to its increasing attractiveness to retirees, most of them from the frigid Northeast. Indeed, in some places, chief among them Hilton Head, the most common accent is a New York or New Jersey one, and a Southern accent is rare.

In any case, don't make the common mistake of assuming you're coming to a place where footwear is optional and electricity is a recent development (though it's true that many of the islands didn't get electricity until the 1950s and 1960s). Because so much new construction has gone on in the South in the last quarter-century or so, you might find

# Voodoo and Hoodoo

The spiritual system we know as voodoo—the word is a corruption of various West African spellings—came to the Western Hemisphere with the importation of slaves. Contrary to popular belief, voodoo isn't a mere collection of primitive superstitions but is a clearly defined religion in its own right and is still the dominant religion of millions of West Africans.

Like many ancient belief systems, voodoo is based on the veneration of ancestors and the possibility of continued communication with them, and it's perhaps this characteristic that is responsible for so much misunderstanding. For example, up until fairly recently the African American Gullah and Geechee populations of the South Carolina and Georgia Sea Islands still had a common belief that the older slaves who were born in Africa could actually fly in spirit form back to the continent of their birth and back again.

While voodoo has always been unfairly sensationalized—the most notable recent example being the "voodoo priestess" Minerva in *Midnight in the Garden of Good and Evil*—it's not necessarily as malevolent in actual practice as in the overactive imaginations of writers and directors. For example, the stereotypical practice of sticking pins in dolls to bring pain to a living person actually has its roots in European and Native American folklore. But sensationalism sells, so you'll sometimes find such items being hawked to the gullible as "voodoo dolls."

Much of what the layperson thinks is voodoo is actually hoodoo, a body of folklore—not a religion—indigenous to the American South. Hoodoo combines elements of voodoo (communicating with the dead) and fundamentalist Christianity (extensive scriptural references). In the United States, most African American voodoo tradition was long ago subsumed within Protestant Christianity, but the Gullah populations of the Sea Islands of South Carolina and Georgia still keep alive the old ways. In the Gullah and Geechee areas of the Georgia and Carolina Sea Islands, the word *conjure* is generally the preferred terminology for this hybrid belief system, which has good sides and bad sides and borrows liberally from African lore and Christian folkways.

The old Southern practice of painting shutters and doors blue to ward off evil comes from hoodoo, where the belief in ghosts, or "haints," is largely a byproduct of poorly understood Christianity (Mediterranean countries also use blue to keep evil at bay, and the word *haint* is of Scots-Irish origin). If you keep your eyes attuned, you can still see this particular shade of "haint blue" on rural and vernacular structures throughout the Lowcountry. (Were you to enter one of these homes, you would almost certainly find a horseshoe tacked over the front door as well.)

Another element of hoodoo that you can still encounter today is the role of the "root doctor," an expert at folk remedies who blends various indigenous herbs and plants in order to produce a desired effect or result. In *Midnight in the Garden of Good and Evil*, this role belongs to the fabled Dr. Buzzard, who teaches Minerva everything she knows about "conjure work." However, a root doctor is not to be confused with a "gifted reader," a fortune-teller born with the talent to tell the future. From the no-doubt embellished account in John Berendt's *Midnight*, scholars would put the late Minerva squarely into the category of root doctor or "conjurer" rather than the undeniably more compelling "voodoo priestess."

some aspects of the infrastructure—specifically the roads and the electrical utilities—actually superior to where you came from.

## POPULATION

For demographic purposes, Charleston is part of the Charleston-North Charleston Metropolitan Statistical Area (MSA), which includes Berkeley, Dorchester, and Charleston Counties. In the 2010 census, it comprised about 664,000 people. The city of Charleston proper has a population of about 120,000. The Hilton Head-Beaufort MSA includes Beaufort and Jasper Counties and comprised about 180,000 people in the 2010 census. The town of Hilton Head had about 37,000 residents in 2010, and Beaufort had about 13,000. The Savannah MSA, which includes Chatham, Bryan, and Effingham Counties, numbered about 347,000 people in the 2010 census. The city of Savannah itself has a

# Sephardic Jews in the South

Visitors are sometimes surprised to discover that two of the oldest cities in the Anglo-Saxon Protestant South have rich and early histories of an active Jewish presence—specifically, **Sephardic Jews** (those with a Spanish or Portuguese background). Contrary to modern trends, Jews and Muslims on the Iberian Peninsula got along quite well while the Islamic Moors of North Africa dominated the area. But after Ferdinand and Isabella's completion of the Reconquista in that pivotal year of 1492—also the date of Columbus's famous voyage—the Jews of Spain went from being respected citizens to persecuted pariahs nearly overnight. Five years later, Portugal followed suit, expelling all Jews on pain of death unless they became "New Christians," or *conversos*. A sizeable proportion of *conversos*, however, were actually so-called crypto-Jews, who publicly practiced Roman Catholicism while secretly remaining devout Jews. Many synagogues of Sephardic origin today have their floors covered in sand to remember that dark time when Jewish congregations practiced their faith in basements covered with sand to muffle the sounds of their feet.

The diaspora of the Sephardic Jews, ironically, contributed greatly to the health of the global Jewish community, as skilled tradesmen, doctors, and men of letters spread out to Spanish, Portuguese, English, and Dutch colonies where the Inquisition had little sway. It was primarily from the ranks of this Sephardic diaspora that the Jewish settlers of the Lowcountry and Georgia coast came.

The first Jewish presence in Charleston was recorded in 1695, with Jews voting in local elections as early as 1702. Stimulated by the busy port, the Charleston Jewish community quickly grew with the addition of **Ashkenazi**, or Eastern European, Jews in the late 1700s. By 1820, Charleston boasted the biggest Jewish population in the United States. Savannah wasn't the first colonial town to host Jewish settlers, but the group of 42 Sephardic Jews that arrived five months after Oglethorpe's landing in 1733 was by far the largest contingent to travel to North America up to that time. All but eight of this core group were Spanish and Portuguese Jews who immi-

population of about 136,000. The Brunswick MSA includes Brantley, Glynn, and McIntosh Counties and has about 100,000 people.

## Racial Makeup

Its legacy as the center of the U.S. slave trade and plantation culture means that the Charleston-Savannah region has a large African American population. The Charleston MSA is about 31 percent African American, and the Savannah MSA about 35 percent. In the cities proper, the black population is higher, about 35 percent in Charleston's case and nearly 60 percent in Savannah's.

The Hispanic population, as elsewhere in the United States, is growing rapidly, but statistics can be misleading. Though Hispanics are growing at a triple-digit clip in the region, they still remain less than 3 percent of each state's population. Bilingual signage is becoming more common but is still quite rare.

## RELIGION

The area from Charleston to Savannah is unusual in the Deep South for its wide variety of religious faiths. While South Carolina and Georgia remain overwhelmingly Protestant—at least three-quarters of all Christians in both states are members of some Protestant denomination, chief among them Southern Baptist and Methodist—Charleston and Savannah's cosmopolitan, polyglot histories have made them real melting pots of faith.

Both cities were originally dominated by the Episcopal Church (known as the Anglican Church in other countries), but from early on they were also havens for those of other faiths. Various types of Protestant offshoots soon arrived, including the French Huguenots and Congregationalists in Charleston and the Scottish Presbyterians and German Salzburger Lutherans in the Savannah area.

grated to London after spending years as crypto-Jews in their home countries. Accepted without question by Oglethorpe, the Jews of Savannah quickly rose in power and influence. In fact, the first white male child born in Georgia was a Jewish boy, Philip "Uri" Minis.

In one of the great tales of the American melting pot, the assimilation of the Jews into Southern society was so complete that the Secretary of State of the Confederate States of America, Judah Benjamin, was a practicing Jew of Sephardic origin. This assimilation also had a flip side, however, in that the Sephardic Jews were generally just as enthusiastic about owning slaves as any other white citizens of the area. In 1830 about 83 percent of Jewish households in Charleston had slaves, compared to an almost-identical percentage of 87 percent of white Christian Charlestonians.

The center of Jewish culture in Charleston is **Kahal Kadosh Beth Elohim Reform Temple** (90 Hasell St., 843/723-1090, www.kkbe.org, service Sat. 11am, tours Mon.-Fri. 10am-noon, Sun. 10am-4pm), birthplace of Reform Judaism in the United States and the oldest

Temple Mickve Israel in Savannah

continuously active synagogue in the nation. In Savannah, the key Judaic attraction is **Temple Mickve Israel** (20 E. Gordon St., 912/233-1547, www.mickveisrael.org, 30-minute tours Mon.-Fri. 10am-12:30pm and 2pm-3:30pm, $6 suggested donation), the only Gothic synagogue in the country and the third-oldest Jewish congregation in North America.

The seeds of Methodism and the "Great Awakening" were planted along the coast from Savannah up to Charleston.

Owing to vestigial prejudice from the European realpolitik of the founding era, the Roman Catholic presence on the coast was late in arriving, but once it came it was there to stay. Savannah, in particular, has quite a large Roman Catholic population by Southern standards, mostly due to the influx of Irish in the mid-1800s.

But most unusually of all for the Deep South, Charleston and Savannah not only have large Jewish populations but ones that have been key participants in the cities from the very first days of settlement. Sephardic Jews of primarily Portuguese descent were among the first settlers of both Charleston and Savannah, and they kept up an energetic trade between the two cities for centuries afterward, continuing to the present day.

# MANNERS

The prevalence and importance of good manners is the main thing to keep in mind about the South. While it's tempting for folks from more outwardly assertive parts of the world to take this as a sign of weakness, that would be a major mistake. Southerners use manners, courtesy, and chivalry as a system of social interaction with one goal above all: to maintain the established order during times of stress. A relic from a time of extreme class stratification, etiquette and chivalry are ways to make sure that the elites are never threatened—and, on the other hand, that even those on the lowest rungs of society are afforded at least a basic amount of dignity. But as a practical matter, it's also true that Southerners of all classes, races, and backgrounds rely on the observation of manners as a way to sum up people quickly. To any Southerner, regardless of class or race, your use or neglect of basic manners and proper respect indicates how seriously they should take you—not in a socioeconomic sense, but in the big picture overall.

The typical Southern sense of humor—equal parts irony, self-deprecation, and good-natured teasing—is part of the code. Southerners are loath to criticize another individual directly, so often they'll instead take the opportunity to make an ironic joke. Self-deprecating humor is also much more common in the South than in other areas of the country. Because of this, conversely you're also expected to be able to take a joke yourself without being too sensitive.

Another key element in Southern manners is the discussion of money—or rather, the nondiscussion. Unlike some parts of the United States, in the South it's considered the height of rudeness to ask someone what their salary is or how much they paid for their house. Not that the subject is entirely taboo—far from it; you just have to know the code. For example, rather than brag about how much or how little they paid for their home, a Southern head of household will instead take you on a guided tour of the grounds. Along the way they'll make sure to detail: (a) all the work that was done; (b) how grueling and unexpected it all was; and (c) how hard it was to get the contractors to show up.

Depending on the circumstances, in the first segment, (a) you were just told either that the head of the house is made of money and has a lot more of it to spend on renovating than you do, or that they are a brilliant negotiator who got the house for a song. In part (b) you were told that you are not messing around with a lazy deadbeat here, but with someone who knows how to take care of themselves and can handle adversity with aplomb. And with part (c) you were told that the head of the house knows the best contractors in town and can pay enough for them to actually show up, and if you play your cards right, they might pass on their phone numbers to you with a personal recommendation. See? Breaking the code is easy once you get the hang of it.

## Walter Edgar's Journal

He's originally from Alabama, but you could call University of South Carolina (USC) professor Walter Edgar the modern voice of the Palmetto State. From the rich diversity of barbecue to the inner workings of the poultry business and the charms of beach music, Edgar covers the gamut of South Carolina culture and experience on his popular weekly radio show *Walter Edgar's Journal*, airing on South Carolina public radio stations throughout the state.

Currently director of the USC Institute of Southern Studies, the Vietnam vet and certified barbecue contest judge explains the show like this: "On the *Journal* we look at current events in a broader perspective, trying to provide context that is often missing in the mainstream media." More specifically, Edgar devotes each one-hour show to a single guest, usually a South Carolinian—by birth or by choice—with a unique perspective on some aspect of state culture, business, arts, or folkways. By the time the interview ends, you not only have a much deeper understanding of the topic of the show but of the interviewee as well. And because of Edgar's unique way of tying strands of his own vast knowledge and experience into every interview, you also leave with a deeper understanding of South Carolina itself.

In these days of media saturation, a public radio show might sound like a rather insignificant perch from which to influence an entire state. But remember that South Carolina is a small close-knit place, a state of Main Street towns rather than impersonal metro areas. During any given show, many listeners in Edgar's audience will know his guests on a personal basis. And by the end of the show, the rest of the listeners will feel as if they do.

Listen to "Walter Edgar's Journal" each Friday at noon on South Carolina public radio, with a repeat each Sunday at 4pm. Hear podcasts of previous editions at www.scetv.org.

## Etiquette

As we've seen, it's rude here to inquire about personal finances, along with the usual no-go areas of religion and politics. Here are some other specific etiquette tips:

- **Basics:** Be liberal with "please" and "thank you," or conversely, "no thank you" if you want to decline a request or offering.

- **Eye contact:** With the exception of very elderly African Americans, eye contact is not only accepted in the South, it's encouraged. In fact, to avoid eye contact in the South means you're likely a shady character.

- **Handshake:** Men should always shake hands with a *very* firm, confident grip and appropriate eye contact. It's OK for women to offer a handshake in professional circles, but otherwise not required.

- **Chivalry:** When men open doors for women here—and they will—it is not thought of as a patronizing gesture but as a sign of respect. Accept graciously and walk through the door.

- **The elderly:** Senior citizens—or really anyone obviously older than you—should be called "sir" or "ma'am." Again, this is not a patronizing gesture in the South but is considered a sign of respect. Also, in any situation where you're dealing with someone in the service industry, addressing them as "sir" or "ma'am" regardless of their age will get you far.

- **Bodily contact:** Interestingly, though public displays of affection by romantic couples are generally frowned upon here, Southerners are otherwise pretty touchy-feely once they get to know you. Southerners who are well acquainted often say hello or good-bye with a hug.

- **Driving:** With the exception of the interstate perimeter highways around the larger cities, drivers in the South are generally less aggressive than in other regions. Cutting sharply in front of someone in traffic is taken as a personal offense. If you need to cut in front of someone, poke the nose of your car a little bit in that direction and wait for a car to slow down and wave you in front. Don't forget to wave back as a thank-you. Similarly, using a car horn can also be taken as a personal affront, so use your horn sparingly, if at all. In rural areas, don't be surprised to see the driver of an oncoming car offer a little wave. This is an old custom, sadly dying out. Just give a little wave back; they're trying to be friendly.

## THE GUN CULTURE

One of the most misunderstood aspects of the South is the value the region places on the personal possession of firearms. No doubt, the 2nd Amendment to the U.S. Constitution ("A well-regulated Militia, being necessary to the security of a free State, the right of the people to keep and bear Arms, shall not be infringed") is well known here and fiercely protected, at the governmental and at the grassroots levels.

State laws do tend to be significantly more accommodating of gun owners here than in much of the rest of the country. It is legal to carry a concealed handgun in South Carolina and Georgia with the proper permit, and you need no permit at all to possess a weapon in your house or car for self-defense.

Both states now have so-called (and controversial) "stand your ground" laws, whereby if you're in imminent lethal danger, you do not have to first try to run away before resorting to deadly force to defend yourself.

In 2014, Georgia passed what is widely considered to be the most permissive new gun law in the country, allowing those with the proper license to carry an open or concealed handgun into a bar (though if you do, you're not supposed to drink alcohol).

# Essentials

# Transportation

## AIR

The most centrally located airport for the region covered in this guide is **Savannah/ Hilton Head International Airport** (SAV, 400 Airways Ave., 912/964-0514, www.savannahairport.com), directly off I-95 at exit 104, about 20 minutes from downtown Savannah, 45 minutes from Hilton Head Island, and less than two hours from Charleston. Airlines with routes to SAV include American Airlines (www.aa.com), Allegiant (www.allegiant.com), Delta (www.delta.com), JetBlue (www.jetblue.com), Sun Country (www.suncountry.com), and United (www.ual.com).

A bit less convenient to the rest of the region because of its location well north of town is **Charleston International Airport** (CHS, 5500 International Blvd., 843/767-1100, www.chs-airport.com), served by American Airlines (www.aa.com), Delta (www.delta.com), JetBlue (www.jetblue.com), and Southwest (www.southwest.com).

Many travelers to the region are using **Jacksonville International Airport** (JAX, 2400 Yankee Clipper Dr., 904/741-4902, www.jia.com), about 20 miles north of Jacksonville, Florida. While it's a two-hour drive from Savannah, this airport's proximity to the attractions south of Savannah makes it attractive for some visitors, who can often find a good deal on airfare that makes it worth their while to make the drive.

## CAR

The main interstate highway arteries into the region are the heavily traveled north-south I-95, the east-west I-26 to Charleston from Columbia, South Carolina, and the east-west I-16 to Savannah from Macon, Georgia. A common landmark road through the entire area covered by this guide is U.S. 17, which used to be known as the Coastal Highway and which currently goes by a number of local incarnations as it winds its way down the coast, roughly paralleling I-95. Charleston has a "perimeter" interstate, I-526 (the Mark Clark Expressway), while Savannah has a much smaller version, I-516 (Lynes Parkway).

## Rental Car

You don't have to have a car to enjoy Charleston and Savannah, but to really explore the areas surrounding those cities you'll need your own vehicle. Renting a car is easy and fairly inexpensive, as long as you play by the rules, which are simple. You need either a valid U.S. driver's license from any state or a valid International Driving Permit from your home country, and you must be at least 25 years old.

If you do not either purchase insurance coverage from the rental company or already have insurance coverage through the credit card you rent the car with, you will be 100 percent responsible for any damage caused to the car during your rental period. While purchasing insurance at the time of rental is by no means mandatory, it might be worth the extra expense just to have that peace of mind.

Some rental car locations are in cities proper, but the vast majority of outlets are in airports, so plan accordingly. The airport locations have the bonus of generally holding longer hours than their in-town counterparts.

## TRAIN

Passenger rail service in the car-dominated United States is far behind other developed nations, both in quantity and quality.

Charleston and Savannah are both served by the New York-Miami *Silver Service* route of the national rail system, **Amtrak** (www.amtrak.com), which is pretty good, if erratic at times—although it certainly pales in comparison with European rail transit. Both cities' Amtrak stations are in light industrial parts of town, nowhere near the major tourist centers. Charleston's station is at 4565 Gaynor Street (843/744-8263), while Savannah's is at 2611 Seaboard Coastline Drive (912/234-2611).

## BOAT

One of the coolest things about the Charleston and Savannah area is the presence of the Intracoastal Waterway, a combined artificial and natural sheltered seaway from Miami to Maine. Many boaters enjoy touring the coast by simply meandering up or down the Intracoastal, putting in at marinas along the way. There's a website for **Intracoastal information** at www.cruiseguides.com and a good resource of area **marinas** at www.marinamate.com.

# Recreation

## BEACHES

Some of the best beaches in the United States are in the region covered by this guide. While the upscale amenities aren't always there and they aren't very surfer friendly, the area's beaches are outstanding for anyone looking for a relaxing, scenic getaway.

By law, beaches in the United States are fully accessible to the public up to the high-tide mark during daylight hours, even if the beach fronts private property and even if the only means of public access is by boat. While certain seaside resorts have over the years attempted to make the dunes in front of their properties exclusive to guests, this is actually illegal, although it can be hard to enforce. On federally run National Wildlife Refuges, access is limited to daytime hours, sunrise to sunset.

It is a misdemeanor to disturb the **sea oats,** those wispy, waving, wheat-like plants among the dunes. Their root system is vital to keeping the beach intact. Also, never disturb a turtle nesting area, whether it is marked or not.

### South Carolina

The barrier islands of the Palmetto State have seen more private development than their Georgia counterparts. Some Carolina islands, like Kiawah, Fripp, and Seabrook, are not even accessible unless you are a guest at their affiliated resorts, which, of course, means that the only way to visit the beaches there if you're not a guest is by boat, which I really don't advise. Charleston-area beaches include **Folly Beach, Sullivan's Island,** and **Isle of Palms.** Folly Beach has a county recreation area with parking at **Folly Beach County Park.** Isle of Palms has a county recreation area with parking at **Isle of Palms County Park.**

Moving down the coast, some delightful beaches are at **Edisto Island** and **Hunting Island,** which both feature state parks with campgrounds. **Hilton Head Island** has about 12 miles of beautiful family-friendly beaches, and while most of the island is devoted to private golf resorts, the beaches remain accessible to the general public at four convenient points with parking: **Driessen Beach Park, Coligny Beach Park, Alder Lane Beach Access,** and **Burkes Beach Road.**

### Georgia

The main beach in Georgia is outside Savannah at **Tybee Island,** with full accessibility from end to end. The beach on the north end is smaller and quieter, while the south end is wider, windier, and more populated. There are public parking lots, but you can park at metered spots near the beach as well.

Farther south, a very good beach is at **Jekyll Island,** a largely undeveloped barrier island owned by the state. There are three picnic areas with parking: **Clam Creek, South Dunes,** and **St. Andrew.** Nearby **St. Simons Island** does have a beach area, but it is comparatively narrow and small. Adjacent **Sea Island** is accessible only if you're a guest of the Sea Island Club.

The rest of Georgia's barrier islands are only accessible by ferry, charter, or private boat. Many outfitters will take you on a tour to barrier islands such as Wassaw or Sapelo; don't be shy about inquiring. The most gorgeous beach of all is at **Cumberland Island National Seashore.**

## Surfing

By far the most popular surfing area in the region is the **Washout** at Charleston's Folly Beach. The key surf shop on Folly is **McKevlin's.** For Folly surf conditions, go to www.mckevlins.com or www.surfline.com. The only other surfing of note in the area is on the south end of **Tybee Island** near the Pier and Pavilion. The key surf shop on Tybee is **High Tide Surf Shop.** For a surf report go to www.hightidesurfshop.com.

## ON THE WATER
### Kayaking and Canoeing

Some key kayaking and canoeing areas in the Charleston area are **Cape Romain National Wildlife Refuge, Shem Creek, Isle of Palms,** and the **Charleston Harbor.** The best outfitter and tour operator in the area is **Coastal Expeditions.** Farther south in the Lowcountry are the Ashepoo, Combahee, and Edisto blackwater rivers, which combine to form the **ACE Basin.** Next is **Port Royal Sound** near Beaufort; a good outfitter and tour operator in this area is **Carolina Heritage Outfitters.** The Hilton Head/Bluffton area has good kayaking opportunities at Hilton Head's **Calibogue Creek** and Bluffton's **May River.** The best outfitter and tour operator here is **Outside Hilton Head.** The Savannah area has rich kayaking

and canoeing at **Tybee Island, Skidaway Island,** and the blackwater **Ebenezer Creek.** The best local outfitter and tour operator in this area is **Savannah Canoe and Kayak.** Farther south, down the Georgia coast, the richest kayaking and canoeing area is in the **Altamaha River** estuary, a hybrid blackwater-alluvial river. Good kayaking can be found in the **St. Simons Island** area. The best outfitter and tour operator in the area is **SouthEast Adventures.** Kayaking to **Cumberland Island** is a special experience; contact **Up the Creek Xpeditions** in St. Marys.

### Fishing and Boating

Because of the large number of islands and wide area of salt marsh, life on the water is largely inseparable from life on the land in the Lowcountry and Georgia coast. Fishing and boating are very common pursuits here, with species of fish including spotted sea trout, channel bass, flounder, grouper, mackerel, sailfish, whiting, shark, amberjack, and tarpon. Farther inshore you'll find largemouth bass, bream, catfish, and crappie, among many more. While entire books can be and are devoted to the area's fishing opportunities, here is an overview.

It's easy to fish on piers, lakes, and streams, but if you're over age 16, you have to get a nonresident fishing license from the state. These are inexpensive and available in hardware stores, marinas, and tackle shops anywhere. In Georgia, a regular license is $9, a one-day license $3.50. A separate license is required for trout fishing. Go to http://georgiawildlife.dnr.state.ga.us for more information or to purchase a license online. In South Carolina, a nonresident seven-day license is $11. Go to www.dnr.sc.gov for more information or to purchase a license online.

The most popular places for casual anglers are the various public piers throughout the area. There are public fishing piers at **Folly Beach, Hunting Island, Tybee Island, St. Simons Island,** and **Jekyll Island.** Two nice little public docks are at the **North**

Charleston Riverfront Park on the grounds of the old Charleston Navy Yard, and the **Bluffton public landing** on the May River. Many anglers cast from abandoned bridges, unless signage dictates otherwise. Fishing charters and marinas are ample throughout the region, for both inshore and offshore trips.

## ON THE LAND
### Golf and Tennis

The first golf club in the country was formed in Charleston, and that area has more than its share of fine courses. As far as quality is concerned, the consensus pick for best course in South Carolina is definitely the Pete Dye-designed Ocean Course at the **Kiawah Island Golf Resort**, which is open to guests of the club. Coming in second would almost certainly be **Harbour Town** on Sea Pines Plantation in Hilton Head. Not coincidentally, both courses host PGA events.

In Georgia, the Ocean Forest Course at the **Sea Island Club** on Sea Island is a gem—though you must be a guest at the club to play—as is the affiliated Seaside Course. For value, go in the off-season, in the colder months, when prices are lowest. Not all courses close, and most are in great shape because of the reduced traffic.

The premier tennis facility in the Charleston area is the new **Family Circle Cup Tennis Center** on Daniel Island, home of the eponymous women's event and some great public courts. Other key tennis facilities are at the **King and Prince** on St. Simons and **Jekyll Island Tennis Center.**

### Hiking and Biking

Due to the flat nature of the Lowcountry and Georgia coast, hiking and biking here are not very strenuous. However, the great natural beauty and prevalence of a rich range of plant and animal life make hiking and biking very rewarding experiences. Probably the best trails can be found at state parks in the region, such as **Edisto Island State Park, Hunting Island State Park,** and **Skidaway Island State Park.** Many National Wildlife Refuges (NWRs) in the area also feature excellent trails, such as **Pinckney Island NWR, Harris Neck NWR,** and **Cape Romain NWR.**

There are a couple of "rails to trails" projects that might appeal: the **James Island Trail** outside Charleston and the **McQueen Island Trail** on the way to Tybee Island outside Savannah. Some areas are almost defined by the plethora of bike and pedestrian trails running nearly their entire length and breadth, such as Jekyll Island and Hilton Head Island.

Wide beaches, very conducive to biking on the sand, are one of the great pleasures of this area. Most bikes you rent in the area will have fat enough tires to do the job correctly. The best beach rides are on **Sullivan's Island, Hilton Head Island, Jekyll Island, St. Simons Island, Cumberland Island,** and **Tybee Island.**

# Travel Tips

## TRAVELING WITH CHILDREN

The Lowcountry and Georgia coast are very kid friendly, with the possible exception of some B&Bs that are clearly not designed for younger children. If you have any doubts about this, feel free to inquire. Otherwise, there are no special precautions unique to this area. There are no zoos per se in the region, but animal lovers of all ages will enjoy **Charles Towne Landing** in Charleston and **Oatland Island Wildlife Center** in Savannah. Better still, take the kids on nature outings to the amazing National Wildlife Refuges in the area.

# WOMEN TRAVELING ALONE

Women should take the same precautions they would take anywhere else. Many women traveling to this region have to adjust to the prevalence of traditional chivalry. In the South, if a man opens a door for you, it's considered a sign of respect, not condescension. Another adjustment is the possible assumption that two or three women who go to a bar or tavern together might be there to invite male companionship. This misunderstanding can happen anywhere, but in some parts of the South it might be slightly more prevalent. Being aware of it is the best defense; otherwise no other steps need to be taken.

# ACCESS FOR TRAVELERS WITH DISABILITIES

While the vast majority of attractions and accommodations make every effort to comply with federal law regarding those with disabilities, as they're obliged to do, the very historic nature of this region means that some structures simply cannot be retrofitted for maximum accessibility. This is something you'll need to find out on a case-by-case basis, so call ahead. The sites administered by the National Park Service in this guide (Charles Pinckney National Historic Site, Fort Sumter, Fort Moultrie, Fort Pulaski, Fort Frederica, and Cumberland Island National Seashore) are as wheelchair-accessible as possible.

Some special shuttles are available. In Charleston, call the "Tel-A-Ride" service (843/724-7420). A couple of cab companies in town to check out are Express Cab Company (843/577-8816) and Flag A Cab (842/554-1231). In Savannah, Chatham Area Transit (www.catchacat.org) runs a Teleride service (912/354-6900). For the visually impaired, in Charleston there's the Association for the Blind (1071 Morrison Dr., 843/723-6915, www.afb.org) and in Savannah the Savannah Association for the Blind

(214 Drayton St., 912/236-4473). Hearing-disadvantaged individuals can get assistance in Charleston at the Charleston Speech and Hearing Center (843/552-1212).

# GAY AND LESBIAN TRAVELERS

Don't believe all the negative propaganda about the South. The truth is that the metropolitan areas of Charleston, Beaufort, and Savannah are tolerant, and gay and lesbian travelers shouldn't expect anything untoward to happen. Outside the metro areas, locals are less welcoming to gay men and lesbian women, although overt hostility is rare. The best approach is to simply observe dominant Southern mores for anyone, gay or straight. In a nutshell, that means keep public displays of affection and politics to a minimum. Southerners in general have a low opinion of anyone who flagrantly espouses a viewpoint too obviously or loudly.

# SENIOR TRAVELERS

Both because of the large proportion of retirees in the region and because of Southerners' traditional respect for the elderly, the area is quite friendly to senior citizens. Many accommodations and attractions offer a slight senior discount, which can add up over the course of a trip. Always inquire about such discounts before making a reservation, however, as checkout time is too late to do so.

# TRAVELING WITH PETS

While the United States is very pet friendly, that friendliness rarely extends to restaurants and other indoor locations. More and more accommodations are allowing pet owners to bring pets, often for an added fee, but inquire before you arrive. In any case, keep your dog on a leash at all times. Some beaches in the area permit dog walking at certain times of the year, but as a general rule, keep dogs off of beaches unless you see signage saying otherwise.

# Health and Safety

## CRIME

While crime rates are indeed above national averages in many of the areas covered in this guide, especially in inner-city areas, incidents of crime in the more heavily trafficked tourist areas are no more common than anywhere else. In fact, these areas might be safer because of the amount of foot traffic and police attention.

By far the most common crime against visitors here is simple theft, primarily from cars. (Pickpocketing, thankfully, is rare in the United States.) Always lock your car doors. Conversely, only leave them unlocked if you're absolutely comfortable living without whatever's inside at the time. As a general rule, I try to lock valuables—such as CDs, a recent purchase, or my wife's purse—in the trunk. (Just make sure the "valet" button, allowing the trunk to be opened from the driver's area, is disabled.)

Should someone corner you and demand your wallet or purse, just give it to them. Unfortunately, the old advice to scream as loud as you can is no longer the deterrent it once was, and in fact may hasten aggressive action by the robber.

If you are the victim of a crime, *always call the police.* Law enforcement wants more information, not less, and at very least you'll have an incident report in case you need to make an insurance claim for lost or stolen property.

Remember that in the United States, as elsewhere, no good can come from a heated argument with a police officer. The place to prove a police officer wrong is in a court of law, perhaps with an attorney by your side, not at the scene.

For emergencies, always call 911.

## AUTO ACCIDENTS

If you're in an auto accident where there's injury or damage to one or both cars, you must at minimum exchange insurance information with the other driver. It's always prudent to wait for police. Unless there is personal injury involved, you should move your car just enough to clear the way for other traffic if able to do so.

Since it's illegal to drive in these states without auto insurance, I'll assume you have some. And because you're insured, the best course of action in a minor accident, where injuries are unlikely, is to patiently wait for the police and give them your side of the story. In my experience, police react negatively to people who are too quick to start making accusations against other people. After that, let the insurance companies deal with it; that's what they're there for. If you suspect any injuries, call 911 immediately.

## ILLEGAL DRUGS

Marijuana, heroin, methamphetamine, and cocaine and all its derivatives are illegal in the United States with only a very few select exceptions, none of which apply to the areas covered by this guide. The use of ecstasy and similar mood-elevators is also illegal. The penalties for illegal drug possession and use in South Carolina and Georgia are quite severe.

## ALCOHOL

The drinking age in the United States is 21. Most restaurants that serve alcoholic beverages allow those under 21 inside. Generally speaking, if only those over 21 are allowed inside, you will be greeted at the door by someone asking to see identification. These people are often poorly trained and anything other than a state driver's license may confuse them, so be forewarned.

Drunk driving is a problem on the highways of the United States, and South Carolina and Georgia are no exceptions. Always drive defensively, especially late at night, and obey all posted speed limits and road signs—and never assume the other driver will do the same. You may never drive with an open alcoholic beverage in the car, even if it belongs to a passenger.

As far as retail purchase goes, in South Carolina you may only buy beer and wine, not hard liquor, on Sundays. In most parts of Georgia, no alcoholic beverages are sold at the retail level on Sundays, other than in restaurants that also sell food.

## MEDICAL SERVICES

Unlike most developed nations, the United States has no comprehensive national health care system (although there are programs for the elderly and the very poor, as well as the new Affordable Care Act, or "Obamacare," for those who work but have no access to insurance). Visitors from other countries who need nonemergency medical attention are best served by going to freestanding medical clinics. The level of care is typically very good, but unfortunately you'll be paying out of pocket for the service. For emergencies, however, do not hesitate to go to the closest hospital emergency room, where the level of care is generally also quite good, especially for trauma. Worry about payment later; emergency rooms in the United States are required to take true emergency cases whether or not the patient can pay for services. Call 911 for ambulance service.

### Pharmaceuticals

Unlike many other nations, antibiotics are available in the United States only on a prescription basis and are not available over the counter. Most cold, flu, and allergy remedies are available over the counter. While homeopathic remedies are gaining popularity in the United States, they are nowhere near as prevalent as in Europe.

Drugs with the active ingredient ephedrine are available in the United States without a prescription, but their purchase is tightly regulated to cut down on the use of these products to make the illegal drug methamphetamine.

## STAYING HEALTHY
### Vaccinations

As of this writing, there are no vaccination requirements to enter the United States. Contact your embassy before coming to confirm this before arrival, however. In the autumn, at the beginning of flu season, preventive influenza vaccinations, simply called "flu shots," often become available at easily accessible locations like clinics, health departments, and even supermarkets.

### Humidity, Heat, and Sun

There is only one way to fight the South's high heat and humidity, and that's to drink lots of fluids. A surprising number of people each year refuse to take this advice and find themselves in various states of dehydration, some of which can land you in a hospital. Remember: If you're thirsty, you're already suffering from dehydration. The thing to do is keep drinking fluids *before* you're thirsty as a preventative action rather than a reaction.

Always use sunscreen, even on a cloudy day. If you do get a sunburn, get a pain-relief product with aloe vera as an active ingredient. On extraordinarily sunny and hot summer days, don't even go outside between the hours of 10am and 2pm.

## HAZARDS
### Insects

Because of the recent increase in the mosquito-borne West Nile virus, the most important step to take in staying healthy in the Lowcountry and Georgia coast—especially if you have small children—is to keep **mosquito bites** to a minimum. Do this with a combination of mosquito repellent and long sleeves and long pants, if possible. Not every mosquito bite will give you the virus; in fact, chances are quite slim that one will. But don't take the chance if you don't have to.

The second major step in avoiding insect nastiness is to steer clear of **fire ants,** whose large gray or brown dirt nests are quite common in this area. They attack instantly and in great numbers, with little or no provocation.

They don't just bite; they inject you with poison from their stingers. In short, fire ants are not to be trifled with. While the only real remedy is the preventative one of never coming in contact with them, should you find yourself being bitten by fire ants, the first thing to do is to stay calm. Take off your shoes and socks and get as many of the ants off you as you can. Unless you've had a truly large number of bites—in which case you should seek medical help immediately—the best thing to do next is wash the area to get any venom off, and then disinfect with alcohol if you have any handy. Then a topical treatment such as calamine lotion or hydrocortisone is advised. A fire ant bite will leave a red pustule that lasts about a week. Try your best not to scratch it so that it won't get infected.

Outdoor activity, especially in woodsy, undeveloped areas, may bring you in contact with another unpleasant indigenous creature, the tiny but obnoxious **chigger,** sometimes called the redbug. The bite of a chigger can't be felt, but the enzymes it leaves behind can lead to a very itchy little red spot. Contrary to folklore, putting fingernail polish on the itchy bite will not "suffocate" the chigger, because by this point the chigger itself is long gone. All you can do is get some topical itch or pain

relief and go on with your life. The itching will eventually subside.

## Threats in the Water

While enjoying area beaches, a lot of visitors become inordinately worried about **shark attacks.** Every couple of summers there's a lot of hysteria about this, but the truth is that you're much more likely to slip and fall in a bathroom than you are to even come close to being bitten by a shark in these shallow Atlantic waters.

A far more common fate for area swimmers is to get stung by a **jellyfish,** or sea nettle. They can sting you in the water, but most often beachcombers are stung by stepping on beached jellyfish stranded on the sand by the tide. If you get stung, don't panic; wash the area with saltwater, not freshwater, and apply vinegar or baking soda. A product called Jellyfish Squish is also available and seems to work well.

## Lightning

The southeastern United States is home to vicious, fast-moving thunderstorms, often with an amazing amount of electrical activity. Death by lightning strike occurs often in this region and is something that should be taken

lightning on Tybee Island

quite seriously. The general rule of thumb is that if you're in the water, whether at the beach or in a swimming pool, and hear thunder, get out of the water immediately until the storm passes. If you're on dry land and see lightning flash a distance away, that's your cue to seek safety indoors. Whatever you do, do not play sports outside when lightning threatens.

# Information and Services

## VISITOR INFORMATION

### Charleston

The main visitors center is the Charleston Visitor Reception and Transportation Center (375 Meeting St., 800/774-0006, www.charlestoncvb.com, Mon.–Fri. 8:30am-5pm). Outlying visitors centers are the Mt. Pleasant-Isle of Palms Visitor Center (99 Harry M. Hallman Jr Blvd., 800/774-0006, daily 9am-5pm) and the North Charleston Visitor Center (4975-B Centre Pointe Dr., 843/853-8000, Mon.-Sat. 10am-5pm).

### Beaufort and the Lowcountry

The Beaufort Visitors Information Center is within the Beaufort Arsenal building (713 Craven St., 843/986-5400, www.beaufortsc. org, daily 9am-5:30pm). In Hilton Head, get information, book a room, or secure a tee time just as you come onto the island at the Hilton Head Island Chamber of Commerce Welcome Center (100 William Hilton Pkwy., 843/785-3673, www.hiltonheadisland. org, daily 9am-6pm), in the same building as the Coastal Discovery Museum. You'll find Bluffton's visitors center in the Heyward House Historic Center (70 Boundary St., 843/757-6293, www.heywardhouse.org, Mon.-Fri. 10am-3pm, Sat. 11am-2pm).

### Savannah

The main place for visitor information in Savannah is the downtown Savannah Visitors Center (301 MLK Jr. Blvd., 912/944-0455, Mon.-Fri. 8:30am-5pm, Sat.-Sun. and holidays 9am-5pm). The Savannah Convention and Visitors Bureau (101 E. Bay St., 877/728-2662, www.savcvb.com, Mon.-Fri. 8:30am-5pm) keeps an up-to-date list of lodgings at its website. Other visitors centers in the area include the River Street Hospitality Center (1 River St., 912/651-6662, daily 10am-10pm), the Tybee Island Visitor Center (S. Campbell Ave. and U.S. 80, 912/786-5444, daily 9am-5:30pm) and the Savannah Airport Visitor Center (464 Airways Ave., 912/964-1109, daily 10am-6pm).

### The Golden Isles

The Brunswick-Golden Isles Visitor Center (2000 Glynn Ave., 912/264-5337, daily 9am-5pm) is at the intersection of U.S. 17 and the Torras Causeway to St. Simons Island. A downtown information station is in Old City Hall, at the corner of Mansfield and Newcastle Streets (912/262-6934, daily 8am-5pm).

The Jekyll Island Visitor Center (901 Downing Musgrove Causeway, 912/635-3636, daily 9am-5pm) is before you get to the island, on the long causeway along the marsh. The St. Simons Visitor Center (530-B Beachview Dr., 912/638-9014, www.bgivb.com, daily 9am-5pm) is in the St. Simons Casino building near Neptune Park and the Village.

The Darien Welcome Center is at the corner of U.S. 17 and Fort King George Drive (912/437-6684, Mon.-Sat. 9am-5pm). The Sapelo Island Visitors Center (912/437-3224, www.sapelonerr.org, Tues.-Fri. 7:30am-5:30pm, Sat. 8am-5:30pm, Sun. 1:30pm-5pm) is actually not on Sapelo but at the dock where you take the ferry, in Meridian, Georgia, on Highway 99 from Darien.

The St. Marys Visitor Center is located at 406 Osborne Street (912/882-4000, www. stmaryswelcome.com, Mon.-Sat. 9am-5pm,

Sun. noon-5pm). The **Cumberland Island Visitors Center** is at 113 St. Marys Street (912/882-4336, daily 8am-6pm).

There are several entrances to the Okefenokee Swamp, with the closest thing to a visitors center being the U.S. Fish and Wildlife Service's **Richard S. Bolt Visitor Center** (912/496-7836, daily 9am-5pm) at the eastern entrance near Folkston, Georgia.

## MONEY

Automated teller machines (ATMs) are available in all urban areas covered in this guide. Be aware that if the ATM is not owned by your bank, not only will that ATM likely charge you a service fee, but your bank may charge you one as well. While ATMs have made traveler's checks less essential, traveler's checks do have the important advantage of accessibility, as some rural and less-developed areas covered in this guide have few or no ATMs. You can purchase traveler's checks at just about any bank.

Establishments in the United States only accept the national currency, the U.S. dollar. To exchange foreign money, go to any bank.

Generally, establishments that accept credit cards will feature stickers on the front entrance with the logo of the particular cards they accept, although this is not a legal requirement. The use of debit cards has dramatically increased in the United States. Most retail establishments and many fast-food chains are now accepting them. Make sure you get a receipt whenever you use a credit card or a debit card.

## MEDIA AND COMMUNICATIONS
### Newspapers

The closest thing to a national newspaper in the United States is *USA Today,* which you will find at diverse locations from airports to gas stations. The national paper of record is the *New York Times,* which is available in larger urban areas but only rarely in outlying areas.

In Charleston, the paper of record is the *Post and Courier* (www.charleston.net). Its entertainment insert, "Preview," comes out on Thursdays. The free alternative weekly is the *Charleston City Paper* (www.charlestoncitypaper.com), which comes out on Wednesdays and is the best place to find local music and arts listings. A particularly well-done and lively metro glossy is *Charleston* magazine (www.charlestonmag.com), which comes out once a month.

In Beaufort, the daily newspaper of record is the *Beaufort Gazette* (www.beaufortgazette.com). An alternative weekly focusing mostly on the arts is *Lowcountry Weekly* (www.lcweekly.com). Hilton Head's paper of record is the *Island Packet* (www.islandpacket.com). A good Bluffton publication is *Bluffton Today* (www.blufftontoday.com).

In Savannah, the daily newspaper of record is the *Savannah Morning News* (www.savannahnow.com). It puts out an entertainment insert on Thursdays called "Do." The independent free weekly newspaper in town is *Connect Savannah* (www.connectsavannah.com), hitting stands each Wednesday.

The main paper in the much more sparsely populated Golden Isles region is the *Brunswick News* (www.thebrunswicknews.com), but many people read the newspaper of record of nearby Jacksonville, Florida, the *Florida Times-Union* (www.jacksonville.com).

### Internet Access

Visitors from Europe and Asia are likely to be disappointed at the quality of Internet access in the United States, particularly the area covered in this guide. Fiber-optic lines are still a rarity, and while many hotels and B&Bs now offer in-room Internet access—some charge, some don't, make sure to ask ahead—the quality and speed of the connection might prove poor. Wireless (Wi-Fi) networks are also less than impressive, but that situation continues to improve on a daily basis in coffeehouses, hotels, and airports. Unfortunately, many hotspots in private establishments charge fees. Charleston does have a municipal free Wi-Fi network, however. While Savannah does not yet have a citywide Wi-Fi network, you can get a list of free Savannah Wi-Fi hotspots at www.thecreativecoast.org/datainfo/hotspots.

## Phones

Generally speaking, the United States is behind Europe and much of Asia in terms of cell phone technology. Unlike Europe, where "pay as you go" refills are easy to find, most American cell phone users pay for monthly plans through a handful of providers. Still, you should have no problem with cell phone coverage in urban areas. Where it gets much less dependable is in rural areas and on beaches. Bottom line: Don't depend on having cell service everywhere you go.

As with a regular landline, any time you face an emergency, call 911 on your cell phone.

All phone numbers in the United States are seven digits preceded by a three-digit area code. You may have to dial "1" before a phone number if it's a long-distance call, even within the same area code. The area code for the part of South Carolina covered in this guide is 843. The area code for the part of Georgia covered in this guide is 912.

# Resources

## Suggested Reading

### NONFICTION
#### Georgia

Calonius, Erik. *The Wanderer: The Last American Slave Ship and the Conspiracy That Set Its Sails.* New York: St. Martin's Press, 2006. A page-turning tale of the last illegal slave shipment to land in the United States, on Jekyll Island, Georgia.

Fraser, Walter J. Jr. *Savannah in the Old South.* Athens, GA: University of Georgia Press, 2005. An insightful and balanced history of Georgia's first city, from founding through Reconstruction.

Georgia Writers Project. *Drums and Shadows: Survival Studies Among the Georgia Coastal Negroes.* Athens, GA: University of Georgia Press, 1986. Arising from a government-funded research project during the Depression, this still ranks as one of the best oral histories ever assembled, using firsthand accounts from African American residents of Georgia's Sea Islands to paint a picture of a lifestyle gone by.

Greene, Melissa Fay. *Praying for Sheetrock.* New York: Ballantine, 1992. In this modern classic, Greene explores the racism and corruption endemic in McIntosh County, Georgia, during the era of the civil rights movement.

Kemble, Fanny. *Journal of a Residence on a Georgian Plantation in 1838-1839.* Athens, GA: University of Georgia Press, 1984. A famed English actress's groundbreaking antislavery account of her stay on a rice plantation in McIntosh County, Georgia.

Morgan, Philip, ed. *African American Life in the Georgia Lowcountry: The Atlantic World and the Gullah Geechee.* Athens, GA: University of Georgia Press, 2010. The best book I've come by on the history and folkways of Georgia's Gullah or Geechee people. Balanced, scholarly, yet still readable in the extreme.

Seabrook, Charles. *Cumberland Island: Strong Women, Wild Horses.* Winston-Salem, NC: John F. Blair, 2002. An even-handed, journalistic look inside the tension between environmentalists and the residents of Cumberland Island.

Wood, Betty, ed. *Mary Telfair to Mary Few: Selected Letters, 1802-1844.* Athens, GA: University of Georgia Press, 2007. The revealing, chatty letters of a great arts patron and member of a major Savannah slave-owning family, to her best friend who left the city and moved north because of her abolitionist leanings. We know that Mary Few replied, but her letters remain undiscovered.

#### South Carolina

Fraser, Walter J. Jr. *Charleston! Charleston! The History of a Southern City.* Columbia, SC: University of South Carolina Press, 1991. Another typically well-written and balanced tome by this important regional historian.

Gessler, Diana Hollingsworth. *Very Charleston: A Celebration of History, Culture, and Lowcountry Charm.* Chapel Hill, NC: Algonquin Books, 2003. A quick, visually appealing insider's perspective with some wonderfully whimsical cartoon-style illustrations.

Klein, Maury. *Days of Defiance: Sumter, Secession, and the Coming of the Civil War.* New York: Vintage, 1999. A gripping and vivid account of the lead-up to war, with Charleston as the focal point.

Rogers, George C. Jr. *Charleston in the Age of the Pinckneys.* Columbia, SC: University of South Carolina Press, 1980. This 1969 history is a classic of the genre.

Rosen, Robert. *A Short History of Charleston.* Columbia, SC: University of South Carolina Press, 1997. Quite simply the most concise, readable, and entertaining history of the Holy City I've found.

Woodward, C. Vann, ed. *Mary Chesnut's Civil War.* New Haven, CT: Yale University Press, 1981. The Pulitzer Prize-winning classic compilation of the sardonic and quietly heartbreaking letters of Charleston's Mary Chesnut during the Civil War.

## General Background

Aberjhani and Sandra West. *Encyclopedia of the Harlem Renaissance.* New York: Checkmark Books, 2003. A brilliantly researched account of the great African American diaspora out of the South that eventually gave birth to the Charleston dance craze of the 1920s.

Lewis, Lloyd. *Sherman: Fighting Prophet.* Lincoln, NE: University of Nebraska Press, 1993. Though first published in 1932, this remains the most thorough, insightful, and well-written biography of General William Sherman in existence.

Robinson, Sally Ann. *Gullah Home Cooking the Daufuskie Island Way.* Chapel Hill, NC: University of North Carolina Press, 2007. Subtitled "Smokin' Joe Butter Beans, Ol' 'Fuskie Fried Crab Rice, Sticky-Bush Blackberry Dumpling, and Other Sea Island Favorites," this cookbook by a native Daufuskie Islander features a foreword by Pat Conroy.

Stehling, Robert. *Hominy Grill Recipes.* Charleston, SC: Big Cartel, 2009. This humble, hand-illustrated, self-published little tome features 23 great recipes from one of Charleston's most respected Southern cooking joints, Hominy Grill on Rutledge Avenue. At only $12.95, one of the best cookbooks for the money you'll find.

## FICTION

Berendt, John. *Midnight in the Garden of Good and Evil.* New York: Vintage, 1999. Well, not exactly fiction, but far from completely true, nonetheless this modern classic definitely reads like a novel while remaining one of the unique and readable travelogues of recent times.

Caskey, James. *Haunted Savannah: The Official Guidebook to Savannah Haunted History Tour.* Savannah: Bonaventture Books, 2012. The author may quibble with this being in the "fiction" section, but this is an entertaining and also quite educating look at Savannah's various paranormal tales.

Conroy, Pat. *The Lords of Discipline.* New York: Bantam, 1985. For all practical purposes set at the Citadel, this novel takes you behind the scenes of the notoriously insular Charleston military college.

Conroy, Pat. *The Water is Wide.* New York: Bantam, 1987. Immortal account of

Conroy's time teaching African American children in a one-room schoolhouse on "Yamacraw" (actually Daufuskie) Island.

Hervey, Harry. *The Damned Don't Cry.* Marietta, GA: Cherokee Publishing, 2003. The original *Midnight,* this bawdy 1939 potboiler takes you into the streets, shanties, drawing rooms, and boudoirs of real Savannahians during the Depression.

O'Connor, Flannery. *Flannery O'Connor: Collected Works.* New York: Library of America, 1988. For a look into Savannah's conflicted, paradoxical soul, read anything by this native-born writer, so grounded in tradition yet so ahead of her time even to this day. This volume includes selected letters, an especially valuable (and entertaining) insight.

# Internet Resources

## RECREATION

### South Carolina Department of Natural Resources
www.dnr.sc.gov

More than just a compendium of license and fee information—though there's certainly plenty of that—this site features a lot of practical advice on how best to enjoy South Carolina's great outdoors, whether you're an angler, a kayaker, a bird-watcher, a hiker, or a biker.

### Georgia Department of Natural Resources
www.gadnr.org

Ditto for this site, which has lots of great information on the wildlife and geology of Georgia's beautiful and largely undeveloped barrier islands.

### Savannah Bicycle Campaign
www.bicyclecampaign.org

The clearinghouse for routes and rides by Savannah's most dedicated cyclists.

### Georgia State Parks
www.gastateparks.org

Vital historical and visitor information for Georgia's underrated network of historical state park sites along the coast, including camping reservations.

### South Carolina State Parks
www.southcarolinaparks.com

Ditto for this site all about South Carolina's state parks.

### Dozier's Waterway Guide
www.waterwayguide.com

A serious boater's guide to stops on the Intracoastal Waterway, with a lot of solid navigational information.

## NATURE AND ENVIRONMENT

### Ocean Science
http://oceanscience.wordpress.com

A blog by the staff of Savannah's Skidaway Institute of Oceanography, focusing on barrier island ecology and the maritime environment.

## CUISINE AND ENTERTAINMENT

### Savannah Foodie
www.savannahfoodie.com

An insider's look at the Savannah restaurant scene, with an emphasis on breaking news.

### Charleston City Paper blogs
http://ccpblogs.com

The collected staff blogs of the Charleston City Paper, dealing with the latest foodie news in town and entertainment options.

## HISTORY AND BACKGROUND

### South Carolina Information Highway
**www.sciway.net**

An eclectic cornucopia of interesting South Carolina history and assorted background facts, which makes for an interesting Internet portal into all things Palmetto State.

### New Georgia Encyclopedia
**www.georgiaencyclopedia.org**

A mother lode of concise, neutral, and well-written information on the natural and human history of Georgia from prehistory to the present.

## TOURISM INFORMATION

### Charleston Convention and Visitors Bureau
**www.charlestoncvb.com**

This very professional and user-friendly tourism site is perhaps the best and most practical Internet portal for visitors to Charleston.

### Visit Savannah
**www.visitsavannah.com**

Savannah's Convention & Visitors Bureau is particularly adept at social media.

# Index

# C

# List of Maps

# Photo Credits

Title Page © Jim Morekis; page 4 © Jim Morekis; page 5 (top) © Jim Morekis, (lower right) © Cvandyke | Dreamstime.com; pages 6-9 © Jim Morekis; page 10 © William Manning | Dreamstime.com; page 12 (top) © Jim Morekis; (lower right) © Darryl Brooks | Dreamstime.com; page 13 © Rolf52 | Dreamstime.com; page 14 (top) © Americanspirit | Dreamstime.com, (lower right) © Realitytimes | Dreamstime.com; page 15 courtesy of the Glass Onion; page 16 © Brian Welker | Dreamstime.com; page 17 © Visions of America LLC | Dreamstime.com; page 18 © Bddigitalimages | Dreamstime.com; page 19 © Jim Morekis; page 20 (top) © Kongomonkey | Dreamstime.com, (lower right) © Jim Morekis; page 21 © Smvphotos | Dreamstime.com; page 22 © Jim Morekis; page 23 (top) © dndavis/123rf.com; (lower right) © Famfinder | Dreamstime.com; page 24 © Brian Welker | Dreamstime.com; page 25 (top) © Jon Bilous | Dreamstime.com, (bottom) © Jf Halbrooks | Dreamstime.com; page 27 © Jerry Coli | Dreamstime.com; pages 36-46 © Jim Morekis; page 47 © Jerry Coli | Dreamstime.com; pages 49-66 © Jim Morekis; page 72 © Tinamou | Dreamstime.com; page 74 © Ron Cogswell; page 76 © Jim Morekis; page 85 © Jerry Coli | Dreamstime.com; pages 89-112 © Jim Morekis; page 113 © Jerry Coli | Dreamstime.com; pages 120-121 © Jim Morekis; page 126 (top) © Jim Morekis (bottom) © Cvandyke | Dreamstime.com; page 127 © Alex Grichenko | Dreamstime.com; page 130 © John Wollwerth | Dreamstime.com; page 132 © Jim Morekis; page 133 © John Wollwerth | Dreamstime.com; page 134-179 © Jim Morekis; page 181 © Cmoulton | Dreamstime.com; page 182 (top) © Sean Pavone | Dreamstime.com, (bottom) © Jim Morekis; page 183 © Dbvirago | Dreamstime.com; page 196 © Kongomonkey | Dreamstime.com; pages 200-210 © Jim Morekis; page 212 © Britt Scott; page 215 © Jim Morekis; page 217 © Britt Scott; page 218 © Jim Morekis; page 219 © Dndavis | Dreamstime.com; page 222 © Dhsnover | Dreamstime.com; page 225 © dndavis/123rf.com; pages 226-254 © Jim Morekis; page 257 © Fotoluminate | Dreamstime.com; pages 269-273 © Jim Morekis; page 280 (top) © Brian Lasenby | Dreamstime.com, (bottom) © Jim Morekis; page 281 © Brian Lasenby | Dreamstime.com; pages 288-314 © Jim Morekis; page 324 © Stockage | Dreamstime.com; page 325-340 © Jim Morekis; page 342 © Brian Lasenby | Dreamstime.com; pages 364-367 © Jim Morekis; page 370 (top) © Kclarksphotography | Dreamstime.com, (bottom) © Sean Pavone | Dreamstime.com; page 378 © Alex Grichenko | Dreamstime.com.

# Also Available